CHINA LEARNS FROM THE SOVIET UNION, 1949–PRESENT

THE HARVARD COLD WAR STUDIES BOOK SERIES
SERIES EDITOR: MARK KRAMER, HARVARD UNIVERSITY

CHINA LEARNS FROM THE SOVIET UNION, 1949–PRESENT

Edited by
Thomas P. Bernstein and Hua-yu Li

LEXINGTON BOOKS
A division of
ROWMAN & LITTLEFIELD PUBLISHERS, INC.
Lanham • Boulder • New York • Toronto • Plymouth, UK

Published by Lexington Books
A division of Rowman & Littlefield Publishers, Inc.
A wholly owned subsidiary of The Rowman & Littlefield Publishing Group, Inc.
4501 Forbes Boulevard, Suite 200, Lanham, Maryland 20706
http://www.lexingtonbooks.com

Estover Road, Plymouth PL6 7PY, United Kingdom

Published with the generous support of the Weatherhead East Asian Institute and the
Harriman Institute for Russian, Eurasian, and Eastern European Studies.

British Library Cataloguing in Publication Information Available

Library of Congress Cataloging-in-Publication Data
China learns from the Soviet Union, 1949–present / edited by Thomas P. Bernstein and
Hua-yu Li.
    p. cm. — (Harvard Cold War studies book series)
  Includes index.
  ISBN 978-0-7391-4222-6 (cloth : alk. paper) — ISBN 978-0-7391-4224-0 (electronic :
alk. paper)
  1. China—Foreign relations—Soviet Union. 2. Soviet Union—Foreign relations—
China. 3. Communism—China—History—20th century. 4. Communism and culture—
China. 5. China—Politics and government—1949- 6. China—Economic conditions—
1949- 7. China—Social conditions—1949- 8. Education—China—History—20th
century. I. Bernstein, Thomas P. II. Li, Hua-Yu.
  DS740.5.S65C477 2010
  303.48'251047—dc22
                                                                2009025629

Printed in the United States of America

To Dorothy J. Solinger and Jim McLendon

Contents

Part Seven: The Era of Reform and the Impact of the Soviet Collapse

Acknowledgments

THIS BOOK IS THE RESULT OF AN international conference on "The Soviet Impact on China: Politics, Economy, Society, and Culture, 1949–1991," held at Columbia University in June 2007 and organized by the two co-editors.

In the course of editing the chapters, we changed the title to "China Learns from the Soviet Union, 1949–Present" in order to highlight China's active role in the evolution of the relationship between the two countries and in the process of adopting and adapting Soviet models of socialist construction and governance. As is well known, China chose to emulate the Soviet Union most closely in the first half of the 1950s, followed by increasing rejection of Nikita Khrushchev's efforts to reform Stalinism, but also by Maoist critiques of Stalin's rule. As the Sino-Soviet conflict deepened, the Soviet Union became *fanmian jiaocai*, a case of negative teaching material. In the 1980s, as Mikhail Gorbachev's reforms gathered steam, Chinese interest in what was transpiring in the Soviet Union revived. However, after the end of Communist rule and the disintegration of the Soviet Union, China turned harshly against the Gorbachev reforms, especially against his pursuit of political liberalization. This stance has continued to this day. China thus once again regards the Soviet Union as a teacher by negative example.

We would like to express our sincere gratitude to the funding provided by the Harriman Institute for Russian, Eurasian, and Eastern European Studies and the Weatherhead East Asian Institute, both at Columbia.

We are grateful to the anonymous reviewer for making very helpful and detailed comments on the manuscript. And we would like to express our appreciation to our contributors for bearing with us during the editing process.

Some of the authors were not accustomed to writing western-style academic papers but they responded readily to our requests for changes.

And last but not least, we would like to thank Mark Kramer, the director of Cold War Studies at Harvard University and the editor of the *Journal of Cold War Studies*, as well as Sylvana Kolaczkowska, the journal's managing editor, for their continued support and encouragement. And we also thank the editors at Rowman & Littlefield, and Lexington Books–Julie E. Kirsch, Paula Smith-Vanderslice, and Melissa McNitt.

Introduction: The Complexities of Learning from the Soviet Union

Thomas P. Bernstein

WHEN THE CHINESE COMMUNISTS CAME to power in 1949, they were determined to learn from the Soviet Union. As Mao Zedong put it:

> the Communist Party of the Soviet Union, under the leadership of Lenin and Stalin . . . learned not only how to make the revolution but also how to carry on construction. It has built a great and splendid socialist state. The [CPSU] is our best teacher and we must learn from it.[1]

Four years later, he made the same point even more emphatically:

> In front of us lie very difficult tasks and we do not have enough experience. Therefore, we must seriously study the advanced experiences of the Soviet Union. Whether within or without the Communist Party, whether old or new cadres, technicians, intellectuals, worker or peasant masses, all must learn sincerely from the Soviet Union. We must . . . study . . . the advanced science and technology of the Soviet Union. In order to build up our great country, we must launch a nationwide upsurge of studying the Soviet Union.[2]

Between 1949 and 1956, China intensively emulated Soviet experiences and practices in a wide variety of fields, often, but not always quite uncritically. Especially in the first few years, Chinese leaders personally asked for instructions and advice on political and developmental issues. One indicator of Soviet influence is that roughly ten thousand advisors served in China, mainly from 1953 to 1957, quite a few remaining until Khrushchev abruptly pulled them out in 1960. They served in a large variety of capacities. In the first quarter of

1954, 403 specialists served in twenty-eight ministerial-level units. The largest group of 127 was in the Ministry of Education followed by 49 in the Ministry of Fuel Industry and 45 in the Ministry of Heavy Industry.[3]

In 1956, however, Mao Zedong struck a rather different tone about learning from the Soviets and the Eastern Europeans:

> we mustn't copy everything indiscriminately and transplant mechanically. Naturally, we mustn't pick up their shortcomings and weak points. . . . Some of our people were not clear about this and even picked up their weaknesses. While they were swelling with pride over what they had picked up, it was already being discarded in those countries; as a result they had to do a somersault like the Monkey [King], Sun Wu-kung.[4]

And during the Great Leap Forward, China became even more critical as it struck out on its own in a search for a more suitable developmental and ideological model. As noted below, however, the new approaches continued to be significantly influenced by core aspects of the Stalinist experience. In the 1960s, the Soviet Union was treated largely as "negative" teaching material (*fanmian jiaocai*), as indicated by anti-Soviet polemics such as "On Khrushchev's Phony Communism and its Historical Lessons for the World," published in 1964 and probably authored by Mao.[5] It contained detailed prescriptions for China on how to avoid falling into the Soviet revisionist abyss. This negative view persisted until the Chairman's death in 1976.

During the late 1970s and 1980s, Chinese interest in Soviet experience revived. When Mikhail Gorbachev began his efforts to revitalize Soviet socialism, Chinese analysts once again examined what appeared as positive aspects of Soviet policies and which seemed to converge with those underway in China (see Gilbert Rozman's chapter). But as Gorbachev's *glasnost'* (openness) and *perestroika* (restructuring) increasingly undermined the CPSU's monopoly of power, Chinese observers became alarmed. After the collapse and disintegration of the Soviet Union in 1991, a veritable cottage industry arose as Chinese Soviet specialists were mobilized to provide explanations for this catastrophic outcome and of its implications for China. Once more, the Soviet Union became a teacher by negative example (see chapters by Rozman, Zhou Minglang, and Guan Guihai).[6]

These remarkable ups and downs in the Chinese view of the value of Soviet experience reflected the relevance of the Soviet Union to China's own course. As Gilbert Rozman puts it,

> Discussions of the Soviet Union are of such importance because China's communist leaders have continuously measured their country against the yardstick

of their neighbor to the north; their worldview has been intimately related to their view of Soviet socialism . . .[7]

This book seeks to shed additional light on the history of China's adoption, adaptation, and rejection of the Soviet model. Over time, a significant literature has appeared on the topic.[8] But a new look at the issue is warranted because of the large increase in documentation that became to available from the early 1990s to the present, and which earlier studies were not able to use. Following the Soviet collapse, Russian, Chinese, and western scholars gained varying degrees of access to Soviet archives. Within China, a large academic literature has appeared on Sino-Soviet relations, based also on varying degrees of access to Chinese primary sources.[9]

As the table of contents of the book indicates, the authors, who come from the People's Republic of China, the United States, Europe, Australia, and Taiwan contribute case studies on the role of the Soviet model in the political, economic, social and cultural spheres. The book aims to provide a picture of the range, diversity, and complexity of Soviet influences. Two examples illustrate the point: Professor Zang Jian's chapter on Chinese women emphasizes an important source of attractiveness of the Soviet model to women, namely that women should work outside the home, an ideal that in the reform period was significantly attenuated, contributing to nostalgia for the 1950s. In contrast to this welcome feature of the Soviet model, Soviet efforts to export Trofim Lysenko's dogmas in biology and genetics ran into resistance from western-trained scientists and were largely abandoned already in 1956 (see Lawrence Schneider's chapter).

Influences on Chinese Choices of the Soviet Model

Sino-Soviet Relations

The evolution of Sino-Soviet relations strongly influenced Chinese attitudes toward the Soviet model. Hence, we include several chapters on Sino-Soviet relations—chapter 1, by Lorenz Luthi on the relationship from 1949 to 1969; a case study by Zhang Shengfa on the importance of the return to China in 1952 of the jointly owned and managed Chinese Eastern Railway for increasing China's trust in Stalin, and Péter Vámos on the rapprochement in the 1980s.[10] When relations were generally good as in the first half of the 1950s, Chinese were strongly in favor of learning from Soviet "advanced experiences." Relations cooled somewhat from 1956 on, and in 1958 deteriorated sharply as Mao concluded that Nikita Khrushchev was seeking to control China (see You Ji's chapter). The work of Soviet advisors in China was terminated in mid-1960, and a long period of adversary relations ensued. The gradual warming of Sino-Soviet relations in the 1980s, culminating in Gorbachev's visit to China in May 1989, was also, as noted, accompanied by renewed interest in the changing Soviet domestic scene.

Influence of Legacies

Chinese borrowing from foreigners did not of course start with the Soviet Union in 1949, but began in the last third of the 19th century, when the famous formula, "Chinese learning as the essence; foreign learning for use" prevailed (*zhongxue wei ti, waixue wei yong*). Efforts to confine foreign models to technology, especially military, lasted until China's disastrous defeat by Japan in 1895. After the anti-western Boxer uprising in 1900 and the victorious intervention by eight foreign powers, China seriously began to import political, legal, social, and cultural institutions from France, Japan, Germany, and the United States, and from 1949 on, from the Soviet Union.

With regard to the People's Republic's progression from acceptance to rejection of the Soviet model, Suzanne Pepper finds a direct link to the past, particularly in education:

> Certain key features that had marked the initial experience of learning from the outside world during the early decades of the century now reappeared: a sudden enthusiastic rush to learn the secrets of the foreigners' success, mechanical copying, followed by a backlash against the ensuing dislocations and unseemly desire to emulate foreigners in so uncritical a manner.[11]

It should be noted that some of the Chinese contributors distinguish sharply between imported models adopted under military pressure, characteristic of the Eastern European states, and the voluntary, selective adoption of learning from the Soviet Union in China. Izabella Goikhman's chapter also argues that the Chinese side safeguarded its autonomy after 1949 in educational matters.

A second set of legacies arose from the road to power of the Chinese Communist Party, 1921–1949. Shortly after the Bolshevik Revolution, Chinese intellectuals, disillusioned by the West, turned to Marxism and found inspiration and guidance in the successes of the Bolshevik revolution and in Soviet Russia's anti-imperialist stance. Transmitted via the Communist International or Comintern (1919–1943), the organization of worldwide communist parties led by Moscow, the young CCP, founded in 1921, readily adopted Leninist organizational structures and behavioral models.

As a member of the Comintern, the CCP was subordinate to Moscow and obliged to follow its directives. This was problematic since Stalin viewed the international communist movement through the prism of Soviet national interests. Orders by Stalin and the Comintern in 1927 led to the virtual destruction of the CCP.[12] In the early 1930s, bitter disputes arose between Mao Zedong's faction and that of the leftist "Soviet returned students." This was one of a series of struggles with Moscow-trained communists that Mao eventually won during the Yan'an period (1935–45). His victory enhanced Mao's independence from Soviet tutelage. He did so on a platform that signified pursuit of an independent road to power via the "Sinification" of Marxism-Leninism and the development of an indigenously appropriate rural base area strategy. Ironically, Mao legitimated this stance by referring to the Stalin era's canonical work, *The History of the All-Union Communist Party (Bolshevik)— Short Course*, which emphasized Lenin's own innovation in adapting Marxism to Russia (see below for more on the *Short Course*).

Mao's independence was shown in 1941 and 1942, when he repeatedly turned down Stalin's urgent requests for the CCP to engage Japanese forces directly, at a time when the Soviet Union was on the brink of defeat by Nazi Germany, but also at a time when Mao felt that complying would put CCP's survival in jeopardy.[13] For his part, Stalin put his bets on the Nationalist government, signing a treaty with it in 1945 that was bitterly resented by the Chinese Communists. Stalin also advised the Chinese to make peace with the Nationalists, once in 1945 and more controversially, in l949 when he warned them not to cross the Yangzi lest the United States intervenes in the Chinese Civil War.[14]

Both parties put this legacy of distrust aside when they decided to put Sino-Soviet relations on a new footing in 1949–50. As Zhang Shengfa notes in his chapter, Stalin's overriding interest in an alliance that would vastly expand the socialist camp in the context of bipolarity overrode his reservations. Mao, of course, needed an ally against the United States.

Against this background of the CCP's largely independent rise to power and the merger of Marxist-Leninist ideology with Chinese nationalism, the first stage of the relationship in the first half of the 1950s is remarkable for the explicitly subordinate status vis-à-vis Stalin and the Soviet model that Chinese leaders seemed to accept. In Chinese culture, a relationship defined as this one between the Soviet elder brother (*laodage*) and of China as the younger brother implied an obligation on the part of the younger to accept the authority of the older, but also an obligation of the older brother to nurture and protect the younger. This stance did make sense as long Joseph Stalin, the acknowledged and legitimate leader of the world communist movement, was still alive. But the deference due him naturally disappeared after the dictator's death in 1953 and helps account for Mao's increasing assertiveness in the years to come.

Memories of the past did not of course disappear during China's "elder brother" phase. When relations turned sour, the Chinese felt free to bring up grievances about the past. At the Chengdu Conference in early 1958, for example, Mao recalled that Stalin had favored the leftists in the early 1930s, and more recently, trusted Mao Zedong as a real communist only after China entered the Korean War.[15]

One Model or Several?

At a high level of generality, China accepted the entire Stalinist model of socialist construction, including the basic components of a socialist state such as state ownership and central planning. This included the necessity of terminating private ownership of the means of production and hence of class struggle against the urban bourgeoisie and against rich peasants in the villages. The necessity for the collectivization of agriculture based on the assumption that large units farmed in common were inherently superior to family farming was also accepted, as was an industrialization program that gave absolute priority to heavy and defense industry and that relied to a large extent on the extraction from agriculture of a surplus for urban-industrial investments.

The existence of a successful Soviet (Stalinist) model of socialist development, one that had proven itself in practice, was a major source of inspiration, confidence, and certainty as to the correctness of the Soviet course and its outcome, as many analysts have noted.[16] The popular slogan, "The Soviet Union of today is our tomorrow" (*Sulian de jintian shi women de mingtian*) signified this optimistic attitude.

As Kong Hanbing puts it in his chapter, "The Chinese equated the sacred cause of socialism with the Soviet Stalinist Model, believing that it represented the material embodiment of Marxism and the truth of socialism." In order to inculcate the correct strategy of Soviet-style socialist construction, China's cadres and intellectuals were mobilized to study The *Short Course* of the history of Soviet Communism, a distillation of the Soviet experience written at Stalin's behest and with his participation.[17] The work was designed to glorify the great man as Lenin's only worthy successor. The *Short Course* was published in 1938 and shortly thereafter translated into Chinese. The work was studied already during the 1942–44 Rectification Campaign. Mao Zedong considered the book to be an "encyclopedia of Marxism and Leninism," an authoritative source and a model of integration of theory and practice. It conveyed the Soviet emphasis on class struggle and showed how the Soviets had succeeded in their tasks of industrialization and collectivization. As shown in Hua-yu Li's chapter, the *Short Course* played a major role in orienting the country's elite to the concepts and methods that came to be known in late 1953 as the "General Line of the Transition to Socialism."

The unquestioning acceptance of the Soviet model at this general level during the first half of the 1950s did not, however, free Chinese leaders from having to make judgments about how it should be applied in practice, simply because Chinese conditions differed in key respects. For instance, since China lacked the capacity to mechanize agriculture until industrialization had made a great deal of progress, China had to decide whether to defer the collectivization of agriculture. This, as noted below, caused disputes among the leaders but was resolved by Mao Zedong in favor of plunging ahead. Interestingly, as Hua-yu Li shows in her excellent study, *Mao and the Economic Stalinization of China, 1948–1953*, plunging ahead was very much contrary to the advice that Stalin conveyed to Chinese leaders from 1949 on. He recommended a cautious, gradual course that would maintain a mixed economy for a prolonged period preparatory to the socialist stage. As Li shows, Mao formally accepted this advice but actually circumvented it.[18] On other issues, Soviet advice coincided with Chinese preferences, as in the case of whether China should establish a unitary or a federal state, as the Soviet Union had done. Thus China explicitly diverged from this aspect of the "Soviet model" (see Zhou Minglang's chapter).

The preceding discussion points to the complexity of the Soviet model. Looked at more closely it is possible to distinguish three models, using the term loosely, which overlapped but were nonetheless distinct and that influenced Chinese choices (see Lorenz Luthi's chapter). One was a moderate strategy similar to the advice that Stalin gave to the Chinese from 1949 on. It was relevant especially to the initial stage of socialist construction but also emerged at later stages of China's development. A second one was "revolutionary Stalinism" as embodied in the Soviet "socialist offensive" of 1929–1934. And a third was "bureaucratic and middle class Stalinism," approaches that emerged in the late Stalinist period, and which were in profound conflict with the Maoist effort to maintain and foster revolutionary values in the Great Leap Forward and the Cultural Revolution.

The Soviet moderate model drew its inspiration from one of Lenin's last articles, "On Cooperation," published in early 1923 during the first years of the Soviet New Economic Policy (NEP), 1921–27 adopted after the Civil War and the radical practices of "War Communism."[19] Lenin focused on the most problematic social group in the Soviet Union, the peasantry. He argued that the socialist transformation of the peasantry would require several decades. During these years the peasantry should be drawn into the orbit of the socialist urban-industrial sector by means of marketing, consumer, and credit cooperatives. Together with a rural cultural revolution that would eliminate illiteracy, peasants would gradually become accustomed to socialist ways, paving the way toward eventual collectivization.

During the Soviet industrialization debates and power struggles of the mid-1920s, Nikolai Bukharin elaborated on Lenin's ideas, emphasizing the need for conciliating the peasants rather than waging class struggle in the countryside, and taking an interdependent, mutually reinforcing approach to agricultural and industrial development so as to maintain peasant incentives. Bukharin was shot as an enemy of the people in 1938 and could not be mentioned by name, but his approach was known to some Chinese leaders (see Hou Xiaojia's chapter), and because Stalin had publicly sided with him until 1927.[20] The moderate approach thus emphasized markets, incentives, and a mixed economy. Beginning in the later 1920s, Stalin reinterpreted Lenin's article as calling for the establishment of producers' collectives, that is, collective farms.

Revolutionary Stalinism was a stage that started in 1929 during which the Soviets launched all-out campaigns to collectivize agriculture and eliminate the so-called kulaks or rich peasants as part of the forcible seizure of presumed peasant surpluses and to industrialize and urbanize at breakneck speed. An additional component of these campaigns was a "cultural revolution," which aimed at literacy and technical training, but which also had anti-authoritarian themes somewhat similar to the Chinese Cultural Revolution.[21] The process of mobilizing the country generated enormous dynamism and a sense of forward momentum that inspired many young urbanites. The cost in human life and suffering, especially in the countryside, was prodigious but the country did rapidly industrialize. It should not be surprising that Mao Zedong was attracted to the core values of "Revolutionary Stalinism."

The third approach, "bureaucratic and middle-class Stalinism," reflected a turn toward stability. Under the aegis of central planning and centralized management of the economy, large bureaucracies emerged, which relied heavily on rules, routines, regulations, and material incentives. Technological elitism was greatly valued and a high degree of inequality arose. Western scholars saw a loss of revolutionary momentum and signs of petrification.[22] Vera Dunham's superb study, *In Stalin's Time: Middle Class Values in Soviet Fiction*, demonstrates the emergence of an acquisitive class that constituted an important prop of the regime.[23]

The Soviet specialists who came to China in the early 1950s were to varying degrees the product of the bureaucratic mentality. A telling example of this was the attitude of Soviet police specialists toward the 1951 Campaign to Suppress Counterrevolution, which relied on mass mobilization rather than on Stalinist "stability, formality, and professionalism." A campaign program that entailed ongoing and intense populist politicization worried Soviet advisors "who had not seen such actions since the days of their own first five-year plan," that is, the days of revolutionary Stalinism. In this case, reportedly, the Soviet advisors became convinced of the merits of the Chinese approach.[24] It is not surprising that later, during the Great Leap Forward, Mao directed his ire at bureaucratic Stalinism. All three approaches were the subject of political disputes and manipulation in China.[25]

The Soviet Model and Socialist Transformation

In the very early 1950s, the PRC defined itself as a "New Democracy" consisting of a mixed economy, in which the major industries were already state-owned but coexisted with a sizeable sector of private manufacturing and trading enterprises, as well as a private handicrafts industry. Agriculture, once landlords had been violently dispossessed, was dominated by the individual, private-property owning small-holder peasantry. CCP leaders agreed that in due course, private property in the means of production would be abolished. The question was how long the stage of New Democracy should last.

Chinese leaders looked at the Soviet NEP, which in key respects resembled New Democracy. In the summer of 1950, Mao Zedong, in line with Lenin's ideas, claimed that full socialist transformation should occur in the distant future. At a June meeting of the Chinese People's Political Consultative Conference (CPPCC), Mao stated that New Democracy would take a long time during which conditions for socialist transition would gradually mature. He told anxious businessmen that it would take twenty to thirty years. Actually, intra-party discussions had already shortened this estimate to ten, fifteen or twenty years.[26] And within a year, Mao started to short-circuit this long-term perspective.

Other leaders, however, such as Liu Shaoqi, continued to adhere to NEP-type policies and to Stalin's moderate advice. As Bo Yibo reports in his *Recollections*, Liu believed that the order of priority of the three branches of the economy should be agriculture first; with light and heavy industry coming in second and third, which resembled Bukharin's project. Liu also believed that agriculture could not be collectivized before industry could supply machinery. Instead, Liu advocated the promotion of supply and marketing cooperatives, also very much in line with the Lenin-Bukharin project. This approach had long been advocated by Zhang Wentian, a former "returned student," a Politburo member and Heilongjiang Party secretary (see Hou Xiaojia's chapter). Liu thus wanted to encourage the individual economy, including rich peasants, in order to maintain the incentives necessary for agricultural growth, until the conditions for a rapid future transition to socialism had been created.[27]

At the same time in 1950–51 that these NEP-type ideas were being discussed, the establishment of small mutual aid teams was promoted, which were based on private property but used draft animals and large tools in common. When in 1951 party leaders in Shanxi province sought to go further by elevating small teams to the level of larger, "semi-socialist producers' coops" with a higher level of socialized property, Liu condemned these efforts as "utopian agrarian socialism," since there was no corresponding change in the productive forces. The authors of a two-volume Chinese biography of Mao Zedong published in 2003 comment that "Liu Shaoqi's opinion had a certain representativeness within the Party."[28]

Stalin himself continued to prefer the moderate course. In the fall of 1952, he told a delegation to the 19th Congress of the CPSU led by Liu Shaoqi that "Your ideas are correct. After we seized political power, the transition to socialism should have been done with a step-by-step approach (*yinggai caiqu zhubu de banfa*). Your attitude toward China's capitalists is correct."[29]

Mao Zedong, however, as Hou Xiaojia shows in her chapter, had long come to believe in the potential of even small rural collectives to serve as the bridge to fully socialist agriculture. He also claimed that an organizational change could by itself increase output and that therefore China could move toward collectivization before agriculture could be mechanized. Mao criticized Liu, together with Bo Yibo and others, and in the end Mao reportedly convinced them. "Under the prevailing conditions and since there was a lack of experience, such disputes over differing opinions were normal."[30] From them on, Mao pressed vigorously for the implementation of "Mutual-Aid and Cooperation," intensively pressuring his subordinates from 1952 on.

Mao believed that the rural situation after land reform was sufficiently fluid so that it was possible "to strike while the iron is hot." Most likely he was also influenced by the society-wide radicalization that began in late 1950 after China's entry into the Korea War, and continued to 1952.[31] This included the bloody Campaign to Suppress Counterrevolution, and urban campaigns that aimed at bringing the bourgeoisie under full control and "reeducate" those who still held pro-U.S. or pro-Nationalist views, especially intellectuals. In this atmosphere of intolerance, policies that called for preserving the rich peasants, that is, class enemies, could not thrive.

In this context, Mao repudiated the Soviet moderate model. In February 1953, Mao remarked to provincial officials that Soviet methods shouldn't necessarily be imitated (*fangzhao*). Contrary to Stalin's advice to retain the rich peasant economy lest production be harmed, he said, China was instead relying on mutual-aid and cooperation to increase output.[32] Mao's biographers claim that in this way, Mao "broke through the Soviet model," charting a new road to the transformation of agriculture.[33]

How long the transition to socialism should take was also in dispute and subject to manipulation. Mao, for instance, formally accepted the time period required for socialist transformation in the *Short Course* as that is largely valid for China. The *Short Course* claimed that by the end of 1925, that, four years after the onset of the NEP, the Soviet Union, having recovered from its civil war, began to industrialize already in 1926. It attained a "decisive victory" in 1933, so that eight years were required for the transition.[34]

Mao publicly accepted such long time periods, which conveyed an impression of caution. Moreover, at times he agreed to slowdowns in the pace of cooperativization, only to change his mind later and to blame subordinates for rightism.[35] Even in July 1955, when he predicted that a great upsurge in agricultural transformation was about to commence, he noted that agricultural collectivization in the SU had taken seventeen years from 1921 to 1937 and that China's would also take that long, that is, until 1967, to complete the process.[36] Yet, by unleashing China's mobilizational assets in the "High Tide" of socialist transformation in 1955–56 China completed collectivization by the end of 1956, together with the equally unexpectedly rapid socialization of private business and handicrafts.

Bo Yibo's Recollections written during the reform period contained this regretful assessment:

> . . . we only used the time frame of the Soviet Union for carrying out socialist transformation from 1924 on. But if we had paid attention to what Lenin said about the New Economic Policy, and if we had done a political and economical calculus, perhaps we might have maintained a more sober outlook and the entry into the transition and the procedural arrangements might have been done somewhat more carefully and stably.[37]

Chinese leaders, including Mao, were aware of the costs of excessive speed, since the *Short Course* had reported on the disastrous "leftist" mistakes that Stalin labeled "Dizzy with Success" during the all-out collectivization drive in early 1930. On the eve of the "High Tide," Mao noted that during Soviet collectivization production had gone down, peasants had slaughtered livestock, and Soviet agriculture down to the present had not reached pre-revolutionary levels.[38] But Mao insisted that "what we should not do is to allow some comrades to cover up their dilatoriness by quoting the experience of the Soviet Union." Yes, he said, there were lessons for China in the losses of Soviet collectivization, namely that the Chinese must make great efforts to secure increased output and should not allow livestock to be slaughtered. "Our cooperatives must be better than those of the Soviets." Alas, Mao's hopes were not realized.[39]

The Soviet Model and Heavy Industrialization

The Chinese Communists inherited legacies from the state industrialization plans and programs of the Nationalist Government. Several vice-chairmen of the National Resources Commission, a planning agency, later served in the Communist State Council planning apparatus. Thus, as William Kirby has pointed out, China was not totally dependent on the Soviet Union.[40] But overall, the Soviet model of industrialization and Soviet assistance were extremely important to China, since much had to be learned about centralized economic planning, management of large-scale enterprises, together with the acquisition of technical knowledge and skills. In this sphere, as Kong Hanbing's chapter makes clear, China transplanted the industrial model in its entirety. Kong provides a detailed description of the activities of a Chinese delegation of top-level industrial and planning officials, which, initially led by Zhou Enlai, spent almost eight months, from August 1952 to May 1953, in the SU. Their goal was to learn how the Soviets drew up the various components of a five-year plan. Its members listened to authoritative lectures, which then became embodied in successive drafts of the Chinese first five-year plan. And they visited Soviet enterprises to learn the specifics of the operations of large-scale industrial undertakings. Their activities were of vital importance because the core of the Chinese industrialization program of the First Five-Year Plan relied on Soviet assistance, including the delivery of an estimated 156 plants.

Kong Hanbing observes that as each major project came to fruition, the Soviet role in China's initial industrialization "made a deep impression on Chinese people." It validated their faith in socialism. A U.S. analyst, writing in 1975, appraised Soviet technical assistance in these glowing terms:

> In the 1950s . . . China eagerly accepted . . . the most comprehensive technology transfer in modern history. . . . The Chinese obtained from the Soviet Union the foundation of a modern industrial system . . . This was invaluable to China's subsequent development. It would have taken the Chinese decades to evolve such a comprehensive industrial system on its own.[41]

Bureaucratic and Middle Class Stalinism

During the first half of the 1950s, bureaucratic Stalinism together with middle class life styles made them felt in Soviet educational and cultural exports to China. These themes are present in a number of chapters in this volume. Douglas Stiffler emphasizes the degree to which the rigid approach characteristic of Soviet higher education dominated Chinese People's University, especially in the first three years, although there was more give and take in the later years. Likewise, Lawrence Schneider's chapter on Lysenkoism illustrates the export to China of a rigid dogma but one that encountered resistance within China. At the same time, Izabella Goikhman's chapter suggests that even during the years of intense emulation of the Soviet model in education, the Chinese always kept their goal of achieving self-reliance in view. You Ji's chapter on the military strikingly illustrates the contrast between the "fine traditions" cultivated in the PLA during the pre-1949 period and the formalistic, rule-bound training manuals and practices introduced by Soviet advisors in the military academies in the first half of the 1950s. Similarly, Greg Rohlf's chapter on China's state farms emphasizes the complex bureaucratic procedures that were required to set up state farms along Soviet lines.

With regard to material incentives, which, as is well known, were downgraded or even eliminated during the Great Leap and later as well, it is noteworthy that a Chinese delegation which included rural labor heroes visited Soviet model collective farms in 1952 and found a strong bias against egalitarianism (see Hou Xiaojia's chapter). An article published in the People's Daily in 1952 about their visit was titled: "The Incompatibility of Socialism and Egalitarianism."[42] The Chinese visitors returned with reports of a highly differentiated reward system on the mechanized farms and the good life of Soviet collective farmers, which included ownership of modern personal property and ample private plots. The theme of material incentives also appears vividly in Mingling Yu's chapter on the import to China of the Soviet model of Stakhanovite labor heroes, who were also lavishly rewarded for their deeds.

While China was in the throes of revolutionary Stalinism, Soviet mentalities had absorbed the middle-class themes of late Stalinism. This dissonance between revolutionary stages is strikingly displayed in Elizabeth McGuire's chapter on Chinese students in the Soviet Union. While Khrushchev sought to revitalize the revolutionary spirit by such campaigns as the Virgin Lands beginning in 1954, the fundamental ethos of the Soviet students clashed with that of their Chinese counterparts:

> Once, a Chinese student asked a Russian friend why the Soviet students didn't do more political study, and the friend replied that as far as he knew, the USSR had gone through a similarly intense period just after the Russian Revolution but then had relaxed, and that the same thing would happen eventually in China. The Chinese student took offense, but years later came to believe his Russian friend had been right.

The chapters by Zang Jian on women and by Tina Chen on Soviet films further illustrate the export of middle class values in the 1950s. Zang's chapter highlights the attractiveness of Soviet fashions and Chen's the attractiveness of Soviet film stars. To be sure, Soviet films were mainly epics about the

Revolution or World War II, but even here, the stereotype of socialist heroes unmotivated by personal concerns is qualified. At the same time, He Dong-hui's chapter conveys a sense of the enormous impact on young people of the quintessential Soviet novel of socialist realism, *How the Steel Was Tempered*, in which the hero renounces bourgeois love for revolutionary commitment. The general image of the Soviet Union as a well-off and successful state, on the other hand, also showed the young that emulating the Soviet Union did not just entail sacrifice.

When China turned left during the Great Leap Forward, revolutionary purity came to the fore and values that were part of the late Stalinist message could no longer be heard. Neither could the Khrushchev era's relatively more liberal and humanistic films, which violated the black and white canons of China's official morality.

Toward Repudiation of the Soviet Model

Beginning in 1956, a more critical attitude emerged toward learning from the Soviet Union in terms of both the forms it had taken and the substance. In his January 1956 "Report on the Question of Intellectuals" Zhou Enlai complained of a "dependent mentality" (*yilai sixiang*) with regard to the Soviets. He criticized "blind emulation, undue haste, mechanical application, and arbitrary rejection by "some comrades" of the achievements of the capitalist countries in science and technique. These defects should henceforth be avoided." Zhou added that henceforth Soviet specialists should only be engaged in the most advanced fields and that China could not indefinitely rely on Soviet experts.[43]

Khrushchev historic indictment of Stalin's "cult of the personality" and of his crimes against the Party at the 20th Congress the CPSU induced a more skeptical attitude among Chinese toward the Soviets. Khrushchev undertook this momentous step for domestic political reasons, failing to consult with the fraternal parties or to consider the impact of his denunciation of Stalin on them.[44] The attack on the "cult" in essence removed a pillar from the Soviet political system and hence from the Soviet political model, which could not but affect China's politics, since Mao had fostered his own cult and thus felt personally challenged. In response, a People's Daily editorial praised Stalin as a "great Marxist-Leninist" but one who made serious errors. This watershed episode caused Chinese to distrust Khrushchev's judgment and impaired their confidence in the Soviet model.[45]

Mao's "On the Ten Great Relationships" (April 1956) not only repudiated uncritical acceptance of Soviet advice, but also called into question the Stalinist policy of assigning absolute priority to heavy industry. Mao suggested that heavy industry should continue to occupy pride of place but that more investments should go to light industry and agriculture. He criticized the SU for squeezing the peasants too hard, hence hurting incentives. "You want the hen to lay more eggs and yet you don't feed it . . . what kind of logic is that?" China should learn a lesson from the "grave mistakes" made by the Soviet Union in agriculture.[46]

Other leaders, notably Chen Yun, also argued for more balanced development between the three economic sectors and for stimulating the growth of an agricultural surplus by offering greater incentives to peasants, for example, reopening markets and producing more light industrial goods. All this seemed to augur in a policy of moderation, the spirit of which bore some resemblance to the NEP and Bukharin's preferences. Had these policies been pursued, China would have significantly moved away from the Stalinist model. Instead, Mao pushed his country into the extremes of the Great Leap Forward.

The Soviet Model during the GLF and the Cultural Revolution

The Great Leap Forward (GLF) is widely seen as signifying abandonment of the Soviet model by the Chinese and its replacement by a new, Maoist model. This is not incorrect but if we recall the distinction between revolutionary and bureaucratic Stalinism, it becomes clear that Mao repudiated the latter but not the former.

The GLF consisted of nationwide mobilization of society to break through all obstacles on the industrial and agricultural fronts. Utopian visions of "three years of hardship and a hundred years of happiness" sought to fire up the masses, accompanied by class struggle against recalcitrant, conservative forces. For a time, the new people's communes seemed to augur a quick rural transition from collective to state ownership and even entry into communism ahead of the Soviet Union.[47]

Some of these GLF themes owed a debt to revolutionary Stalinism and even to the extreme radicalism of "War Communism" in 1918–1920. Beginning in 1929, enormous mobilizational enthusiasm was aroused, especially among workers and young people sent to tackle the gigantic tasks of breaking through to socialism. A spirit of instant progress and of utmost tempo was boosted by such slogans as "there is no fortress that Bolsheviks cannot conquer." Goals and the objective limits of what could be achieved often collided, as in China during the GLF.[48] In agriculture, some communes were set up not only during War Communism but also in the early stages of collectivization, while many ordinary collective farms initially practiced a level of egalitarianism that was quite similar to those of the Chinese communes. And the theme of class struggle against societal enemies was pervasive.

At the same time, the GLF differed in important respects from "revolutionary Stalinism." Mao Zedong took utopian goals much more seriously than Stalin, who in 1931 coldly rejected egalitarianism as a petty bourgeois deviation.[49] The ideologies of the GLF and later of the Cultural Revolution sought to downgrade differentiated material incentives and to overcome bourgeois or capitalist mindsets through constant political struggle. Contrary to the argument put forth in Richard Lowenthal's famous book chapter, "Development vs. Utopia in Communist Policy," Stalin pragmatically abandoned efforts to incorporate communist practice into current policy of building socialism whereas Mao did not.[50]

In his lengthy comments on a *Soviet Textbook of Political Economy* and on Stalin's 1952 booklet, *Economic Problems of Socialism in the U.S.S.R.*, penned during the GLF, Mao criticized Stalin's preoccupation with the economy at the expense of political motivation. Stalin, Mao charged, was not interested in raising consciousness, in cultivating the "new man," in practicing the mass line, or in spontaneous mass participation. Instead he put his faith in elites, technology, and material incentives rather than in spiritual transformation. Stalin failed to realize that even worker-peasant intellectuals might succumb to bourgeois influences and that remolding of intellectuals is a long-term, core task.[51] In contrast, Chinese cadres were taking part in labor and were being "sent down" for tempering. Workers participated in management. Stalin distrusted peasants, not allowing them to own machinery.

Mao thus formed an opinion of late-Stalinism as a stultifying bureaucratic strait-jacket and as lacking a spirit of forward movement, which he labeled "dogmatism," and which he claimed was present in the Chinese economy, the cultural arena, and in education:

> In economic work dogmatism primarily manifested itself in heavy industry, planning, banking and statistics, especially in heavy industry and planning. . . . The socialist revolution and the cooperativization of agriculture were not influenced by dogmatism because the Centre [Mao] had a direct grasp of them.[52]

Dogmatism consisted not just of following Soviet prescriptions—Mao railed against Soviet doctors who wouldn't let him eat eggs and chicken soup—but of fundamental misconceptions of how change should occur. Mao charged that Stalin failed to understand the dynamics of change: balance is relative, imbalance is absolute. Contradictions and struggle are absolutes and always exist. The *Textbook* opposed crash programs and demanded adherence to predetermined schedules: "This utter repudiation of crash programs and accelerated work is too absolute."[53]

At the same time, China, despite Mao's critical comment in the "Ten Great Relationships," retained major features of the Stalinist system as whole, whether revolutionary or bureaucratic. This was the case with regard to maintaining absolute priority for heavy industry, which, during the Leap, received the largest share ever of investment funds.[54] During the Leap, moreover, agriculture was more harshly exploited than at any time before or since, the prime cause of a ghastly famine. During a period of GLF retrenchment in early 1959, Mao remarked: "We should make a comparison between Stalin's policies and our own. Stalin had too much enthusiasm. With the peasants, he drained the pond to catch the fish. Right now we have exactly the same illness."[55] In fact extraction from the countryside reached a peak in 1959–60.[56] But it should be noted that GLF industrial strategy also differed from Soviet patterns, especially in the policy of building large, medium, and small enterprises controlled by various levels of the hierarchy and by industrializing the countryside. This approach failed in the short run but bore fruit in later years, especially the reform era.

Professor Kong Hanbing concludes that Mao, if anything, intensified the application of the Stalinist model. Even during the Cultural Revolution, he argues, a distorted form of Stalinist economics was practiced. Despite all the changes of the late Mao era, in essence, structurally, China retained its Stalinist-type economic system.

In the context of Mao's efforts to revitalize the revolution, it is noteworthy that Nikita Khrushchev was also concerned with reinvigorating Soviet socialism in the middle and late 1950s. Some of his experiments had strong "Chinese" overtones, such as his Virgin Lands campaign (see Elizabeth McGuire's chapter) and the decentralization of the economy in the form of the regional economic councils. In education, Khrushchev complained from 1956 on that Soviet schools were divorced from life and that there was a need to combat the elitism inherent in fulltime academic education. Hence, in 1958, Khrushchev proposed introduction of a labor requirement between graduation from secondary school and entry into higher schools at the very same time that the principle of combining labor with education was also being introduced in China. Chinese educators were aware of Soviet thinking in the realm of education.[57] The Soviet leader also called for increased mass participation, as in promotion of "comrades' courts" and citizens' militias, which were seen as tangible steps toward the withering away of the state, in which state functions would gradually be turned over to public bodies in the transition to communism. All these innovations, however, were eventually abandoned.

For Mao, what counted was not Khrushchev's effort to revitalize the revolution, but his revisionism, especially his "state of the whole people," which signified the abandonment of class struggle. Giving up on the dictatorship of the proletariat meant allowing a "privileged stratum" within the CPSU to engineer a capitalist restoration, which is what Mao claimed, was in fact happening in the 1960s in the SU. The 1964 pamphlet, "On Khrushchev's Phony Communism" contains fifteen theses that summarize Mao's ideas about socialism and strategies for the prevention of capitalist restoration, including requirements that cadres take part in labor and that wage differences should be narrowed to the extent possible.[58]

The Cultural Revolution (CR) is also widely regarded as the apotheosis of Chinese rejection of things Soviet. Yet, Andrew Walder's important book chapter, "Cultural Revolution Radicalism: Variations on a Stalinist Theme," demonstrates similarities between the CR and Stalin's terror of 1936–38. As in the Soviet Union, in China, "hidden enemies and traitors within Chinese intellectual circles and within the Party—right up to its highest reaches—were claimed to have conspired to overthrow Communist political power and restore capitalism," all the while, as in the Soviet Union, conspiring with foreign forces. Walder suggests that the theme of conspiracy "is borrowed directly . . . from the Stalinist political culture . . ." Stalin's thesis that class struggle would become fiercer the closer the SU comes to socialism found its echo in Mao's thesis "Never forget class struggle."

Walder recognizes the un-Stalinist way in which Mao's purges were implemented, namely by mobilizing the masses, calling on them to rebel against constituted authority. Moreover, what was new in Maoism was the assertion that a new bourgeoisie was forming within the Party and government, "something that Soviet Stalinists had not claimed in their own class-conspiracy theory." Still, Walder rightly concludes that "Even in their most radical departure from historical Stalinism, Maoists betrayed their Stalinist heritage."[59]

The Reform Period, 1978–

Early on, China's leaders jettisoned Mao's radical legacy but soon thereafter began to do away with much of their Soviet style economic system. During this period, some Chinese scholars started to examine their own experience with building socialism, voicing regret that New Democracy had been aborted prematurely. Su Shaozhi, until 1987 the head of the Marxism-Leninism Institute of the Chinese Academy of Social Science, argued for a reassessment of the NEP, Stalin's approach to industrialization, and his magnification of the class struggle. Su quoted Lenin on the long-term nature of socialist transition, which, he argued required even more time in China.[60] Such formulations presaged the thesis put forth at the 13th Party Congress by the then Party Secretary, Zhao Ziyang, that China was only in the primary stage of socialism. Realization that the aura of certitude surrounding the Stalinist model had foreclosed alternatives more in line with Chinese conditions was most clearly displayed in the dramatic return to family farming under the label of the "household responsibility system."

As Gilbert Rozman shows in his chapter, there was intense interest among Chinese observers as Gorbachev's political reforms got underway and as Soviet scholars and journalists examined China's reforms. The discourse in both came to be defined in terms of socialist reform, since both now once more recognized the other as socialist. Prospects of fruitful mutual learning loomed, especially as the process of normalization of Sino-Soviet relations matured (see chapter by Péter Vámos).[61] After the end of a short-lived campaign against bourgeois liberalization in the spring of 1987, Chinese scholars displayed strong interest in Soviet reforms in the realms of democratization, party-state relations, social justice, and legal reform. The suppression of the Tiananmen movement terminated such discussions, and as Gorbachev's reforms radicalized, Chinese analysts turned hostile.

The Soviet collapse gave rise to many years of intensive state-directed research in China. Specialist opinion, analyzed in fascinating detail by Guan Guihai, divided into two schools of thought. One primarily blamed the collapse on Gorbachev's voluntaristic willfulness, including his conversion to social democratic values. The other concluded that he made fatal mistakes but that these occurred during the process of tackling long-standing systemic problems in the Soviet system, problems that went back to the very nature of the Stalinist system. Many publications resulted from these inquiries. An eight-part DVD series was made in 2004, titled, "Be Vigilant in Peacetime: The Historical Lessons of the Death of the CPSU." This film was not publicly shown but was widely disseminated among the Chinese elite and reportedly deeply impressed many of them. It sided more with the voluntarist school.

The Soviet collapse had a direct impact on China's domestic political trajectory.[62] Most specifically, as demonstrated in the second half of Zhou Minglang's chapter, the key role that Soviet republics and nationalities played in the collapse prompted significant changes in China's nationality policies that were enacted into law in the late 1990s and in the early 21st century. These changes aimed at greater control of the kinds of centrifugal political forces that had undermined and destroyed the USSR. They were accompanied by socio-economic policies designed to win over restive minorities, including the Western Development Program.

More generally, the lessons of the collapse of the Soviet Union played a significant role in re-enforcing the longstanding current in Chinese policies, which opposed political liberalization, such as the freeing up of the media and of broadening public participation. This opposition began with Deng Xiaoping's promulgation of the "Four Principles" in 1979, following the suppression of the "Democracy Wall Movement," continued in short-lived campaigns against bourgeois liberalization in the 1980s culminating in the suppression of the Tiananmen demonstrations in 1989. The Soviet collapse solidified the determination of Chinese leaders not to risk potentially desta-bilizing moves to open up the political system and instead to confine political reforms to non-threatening realms.

Whether the CCP can succeed in staving off the rising pressures from a rapidly modernizing society for political liberalization is a crucial issue that is widely debated in the West. But as long as China does not liberalize politically, the lessons of the Soviet Union under Gorbachev will continue to influence China into the future. Put differently, the political system of China continues to exhibit strong structural and institutional similarities to that of the pre-Gorbachev Soviet Union.

Notes

1. "On the People's Democratic Dictatorship," *Selected Works of Mao Zedong*, vol. IV (Peking: Foreign Language Press, 1961), 423.

2. *Xinhua yuebao* [Xinhua monthly], no. 3, (1953): 13.

3. Deborah A. Kaple, "Soviet Advisers in China in the l950s," in Odd Arne Westad, ed., *Brothers in Arms: The Rise and Fall of the Sino-Soviet Alliance, 1945–1963* (Washington, DC: Woodrow Wilson Center Press, 1998), 117–40. A full-length study is by Shen Zhihua, *Sulian zhuanjia zai Zhongguo* [Soviet experts in China] (Beijing: Zhongguo guoji guangbo chubanshe, 2003).

4. "On the Ten Major Relationships," 25 April 1956, in *Selected Works of Mao Zedong* (Beijing: Foreign Languages Press, 1977), vol. 5, 303. "Somersault" was a reference to the dismissal of Trofim Lysenko from his major post. See Chapter 14 by Lawrence Schneider.

5. Reprinted in William E. Griffith, *Sino-Soviet Relations, 1964–65* (Cambridge: MIT Press, 1967), 314–50.

6. Lessons for China are analyzed carefully in David Shambaugh, *China's Communist Party: Atrophy and Adaptation* (Washington, DC: Woodrow Wilson Center Press, 2008).

7. Gilbert Rozman, *The Chinese Debate about Soviet Socialism, 1978–1985* (Princeton: Princeton University Press, 1987), 3.

8. See, for example, Lowell Dittmer, *Sino-Soviet Normalization and Its International Implications, 1945–1990* (Seattle: University of Washington Press, 1992), especially Part I; also, Frederick C. Teiwes, "The Establishment and Consolidation of the New Regime, l949–57," (hereinafter as The Establishment) in Roderick MacFarquhar, ed., *The Politics of China* (New York: Cambridge University Press, 1997), 15–18; and elsewhere; Suzanne Pepper, *Radicalism and Education Reform in 20th Century China* (hereinafter as *Radicalism and Education*) (New York: Cambridge University Press, 1996), Part II, "Learning from the Soviet Union."

9. See, for instance, Shen Zhihua, Mao Zedong, *Sidalin yu Chaoxian zhanzheng* [Mao Zedong, Stalin, and the Korean War] (Guangzhou: Guangdong renmin chubanshe, 2003).

10. The recent literature on Sino-Soviet relations and especially on the sub-periods is rapidly growing. For one example, see Chen Jian, *Mao's China and the Cold War* (Chapel Hill: University of North Carolina Press, 2001) and Elizabeth Wishnick, *Mending Fences: The Evolution of Moscow's China Policy from Brezhnev to Yeltsin* (Seattle: University of Washington Press, 2001).

11. Suzanne Pepper, *Radicalism and Education*, 158.

12. See Tony Saich, ed., *The Rise to Power of the Chinese Communist Party: Documents and Analysis* (Armonk, NY: M.E. Sharpe, 1996).

13. See Dieter Heinzig, *The Soviet Union and Communist China: The Arduous Road to the Alliance* (hereinafter as *The Soviet Union and Communist China*) (Armonk, NY: M. E. Sharpe, 2004), 33–37. Mao did promise that if Japan actually attacked the Soviet Union, the Communists would change their minds.

14. For analysis of various views on the 1949 episode, see Dieter Heinzig, *The Soviet Union and Communist China*, 171–74.

15. See "Talks at the Chengdu Conference," in Stuart Schram, ed., *Chairman Mao Talks to the People: Talks and Letters: 1956–71* (hereinafter as *Chairman Mao Talks to the People*) (New York: Pantheon Books, 1974), 102–3.

16. See Nina P. Halpern, "Creating Socialist Economies: Stalinist Political Economy and the Impact of Ideas," in Judith Goldstein and Robert O. Keohane, eds., *Ideas and Foreign Policy: Beliefs, Institutions and Political Change* (Ithaca: Cornell University Press, 1993), 87–110.

17. For the English language version, see Edited by a Commission of the Central Committee of the CPSU(B), (Moscow: Foreign Languages Publishing House, 1943).

18. See especially Chapter 2 (Lanham, MD: Rowman & Littlefield, 2006). Why Stalin recommended moderate policies to the Chinese is not very clear, all the more since in Eastern Europe, revolutionary Stalinism was being practiced with a vengeance between 1948 and l953.

19. See V. I. Lenin, *Alliance of the Working Class and the Peasantry* (Moscow: Foreign Languages Publishing House, 1959), 386–94.

20. For the definitive study, see Stephen F. Cohen, *Bukharin and the Bolshevik Revolution* (New York: Vintage Books, 1971).

21. See Sheila Fitzpatrick, ed., *Cultural Revolution in Russia, 1928–1931* (Bloomington: Indiana University Press, l978).

22. See, Jerry F. Hough and Merle Fainsod, *How the Soviet Union is Governed*, (Cambridge: Harvard Univrsity Press, 1979), 178 ff.

23. Vera Dunham, *In Stalin's Time: Middle Class Values in Soviet Fiction* (Durham, NC: Duke University Press), 1990.

24. Michael Dutton, *Policing Chinese Politics* (Durham, NC: Duke University Press, 2005), 163. For discussion of CCP resistance to the Soviet practice of independence of security organs from local party control Murray Scot Tanner and Eric Green, "Principals and Secret Agents: Central versus Local Control over Policing and Obstacles to the 'Rule of Law' in China," *China Quarterly*, no.191, September 2007: 651. See also

Robin Munro, *China's Psychiatric Inquisitions: Dissent, Psychiatry and the Law in Post-1949–China* (London: Wildly, Simmonds and Hill Publishing, 2006), for analysis of Soviet influence of the use of psychiatry to deal with political dissent.

25. Cf Dorothy J. Solinger, ed., *Three Visions of Chinese Socialism* (Boulder, CO: Westview Press, 1984) for analyses of market, radical, and bureaucratic models of governance.

26. Peng Xianzhi and Jin Chongji, eds., *Mao Zedong zhuan, 1949–1976* (shang) [Mao Zedong Biography, vol. 1] (hereinafter as *Mao zhuan 1*) (Beijing: Zhongyang wenxian chubanshe, 2003), 239–40, and Hu Sheng, ed., *Zhongguo Gongchandang de 70 nian* [70 Years of the CCP], (Beijing: Zhonggong dangshi chubanshe, 1991), 287.

27. Bo Yibo, *Ruogan zhongda juece yu shijian de huigu* [Recollections of certain major decisions and events] (herein after as Bo Yibo) (Beijing: Zhonggon dangxiao chubanshe, 1991), 59 ff. See also Hou Xiaojia's Chapter.

28. *Mao zhuan 1*, 346.

29. Bo Yibo, 221.

30. *Mao zhuan 1*, 347.

31. Cf Frederick C. Teiwes, "The Establishment," 37–40.

32. *Mao zhuan 1*, 247.

33. *Mao zhuan 1*, 246, 347.

34. Bo Yibo, 217. Bo reports another calculus: according to a Stalin speech given in November l936, socialist transformation in the Soviet Union began already in 1924.

35. See Frederick C. Teiwes and Warren Sun, *The Politics of Agricultural Cooperativization in China: Mao, Deng Zihui and the 'High Tide' of l955* (Armonk, NY: M. E. Sharpe, l993).

36. Mao Tse-tung, *On the Question of Agricultural Co-operation* (Beijing: Foreign Languages Press, l956), 33–34.

37. Bo Yibo, 218.

38. *Mao zhuan 1*, 383.

39. *Mao zhuan 1*, 383.

40. William C. Kirby, "Continuity and Change in Modern China: Economic Planning on the Mainland and on Taiwan, 1943–58," *Australian Journal of Chinese Affairs*, no. 24 (July 1990): 121–42.

41. Hans Heyman, "Acquisition and Diffusion of Technology in China," in China: A Reassessment of the Economy (Washington, DC: US Government Printing Office, 1975), 678, 687.

42. *Renmin ribao*, September 14, 1952, in Survey of the China Mainland Press, no. 427, October 1, 1952, 34–37.

43. Zhou Enlai, "Guanyu zhishi fenzi wenti de baogao," [Report on questions concerning intellectuals] January 14, 1956, in *Zhou Enlai tongyi zhanxian wenxuan* [Selected works of Zhou Enlai on the united front] (Beijing: Renmin chubanshe, l984), 298–99.

44. See William Taubman, *Khrushchev: The Man and the Era* (New York: W.W. Norton, 2003), Chapter 11.

45. "On the Historical Experience of the Dictatorship of the Proletariat," April 16, 1956, *Renmin ribao* editorial, in *Communist China 1955–1959: Policy Documents with*

Analysis, ed., trans. R. R. Bowie and John K. Fairbank (Cambridge, MA: Harvard University Press, 1962), 129. *Renmin ribao*, April 5, 1956. Two years later, at the Chengdu Conference, Mao explicitly approved of "correct" cults of the personality. And in l964, Mao attributed Khrushchev's fall from power due failure to promote his own cult. Stuart Schram, *Chairman Mao Talks to the People*, 99–100; Roderick MacFarquhar, *The Origins of the Cultural Revolution*, vol.3, The Coming of the Cataclysm (New York: Columbia University Press, l997), 417.

46. *Selected Works of Mao Tse-tung*, vol. 5 (Beijing: Foreign Languages Press, 1977), 291.

47. See, for instance, Alfred L. Chan, *Mao's Crusade: Policies and Policy Implementation in China's Great Leap Forward* (New York: Oxford University Press, 2001).

48. For a telling example of impossible goals in the oil industry, see Alexandre Barmine, *One Who Survived* (New York: Putnam and Sons, l945), 199–200.

49. See J. Stalin, *Works*, vol. 13, 53ff.

50. Chalmers Johnson, ed., *Change in Communist Systems* (Palo Alto, CA: Stanford University Press, 1970), 33–116.

51. See *A Critique of Soviet Economics by Mao Tse-tung*, Translated by Moss Roberts, with Annotations by Richard Levy and an Introduction by James Peck (New York: Monthly Review Press), 47.

52. See Stuart Schram, *Chairman Mao Talks to the People*, "Talks at Chengtu," 99.

53. Mao Tse-tung, *A Critique of Soviet Economics*, 87.

54. Yang Jianbai and Li Xuezeng, "The Relation between Agriculture, Light Industry and Heavy Industry in China," *Social Sciences in China*, no. 2 (1980): 182–212.

55. Mao Tse-tung, "Speeches at the Chengchow Conference," (February and March l959), in *Chinese Law and Government*, vol. IX, no. 4 (Winter 1976–77): 18.

56. See Thomas P. Bernstein, "Stalinism, Famine, and Chinese Peasants: Grain Procurement during the Great Leap Forward," *Theory and Society*, vol. 13, no. 3, May l984: 339–77 and Bernstein, "Mao Zedong and the Famine of 1959–60: A Study in Wilfulness," *China Quarterly*, no. 186 (June 2006): 421–45.

57. According to Suzanne Pepper, some of his ideas for education harkened back to the "Cultural Revolution" of 1928–31. See Chapter 11 of her book, *Radicalism and Education Reform*.

58. See note 5.

59. William A. Joseph, et. al., eds., *New Perspectives on the Cultural Revolution* (Cambridge: Harvard University Press, 1991), 41, 43, 54.

60. Gilbert Rozman, *The Chinese Debate about Soviet Socialism, 1978–1985* (Princeton, NJ: Princeton University Press, 1987), see especially, 154–83 and 310–32.

61. See also Elizabeth Wishnick, *Mending Fences* (Seattle: University of Washington Press, 2001).

62. See David Shambaugh, *China's Communist Party: Atrophy and Adaptation* for close analysis of how the lessons of the Soviet collapse are being applied to boost the CCP's chances of survival.

I
THE UPS AND DOWNS
OF SINO-SOVIET RELATIONS

1

Sino-Soviet Relations during the Mao Years, 1949–1969

Lorenz M. Lüthi

IN THE TWO DECADES FROM 1949 TO 1969, Sino-Soviet relations followed a circular path. Apart from official diplomatic relations with the Nationalist government of China, Soviet contacts with Chinese leaders of any color were relatively rare before 1949. The unexpected 1941 Soviet non-aggression treaty with Japan left China without an effective deterrence against Japanese aggression. Immediately after the end of World War II, it was national interests, not revolutionary aims or ideological affinity that drove Stalin's policy toward China. Following difficult negotiations in the summer of 1945, the Soviet Union formally allied with the Nationalists who headed the internationally recognized government and had traded economic concessions in Manchuria and Xinjiang for political support from the Soviet Union.[1] Stalin looked down on what he called China's margarine communists. It was only in 1949, just before its victory in the civil war that his interests in Chinese Communism reawakened. After the alliance of February 14, 1950, Moscow's relations with the new regime in Beijing developed rapidly, reaching their apex in the mid-1950s. Once disagreements developed, the alliance underwent a slow but steady decline. By 1966, only low-level governmental contacts remained of what once was a rich and multifaceted set of political, economic, party, and military relations. Three years later, both sides engaged in a brief military conflict over disputed, but otherwise insignificant, islands and grasslands. In contrast to the mid-1940s, China's Communists now looked down on the Soviet traitors against world revolution.

The Sino-Soviet relationship rose on the basis of their shared ideology, yet fell as a result of interpretative disagreements about it. Both sides were dedicated to communism, or what they believed communism represented. Both saw the world in terms of a struggle between good and evil, between a shining communist future and a sinister capitalist past, between peace and aggression, and between Marxism and imperialism. As disagreements emerged over the course of the 1950s and early 1960s, it became clear that each had different ideas about how to achieve the good, the shining future, peace, and Marxism, and how to deal with evil, capitalism, aggression, and imperialism. These disagreements were rooted in the theoretical deficiencies of Marxism itself, the inadequate understanding of this ideology, or its misuse for domestic purposes and even for personal gain. Below, we will briefly sketch Sino-Soviet relations from 1949 to 1969 before focusing on the sources of cohesion and conflict of this partnership.

Chronology, 1949–1969

In early 1949, after two decades of neglect, Stalin decided to re-establish good relations with the Chinese Communists, who were poised to win the civil war, by sending Anastas Mikoyan to China.[2] Although the Comintern had initiated the foundation of the Chinese Communist Party (CCP) in 1921, relations after 1927 had been negligible. For some years before Mikoyan's arrival in China, the CCP leaders themselves had worked for rapprochement. The ideological movement toward Stalin's positions in the emerging Cold War aimed at securing economic, military, technological, and political assistance for the period after the expected establishment of the People's Republic, which occurred on October 1, 1949.[3] By early December that year, Mao Zedong was on his way to Moscow to lobby Stalin for a general agreement on the cooperation between the two largest socialist states. On February 14, 1950, after two months of maneuvering and negotiating, the two sides signed the Alliance and Friendship Treaty, which provided China with Soviet military support against outside aggression. Several agreements on economic aid financing followed in early spring, forming the basis of what would eventually become the largest ever socialist development project. In return, the PRC had to grant economic and military concessions in Xinjiang and Manchuria to the Soviet Union, accept unfavorable terms of trade, and consent to loan conditions in hard currency.[4]

The following three years witnessed both the Stalinization of the PRC, and friction over the Korean War. While Soviet aid was less significant than expected during the Korean War from mid-1950 to mid-1953,[5] China's political system and official ideology was effectively Stalinized.[6] At that time, the Soviet Union was particularly engaged in the modernization of the People's Liberation Army (PLA),[7] while the chaotic state of China's economy in the immediate post-civil war period and during the Korean War did not yet allow for massive Soviet economic aid.[8]

The years 1953–56 were the golden period of the alliance. In need to shore up support in the socialist camp for his leadership, Khrushchev reversed some of Stalin's policies toward China, and corrected unfavorable terms of trade.[9] At the same time, the PRC tried to break out from its international isolation by establishing relations with India in 1954[10] and attending the Bandung Conference of the Afro-Asian Movement the following year.[11] China's major diplomatic breakthrough, however, was its momentous role at the 1954 Geneva Conference on Indochina and Korea, where its foreign minister Zhou Enlai contributed much to the success of the negotiations.[12] Yet, the mid-1950s also witnessed the first Chinese dissatisfactions with the status quo in international and inter-socialist affairs. The first Taiwan Strait Crisis in 1954–55—the shelling by the PRC of a small Nationalist-held island, Jinmen, in Xiamen Bay—came as a surprise to the world, in general, and to the Soviet Union, in particular. Khrushchev's refusal to unfold the nuclear umbrella over the island to deter American countermoves revealed the limits of the alliance to Mao Zedong. Moscow did, however, help Beijing to develop its own nuclear capabilities in the aftermath of the crisis.[13] Moreover, disagreements over economic development emerged in the mid-1950s, even if Soviet economic assistance reached its peak in these years.[14]

Khrushchev's announcements, at the twentieth congress of the Communist Party of the Soviet Union (CPSU) in February of 1956, of de-Stalinization and the policy of peaceful coexistence with the United States increased the existing disagreements. While initially embracing peaceful coexistence, Mao rejected de-Stalinization for ideological and personal reasons. Although his fellow leaders eventually forced him to accept de-Stalinization in China—and thereby a partial loss of his own power during the eighth CCP Congress in September of 1956—he managed to recapture his influence the following year and, afterward, to roll back de-Stalinization in China. Simultaneously, the PRC, under Mao's ideological leadership, also defined its own, highly critical position on de-Stalinization. Nevertheless, none of these disagreements became public at the first Moscow Conference of the world's communist parties.[15]

Disagreements steadily intensified from diplomatic skirmishes to public attacks in print and on radio throughout the 1958–60 period. In international affairs, rifts emerged as a result of Mao's radical rejection of peaceful coexistence, during the second Taiwan Strait Crisis in 1958, the first Sino-Indian Border War and Khrushchev's visit to the United States in 1959, and the Paris Summit in 1960.[16] Beijing saw Moscow's embrace of peaceful coexistence as treason against world revolution.[17] Domestically, Mao's Great Leap Forward was a deliberate challenge to Khrushchev's adherence to the late Stalinist development model (although, in fairness, the new Soviet leader did tinker with it), thus signifying the Chinese attempt to surpass the Soviet Union in the construction of communism.[18] While ideological radicalism destroyed Sino-Soviet economic relations by the summer of 1960—the sudden withdrawal of the Soviet specialists followed a month-long Chinese campaign attempting to indoctrinate them against their own government—the subsequent collapse of the Great Leap Forward (GLF) undermined much of Mao's ideological claims. By the fall of 1960, hubris reigned in the Sino-Soviet alliance, although both sides did decide, at the second meeting of the world's communist parties in Moscow in November 1960 to pull back from the brink and come to a temporary truce in the ideological debates.[19]

The famines caused by the GLF and the ensuing relative demise of Mao's power in daily decision making, led to more sensitive policies approaches by his fellow leaders. The year of 1961 and the first half of 1962 marked an ambiguous truce in Sino-Soviet relations. Ideological radicalism yielded the political stage to pragmatic economic and foreign policies, including a limited restoration of cooperation between Beijing and Moscow.[20] Yet, to keep the flame of ideological radicalism alive, Mao seized on the Soviet-Albanian split in 1960–61, and the Soviet removal of Stalin's body from the Lenin Mausoleum in 1961.[21]

Mao returned to supreme power in late summer 1962 determined to radicalize his country's foreign policy toward the alleged Soviet traitors by instrumentalizing the supposed capitalist methods that had helped to restore China's economy after the collapse of the GLF. Turning away from moderation in relations with the Soviet Union, he advocated for China to lead the developing world in the pursuit of world revolution.[22] Khrushchev's humiliation during the Cuban Missile Crisis in October of 1962 and his vacillation during the simultaneous second Sino-Indian Border War allowed Mao to implement his radical views in China's foreign policy.[23] Starting in early 1963, he worked for the Sino-Soviet split in order to discredit Soviet leadership in the socialist world abroad and at home.[24] By early 1966, Mao decided to sever party relations with the Soviet Union in the run-up to the Cultural Revolution, during which his internal enemies, real and imaginary, were purged as Soviet-style traitors of the communist cause.[25]

China's international self-isolation in the early Cultural Revolution years paralleled the nadir of Sino-Soviet relations. Only low-level governmental relations remained of what was once a multi-faceted alliance.[26] Cultural Revolution excesses not only targeted western diplomatic representations in Beijing as imperialist agents, but also the Soviet embassy as the legation of the world revolution's traitors.[27] The near collapse of relations triggered the militarization of the common border, including the disputed territories.

Soviet encroachment of such areas convinced China of the need to defend its borders with greater assertiveness.[28]

The March clashes of 1969, which triggered a major crisis including the threat of nuclear war, originally were a limited Chinese punitive action against Soviet infringement of what the PRC believed to be its own territory. Skirmishes on the frozen border river occurred as early as November 1967; fatalities, on the Chinese side, occurred for the first time the following month.[29] The March 2, 1969, clash was an ambush prepared by the Chinese side to reassert claims against Soviet encroachment on Zhenbao/Damanskii Island on an isolated stretch of the Ussuri River.[30] The Soviet counterattack on March 15 did not go as planned, and eventually led to veiled Soviet threats that nuclear weapons might be used.[31]

Sources of Cohesion in Sino-Soviet Relations

Despite the subsequent sharp deterioration of the relationship, the Sino-Soviet alliance started on firm foundations in the early 1950s. They included a common ideology, comparable life-experiences of their supreme leaders, a similar view on the international situation in the late 1940s, and shared commitments to world revolution. Both Stalin and Mao were dedicated communists, not window-dressing opportunists or outright cynics. That they adhered to crude and simplified versions of Marxist-Leninist ideology is beside the point. They were firmly convinced that they had understood the complexity of its ideas correctly. Each had devoted their lives to the creation of a political utopia early in their careers, at a time when this had not been opportune. Stalin had joined the Russian Social Democratic Party at the turn of the century when it was a splinter party. In 1903, it split into the larger Menshevik and tiny Bolshevik party, with Stalin becoming a member of the latter's Central Committee.[32] Mao was a founding member of the CCP in 1921, when the future of any aspiring politician in China lay with the Nationalist Party.[33] Both experienced hardship and political exclusion as a result of their choices; one faced repeated penal exile in Siberia in the 1910s,[34] the other spent the period from 1927 to 1945 in virtual internal self-exile where he experimented with early forms of communist state building.[35] Both experienced a brutal and scarring civil war.[36] In brief, both had joined fledgling parties that survived, miraculously, to take power after a long and brutal struggle.

Both parties were committed to the overhaul of the contemporaneous bourgeois and imperialist international system. The Bolshevik party aimed for world revolution that would bring about socialism and then communism in the developed world (Europe and North America). Its first leader, Vladimir

Lenin, believed that the European colonies in much of what is now called the Third World, and especially China, could play a crucial role in the defeat of imperialism and thereby in the internal collapse of capitalism. National revolutions in the colonies, he believed, were precursors to socialist revolutions in Europe.[37] Similarly, the CCP adhered to ideas that challenged the existing world order, dividing the world's nations into imperialist exploiters and subjugated colonies. It was no wonder that the Chinese Communists were open to Lenin's idea about the central role of national revolutions in the colonies and their importance to world revolution.[38] Thus, Stalin and Mao alike adhered to an ideology that was both radical and anti-establishment.

Despite the loose political and ideological relationship between Soviets and the Chinese Communists between 1927 and 1945, Stalin and Mao saw eye-to-eye on the basic nature of international affairs. As early as 1919, even before he ascended to supreme power, Stalin had argued that the world was split into two hostile camps—imperialism and communism.[39] Against the background of the emerging division of Europe and the Soviet refusal to participate in the Marshall Plan, Andrei Zhdanov revived Stalin's views at the founding meeting of the Cominform in September of 1947. He claimed that the world was split into two hostile camps: "The imperialist and anti-democratic camp, on the one hand, and the anti-imperialist and democratic camp, on the other."[40]

It is not clear how much Mao borrowed from Stalinist thinking. In January 1940, for example, he wrote that "once conflict between the socialist Soviet Union and the imperialist powers grows sharper, China will have to take her stand on one side or the other . . . The whole world will be swept into one or the other of these two fronts . . . However, whether you like it or not, the Western imperialists are determined to oppose the Soviet Union and communism. . . . All these circumstances make it essential for the revolutionary . . . [China to conclude an] alliance with Russia, and under no circumstances [an] alliance with imperialism against Russia."[41] In August of 1946, he refined his views when he formulated the theory of the intermediate zone, arguing that there was an American-Soviet contest for the intermediate zone—the capitalist, colonial, and semi-colonial countries of West Europe, Africa, and Asia (including China), respectively. Both texts had surprising similarities with Stalin's views in 1919, and Zhdanov's views in 1947.[42] Believing that the Soviet Union was the defender of world peace, and thereby of the interests of the intermediate zone, it comes as no surprise that the Chairman led Communist China into an alliance with the Soviet Union.[43] Thus, Moscow and Beijing established the alliance on the basis of a shared, anti-imperialist worldview; it was directed, despite its convoluted wording about Japanese aggression, against the United States.[44]

Apart from the defensive purpose of the alliance, the two signatories also shared an offensive goal: the spread of world revolution. Despite Stalin's promulgation of "socialism in one country" in the late 1920s, the Soviet dictator had never given up the idea of exporting revolution.[45] The defeat of Germany in 1945 left Soviet armies standing in Eastern Europe, providing Stalin with the opportunity to install Soviet-style, communist regimes. Yet the escalation of conflict with the United States in the following years foreclosed any prospects of expanding further into West Europe or the Middle East.[46] By late 1948, with the CCP on the road to victory in the Chinese civil war, Asia presented itself as the new revolutionary frontier.[47] While negotiating the alliance with Stalin at the turn of 1949/50, Mao extended recognition to a fellow revolutionary movement—the Vietnamese Communists under Ho Chi Minh, who were barely surviving against the French colonial armies.[48] Similarly, the Korean War that started in mid-1950 supplied Mao with the means to deepen the revolution in China, to secure it in northern Korea, and to expand it to that country's south.[49]

Apart from these ideological factors, Stalin as a leader played a centripetal role in the socialist world. The man who headed the first socialist state, who had industrialized it in the 1930s, and defended it against the near-fatal German assault soon thereafter, and who established the socialist camp at the end of World War II, was the iron clamp that kept the international communist movement together. Communists in virtually every country—from the United States to France, Poland, Iran, and China—submitted to the man in the Kremlin, especially once the Cold War had made ideological conflict central to world affairs. He was, at turns, the source of political strength, ideological inspiration, philosophical wisdom, or just financial and military aid. His very existence and exalted political standing was unique in the history of international political movements. The Russian transcripts of Mao's first personal meeting with Stalin in late 1949 bear witness to the awe and deference that the Soviet leader inspired in his guests, not only in his East European puppets, but also in visitors from farther afield.[50]

Thus the alliance, as it emerged in early 1950, was not an accidental event or the result of opportunist thinking on the part of Mao and his fellow Chinese Communists. It was rooted in biographical, ideological, and political commonalities that were vibrant and deep. Yet, as the following section reveals, they were not robust enough to keep the alliance together.

Sources of Conflict in Sino-Soviet Relations

Since, historically speaking, very few alliances have been enduring, the end of the Sino-Soviet alliance, at first view, appears to be nothing out of the ordinary. China's economic development over the course of the 1950s, its slow diplomatic rise on a global scale, and military growth all naturally transformed the country's needs and dedication to the partnership. Given the commitment of the CCP leaders to China's restoration to former glory and greatness in international affairs, one might have expected a slow loosening of the country's asymmetrical ties to its superpower ally. But this still leaves the historian with the task to explain the *nature* of the partnership's speedy and bitter collapse which is *atypical* in the history of alliances.

The roots of Sino-Soviet hostility in the mid-1960s lie in the dynamics of the relationship. No single sufficient cause exists; a complex web of factors ultimately led to the downfall of the alliance. There is also no ground to see the collapse as a foregone conclusion at any time before 1962. Reasons for and against the maintenance of the alliance aligned with, competed against, or replaced each other over the period from the mid-1950s to the mid-1960s.

Ideological Disagreements

Ideological disagreements were fundamental to the foundering of the alliance. They are related to the intrinsic nature of Marxist ideology and to the ensuing disputes on substantial theoretical issues. While Marxism supplies a supposedly sensible interpretation of the historical, stage-like development of human society, it only provides rough suggestions about future stages (socialism and communism), without laying out clear pathways of political action to realize them. Thus, revolutionary practitioners are left to their own devices to formulate courses of action.[51] This deficiency in Marxist ideology provided a fertile breeding ground for the formulation of competing political programs throughout the international communist movement, but particularly for the ideological debates of the Sino-Soviet split.

In concrete terms, ideological disagreements emerged over the correct economic development path as early as the mid-1950s, at the high-point of the relationship, and lasted into late that decade. Arguments over de-Stalinization erupted shortly after Khrushchev's famous Secret Speech on February 25, 1956, and went on, intermittently, until 1961. Finally, clashes over the correct handling of imperialism, triggered, as well, by Khrushchev's Secret Speech, rose to prominence in the ideological debates the late 1950s and dominated the 1960s.

Ideological Disagreements on Economic Development

The disagreements over economic development stemmed from different needs and outlooks of the two allies. When, after a period of economic consolidation, the PRC turned to the Soviet Union in 1952 with requests for advice and aid for its 1st Five-Year Plan (FYP; 1953–57), it calculated yearly industrial development growth rates of 15 or more percent. The backward state of the country's economy and the can-do attitude of the Chinese leadership induced the PRC to propose economic solutions similar to those that Stalin had pursued in the late 1920s and early 1930s (*Revolutionary Stalinism*). The prospect of large-scale Soviet aid and boundless advice seemed to support such a bold approach. The Soviet dictator, however, had abandoned shocklike, unbalanced development strategies by the mid-1930s and had settled on bureaucratically controlled and more balanced economic development (*Bureaucratic Stalinism*). Thus, in the weeks before his death, Stalin cut down on Chinese growth rates and requests for Soviet economic and financial assistance. The Chinese leaders eventually implemented a downwardly revised first Chinese FYP in mid-1953, half a year after its official start.[52]

While Revolutionary and Bureaucratic Stalinist methods worked in the Soviet Union to a greater or lesser extent, they were a difficult fit for the Chinese economy. Both socialist countries started their economic development programs (the Soviet Union in the 1920s, China in the 1950s) with a small industrial sector and a large, subsistent agriculture. However, mechanization and the availability of some arable land reserves provided the Soviet Union with the chance to increase agricultural production while using rural surpluses to buy technology from abroad and shift labor, freed from the farmland, to newly erected industrial projects.[53] At the same time, the lack of foreign investment naturally dampened economic overexpansion, as resources for investment had to be produced internally. However, this did not prevent Stalin's megalomaniacal miscalculations of economic expansion in the early 1930s.[54] Nor did agriculture do well in the Soviet period—in many respects, it was a spectacular failure. Although it eventually did become more labor-efficient—thereby freeing much needed labor for industrialization—overall output did not increase significantly beyond the production levels of the late 1920s.[55]

The parameters of the Chinese economy in the 1950s were fundamentally different. The country did not command arable land reserves; on the contrary, its peasants operated near the limits of the country's natural capacities.[56] As a result, Soviet loans, to a large degree, and a slightly more efficient agriculture fuelled industrial development.[57] This situation created a bifurcated Chinese economy with an industrial sector heavily dependent on continued outside investment, and an agricultural sector operating at low levels that was unable, despite a more forceful requisition regime introduced in late 1953, to support the ambitious long-term industrial expansion plans of the CCP.[58]

Thus by the mid-1950s, China was heading for troubled economic waters. Soviet loan disbursements—the main fuel of industrial development—were scheduled to end by the second half of the 1950s. There was little hope that Moscow would be able or willing to spend more money to satisfy Beijing's appetite for further investment. China, moreover, was then contractually obligated to start repaying the loans—primarily in raw materials and *agricultural products*. The prospect that China's agriculture had to support industrial development alone *and* satisfy loan repayment created a significant problem.[59] By mid-1955, the Chinese leaders discussed alternative development plans. Prime Minister Zhou Enlai proposed a Yugoslav solution that replaced the central and administrative planning of *Bureaucratic Stalinism* with a limited, socialist market economy. Vice-Chairman of the PRC Liu Shaoqi recommended economic reforms along the lines of Lenin's *New Economic Policy* (NEP). Introduced in the early 1920s, NEP, aiming to jumpstart an economy that had been ruined in the civil war, had allowed independent peasant markets. The economic planner Chen Yun advocated a mix of NEP and Bureaucratic Stalinist methods.[60]

Mao discarded all these suggestions for ideological reasons: Tito was a traitor, Stalin had dismissed NEP policies as the return of capitalism to the countryside, and Bureaucratic Stalinism had created a new class society that was a mockery of the egalitarian and anti-bourgeois ideals of the PRC.[61] Instead, the Chairman started to toy with ideas similar to those of Revolutionary Stalinism. It is not clear whether he borrowed directly from Stalin's early economic ideas, or whether he arrived at similar conclusions after setting out from a different starting point. Whatever the case may be, when Mao wrote his seminal texts on revolution and political organization in the 1930s, he in fact had used Soviet texts from the Revolutionary Stalinist period to form his own theoretical ideas, which suggests that there is more than just an accidental ideological resemblance with Revolutionary Stalinism.[62] It is, anyway, obvious that the Chairman's economic decisions in the mid-1950s were ideologically motivated, because he did not consider development models outside of the Marxist-Leninist mindset.

Consequently, Mao pushed for faster agricultural collectivization of the peasantry.[63] Although his proposals were by no means as radical as Stalin's forced collectivization a quarter of a century before, he took his cue from Stalin's *Short Course*, the 1938 bible of socialist political and economic development: "by a great effort the Soviet Union successfully accomplished the socialist transformation of the whole of its agriculture and at the same time achieved a massive technical reconstruction of agriculture. *This road traversed by the Soviet Union is our model.*"[64] Even if the goal of making agriculture more efficient and less labor-intensive was apparent, Mao's policy proceeded from unrealistic economic assumptions. The closing of rural markets, the removal of incentives for peasants to work harder, and the misappropriation of scarce industrial resources to his collectivization drive led to bottlenecks in agricultural supplies, production stoppages in the industry, a bloated state budget and inflation, and, by 1956, the recurrence of spring famines. Yet, since the range of Mao's Revolutionary Stalinist policies was not as sweeping as the scope of transformation Stalin had envisioned 25 years earlier, the disasters were also not as appalling. All the same, the destruction of an economically autonomous peasantry produced, as it had in the Soviet Union of the 1930s, an obedient, phlegmatic and hardly enterprising rural society.[65]

The negative results of Mao's hasty economic drive became apparent just as Khrushchev, at the 20th CPSU congress in February of 1956, criticized Stalin for criminal rule and political mistakes. The new Soviet leader called for the political and ideological, not economic, de-Stalinization of the Soviet Union. The fact that Stalin, who once had occupied a quasi-divine position within and without his own country, had become a fair target of criticism put Mao into a delicate situation at home. While the Chairman tried to come up with his own interpretation of Stalin's mistakes—one that was supposed to shield him from criticism at home—he simultaneously tried to limit the wider discussion of Khrushchev's Secret Speech in China.[66] Nevertheless, the economic problems he had brought upon China forced him to backtrack on his own development ideas. Khrushchev's removal of Trofim Lysenko—a pseudo-agrobiologist who had convinced Stalin of his ideas on dialectic genetics—from his official positions shortly after the Secret Speech, quickly led, over the course of the spring and summer of 1956, to the abolition of his agricultural policies and Lysenkoist genetics in China.[67] This development preceded the return, at the 8th CCP congress the following September, from Mao's recent economic adventures to the basic ideas of the first FYP.[68]

In less than two years, however, Mao's economic ideas reappeared in more extreme forms. After the Hungarian Revolution in October of 1956, the Chairman discerned that Bureaucratic Stalinism was too rigid and incapable of addressing, and thereby defusing, internal conflicts.[69] In response, he was willing to embark on liberal policies at home.[70] While Chen Yun exploited the opportunity to re-introduce NEP-style peasant markets,[71] Mao embarked on what would become the Hundred Flowers Campaign in the spring of 1957: the creation of controlled discussion fora in which invited party members and technical cadres were permitted to voice constructive criticism of the Chinese political system.[72] But once the lid had been removed from the boiling pot of political dissatisfaction, the Chairman, in May of 1957, faced a storm of fundamental criticism that, so he believed, threatened to undermine CCP rule.[73] As a result, neither the continuation of the liberal experiment, nor the return to Bureaucratic Stalinism, which had to rely on the expertise of the very cadres that had turned out to be politically unreliable, remained as live options for the future economic development. Seemingly without an alternative, Mao returned to radical economic ideas—this time on a grander scale.[74]

The GLF was a deliberate challenge to Soviet leadership in socialist economic development. What had originally started as a friendly boasting match between Khrushchev and Mao at the Moscow Meeting of the world's communist parties in November of 1957—the Soviet leader claimed that the Soviet Union would economically overtake the United States in 15 years, while the Chairman promised to achieve a similar feat with regard to the United Kingdom—grew into a Chinese attempt to overtake the Soviet Union economically.[75] Resurrecting ideas from the failed collectivization drive two years earlier, Mao asserted that the mobilization of mass labor not only would help to transcend Stalinist economic achievements, but also would allow China to enter the final stage of history—communism—before the Soviet Union.[76] The GLF proceeded on the basis of bumper crops in 1958 which led to increased procurement quotas, unrealistic assumptions about human behavior in communal living and working arrangements, and the sheer lack of planning.[77] Again, the available evidence does not allow conclusions regarding the extent of Mao's usage of Revolutionary Stalinist ideas, although it is clear that he criticized the late Soviet leader for abrogating supposedly correct policies when the latter adopted Bureaucratic Stalinist methods in the mid-1930s.[78]

The Soviet Union witnessed China's economic radicalization from the sideline without making any public comments throughout most of 1958. During Khrushchev's visit to Mao in Beijing in late July and early August, the Soviet visitors told their Chinese hosts that experimental communes in the Soviet Union had not worked in the 1920s, and that Chinese production targets were wholly unrealistic.[79] This was certainly appropriate criticism; more importantly, Beijing's economic claims and targets were thorns in Moscow's side.[80] In the fall of 1958, the Soviet Union had abrogated its own, ambitious, sixth FYP (1956–60) as a result of unexpected expenses in the wake of the Hungarian Revolution, faulty investments patterns, and problems in agricultural production.[81] It seemed that China was indeed overtaking the Soviet Union.

The fundamental design faults of the GLF showed quickly. Over the fall of 1958, ever increasing production quotas, the use of farm labor for giant infrastructure projects to the detriment of agricultural production, the misappropriation of resources on every level, and the lack of basic planning took its toll. Late in the year, the specter of famines threatened the country.[82] Although dragging his feet, Mao decided in late 1958 and the first half of 1959 to moderate the extremes of the GLF without abandoning it.[83] Aware of the strained relations with the Soviet comrades, he also banned propaganda that claimed China would enter communism before the Soviet Union, and ordered public praise of the new, downwardly revised, Soviet economic targets for the following seven years as the correct path to communism.[84] Once Beijing had announced modifications to the GLF, Moscow gave its first critical public comment on China's economic radicalism.[85]

The scope of the GLF disasters, especially the deadly famines, set in only over time. Mao's inability to admit mistakes and take responsibility, as well as his paranoia about a supposed leadership challenge at the Lushan work conference that gathered central and important provincial leaders in the summer of 1959 further delayed the end of the GLF and the return to sensible economic policies.[86] It was only under the pressure of deadly famines and the complete economic collapse in late 1960 that Mao gave up his radical development visions.[87] The PRC did not launch another challenge to the Soviet Union in the field of economic development until the 1980s—on the one hand, because Mao's economic ideas had been discredited to the core, and, on the other, since his fellow leaders focused on economic consolidation and recovery in the first half of the 1960s.

Ideological Disagreements on De-Stalinization

Shortly after disagreements on economic development erupted, de-Stalinization added a second aspect to the ideological struggle between Mao and Khrushchev. As mentioned above, the general direction of the criticism about Stalin's personality cult in the Secret Speech also applied to Mao's supreme leadership. Despite the Chairman's attempts to prevent an open debate in China, his fellow leaders used the opportunity to limit his prerogatives and skip the reference to Mao Zedong Thought from the new party constitution at the 8th CCP congress in September.[88]

In the wake of the Hungarian Revolution, Mao reassessed de-Stalinization once more. In the belief that Khrushchev's Secret Speech had sown confusion among the socialist states, he blamed the Soviet leader for throwing away the "sword" of Stalin. Although he was willing to embark on liberal economic policies to avoid the mistakes of a rigid application of Bureaucratic Stalinism to China, as they had supposedly occurred in Hungary, he moved further away from Khrushchev's ideological and political de-Stalinization.[89] The purge of Stalin's long-time lieutenants, Vyacheslav Molotov, Lazar Kaganovich, and Georgy Malenkov, during the so-called Anti-Party Incident in the summer of 1957, led Mao to conclude that these plotters against Khrushchev had not committed a grave error at all, but that, in fact, their purge was counter to their revolutionary contributions and CPSU norms.[90] While the incident insured both Khrushchev's political survival as the supreme Soviet leader and the continuation of de-Stalinization, it reconfirmed Mao's most recent decisions to follow once more radical economic policies, as mentioned further above, that led him to further ideological conflict with the Soviet comrades.

Over the course of 1957 and early 1958, Mao was able to claw his way back into supreme leadership. By March 1958, he announced a new personality cult which was designed to help him push through his radical GLF ideas.[91] At the Beidaihe Politburo meeting in August, he even arrogated supreme decision making power to himself when he announced the launching of radical economic policies, thereby abolishing the last remnants of the sensible economic decisions taken at the 8th party congress.[92] After the supposed challenge to his leadership at the Lushan Conference in mid-1959, Mao, with the help of Lin Biao and the PLA, amplified his personality cult as a means to shield him from further challenges.[93]

Since the Chinese leadership had greatly reduced the flow of information to Moscow's embassy in Beijing, the Soviet leaders were not completely aware of the growing personality cult.[94] The contentious (and last) meeting between the first leaders of the two countries during the tenth anniversary celebrations of the PRC around October 1, 1959 left both Mao and Khrushchev with a bad impression of the other.[95] While the Chairman decided not to take the revisionist Soviet general secretary seriously, the CPSU leaders internally complained about the sickly Stalin-like personality cult in the PRC.[96] The outbreak of open ideological disputes in April of 1960, when the CCP published the so-called Lenin Polemics, and the subsequent public clashes at the meeting of the World Federation of Trade Unions in Beijing and the third Romanian Party Congress in Bucharest in June, caused Khrushchev to conclude: "When I look at Mao Zedong, I just see Stalin, an exact copy."[97]

Against the background of Mao's rising personality cult and the increasing official adoration of Stalin by the CCP, the twenty second CPSU congress in October of 1961 decided to remove the late dictator's body from the Lenin Mausoleum and inter it behind that building, close to the Kremlin Wall.[98] It was the symbolic end of Stalin's personality cult in the Soviet Union, but also a political signal to the Chinese Communists who had made the mausoleum a pilgrimage site in an open refusal of de-Stalinization.[99] This contentious political issue briefly reappeared during the nine Chinese polemics in the second half of 1963 and the first half of 1964, but largely in the context of Chinese attacks on Khrushchev for supposed mistakes committed in domestic and foreign policies in general, and in relations with the Chinese Communists in particular.[100] Paradoxically, at this point, the Chinese Communists had worked out their own criticism of Stalin; while Khrushchev chided his predecessor for ideological orthodoxy, the Chinese accused him of lack thereof.[101]

Ideological Disagreements on International Affairs

Apart from disagreements on economic development and de-Stalinization, Beijing and Moscow increasingly disagreed on the handling of imperialism. At the twentieth CPSU congress, Khrushchev had also announced the new Soviet policy of peaceful coexistence with the United States, arguing that the competition between communism and capitalism should move from a worldwide military standoff to a nonviolent contest of the two rival, socio-economic systems. To a certain degree, the proposal resembled the 1954 proclamation of Sino-Indian *Pancha Shila*, which had promulgated peaceful coexistence between the two countries, including mutual respect for sovereignty and non-intervention in internal affairs.[102] In early 1956, the Chinese Communists embraced Khrushchev's peaceful coexistence among the super-powers, in the hope that the reduction of international tensions might bring the reunification of Taiwan with China.[103]

The ideological perception that imperialism had instigated both the Hungarian Revolution and the simultaneous Suez Crisis led Mao to abrogate Chinese support for Khrushchev's peaceful coexistence.[104] However, from late 1956 to late 1957, he considered a resolution to the problem of de-Stalinization more important than the growing dispute over Soviet-style peaceful coexistence. Even when the CPSU requested a public endorsement of the decisions of its 20th congress in the final documents by the world's communist parties gathering at the Moscow Meeting in November of 1957, the CCP did not lodge a protest against peaceful coexistence except in the form of a secret memo confidentially handed over to the host party.[105]

The dispute over peaceful coexistence erupted into the public spotlight the following year. Frustrated by the lack of progress on Taiwan in the ambassadorial talks with the United States in Geneva, disappointed by their sudden American downgrading, and concerned about supposed U.S. attempts to divide China permanently into Taiwan and the mainland, Mao planned the second Taiwan Strait Crisis as early as December of 1957.[106] Against the ideological radicalization occurring during the run-up to the GLF, Beijing came to believe that Moscow was colluding with Washington in the Middle East.[107] The second Taiwan Strait crisis was closely timed to mobilize the Chinese people for the launch of the radical GLF policies, adopted at the August Beidaihe Politburo meeting.[108] While the timing of the two had primarily instrumental reasons, their simultaneity nevertheless symbolized a double challenge to the Soviet Union with regard to economic development and peaceful coexistence with United States.

The crisis, which lasted for a couple of weeks, led to a quick and unexpected escalation of the Sino-American conflict in the Taiwan Strait, including veiled U.S. nuclear threats and Soviet counterthreats.[109] Washington's offer to resume the informal ambassadorial talks in Warsaw and generally defensive American behavior in the Taiwan Strait convinced Beijing to terminate the crisis.[110] Yet the lack of prior notification and the ease with which the PRC had committed the Soviet Union to near nuclear war raised concern in the Kremlin about the Chinese ally.[111] While the crisis was still going on, Moscow had agreed to Washington's long-standing proposal to convene nuclear arms limitation talks, which eventually led to the Limited Nuclear Test Ban treaty in mid-1963.[112] Simultaneously, it also decided to reduce, and eventually abrogate, the transfer of Soviet know how and technology to the Chinese nuclear weapons project, including the delivery of a promised model A-bomb by 1959.[113]

The crisis in Sino-Indian relations in 1959 and the simultaneous Soviet-American rapprochement provided additional fuel to Sino-Soviet disputes on peaceful coexistence. The Tibetan Uprising early that year and China's ideological hard-line accusation that India had instigated it, not only brought about a swift collapse of *Pancha Shila*, but also led to the militarization of the Sino-Indian border and, eventually to war in the Himalayas.[114] This unexpected turn of events posed a serious dilemma to the Soviet Union: should it side with an ally or with its most important friend outside of the socialist world? Moscow's declaration of neutrality in the conflict did not go down well in Beijing.[115] Likewise, simultaneous but unrelated Soviet attempts to seek a rapprochement with the United States were not warmly received in the PRC, because Mao believed that Khrushchev was selling out socialist positions.[116] Conversely, the outbreak of the Sino-Indian border war in the summer of 1959, although triggered by New Delhi, led Moscow to believe that Beijing was trying to sabotage Khrushchev's impending, and seminal visit to Washington.[117]

These developments provided the stage for the final meeting between Khrushchev and Mao on the occasion of the 10th anniversary of the PRC. The celebrations followed Khrushchev's visit to the United States and the contentious Lushan Work Conference, from which Mao had emerged more radicalized and more committed to develop his own personality cult. While the Soviet leader lauded the Soviet-American rapprochement and tried to encourage the PRC to end the conflict with the equally anti-imperialist India, the Chinese leaders accused Khrushchev of abandoning the communist cause and of ideological revisionism.[118] By the end of the year, Moscow and Beijing assessed each other. While Mao gave up on Khrushchev as a credible leader of the anti-imperialist socialist world,[119] Moscow grew concerned over the ideological radicalism in Beijing and its divisive influence on the socialist world.[120]

Convinced to represent true communist positions in world affairs, the CCP stoked conflict in 1960, causing a CPSU overreaction. When Kang Sheng criticized Soviet policy toward the United States at the consultative meeting of the Warsaw Pact in February of 1960,[121] Khrushchev lost his temper and called Mao "a pair of worn-out galoshes."[122] The Chairman for his part redoubled efforts with the publication of the so-called Lenin Polemics in April, in which the Chinese side, for the first time, made supposed Soviet mistakes in international relations public.[123] The U-2 incident on May 1st and the cancellation of the Soviet-American-British-French summit in Paris two weeks later was additional grist for his mill.[124] At the meeting of the leftist World Federation of Trade Unions in early June, the CCP delegates tried—unsuccessfully, as it turned out—to impose Chinese views on peaceful coexistence and world revolution on the agenda.[125] Khrushchev reacted at the 3rd congress of the Romanian party in Bucharest later that month by bullying the Chinese representative, Peng Zhen, to accept Soviet ideological positions.[126] Following that meeting, after Khrushchev had heard that the CCP had tried to impose its views on Soviet military and economic specialists working in the PRC, he recalled all of them before the end of August.[127] The ideological dispute thereby had spread to other aspects of the relationship, damaging the once close economic relations beyond repair.[128]

While the two allies were moving toward the precipice, the Vietnamese party tried to mediate in August of 1960.[129] At that point, both sides realized that they each had reason to pull back from the brink. The crumbling of the GLF undermined Chinese claims to international ideological leadership, while the collapse of the Soviet-American rapprochement following the U-2 incident weakened Khrushchev's policy of peaceful coexistence.[130] The two sides managed to come to an ideological armistice at the Moscow Conference of the world's communist parties in November of 1960.[131]

The collapse of the GLF discredited Mao's leadership in China's daily affairs. From early 1961 to mid-1962, his less radical fellow leaders managed, initially with the Chairman's acquiescence, to introduce sensible economic recovery policies and even encouraged the formulation of less ideological and confrontational foreign policies. Moscow, for its part, was willing to provide both food aid, to alleviate the GLF famines, and advanced military aid.[132]

However, Mao was waiting in the background to seize any opportunity to retake the political initiative and reverse the domestic recovery politics he increasingly considered treason against socialist principles. The Soviet-Albanian split, which peaked in the withdrawal of Warsaw Pact submarines and ships from the small Mediterranean country in the summer of 1961, provided him with the opportunity to seize the initiative in foreign affairs and unite the Chinese leadership against perceived Soviet ideological attacks.[133] Khrushchev's unplanned rants against Albania and Stalin at the twenty second CPSU congress in the early fall provided Mao with additional ammunition.[134] However, the Chairman had to wait another year to grab leadership in domestic affairs. At the Beidaihe work conference in the late summer of 1962, exploiting the ideological conflicts with the Soviets on international affairs, he painted his fellow leaders as Khrushchevite revisionists in domestic affairs, thereby forcing the end of non-socialist recovery policies.[135]

Back in the saddle of daily policy making, Mao benefited from Khrushchev's ill-advised Cuban adventure and the simultaneous Sino-Indian border conflict in October and November of 1962. It provided him with the opportunity to accuse Khrushchev both of buckling under imperialist pressure and of treason against a revolutionary ally, and to portray himself as the only credible anti-imperialist leader and promoter of world revolution.[136] However, much of this revolutionary and anti-Soviet rhetoric was increasingly linked to his domestic needs against what he perceived to be possible rivals to his supreme position in China, thus belonging to the category of domestic sources of the Sino-Soviet split, covered below.

Secondary Disagreements

Aside from ideological conflicts, secondary factors helped to accelerate the Sino-Soviet split. They included changed needs within the alliance, territorial conflicts, and the role of the United States. Most of them however, emerged subsequent to, and were possibly augmented by, the outbreak of ideological disputes.

Despite its crushing victory in the civil war, the Chinese Communists established a new state in late 1949 that was militarily and economically a dwarf. The decision to seek an alliance with Moscow stemmed from the need to acquire an instant security shield against the perceived American threat and open access to economic aid and know how. Despite Stalin's hesitant support during the Korean War,[137] Soviet military aid quickly provided the PRC with a modern land-based army, an advanced air force, a respectable navy, and a nuclear weapons project.[138] Likewise, despite the problems with the Stalinist development model as outlined above, Soviet economic assistance supplied China with the heavy industrial backbone, on which the country could develop further.[139]

The scale of its assistance, however, made the Soviet Union quickly less important to the military and economic survival of the People's Republic. During the late Stalin and early Khrushchev years, Beijing had remained Moscow's loyal ally; Chinese needs, Stalin's centrality to the socialist world, and Khrushchev's attempts to play the China card in its struggle against the remaining Stalinists at home had provided the basis for a solid partnership. Yet, once ideological disagreements flared up in the mid-1950s, Soviet military and economic aid became less central to the well-being of China, especially since the prospect for more Soviet loans was waning. It was precisely this development that allowed Mao to downgrade relations with the Soviet comrades in late 1959 when he became convinced that Khrushchev had become an ideological revisionist. At this moment in time, Beijing was in the position to afford trading good relations with Moscow for ideological independence from it.[140] The continued maintenance of a close partnership would have required ideological concessions on Mao's part while providing only marginal improvements in economic and military aid. Indeed, the Soviet refusal to deliver a model A-bomb in 1959 did not greatly delay Chinese successes in its own nuclear weapons program.[141] Thus, greater independence was a price worth paying, given that Mao considered the Soviet behavior to have been unreliable during the second Taiwan Strait Crisis in 1958 and the Sino-Indian border war the following year.

The rise of territorial conflicts followed the emergence of ideological conflicts in the same fashion. The Chinese side initiated border disputes over grazing rights in the Taishan region in the summer of 1960 after it had made its lingering ideological disagreements public with the release of the Lenin Polemics in April. Once the two sides had come to an agreement on ideological issues at the Moscow Conference the following November, the border disputes disappeared as quickly as they had emerged.[142] Regardless of the collapse of the Sino-Soviet reconciliation talks in Moscow during the summer of 1963, both sides agreed to negotiate on the eastern sector of their common border (from Vladivostok to the Ussuri) in early 1964; by the late summer, they even had reached an understanding over most of the disputed islands and territories.[143] Yet, despite the fact that Mao had promised Stalin in early 1950 that China would relinquish all claims on Outer Mongolia, he instigated a propaganda war in the summer of 1964 by raising supposedly historical claims on that country as well as on large parts of Eastern Siberia and the Soviet maritime provinces.[144] These territorial issues remained unresolved for the following quarter of a century, largely as a result of Khrushchev's removal from power in October of 1964 and Mao's subsequent turn toward internal conflict. But there is little doubt that Mao stoked territorial disputes, playing on Moscow's fears of a territorial disintegration of the Soviet Union, as a means to pressure the erstwhile ally on ideological disagreements.

Conventional wisdom has it that the United States helped to further the Sino-Soviet split. Given that the alliance was directed against imperialism, American actions certainly had the potential to undermine that partnership. Washington's hard-line policy toward Beijing in the 1950s was designed to tax Moscow's resources and thereby undermine the alliance.[145] Apart from the two Taiwan Strait crises (1954–55 and 1958), however, the United States did not have any opportunities in the 1950s to destabilize the Sino-Soviet alliance. Once the CCP made the disputes public in the spring of 1960, the subsequent worsening of Soviet-American relations and the continued Sino-American antagonism also did not allow the United States to apply pressure on the alliance. It was only in the wake of Mao's political resurgence in the summer of 1962 and the radicalization of ideological disputes following the Cuban Missile Crisis in October, that Washington was able to exploit the So-viet-American-British negotiations on the Limited Nuclear Test Ban Treaty to isolate the PRC and tax Sino-Soviet relations. However, American actions only helped to widen the pre-existing rift.[146]

Despite the long-standing policy of splitting the alliance, American actions in the mid-1960s seemed to provide a rallying point for the alliance. The U.S. escalation of the war in Vietnam after August of 1964 threatened Chinese security and triggered a Soviet about-face, from Khrushchev's hands-off policy to the military and economic support provided by his successors. Yet, despite this threat to security, Beijing refused to cooperate with Moscow in aiding Hanoi, largely because mistrust and ideological hyperbole prevented Mao from doing so.[147]

Other Explanations for Conflict

Factors outside of the narrow realm and purpose of the alliance addition-ally helped to undermine the Sino-Soviet partnership. These included Chinese domestic politics, self-perceptions, and personality issues. Again, none of these caused the disputes, but they helped to augment their impact.

Once Mao had decided, by late 1959, that Soviet economic and military aid would no longer come forth in large quantities, and thus China should pursue a more independent path, he exploited the decline in the partnership for his domestic needs. This major decision regarding China's strategic reori-entation closely followed the leadership clashes over the GLF at the Lushan Conference in the preceding summer.[148] Over the course of the following years, the Chairman rhetorically linked his internal enemies—real and in-vented—to Khrushchev's supposed treason in international relations. After his resurgence in domestic politics in the summer of 1962, he micromanaged the collapse of Sino-Soviet relations in view of what he perceived to be a do-mestic leadership struggle.[149] Thus, the Sino-Soviet split grew into a function of domestic politics; to launch the Cultural Revolution in mid-1966 with its purges of supposedly unreliable Chinese leaders, Mao needed a complete break with the Soviet Union. His refusal to send a delegation to the twenty third CPSU Congress in the spring of that year signified the definitive collapse of communist unity between the two countries.[150]

Less tangible is the role of self-perceptions in the breakdown of the Sino-Soviet relationship. Mao's China suffered from an overestimation of its own importance to the outside world. Stalin's death caused the Chairman to see himself as one of the senior revolutionaries in the communist world. Khrushchev's invitation to the Chinese Communists to send a delegation to Moscow during the critical days of the Polish October and the Hungarian Revolution in late 1956 combined with the Chinese misperception that the CCP had saved the unity of the socialist world by providing correct advice to the CPSU during these days critically increased Mao's belief that his PRC was equal with the Soviet Union.[151] This in turn supported his willingness to proceed with his own policies, as outlined above.

Despite this perceived equality, Beijing never was on par with Moscow in affairs on a global level or within the socialist world. While the Soviet Union was a true superpower with increasingly global commitments, the PRC was an international pariah. Furthermore, Mao's economic visions and ideological radicalism even alienated much of the socialist world from his country.[152] The claim to equality was a mirage; a closer look reveals only scaffolding, no concrete. It was this misperception that reinforced Mao's belief that his ideological views would prevail in the struggle for a majority within the communist world.

Equally elusive is the impact of personality conflicts on the Sino-Soviet alliance. Both Mao and Khrushchev were overconfident and difficult-to-work-with leaders. Mao's apparent seniority in world revolution led him to believe that he was a more mature and suitable leader of world revolution. He had no qualms about lecturing Khrushchev on his supposed deficiencies in character and manners.[153] Likewise, Khrushchev lacked magnanimity when Mao's exalted economic and revolutionary visions floundered in the late 1950s.[154] These personality issues, however, only added complexity to the Sino-Soviet split.

Finally, national interest explanations for the split have also attracted much scholarly attention over the past half century, although many are speculative and not based on Chinese evidence. For example, it seems reasonable, on the surface, to argue that the second Taiwan Strait Crisis was Mao's challenge to Khrushchev's peaceful coexistence because Soviet-American rapprochement seemed to undermine the fulfillment of one of China's most important national aspirations—reunification. Although fragmentary, Chinese sources not only fail to corroborate such an argument but also provide evidence against it. Most importantly, Beijing had initiated a similar—and much longer—crisis in the Taiwan Strait already in 1954, that means, *before* the post-Stalin leadership in Moscow had pronounced the policy of peaceful coexistence. Shortly after Khrushchev's Secret Speech in early 1956, the Chinese leadership in fact *welcomed* peaceful coexistence because it seemed to provide an opportunity to find a peaceful solution to China's division.[155] The PRC gave up on the novel Soviet policy in late 1956, in the wake of the Hungarian Revolution and the Suez Crisis, which it grossly misperceived—thanks to ideological blinders—as initiated by U.S. imperialism.[156] The planning for the second Taiwan Strait Crisis itself started a year later, and underwent a series of changing and very different justifications within eight months—none of them, however, related to a Chinese grudge about peaceful coexistence undermining the country's national aspirations.[157] In fact, the Soviet Union initially supported the Chinese-initiated crisis, believing that it was designed to lead to the liberation of Taiwan.[158]

It is crucial to see Chinese foreign policy in the context of the ideological makeup of the Chinese Communist regime—and not as a construct occurring in an ideological void. It is hard to believe that Mao's policy of breaking with the Soviet comrades, of throwing his country into economic agony, and of leading China into self-isolation was in the national interest of the PRC. Yet, all of it emerged against the background of ideological conflict. One might argue that Mao misperceived the national interest of his country, but that just seems to strengthen further the argument that the formulation of national interest is inherently dependent on other factors and thus does not occur in a void. In the end, Chinese evidence does not allow us to make the case for a Sino-Soviet conflict over national interest that eventually led to the split.

Conclusion

Although, historically speaking, only very few alliances were enduring, the Sino-Soviet partnership disintegrated quickly and, primarily, for ideological reasons. Despite the fact that the leaders of both countries shared similar life experiences and ideological view points, their understanding of Marxist-Leninist ideology was sufficiently disparate to undermine the alliance. Disagreement on economic development strategies emerged early on, followed by disputes over de-Stalinization and the course of world revolution. A handful of other factors, ranging from external influences, to domestic issues, to personality problems, further pushed the alliance toward collapse, but acted only as catalysts.

The rise and fall of the Sino-Soviet alliance was one of the defining moments of the Cold War. While obliterating the rigid bipolarity of the early superpower conflict, it provided other socialist states with the opportunity to follow their own policies, most importantly Romania, Albania, and North Korea. The split presented the PRC and the United States with room to maneuver, and, with the Sino-American rapprochement of 1971–72, to realign the international system. China's seminal progression from Soviet ally to American friend had a direct influence on the Vietnam War and the emergence of Euro-Communism, but it also reverberated in nuclear disarmament talks in the 1960s and 1970s, and the simultaneous German-German rapprochement.

For China itself, the collapse of the alliance had an enormous impact. Starting in 1959, Mao Zedong systematically exploited the split for his domestic needs. Linking his internal rivals—some real but most of them imaginary—to the Soviet ideological revisionists and traitors of world revolution, he created the conditions to unleash the Cultural Revolution. The ten years of great disaster, as the CCP has come to call the Cultural Revolution, not only brought great human suffering on the Chinese people, but also delayed, if not reversed, the development of the PRC.

The emergence and collapse of the alliance from 1949 to 1969 also calls for a reassessment of alliance theory. Dominated by Realist and Neo-realist interpretations, alliance theory has often neglected to take ideology, economics, and domestic politics seriously. States do not act according to abstract ideas of national interests and security, but their leaders formulate these on the basis of ideological preferences. The Sino-Soviet alliance would have hardly occurred without Mao's and Stalin's ideological commitments; similarly, the increasingly disparate interpretations of Marxism-Leninism were primarily responsible for the Sino-Soviet split.

Notes

Acknowledgments: I owe thanks to Thomas Bernstein, Li Hua-yu, Catherine Lu, and one anonymous reviewer for graciously providing comments on an early draft. I am grateful to Ryan Griffiths for proofreading the final draft.

1. John W. Garver, *Chinese-Soviet Relations, 1937–1945: The Diplomacy of Chinese Nationalism* (New York: Oxford University Press, 1988), 214–28.

2. Chen Jian, *Mao's China and the Cold War* (hereinafter as *Mao's China*) (Chapel Hill: University of North Carolina Press, 2001), 44–45.

3. Niu Jun, "The Origins of the Sino-Soviet Alliance," in *Brothers in Arms: The Rise and Fall of the Sino-Soviet Alliance, 1945–1963*, ed. O. Arne Westad (hereinafter as *Brothers in Arms*) (Washington, DC: Woodrow Wilson Center, 1998), 61–69.

4. Chen Jian and Yang Kuisong, "Chinese Politics and the Collapse of the Sino-Soviet Alliance" (hereinafter as "Chinese Politics"), in *Brothers in Arms*, 249–50. Wu Xiuquan, *Eight Years in the Ministry of Foreign Affairs: Memoirs of a Diplomat* (hereinafter as *Eight Years*) (Beijing: New World, 1985), 23–24.

5. Sergei N. Goncharov, John W. Lewis, and Xue Litai, *Uncertain Partners: Stalin, Mao, and the Korean War* (hereinafter as *Uncertain Partners*) (Palo Alto, CA: Stanford University Press, 1993), 130–202.

6. Li Hua-yu, "The Political Stalinization of China: The Establishment of One-Party Constitutionalism, 1948–1954," in *Journal of Cold War Studies* 3/2 (2001): 28–47. Nikita S. Khrushchev, *Khrushchev Remembers: The Last Testament* (hereinafter as *Testament*) (Boston: Little, Brown, 1974), 241–42.

7. Sergei Goncharenko, "Sino-Soviet Military Cooperation," *Brothers in Arms*, 152–60.

8. Jiang Hongxun and Zhou Guohua, "50niandai Sulian yuanzhu Zhongguo meitan gongye jianshe xiangmu de youlai he bianhua" [Origins and change of soviet assistance to the chinese coal industry in constructing projects in the 1950s] (hereinafter as "50niandai"), *Dangdai Zhongguo shi yanjiu* [Studies in Contemporary chinese History] 4 (1995): 13–14.

9. Nikita S. Khrushchev, *Khrushchev Remembers* (Boston: Little, Brown, 1970), 463. Zhang Shuguang, "Sino-Soviet Economic Cooperation," *Brothers in Arms*, 201–3.

10. Xinhua News Agency, *China's Foreign Relations: A Chronology of Events, 1949–1988* (Beijing: Foreign Languages, 1989), 258.

11. William T. Tow, "China and the International System," in *Chinese Foreign Policy: Theory and Praxis*, ed. Thomas W. Robinson and David Shambaugh (Oxford: Clarendon, 1994), 125–26.

12. Chen Jian, "Chinese Politics," 258.

13. Dimitrii T. Shepilov, *Neprimknuvshii* [Not having sided] (Moskva: Vagryus, 2001), 380–84. Li Lianqing, *Lengnuan suiyue: yibosanzhe de ZhongSu guanxi* [Years of changing temperature: the twists and turns of Sino-Soviet relations] (hereinafter as Lengnuan) (Beijing: Shijie zhishi chubanshe, 1998), 319.

14. Lorenz M. Lüthi, *The Sino-Soviet Split: Cold War in the Communist World* (hereinafter as *The Sino-Soviet Split*) (Princeton: Princeton University Press, 2008), 41–44.

15. Lorenz M. Lüthi, *The Sino-Soviet Split*, 46–79.

16. A. A. Brezhnev, *Kitai: Ternistyi put' k dobrososedstvy: vosponminaniya i razmyshleniya* [China: the thorny path to good neighborhood: reminiscences and reflections] (hereinafter as *Kitai*) (Moskva: Mezhdunarodnye otnosheniya, 1998), 52–70. "Kang Sheng's Speech at Moscow Conference," February 4, 1960, in *Survey of China Mainland Press* (hereinafter as *SCMP*), 2194, 42–46.

17. Wu Lengxi, *Shinian lunzhan, 1956–1966: ZhongSu guanxi huiyulu* [Ten years of debate, 1956–1966: recollections of Sino-Soviet relations] (hereinafter as *Shinian lunzhan*) (Beijing: Zhongyang wenxian chubanshel, 1999), 236–46.

18. Bo Yibo, *Ruogan zhongda juece yu shijian de huigu*, (shangjuan) [Recollections of some important decisions and events, vol. 1] (hereinafter as *Ruogan 1*) (Beijing: Zhonggong zhongyang dangxiao chubanshe, 1991), 704. Veljko Micunovic, *Moscow Diary* (Garden City: Doubleday, 1980), 421–23.

19. Lorenz M. Lüthi, *The Sino-Soviet Split*, 174–91.

20. Lorenz M. Lüthi, *The Sino-Soviet Split*, 195–201.

21. Lorenz M. Lüthi, *The Sino-Soviet Split*, 201–209.

22. "Communication of the Main Points of the 6th All-Country Foreign Affairs Conference," no date, in *Jiangsu sheng dang'anguan* [Jiangsu Provincial Archive] (hereinafter as *JSSDAG*), 3124, zhang 145, 2–13.

23. John Gittings, *Survey of the Sino-Soviet Dispute* (hereinafter as *Survey*) (London: Royal Institute of International Affairs, 1968), 176.

24. Lorenz M. Lüthi, *The Sino-Soviet Split*, 236–44.

25. Wu Lengxi, *Yi Mao zhuxi* [Remembering Chairman Mao] (hereinafter as *Yi Mao zhuxi*) (Beijing: Xinhua chubanshe, 1995), 151–52. Wu Lengxi, *Shinian lunzhan*, 937–39. *Peking Review* (hereinafter as *PR*) 13 (March 25, 1966), 6.

26. "Inter-Governmental Relations of the PRC with the Soviet Union," November 11, 1966, in *Arkhiv Vneshnei Politiki Rossiiskoi Federatsii* [Foreign Policy Archive of the Russian Federation] (hereinafter as *AVPRF*), f.0100, o.59, d.16, p.526, 117.

27. Barbara Barnouin and Yu Changgen, *Chinese Foreign Policy during the Cultural Revolution* (London: Kegan Paul, 1998), 69–71. Ma Jisen, *The Cultural Revolution in the Foreign Ministry of China* (Hong Kong: Chinese University Press, 2004), 163–64, 168–72, 187–89.

28. Yang Kuisong, "The Sino-Soviet Border Clash of 1969: From Zhenbao Island to Sino-American Rapprochement" (hereinafter as *Sino-Soviet Border Clash*), *Cold War History* 1/1 (2000), 24–25.

29. Li Ke and Hao Shengzhang, *Wenhua dageming zhong de renmin jiefangjun* [The People's Liberation Army during the Cultural Revolution] (hereinafter as *Wenhua dageming*) (Beijing: Zhonggong dangshi ziliao chubanshe, 1989), 317. Gong Li, "Chinese Decision Making and the Thawing of U.S.-China Relations," in *Re-examining the Cold War: U.S.-China Diplomacy, 1954–1973*, eds. Robert S. Ross and Jiang Changbin (Cambridge: Harvard University Press, 2001), 329.

30. Yang Kuisong, *Sino-Soviet Border Clash*, 27, 30.

31. Li Ke, *Wenhua dageming*, 321–23. *Guardian*, March 20, 1969, 1.

32. Robert Conquest, *Stalin: Breaker of Nations* (hereinafter as *Stalin*) (New York: Viking, 1991), 27–49.

33. Phillip Short, *Mao: A Life* (hereinafter as *Mao*) (New York: Henry Holt, 2000), 117–24.

34. Robert Conquest, *Stalin*, 51, 54–57.

35. Phillip Short, *Mao*, 318–407.

36. Robert Conquest, *Stalin*, 72–95. Phillip Short, *Mao*, 265–317, 408–38.

37. Vladimir I. Lenin, *Imperialism, the Highest Stage of Capitalism* (Moscow: Progress, 1978).

38. Tony Saich, *The Rise to Power of the Chinese Communist Party* (Armonk, NY: M.E. Sharpe, 1996), xlv–xlvi.

39. Harry Overstreet, and Bonaro Overstreet, *The War Called Peace: Khrushchev's Communism* (New York: W.W. Norton, 1961), 14.

40. Andrei Zhdanov's speech, available at: http://www.cnn.com/SPECIALS/cold.war/episodes/04/documents/cominform.html. Levering, 133.

41. Mao Zedong, "On New Democracy," January 1940, in *Selected Works* (hereinafter as *SW*) vol. 2 (Beijing: Foreign Languages Press, 1961), 364–65.

42. Mao Zedong, "Talk with the American Correspondent Anna Louise Strong," August 1946, in *SW*, vol. 4, 97–101.

43. Bo Yibo, "The Making of the 'Lean-to-One Side' Decision," in *Chinese Historians* 5/1 (Spring 1992), 57–62.

44. "Sino-Soviet Treaty of Friendship, Alliance, and Mutual Assistance," February 14, 1950, in *Current Background* (hereinafter as *CB*), 545, 1.

45. Robert Conquest, *Stalin*, 122. Dmitri A. Volkogonov, *Stalin: Triumph and Tragedy* (London: Weidenfeld and Nicolson, 1991), 104–5, 109–10, 113.

46. Vojtech Mastny, *The Cold War and Soviet Insecurity* (hereinafter as *The Cold War*) (New York: Oxford University Press, 1996), 11–79.

47. Vojtech Mastny, *The Cold War*, 85–91.

48. Dieter Heinzig, *Die Sowjetunion und das kommunistische China 1945–1950* [The Soviet Union and communist China, 1945–1950] (Baden-Baden: Nomos, 1998), 494–501.

49. Chen Jian, *China's Road to the Korean War: the Making of the Sino-American Confrontation* (New York: Columbia University Press, 1994).

50. "Conversation between Stalin and Mao, Moscow, 16 December 1949," in "Stalin's Conversations with Chinese Leaders," ed. Chen Jian, Vojtech Mastny, O. Arne Westad, and Vladislav M. Zubok, in *Cold War International History* (hereinafter as *CWIHP*) Bulletin 6–7 (Winter 1995/96): 5–7.

51. Lorenz M. Lüthi, *The Sino-Soviet Split*, 8.

52. Li Hua-yu, *Mao and the Economic Stalinization of China, 1948–1953* (Lanham, MD: Rowman & Littlefield, 2006), 64, 88–89, 109. Yuan Baohua, "Fu Sulian tanpan de riri yeye" [Going to Moscow to negotiate day and night] (hereinafter as *Fu Sulian*), in *Dangdai Zhongguo shi yanjiu* (Studies of contemporary Chinese history), no. 1 (1996): 23–26. Li Yueran, "Woguo tong Sulian shangtan: diyi ge wunian jihua qingkuang the huiyi" [Negotiations between our country and the Soviet Union: recollections on the circumstances of the First Five-Year Plan] (hereinafter as *Woguo*), in *Xin Zhongguo waijiao feng yun* [The stormy diplomacy of the new China], vol. 2, ed. Pei Jianzhang (Beijing: Shijie zhishi chubanshe), 1991, 15–18. Wang Taiping, *Zhonghua renmin gongheguo waijiaoshi* [A diplomatic history of the People's Republic of China] (hereinafter as *Zhonghua*), vol. 2 (Beijing: Shijie zhishi chubanshe, 1998), 40. Bo Yibo, *Ruogan 1*, 296, 299.

53. Robert C. Tucker, *Stalin in Power: The Revolution from Above, 1928–1941* (hereinafter as *Stalin in Power*) (New York: W.W. Norton, 1990), 70–74.

54. Robert C. Tucker, *Stalin in Power*, 200–204.

55. Sheila Fitzpatrick, *Stalin's Peasants: Resistance and Survival in the Russian Village after Collectivization* (New York: Oxford University Press, 1994), 69–76. Martin Malia, *The Soviet Tragedy: A History of Socialism in Russia, 1917–1991* (hereinafter as *Soviet Tragedy*) (New York: Free, 1994), 198–99.

56. Vaclav Smil, "China's Agricultural Land," in *The China Quarterly* 158, 414–29.

57. "Soviet-Chinese Relations (Reference)," May 1965, in *AVPRF*, f.0100, o.56, d.22, 498, 223–24. Wu Lengxi, *Shinian lunzhan*, 336.

58. Mark Selden, "Cooperation and Conflict: Cooperative and Collective Formation of China's Countryside" (hereinafter as *Cooperation*), *Transition to Socialism in China*, ed. Mark Selden and Victor Lippit (Croom Helm: M.E. Sharpe, 1982), 59. David Bachman, *Chen Yun and the Chinese Political System* (hereinafter as *Chen Yun*) (Berkeley: University of California Press, 1985), 48–49, 54, 59.

59. Bo Yibo, *Ruogan 1*, 299. Zhang Shuguang, *Economic Cold War* (Palo Alto, CA: Stanford University Press, 2001), 166–68, 282–83. About loan and debt repayment: "Soviet-Chinese Relations (Reference)," February 13, 1961, in *AVPRF*, f.0100, o.54, d.27, p.470, 29, 30. Wu Lengxi, *Shinian lunzhan*, 336. Nicholas Lardy, "Chinese Economy under Stress, 1958–1965," *Cambridge History of China*, vol. 14, ed. Roderick MacFarquhar and John K. Fairbank (hereinafter as *Cambridge History of China*) (Cambridge: Cambridge University Press, 1987), 361. Li Rui, *Li Rui wenji*, vol. 3/1 (Haikou: Nanfang chubanshe, 1999), 37.

60. Edward Friedman, "Maoism, Titoism, Stalinism: Some Origins and Consequences of the Maoist Theory of the Socialist Theory," (hereinafter as *Maoism*) in *The Transition to Socialism in China* (Armonk, NY: M. E. Sharpe, 1982), 160–76. Jan Prybyla, *Political Economy of Communist China* (hereinafter as *Political Economy*) (Scranton, PA: International Textbook Co., 1970), 111. Deborah Milenkovitch, *Plan and Market in Yugoslav Economic Thought* (New Haven, CT: Yale University Press, 1971), 62–77. Carol L. Hamrin, "Yang Xianzhen," in *China's Establishment Intellectuals*, ed. Carol L. Hamrin and Timothy Cheek (Armonk, NY: M.E. Sharpe, 1986), 61–62. Barry Naughton, "Deng Xiaoping: the Economist," *Deng Xiaoping: Portrait of a Chinese Statesman*, ed. David Shambaugh (Oxford: Clarendon Press, 1995), 131. David Bachman, *Chen Yun*, 33–34, 37–38, 48.

61. Edward Friedman, *"Maoism,"* 160–70. Mao Zedong, "Two Talks on Mutual Aid and Cooperation in Agriculture," October and November 1953, in *SW*, vol. 5, 132. Mao Zedong, "Combat Bourgeois Ideas in the Party," August 12, 1953, in *SW*, vol. 5, 104. Kenneth Lieberthal, "The Great Leap Forward and the Split in the Yenan Leadership," *Cambridge History of China*, vol. 14, 303–4.

62. Raymond F. Wylie, *The Emergence of Maoism: Mao Tse-tung, Ch'en Po-ta and the Search for Chinese Theory, 1935–1945* (Palo Alto, CA: Stanford University Press, 1980), 114–18, 121–22, 124–25.

63. Zhonggong zhongyang wenxian yanjiushi bian, *Mao Zedong zhuan (1949– 1976)* [Biography of Mao Zedong (1949–1976)] (hereinafter as *Mao Zedong zhuan*) (Beijing: Zhongyang wenxian chubanshe, 1997), vol. 1, 508.

64. Mao Zedong, "On the Cooperative Transition of Agriculture," July 31, 1955, in *SW*, vol. 5, 199.

65. Edward Friedman, Paul G. Pickowicz, and Mark Selden, *Chinese Village, Socialist State* (hereinafter as *Chinese Village*) (New Haven, CT: Yale, 1991), 186–87. Mark Selden, *Cooperation*, 70–73. Jan Prybyla, *Political Economy*, 156. Craig Dietrich, *People's China*, 2nd ed. (New York: Oxford University Press, 1994), 100–101. Jean-Luc Domenach, *Origins of the Great Leap Forward* (Boulder, CO: Westview University Press, 1995), 41, 43, 56. Edward Friedman, *Chinese Village*, 192–203. Lowell Dittmer, *China's Continuous Revolution* (Berkeley: University of California Press, 1987), 17–18.

Roderick MacFarquhar, *The Origins of the Cultural Revolution*, vol. 1 (hereinafter as *Origins*) (New York: Columbia University Press, 1974), 59, 347, n. 27. David Bachman, *Chen Yun*, 60. Mark Selden, *Cooperation*, 79–80. Jan Prybyla, *Political Economy*, 156–58.

66. Wu Lengxi, *Shinian lunzhan*, 12–20. "Soviet-Chinese Relations," March 11, 1957, in *AVPRF*, f.0100, o.50, d.29, p.426, 26. A. A. Brezhnev, *Kitai*, 49–50. Also, Jan Rowi ski, "China and the Crisis of Marxism-Leninism," in *Communist China in Retrospect*, ed. Marie-Luise Näth (Frankfurt/Main: Lang, 1995), 71.

67. Valery Soyfer, *Lysenko and the Tragedy of Soviet Science* (New Brunswick, NJ: Rutgers University Press, 1994). Laurence Schneider, "Lysenkoism in China," *Chinese Law and Government* (hereinafter as *CLG*) 19/2, iv–xi.

68. Wu Xiuquan, *Eight Years*, 125. Roderick MacFarquhar, *Origins*, vol. 1, 100–101, 122–38.

69. Mao Zedong, "Speech to the Personages of Industrial and Commercial Circles," November 8, 1956, in *Mao Zedong wenji* (diqijuan) [Selected Writings of Mao Zedong, vol. 7] (Beijing: Renmin chubanshe, 1999), 178. Mao Zedong, "Speech at the Second Plenary Session of the Eighth CCP CC," November 14, 1956, in *SW*, vol. 5, 337–39.

70. Li Rui, *Li Rui wenji*, 48. Li Rui, "An Initial Study of Mao Zedong's Erroneous 'Left' Thinking in His Later Years [Part I]" (hereinafter as "Study [I]"), in *CLG* 29/4, 36. Li Zhisui, with Anne F. Thurston, *The Private Life of Chairman Mao* (New York: Random House, 1994), 197–99. Roderick MacFarquhar, *Origins*, vol. 1, 169, 177–80.

71. Nicholas Lardy et al., *Chen Yun's Strategy for China's Development* (Armonk, NY: M.E. Sharpe, 1983), 7–22, 30–38. David Bachman, *Chen Yun*, 117–30.

72. Li Rui, "Study [I]," 37–38. Roderick MacFarquhar, *Origins*, vol. 1, 218.

73. Mao Zedong, "Things Are Beginning to Change," May 15, 1957, in *SW*, vol. 5, 444.

74. Roderick MacFarquhar, *Origins*, vol. 1, 312–13, and vol. 2, 4, 16–17. Li Rui, "Study [I]," 49.

75. Mao Zedong, "[Speech Held in Moscow, November 18, 1957]," in *Jianguo yilai Mao Zedong wengao* (diliuce) [Selected writings of Mao Zedong since the founding of the PRC, vol. 6] (hereinafter as *JYMW 6*) (Beijing: Zhongyang wenxian chubanshel, 1993), 635. Li Rui, *Li Rui wenji*, 53–54. Li Yueran, *Waijiao wutai shang de Xin Zhongguo lingxiu* [New China's leaders on the diplomatic stage] (hereinafter as *Waijiao*) (Beijing: Jiefangjun chubanshe, 1989), 162–63. Zhang Shuguang, "Sino-Soviet Economic Cooperation," 203.

76. Li Rui, "Study [I]," 46. Bo Yibo, *Ruogan 1*, 704. Veljko Micunovic, *Moscow Diary*, 421–23.

77. Roderick MacFarquhar, *The Origins of the Cultural Revolution*, vol. 2 (hereinafter as *Origins 2*) (New York: Columbia University Press, 1983), 124. *SCMP* 1846, 1. Mao, "Talk at Beidaihe Conference (Draft Transcript)," August 30, 1958, in *The Secret Speeches of Chairman Mao: From the Hundred Flowers to the Great Leap Forward* (hereinafter as *SS*), ed. Roderick MacFarquhar, Timothy Cheek, and Eugene Wu (Cambridge: Harvard University Press, 1989), 434–37. Jürgen Domes, *Peng Te-huai:*

The Man and the Image (hereinafter as *Peng*) (Palo Alto, CA: Stanford University Press, 1985), 80. Li Rui, "Study [I]," in *CLG* 29/4, 7.

78. Mao, "Speech at the Chengdu Meeting," March 22, 1958, in *Mao Zedong xuanji* (sanjuan) [Selected works of Mao Zedong, vol. 3] (Hong Kong: Mingbao yuekan, 1971), 182. "Record of Conversation with Mao Zedong," February 28, 1958, in *AVPRF*, f.0100, o.51, d.6, p.432, 95.

79. Referred to as "Short Record of Conversation," December 4, 1960, in *AVPRF*, f.0100, o.53, d.6, p.453, 52. Bo Yibo, *Ruogan 1*, 704.

80. Bo Yibo, *Ruogan 1*, 704. Veljko Micunovic, *Moscow Diary*, 421–23. Ding Ming, ed., "Huigu ge sikao: Yu ZhongSu guanxi qinlizhi de duihua" [Review and reflections: interviews with those who witnessed personally Sino-Soviet relations], in *Dangdai Zhongguo shi yanjiu* [Studies in contemporary Chinese history], no. 2 (1998): 22, 31. Lev P. Delyusin, "Guanyu SuZhong chongtu qiyin de ruogan sikao" [Some reflections on the causes for the Soviet-Chinese conflict], *Dangdai Zhongguo shi yanjiu* [Studies in contemporary Chinese history], no. 3 (1998): 101.

81. Manfred Hildermeier, *Geschichte der Sowjetunion, 1917–1991: Entstehung und Niedergang des ersten sozialistischen Staates* [History of the Soviet Union, 1917–1991: formation and demise of the first socialist state] (hereinafter as *Geschichte*) (Munich: C. H. Beck, 1998), 791. Martin Malia, *Soviet Tragedy*, 330. Abram Bergson, *The Economics of Soviet Planning* (New Haven, CT: Yale University Press, 1964), 83. Harry Schwartz, *Soviet Economy since Stalin* (London: Gallancz, 1965), 85–95. "Stenographic Account of the CPSU CC Plenum" (November 5, 1958), in *Rossiiskii Gosudarstvennyi Arkhiv Noveishei Istorii* [Russian state archive of contemporary history] (hereinafter as *RGANI*), f.2, o.1, d.332, 3a, 8a.

82. Xiao Donglian, *Qiusuo Zhongguo: Wenge qian shinian shi* [In search of China: the history of the decade before the Cultural Revolution, vol. 1] (hereinafter as *Qiusuo*) (Beijing: Hongqi Chubanshe, 1999), 437–39, 639.

83. Xu Zehao, *Wang Jiaxiang zhuan* [Biography of Wang Jiaxiang] (hereinafter as *Wang*) (Beijing: Dangdai zhongguo chubanshe, 1996), 539. Hu Qiaomu, *Hu Qiaomu huiyi Mao Zedong* [Hu Qiaomu remembers Mao Zedong] (Beijing: Renmin chubanshe, 1994), 15. Xiao Donglian, *Qiusuo*, vol. 1, 477–78. Peng Dehuai, *Memoirs of a Chinese Marshal: The Autobiographical Notes of Peng Dehuai (1898–1974)* (Beijing: Foreign Languages Press, 1984), 486–87. Wu Lengxi, *Yi Mao zhuxi*, 111–12.

84. Li Rui, *Li Rui wenji*, vol. 3/2, 345. Mao, "Talk at Wuchang Conference," November 21, 1958, morning, in *SS*, 486.

85. Roderick MacFarquhar, *Origins*, vol. 2, 135. Wu Lengxi, *Shinian lunzhan*, 191.

86. Lorenz M. Lüthi, *The Sino-Soviet Split*, 126–35.

87. Lorenz M. Lüthi, *The Sino-Soviet Split*, 194–201.

88. Wu Xiuquan, *Eight Years*, 125. Roderick MacFarquhar, *Origins*, vol. 1, 100–101, 122–38.

89. Mao Zedong, "Speech at the Second Plenary Session of the Eighth CCP CC," November 14, 1956, in *SW*, vol. 5, 341.

90. Harrison Salisbury, *The New Emperors: China in the Era of Mao and Deng* (Boston: Little, Brown, 1992), 138. Shi Zhe, and Li Haiwen, *Zai lishi juren shenbian:*

Shi Zhe huiyilu [At the side of historical giants: Shi Zhe memoirs] (hereinafter as *Zai lishi*), rev. and exp. ed. (Beijing: Zhongyang wenxian chubanshe, 1998), 509. Liu Xiao, *Chushi Sulian banian* [Eight years as ambassador to the Soviet Union] (Beijing: Dangshi ziliao chubanshe, 1998), 58.

91. Mao Zedong, "Zai Zhongyang Chengdu huiyi shang de jianghua" [Speech at the Chengdu Work Conference], March 1958, in *Mao Zedong daguan* [The grand sight of Mao Zedong] (Beijing: Renmin daxue chubanshe, 1993), 605. Mao Zedong, "Zai Chengdu huiyi shang de jianghua" [Speech at the Chengdu Conference], March 10, 1958, in *Mao Zedong sixiang wansui* [Long live Mao Zedong thought] (n.p., 1969), 162.

92. Mao Zedong, "Beidaihe Zhongyang zhengzhiju kuada huiyi zhunbei taolun de wenti" [Problems to be prepared for discussion at Beidaihe enlarged politburo meeting], August 1958, in *JYMW* 7, 343. Mikhail I. Sladkovskii et al., eds., *Ocherki kommunisticheskoi partii Kitaya, 1921–1969* [Essays on the history of the Communist Party of China, 1921–1969] (Moskva: SSSR AN, Institut Dal'nego Vostoka, 1971), 352.

93. Xiao Donglian, *Qiusuo*, vol. 1, 570–71.

94. "On the Condition of the Exchange of Information," February 18, 1960, in *AVPRF*, f.0100, o.53, d.24, p.457, 7–33.

95. Dmitri A. Volkogonov, *Autopsy of an Empire: The Seven Leaders Who Built the Soviet Regime* (New York: Free Press, 1998), 233. Wu Lengxi, *Shinian lunzhan*, 227–28.

96. Si Fu, "Zhonggong duidai Dulese 'heping yanbian' zhanlue de qianqian houhou" [The whole story of how China handled Dulles's strategy of "peaceful evolution"] (hereinafter as "Zhonggong"), in *Zhiqingzhe shuo* [Those who know the facts speak], vol. 8, ed. Chang Cheng (Zhongguo qingnian chubanshe, 1999), 42–71. Mao Zedong, "Guanyu guoji xingshi de jianghua tigang" [Outline of a speech on the international situation], December 1959, *JYMW 8*, 600. Wu Lengxi, *Shinian lunzhan*, 233–34. "To the Presidium of the CPSU CC," December 18, 1959, in *RGANI*, f.2, o.1, d.415, 19–33, 43–44.

97. For the events from April to June: Lorenz M. Lüthi, *The Sino-Soviet Split*, 160–74. "Report," July 16, 1960, in *RGANI*, f.2, o.1, d.484, 69–87a (quote).

98. William Taubman, *Khrushchev: The Man and his Era* (hereinafter as *Khrushchev*) (New York: W.W. Norton, 2003), 515. Rudolf G. Pikhoya, *Sovetskii Soyuz: istoriya vlasti, 1945–1990* [The Soviet Union: a history of power, 1945–1991] (Novosibirsk: Sibirskii Khronograf, 2000), 215, 217. Liu Xiao, *Chushi*, 25.

99. *SCMP* 2605, 35. Zhonggong zhongyang wenxian yanjiushi bian [CCP, Central Documents Research Office], *Zhou Enlai nianpu, 1949–1976* (xiajuan) [A chronicle of Zhou Enlai's life: 1949–1976, vol. 2] (Beijing: Zhongyang wenxian chubanshe, 1997), 440–41.

100. The polemics are in *PR* 37 (September 13, 1963), 6–23; 38 (September 20, 1963), 8–15; 39 (September 27, 1963), 14–27; 43 (October 25, 1963), 6–15; 47 (November 22, 1963), 6–16; 51 (December 20, 1963), 6–18; 6 (February 7, 1964), 5–21; 14 (April 3, 1964), 5–23; 29 (July 17, 1964), 7–28.

101. Wu Lengxi, *Shinian lunzhan*, 339–42.

102. John L. Gaddis, *We Now Know* (Oxford: Clarendon Press, 1997), 108, 207. Matthew Evangelista, "Why Keep Such an Army?" in CWIHP Working Paper 19, 17–26. Hildermeier, *Geschichte*, 762–63. Adam Ulam, *Expansion and Coexistence* (New York: Praeger, 1968), 132.

103. Zhou Enlai, "Taiwan jiang bei jiefang" [Taiwan will be liberated], June 29, 1956, in *Zhou Enlai xuanji* (xiajuan) [Selected works of Zhou Enlai, vol. 2] (Xianggang: Yishan tushu gongsi, 1976), 206.

104. Wu Lengxi, *Shinian lunzhan*, 80. *SCMP* 1233, 45.

105. Wu Lengxi, *Shinian lunzhan*, 138. Yan Mingfu, "Huiyi liangci Mosike huiyi he Hu Qiaomu" [Recollecting Hu Qiaomu attending two Moscow conferences], in *Dangdai Zhongguo shi yanjiu* [Studies in contemporary Chinese history], no. 3 (1997): 9. The Chinese published an outline of the memo in 1964: *PR* 14, April 3, 1964, 22–23.

106. Chen Jian, *Mao's China*, 167–71. Zhai Qiang, *The Dragon, the Lion, and the Eagle: Chinese-British-American Relations, 1949–1958* (hereinafter as *Dragon*) (Kent, OH: Kent State University Press, 1994), 173–74. U. Alexis Johnson, *Right Hand of Power* (Englewood Cliffs, NJ: Prentice Hall, 1984), 236, 243, 260–61. Ronald Keith, *Diplomacy of Zhou Enlai* (Basingstoke: Macmillan, 1989), 90. Zhang Baijia and Jia Qingguo, "Steering Wheel, Shock Absorber, and Diplomatic Probe in Confrontation," *Re-Examining the Cold War: U.S. Diplomacy, 1954–1973*, ed. Robert S. Ross and Jiang Changbin (Cambridge: Harvard University Press, 2001), 187.

107. Li Zhisu, *Private Life*, 262.

108. Mao Zedong, "Talk at Beidaihe Conference (Draft Transcript)," August 17, 1958, in *SW*, 402. Also, "Statements by Leaders of the PRC on Important Questions of Foreign Policy," December 9, 1960, in *AVPRF*, f.0100, o.53, d.24, p.457, 236.

109. "White House Press Release," September 4, 1958, in *Foreign Relations of the United States* (hereinafter as *FRUS*), *1958–1960*, XIX, ed. United States, Department of State (Washington, DC: GPO, 1996), 135–36. Soviet counter threat in: "Telegram From the Embassy in the Soviet Union to the Department of State," September 19, 1958, in *FRUS 1958–1960*, XIX, 231–38.

110. U.S. offer in "Radio and Television Report," September 11, 1958, in *The Public Papers of the President: Dwight D. Eisenhower*, vol. 6 (Washington, DC: GPO, 1960), 699–700. PRC understanding of American defensive positions in "Written Report by Petr Panchevski—Ambassador in the PRC," November 12, 1958, in *Arkhiv na Ministerstvoto na Vunshnite Raboti* [*Archive of the Ministry of Foreign* Relations] (hereinafter as AMVR), o.14p, a.e.491, 158–61.

111. Mikhail S. Kapitsa, *Na raznykh paralleliakh: zapiski diplomata* [On different parallels: notes of a diplomat] (Moskva: Kniga i biznes, 1996), 61–63. A. A. Brezhnev, *Kitai*, 57–58. O. Arne Westad, "Introduction," *Brother in Arms*, 21–22.

112. Zhai Qiang, *Dragon*, 197–99.

113. Wang Taiping, *Zhonghua*, vol. 2, 221–22. Sergei Goncharenko, "Sino-Soviet Military Cooperation," 157. Zhang Shuguang, "Sino-Soviet Economic Cooperation," 207. A. A. Brezhnev, *Kitai*, 58–59.

114. Lorenz M. Lüthi, *The Sino-Soviet Split*, 138–46.

115. *Pravda*, September 10, 1959, 3.

116. Li Lianqing, *Lengnuan*, 297–98. Wu Lengxi, *Shinian lunzhan*, 206–07, 218. Xiao Donglian, *Qiusuo*, vol. 1, 576.

117. Nikita S. Khrushchev, *Testament*, 263, 307, 311.

118. Si Fu, "Shi pengyou haishi diren—Zhonggong dui Heluxiaofu zai ZhongYin guanxi shang" [Friend or foe—the CCP with regard to Khrushchev in Sino-Indian relations], in *Zhiqingzhe shuo*, vol. 8, 288–92. Li Yueran, *Waijiao*, 179–83. Wu Lengxi, *Shi nian lunzhan*, 223–27. "Record of Conversation of Comrade Khrushchev N.S. with CC CCP Chairman Mao Zedong, Vice Chairman CC CCP Liu Shaoqi, Zhou Enlai, Zhu De, Lin Biao, Politburo Members Peng Zhen and Chen Yi, and Secretariat Member Wang Jiaxiang," October 2, 1959, in "'One Finger's Worth of Historical Events': New Russian and Chinese Evidence on the Sino-Soviet Alliance and Split, 1948–1959," ed. David Wolff, CWIHP Working Paper 30 (2000), 65–68.

119. Si Fu, "Zhonggong," 57–58. Mao Zedong, "Guanyu guoji xingshi de jianghua tigang" [Outline of a speech on the international situation], December 1959, in *JYMW* 8, 600.

120. *New York Times* [*NYT*], December 2, 1959, 4. "To the Presidium of the CPSU CC," December 18, 1959, in *RGANI*, f.2, o.1, d.415, 19–33, 43–44.

121. "Speech of Comrade Kang Sheng on the Meeting of the Political Consultative Committee of the Members of the Warsaw Pact," [February 4, 1960], in *Stiftung Archiv der Parteien und Massenorganisationen der DDR im Bundesarchiv* [*Archive of the Parties and Mass Organizations of the GDR in the Federal Archives*] (hereinafter as *SAPMO-BArch*), DY 30/3386, 87–99.

122. Wu Lengxi, *Shinian lunzhan*, 251.

123. Wu Lengxi, *Shinian lunzhan*, 258–59. *CB* 617, 1–29, 30–45. *SCMP* 2246, 12.

124. *Mao Zedong zhuan*, vol.2, 1075.

125. "Report on the Preparation and Course of the Eleventh General Meeting of the WFTU," June 9, 1960, in *SAPMO-BArch*, DY 30/3671, 16–24.

126. Lorenz M. Lüthi, *The Sino-Soviet Split*, 169–74.

127. "[Letter by Chervonenko]," July 9, 1960, in *AVPRF*, f.0100, o.53, d.24, p.457, 96–98. "Note: The Soviet Embassy in Beijing to the Ministry of Foreign Affairs of the PRC," July 18, 1960, in "A Crucial Step toward the Breakdown of the Sino-Soviet Alliance: The Withdrawal of Soviet Experts from China in July 1960," ed. Chen Jian, *CWIHP Bulletin* 8–9, 249–50.

128. Lorenz M. Lüthi, *The Sino-Soviet Split*, 174–80.

129. Ilya V. Gaiduk, *Confronting Vietnam: Soviet Policy toward the Indochina Conflict, 1954–1953* (Palo Alto, CA: Stanford University Press, 2003), 105–17. "Telegram No. 165 from Claudius to Ulbricht and Schwab," August 24, 1960, in *SAPMO-BArch*, DY 30/3667, 13–17.

130. Lorenz M. Lüthi, *The Sino-Soviet Split*, 160–67.

131. Lorenz M. Lüthi, *The Sino-Soviet Split*, 182–91.

132. Lorenz M. Lüthi, *The Sino-Soviet Split*, 194–218.

133. Wu Lengxi, *Shinian lunzhan*, 457.

134. "Summary Report of the CPSU CC," October 17, 1961, in *RGANI*, f.1, o.4, d.89, 26–222 and f.1, o.4, d.90, 1–99. Taubman, *Khrushchev*, 515. Lev P. Delyusin, "Nekotorye razmyshleniya o nachale sovetsko-kitaiskogo konflikta" [Some reflections

on the beginning of the Soviet-Chinese conflict], paper presented at the conference "Sino-Soviet Relations and Cold War: International Scientific Seminar," Beijing, China, October 1997, 19.

135. Lorenz M. Lüthi, *The Sino-Soviet Split*, 220–24.

136. John Gittings, *Survey*, 176.

137. Sergei N. Goncharov, *Uncertain Partners*, 130–202.

138. Sergei Goncharenko, "Sino-Soviet Military Cooperation," 147, 152, 160.

139. Yuan Baohua, "Fu Sulian," 23–26. Li Yueran, "Woguo," 15–18. Wang Taiping, *Zhonghua*, vol. 2, 40. Bo Yibo, *Ruogan 1*, 296, 299. "Reference of the Trade Representative of the USSR in the PRC," September 22, 1960, in *AVPRF*, f.0100, o.53, d.24, p.457, 188–92. Su Shifang, "Guanyu 50niandai wo guo cong Sulian jinkou jishu he chengtao shebei de huigu," in *Dangdai Zhongguo shi yanjiu* [Studies in contemporary Chinese history], no. 5, 1998, 14, 49–50. Dangdai Zhongguo congshu [Contemporary China series], *Dangdai Zhongguo waijiao* [Contemporary China: foreign relations] (Beijing: Zhongguo shehui kexue chubanshe, 1988), 29. Jiang Hongxun, "50niandai," 13–14.

140. Lorenz M. Lüthi, *The Sino-Soviet Split*, 151–53.

141. A. A. Brezhnev, *Kitai*, 58–59.

142. Lorenz M. Lüthi, *The Sino-Soviet Split*, 180–82.

143. Lorenz M. Lüthi, *The Sino-Soviet Split*, 274–77.

144. Pei Jianzhang, *Zhonghua Renmin Gongheguo Waijiaoshi* [A diplomatic history of the People's Republic of China, vol. 1] (Beijing: Shijie zhishi chubanshe, 1994), 20–21. O. Arne Westad, ed., "Fighting for Friendship," in *CWIHP Bulletin* 8–9, 229. Shi Zhe, *Zai lishi*, 400–3. Xu Zehao, *Wang*, 497. Mao Zedong, "Jiejian Riben shehuidang renshi deng de tanhua" [Meeting with personage of the Japanese Socialist Party], July 10, 1964, in *MZDSW 1969*, 532–45.

145. John Gaddis, *Long Peace* (New York: Oxford University Press, 1987), 164–87.

146. Lorenz M. Lüthi, *The Sino-Soviet Split*, 246–72.

147. Lorenz M. Lüthi, *The Sino-Soviet Split*, 302–39.

148. Lorenz M. Lüthi, *The Sino-Soviet Split*, 126–35, 151–53.

149. Lorenz M. Lüthi, *The Sino-Soviet Split*, 219–45.

150. Wu Lengxi, *Yi Mao zhuxi*, 151–52. Wu Lengxi, *Shinian lunzhan*, 937–39. *PR* 13 (March 25, 1966), 6.

151. Lorenz M. Lüthi, *The Sino-Soviet Split*, 62–70.

152. Lorenz M. Lüthi, *The Sino-Soviet Split*, 299.

153. Li Yueran, *Waijiao*, 152.

154. Wu Lengxi, *Shinian lunzhan*, 474, 480.

155. Zhou Enlai, "Taiwan will be liberated," June 29, 1956, 206.

156. Wu Lengxi, *Shi nian lunzhan*, 80. *SCMP* 1233, 45.

157. Lorenz M. Lüthi, *The Sino-Soviet Split*, 96–99.

158. Nikita S. Khrushchev, *Testament*, 262.

2

The Main Causes for the Return of the Changchun Railway to China and Its Impact on Sino-Soviet Relations

Shengfa Zhang

Introduction

ON FEBRUARY 14, 1950, DURING Mao Zedong's visit to the Soviet Union, China and the Soviet Union signed the Treaty of Friendship, Alliance and Mutual Assistance, as well as separate agreements on the Chinese Changchun Railway (CCR), *Lushun*, and *Dalian*. Under the Treaty, China and the Soviet Union formally established a political allianceL "In the interests of consolidating peace . . . both contracting parties will consult with each other in regard to all important international problems affecting the common interests of China and the Soviet Union."[1]

The Agreement on the CCR stipulated that "Both Contracting parties agree that the Soviet government transfer without compensation to the government of the People's Republic of China all its rights to joint management of the Chinese Changchun Railway with all property belonging to the Railway. The transfer shall be effective immediately after the conclusion of a peace treaty with Japan, but not later than the end of 1952."[2] This railway was an extremely important part of China's Northeastern economy. It ran from the Soviet borders at Manzhouli in the East to *Suifenhe* in the West and from *Harbin* south to *Dalian*. At the time the worth of the CCR together with associated and ancillary equipment was given as US$600 million or 2.28 billion new yuan (or 22.8 trillion old yuan).[3]

In December 1952, the Soviet Union in fact returned its share of the Chinese Changchun Railway to the PRC. Why did Stalin agree to this? After all, in the early 1950s, the disparity in strength between China and the Soviet Union was very clear: the Soviet Union was strong China was weak. Why did Stalin make such a great concession to China when the Soviet Union was in such a strong position? Most Chinese and foreign scholars believe that the primary reason the Soviet Union abandoned the rights and interests in the CCR was to establish Sino-Soviet friendship on a reliable basis and turn China into a Soviet strategic ally in Far East.[4]

I fully agree with this view. However, I also believe that this view focuses mainly on the negotiations on the CCR's return in 1949–1950, but not on the process that led to the actual return of CCR in 1952. If this is done, we obtain a more comprehensive and complete picture. Therefore, this chapter attempts to analyze the reasons for the CCR's return to China by the Soviet Union in terms of two different stages: the first was the period of the negotiations of the Sino-Soviet treaties and agreements from December 1949 to early 1950; the second the period in the latter half of 1952, when the CCR was finally returned to China. Most studies have not analyzed the final return in depth. Using both Russian and Chinese documents and materials, this chapter also analyzes the impact of the CCR's return to China on Sino-Soviet relations.

The Primary Cause: Stalin's Need for China in the Cold War with the United States

In the early postwar period Stalin adopted the policy of cooperation among big powers. The main contents of the policy were to maintain the cooperation with Western countries to a certain degree and on the basis of the Yalta system, and temporarily stop or restrain supporting and helping foreign revolutionary movements. Because the Yalta system, which basically satisfied the Soviet requirements for territory, security and spheres of influence, was a product of cooperation and compromise with the Western countries. It was necessary for Moscow to continue to cooperate with the West to protect the vested interests which the Yalta system brought to the Soviet Union.

In the later stages of the war and early post-war period, Stalin's Far East strategy was to build broad security zones around the Soviet Union by implementing the terms of the Yalta Agreement. This strategy considered of the following elements: turning Outer Mongolia into a state that was legally independent of China, so that the Soviet Union would be able to build reliable military bases in Mongolian territory; restoring the Russian sphere of influence in northeastern China to ensure for the Soviet Union an outlet to the Pacific and an ice-free port; regaining the southern Sakhalin and Kurile Islands lost during the war with Japan in 1904–1905 by Tsarist Russia, thereby guaranteeing the sea lanes that served to connect the Soviet ports in the Pacific region.

In addition, in order to preserve cooperation between the Soviet Union and the Western countries within the Yalta system and use it to guarantee Soviet rights and interests, Stalin, who was prejudiced against the Chinese Communists,[5] took a passive and negative attitude toward the Chinese Communist Party (CCP) and the Chinese revolution in the early postwar period. However, from 1947 onwards, as a result of the outbreak of the U.S.-Soviet Cold War and the strategic counterattack of the CCP's forces in the civil war, Stalin's attitude and stance toward the CCP and the Chinese revolution changed gradually from passive indifference to active support.

In the late 1940s and early 1950s, the Soviet Union was in a disadvantageous position generally in the Cold War. In Europe, in the year-long period from 1948 to 1949, the crisis resulting from the Soviet blockade of Berlin did not bring the Soviet Union any benefits. The blockade was proved unable to stop the founding of the Federal Republic of Germany, nor did it drive the Western allies out of Berlin. Instead, it sped the pace of the Western formation of the NATO alliance in April 1949. Meanwhile, owing to the deterioration of the relationship between the Soviet Union and Yugoslavia, the latter was expelled from the Soviet-led socialist camp, causing the Soviet Union to lose its first ally in Europe. In Asia, the situation in which the United States alone was occupying and managing Japan seemed to be irreversible.

It was precisely when the Soviet Union was plunged into the hard situation of the Cold War with the United States that in the Far East, the Chinese revolution unexpectedly achieved victory. This meant that the geopolitical situation and the power structure in the Far East would be reshaped and rebuilt in favor of the Soviet Union.

Stalin realized that after the victory of the Chinese revolution, China would be able to become an important Soviet ally in the Far East, which undoubtedly would be of crucial significance if the Cold War heated up. In mid-May 1948, Stalin told Kovalev, the head of the Soviet experts group that would soon be dispatched to the Chinese liberated areas, "We certainly will provide the new China with all possible assistance. If socialism succeeds in China, and our two countries move ahead along the same road, it could be possible that the worldwide socialist victory would be guaranteed. In this case, we will not fear the threats of any sudden incidents. So, we can not begrudge our own strength for the assistance to the Chinese communists."[6]

From then on, the relations between the two parties began to improve. Mikoyan visited Xibaipo, the then location of the CCP headquarters, in January–February 1949; Liu Shaoqi visited the USSR in June–August 1949, deepening Stalin's resolve that China should become a strategic ally of the Soviet Union after the CCP came to power.

On the issue of the Chinese revolution, in the process of the exchange of messages between Stalin and Mao Zedong, a consensus was reached. On January 14, 1949, Mao Zedong in his telegram to Stalin wrote: "in speaking of the basic policy, namely, to prevent extensive negotiations with the Guomindang (GMD) and of carrying the revolutionary war through to the end, we are in complete agreement with you."[7]

With regard to the relations between the CCP and the CPSU, Mao Zedong expressed an attitude of loyalty and obedience toward it. Mikoyan reported to Stalin that "Mao Zedong always said that they [the CC CCP] were waiting for instructions and leadership from our Central Committee."[8] In a talk with Mikoyan on 30 January, Mao Zedong humbly assumed the status of Stalin's disciple:

> raising a glass to Comrade Stalin's health, Mao Zedong stressed that the Lenin – Stalin's theory on China is the basis of the present triumph of the Chinese revolution. Stalin is not only the teacher of the Soviet people, but also the teacher for the Chinese people and the peoples of the world. When talking about himself, Mao Zedong said that he is Stalin's disciple.[9]

Mao Zedong made it clear that new China would become a firm ally of the Soviet Union. On February 4, 1949, again in talking with Mikoyan,

> Mao Zedong openly expressed his pro-Soviet feelings. He presented the evidence that on the occasion of the anniversary of the October Revolution, they stressed that China should stand on the Soviet-led anti-imperialist camp. Mao Zedong said finally that the middle road does not exist for us.[10]

As for the CCP's relations with the United States, Zhou Enlai clearly expressed the CCP's firm anti-U.S. stance. In his conversation with Mikoyan on February 1, Zhou Enlai indicated that "Since then (out break of Civil War), we have begun to expose the U.S. more actively. Although we have suspended relations with the Americans, they have attempted many times to establish contact with us through those who do have relations with us. But we restricted ourselves to listening to the American desires to establish contact with us."[11] Zhou Enlai added that:

> After our troops seized *Shenyang* last year, there was a new problem with U.S. relations. Their foreign consulates (of the United States, Britain and France) suggested that they did not plan to retreat and wanted to establish diplomatic relations with us. We know that these consulates remained open in order to spy on us and the Soviet Union. We do not want to see them in *Shenyang*, therefore we are taking measures to isolate them and making it impossible for them to stay

in order to force them to evacuate from *Shenyang*. . . . Americans are destroying our system, so we must isolate the U.S. in our country. [12]

Concerning the Yugoslav question, Mao Zedong condemned Tito for his anti-Soviet behavior. On February 3, responding to Mikoyan's introduction of the Yugoslavian situation, Mao Zedong said that Tito is a Zhang Guotao who became a turncoat and traitor to the CCP. [13]

During his visit to the Soviet Union, on July 4, 1949, Liu Shaoqi, a Secretary of the CC CPC, presented to the CPSU and Stalin a detailed report on the situation of the Chinese revolution and on new China's domestic and foreign policies. Liu's report pointed out that the new regime "will be a people's democratic dictatorship led by the proletariat and based on the worker-peasant alliance." With regard to China's foreign relations, Liu indicated that:

China's revolution must thoroughly abolish the imperialists' dominance in China in the military, political, economic and sphere. . . . In the field of international relations, we definitely will maintain a consistent policy with Soviet Union. We had already made some explanations in this regard to the democratic parties. Some non-party personages criticize us for the policy which leans-to-one-side, that is, to the side of the Soviet Union, but comrade Mao Zedong replied to them: our policy will be just that, to lean-to-one-side, because if we do not join together with the Soviet Union and struggle against the imperialists, if we try to take the middle road, it would be wrong. After these explanations, all the democratic parties together with the CCP have signed and issued a statement opposing the North Atlantic Treaty.

About the relations between the CPSU and the CCP, the report declared, "Comrade Mao Zedong and the CC CCP think that the CPSU is the high command of the world communist movement, while the CCP is only in command of a front army. Local interests should be subordinated to the international interests, therefore, we, the CCP, are subordinated to the decision of the CPSU." [14]

Through the exchanges of the telegrams between Stalin and Mao Zedong, as well as the Mikoyan and Liu Shaoqi visits, Stalin obtained a more comprehensive understanding and judgment regarding Mao Zedong, the CCP and the future new China. Stalin believed basically that Mao Zedong and the CCP leaders were Lenin's and Stalin's students; that the CCP was like-minded in the ideological aspect; that the future of New China in the aspect of international relations could become a friendly allied country similar to the people's democratic countries in Eastern Europe. Given the tense situation of the Cold War, Stalin prepared to give up the majority of the Soviet rights and interests in Northeast China so as to obtain an important strategic ally, thereby creating a more reliable foundation to safeguard the Soviet geopolitical interests in the Far East.

During his visit to the Soviet Union from December 1949 to February 1950, Mao Zedong expressed certain dissatisfactions with the Soviet Union concerning the problems of a new Sino-Soviet treaty and other issues; he nevertheless manifested his loyalty to Stalin and the Soviet Union both in face-to-face meetings and behind the scenes. This was also reflected in Kovalev's report. In his January 2 report to Stalin after having met with Mao Zedong, Kovalev informed Stalin that Mao Zedong highly praised the October Revolution and the CPSU: "The gunfire of the October Revolution has sent Marx-Lenin-Stalin's doctrine to China. There would not be the CCP or the victory of the Chinese revolution without the CPSU. Long live the Lenin-Stalin doctrines."[15]

On the basis of the exchange of opinions on the CCR and *Lushun* between two sides during Mikoyan's visit to Xibaipo in January–February 1949, Stalin officially agreed to return the CCR to China in the negotiations between the two nations, and the two countries reached the corresponding agreements on the CCR and other issues.

1952: Stalin's Recognition That China Had in Fact Become a Reliable Strategic Ally and That Mao Zedong Was a True Marxist

Although the Sino-Soviet agreement in 1950 stipulated that the CCR would be given back to China after the signing of a peace treaty with Japan (but no later than the end of 1952), in view of the respected status that Stalin enjoyed as a revolutionary leader worldwide, the dominant position which the Soviet Union occupied in the relations between the two countries, and the complexity and the variability of the international situation at that time, it was still uncertain whether Stalin would scrupulously follow his promise. It was to a large extent to be dependent on the actual development of the bilateral relations whether the CCR could be transferred to China as scheduled. The key question, in the eyes of Stalin was whether China was or was not a reliable strategic ally and whether Mao Zedong was or was not a true Marxist.

Precisely on this issue, the Korean War, which broke out in June of 1950, became the touchstone of the Sino-Soviet alliance. In early October, when the North Koreans were in a critical situation, Stalin twice sent telegrams to Mao Zedong, suggesting that China dispatch troops to assist North Korea.[16] Despite the just-concluded civil war, when new China was faced with the urgent task of economic reconstruction, Mao Zedong made a quick decision to send troops after that matter was considered and discussed repeatedly in the

CC of the CCP.[17] On October 13, Mao Zedong informed Stalin of the Chinese decision.[18] On October 19, the main forces of the Chinese People's Volunteers crossed the Yalu River and entered North Korea. On October 25, the Volunteers officially engaged in battle.

The Korean War was the extension on the Korean Peninsula of the U.S.-Soviet competition and confrontation in Europe. During the Korean War, Stalin utilized the Sino-Soviet alliance to fight a proxy war with the United States, following the principle that the Soviet Union must not engage in direct military conflict with the United States. China and the Soviet Union closely cooperated during the Korean War. The Soviet Union provided China with weapons and ammunitions, while Mao Zedong informed Stalin of the operational plans and consulted with him about the strategy of the armistice negotiations and on other issues.

From the perspective of the Soviet Union, China's intervention in the Korean War proved that Mao Zedong was faithfully implementing the policy of "leaning to one side," and showed by practical deeds that China was a loyal ally of the Soviet Union. This is what paved the way for the smooth return of the CCR's to China.

In addition, a report on the domestic Chinese situation from Yudin, the Soviet Ambassador,[19] sent on January 20, 1951, led Stalin to trust Mao and China even more. The report consisted of the three parts: 1) on the anti-American movement relating to the Korean War, 2) on Mao Zedong's strategy and plan for the Korean War, and 3) on Mao Zedong's request regarding consultation and cooperation between the CCP and the CPSU with regard to the affairs of the Asian Communist parties. A summary follows:

1) With regard to the first, the anti-American movement, on December 15, 1950, Yudin reported to Mao on an inspection tour that he made of the situation in major Chinese cities.[20] (Yudin also sent this report to Stalin.) Yudin commented on the political tendencies among Chinese intellectuals, and in accordance with Stalin's way of thinking proposed a guiding opinion. Yudin divided Chinese intellectuals into three categories: Marxists; intellectuals who wanted to learn Marxism but seldom read Marxist works and knew little of Marxism; and non-Marxist intellectuals. Yudin accused the latter of "almost openly hostility to Marxism, and of unwillingness to recognize or not wanting to recognize Marxism." He wrote: "I have run into this kind of intellectual in the missionary (American) universities in Hangzhou and Guangzhou. They openly believe that U.S. culture is the highest level of culture, and, in their view, what the Chinese people most need is this kind of 'culture.' They train the college students in taking a hostile attitude to

communism and the new China. Yudin concluded that while "I cannot judge how many missionary universities are training experts whom China needs, however, there is no doubt that they cultivate the culture of communist's enemies and of new China's political opponents."[21] Yudin's report ended on a Stalinist tone: "the lesson of history is that the ruling class will not voluntarily withdraw from the stage of history, and the resistance will reach this level: the more certain it is that the ruling class will perish, the more intense will be its resistance."[22]

Although Mao Zedong's response to Yudin's report has not been made available, Yudin's opinion very quickly produced concrete results. On December 29, in a conference of the Government Administrative Council (the Chinese Cabinet), Vice Premier Guo Moruo delivered a "Report on Principles of Dealing with the Cultural and Educational Organs, Relief Agencies and Religious Groups which Accept American Funds." It was approved by the Cabinet. The report pointed out that "for more than 100 years, in addition to political, economic and armed aggression against our country, U.S. imperialism, for a long time, has paid great attention to . . . cultural aggression." "The Cultural and Educational Organs, Relief Agencies and Religious Groups which accept American funds account for about half the total of all similar organs that receive foreign grants." In order to wipe out the influence of U.S. imperialism in China, the report proposed taking over the above organs and bodies. The report concludes that it is necessary to finally, completely and forever eliminate the 100 years of cultural aggression of U.S. imperialism against the Chinese people.[23] The State Administrative Council asked its subordinate Committee on Culture and Education to formulate plans to implement the above policy and called on the nation "to struggle for wiping out completely the cultural aggressive influence of U.S. imperialism in China."[24]

In the spirit of these decisions, China started a movement against pro-American attitudes, against worship of America and against fear of America. In January 1951, the Chinese Ministry of Education met to deal with the colleges and universities that accepted foreign funds and decided that the state would completely take over colleges and universities which were subsidized by foreign countries. In April, the Religious Affairs Department of the Culture and Education Committee convened to deal with Christian groups that accepted grants from the United States. According to the policy of the State Administrative Council, Christian, autonomous, self-supporting and self-sustaining movements were encouraged, but Christian groups receiving U.S. money were specifically singled out and were to be completely managed by Chinese believers.[25]

On January 4, 1951, Zhou Enlai informed Yudin about China's anti-U.S. campaign. Yudin wrote:

> Zhou Enlai elaborated on the movement against U.S. imperialism launched in China. He pointed out that important political achievements had already resulted from the movement. Even a majority of the urban bourgeoisie positively participated in this movement. He said that in China there had never been such movement. Since we are forced to go to war against the United States, then we will seriously prepare our people for it.[26]

Through Yudin's report to Stalin together with the attached report to Mao Zedong, Stalin now understood that China was developing a vigorous campaign against American imperialism, which was linked to the Korean War. For Stalin who wanted to eliminate U.S. influence in China and who was familiar with U.S. attempt to undermine the Sino-Soviet alliance, the movement against the U.S. imperialism in China was very gratifying and satisfactory.

2) With regard to China's position and strategy in the ongoing Korean War, Yudin reported that Mao Zedong told him on December 31, 1950, that "Our main task in Korea is to eliminate American effective strength as much as possible . . . We do not oppose the fact that the war has been dragging on, because the U.S. military presence in Korea will torment the United States every day, bring about internal disputes within the imperialist ruling clique, and arouse public opinion against it."[27] Given the impossibility of winning the Korean War, Stalin's basic strategy was to leave the United States deeply bogged down in Korea, consume a great deal of U.S. strength, thereby containing and weakening U.S. ability to act in Europe. Mao's firm anti-U.S. stance indeed coincided with Stalin's strategy.

3) On China's request for consultation and cooperation with the CC of the CPSU on the affairs of Asian Communist parties, Yudin's reported that Mao told him that "Now all of Asian communist parties are seeking his advice and asking for his help. Now, except for the Communist Party of India, all Asian communist parties have permanent representatives in Beijing. It is necessary to examine their different conditions, put forward proposals to them, and provide them with help. We are not competent to do this." Therefore, Mao Zedong proposed, "we hope that the CC of the CPSU study our problems and our work." He added, "We seriously propose that Central Committee of the CPSU send permanent representatives to the CCP Central Committee. These representatives should have some assistants who will study the Asian issues together with our staff, and bring them to the attention of both Central Committees in order to resolve them together."[28]

It must have been gratifying for Stalin that China on its own initiative complied with the unwritten stipulation that "Big Brother" should play a leading role in dealing with affairs relating to the regional communist parties, thereby demonstrating the complete adherence to China's policy of "leaning to one side." This was in striking contrast to the Communist Party of Yugoslavia, which, often provided advice and assistance to other Eastern Europe countries on its own establishing itself as a secondary leadership center of the Eastern European Bloc.

Yudin's report reassured Stalin about the firm anti-U.S. stance of Mao Zedong and the Chinese Communists and he was pleased with the practice of consultation with the CPSU on major issues. Therefore, Yudin's report convinced Stalin that China firmly abided by its pledge and commitment to subordinate itself to the leadership of the CPSU and that Mao Zedong was a loyal Marxist,[29] unlike Tito who had betrayed Stalin and the Soviet-Eastern bloc. This undoubtedly contributed to Stalin's ultimate confidence that the CCR could be returned to China, a reliable ally deserving the trust of Soviet Union.

During the Chinese Premier's visit to Soviet Union in August and September 1952, Zhou Enlai once again expressed to Stalin China's firm stance of fighting with the United States in Korea. On August 20, Zhou Enlai introduced the Korean situation, saying that there was some kind of balance of power on the Korean battlefield. At the same time he told Stalin, "Mao Zedong believed that the war is advantageous to us, because it had disrupted U.S. preparations for the third world war." Stalin said with satisfaction: "Mao Zedong is right. This war has hurt the U.S. vitality."[30]

Also during Zhou Enlai's visit, on September 15, China and the Soviet Union issued an announcement regarding the return of the CCR before December to China before December 31, 1952.[31]

Impact of the CCR's Return to China on Sino-Soviet Relations

On December 31, 1952, a handover ceremony was held in Harbin, the capital of *Heilongjiang* province, and the CCR was thus finally returned to China.

As noted earlier, the value of the fixed and liquid assets transferred without compensation was 2.28 billion yuan or US$600 million. A partial list of the CCR's assets includes the following: 3,282.7 km of railroad lines, including the trunk lines from *Manzhouli* to *Suifenhe* and from *Manzhouli* to *Dalian* and *Lushunkou*; 880 locomotives, 10,200 trucks; repair facilities, power plants, telegraph offices, signaling and communications equipment; administrative buildings; and subsidiary enterprises, such as coal mines, tree farms and lumber yards. Associated facilities included 1.85 million square meters of housing; 121 hospitals, clinics, and epidemic prevention stations; 69 schools, 25 cultural centers and clubs, 322 "Red Corners" (entertainment rooms); as well as shops and other commercial enterprises.[32]

Indeed, the returned CCR was a huge asset for the new China with its weak economic base. The figure of $600 million was twice the size of the Soviet loan to China that was part of the Sino-Soviet Treaty.[33] These immensely valuable assets allowed China to enhance the development of the railroad industry and economy, in particular in the Northeast region.

What was even more important was that the handover of this railway, together with giving up of the Soviet rights and interests in Chinese *Dalian* and *Lushun*, removed the fetters imposed on China by the Yalta Agreement and the Sino-Soviet Treaty and agreements of 1945, restored China's full sovereignty, thereby ending the last humiliation of the Chinese nation and rehabilitating the national self-esteem and self-confidence of the Chinese people. The transfer of the CCR from the Soviet Union to China made the Chinese people feel satisfied and happy, and won high praise for the Chinese government.

The return of the CCR as scheduled to China by the Soviet Union, from the Soviet side, indicated that Soviet Union had scrupulously followed its pledge which was made in the Sino-Soviet agreement in 1950, and enhanced Stalin's credibility in China and Stalin's prestige in the hearts of the Chinese leaders and people. On the part of China, the handover of the CCR allowed Stalin and the Soviets to gain the trust and gratitude from Mao and China, and increased Chinese willingness to cooperate with and learn from the Soviet "Big Brother." Therefore, the transfer of the CCR greatly promoted and strengthened the friendship and trust between two nations, and made positive and significant impact on the development of bilateral relations. As Chinese Premier and Foreign Minister Zhou Enlai on the handover ceremony said, "The Soviet government fulfills generously and selflessly its obligations which it shoulders. This shows that the Soviet government is infinite loyal to the fraternal Sino-Soviet alliance cause . . . The great friendship between China and the Soviet Union becomes more consolidated and developed."[34]

Specifically speaking, the significant impact, which the return of the CCR to China by the Soviet Union had on Sino-Soviet relations, consisted of the following.

First, the return of the CCR on schedule to China gave a further impetus to the tide of learning from the Soviet Union. In the eyes of the Chinese people the Soviet "Big Brother" proved trustworthy, as the return of the CCR showed. The Chinese were strongly fascinated by the slogan, "the Soviet Today Is China's Tomorrow." They believed in it without a doubt.

In the process of jointly managing the CCR, the Soviet patterns of railway administration in different degrees were also adopted. In the initial period after the railway was transferred to China, the general direction of learning from the Soviet "Big Brother" was further enhanced. In August 1954, the Chinese Ministry of Railways in its "work arrangement" stated:

> Learning from and the promotion of the CCR's experience is to substantively carry out socialist transformation of the national railway in operation and management. It must be recognized that . . . the CCR is an advanced example, which is created with the help of more than 1500 Soviet experts, and with the use of Soviet advanced experience, and according to China's railroad special situation. With the help of Soviet experts stationed in China's Ministry of Railways, the CCR's experience has been consolidated, therefore the national railroad must learn from the CCR.[35]

In other words, the CCR needed to learn from the Soviet model of railway management, and that model spread throughout an widely in all-China railway system. The CCR's fundamental directions to use the Soviet railway model included:

> The leading cadre must study the Lenin—Stalin work style; establish a comprehensive financial plan of production; formulate of technical and organizational measures; carrying out the patriotic labor competition among the staffs; implement an economic accounting system; organize technological learning and training of cadres; and care about staff's material and cultural life.[36]

Second, the return of the CCR, contributed to the development of the strategic alliance between the two countries and to consolidation of Sino-Soviet cooperation in the Korean War. Since July of 1951, when the Korean armistice negotiations began, although Stalin did not expect to win the war, it was clear for him that the Korean War would consume American military and economic strength, create tensions between the United States and its allies, undermine the political prestige of the United States, and thus restrict and weaken indirectly American position in Europe. Accordingly, Stalin encouraged China and North Korea to take a tough stance in the armistice negotiation.[37] The Soviet Union continued to provide China with weapons and equipment, and Mao Zedong not only informed Stalin about the development of the Korean War, but also listened to and obeyed Stalin's suggestions concerning the armistice negotiations.

The transfer of the CCR was completed against the background of the armistice talks in Korea. The Soviet Union did not directly join the armistice negotiation, but Stalin always played the dominant role in guiding and controlling China and North Korea. Almost all Chinese and North Korean strategies and tactics of the negotiation were decided by Stalin until his death in March 1953.

However, while in the short term the return of the CCR strengthened Sino-Soviet relations and China's eagerness to learn from the Soviets, in the longer term, the Soviet handover of the CCR to China also weakened the Soviet position and influence in China. This was mainly manifested in the following aspects:

- China's Northeast was China's most important heavy industrial base and the CCR was its key railway line. The return of the CCR to China meant that the Soviet Union in fact lost a major source of leverage on China's economy.
- After the death of Stalin, especially after the 20th Congress of the Communist Party of Soviet Union in February 1956, the uncritical copying of the Soviet model began to be questioned in China. In line with this change, the use of Soviet experience in the management of the CCR was no longer worshipped. The Chinese Ministry of Railways proposed that from 1957 onward learning and promoting "the CCR's experience" would no longer govern the way in which railways nationwide were managed.[38]
- Many Soviet alien residents in the Northeastern railway areas did not immediately leave Chinese territory in 1949, the handover of the CCR foreshadowed this development, thereby gradually undermining the Soviet immigrant community. As N.E. Ablova pointed out, "by the early 1960s, almost all Russian residents in *Harbin* and *Manchuria* had left. It is certain that the signing of the final Protocol on the handover of the CCR predecided the departure from China of former Russian citizens, thereby ending the history of Russian immigrants in the Far East."[39] Thus, the return of the CCR weakened the firm position and great influence of the Soviet Union on China's Northeast. In the late 1950s and early 1960s, when Sino-Soviet relations deteriorated and especially when armed conflict between the two countries took place in 1969, fortunately, there was no possibility that the problem of the Soviet immigrants in China's Northeast could exacerbate the tension between the two countries.[40]

Conclusion

To sum up, I believe that the main cause that led Stalin to agree to return the CCR to China and eventually give it back as scheduled are as follows: The difficult Soviet position in the cold war, it urgently needed China as a strategic ally. Mao Zedong reiterated repeatedly his loyalty and obedience to Stalin and the CPSU and promoted a policy of "leaning-to-one-side," causing Stalin to believe that China might become a Soviet reliable ally. China's entry into the Korean War indicated that China truly had become a Soviet strategic ally. Moreover, Yudin's report on the anti-U.S. movement in China further assured Stalin that Mao Zedong was a firm Marxist, not a second Tito.

At the same time, Stalin's giving up the Soviet special rights and interests in Northeast China was not an irreparable strategic loss for the Soviet Union. The strategic alliance between the Soviet Union and the People's Republic of China not only enhanced Soviet security in the Far East, but also to a great extent compensated for the losses which the Soviet Union suffered in the European Cold War during 1948–1949. The alliance with China thus greatly strengthened the Soviet Union's capacity to struggle with the United States in the Cold War. This was a great gain for the Soviet Union.

The return of the CCR to China by the Soviet Union had a great impact on Sino-Soviet relations. In some respects the impact was direct and immediate; in others it was indirect and gradual. From a short-term perspective, the return of the railway had basically a positive impact on the Sino-Soviet relations; from a long-term perspective, it weakened the Soviet position and influence in China.

Notes

1. For the Chinese version of the Treaty, see Chinese Institute of International Relations, ed., *Xiandai guoji guanxishi cankao ziliao* (Reference Materials Relating to the History of Modern International Relations), vol. 1, 1950–1953 (Beijing: Remin jiaoyn chubanshe, 1960), 9–11. For the Russian version of the Treaty, see *Sovetsko-kitayskie otnosheniya*, t. 5, kn. 2, (Sino-Soviet Relations, vol. 5, part 2), (Moskva: Pamyatniki istoricheskoy mysli, 2005), 296–304.

2. For the Chinese version of the Agreement, see *Xiandai guoji guanxishi cankao ziliao: 1950–1953*, 11–13; for the Soviet version of the Agreement, see *Sovetsko-kitayskie otnosheniya*, 305–7.

3. The $600 million is in N.E. Ablova, *Istoriya KVCD i rosiiskaya emigratsiya v Kitae: mezhdunarodnye i politicheskie aspekty istori* [The Chinese Eastern Railway and The Russian Immigration in China: International and Political History] (Moscow: Russian Panorama, 2005), 378. The yuan figure is in *Zhongguo waijiaobu dangan* (Archive of Chinese Foreign Ministry), 109-00175-01, 035.

4. See Yang Kuisong, "Zhongsu zhijian guojia liyi yu minzu qinggan de zuichu pengzhuang" [The initial collision of national interests and national sentiments between China and the Soviet Union] in *Lengzhan yu Zhongguo* [The cold war and china], eds. Zhang Baijie and Niu Jun (Beijing: Shijie zhishi chubanshe, 2002), 128–29, 130; Shen Zhihua, ed., *Zhongsu guanxi shigang* [A History of Sino-Soviet

Relations, 1917–1991] (Beijing: Xinhua chubanshe, 2007), 109–11; A. Ledovskii, "Peregovory Stalina s MaoTszedunom v dekabre 1949–fevrale 1950 g., novye arkhivnye dokumenty" (Negotiations between Stalin and Mao Zedong in December 1949 to February 1950, new archival documents), *Novaya i noveyshaya istoriya*, 1997, no. 1, .46–47; N. E. Ablova, *Istoriya KVCD i rosiiskaya emigratsiya v Kitae*, 398; S. N. Goncharov, et al., *Uncertain Partners: Stalin, Mao, and the Korean War* (Palo Alto, CA: Stanford University Press, 1993), 111–29, 203–25; D. Heinzig, *The Soviet Union and Communist China, 1945-1950: The Arduous Road to the Alliance* (Armonk, NY: M. E. Sharpe, 2004), 263–384, 385–402. However, the author of a diplomatic history of the PRC concluded that it was only natural for the Soviet Union to return the CCR. As he puts it: "During the Russo-Japanese War in 1904 Japan had taken away the 'Southern Manchurian Railroad' from Russia. In 1935, the Soviet Union sold the Chinese Eastern Railway to Japan. Therefore, the Soviet rights to 'common ownership, common management' of the CCR set by 1945 Sino-Soviet agreement did not have any legal basis. After new China was established, the Soviet Union should have returned the CCR to China on its own initiative." See Pei Jianzhang, *Zhonghua renmin gongheguo waijiaoshi* [The diplomatic history of the People's Republic of China] (Beijing: Shijie zhishi chubanshe, 1994), vol.1, 1949–1956, 23.

5. In a talk regarding China in June 1944 with Harriman, the U.S. ambassador to the Soviet Union, Stalin said that "the Chinese Communists are not real Communists, they are 'margarine' Communists," *Foreign Relations of the United States*, 1944, vol. VI (Washington, DC: GPO, 1967), 799.

6. See I. V. Kovalev, "Dialog Stalina s Mao Tszedunom (Okonchanie)" [Stalin's dialogue with Mao Zedong, Conclusion], *Problemy Dal'nego Vostoka*, 1992, no. 1–3, 77.

7. Archive of the President, Russian Federation (hereinafter APRF), fond 45, opis 1, delo 330, listy 104–5. See S. Tihvinskiy, "Perepiska I.V. Stalina s Mao Tszedunom v yanvare 1949 g" [Correspondence of I. V. Stalin with Mao Zedong in January 1949], *Novaya i noveyshaya istoriya*, 1994, no. 4–5, 138–39.

8. A. I. Mikoyan's Report about his conversations with the leaders the CPC in 1949, September 22, 1960, *Sovetsko-kitayskie otnosheniya*, t. 5, kn. 2, 342.

9. APRF, fond 39, opis 1, delo 39, listy 5, *Sovetsko-kitayskie otnosheniya*, t. 5, kn. 2, 36.

10. APRF, fond 39, opis 1, delo 39, listy 63, *Sovetsko-kitayskie otnosheniya*, t. 5, kn. 2, 72.

11. APRF, fond 39, opis 1, delo 39, listy 18, *Sovetsko-kitayskie otnosheniya*, t. 5, kn. 2, 44.

12. APRF, fond 39, opis 1, delo 39, listy 19, *Sovetsko-kitayskie otnosheniya*, t. 5, kn. 2, 45.

13. APRF, fond 39, opis 1, delo 39, listy 48, *Sovetsko-kitayskie otnosheniya*, t. 5, kn. 2, 62.

14. APRF, fond 45, opis 1, delo 328, listy 32–50, *Sovetsko-kitayskie otnosheniya*, t. 5, kn. 2, 154, 158, 160, 162. On June 30, in his famous article "On the people's democratic dictatorship," Mao Zedong announced and elaborated on the policy of "lean-

ing-to-one-side" in relation to the Soviet Union. *Mao Zedong xuanji* [Selected works of Mao Zedong], vol. 4 (Beijing: Renmin chubanshe, 1991), 1473.

15. APRF, fond 3, opis 65, delo 533, listy 61–62, *Sovetsko-kitayskie otnosheniya*, t. 5, kn. 2, 254.

16. APRF, fond 45, opis 1, delo 334, listy 112–15, Quoted in A. V. Torkunov, *Zagadochnaya voina: koreskiy konflikt 1950–1953 godov* [Mysterious War: The Korean Conflict, 1950–53] (Moscow, ROSSPEN, 2000), 113–14, 116–17.

17. On October 8, Mao Zedong informed Kim Il Sung of the Chinese decision to send troops into Korea. On that day, Mao Zedong issued a formal order to organize the Chinese People's Volunteers. See *Jianguoyilai Maozedong wengao* [Mao Zedong's manuscripts since the FOUNDING of the PRC] (Beijing: Zhongyang Wenxian chubanshe, 1987), vol.1, 543–45.

18. APRF, fond 45, opis 1, delo 334, listy 111–112, Quoted in A.V.Torkunov, *Zagadochnaya voina: koreskiy konflikt 1950–1953 godov*, 118.

19. After Mao Zedong visited the Soviet Union, according to Mao Zedong's request, Stalin dispatched Yudin, a famous philosopher and Chief Editor of the Cominform's official magazine, *For a Lasting Peace and for the People's Democracy*, to China to help with the editing of *Selected Works of Mao Zedong*. Yudin's role was not only restricted to editing work. During his stay in China, Yudin held in-depth and detailed conversations with Mao on a wide range of problems, and carried on the widespread on-the-spot investigation in accordance with Mao's proposal. In fact, Yudin acted in China as Stalin's personal representative, and his reports on the Chinese situation constituted an important basis for Stalin's understanding of China.

20. From October 29 to December 3, 1950, Yudin went to Nanjing, Shanghai, Hangzhou, Guangzhou, Hankou, Wuchang and Xi'an, visited some universities in Shanghai, Hangzhou, Guangzhou and Wuchang, and gave speeches and lectures. He also visited some factories and the countryside and held discussions with local intellectuals, workers and farmers. See "P. F. Yudin o besedakh s Mao Tszedunom: dokladnye zapiski I. V. Stalinu i N. S. Khruschevu, 1951–1957 gg." [P. F. Yudin's Report to I. V. Stalin and N. S. Khrushchev in 1951–1957 about his CONVERSATIONS with Mao Zedong], *Istoricheskiy Arkhiv*, 2007, no. 4, 19.

21. "P. F. Yudin o besedakh s Mao Tszedunom: dokladnye zapiski I. V. Stalinu i N. S. Kruschevu, 1951–1957 gg.," 20–22.

22. "P. F. Yudin o besedakh s Mao Tszedunom: dokladnye zapiski I. V. Stalinu i N. S. Kruschevu, 1951–1957gg," 23.

23. *Jianguoyilai zhongyao wenxian xuanbian* (Selected important documents since fondation of the PRC (Beijing: Zhongyang wenxue chubanshe, 1992), vol.1, 511–15.

24. *Jianguoyilai zhongyao wenxian xuanbian*, vol. 1, 510.

25. See Xie Yi, ed., *Zhongguo waijiaoshi: Zhonghua renmin gongheguo shiqi, 1949–1979* [A diplomatic history of China: The People's Republic of China, 1949–1979] (Kaifeng: Henan renmin chubanshe, 1988), 54.

26. "P. F. Yudin o besedah s Mao Tszedunom: dokladnye zapiski I. V. Stalinu i N. S. Khruschevu 1951–1957 gg.," 18.

27. "P. F. Yudin o besedah s Mao Tszedunom: dokladnye zapiski I. V. Stalinu i N. S. Khruschevu 1951–1957 gg.," 15.

28. "P. F. Yudin o besedah s Mao Tszedunom: dokladnye zapiski I. V. Stalinu i N. S. Khruschevu 1951–1957 gg.," 15–16.

29. After Stalin passed away, Yudin told Mao Zedong that after he returned to his homeland Stalin had asked him, "Are the Chinese comrades (true) Marxists?" When Yudin gave the affirmative reply, Stalin said, "This is very good! I might feel relieved," Yudin's diary, "Zapis besedy s tovarishchem Mao" [Record of Talks with Comrade Mao Zedong], *Problemi Dal'nego Vostoka,* 1994, no. 5, 106–7.

30. A. Ledovskii, "Stenogrammy peregovorov Stalina s Zhou Enlai v avguste-septyabre 1952 g" [Record of talks between Stalin and Zhou Enlai in August-September 1952], *Novaya i noveyshaya istoriya,* 1997, no. 2, 75.

31. See *Zhonghua renmin gongheguo duiwaiguanxi wenjianji, dierji, 1951–1953* [Documents of foreign relations of the People's Republic of China, 1951–1953] (Beijing: Shijie zhishi chubanshe, 1958), vol. 2, 88–89.

32. "Zhongchang tielu yijiuwuer nian daijie pinghenbiao ji shengchan caiwu gongzuo juesuan shuomingx shu" [The balance sheet of loan and final account specification on production and financial work of the CCR in 1952], Archive of Harbin, 10–12.

33. It should also be remembered that in the early postwar period, when the Soviet army occupied Northeast China, many enterprises and their equipment were plundered as war booty and sent back to the Soviet Union. According to a report by Edwin Pauley, a personal representative of President Truman on the Allied Commission on Reparations, the value of machinery and equipment moved out of the Northeast was $895 million. See Wang Zhao, "Zhongdong tielu shimo" [Story of the Chinese Eastern Railway], *Problems of Soviet Union and East Europe, 1983,* no. 3. Another view claims that the equipment taken away by the Soviets was worth about $2 billion. See Wu Dongzi, ed., *Zhongguo weijiaoshi: Zhonghuaminngguo shiqi, 1919–1949* [A diplomatic history of China: The Era of the Republic of China, 1919–1949] (Kaifeng: Henan Renmin chubanshe, 1990), 698.

34. *Zhongguo waijiaobu dangan,* 109-00175-01, 31–32.

35. See Chinese Academy of Social Sciences and Central Archive, ed., *Zhonghua renmin gongheguo jingji dangan ziliao xuanbian* [Economic reference material collections of People's Republic of China, 1953–1957: volume of transportation and communication] (hereinafter *Zhonghua renmin*) (Beijing: Zhongguo wujia chubanshe, 1998), 254.

36. Chinese Academy of Social Sciences and Central Archive, ed., *Zhonghua renmin,* 275.

37. During his August 1952 talks with Premier Zhou Enlai, Stalin said provocatively, "Chinese comrades must understand that if the United States does not lose the war, China would never reoccupy Taiwan."(APRF, fond 45, opis 1, delo 329, listy 68–71, *Sovetsko-kitaiskie otnosheniya,* t. 5, kn. 2, 322–23.)

38. See Li Wenyao, "Tui guang 'zhongdong tielu jingyang' shimo" [Story about promoting 'experience in the CCR'], *People's Railway,* August 18, 2006, http://www.rmtd.com.cn/Article/2006/200608/2006-08-16/20060816094335.html.

39. N. E. Ablova, *Istoriya KVCD i rosiiskaya emigratsiya v Kitae,* 386.

40. In contrast, the problem of the Soviet immigrants in Xinjiang became a key element in the tense relations between the two countries in the same period. See Li Danhui, "Historical Review on the Problem of the Soviet Immigrants in Xinjiang (1945–1965)," http://www.coldwarchina.com/zwxz/zgxz/ldh/001647.html. </notes>

3

"Only a Handshake but No Embrace": Sino-Soviet Normalization in the 1980s

Péter Vámos[1]

The International Political Framework of Sino-Soviet Relations

IN THE LAST DECADE OF THE COLD WAR, the People's Republic of China (PRC) was a "virtual great power,"[2] perceived by political and business circles around the world as having achieved global power status, but not carrying the same strategic weight as the two superpowers. In the 1980s, China lagged far behind the two superpowers in military technology and its economy was not yet of global significance. It is fair to say that whereas the United States and the Soviet Union were global powers with a regional interest in the Asia-Pacific, China was a regional power with global influence.[3]

The global political framework continued to center on the United States and the Soviet Union, and the "loose bipolar" character of the international system remained constant. Although China was only a "complicating factor"[4] in the relationship between the two superpowers, the Soviets had less room for maneuver in the strategic triangle than the other two. Soviet ambitions in the 1970s to use military force to establish and support regimes in Africa, Central America, and the Middle East had contributed to the souring of relations with the United States and the decay of détente on the one hand, and, as a consequence, the arms race and an oversized imperial periphery, which became as much a liability as a strategic asset, had consumed the economic reserves of the Soviet Union on the other. Moreover, as a result of Soviet support of the Vietnamese invasion of Cambodia and the Soviet invasion of Afghanistan, Moscow became diplomatically isolated in Asia.

As in the 1970s the principal conflict in the Asia-Pacific region had become that between China and the Soviet Union, it was only a logical consequence that changes occurred in the Sino-American policy.[5] Following the Soviet invasion of Afghanistan and the Vietnamese invasion of Cambodia and the official normalization of bilateral relations in 1979, the Sino-American relationship could be described as a "tight alignment, close to being a de facto alliance."[6] As a result of the transformation of China's position from being a target for American containment policies to a quasi-alliance with the United States and its allies, Beijing's role in international politics was transformed.

Deng Xiaoping's Reforms and Their Political Implications

In the late seventies, profound changes occurred in Chinese domestic politics. In December 1978 Deng Xiaoping embarked on his ambitious reform program, which resulted in the replacement of Maoist radicalism by pragmatic moderation and the corresponding shift from the primacy of politics to that of economics. In Thomas Robinson's words, "whatever appeared good for China's domestic economic development became Beijing's foreign policy."[7]

The Chinese policy of opening was designed to facilitate integration into international markets. For the PRC, the relationship with the United States was of primary importance. First, Deng showed willingness for a compromise with the Americans on the Taiwan issue which resulted in the establishment of diplomatic relations between the United States and the PRC on January 1, 1979. Washington and its allies (including Japan and EEC member states) served for Beijing as major sources of advanced technology and foreign investment. Furthermore, it was the United States that with its military presence was a key factor in providing the strategic stability in the Asia-Pacific that had proven beneficial to China.

Having normalized its relations with the United States, for the purpose of providing a peaceful environment, Deng also sought improved relations with the Soviet Union. The Chinese had good reasons to seek normalization with the Soviet Union. The Sino-Soviet conflict remained a destabilizing factor for China. With the border issue unsettled and Soviet military deployments in Siberia and Mongolia, the Soviet Union was perceived as the gravest threat to China's security. Moreover, as there existed a functional interdependence and regional complementarity between the two economies, both sides were interested in the normalization of relations.[8]

In April 1979, a month after the withdrawal of Chinese troops from Vietnam, Beijing sent the first signal to Moscow of its willingness to take steps toward the normalization of political relations. The PRC announced that

China intended to let the 1950 Treaty of Friendship, Alliance and Mutual Assistance expire without seeking an extension. However, in contrast to China's sharp rejection of Soviet initiatives following Mao's death, Foreign Minister Huang Hua emphasized China's "consistent stand" for "the maintenance and development of . . . normal state relations," and called for "negotiations . . . of outstanding issues and the improvement of relations between the two countries."[9]

Moscow responded positively to the Chinese initiative, but tensions did not ease immediately. The two parties started negotiations in September 1979, but they could not agree even on the agenda. The Soviet Union wished to negotiate on "bilateral issues" whereas the Chinese put forward Soviet foreign policies that concerned "third countries" (Vietnam, Mongolia, and starting from early 1980 Afghanistan). In late November the parties agreed to continue the dialogue next spring.

The Hungarian Ambassador in Beijing, Róbert Ribánszki reported in early 1980 that there were contradictions among Chinese leaders concerning the aims, depth and timing of negotiations. According to the evaluation of the Hungarian embassy in Beijing, propaganda considerations played an important role in the Chinese proposal.[10] Beijing did not intend to break the negotiation process, but did not aim at fast and substantive achievements either. Chinese leaders considered that conducting negotiations with the Soviets could provide considerable room for maneuver against the West, exert pressure on Vietnam, and, most important, could calm down the "Muscovites." (Chen Yun, vice-chairman of the CCP CC, who returned to power in December 1978, at the 3rd plenum of the CCP CC, was the emblematic figure among those leaders who considered it necessary to normalize relations with the Soviet Union.)

On January 19, 1980, three weeks after the Soviet invasion of Afghanistan, Beijing announced that it would not continue negotiations, as they were not appropriate under the new circumstances. In American China-specialist Jonathan Pollack's opinion the reason for the delay was that some Chinese officials viewed the invasion as an act of weakness and desperation, whereas the majority believed that hints of accommodation and flexibility toward the Soviet Union would send the wrong signal to both Washington and Moscow.[11]

The Soviet invasion of Afghanistan set in motion a train of political and strategic consequences. President Carter announced a grain embargo against the Soviet Union, withdrew the SALT II agreement from the Senate, and announced that the United States would not participate in the Olympic Games in Moscow. What is important for us in this respect is that the Carter administration decided to establish closer relations with China, which also included military cooperation.[12] Following Carter's proposal for an "embryonic

U.S.-Chinese military relationship" Deng may have concluded that U.S. policy was moving in the directions that he sought.[13] In order to gain a better position, and based on his successful negotiation strategy of raising "three obstacles" to the establishment of official diplomatic relations with the United States,[14] Deng identified three issues as "major obstacles" to the normalization of relations with the Soviet Union, including the Soviet military presence along its northern borders and in Mongolia, and Soviet support for Vietnam's invasion of Cambodia. In January 1980, the Soviet invasion of Afghanistan—which began in December 1979, less than two weeks after the conclusion of the initial round of Sino-Soviet negotiations in Moscow—was added to the list.

The Soviet military presence had been immense in the Russian Far East and in Mongolia since the mid-1960s. The People's Republic of Mongolia and China had signed a border agreement in 1962, and by 1964 the demarcation of the border had been completed. However, following the increase in the numbers of border incidents, the Soviets signed a new defense agreement with Mongolia giving them the right to station military units and maintain bases there, which upset the military balance between the opposing sides. In the early 1980s, about one fourth of Soviet ground forces and one third of its air force were stationed along or in the region of the Sino-Soviet border.

In December 1978, only days before the official announcement of the establishment of Sino-American diplomatic relations, Vietnam, with heavy Soviet support, invaded Cambodia and replaced the Chinese-supported Pol Pot regime with that of Heng Samrin. Having returned from a successful tour of the United States and Japan, in February 1979 Deng launched a "pedagogical attack" against Vietnam. From a strictly military point of view the war was a failure for the Chinese, as they did not succeed in diverting Vietnamese forces from Cambodia. However, as Michael Yahuda notes, the Chinese did in fact teach the Vietnamese a lesson in geopolitics, in the sense that unlike their former adversaries, France and the United States, or indeed its then ally, the Soviet Union, China was a constant presence as a more powerful neighbor.[15] In the next ten years, Vietnam was dependent upon the Soviet Union to sustain its dominant position in Cambodia. Vietnam's geopolitical importance was obvious for both the Soviet Union and China. The Soviet navy gained access to the former American bases in Vietnam, and for ten years was not willing to retreat, since to do so would weaken its positions in Southeast Asia. On the other side, Soviet support for Vietnam added to Chinese fears of the Soviet threat of encirclement. This then resulted in a stalemate, which was only broken a decade later when the Soviet Union was no longer able to continue to supply Vietnam with the materiel it needed to prosecute the war and underwrite its economy.[16]

Gradual Thaw (1979–1982)

The Soviet invasion of Afghanistan, which had initially seemed so threatening to China's security, led to a change in the balance of forces between the superpowers and made the prospects of war seem more distant, partly as a result of a tacit strategic partnership between China and the United States described euphemistically as the pursuit of parallel actions.[17] Washington adopted a more confrontationist policy toward the Soviet Union, and embarked on a course of rapid military buildup and the SDI program. On the other hand, the United States followed a more favorable policy toward China, which had military aspects as well, including the export of "non-lethal" military equipment, and the replacement of American electronic intelligence collection stations from Iran to Western China which were used to monitor Soviet missile tests and other military activities in the USSR.[18] Although the period until 1981 was for China a time of search for a united front to resist alleged Soviet expansionism, the American support for the Afghani resistance forces, the isolation of the Soviet Union in the Third World, and its growing economic problems, persuaded Deng that the immediate danger of a Soviet attack had receded.[19] As perhaps the most skilful practitioners of real-politik, the Chinese were ready by 1982 to distance themselves from the United States and explore openings to Moscow. China's new policies of economic reform and openness, parallel to ideological changes that involved the abandonment of the Maoist ideology of class struggle and the redefinition of Chinese political priorities and national interests also assisted this process.

During the first period of Sino-Soviet normalization between 1979 and 1982, although there were no significant improvements, both sides initiated some small steps toward enlarged relations. As the Chinese leadership downgraded the Soviet threat and concluded that the prospects for conflict with the Soviets were less than previously estimated, two major foreign policy implications followed: the reduction of the need to stress the strategic link with the United States and a gradual turn back toward the Soviet Union, at least "to test the waters of Sino-Soviet détente, if not actual rapprochement."[20]

Mutual perceptions of the two opposing powers were all but favorable, at least on the propaganda level. The first issue of the principal Chinese periodical on Soviet issues stated in 1981 that "obviously, the military threats and hegemonic policy of the Soviet Union against China are the fundamental obstacles to the settlement of the Sino-Soviet boundary question and the normalization of Sino-Soviet state relations."[21] Meanwhile, Soviet assessments of Chinese foreign policy still emphasized the Chinese ambitions to establish an alliance of anti-Soviet forces, including the United States and its Western European allies, Japan, ASEAN countries and some Muslim states, including Saudi Arabia, "to keep Soviet hegemony from starting a new world war."[22]

In the course of the decade, Beijing on the level of principle continued to appear unyielding by maintaining its preconditions for normalizing relations with Moscow, but for the sake of practical advantages and based on a pragmatic and more flexible approach, it started a slow thaw of its relations with the Soviet Union. As a result, "Sino-Soviet relations were advancing on two distinct tracks. They were progressing rapidly on the state-to-state track of economic, scientific, and cultural exchanges, while the Chinese were awaiting Soviet action on one of the 'three obstacles' before proceeding with the track of strategic cooperation and party-to-party relations."[23] This was a carefully constructed scenario, as the three obstacles did not prevent distinct improvements in bilateral relations, but they did signify to the Americans that the Chinese were not in danger of re-aligning with the Soviet Union.

Parallel to the establishment of procedurally formalized diplomatic channels of communication, two-way trade expanded from 223 million rubles in 1982 to 1.6 billion rubles in 1985.[24] Although trade increased more than tenfold between 1982 and 1989, far outpacing the rate of both China's overall trade expansion and its trade growth with any other single trading partner,[25] Chinese trade relations with the Soviet Union were still secondary compared to those with Western countries, and lagged far behind Soviet trade relations with its satellites.[26]

As to the apparent reluctance of both sides to go about political normalization, there are at least two reasons to be mentioned. First, having normalized its relations with the United States in 1979, it was not urgent for China to reconcile with the Soviet Union. On the other hand, Moscow made it clear that the Soviet Union was not willing to make concessions to the Chinese although Beijing connected the resumption of consultations to practical actions from the Soviet side toward the removal of the three obstacles.[27] Since the United States and its Western allies, including Japan, could be used as sources for advanced technology that China needed so badly for its modernization goals, the need for Soviet support was not urgent; trade, credit, or technology pressures did not exist in relation to the USSR. As M. S. Kapitsa, head of the First Far Eastern Department at the Soviet Ministry of Foreign Affairs (MFA) and one of the leading China experts in Moscow put it in the spring of 1981, the Chinese "wish to modernize their economy using Western technological help and credits, and have no other capital to pay for this help but anti-Sovietism."[28]

Constant military pressure was part of the game. As O. B. Rakhmanin, first deputy head of the CPSU CC International Department told the Hungarian ambassador in Moscow in August 1980, although "the Soviet Union was not interested in the escalation of the situation, but in order to avoid a new war, the Chinese had to understand what the Soviet Union was capable of."[29] In Kapitsa's words: "it has been our resolution to become a strong power in the

Pacific, and it cannot be obstructed by anyone. Why should the Pacific Ocean remain an American sea?" The Soviets who enjoyed absolute superiority over China in conventional firepower and nuclear capacity undertook a second stage in their Far Eastern arms buildup, focusing primarily on air and naval forces. Against this background, the Soviets also proposed small steps, including local cross-border trade, renewal of scientific-technological cooperation and border talks, even inviting a Chinese ping-pong team to the Soviet Union. In most cases the Chinese showed willingness to take steps forward, but Deng refused to admit the possibility of any lasting improvement in Sino-Soviet relations unless Moscow would give way on the three obstacles. This dual approach remained a characteristic element of both Beijing's and Moscow's tactics throughout much of the decade.

American determination to counterbalance Soviet military superiority to China enabled the Chinese to center their foreign policy on economic development. Although Beijing repeatedly emphasized the importance of its economic relationship with the West, the Chinese interest in a peaceful environment and in economic relations with both superpowers led to further broadening of Sino-Soviet relations. Deng realized the economic difficulties the Soviet Union had to face, but remained suspicious toward Moscow, repeatedly asserting that the Soviet Union constituted China's principal security threat. However, he showed more flexibility and patience to navigate contacts toward gradual institutionalization and to elevate the level of political relations.

Resumption of Political Consultations, Progress in Practical Issues (1982–1985)

The Soviets took the first big step with Brezhnev's March 1982 speech in Tashkent to pave the way for the resumption of talks. The Soviet leader called China a socialist country, supported China's position on Taiwan, expressed his willingness to improve relations with China, and proposed consultations between the two sides. Deng instructed the MFA to react to the Tashkent speech immediately. Qian Qichen, then head of the Information Department, arranged the first press conference in the history of the MFA for March 26, 1982. The Chinese reaction consisted of only three sentences: "We paid attention to the sections concerning Sino-Soviet relations in President Brezhnev's speech in Tashkent on March 24. We categorically refute its attacks against China. In Sino-Soviet relations and in international affairs, we attach importance to the Soviet Union's real actions." The announcement was received with a standing ovation, as there were no seats for the journalists, and all guests were standing in the lobby surrounding Qian and his interpreter, Li Zhaoxing. The two important phrases in the text were "paid attention to" and "attached importance to," which signaled the positive attitude of the Chinese. The next day, those three sentences were published in the center of the cover page of *Renmin Ribao*, underlining its importance.[30]

In the summer, Deng Xiaoping summoned senior leaders and MFA senior officials, including Chen Yun, Li Xiannian and Qian Qichen to discuss further actions. Deng said that a big step should be made toward the improvement of bilateral relations, but added that the principal Chinese position concerning the Soviet removal of the three obstacles had to be maintained. As to the transmission of the message to Moscow, Chen Yun proposed that a form must be found which raised the counterpart's attention, but did not raise concerns in the West. Sending a special envoy seemed the only feasible option, since at the time no other channels of direct contact existed. Deng proposed that Yu Hongliang, head of the MFA USSR and East European Department be sent to Moscow and Warsaw with the purpose of inspecting Chinese embassies there. The first and most important stop was Moscow, where he met with his counterpart, Head of Department Kapitsa (who interrupted his vacation and returned to Moscow for the meeting) and Vice-Foreign Minister Leonid Ilichev on August 10 at the Chinese embassy.

Yu Hongliang transmitted Beijing's message orally, speaking without notes. Qian Qichen recalls the text in his memoirs as follows:

There has been an abnormal relationship between China and the Soviet Union for many years, and the two peoples do not want to see the continuation of such a situation. Now it is time to do something to improve Sino-Soviet relations. Of course, the problems cannot be solved in one day, but the Chinese side holds that the important thing is the existence of true willingness to improve relations. It is fully possible to find a fair and reasonable solution through negotiations. The Chinese side proposes that the Soviet Union should persuade Vietnam to withdraw its troops from Cambodia as a starting point, or it is also possible to start with other problems that influence the relationship between our two countries, such as the reduction of military force in the border region. At the same time, both sides should work on finding mutually acceptable measures in order to solve the problem of withdrawal of Soviet troops from Mongolia. The Chinese side also hopes that a fair solution can be found for the Afghan issue. To sum up, only if both sides think about the prospects for the development of the relationship, are willing to resume good neighborly relations between our two great countries, start with solving one or two of the important problems, will it then be possible to open up a new phase in bilateral relations. As to the form of exchanging views, it can be done by consultations between the two sides.[31]

The Chinese showed flexibility in their position on the three obstacles to normalization. They did not call for simultaneous Soviet actions on all three problems, and indicated that they did not expect that any one obstacle would be removed at once. What mattered to the Chinese was that the Soviets take a constructive attitude. With the emphasis on Cambodia, Yu hinted that that the primary concern for China was Southeast Asia, its traditional sphere of interest.

After the meeting Yu left for Warsaw, in order to give time for the Soviets to form their opinion. On August 18, a day after the signing of the Sino-American Joint Communiqué,[32] Yu on his way back to China made a stopover in Moscow and met Ilichev for a second time. There he was informed that an official response was under preparation. On August 20, Soviet First Vice-Foreign Minister Maltsev summoned Chinese chargé d'affaires Ma Xusheng and informed him that the Soviet Union was ready to continue negotiations at any time, anywhere and on any level in order to "remove the obstacles for normalization of relations." The phrase "removal of obstacles" signaled the positive attitude of the Soviets. Having received the Soviet response, Deng agreed to the resumption of negotiations. Before the opening of the Twelfth Party Congress on September 1, 1982, the two sides agreed to conduct political consultations on the vice-foreign ministerial level.[33]

In 1982, following a comprehensive reassessment of the international strategic environment, the Chinese leadership began to distance itself from Washington in strategic terms, claimed that the United States and the Soviet Union had reached essential strategic parity, and that the two superpowers posed an equal hegemonic threat to the world. Under these circumstances, China announced that it would follow an independent foreign policy. At the party congress, General Secretary Hu Yaobang explained that henceforth China would not "attach itself to any big power or group of powers." After 1982, in the era of an "independent foreign policy," China would avoid confrontation or alignment with either superpower, reserved the right to criticize some aspects of both countries' policies, and endorsed those initiatives with which it agreed. However, the declaration of an "independent foreign policy" should not be taken at face value, as the distance that China sought to establish from the two superpowers was more hypothetical than real.[34] Chinese propaganda continued to assert that the USSR remained on the offensive, posing a direct threat to the security of China, while, in spite of a growing concern over Washington's Taiwan policy and limitations on transfer of technology, China still tilted strongly toward the United States on the important strategic questions, including Cambodia and Afghanistan.

The solid Sino-American relationship, which also manifested itself in the signing of the 1982 joint communiqué, had increased Chinese self-confidence toward Moscow, while the new policy line which substantially increased the Chinese sphere of independent maneuver provided a basis for gradually improving relations with the Soviet Union. The dropping of "social imperialism" and "contemporary revisionism" from the 1982 Constitution of the PRC was as much a gesture to Moscow as a reflection of the major ideological changes that had taken place since Deng launched his policy of reform and openness.

The first round of vice-foreign ministerial consultations took place in Beijing and lasted for two weeks between 5 and 21 October 1982. The phrase "consultation" was proposed by the Chinese. According to the Soviets this was an obvious face-saving maneuver as the Chinese side had been insisting for three years that they would not start negotiations unless the Soviets fulfilled their preconditions.[35]

Between 1982 and 1988, twelve rounds of Sino-Soviet political consultations took place on the vice-ministerial level. This time the Chinese proposed that negotiations take place twice a year, one round in the spring in Moscow and one in the fall in Beijing. Each round comprised six (later five, then four) meetings followed by an unofficial part, when the two negotiating partners made trips in the host country. As both sides had made their positions known before the actual round, the first two rounds resembled a series of monologues rather than real dialogues. Even later on, mostly in the first half of the 1980s both sides regularly resorted to political or ideological diatribes during the negotiations. By the mid-1980s the atmosphere became more friendly and bridges of trust had been built between the two sides. Political and especially ideological lectures disappeared, and were substituted with more businesslike negotiations. In spite of fundamental differences of opinion on principal issues, both parties agreed from the beginning on the necessity of the further improvement of economic, trade, cultural, sports, scientific and technological relations.

In the course of the decade, Deng Xiaoping kept on reciting his "political credo" that without settlement on the three obstacles it was not possible to improve relations with the Soviet Union and that relations with the USSR would not come at the expense of China's ties to the West. From the beginning, the Chinese were also insisting on the principle that peaceful coexistence should serve as the basis for Sino-Soviet relations. That Pancha Shila—the five principles of peaceful coexistence drawn up in 1954, which the Chinese and the Indian Premiers had agreed should form the basis for relations between the two states with different social systems—should be extended to relations between all countries irrespective of social system, was a point that appeared already in the Chinese statement of November 1, 1956, a response to the Soviet government's declaration issued on October 30. When the Soviets inquired about the reason for the Chinese demand already before the first round of consultations, the Chinese replied that "there existed contradictions, and sometimes even sharp conflicts between socialist countries," and mentioned Vietnam's attack on and occupation of Cambodia as an example.[36]

In 1984, the two foreign ministers met in New York at the UN for the first time in several years. First deputy Prime Minister Ivan V. Arkhipov's tour of China in December 1984 was the highest level visit of a Soviet leader since Kosygin's 1969 negotiations with Zhou Enlai at Beijing airport.[37] The Chinese emphasized the friendly nature of the visit and fulfilled all Arkhipov's requests, including a meeting with Peng Zhen, and visits to Wuhan and Shenzhen. Hinting at Hungarian Deputy Prime Minister József Marjai's visit to China in August 1984, the Chinese evaluation of Arkhipov's visit mentioned that it "ended the illusion that certain socialist countries 'ran ahead' compared to the Soviet Union in building relations with China."[38]

By 1984 there were two important new elements in Chinese behavior toward the Soviet Union. First, the Chinese acknowledged that the two sides shared identical or very close opinions on certain international issues, and expressed their willingness to engage in diplomatic consultations on those issues. However, they excluded the possibility of a joint or parallel action unless progress was made by the Soviet Union in relation to the three obstacles.[39] Second, they told diplomats of socialist countries that if the Soviet Union were willing to remove at least one of the three obstacles (they mentioned the Soviet support for Vietnam), China would be ready to re-establish inter-party relations with the Soviet Union and other socialist countries.[40]

As part of Beijing's "funeral diplomacy," Li Peng in March 1985 made another gesture toward the Soviets when during his meeting with Gorbachev he said that "we are two neighboring great socialist countries. If we cannot be friends, let us at least be good neighbors." Li also emphasized that China did not strive for strategic cooperation with the United States. In his response Gorbachev said that the Soviet Union wanted to normalize its relations with China, wished to continue dialogue and to raise the level of negotiations.[41] The Gorbachev–Li Peng meeting had a favorable effect on bilateral relations and their atmosphere. The Chinese greetings sent to Gorbachev, unexpectedly, also touched upon party-to-party relations, and China officially acknowledged the Soviet Union as a socialist country. Although the Soviets regarded the last two actions as corrections of the previously mistaken policy line and not as steps forward (Kapitsa even labeled them as a misleading maneuver), nevertheless, they appreciated the fact that such steps had been taken at all.[42]

Kapitsa told the Hungarian counselor in Moscow that the Chinese considered Gorbachev as a man to be reckoned with in the long run, therefore they did not want to put all their cards on the table at the negotiations.[43] A

Soviet diplomat in Beijing expressed a more pessimistic view when he concluded that a "more realistic approach" was needed and the Soviets had to give up illusions concerning fast improvement. The Chinese evaluated Gorbachev as a flexible leader, but added that he would need at least two years before his influence became strong enough to make the necessary personnel changes and alterations in its foreign policy line, so that substantial development in political relations could occur only after that.[44]

Meanwhile, new channels of regular contact between the two countries were opened. Vice-ministerial consultations on international issues were begun in September 1983, a third series of talks was commenced in December 1984 with the Chinese visit of Ivan V. Arkhipov, the first Vice-Chairman of the USSR Council of Ministers and, as former leader of the Soviet advisory staff during the heyday of Sino-Soviet cooperation, "an old friend of China." A fourth channel was opened with the establishment of the Sino-Soviet Committee on Economic, Trade, Scientific and Technological Cooperation in 1985. As an important new development between the two MFAs in 1985, the Soviets briefed the Chinese ten times on confidential political events. At first, the Chinese received the information with suspicion, but later showed interest in topics such as the Geneva summit meeting. In the course of the year, the Chinese also briefed the Soviet ambassador in Beijing on five occasions.[45] By the mid-1980s, the two sides had established a network of diplomatic, scientific, cultural, sports, health, and other exchanges.

By the time of Mikhail S. Gorbachev's accession to power in March 1985, in Gilbert Rozman's words, "there was no longer any doubt that two socialist neighbors with some nostalgic memories were working to resolve their serious differences."[46] In spite of the slow improvement that had been achieved in political normalization, there were few signs in Chinese writings on most subjects of the hostility that had been expressed toward Moscow only a year or two earlier.[47]

During his first year in office, Gorbachev did not show any intention to proceed with the problem of the three obstacles. Ambassador Shcherbakov, upon his return from Moscow where he had consulted with Gorbachev and Shevardnadze, told friendly ambassadors that there was no change in the Soviet attitude toward China. Moscow followed the old pattern by stressing that the main controversies between the Soviet Union and China were ideological and inter-party in nature and that the SU wanted China to become a force for socialism in the USSR-USA-PRC triangle.[48]

In sum, negotiations before 1986 did not produce any breakthroughs, and there were no obvious signs of one. Although the overall tone on both sides was softening, and an increasing number of concrete results had been achieved, the Chinese were cautious not to give an impression that they would yield an inch on the three obstacles.

Breakthrough in Bilateral Relations (1986–1989)

The economic stagnation of the Soviet Union had become evident even before Brezhnev's death, but by the mid-1980s it reached a level when chances for drastic improvements seemed rather slim in a socialist economic system that had shown itself to be extremely ineffective.[49] At the CPSU's Twenty-seventh Congress in February 1986, Gorbachev called for "radical economic reform" at home, and at the same time praised Chinese reform and expressed satisfaction with the improvement in relations. From this time on, Chinese interest in the Soviet Union began to focus on the nature of Gorbachev's efforts, with special concern for his commitment to reforming the economic management system.

Furthermore, Gorbachev recognized that there was a foreign policy dimension to the critical economic situation at home. He sought to reverse the excessive reliance that had been placed on military force. As documented in the notes from CPSU Politburo meetings in 1986, Gorbachev acknowledged the costly failures of the Kremlin in relation to Afghanistan, and expressed the resolute determination to conclude the war and withdraw Soviet troops.[50]

The first breakthrough in Soviet China-policy occurred in July 1986, when in a speech in Vladivostok the general secretary made a series of unilateral concessions to the Chinese. He addressed two of the "three obstacles," troop withdrawals from Mongolia and the Russian Far East and from Afghanistan, and practically accepted the Chinese position on the border issue, recognizing that the border between the two countries should run along the main navigation channels of the Ussuri and the Amur, and not along the line of the Chinese bank of the two border rivers. During the year, Kapitsa was removed from his post of vice-foreign minister in charge of East Asian affairs, and replaced by Igor Rogachev, who from 1986 onwards also served as Soviet chief negotiator at the political consultations with China.[51]

All these developments facilitated a further acceleration of the rapprochement process. In 1986 the Chinese opened a consulate in Leningrad, and the Soviets in Shanghai. In May of the same year, the two countries concluded a two-year cultural accord to expand cooperation in science, education, culture, art, film, journalism, publishing, broadcasting, television, sports, health, and other areas. In June, the two academies signed an agreement on scientific cooperation, and a month later, the PRC held its first large-scale industrial and trade exhibition in Moscow in thirty-three years, reciprocated by a Soviet exhibition in Beijing in December. Exchanges of journalists, academics, and officials quickly ensued.[52] The Chinese also agreed to reopen border talks in early 1987. At the same time, Beijing, faithful to its previous position and seeking to maintain and even increase pressure on Moscow to make real practical steps, rejected Soviet offers of a mutual non-aggression treaty, and repeatedly warned its counterpart of a possible deterioration of relations without political normalization.

The Soviets nevertheless moved cautiously toward fulfilling the promises made by Gorbachev. As Hungarian historian Csaba Békés notes, the reform-minded new leadership did not adequately assess the severity of the looming crisis of the Soviet Union, and refused, up until the summer of 1988, to take any major unilateral steps in disarmament. Furthermore, the reforms did not significantly improve either the political conditions or the efficiency of the economy.[53] It was no sooner than at a closed session of the foreign ministers at the Warsaw meeting of the Political Consultative Body of the Warsaw Treaty on July 15–16, 1988, that Eduard Shevardnadze openly admitted that the Soviet Union was "facing a critical situation," and it could no longer afford to run a permanent arms race with the West, given that it exceeded the Eastern bloc "in every possible respect."[54] He stressed that the termination of the arms race had to be given absolute priority and every chance had to be grasped in order to come to an agreement.[55]

The Soviet "new thinking" recognized peace as of highest value, preceding class, social, political, and ideological considerations. The new Soviet leadership considered the promotion of freedom of choice based on international law and legality as the main task of Soviet diplomacy and recognized the right of each nation to decide its own fate, the ways of its own development and how to safeguard it own achievements. In a January 1988 issue of the Beijing journal *Liaowang* (Observer), Gorbachev spoke about the foreign policy aspect of the new Soviet concept which emphasized building long-term policies that seek to balance various national interests and that settle regional conflicts by political means.[56] This new attitude led to a series of changes in the Asia-Pacific policy of the Soviet Union, including the Cambodian issue.

Based on currently available sources, it can be clearly established that no significant change in Soviet attitude toward a settlement with China occurred before the middle of 1988. As a next major step, Gorbachev reiterated his willingness in an address in Krasnoyarsk in September 1988 to participate in confidence-building arrangements and discussions with China on both territorial and military issues.

Gorbachev's Krasnoyarsk speech mirrors the realization that the Soviet Union could give weight to its initiatives only if it effectively joined the regional economic system, and for that it needed a substantial development of its domestic economy and the improvement of the level of technology. One of the messages of the Krasnoyarsk speech was that the Soviet Union wanted to take part in Asian issues as a partner equal to the United States, and that the Soviet Union was also an Asian power. Therefore without or against it there was no possibility for a settlement of regional problems. For that, as we have seen, Gorbachev was willing to make unilateral concessions. The unilateral steps for disarmament were announced by Gorbachev at the UN General Assembly on December 7, 1988.[57]

At the twelfth round of vice-ministerial consultations, held between 13 and 20 June 1988 in Moscow, the Chinese related the possibility of any substantial improvement in political relations to the removal of the three obstacles, and especially to the solution of the Cambodian problem, which the Chinese side called the precondition for a Sino-Soviet summit meeting. According to a Soviet source, this was the first time that the Chinese acknowledged the existence of common elements in Soviet and Chinese positions: first, only a political solution was possible; second, Cambodian domestic issues should be decided by the Cambodian people; third, a quadrilateral coalition government had to be formed; Cambodia should become an independent, neutral, non-aligned state, and finally, the agreement should be provided with international guarantees. An international forum similar to the Geneva conference in 1954 should be convened to discuss the guarantees. The Soviets proposed the establishment of a separate forum for further discussion on the Cambodian issue.[58] Finally, then, in 1988 Gorbachev showed willingness to respond positively to Chinese demands to cease Soviet assistance to Vietnam and press Hanoi to withdraw from Cambodia.

The accommodation process between the Soviet Union and the United States on a series of issues was an important precondition for China's own ambitions for "peace and development" and thus was welcomed by Beijing in spite of the fact that it resulted in the marginalization of China in global affairs.[59] In August 1987, Qian Qichen in an interview accentuated the common interest of the Chinese and Soviet leaderships: "China believes that Gorbachev is serious about reforming the Soviet system, which is good news for the improvement of bilateral relations, as reform on that scale needed a long period of relative peace in the world, just like the Chinese modernization efforts."[60] The Chinese were able to sustain sufficient pressure upon the weakening Soviet Union for further concessions, both in foreign policy—first of all with regard to the primary concern for the Chinese, the Cambodian issue—and in theoretical, ideological terms. Moscow finally gave up its attempt to redirect China to the family of socialist countries, and agreed to conduct its relations with Beijing on the basis of the five principles of peaceful coexistence and mutual benefit. Qian Qichen's visit to Moscow as foreign minister in December 1988 was reciprocated by Shevardnadze in February 1989. Parallel to negotiations on the Cambodian issue, the two sides agreed on the date and schedule of Gorbachev's visit to China and his meeting with Deng Xiaoping, which was considered as the symbolic act of normalization.

Preparations for the Summit Meeting

As long-awaited Soviet practical actions were on the way, in the last months of 1988 Chinese negotiating tactics, including their views related to the summit meeting, had undergone a profound change. While earlier Beijing had identified the removal of the three obstacles as a precondition, now it accepted the principle that preparations for the summit could proceed parallel to the settlement of the remaining issues. Meanwhile, in order to ease Western concerns that the fast normalization of Sino-Soviet relations could affect the relations of their countries with China, which had only been reinforced by Li Peng's designation to the post of prime minister, Chinese leaders used every opportunity to emphasize that there was no return to the alliance of the fifties. The basis of relations between socialist countries could be nothing else than the five principles of peaceful coexistence. China's interest in acquiring Western technology and machinery had not changed; and that stable relations with the United States, Japan and Western Europe were an integral and unshakable part of China's foreign policy, and were not merely based on economic considerations.[61]

The first official meeting of the two foreign ministers took place on December 1-3, 1988 in Moscow. Both sides agreed that the visit, which was reciprocated by Shevardnadze's visit to Beijing in February 1989, opened a new phase in the normalization of bilateral relations, and that the former practice of vice-ministerial meetings had exhausted itself and therefore had to be concluded and replaced by normal diplomatic channels.[62] The two leaders declared that their countries did not pose a threat to the other's security. Qian Qichen outlined the idea of a "new international order" proposed by Deng Xiaoping. As the concept identified cooperation as the basic principle for international relations, in Moscow's opinion it showed many similarities to the Soviet concept of "new thinking," moreover, Soviet leaders spoke about a basic change in Chinese foreign policy and called it the first Chinese concept which included normalization of relations with the USSR.[63]

Soviet sources stressed that the Chinese made principal concessions on the Cambodian issue.[64] As to the basic principles for bilateral relations, Qian, referring to the October 30, 1956, Soviet government declaration and the

November 1 Chinese statement, said that between the two great socialist countries the five principles of peaceful coexistence as well as friendship and good neighborly relations should be observed. It meant a slight alternation compared to the previous Chinese position in which they stuck to the narrow understanding of Pancha Shila.

During Shevardnadze's visit to China on February 2–4, 1989, the two sides agreed on the date and timetable of Gorbachev's visit. Gorbachev was invited by Chairman Yang Shangkun, but the meeting with Deng Xiaoping, the "main architect of Chinese policy" was considered as the summit meeting symbolizing the normalization of state-to-state relations. The Chinese were cautious on the question of restoration of inter-party relations. They argued that the meeting between Zhao Ziyang and Gorbachev would automatically mean the restoration of party relations, but there was no need to issue an extra statement on that.[65] Commenting on Shevardnadze's visit, Chinese politicians reiterated that normalization of party relations would not mean the return to the dominance of CPSU, and that emphasis would be laid on state-to-state relations. They stressed that party-to-party relations had to be based on equality, independence, and sovereignty; there could be no center or leading force for the international communist movement; and there was no unified model for building socialism. The Chinese regarded the whole socialist world as a large laboratory in which each party played an independent, sovereign role, and was responsible only to its own nation.[66] The two sides agreed that relations should be based on peaceful coexistence as well as equality and mutual benefit.[67]

The Summit Meeting, May 15–18, 1989

During the highpoint of the Tiananmen demonstrations, on May 16, 1989, between 10 am and 12:30 pm, the historic meeting of Deng Xiaoping and Mikhail S. Gorbachev took place in the Great Hall of the People. Deng's instruction for the reception ceremony was: "only handshake but no embrace," which was also a symbolic description of the state of bilateral relations.[68] At the meeting, four topics were raised by Deng. Concerning normalization of bilateral relations, the Chinese leader stated that this had been a long process which began with Gorbachev's Vladivostok speech. Second, he reviewed the behavior of imperialist powers toward China in the past one and a half centuries and said that Tsarist Russia robbed the largest territories from China and the Soviet Union also occupied parts of China's territory. Deng mentioned inequality as the basic problem in the Soviet treatment of China, and added that the USSR had posed a constant threat to China's security in the past thirty years. However, Deng added that China had no territorial claims toward the Soviet Union. Deng recalled the times of ideological disputes and acknowledged that he himself was not always correct. Gorbachev also acknowledged that the Soviet Union had its share of mistakes in the "not distant past," and agreed with Deng's proposal to "end the past and open up the future." Third, analyzing the practice of building socialism, he declared that a dogmatic approach to Marxism-Leninism was incorrect and that classical teachings on the theoretical basics of socialism should be renewed by present generations. Fourth, concerning the Cambodian issue he expressed his doubts about Vietnam's genuine willingness to withdraw. As to the future of Cambodia, no agreement was reached. The Chinese supported a quadrilateral coalition government headed by Prince Sihanouk, while the Soviets considered Cambodian national reconciliation a domestic issue which should be decided by Cambodians themselves.[69]

Gorbachev's meeting with Zhao Ziyang meant the normalization of party-to-party relations between the CCP and CPSU. Soviet sources emphasized two elements in Zhao Ziyang's remarks: first, that Deng's retirement after the 13th party congress had been only formal and he remained the supreme leader of the country. The Soviet assessment was that Zhao by this statement distinguished himself from Deng and shifted responsibility for the escalation of the domestic situation onto him. Second, Zhao spoke about the huge gap that existed between political and economic reforms and stressed the necessity to carry on political reforms. He also welcomed Gorbachev's statement about the necessity to strengthen the rule of law and develop the Soviet Union in the direction of a legal state.[70]

The main concern for the Chinese was the restoration of party relations. They considered it as a strictly bilateral issue, and declared that the CCP would not participate in any multilateral party conferences or other events and the two parties would exchange information and experience but would not harmonize their policies.[71] The Soviets noticed that Chinese ideas concerning the method and pace of the development of inter-party relations were not clear and pointed out that Beijing considered party relations as secondary to state relations.

With Prime Minister Li Peng, his main negotiating partner, Gorbachev discussed the future development of economic cooperation. The Soviets proposed among others cooperation in metallurgy, the energy sector and transport, whereas the Chinese put forward the idea of a broader utilization of Chinese labor forces in Siberia.[72] They also discussed the border issue and the reduction of military forces in the border region. The establishment of Sino-Soviet bilateral relations on the five principles of peaceful coexistence was considered as a symbolic action and a model for a "new type" of relations by the Chinese, all the more because earlier the Soviet Union had been reluctant to accept those principles as the basis of its relations with socialist countries. This move equaled the rejection of the Brezhnev doctrine.[73]

The timing of Gorbachev's visit could not have been more unsuitable because of the students demonstrations in the Chinese capital. Nevertheless, neither side proposed the postponement of the visit.[74] The Soviets did not make any attempt to exploit the difficult situation of the Chinese leadership. In the first live broadcast on Chinese state radio and television of the speech by a foreign statesman, Gorbachev said exactly what the majority of Chinese wanted to hear: no compulsory model for socialism existed; no party had the right to the only truth; and the Soviet Union did not strive for a leading role in this respect.[75] The Soviet ambassador in Beijing was unwilling to comment on the impact of Chinese domestic situation on Gorbachev's visit.[76] However, we know from other Soviet sources that Gorbachev was deeply shocked by the mass demonstrations that culminated during his visit in Beijing, and feared that similar events could take place in the Soviet Union as well.[77]

Conclusion

History proved that time was on Deng's side in his dealings with the Soviet Union. Deng played on his country's improving international position and influence in the 1980s. The priority on domestic economic reform in both countries was the principal reason for the improvement in Sino-Soviet relations. Although the Soviet Union served as an important model for China in many respects, as a result of opposite developments in the two countries— Chinese economic growth and increase in output versus Soviet economic regression and mounting domestic problems—Chinese patience prevailed, and similar to the case of Sino-American normalization, China's counterpart had to give in and make concessions in order to improve its relations with the PRC. Deng's confidence was based on the strength of the Chinese economy which profited from Western investments and technology transfer throughout the whole period. In the case of the Soviet leadership, which emphasized its principal positions all along, it took seven years and four general secretaries to realize that it served their interest to normalize political relations with their neighbor as the Soviet Union could not be successful against but only with China. The Chinese welcomed Gorbachev's declared willingness to rely less on the threat or use of force in Soviet foreign policy and strive for a peaceful international climate. However, the Tiananmen incident and its international consequences and the collapse of the Soviet Union served as an enlightening lesson for China not to commit the same mistakes as Gorbachev. The key point for the CCP was to take economic development as a core, and to seek to improve productivity and the standard of living before embarking on political reform.

Notes

1. Péter Vámos is senior research fellow at the Institute of History of the Hungarian Academy of Sciences, Budapest. He can be reached at *pvamos@tti.hu*. The author would like to thank the Chiang Ching-kuo Foundation for International Scholarly Exchange for its support of research into Hungarian archival documents on China's foreign relations.

2. A phrase used by Kay Möller in his book on the foreign policy of the PRC for the period after 1990. See Kay Möller, *Die Aussenpolitik der Volksrepublik China 1949–2004* (Wiesbaden: VS Verlag für Sozialwissenschaften, 2005), 113.

3. Michael Yahuda, *The International Politics of the Asia-Pacific, 1945–1995* (hereinafter as *International Politics*), (London and New York: Routledge, 1996), 186. Yahuda quotes from *The Chinese View of the World* (New York: Pantheon Books, 1989), edited by Yufan Hao and Guocang Huan, and written by Chinese scholars who studied in the United States. The editors describe China as "a regional power with global strategic significance and political influence," xxix.

4. Michael Yahuda, *International Politics*, 77–78.

5. David Shambaugh, "Patterns of Interaction in Sino-American Relations," in *Chinese Foreign Policy: Theory and Practice*, eds., Thomas W. Robinson and David Shambaugh (hereinafter as *Theory and Practice*) (Oxford: Clarendon Press, 1994), 198–99.

6. David Shambaugh, *Theory and Practice*, 203.

7. Thomas W. Robinson, "Chinese Foreign Policy from the 1940s to the 1990s," in *Theory and Practice*.

8. On the relationship between the two economies, see Lowell Dittmer, *Sino-Soviet Normalization and Its International Implications, 1945–1990* (hereinafter as *Sino-Soviet Normalization*) (Seattle and London: University of Washington Press, 1992), 80–88.

9. *Beijing Review*, 6 April 1979, 3–4, quoted by Jonathan D. Pollack in "The Opening to America," 450, in *The Cambridge History of China*, vol. 15, *The People's Republic: Revolutions within the Chinese Revolution, 1966–1982*, eds., Roderick MacFarquhar and John K. Fairbank (hereinafter as "The Opening to America") (Cambridge: Cambridge University Press, 1991), 450.

10. Ambassador Róbert Ribánszki's report (reporter: Sándor Mészáros): Relations between the PRC and socialist countries in 1979. Beijing, January 24, 1980. HNA XIX-J-1-j-Kína-103-001096-1980 (81. d.) Hungarian diplomatic records kept in the Hungarian National Archives (hereinafter as HNA) serve as a unique source for the study of Sino-Soviet relations. Hungarian diplomats made their evaluations based on first-hand information received from both sides. The Soviets regularly briefed their allies,

the "friendly" or "closely coordinating" countries, both in Moscow and in Beijing, either orally or in the form of Russian language information memoranda. In some cases the original Russian language document is also available at HNA. At first, information was rather one-sided as all the contents of the memoranda had to suit Moscow's interests, and secondly they were not much different from official reflections and public announcements. From the mid-1980s onwards, however, information became more objective since the Chinese also briefed the representatives of East European socialist countries concerning the new developments of Sino-Soviet bilateral relations.

11. HNA, 454–55.

12. HNA, 457.

13. HNA, 452–53.

14. Washington's diplomatic relations with Taiwan; the 1954 US-ROC mutual defense treaty; and the presence of American troops on Taiwan.

15. Michael Yahuda, *International Politics*, 206.

16. Michael Yahuda, *International Politics*, 91.

17. Michael Yahuda, *International Politics*, 207.

18. The reason for the surprisingly harsh U.S. reaction to the invasion of Afghanistan by Soviet troops in December 1979 was that the Soviet Union, for the first time since 1945, occupied a country which did not belong to the Soviet sphere of influence tacitly accepted by the West. During the 1956 and 1968 Eastern European crises, the West tacitly acknowledged the Soviet Union's right to restore order within its empire. This step, however, was considered a unilateral and violent extension of the Soviet sphere of influence. In Western interpretations, Moscow disregarded the tacit agreement based on status quo policy which had functioned well since the end of the Second World War. See Csaba Békés, *Európából Európába. Magyarország konfliktusok kereszttüzében, 1945–1990* [From Europe to Europe: Hungary in the cross-fire of conflicts, 1945–1990] (hereinafter as *Európából Európába*) (Budapest: Gondolat, 2004), 265–66. Although Hafizullah Amin was considered an ally of the Soviet Union, the invasion of Afghanistan could not be considered as the imposition of the Brezhnev Doctrine, since Afghanistan was not part of the Soviet sphere of influence. Hungarian reservation in relation to the Soviet step also supports this argument. "According to the official Hungarian position, the Soviet support for revolutionary forces in Afghanistan was not a Warsaw Pact action, but an issue only between the Soviet Union and Afghanistan." Békés, 260–61.

19. Michael Yahuda, "Deng Xiaoping: The Statesman," in *Deng Xiaoping: Portrait of a Chinese Statesman*, ed. David Shambaugh (hereinafter as *Deng Xiaopiug*) (Oxford: Clarendon Press, 1995), 152–53.

20. Thomas W. Robinson, *Theory and Practice*, 572–74.

21. The Chinese article is quoted by Gilbert Rozman, *The Chinese Debate about Soviet Socialism, 1978–1985* (hereinafter as *Chinese Debate*) (Princeton: Princeton University Press, 1987), 91–92.

22. Head of Department Ferenc Szabó's memorandum on his meeting with Soviet Counselor in Budapest Kokeiev, "Soviet assessment of the 'changes' in Chinese foreign policy," Budapest, Februar 11, 1981. HNA XIX-J-1-j-Kína-57-001088/1-1981 (84. d.).

23. Gilbert Rozman, *Chinese Debate*, 139–40.

24. Ambassador Sándor Rajnai's report (reporter: András Dunajszki): Report on Soviet-Chinese economic relations. Moscow, May 14, 1985. HNA XIX-J-1-j-SZU-51-002842-1985 (140. d.).

25. Lowell Dittmer, *Sino-Soviet Normalization*, 80–81.

26. The five-year trade agreement signed by Arkhipov and Yao Yilin in July 1985 in Moscow called for 12 billion rubles (equal to 14 billion USD or 35 billion SFR) of trade for the years between 1986 and 1990, and the duplication of the amount of bilateral trade by the end of the five-year period from 1.8 billion dollars in 1985 to about 3.6 billion in 1990. (Ambassador László Iván's cable: Latest developments of Soviet-Chinese relations. Beijing, June 6, 1985. No. 99. HNA XIX-J-1-j-Kína-103-001677/7-1985 [87. d.]) In comparison, when the amount of Sino-Soviet bilateral trade between 1986–1990 was proposed to reach 3-3.5 billion rubles in 1985, the Soviet Union signed a 51 billion ruble agreement with Hungary for the same time period. Vice-Foreign Minister Miklós Barity's report on his consultations with Vice-Foreign Minister Vadim Petrovich Loginov on December 9–10, 1985, in the Soviet Union. Budapest, December 16, 1985. HNA XIX-J-1-j-SZU-144-005246/2-1985 (139. d.).

27. Ambassador Mátyás Szárös's cable: Cde. Rakhmanin on Soviet-Chinese relations. Moscow, August 5, 1980, no. 351. HNA XIX-J-1-j-Szu-10t-002647/4-1980 (125. d.).

28. Memorandum on Kaptisa's talks with Comrade Dr. Vencel Házi (hereinafter as Memorandum on Kaptisa), April 24, 1981. HNA XIX-J-1-j-Szu-144t-002789/1/1981 (138. d.).

29. Memorandum on Kaptisa, (138. d.).

30. Qian Qichen, *Waijiao shiji* [Ten records on foreign relations] (hereinafter as *Waijioa shiji*) (Beijing: Shijie zhishi chubanshe, 2003), 4–6.

31. Qian Qichen, *Waijiao shiji*, 8.

32. The communiqué limited the quantity and quality of U.S. arms sales to Taiwan. In the eyes of the Chinese, this removed the key obstacle to Sino-American relations, but also included a gesture toward the Soviets by making only indirect reference to common strategic goals, in contrast to earlier communiqués which stressed joint opposition to hegemony.

33. Qian Qichen, *Waijiao shiji*, 8–10.

34. Jonathan D. Pollack, "The Opening to America," 467.

35. Ambassador Róbert Ribánszki's cable: The Soviet Ambassador in Beijing on Soviet-Chinese consultations. Beijing, December 1, 1982. No. 238. HNA XIX-J-1-j-Kína-10-005765/7-1982 (76. d).

36. Ambassador Róbert Ribánszki's cable: Chinese official persons on Sino-Soviet relations. Beijing, October 4, 1982. No. 181. HNA XIX-J-1-j-Szu-103-0024/13-1982 (76. d.).

37. Arkhipov's visit was first initiated by the Soviets in October 1983, and the Chinese proposed April 1984 as a suitable date for the visit. The visit was first postponed by the Soviets because of President Reagan's visit to China, and for the second time in May as a result of the situation at the Sino-Vietnamese border. According to Soviet

sources, the Chinese understood well the message of the postponement, and promised not to take any steps that would escalate tension.

38. Chargé d'affaires Sándor Jolsvai's cable: Chinese assessment of Arkhipov's visit. Beijing, January 7, 1985. No. 3. HNA XIX-J-1-j-SZU-51-00156-1985 (140. d.).

39. Head of Department Bálint Gál's memorandum: Consultation in Moscow on China, Indochina and Korea. Budapest, December 1984. HNA XIX-J-1-j-SZU-144-006143-1984 (135. d.).

40. Head of Department Bálint Gál's memorandum: Soviet information on China and Soviet-Chinese relations. Budapest, December 3, 1984. HNA XIX-J-1-j-Kína-10-00974/6-1984 (82. d.).

41. Ambassador László Iván's report (reporter: Sándor Jolsvai): Soviet preliminary assessment of the latest development of Soviet-Chinese relations. Beijing, March 28, 1985. HNA XIX-J-1-j-Kína-103-001677/3-1985 (87. d.).

42. Ambassador László Iván's cable: The sixth round of Soviet-Chinese consultations (preliminary information from the Soviet ambassador in Beijing). Beijing, April 9, 1985. No. 63. HNA XIX-J-1-j-SZU-103-002228/1985 (138. d.).

43. Chargé d'affaires János Barabás's report (reporter: László Sz cs): Vice-Foreign Minister M. S. Kapitsa on the latest round of Soviet-Chinese political consultations. Moscow, April 29, 1985. HNA XIX-J-1-j-SZU-103-002228/2-1985 (138. d.).

44. Ambassador László Iván's cable: The latest developments of Soviet-Chinese relations. Beijing, June 6, 1985. No. 99. HNA XIX-J-1-j-Kína-103-001677/7-1985 (87. d.).

45. Vice-Foreign Minister Miklós Barity's report on his consultations with Vice-Foreign Minister Vadim Petrovich Loginov on December 9-10, 1985 in the Soviet Union. Budapest, December 16, 1985. HNA XIX-J-1-j-SZU-144-005246/2-1985 (139. d.).

46. Gilbert Rozman, *Chinese Debate*, 6.

47. Gilbert Rozman, *Chinese Debate*, 133.

48. Ambassador László Iván's cable: Information from the Soviet Ambassador in Beijing on Soviet-Chinese Relations. Beijing, September 25, 1985. No. 139. HNA XIX-J-1-j-Kína-103-001677/12-1985 (87. d.).

49. For the details see Csaba Békés, "Back to Europe: The International Background of the Political Transition in Hungary, 1988–1990," in *The Roundtable Talks of 1989: The Genesis of Hungarian Democracy*, ed. András Bozóki (hereinafter as "Back to Europe") (Budapest: CEU Press, 2002), 237–72.

50. Christian F. Ostermann, ed., "Gorbachev and Afghanistan," *Cold War International History Project Bulletin*, no. 14/15, 143. Notes from Politburo Meetings: June 26, July 24, and November 13, 1986.

51. Rogachev, just like Kapitsa, was an old China-hand with an excellent command of Chinese, and had served as interpreter at the Sino-Soviet negotiations of the 1950s. Lowell Dittmer, *Sino-Soviet Normalization*, 59.

52. Lowell Dittmer, *Sino-Soviet Normalization*, 70–77.

53. Csaba Békés, *Európából Európába*, 277–78.

54. Report to the Politburo and the Council of Ministers on the Warsaw meeting of the Political Consultative Body of the Warsaw Pact Member States, July 18, 1988. HNA 288. f. 11/4453 ö.e. Quoted by Békés (2002).

55. Csaba Békés, *Európából Európába*, 278.
56. *Liaowang* [Observe], no. 2 (1988).
57. Csaba Békés, *Európából Európába*, 279. As Békés noted, this decision, was not free from inconsistency, as it did not signify a cut in military spending. Quite the contrary, however surprising it might seem, in the summer of 1988 the Moscow leaders intended to *increase* the defense budget by 43%(!), including the use of the state reserves as well. Comment by Károly Grósz at the July 22, 1988 meeting of the HSWP CC, HNA M-KS- 288. f. 5/1031. ö.e. See Békés (2004), 279 (in Hungarian). For the English version see Békés (2002). The ambivalent nature of Soviet disarmament is well illustrated by a remark made by a Mongolian diplomat in Moscow on the withdrawal of Soviet troops from Mongolia. The first counselor told his Hungarian colleague that although half of Soviet troops had been withdrawn, but their weapons were still stored in Mongolia, and that Soviet military bases and facilities would also remain, "naturally operated and controlled by Soviet personnel." Ambassador Sándor Rajnai's cable. Moscow, December 2, 1986. No. 295. HNA XIX-J-1-j- SZU-40-005630/1986 (138. d.).
58. The Soviets presented the proposal as a Soviet "attempt to involve the Chinese representatives in discussion on practical questions related to the Cambodian settlement." Vice-Foreign Minister István szi's memorandum: Soviet information on the twelfth round of Soviet-Chinese political consultations. Budapest, June 28, 1988. HNA XIX-J-1-j-SZU-14-003513/1988 (96. d.) In Qian Qichen's interpretation, "in that situation, in order to push the Soviet Union to exert more influence on Vietnam, the Chinese decided to accept the Soviet proposal." Qian Qichen, *Waijiao shiji*, 28. As a result, the vice-foreign ministers reconvened between 27 August and 1 September in Beijing to negotiate on the Cambodian issue. Sino-Soviet negotiations on the Cambodian issue continued through 1988–89. Meanwhile, Vietnam made concessions based on its own considerations. Hanoi pulled out 20,000 troops from Cambodia in November 1987, and in July 1988 announced that its forces would be withdrawn from Cambodia by early 1990.
59. In 1987–88, China was not involved either in the negotiations that resulted in the signing of the INF agreement on eliminating medium- and short-range nuclear missiles, or in the Geneva agreements that led to the Soviet military withdrawal from Afghanistan, although the latter was one of the conditions from the Chinese side for normalizing Sino-Soviet relations.
60. *The Economist*, August 15, 1987, 25–26, quoted by J. Richard Walsh: *Change, Continuity and Commitment. China's Adaptive Foreign Policy* (Lanham, MD and London: University Press of America, 1988), 103.
61. Ambassador Iván Németh's report: Information on issues related to Sino-Soviet normalization of relations. Beijing, November 10, 1988. HNA XIX-J-1-j-Kína-10-003203/4-1988 (57. d.).
62. The question of reestablishment of inter-party relations was not on the agenda.
63. Vice-Foreign Minister István szi's memorandum: On Qian Qichen's visit to the Soviet Union. Budapest, December 7, 1988. HNA XIX-J-1-j-Kína-135-004674/1-1988 (57. d.).

64. Starting from late 1987, there were signs of change in the Chinese position concerning the Cambodian issue. Beijing did not insist on Khmer Rouge dominance and the removal of Heng Samrin, but claimed that there was no military solution for the problem, and real results could be attained only through negotiations. They saw a chance for an independent, non-allied Cambodia with a coalition government headed by Sihanouk. (The Hungarian Embassy in Ulanbator's cable: Ulanbator, October 20, 1987. No. 134. HNA XIX-J-1-j-Kína-10-004807/1-1987 [78. d.]) In December 1988, Qian arrived in Moscow with a demand for total Vietnamese troops withdrawal from Cambodia by the end of June 1989. The Soviets were unwilling to agree on a final date of Vietnamese withdrawal, and claimed that "the Soviet Union cannot give orders to Vietnam." Nevertheless, as the Chinese saw the several common elements of the two positions, they proposed that the date of final withdrawal of Vietnamese troops could be postponed to the end of 1989, which was accepted by both sides. Qian Qichen, *Waijiao shiji*, 32–33.

65. Based on information from Vice-Foreign Minister Rogachev. Chargé d'affaires János Barabás's report (reporter: János Barabás, Sándor Mózes): The Soviet foreign minister's negotiations in Beijing. Moscow, February 9, 1989. HNA XIX-J-1-j- SZU-135-001057/1989 (83. d.).

66. Ambassador Iván Németh's cable: Chinese information on Sino-Soviet foreign ministerial negotiations. Beijing, February 14, 1989. No. 36. HNA XIX-J-1-j-SZU-135-001057/1-1989 (83. d.).

67. Hungarian MFA Secretary of State Gyula Horn's memorandum: Soviet information on Foreign Minister Shevardnadze's official visit to China and Pakistan. Budapest, February 14, 1989. HNA XIX-J-1-j- SZU-146-0037/1-1989 (84. d.).

68. Qian Qichen, *Waijiao shiji*, 36.

69. In reality it meant that the Soviets were against the inclusion of the Chinese-supported Khmer Rouge into the government.

70. Ambassador Iván Németh's cable: The Soviet ambassador in Beijing on Gorbachev's visit to China. Beijing, May 22, 1989. No. 138. HNA XIX-J-1-j-Kína-13-002010/2-1989 (49. d.) Later on, Soviet sources indicated that Gorbachev held the most pleasant negotiations with Zhao Ziyang, and that one of the charges against Zhao was that he leaked out a state secret when he told Gorbachev that Deng was still the supreme leader of China, and that it could cast a shadow on Sino-Soviet relations. Ambassador Iván Németh's cable: Statements by Soviet and other socialist ambassadors on the Beijing events. Beijing, June 6, 1989. HNA XIX-J-1-j-Kína-2-001433/8-1989 (49. d.).

71. Parallel to the summit meeting, negotiations between heads of international departments of the two central committees took place. Agreement was reached on the establishment of the system of mutual information and on cooperation in the exchange of experiences of building socialism.

72. According to official statistical data, in the first half of 1989, 8,000 Chinese citizens worked in the Soviet Union.

73. Békés writes that from the middle of 1988, "the *floating* of the Brezhnev doctrine was virtually the only 'weapon' left to the Soviet leadership with which it could, at least for a short time, have an influence on the political processes running

their course in Eastern Europe. After all, by that point Gorbachev and his associates had given up on the possibility of military intervention." See Békés, Csaba, "Back to Europe: The international background of the political transition in Hungary, 1988–1990," in András Bozóki, ed., *The Roundtable Talks of 1989: The Genesis of Hungarian Democracy* (Budapest-New York: CEU Press, 2002), 245.

74. Kapitsa writes that he sent a letter to Gorbachev suggesting the postponement of his trip, but "Gorbachev already then did not listen to suitable advice." Kapitsa (1996), 118. Since the Chinese side did not ask for postponement, a Soviet proposal for postponement would have been considered a very unfriendly move by the Chinese. In a similar situation, a Chinese party delegation decided to visit Moscow on August 19, 1991 (the time of an attempted coup against Gorbachev) and did not propose postponement. The Chinese delegation received information about the incident at Beijing airport before departure, and after some hesitation departed to Moscow as the Soviet side did not ask them not to go. See Xiaoyuan Liu and Vojtech Mastny, eds., *China and Eastern Europe, 1960s–1980s* (Zürich: Forschungsstelle für Sicherheitspolitik, 2004). Yu Hongjun's comment, 203.

75. Chargé d'affaires János Barabás's cable: Cde. Gorbachev's visit to China. Moscow, May 26, 1989. HNA XIX-J-1-j-Kína-13-002010/3-1989 (49. d.).

76. Ambassador Iván Németh's cable: The Soviet ambassador in Beijing on Gorbachev's visit to China. Beijing, May 22, 1989. No. 138. HNA XIX-J-1-j-Kína-13-002010/2-1989 (49. d.).

77. Chargé d'affaires János Barabás's cable: Tensions in the Soviet Union. Moscow, June 8, 1989. HNA XIX-J-1-j-SZU-20-001092/5-1989 (84. d.).

II

IDEOLOGICAL AND MILITARY INFLUENCES

4

Instilling Stalinism in Chinese Party Members: Absorbing Stalin's *Short Course* in the 1950s

Hua-yu Li

The Chinese Communist Party and, for that matter, China were transformed by Stalin's *Short Course*— with the help of Soviet experts—during the 1950s.

—Zheng Yifan

I believe that the *Short Course* reflects the principle ideas of Stalinism, and it had a profound and lasting impact in the theoretical circles of the CCP. In realty, the top leadership of the CCP all learned Marxism and Leninism through reading Stalin's *Short Course*, and that's why I believe that the form of Marxism-Leninism adopted by the Chinese leaders was in fact Stalinism.

—Su Shaozhi

Introduction

IN THIS CHAPTER, I EXAMINE THE INFLUENCE of Stalinism on the ideological transformation of members of the Chinese communist Party (CCP), especially during the 1950s. Specifically, I discuss how Stalin's ideas played an important part in shaping the worldview and mode of thinking of millions of CCP members. This chapter is part of a book project I am working on concerning evolution and change in the CCP between the mid-1940s and the present day. I began my research for this chapter in the summer of 2004, when I interviewed former party leaders, university professors, and researchers, in an attempt to understand, from the perspective of individual members, how they were educated and transformed in accordance with a common Stalinist ideology within the context of the developmental history of the CCP. Instilling Stalinism in party members began systematically in the early 1940s when Mao launched his infamous Rectification Campaign (1941–45). From that time through the Cultural Revolution, several generations of party leaders and rank-and-file members were periodically subjected to similar kinds of political and ideological campaigns.

Drawing upon the rich personal stories of my interviewees, I describe the social, political, and intellectual context in which they studied Stalinist ideas. I also discuss the role played by Soviet experts in the 1950s in China in spreading not only Stalinism, but also Soviet ways of teaching and learning party history and socialist theory—methods that stayed with the CCP well into the years of the Cultural Revolution. I present the evolutionary stages through which my interviewees had passed: from their being unquestioningly devoted to Stalinist ideas; to their becoming doubtful concerning some of these ideas, but unable to voice their doubts openly; to their eventually becoming disillusioned with these ideas during or after the Cultural Revolution. Some of my interviewees, however, remain uncritical adherents of some Stalinist ideas even today.

In this study, I seek to show the importance of understanding the ideological foundations of CCP rule from the perspective of individual party members. The study will also draw attention to a fundamental yet inadequately examined issue concerning the nature of Marxism-Leninism as defined by the CCP and as instilled in the minds of millions of the Chinese communists.

Stalinism Defined

There are many aspects of Stalinism. It is often identified with the ideology and political structures associated with totalitarianism. There are other features of Stalinism, however, such as the victory of socialism in one country, class struggle, state ownership of industry, heavy industrialization, and forced collectivization. Stalinism is further characterized, at least in its Soviet manifestation, by the privileged treatment accorded to specialists and by the resulting social inequalities. Since the 1990s, Western scholars in Soviet/Russian studies have identified Stalinism in other ways: as a "civilization" (Stephen Kotkin, 1995); as the everyday Stalinism that is "made up of the habitat of *Homo Sovieticus* in the Stalin era" (Sheila Fitzpatrick, 1999); as the basis for "mass culture and modern Russian national identity" (David Brandenberger, 2002), and "as the cultural norms of Soviet modernity" (David L. Hoffmann, 2003). In other words, scholars have recently moved beyond the systemic and structural analysis of Stalinism and its impact at the national level to pursue studies of Stalinism as a historical and social phenomenon at the level of everyday life.

In my analysis, I take another approach to defining "Stalinism," viewing it as consisting of Stalin's own distinctive codification of Marx's and Lenin's ideas[1] as expressed in a Soviet party history textbook, *Short Course of the History of the All-Russian Communist Party (Bolshevik)*, or, as it is usually called, the *Short Course*. Both Western and Chinese scholars have examined the importance of this party history textbook for Mao and the CCP, not only during the Yan'an era, but also in the early 1950s.[2] In this chapter, however, I turn my attention to the essential role the book played in shaping the ideological framework and intellectual foundations for CCP members.

To emphasize the unique importance of the *Short Course* is not to diminish the significance of other books. There have been several other important texts worth mentioning. In the 1920s, for example, before the *Short Course* was even written, Bukharin's *The ABC of Communism* was the standard textbook for educating communists around the world, including China. In late 1925, Mao's younger brother, Mao Zemin, was put in charge of publishing and distributing CCP publications as well as Bukharin's *The ABC of Communism*. Mao Zemin was able to establish an effective sales network in China's big cities as well as overseas branch offices in Paris and Hong Kong. Within a half year after Mao Zemin took over this leadership role, more than thirty thousand copies of Bukharin's book were sold in China.[3] *The ABC of Communism* was used as a "key text" for educating party members who were attending a newly established "higher party school" in early 1926.[4] In the 1950s and 1960s, Stalinist texts such as *The Problems of Political Economy in the USSR*, the *Concise Dictionary on Philosophy* (complied by Pavel Yudin under the direction of Stalin), and *The Soviet Political Economy* were all influential. None of them, however, matched the profound and systematic importance of the *Short Course* in shaping the thought and practice of party elites and rank-and-file members in China.

Research Methodology

My study relies heavily on interviews with former Chinese communist officials, academics, and party researchers. I conducted the first round of interviews in Beijing in the fall of 2004. My fifteen interviewees were carefully chosen in close consultation with my main research contact in Beijing, based on their being able to talk about issues with authority and knowledge. They also represented a wide spectrum of political opinions and diverse working experiences in China. I tried to include as many women as possible, but, unfortunately, I was able to interview only one woman. Of the fifteen interviewees, only one, the late Su Shaozhi, was interviewed in the United States, and that interview was conducted by telephone. Su Shaozhi also provided me with written statements.

I did not seek out interviewees who might have been indifferent toward or even suspicious of the book during their careers, for I believed that such people would not have been trusted by the party and, therefore, would not have played any active role in it. In general, I found all fifteen people I interviewed to be easy to talk with, and all spoke candidly with me.

I prepared and distributed to the interviewees ahead of time a nine-item questionnaire. I divided my interview questions into two categories: (1) biographical background of the interviewees; and (2) their recollections and reflections on how they were influenced by Stalinist ideals as embodied in the *Short Course.* In the second part of the questionnaire, I mainly asked the interviewees when they first read the book, their initial reactions to the book, the methods used in studying the book, and the ideas in the book that left the biggest impression on them. When applicable, I also asked them to indicate when they had their first doubts about the ideas presented in the book and to describe the process by which they turned critical. I conducted the interviews in an open-ended fashion. I took notes during the interviews and did not use a tape-recorder. Interviews were typically held at the homes of the interviewees or at coffee shops and restaurants. I sometimes asked follow-up questions by phone while I was still in Beijing, and after returning to the United States, I continued to communicate with my interviewees in Beijing, mainly by e-mail, to pursue follow-up questions and obtain additional information. I was able to have intensive follow-up interviews with one of my interviewees on two occasions when we were both in Cambridge, Massachusetts, in 2005 and again in 2007. I conducted the second round of interviews in Beijing in the summer of 2006, focusing primarily on Chinese scholars specializing in Soviet and Russian studies. I carried out these in-depth interviews in an open-ended manner so as to elicit the interviewees' most candid thoughts.

To analyze my interview data, I organized all the information I obtained into categories. I compared the views presented by the interviewees in each topic category and looked for similarities and differences. I paid particular attention to discrepancies emerging in the answers of officials on the same topic and sought further information to resolve any discrepancies.

The Interviewees

The Eighty-Something Group

Among the fifteen people I interviewed, only one, Li Rui, belongs to the generation of Chinese communists who read the *Short Course* soon after it was published in Moscow in 1938. At age eighty-eight in 2004, the former deputy minister for Hydraulic and Electrical Power and concurrently a secretary to Mao in the late 1950s, he was physically fit and mentally alert. He was also humorous and at peace with what he had endured. He was very happy that he had outlived Mao, and he now writes poetry and attends symposia for poets in China. After all these years, Li still has a copy of the 1939 Moscow edition of the Chinese-language version of the *Short Course*. He first read the book in Yan'an, when he was only in his mid-twenties. He had heard Mao saying that the *Short Course* was an encyclopedia of Marxism, and he said that Mao treated the book as if he had discovered a treasure.[5]

As early as January 1989, Li Rui had told Western scholars of the importance of the *Short Course*, especially its role in educating generations of Chinese communists, during a talk he gave at the Fairbank Center for East Asian Research at Harvard University.[6] In his conversation with me in 2004, Li Rui spoke little about how the book had affected him. Instead, he concentrated on how much the book had influenced the CCP since the Yan'an period.

The Seventy-Something Group

Of the fifteen interviewees, nine were in their seventies. This is the largest group of people I interviewed. They joined the party in the late 1940s and in the early to mid-1950s. I included in this group the late Su Shaozhi (who passed away in 2007), even though he was eight-two years old at the time, because he belonged to the generation that had joined the party around 1949. During his career, he served as the Director of the Institute for Marxism and Leninism of the Chinese Academy of Social Sciences in Beijing, and he was expelled from the CCP in 1987. This group also included Zhu Houze, a soft-spoken man who headed the Department of Propaganda in the mid- to late 1980s; the late Gong Yuzhi, a deputy head of the Department of Propaganda in the early 1990s; Pan Xianzhi, who retired recently as Director of the CCP Document Research Office after writing a two-volume official biography of Mao; Lin Yunhui, a retired professor at the National Defense University, where high-ranking military officers receive political training; Jin Chunming, a retired professor at the Central Party School, where high-ranking civilian officials receive political training; Yao Jianfu, a retired official at an agricultural research institute and senior secretary to Du Runsheng, a prominent agricultural economist; Zheng Yifan, a retired researcher for the Institute of World Socialism of the CCTB (Central Compilation and Translation Bureau); and Xu Tianxin, a retired professor of Russian history at Peking University. Both Zheng and Xu studied in the Soviet Union between 1954 and 1959 and belonged to the very first wave of what became thousands of Chinese university exchange students to participate in long-term programs of study in the Soviet

Union after 1949. They both attended Leningrad University and returned to China in 1959, just before the onset of the Sino-Soviet dispute.

This group of people is special and interesting; they represented the generation of party leaders who were recruited just before or just after the party seized power in China in 1949. They were the kinds of people that the party actively sought to recruit at the time. They were needed to help in building a new China: young, well educated or relatively well educated, capable, energetic, progressive, nationalistic, idealistic, sympathetic to the communist cause, and, perhaps, ambitious. Unlike the Yan'an or the Civil War generation of communist leaders, most of the people in this group reached the pinnacle of their careers only after the Cultural Revolution. They went through a systematic and thoroughgoing ideological indoctrination process in the 1950s and remained loyal and enthusiastic in their support of the communist cause until the Cultural Revolution or, in the case of a few interviewees, shortly thereafter. Some of them suffered horribly during the Cultural Revolution and, together with the earlier generation of leaders, they began to question the many teachings that they had received.

The Sixty- and Fifty-Something Groups

I also interviewed three individuals who were in their early to mid-sixties; the current top leadership in China belongs to this generation. They were: Li Haiwen, a retired party-history researcher who attended Peking University during the Cultural Revolution; Yan Xiajiang, a retired engineer who was a university student attending the Harbin University for Military Industry during the Cultural Revolution; and Fan Linqin, a well-known Peking University student activist during the Cultural Revolution, who was so badly beaten during that time that he still had difficulty walking. All three of them had studied the book and were keenly aware of the influence it had exerted on the CCP. There were only two persons in the fifty-something group: Pi Shenhao, a senior researcher for an economic research institute; and Zhang Shengfa, a senior researcher at the Chinese Academy of Social Sciences, in Beijing. People in these last two groups received less ideological indoctrination through study of the *Short Course* than their elders, but they were taught by people who had received this kind of training in the 1950s. They were nevertheless fully aware of the importance of the book.

The *Short Course*

The *Short Course* is one of the most printed books in world history; the other two are the bible and the *Selected Works of Mao Zedong*. Between 1938 and

1953 more than 42 million copies of the book were issued, in 301 printings and 67 languages.[7] While there is no information available concerning the number of copies of the *Short Course* printed in China, some printing information, however, is available for Hungary. According to one account, in the two-year period from 1948 to 1950, about 530,000 copies of the *Short Course* were printed in Hungary, and at the time there were about 800,000 party members in the country.[8]

Written under the supervision of Stalin and then heavily edited by him, the *Short Course* was first published in Moscow in 1938. Stalin's actual contribution was limited to only one section of Chapter 4, where he wrote about dialectical and historical materialism. After World War II, Stalin, however, claimed sole authorship of the entire work.[9] The Communist Party of the Soviet Union (CPSU), in a propaganda resolution issued on November 14, 1938, at the time of the publication of the *Short Course*,[10] praised the book as an encyclopedia of Marxism and Leninism and an authoritative source for "formal interpretations" of Soviet party history and for basic knowledge of Marxism and Leninism. Between 1938, when the book was first published, and 1956, when de-Stalinization took place, the *Short Course* was revered as a sacred text in the communist world, and it was relied upon as the most authoritative source for answers to all questions concerning ideology, party politics, economic policies, and socialist transformation.[11] Leaders of the communist countries, including Mao, who was particularly enthusiastic about the book, viewed the *Short Course* with unquestioning admiration.

The *Short Course* presents a Stalinist discourse on the history of CPSU between 1883 and 1937. It is filled with accounts of intraparty struggles between the correct line, associated with Lenin and Stalin, and the incorrect line, represented by anti-party groups. The cult of personality is central to the book, and both Lenin and Stalin are given credit for the success of the Russian Revolution, but Stalin alone is praised for achieving socialism. The *Short Course* is full of factual mistakes and false claims. For example, the assassination of S. M. Kirov is described as caused by intensified class struggle as socialist construction progressed, when, in fact, all available evidence indicates that Stalin ordered his assassination because Stalin felt threatened by Kirov's growing popularity within the party. Similarly, collectivization in the Soviet Union was described in the *Short Course* as a revolution from below rather than as a party policy imposed from above, contrary to historical fact. Trotsky was accused of creating his own faction within the CPSU, when, in fact, he never dared to do such a thing.

Most importantly, the *Short Course* allowed Stalin to reinterpret some Marxist and Leninist ideas after his own fashion. Lenin's cooperative ideas, for example, were redefined by Stalin as a two-stage program. In the first stage, according to Stalin, the party would create commercial cooperatives, and, in the second stage, the party would establish producers' cooperatives when "conditions were ready." It was Stalin, of course, who defined when "conditions were ready" for moving to the second stage. Such a two-staged program, however, appears nowhere in Lenin's original writings.

Stalin also put his mark on the ideas that party leaders in other communist countries relied upon beginning in the mid-1940s as they set about building socialism in their countries after they had seized power. In Stalin's definition, socialism meant state ownership and the elimination of all capitalist economic elements. Building socialism, according to Stalin, depended upon forced industrialization and collectivization. Stalin claimed that the *Short Course* was an accurate statement of the ideas of Marx and Lenin, but the book, in fact, consisted of Stalin's reinterpretations, misinterpretations and outright distortions of the ideas of Marx and Lenin in support of his own political and policy agenda. For almost two decades, throughout the communist world, readers of the book were fed false information and twisted ideas, while they thought they were learning true Marxism and Leninism.

The Two Phases of Learning the *Short Course* in China

The study of the *Short Course* in China went through two major phases, and they corresponded to the two learning phases the whole communist world went through. During phase one, between 1939 and 1956, the book was read as if it were a sacred text, like the bible. This period is characterized by what I call the intense Stalinization of the communist world. In China, during the anti-Japanese war (1937–45), for example, the *Short Course* was read not only by party members in Yan'an and the communist occupied areas, but also by party members in the Japanese occupied rural areas.[12] In Paris, the Hungarian communists living in exile and working under the leadership of the French Communist Party, also read the book diligently as they joined with the French underground in fighting against the German occupiers. To avoid the watchful eyes of the Gestapo, the Hungarian communist exiles gave the *Short Course* the code name "uncle Joe's cook book."[13]

During the post-war era, study of the book became even more intense and widespread. According to a memoir written by a Hungarian communist who emigrated to the West in 1956, prior to the de-Stalinization of 1956, the *Short Course* was the most important text used in ideological education. Party members in Hungary were required to learn it almost word for word. Every party resolution and every date had to be memorized. In those years, he wrote, ideological education consisted of relatively little Marx, almost no Engels, much Lenin, and even more Stalin.[14] As will be discussed below, the ideological education of party rank-and-file members in China in the 1950s was equally intense.

The status of the *Short Course* began to change during the CPSU's 20th Party Congress in 1956. For the first time, the *Short Course* was officially criticized by Mikoyan, on February 16, 1956. Eager to replace the *Short Course* as a party history textbook, the Soviet Central Committee Presidium passed a resolution on April 26, 1956, entitled "On the Preparation of a Popular Marxist Textbook on the History of the Communist Party of the Soviet Union."[15] Thus ended the era when the *Short Course* officially defined ideological orthodoxy for the communist world. A new party history textbook was published in Moscow in 1958. The Chinese translation of the new textbook was published in Beijing in 1959, but the new textbook never took root in China[16] because the *Short Course* was never officially repudiated by Mao or the CCP.

The status of the *Short Course* in China after 1956 was more complicated than it was in the Soviet Union and the bloc countries. At first, in China, following the Soviet 20th Party Congress, as elsewhere in the communist world, Stalin's personality cult and the preeminence of the *Short Course* deteriorated rapidly. Soviet experts working at China's Ministry for Higher Education captured the mood of their Chinese colleagues in a report that questioned whether Stalin should continue to be treated as a classic Marxist and Leninist author and whether the *Short Course* should continue to be used as a basic textbook for teaching Marxism and Leninism.[17]

Also in 1956, the CCP under Mao decided to repudiate Stalin's view that "as the socialist revolution deepens, class struggle intensifies." A year later, as a result of the Anti-Rightist Campaign of 1957, however, Mao reinstated this Stalinist principle. Mao asserted his position that the socialist revolution in the superstructure of political thought had to continue. As a result, Mao stayed with Stalin's ideas about the necessity for intensified class struggle.[18]

During phase two, from 1957 to 1978, while the *Short Course* was no longer used to educate party members in China, but it continued to be used to educate university students, especially those majoring in international relations and world history. One of my interviewees, Li Haiwen, while studying as a sophomore at Peking University before the Cultural Revolution, read the *Short Course* for the first time while taking a college-level course on the international communist movement.[19] Most importantly, during the second phase, Mao, because of his admiration for the book, did not allow the book to be repudiated in China. This was especially true after conflict broke out between the CCP and the CPSU in 1960. After the split, Mao decided to oppose Khrushchev and protect the reputation of Stalin.[20] In this context, Stalin's *Short Course* continued to be viewed in a positive light in China.

Since the *Short Course* was never repudiated in China during the second phase, the influence of the *Short Course* was extended to the next generation of Chinese youth in an indirect way. Several interviewees emphasized repeatedly that Stalin's ideas as incorporated in the *Short Course* were passed on to those who grew up in the 1950s but did not have the opportunity to read it formally. They were taught by their teachers and professors who had read the book and been profoundly shaped by Stalin's views.[21]

At a more fundamental level, the de-Stalinization and the repudiation of the *Short Course* in the Soviet Union and the bloc countries did not bring with it a clear-cut repudiation of all Stalinist ideas nor did it eliminate all of the negative influences of the *Short Course*. For example, Stalin's definition of socialism was not challenged in the communist world, and it remained in force, especially in China. While Stalin's Great Purge of the 1930s was condemned in 1956, no one in China, at least, questioned the validity of the theory of the "two-line struggle" in explaining the conflicts within the CPSU. The views of Bukharin and other opposition leaders continued to be regarded as wrong, and these leaders continued to be portrayed as negative historical figures well into the reform era in China.[22]

During the second phase, some Chinese party members and teaching staff at various institutions, however, started to raise questions and express concerns about the contents of the *Short Course*. In particular, they began to question the accuracy of the historical accounts and the emphasis placed upon the personality cult of Stalin in the book. During this phase, the views expressed by these skeptics did not receive much support from others in the party. It was only after 1978 that some scholars and party researchers began to criticize the book openly. They condemned the book for the harmful consequences it had caused China to suffer in the areas of the economy, politics, society, and culture.[23] Others, however, still believed that the book had value as a general reference work. As one interviewee said, "the book is not without value."[24] Still others continue to believe that the book has, for the most part, exercised a positive influence on China.[25]

In 2004, the *Short Course* made a comeback in Russia after almost half a century in official oblivion. Putin, the Russian president, decided to reprint the long-ignored *Short Course* in an attempt to restore some "positive" historical memory of the Soviet past. Russia issued its 302nd printing of the *Short Course* with the same cover page as appeared in the 1945 edition. The book arrived on the book shelves of Russian universities in fall 2004.[26] Putin's action did not go unnoticed in China, but there is no sign yet that the Chinese leaders are planning a new printing of the *Short Course* in China.

The Key Areas of Study

In the 1950s, in order to instill correct ideas and unify the thinking of party leaders and rank-and-file member and the society at large, key chapters of the *Short Course* were identified and carefully studied. They were Chapters 2, 3, 4, 9–12, and the Conclusion.

Chapter 2 talks about the organizational basis of the communist party; it is not a loosely connected alliance of groups, but rather a well-organized, advanced leadership group of the proletariat. Chapter 3 describes Lenin's two basic tactics in carrying out the Russian Revolution, and the chapter was viewed as a particularly important one, for it was believed to be providing guidance for all communist parties in the areas of ideology and theory, organizational principles, and political tactics. According to this chapter, Lenin outlined two stages for carrying out the Russian Revolution. During the first stage of the revolution, the proletariat, taking the leadership role, allied itself with the peasants and carried out the "bourgeois democratic revolution." During the second stage, the proletariat would take the lead in determining when to embark on the transition from the democratic revolution to the socialist revolution. Mao's theory of New Democracy was viewed as the best example of applying Lenin's "two tactics" to China's reality.

Chapter 4 explains the basic theories of dialectical materialism and historical materialism. Section 2 of Chapter 4 was particularly important and had a tremendous impact in theoretical circles in the CCP. The interpretations of dialectical materialism and historical materialism, as formulated by Stalin in Section 2, became guiding principles in philosophy, economics, and all areas of the social sciences in China. Several interviewees indicated that they believed, with the benefit of hindsight, that these interpretations became the bases for dogmatism, and they regretted that they continued to teach these dogmas to their students until just before the Cultural Revolution.

Chapters 9–12 describe the industrialization, collectivization, and class struggle that occurred during the transition from capitalism to socialism. Finally, the Conclusion identifies the six characteristics that define a Bolshevik party. Each of these chapters had a profound impact on China in the areas of party organization, revolutionary strategy, intraparty politics, socialist construction, and party building.

Soviet Study Methods

As more and more Soviet experts came to China beginning in the early 1950s at the request of Mao and the CCP,[27] they played an important role in training China's future political leaders. Throughout the 1950s, they not only helped to spread Stalinist ideas, but also brought with them their ways of learning and teaching. At least two interviewees studied directly with Soviet experts, one at the Central Party School, the other at the newly established People's University, where China's future officials were trained. Neither one of these two interviewees was particularly impressed by the Soviet experts they encountered, and they were particularly critical of the ways the experts taught their classes.

Typically, the Soviet experts read their lecture notes in Russian to their classes, and an interpreter then read the lecture notes to the class in Chinese. The lecture notes were all pre-approved by the Soviet Embassy in Beijing. As a result, the classes lacked interactions between the teachers and students, and there were no discussions among the students in the classroom. At the Institute for Military Affairs, however, the instructional method was more lively. In order to facilitate study, a picture album (translated into Chinese from Russian) was displayed in a special classroom. Students had free access to the picture album. Additional readings relevant to the topics being dealt with in the *Short Course* were also assigned so that students could obtain a better understanding of the historical and intellectual context of the book. In addition, Soviet films—such as *Lenin in October, The Virgin Land,* and *The Great Citizens*—were shown to enrich the educational experience.

Soviet-style examinations were also adopted. Most examinations were oral, and correct answers to the questions had to come directly from lecture notes. Students were asked to draw lots beforehand to determine which questions to answer and then typically given twenty to thirty minutes to prepare for each answer. During the oral exam, students answered questions asked by a main examiner. Most students memorized the book in order to be able to answer the questions fully. It was also important to be able to make intelligent comments about the book in order to pass the exam. If a student could answer a question in a relatively complete fashion, develop an argument, and explain the theoretical and practical significance of the question, it was possible to receive a perfect score of five points. Several interviewees joked about how well they did and about how they received high scores on the exams. Those who did well on the oral exams and passed the political check would be assigned to positions as teaching staff at the institutions where they had just completed their studies.[28]

The Soviet experts also brought with them their approach on how to teach about "negative" historical figures, notable for their absence from the *Short Course.* Some students at the Central Party School asked why the *Short Course* contained so little information about Bukharin and Trotsky. The Soviet experts responded harshly and criticized these students by telling them that there was no need to know about those men.[29] Through such encounters with Soviet experts, the Chinese students learned that they should not ask about "negative" historical figures and that they should accept without question whatever they were told about them. The students who later went on to become teaching staff used the same methods to teach their own students by restricting themselves to only brief negative references to these figures.[30]

There were, however, cases in which Chinese faculty and university officials successfully resisted the Soviet experts. In 1955, when Mao emphasized the importance of drawing lessons from the Soviet experience rather than just blindly copying it, faculty and officials at two military institutions where Soviet models were studied most intensively decided to challenge the continued use of a Soviet-style curriculum. They raised doubts about the validity of studying only the *Short Course* and thereby failing to teach students about the history of the CCP.[31] Zhang Xuesi, president of the Institute for Naval Studies, expressed his concerns directly to the Soviet experts residing at his school. He was successful in persuading the Soviet experts that the Chinese students should learn primarily the history of the CCP.[32]

Some Personal Stories of Ideological Transformation

A Transforming Experience for a Generation

The seventy-something group I interviewed all described the way that they unconditionally accepted the *Short Course* when they first read it and recognized its importance in transforming them into committed communists. They said that they believed that this transforming experience was shared by their generation. In explaining why they read the *Short Course* in the first place, they said that they had read it because they had heard that Stalin and Mao regarded it as a good book. Jin Chunming, for instance, said that Mao had said it was a good book and an encyclopedia of Marxism and Leninism and that is why he read it (*Mao shuo hao jiu du*).[33] Lin Yunhui said that he read the book because Stalin had said that it represented Marxism in action and because Mao had said that the book was an encyclopedia of Marxism and Leninism.[34] Yao Jianfu, however, had a somewhat different explanation: the book was given to him by a communist friend in April 1949, and he viewed it as the first book that the communist party had given to him, and so he read it.[35] Most interviewees had read the book at least three times, and most had studied it first on their own and then later studied it formally in special courses offered at the time. All of the seventy-something interviewees studied it between 1953 and 1954 during a nationwide study campaign[36] that was launched by Mao to compel the whole country to support the building of a socialist China based on Stalinist ideas.

For those committed youth, reading the book for the first time on their own was not an easy task by any means. Several of my interviewees told me that they found the book to be very difficult when they first read it, for they either lacked a knowledge of Soviet history or the theoretical background to understand what was being said. Jin Chuming, for example, read the *Short Course* in April 1949 for the first time. He spent thirty hours in eight days reading it, but he still had areas that he could not comprehend. Like the others, however, he still felt it was a good book.[37] Lin Yunhui shared the same sentiment, and when he first read it, he considered it to be the best textbook on Marxism and Leninism.[38] Pang Xianzhi was the most enthusiastic first-time reader among all the interviewees in the seventy-something group. He began his reading with Section 2 of Chapter 4, which had been published separately in Moscow in a Chinese-language booklet. He read it between 1949 and 1950. For a beginner, Pang felt the idea of historical materialism was difficult to understand, but he nevertheless believed, at that time, that the ideas presented in the booklet were correct. He said he had read it as a theoretical work and did not, at the time, connect the book with the Chinese revolution. Although it was difficult to understand, he nevertheless felt that the section was succinctly written. Pang said it was easy for him to accept the ideas expressed in the booklet and that they played a big part in the formation of his worldview. He said he read it eagerly (*ruji sike*) and felt that every sentence expressed truth (*juju shi zhenli*) and that he absorbed the ideas in the booklet as a sponge absorbs water (*haimian xishui*). As a result of reading the booklet, he felt that his view of the world had been broadened and that the booklet was like a bible or some other sacred text that expressed truth.[39]

Most of the interviewees in the seventy-something group had attended special courses to pursue more systematic study of the *Short Course*. In the early 1950s, the *Short Course* was the basic teaching material for party members to learn Marxism and Leninism. At the time, there were four theory courses for cadres to take: the CCP party history, Marxist philosophy, political economy, and the *Short Course*. Lin Yunhui, for example, came to know about the book in March 1954 when he was transferred to the Institute for Military Studies. He engaged in more systematic study, however, a year later in 1955 when he was admitted to the Political Science Department at the same institute.[40] Su Shaozhi pursued his formal theoretical studies through taking a course entitled "The Foundations of Marxism and Leninism" taught by Soviet experts at People's University. Contrary to what is suggested by the course title, the course was devoted to learning about the *Short Course*, and the lectures basically explained the contents of the book.⁴¹ Zheng Yifan pursued his formal study of the *Short Course* in a political science course he took in 1953 in Beijing. Zheng was, at the time, in Beijing attending a one-year preparatory program before embarking upon his studies in the Soviet Union beginning in 1954. He also used the Russian version of the book to learn the Russian language.⁴²

Jin Chunming obtained more extensive training on the *Short Course* than the other interviewees by attending both regional and central party schools. First, he attended a two-year senior-level theory class at the Northeast Bureau Party School. During his two years there, about one-half year was set aside for the study of the *Short Course*. Jin and the other students were taught by famous Chinese political science professors who had been trained at the Institute for Leninism in Yan'an—including Liu Zhiming, Fu Zhensheng, and Chen Fang—and Jin and his classmates studied the book seriously. Jin said the in-depth lectures delivered by the Chinese professors left a deep impression on him and the other students. In 1955, Jin was chosen to attend another two-year program that trained teaching staff in Marxism and Leninism, but this time he was sent to the Central Party School in Beijing. While there, Jin studied the *Short Course* with Soviet experts for one term. Jin was not particularly impressed by the lectures delivered by the Soviet experts.⁴³ As mentioned before, the Soviet experts read their lectures in Russian, and then their lectures were read again in Chinese by an interpreter.

The Study Campaign of 1953–1954

In 1953, as Mao moved the country from a predominantly private economy to a socialist planned economy, he launched a nationwide study campaign to instill in the minds of party members the "correct" ideas about how to build socialism in China. More fundamentally, this campaign was aimed at unifying the thinking of the party and thus the whole country. Some of my interviewees said rather bluntly that Mao and the CCP Central Committee did not know how to carry out socialist economic construction at the time, so the whole party was told to study Chapters 9–12 of the *Short Course* to learn how to do it. Rank-and-file members of the party were told that those chapters contained practical lessons for China. The seventy-something group that I interviewed went through this intensive learning experience.

This study campaign became one of the rare occasions in post-1949 China when a nationwide, systematic ideological transformation of the party rank-and-file and the party leadership took place. Through reading these chapters of the *Short Course*, the seventy-something group, along with the leaders of earlier generations, learned Stalin's definition of socialism as well as his ideas about how to build socialism, how to accumulate capital in support of industrialization, and how to engage in class struggle while building socialism.

To organize such a large-scale nationwide study campaign effectively, CCP party members were divided into different levels of study groups: elementary, intermediate, and senior. Those in the elementary-level groups attended large lectures and studied Yu Guangyu's simplified writings about political economy. Young college-educated cadres, especially those who had already had revolutionary experience, were asked to join the intermediate-level study groups. The senior-level study groups included ministers and core members of the party leadership. The senior-level groups studied Lenin's New Economic Policy (NEP) and the concept of "capital accumulation carried out internally." They also learned about the need to adopt economic policies that gave priority to heavy industry. In keeping with this priority, they also learned about the need to deprive the peasantry in order to support capital accumulation for industrialization, a policy that came to be referred to as "primitive socialist accumulation."[44]

During this time, according to several people interviewed, the whole party intensively studied Chapters 9–12 of the *Short Course*. Everyone was instructed to emulate the Soviet experience indiscriminately (*ban Sulian*) and that to do so was perfectly justified (*tianjing diyi*)![45] Pang Xianzhi captured the sentiment of the time by saying that everyone studied the chapters conscientiously and in a down-to-earth fashion, chapter by chapter, from beginning to the end, in the evenings after work.[46] He said that the party was unified in its thinking at that time because of the *Short Course* and that the book, in his view, armed cadres with a powerful way of thinking.[47]

At the time that my interviewees were studying the *Short Course*, Mao was proclaiming the "General Line for Socialist Transition," a radical new policy program for transforming China's predominantly private economy into a state-owned economy in accordance with a Stalinist blueprint. According to Li Yunhui, everyone was taught to draw two conclusions from their studies of Chapters 9–12 concerning Mao's "General Line." First, everyone learned that Mao had derived his "theory of New Democracy" from reading Lenin's "Two Tactics." Second, their studies revealed to them that Mao's "General Line for Socialist Transition" was based on Stalin's successful socialist economic construction in the Soviet Union.[48] Jin Chunming, reflecting upon his thinking in those days, said that "reading Chapters 9–12 deepened our understanding of why Mao and the CCP Central Committee had put forward the 'General Line for Socialist Transition;' those chapters not only proved the correctness of the 'General Line,' they also made clear to us the basic concepts of socialism."[49]

Learning about Class Struggle with Actual Cases

Intensive study of the "theory of class struggle" also took place at the time. To make it easier for party members to understand, such study was linked to actual Chinese cases. In their studies, my interviewees were asked to examine the "Gao-Rao Incident" (1954), the "Pan-Yang Incident" (1955), the "Hu Feng Incident" (1955), and other on-going internal purges. After studying these cases, my interviewees were convinced at the time that the party carried out these purges in a manner similar to the way purges were described in the *Short Course* and in accordance with the theories presented in the book. All of the interviewees at that time accepted as true the ideas presented in the book about class struggle.[50]

In addition to learning about the theory of class struggle, party members were also introduced to the principle described in the phrase: "class struggle intensifies as socialist building progresses."[51] One example that was cited from the *Short Course* to support the correctness of this Stalinist concept concerned the assassination of the popular Soviet party leader, S. M. Kirov, a politburo member who was shot to death by Nikolaev, a young party member, in Leningrad in December 1934. Many rumors were flying around in the aftermath of the assassination. Nikolaev and his conspirators were tried, found guilty, and executed in 1935.[52] According to the explanation contained in the *Short Course*, Kirov's assassination was a reflection of the intensified class struggle that was occurring during the course of building socialism. The young assassin, Nikolaev, according to this account, was linked to a group of anti-party conspirators. The Kirov case was so shocking to Chinese communist readers that it left a strong mental imprint on them. Some of them can still cite the exact section (Section 4 of Chapter 11) and the page numbers (the page numbers varied with different editions used at the time) where the case was discussed. The Kirov case continued to be a mystery until 1956 when Khrushchev re-opened the investigation and showed that all evidence pointed to the likely involvement by Stalin and his cronies in the assassination.

No Doubts about the Book

Regardless of their political orientation in 2004 when I first met with my interviewees, none of them said that they ever had any doubts in the 1950s about the ideas expressed in the *Short Course*. For many of them, there was no reason to have any doubts. The book was at the time regarded as a classic and an encyclopedia of Marxism and Leninism. Additionally, the 1950s was a period of warm friendship with the Soviet Union and of great admiration for Stalin and Soviet achievements. Pang Xianzhi expressed his devotion to the book more strongly than most. He did not have any doubts about the book at the time, and he felt the book was like a Holy Bible and expressed the truth.[53] Even with the de-Stalinization in 1956 and the Sino-Soviet conflict in the 1960s, many of my interviewees still believed that Stalin's ideas as found in the *Short Course*, for the most part, continued to be correct.[54]

The Taboo of Doubt

I asked my interviewees why they did not have or express doubts or critical thoughts about the book or about party policies in those days, and their answers were not surprising, although sometimes interesting. According to my interviewees, after 1957, people in China, including party members, began to have doubts about many things, but they could not express them openly. They gave two reasons as to why they could not express any doubts. First, there were external pressures for one not to express doubts or express concerns. One could get into trouble by expressing such thoughts, even when done discreetly. One could come to regret, for example, reporting a doubt to a superior, "opening one's heart" to fellow party members, keeping a diary, or expressing a personal opinion in a letter to a friend. Second, party members were controlled by an intellectual conformity that permeated the party. A self-disciplined communist was not even supposed to harbor critical thoughts (*buneng fubang*) about party ideology or policies. Such mental discipline, i.e., the ability to control one's thoughts, was viewed as a defining trait of a good communist. According to two of my interviewees, they not only exercised such mental discipline, they also taught their student to do so.[55]

Learning to be Critical about the *Short Course* in the Soviet Union

For some exchange students who studied in the Soviet Union between 1954 and 1959, it was easier to learn to be critical about the *Short Course* after de-Stalinization in 1956. It was especially true for those who studied at Leningrad University. Xu Tianxing, for example, studied under Professor Kornatovski, a veteran of the Patriotic War who dared to be critical. He was once arrested for having the courage to speak out, but he was later released. Under the tutelage of Professor Kornatovski, Xu and his Chinese classmates began to read the *Short Course* critically after 1956. Xu began to ponder several questions. Was it true that poor peasants participated in the October Revolution? How should Trotsky be properly evaluated? Why are only the proletarian leaders always correct? And finally, why is class struggle always put in a position of such absolute importance?[56] While it was possible to be critical about Stalin's ideas at the University of Leningrad, Xu soon faced a different reality upon returning to Beijing in 1959. He quickly learned to keep his critical thoughts about the *Short Course* and Stalin to himself.

Growing Qualms

Lin Yunhui, one of my most thoughtful interviewees, expressed some of his candid feelings, not so much about the ideas he learned, but rather about the events he had observed unfolding in China. Being a loyal communist and a true believer in the ideology that had been instilled in him, he accepted all the ideas in the *Short Course* about class struggle, two-line struggle, and Stalin's ideas of socialism as truth, but when confronted with reality, he had his qualms. He, nevertheless behaved in a manner befitting an accomplished communist and tried to ignore his doubts. According to Lin, he felt spiritually troubled about the purges when they occurred, especially the purges of Gao-Rao, Pan-Yang, and Hu Feng in the mid-1950s. In 1956, he, like many others, felt excited when the announcement was made that the socialist transformation had basically been completed and that China had achieved socialism. But as China entered difficult times in the early 1960s, he began to feel puzzled about socialism in China and wondered why increased tensions had emerged in society under socialism. He could not understand what had happened to the plentiful food and goods that used to be available in the past? During the Cultural Revolution, he and many others began to question whether class struggle on a daily basis was a necessary part of building socialism, as Mao had preached. He and many party members began to talk quietly among themselves and to raise doubts about many things that they could not comprehend. Lin, however, only began to experience a serious change in his thinking about the *Short Course* in the early 1980s.[57]

Assessing the Influence of the *Short Course* in China

There is a general consensus among the interviewees that the *Short Course* had a great impact on CCP members, and as a group they gave me a lengthy list of areas where the party had been influenced by the ideas expressed in the *Short Course*. Some of the areas they mentioned are more general and others more specific. Of the more general areas influenced by the *Short Course*, they identified the political system and political organization, modes of thinking, party building, economic management, propaganda, ideological and media control, censorship of books and newspapers, and, finally, writing style.

Why did the interviewees include writing style in their list of areas influenced by the *Short Course*? It is commonly known among well-informed Chinese communists that the CCP has emulated the writing style of the *Short Course* in many contexts. When the CCP had the debates with the CPSU via "open letters" in the 1960s, the CCP attacked the CPSU using provocative language and a condemnatory tone similar to that used in the *Short Course*. Zheng Yifan, one of my interviewees, told me that he consciously emulated the writing style of the *Short Course* at the time he was writing an article critical of the "Gang of the Four." Zheng was asked by his unit superior to write a newspaper article denouncing the Gang of Four. Zheng first checked the section in the *Short Course* where Trotsky was being condemned. In the article criticizing the Gang of Four, he then used language that was provocative and sharply condemnatory in tone, similar to the language used in the section in the *Short Course* condemning Trotsky. Zheng told me that he felt very good after writing the article.[58] He went for the jugular in his denunciation of the Gang of Four, and he had found the proper writing style in none other than the *Short Course.*

At a more specific level, most of the interviewees recognized the negative impact of the ideas contained in the *Short Course* upon the CCP in post-1949 China. Their comments fell into four areas. First, because Stalinist ideas about building socialism presented in the *Short Course* had profoundly shaped the ideological outlook of the Chinese leadership and the party rank-and-file members, the CCP had come to believe that it was appropriate to deprive the peasantry of a substantial portion of its grain in support of a policy of rapid industrialization—a policy called "primitive socialist accumulation." Further, it was taken for granted that the party needed to promote an economic policy that gave priority to heavy industry. More fundamentally, since socialism was viewed as linked to state-ownership, it became essential to eliminate the private economy. Second, Stalin's idea about the need for continuous class struggle during the process of building socialism shaped the thinking of millions of party members; they were made to believe in the inevitability of the intensification of class struggle as socialist construction progresses.

Third, the most influential and most damaging idea for the party and the people was that intraparty struggle is merely an expression of the inevitable two-line struggle that would always exist between the correct line and the incorrect line, with the correct line always being whatever Mao said it was. The intraparty two-line struggle was also considered to be a reflection of the larger societal class struggle. In this view, the capitalist class always had its representatives embedded in the party, and these representatives had to be rooted out and toppled. The Cultural Revolution was, accordingly, seen as

Mao's attempt to eliminate such representatives of the capitalist class from the party.

Fourth, Stalin's ideas about intraparty struggle were put into practice throughout the Maoist era. Since differing ideas expressed by party leaders concerning policies were viewed as a reflection of class struggle and the two-line struggle, it was taken for granted that the party should apply the means of "ruthless struggle and merciless blows" to handle intraparty disputes (*dang-nei douzheng*). The view was also adopted that non-party offenders should be dealt with even more harshly than party offenders. Using ruthless means to deal with internal disputes could be traced back to the 1920s and 1930s when vicious fights and purges took place within the CCP. Since the Yan'an period, however, Stalin's ideas had legitimized those practices, which came to be viewed as part of the process of eliminating internal enemies.

Lastly, party members, following the guidance of the *Short Course*, gave absolute respect and deference to the authority of the party leadership. The cult of personality in the Soviet Union, described in the *Short Course*, was used by Stalin to buttress his drive to establish his absolute authority. Mao, inspired by the example of Stalin, established his own cult of personality. Mao's demand for absolute authority reached its peak during the Cultural Revolution.

Conclusion

There is a general consensus among the fifteen people that I interviewed, regardless of their differing political orientations today, that the *Short Course* has had a profound and lasting impact upon the CCP and China in a wide range of areas. As part of the process of Stalinization of the communist world and China—with the help of Soviet experts in the 1950s—a systematic ideological transformation took place in China and a new generation of party leaders was imbued with a Stalinist worldview. As a result, a Stalinist ideological foundation became part of the fabric of society and helped to sustain communist rule in China. Because, unlike in the Soviet Union and the bloc countries, the *Short Course* was not repudiated in China after 1956, its influence was carried forward by the generation of leaders that was most profoundly shaped by its Stalinist teachings as they trained later generations of leaders.

While this study focuses on personal accounts of ideological transformation and conformity, it is also a historical account of how the CCP was able to sustain party rule through the support and collaboration of docile and committed party rank-and-file members well into the Cultural Revolution years. The fifteen people I interviewed told stories that differed in various ways, but they all described a common experience of ideological and intellectual transformation that, for many of them, approached a spiritual or religious awakening. The essential tragedy for my interviewees and for many Chinese communist members and leaders, however, arose from their having been indoctrinated in and shaped by false ideas disguised as true Marxism and Leninism and by factual misrepresentations pretending to be historical truth. Most of my interviewees, like most communists, carried those beliefs with them, firmly rooted in their psyches, until the Cultural Revolution years. At that point, their belief system was challenged and their worldview shattered by the destructive chaos and cruel excesses of the Cultural Revolution. Like many other communists, most of my interviewees felt that their beliefs and loyalties had been betrayed by what, at Mao's instigation, occurred during the Cultural Revolution. It is ironic that by overplaying his Stalinist hand, Mao inadvertently cured millions of Chinese communists of their Stalinist illusions, which had been instilled in generations of devoted communists through indoctrination based on the Soviet textbook called the *Short Course*.

Notes

1. For a discussion of Stalin's codification of Lenin's ideas after his own fashion, see Leszek Kolakowski, *Main Currents of Marxism 3: The Breakdown* (New York: Oxford University Press, 1981), 22.

2. Benjamin I. Schwartz, *Chinese Communism and the Rise of Mao* (Cambridge, MA: Harvard University Press, 1979), v–vi. Tony Saich, "Writing or Rewriting History? The Construction of the Maoist Revolution on Party History," in *New Perspectives on the Chinese Communist Revolution*, ed., Tony Saich and Hans van de Ven (Armonk, NY: M.E. Sharpe, 1994), 303, 315. Hua-yu Li, *Mao and the Economic Stalinization of China, 1948–1953* (hereinafter as *Mao and the Economic Stalinization of China*) (Lanham, MD: Rowman & Littlefield, 2006), 95–120. Gao Hua, *Hongtaiyang shi zenyang shengqi de: Yan'an zhengfeng de lailong qumai* [How did the sun rise over Yan'an: a history of the Rectification Movement] (Xianggang: Zhongwen daxue chubanshe, 2000), 186–92.

3. Ma Shexiang, *Yige nu gemingzhe de lishi jianzheng* [Historical witness of a female revolutionary] (Beijing: Zhonggong dangshi chubanshe, 2002), 91–92.

4. S. A. Smith, *A Road is Made: Communism in Shanghai, 1920–1927* (Honolulu: University of Hawai'i Press, 2000), 127.

5. Li Rui, interview, September 15, 2004.

6. Li Rui, *Zhiyan: Li Rui liushinian de you yu si* [Speaking candidly: Li Rui's sixty years of concerns and thoughts] (Beijing: Jinri zhongguo chubanshe, 1998), 324.

7. N. N. Maslov, "*Short Course of the History of the All-Russian Communist Party (Bolshevik)*—An Encyclopedia of Stalin's Personality Cult," *Soviet Studies in History* 28, no. 3 (Winter 1989–90): 42.

8. Janos Botos, Gyorgy Gyarmati, Mihaly Korom, and Tibor Zinner, *Magyar hetkoznapok Rakosi Matyas ket emigracioja kozott, 1945–1956* [Everyday life in Hungary between the two emigrations of Matyas Rakosi, 1945–1956] (Budapest: Minerva, 1988), 304.

9. Robert C. Tucker, *Stalin in Power: Revolution from Above* (New York: W.W. Norton & Company, 1992), 531.

10. "*Liangong (bu) dangshi jianming jiaocheng* dui zhonggong dangshi jiaoxue he yanjiu de yingxiang (zuotanhui fayan zhaideng)" [The effect of *History of the Communist Party of the Soviet Union (Bolshevik): Short Course* on teaching and research concerning the history of the CCP (abstract of symposium)], *Zhonggong dangshi yanjiu* [CCP history research], no. 1 (1989): 16.

11. Janos Kornai, interview, Cambridge, MA, February 2, 1994.

12. Hua-yu Li, *Mao and the Economic Stalinization of China*, 98.

13. Balazs Szalontai, a Hungarian scholar, email, June 5, 2003.

14. Balazs Szalontai, a Hungarian scholar, email, June 5, 2003.

15. Alexandre Pantsov, email, June 3, 2003.

16. Zheng Yifan, email, January 19, 2005.

17. Shen Zhihua, *Sulian zhuanjia zai zhongguo: 1948–1960* [Soviet experts in China: 1948–1960] (hereinafter as *Soviet Experts*) (Beijing: Zhongguo guoji guangbo chubanshe, 2003), 261.

18. Lin Yunhui, email, October 13, 2008.

19. Li Haiwen, email, December 13, 2004.

20. See "Guanyu Sidalin wenti: erping Sugong zhongyang de gongkaixin, yijiu liusan nian jiuyue shisanri" [Issues concerning Stalin: second appraisal of the open letter by the central committee of the CPSU, September 13, 1963], in *Guanyu guoji zhongluxian de lunzhang* [Debate on the general guiding principles for the international communist movement] (Beijing: Renmin chubanshe, 1965), 121–48.

21. Lin Yunhui, for example, emphasizes this point repeatedly. He conveyed his view in an email, November 16, 2004. Zheng Yifan takes the same view, email, January 19, 2005.

22. Lin Yunhui, email, November 16, 2004.

23. At least one symposium was held in Beijing in 1989. A number of articles have been written that identified the negative impact of the *Short Course* on China. For a recent article, see Zhang Shihong, "Chongxing shenshi *Lianggong (bu)dangshi jianming jiaocheng*" [Carefully reconsider the *History of the Communist Party of the Soviet Union (Bolshevik): Short Course*], *Yanhuang chuqiu* [Blazing yellow spring and autumn], no. 4 (2003): 17–23.

24. Jin Chunming, interview, August 30, 2004.

25. Pang Xianzhi, interview, September 22, 2004. Also, see Li Wei, "Yibi yushi jujin de Makesi zhuyi zhuzuo—ping *Liangong (bu) dangshi jianming jiaocheng*" [Commenting on the *History of the Communist Party of the Soviet Union (Bolshevik): Short Course*, as a Marxist work for all time], *Zhongguo yu shijie* [China and the world], no. 2 (2004): 1–9.

26. "Eguo chongxin chuban *Linangong (bu) dangshi jianming jiaocheng*" [Republishing the *History of the Communist Party of the Soviet Union (Bolshevik): Short Course* in Russia], *Bainianchao* [A tide of one hundred years], no. 2 (2006): 66.

27. For a comprehensive study of the role played by Soviet experts in China, see Shen Zhihua, *Soviet Experts* in China. For a discussion of the role played by Soviet experts at People's University, see Douglas A. Stiffler's chapter in the present volume.

28. Lin Yunhui, email, November 16, 2004.

29. Jin Chunming, interview, August 30, 2004.

30. Jin Chunming, interview, August 30, 2004.

31. Shen Zhihua, *Soviet Experts*, 253.

32. Shen Zhihua, *Soviet Experts*, 253.

33. Jin Chunming, interview, August 30, 2004.

34. Lin Yunhui, email, December 2, 2004.

35. Yan Jianfu, interview, Cambridge, MA, May 26, 2005.

36. For a similar discussion, see Frederick C. Teiwes, *Politics at Mao's Court: Gao Gang and Party Factionalism in the Early 1950s* (Armonk, NY: M.E. Sharpe, 1993), 49–50.

37. Jin Chunming, interview, August 30, 2004.

38. Lin Yunhui, email, December 2, 2004.

39. Pang Xianzhi, interview, September 22, 2004.

40. Lin Yunhui, email, November 16, 2004.

41. Su Shaozhi, written statement, November 7, 2004.

42. Zheng Yifan, email, January 19, 2005.

43. Jin Chunming, interview, August 30, 2004.

44. Gong Yuzhi, interview, September 21, 2004.

45. Jin Chunming, interview, August, 2004.

46. Pang Xianzhi, interview, September 22, 2004.

47. Pang Xianzhi, interview, September 22, 2004.

48. Lin Yunhhui, email, November 16, 2004.

49. Jin Chunming, interview, August 30, 2004.

50. Lin Yunhui, email, December 2, 2004.

51. Lin Yunhui, email, December 2, 2004.

52. For a detailed discussion of the Kirov assassination and related topics, see Boris. I. Nicolaevsky, *Power and the Soviet Elite* (New York: Frederick A. Praeger, 1965), 69–102. Sarah Davies, *Popular Opinion in Stalin's Russia: Terror, Propaganda, and Dissent, 1934–1941* (Cambridge: Cambridge University Press, 1997), 116–22.

53. Pang Xianzhi, interview, September 22, 2004.

54. Lin Yunhui, email, November 16, 2004.

55. Lin Yunhui and Jin Chunming both emphasized these two points. Interviewed together, August 30, 2004.

56. Xu Tianxing, interview, September 10, 2004.

57. Lin Yunhui, email, November 16, 2004.

58. Zheng Yifan, interview, September 1, 2004.

5

The Soviet Model and the Breakdown of the Military Alliance

You Ji

S OVIET MILITARY INFLUENCE ON CHINA in the 1950s was profound. The primary reason lay in China's need for Soviet military assistance to deal with the acute security threats from the United States and its lack of capabilities to take Taiwan by itself. Moreover, the People's Liberation Army (PLA) faced a tremendous task of transformation from a revolutionary force to a modernized, national, standing military after the end of the civil war. The PLA was not able to accomplish these tasks by itself and had to rely on learning from the Soviet Army (SA). These considerations prompted Mao Zedong to tell his PLA colleagues that the "Soviet Union is our best master teacher."[1] At the same time, as the 1950s unfolded, Mao Zedong became increasingly uneasy about China's rising dependence on Soviet military aid and about what he perceived to be Soviet efforts to control China. By the late 1950s, the bilateral relations registered more and more difficulties. Mao's changing attitudes not only caused worsening tensions between the two communist nations but also triggered internal strife among senior PLA generals. A chain of unwanted events took place in the bilateral relationship which ultimately led to the collapse of the alliance.

This chapter is an attempt to analyze the way in which the mutually beneficial alliance relationship worked and the process of its breakdown. It argues that the ideological factor was not as important as is generally believed. The diverging strategic interests served as the catalyst while Mao's personal judgments played a more crucial role. This was coupled by the mishandling of the dispute on the part of the Soviet leaders. In overall perspective, however, Soviet influence on the PLA remains strong even to this day. Yet there has not been a full appraisal of the subject, especially by the Chinese leadership. With more material available to scholars, this has now become possible.

The Soviet Model and the Transformation of the PLA

It is no exaggeration to state that Soviet military assistance helped lay the foundation for the PLA's modernization. This can be seen in the following areas.

Force Modernization

The failed attempt to capture Jinmen (Quemoy) in 1950 and the huge casualties that the PLA sustained in the Korean War convinced the Chinese commanders that advanced weapons were essential if the military was to be able to fight modern wars, especially with a powerful enemy like the United States. With the West's arms embargo, the USSR became the only foreign source for the purpose. In 1951 the PLA bought Soviet arms that equipped 60 army divisions, 12 air force divisions and 36 naval vessels.[2] Its Air Force and Navy were established largely based on Soviet weapons systems. By the end of the Korean War almost the entire PLA inventory had been purchased from the USSR, enabling the PLA to upgrade equipment for 186 army divisions, a dozen air force armies and nine naval sub-fleets. The equipment included 800,000 guns, 11,000 artillery pieces, 5,000 tanks and armored vehicles, and 5,000 aircraft. When the PLA took over the Lushun Naval Base in May 1955, it obtained at half price a submarine base, equipment for five fighter jet divisions, one bomber division, two infantry divisions, one mechanized army division, three anti-aircraft artillery divisions and three artillery divisions. The bulk of the weapons of the civil war era were phased out and the initial stage of PLA modernization was completed.[3] In a matter of five years the PLA leaped over a generation of weaponry and became one of the most powerful militaries in the world.

Force Regularization

The mission of regularization was a pressing task for the PLA in the early years of the PRC. The civil war had separated PLA field armies in different geographic areas. They had their own command and control systems, discipline standards, force structures and combat principles, mostly according to their own tradition and habits. In late 1949 the Party's Central Military Commission (CMC) decided to unify these institutions by means of centralized regulations, primarily based on the Soviet model. Specifically, this was reflected in three institutions (*sandazhidu*), namely, introduction of compulsory military service, of military ranks and of a salary system, all based on the Soviet model.[4] The force structure of the air force and the navy was almost entirely copied from the USSR, although the ground forces retained some of their pre-1949 characteristics.

In 1950 Mao issued a call for the "five unifications and four standardizations"—unified command, force structure, disciplinary codes, and training programs; and standardized procedures for organization, planning, legal matters, and the administrative hierarchy.[5] To facilitate PLA regularization, the CMC decided in 1950 to use the Soviet corpus of regulations for guidance before it developed its own. Accordingly, the General Staff Department (GSD) formulated eight regulations to run PLA administration: Regulations for Permissions and Reports; for Inspections, for the Conduct of Training Meetings; for Intensive Instruction and Training, for Study Sessions, for the Training of Headquarters, for the Training of Commanders, and Regulations for Officer Parades. Even after the PLA promulgated three major regulations of its own in 1953, the CMC continued to stress that where possible, Soviet regulations would be used for practical reference, especially in the areas of technical management and tactical operations. In this way, a regularized PLA institution emerged based on Soviet practice. It was not until 1958 that the PLA finally drew up its own body of regulations at Mao Zedong's urging, but these were also largely derived from Soviet regulations rather than as Mao preferred, incorporating the PLA's own characteristics to the extent possible.[6]

The following is an incomplete list of the key Soviet military documents translated into Chinese and used by the PLA to realize regularization:

The Soviet Military Regulations, issued to the PLA in January 1950;

The Disciplinary Code of the Soviet Military, issued to the PLA in January 1950;

The Regulations for Internal Management of the Soviet Military, issued to the PLA in January 1950;

The Regulations on Training for the Soviet Army, issued to the PLA in April 1950;

The Regulations on Internal Security in the Soviet Army, issued to the PLA in April 1950;

The Criminal Law of the Soviet Armed Forces, issued to the PLA in April 1950.

On the basis of the last three regulations the PLA formulated its own three major regulations on training; internal security and criminal punishment.

Building a Base of Defense Industries

A modern military requires a foundation of modern defense industries. Soviet assistance helped China lay such a foundation. In the list of the famous 156 Soviet industrial projects built during China's first-five-year plan (1953–1957), 44 were military projects accounting for 28% of the total (12 for aviation, 10 for electronics, 16 for ordnance, 2 for space industry, and 4 for ship-building). During the same period of time the Soviets also helped China to initiate nuclear and missile programs. For instance, the USSR provided a number of prototype missiles according to the Sino-Russian Agreement on New Defense Technology signed in 1957. Although the breakdown of the relationship in 1960 saw the withdrawal of Soviet experts, the work reports that they left behind served as the basis of China's own research. According to Zhu Guangya, the former director of the Commission of the National Defense Industry, the function of the Soviet technological aid was for China to "win time" under enormous external threat.[7]

Tiyong: PLA Traditions as the Foundation and Soviet Learning for Practical Use

From the preceding we see the depth of Soviet influence on the PLA. Using the Soviet model as the guide for the PLA's transformation was a political choice made by the Party based on strategic necessity, namely the lack of alternatives for the PLA to obtain advanced armaments elsewhere. And the aura of invincibility that surrounded the Soviet military was so powerful that few Chinese questioned the validity of this choice. It was also aligned with the PRC's overall national development strategy and its lean-to-one-side foreign policy, which enabled China to acquire precious loans and essential industrial equipment.[8]

However, it turned out that the PLA's tradition and Soviet experience were bound to clash as China sought to fuse them. The PLA had not thought through what role its own model of army building should play, one that was based on decades of war, when it hurried into learning and absorbing a vastly different model. The PLA's own model can be defined as follows: a high level of egalitarianism between officers and soldiers; intensive ideological indoctrination with an emphasis on spiritual commitment; integration with the masses, which was a requirement for waging people's war; and (*shuangzhangzhi*) or the parallel authority of commanders and commissars in combat units, that is, the principle of collective leadership.[9] In contrast, the Soviet model highlighted professionalism, the importance of hardware, the superior position of commanders over commissars and reliance on formal institutions.[10] Fundamentally, the clash centered on whether politics should continue to be in command.

Toward the mid-1950s, internal debates intensified over whether excessive reliance had been placed on the USSR military. At the lower levels more and more PLA officers became uneasy about implementing something they felt was at odds with their egalitarian values. The expedient need to acquire more Soviet weapons could no longer hide their rising doubts about the Soviet model's compatibility with PLA traditions. For instance, the tough Soviet internal management codes caused wide spread complaints from soldiers who could not get used to the detailed and rigid do's and *don'ts* in the regulations. Irritants abounded. The cadets of the Xinyang Infantry Institute complained that they took their clothes off but could not lie on their beds until the whistle was blown. Furthermore, the president of the institute ordered the soldiers to maintain a unified hairdo, and the shortness of haircuts was measured using a ruler.[11] The senior officers in the intensive course for generals in the Nanjing Military Academy (NMA) reported to the CMC expressing their anger at the way the course was organized and taught under the aegis of Soviet advisors. For instance, the Soviet method of daily six-hour, uninterrupted instruction was an irritant for the generals, who complained about not being able to take a nap at noon. And the examination lasted a whole day and was conducted like a courtroom interrogation. All this was presented as evidence of dogmatism in learning the Soviet experience.[12]

Moreover, the Soviet lecturers at PLA educational institutions used exclusively the Red Army's successful campaigns for case analysis to teach Chinese officers and this caused a backlash from PLA generals who believed that the classroom instruction should be mainly based on their war experiences. These views were later politicized and the level of the criticism was raised to the level of principle, namely whether learning the Soviet military was enhancing or undermining the "fine traditions" of the PLA.[13] Mao expressed his bitterness about Soviet advisors in the NMA who did not allow the Chinese teachers to use PLA experience as the main textbook material, which amounted to belittling his military genius. He angrily expressed this to Khrushchev in 1958, forcing the latter to mock the Soviet generals as stupid.[14]

Yet, at the same time, there were powerful champions of learning from the Soviets. One was Politburo member and Marshall Liu Bocheng, one of four marshals in the PLA who had studied in the USSR. As a professional soldier he was highly impressed by the Red Army's great efficiency. He paid particular attention to three points that most symbolized Soviet military professionalism: a rich body of regulations, the key role of the staff at various headquarters, and the dense network of military educational institutions. Even during wartime he kept translating Soviet military codes and regulations which he used to write his own regulations for the Second Field Army. After he left his command post due to poor heath, he asked Mao to allow him to set up a regular PLA military institution to train officers at the army level. In 1950 he became the first president of the NMA and pledged to turn it to be an oriental *Folongzhi* (Frunze) Military Acadamy where he studied from 1928 to 1930.[15] He worked hard to translate the Soviet way of military training and education into PLA practice since he was in charge of the PLA's overall training program. As president of the NMA, he was tolerant of Soviet advisors' insistence on using the Red Army's cases for instruction. In 1954 he was invited to observe the Red Army's exercise of nuclear warfare. After returning home he made admiring speeches about what he had seen in the USSR, speeches that heavily influenced the entire PLA. All this was to be used against him during the anti-dogmatism movement of 1958.

Mao Zedong's Evolving Views

Mao himself had all along been of two minds about learning from the Soviet Union. In the first half of the 1950s, he had enthusiastically called upon the PLA to learn from Soviet advisors and study the advanced experiences of the Soviets, so as to turn the PLA into the "world's second best modernized military."[16] Moreover, despite Mao's displeasure over Soviet chauvinist attitudes toward other communist parties in the world, Moscow did pay enough respect to the CCP leader and did provide China with generous economic and military aid, for which the Chinese were grateful.

But by 1956 Mao became increasingly impatient with the way the Soviet experiences were being copied by the PLA. Negative feelings were reinforced by memories from the 1930s, when the "returned students" from the SU stripped him of power. This is something Mao never forgot or forgave, even though in 1936, Stalin gave him badly needed support to legitimate his struggle against incumbent Party leaders that had begun a year earlier at the Zunyi conference, enhancing his position vis-à-vis Zhang Guotao and Wang Ming.[17] In the Yan'an Rectification movement in 1942–44 dogmatism was used to counter Soviet interference with Mao's leadership.

More fundamentally, Mao had absorbed the tradition of the Hunan School of the late Qing about learning from the West embodied in the slogan of *ti-yong*, Chinese learning as the essence and foreign learning for practical use. The slogan of the Chuanshan Study Society, "Practice is the source of all knowledge," strongly influenced him and guided his later preoccupation of fusing the foreign essence of Marxism with the realities of the Chinese revolution. His struggle with the "returned students" further convinced him of the danger of mechanically learning anything foreign, even when this brought practical benefits, such as economic and military aid. His lifelong opposition to dogmatism was a clear illustration of the *tiyong* mentality.

For Mao, dogmatism represented blind acceptance of foreign ideology, worship of foreign leaders and mechanical adoption of foreign strategies in disregard of Chinese reality. The charge of dogmatism was a serious political label that could be used against perceived opponents. In the mid-1950s, Mao raised the issue of dogmatism and linked it to the dilemmas of how to transform the PLA: should it become more and more dependent on a powerful ally or consciously retain its independence? In Mao's view, the balance between the *ti* and the *yong* had been upset, something not fully understood by overzealous advocates of the Soviet model in the military who did not see the political implications of the learning process. Mao pondered the question of how to cope with the rising Soviet-centric mentality among senior leaders, that is, how to obtain as much Soviet aid as possible yet maintain the "Chinese essence."[18] In this context, it is important to note that Mao understood the need for advanced equipment in modern warfare and tried his best to acquire advanced Soviet weaponry to the very last day of its availability. Nonetheless, he believed that the PLA should preserve its essence, i.e., chart its own path of development but selectively make use of Soviet technology and experiences.[19] In his value system, he saw military technology within a political framework. There were goals more important than simply acquiring hardware.

Political Conflict within the PLA

With Mao's inherently contradictory positions being gradually made known to ranking officials, the debate for and against the Soviet model intensified and evolved into political infighting within the PLA, culminating in the anti-dogmatism movement of May–June 1958. It grew out of bottom-up initiatives by officers who were unhappy with the various consequences of adopting the Soviet military model. One was the literal way in which Soviet military regulations had been copied by the PLA (see above). But there were other, more significant objections. One was that learning the Soviet model had consequences for the distribution of power within the PLA. Since the Soviets practiced the commander responsibility system, political commissars felt marginalized.[20]   According to Li Zuopeng, former Politburo member and commissar of the PLA Navy until the purge of Lin Biao, when Peng Dehuai presided over the formulation of the PLA Management Code in 1953, he de-emphasized political work as the guiding principle for the PLA, causing a lot of thought confusion. Peng transferred large numbers of political affairs officers to other posts, and in 1953–54, the position of political instructor in the tank divisions was abolished. Commissars felt sidelined.[21]

The introduction of formal military ranks in 1955 also caused widespread feelings of unfairness among senior officers. Many generals who were unhappy with their military rank complained to Mao. The competition among his comrades-in-arms led Mao to joke that "men do not tear easily until they are assessed for the award of military ranks." This way of regularization was against the PLA's tradition and worsened the situation of PLA factionalism. And the salary system highlighted the low hierarchical status among the rank and file members who were used to a military culture of egalitarianism.

Learning Soviet experiences thus generated conflict within the PLA, although it would be an exaggeration to claim that there was a fully formed pro-Soviet faction in the PLA. This is in contrast to the pro-Soviet factions that did emerge among those generals trained in the USSR in North Korea and Vietnam. In China, however, there also was a cleavage between those who had studied in the SU and those who had not. In the top PLA command four of the ten marshals (Zhu De, Chen Yi, Nie Rongzhen and Liu Bocheng); and three out ten senior generals (Xiao Jingguang, Xu Guangda and Chen Geng) had studied in the USSR. And at the lower levels 21 senior officers were returnees from the USSR (6 generals, 6 lieut. generals, and 10 major generals) before 1949. After the PRC was founded, the PLA sent 26 promising relatively young senior officers (at the rank of army and divisional commanders) to the USSR. Some of them became top-ranking PLA leaders, such as Admiral Liu Huaqing who was the only professional soldier in the Standing Committee of the Politburo in the early 1990s. The Soviet experience was a visible plus when promotion was considered. For instance, as in every other military in the communist camp, the top leadership promoted senior cadres with rich Soviet experiences as a method to please Moscow. Although Mao did the least in this regard, he still bore this in mind in making personnel arrangements. That Xu Guangda was promoted to senior general was largely due to Mao's consideration of his Soviet connection. He was regarded as the least qualified for the rank. The favoritism caused reportedly caused complaints among the majority of PLA cadres.

And logically, when the relations with the USSR soured in 1959, the Soviet connection became a liability. The purge in 1959 of Marshal Peng was partially justified on the grounds of his "good relations" with his Soviet counterpart. One major accusation was his unauthorized meeting with Khrushchev in Albania in 1959 during which he accepted an invitation to visit Moscow.[22] A piece of "evidence" was that he was given a TV set by Soviet defense minister Georgy Zhukov during his trip to the USSR in 1956.

In March 1956, Mao instructed an enlarged CMC meeting to focus on the issue of how to maintain the PLA's "fine traditions"—including the relations between the army and the society, between officers and men, the mass line, party committee procedures, and political work even after the military rank system had been introduced.[23] The first open call for opposition to dogmatism appeared in five central documents on how to improve cadre education issued by the Party Center in May 1956. It demanded that senior cadres overcome subjectivism, dogmatism, and empiricism when studying Marxism and foreign experiences, and that these should be reflected in academic research, media coverage and classroom instruction.[24] Specific reference was made to the curriculum in PLA schools that bore the imprint of the Soviet experts. The "Ten Great Relationships" in which Mao criticized literal copying of Soviet experience were disseminated as well. A new direction was set for learning from the SU, although it took several years for the documents to show their effect.

In the lead-up to the anti-dogmatism movement, some major international incidents affected Chinese military politics. One was that the Hungarian and Polish militaries had not followed Party orders during the 1956 upheavals. Another was the purge in October 1957 of Soviet Marshall and Minister of Defense Zhukov for Bonapartism, that is, for allegedly trying to seize power, a charge that probably shocked Mao and other CCP leaders.[25] After that Mao issued a number of instructions to strengthen Party control over the generals. For instance, he introduced the institution of appointing local party secretaries as the first political commissars for PLA units deployed in the regions.[26] It was not that Mao did not trust generals under his command but that he became more vigilant than before. Therefore, any sign of PLA internal instability would arouse his attention. And as usual he would see the issue from a strategic angle.

The Unfolding of the Campaign against Dogmatism

In February 1958, Peng Dehuai inspected the Nanjing Military Academy (NMA), during which he severely criticized the Academy for blindly worshiping the Soviet Army. In his report to Mao in April, he said that "whether there is dogmatism in the NMA is not the issue. The issue is that dogmatism is deeply entrenched." Peng was particularly angry about the NMA's continued use of an inscription dating from 1951, "Work hard to build the PLA into a regularized and modernized military," but without Peng's word "revolutionary" which he had added to the PLA's guiding principles in 1953. In his mind, this was a matter of principle and a sign of dogmatism, since the Soviet Army had long stopped using the term.

Peng's criticism of the NMA requires a comment. After all, having experienced the Korean War, Peng Dehuai became an enthusiastic advocate of PLA modernization, meaning it should be equipped with the best hardware possible, which was available only from the USSR. But modernization, in his view, should be in line with the preservation of the "Chinese essence." This meant that he differed from Liu Bocheng, for whom learning the Soviet model meant absorbing its basic approaches and attitudes. Peng was not trained in the Soviet Union, as Liu was in the 1920s and he was not as passionate about the Soviet model as Liu, quite the opposite. His visits to the USSR led him to become uneasy about the model when he witnessed at first hand the rigid hierarchical distance between officers and men, its emphasis on formality, and its reliance on promotions by rank and emphasis on material incentives as ways to boost morale. In his mind these practices ran counter to the traditions of the PLA. To the extent that the PLA had adopted them, to that extent they should be rectified by means of continuing "revolutionization." These views clashed with those of Liu Bocheng, who favored the PLA's transformation along the lines of "formalization." Liu never thought that the above-mentioned inscription which symbolized the Soviet model was problematic. In his view, "revolutionization" was not really necessary and some of the PLA's fine traditions stood in the way of implementing the Soviet model. Actually, when seen from today's vantage point, the differences between the two were more differences of degree than of kind. But they were exacerbated by the personal animosity between the two that dated from the War of Resistance and which helped aggravate the military debate and elevated it to a political level that resulted in the movement against "dogmatism."

Peng's criticism led to a heated political debate in the PLA. In February 1958, General Xiao Ke wrote to Peng disagreeing with his characterization on the grounds that regularization and modernization did not exclude revolutionization. Peng, he wrote, was exaggerating the seriousness of dogmatism in the PLA, since it was at best, a partial phenomenon.[27] In March 1958, Xiao Ke, the head of the Department of Education and Training, decided to hold a meeting to clarify the thinking of his staff because his Department was being labeled as the headquarters of dogmatism. He identified General Zhang Zongxun, his deputy, as the source of the criticism. Zhang had complained that "Soviet experience is poison. The more you learn, the deeper you are poisoned."[28] In contrast, Xiao Ke believed that without a thorough study of the Soviet model, the PLA could not be successfully transformed. This further angered Peng who saw the issue in fundamental terms: continuing the "fine tradition" or "changing color and taking the bourgeois road." Peng sent a summary of the meeting to Mao, who then ordered the convening of an enlarged conference of the CMC.

One element of the "fine traditions" of the PLA was participation in civilian mobilization. As the massive social mobilization of the Great Leap Forward got underway, reaching new heights, Mao began to look askance at the relatively detached posture of the PLA. Mao felt a need to "fire up" the PLA by urging it to catch up with the socialist enthusiasm of the masses. Mao told CCP leaders at the Chengdu Enlarged Politburo conference of March 8-26, 1958, that "we in the past always used the military to push the civilians but this time we will do the reverse. We should do something about the military in 1958."[29] It turned out that this something took the form of the anti-dogmatism movement. Following Mao, Deng Xiaoping, who later was appointed head of the leadership group on the anti-dogmatism movement, also criticized the PLA at the Chengdu conference for failing to integrate with the masses. "There should be a rectification drive to change the situation."[30]

A fierce battle ensued at the enlarged CMC conference held from May 27 to July 22, 1958, which pitted two groups against one another who were sharply divided on the issue of learning from the Soviets. One group was led by Marshal Peng Dehuai and included General Zhang Zongxun. The side that emphasized Soviet learning was led by Marshal Liu Bocheng, president of the NMA, Senior general Su Yu, the chief of staff, General Xiao Ke, the deputy minister of defense and General Li Da, the deputy chief of staff. They insisted that learning the Soviet experience was not only crucial for the transformation of the PLA but had achieved visible success. The excesses were only exceptional cases. The central debating point was whether it was necessary to categorically stress the revolutionary nature of the PLA in addition to modernization and regularization.[31]

But an additional factor was that the dogmatism debate may also have provided an opportunity for Peng to suppress opposition to his leadership in the PLA, but this is a point on which today's PLA historians disagree. In any event, as soon as the conference got under way, chief of staff Su Yu became the target of criticism. Su had commanded the biggest field army during the civil war and made the biggest contribution to victory. Su was in charge of PLA daily administration and operations. His way of management differed from Peng's. Peng believed that Su was deliberately uncooperative with him on the three most important issues: the PLA's strategy, its long-term transformation and current policies. In the conference he even accused Su of being like Georgy Zhukov. One of Su's "crimes" was to complain against Peng's leadership to Soviet advisors in the General Staff Department.[32]

Similar to the case of Su Yu, Liu Bocheng also had had a conflict with Peng Dehuai. Peng and Liu developed tense relations in the late 1930s when Peng was in overall charge of the operations of the 8th Route Army in Shanxi and Liu was commander of the 129th Division. Peng launched the famous "100

Regiments campaign" in 1940, which caused Liu Bocheng's 129th Division to suffer heavy casualties, creating a rift between the two. Liu was a strong voice against Peng in Yanan in 1944 when Peng was "cursed for 40 days." Anti-dogmatism provided a good opportunity for him to settle old scores, using the negative effect of Soviet influence in the PLA as an excuse. However, Peng's forays required Mao's support. For Mao this was not a matter of a personal dispute rooted in PLA "mountaintopism." At the beginning he was hesitant to agree with Peng's view of Su Yu as the PLA's Zhukov, if only because Su had never challenged Mao. Similarly, Mao did not need to support Peng in order to damage Liu Bocheng, who was also his loyal follower.

In any event, the exchange of attacks escalated. On 6 June Mao received a letter from Vice Admiral Fan Qian who requested that anti-dogmatism should be used as guiding principle to evaluate the overall work of the PLA. Mao commented on the letter that "there exist opposing traditions in the PLA: the Marxist fine tradition and anti-Marxist dogmatism. Some comrades are not happy with the way the conference is conducted. Therefore, it should be enlivened."[33] Mao entrusted Deng Xiaoping with coordinating the conference in order for it truly to stimulate the struggle against dogmatism. Mao incited key PLA leaders such as Marshal Lu Ronghuan and General Xiao Hua to raise the dispute between Xiao Ke and Zhang Zongxun to the level of two-line struggle. Inevitably Mao's call led the conference participants to go after the "ultimate source" of dogmatism in the PLA, that is, Marshal Liu Bocheng, who, as noted above, was the leading advocate of learning the Soviet military experience.

As was characteristic of the Mao era, any serious debate on issues of principle that could change the direction of the Party or the military had to be settled through political campaigns, some of which entailed bloodshed. The 1958 anti-dogmatism campaign was one of these incidents in PLA history. Its result was that a relatively large number of senior PLA officers were branded as revisionists and rightists. Marshal Liu was severely criticized. Mao's verdict on him was that he committed errors of "thought" and "direction." Had it not been for Deng's pleading with Mao, Liu would have lost his Politburo membership. Perhaps saving Liu's post also reflected Mao's concern that the Soviets might interpret his purge as an anti-Soviet act, which could have serious ramifications for the alliance, since Mao did want to secure essential technology even while cultivating the PLA's "fine traditions."[34] But Deng was unable to protect General Li Da, his chief of staff in the Second Field Army. He did find it necessary to add a section on rectification of the movement in the Party's "Resolution on CPC History, 1949–1981."[35]

Some argue that the anti-dogmatism movement was part of Mao's effort to enhance party control over the gun.[36] It is true to some extent. Yet Mao's control had never been as firm as it was in the 1950s. The Soviet influence in the military was deepening but it had never come to the degree that would threaten Mao's unshakeable status vis-à-vis the PLA or his absolute control. The cleavages that had developed within the officer corps over the Soviet model, however, were disturbing to Mao and this was a cause of his intervention.

Mao's fundamental principle for absorbing the Soviet military experience was clearly Chinese learning as the foundation and Soviet experience for practical use. In his view, the balance between the two had been upset in the first half of the decade and he concluded that the slogan of self-reliance or (*yiwoweizhu*) should now be emphasized. But the 1958 campaign tilted too far in the opposite direction. It helped build a consensus on how to apply the Soviet model, but at heavy cost for the PLA's professionalization, modernization, and regularization. The campaign marked the end of the internal debate about how much of the Soviet military experience should be translated into PLA practice, but it largely led to the gradual termination of the learning drive.

Resisting Control versus Promoting Further Cooperation

Once the PLA had embarked on a course self-reliant development as the PLA's guiding principle, it would logically affect the Sino-Soviet military alliance which was the most effective medium through which Soviet military influence on the Chinese was transmitted. And indeed, the second half of 1958 saw developments that signaled a breakdown of the alliance. The themes of Chinese fears over excessive dependence on and loss of sovereignty to the SU that were implicit in the anti-dogmatism campaign were reflected in the Chinese handling of two Soviet proposals, one made in April 1958, for a joint long-wave radio station and the other, made in July, for the construction of a joint submarine fleet. And they were reflected in the way Sino-Soviet relations were handled during the bombardment of the Taiwan-controlled offshore island of Quemoy (Jinmen) in August of that year. Both illustrate the nexus between alliance politics and the issue of high technology transfer to China.

The radio station arose from Soviet requirements for long-wave communications link with its budding nuclear submarine fleet in the Western Pacific. A jointly financed station built on Hainan Island would serve this purpose. The Soviets suggested that they would pay the larger part of the estimated cost, 70 million rubles, and the Chinese, 40 million. Mao Zedong agreed but raised the question of ownership, an issue of sovereignty. He decided that China should put up all the funds, while the Soviets supplied the technical equipment, which the Soviets could then use.[37] The Soviets insisted that they would pay for the bulk of the expenses, fearing that the Chinese could deny them access. Even in the absence of a resolution of the issue, Soviet naval experts came to China.

In June, Zhou Enlai asked Khrushchev for Soviet assistance to build nuclear submarines. Soviet naval advisors had indicated that Moscow would respond favorably. Mao supported the initiative. Unexpectedly, on July 21, 1958, the Soviets turned this idea into a proposal for a joint submarine fleet. This would solve the issue of ownership of the radio station, but also enable the SU to use Chinese ice-free ports to guard against the U.S. naval presence in East Asia. China would gain the ability to defend its long coastline, thereby also gaining relief from U.S. pressures. Moreover, China would gain access to highly valuable technology.

Mao, however, reacted angrily, suspecting that Khrushchev intended to control the Chinese military, since inevitably, the weaker Chinese would be the junior partner (*erhbashou*), i.e., command and control would be in Soviet hands.[38] While normal practice in other military alliances, the Soviet proposal reminded Mao of the joint stock companies created under the 1950 Treaty, which he saw as a Soviet effort to establish spheres of influence in China, implying a significant loss of sovereignty. To Mao, this amounted to taking advantage of a friend's weakness. An additional reason was that since the Korean War, Mao had been vigilant against being dragged into an unwanted war by Soviet adventurism. At the global level a relatively tense U.S.-Soviet confrontation was useful for China to pursue its own goals in Asia, but not to the point of real war.[39] In any event, Khrushchev, taken aback by Mao's anger, immediately scrapped the idea when the two met on July 31, 1958.

The proposed joint fleet reenforced Mao's negative perceptions of Khrushchev.[40] More broadly, Mao may never have accepted the idea of alliances, which in the case of the junior partners, do impinge on sovereignty. During wartime, this was permissible, but not during peacetime.[41] On several occasions, Mao attributed the breakdown of the alliance to the dispute over the joint fleet proposal in 1958.[42] Thus, irreparable damage was done to the alliance.

The Impact of the Quemoy Crisis on the Military Alliance and on the Transfer of Technology

China launched an intensive artillery bombardment campaign against Jinmen beginning on August 23, initiating a dangerous crisis in the Taiwan Straits. Mao's evolving calculus appears to have been first, to punish Taiwan for its incursions into Mainland; and second, to send a message to Washington about China's commitment to Taiwan. If in the process of the campaign, Taiwan troops were forced to withdraw from Jinmen, then the PLA would take it, as Mao told the Politburo during the bombardment.[43] If on the other hand the United States reacted strongly, China would desist and in this way tie the Chinese Nationalists permanently to the Mainland, thereby complicating any two-China solution to the Taiwan problem.

Debate lingers on the extent to which Mao informed the Soviets.[44] Mao told Khrushchev during his National Day visit in October 1959 that the chief Soviet advisor to the General Staff Department had been told that China was considering action with regard to Taiwan. "We asked him to report our *Taiwan thing* to the Soviet Ministry of Defense one month prior to the action."[45] Moreover, Soviet advisors were present at the Fujian front and thus knew of the preparations for the campaign.[46] At their 1959 meeting Mao also told Khrushchev that he had only intended to make trouble for the United States rather than occupy the Jinmen.[47]

Failure fully to inform and consult his Soviet ally of his intentions and objectives prior to the campaign was probably due to Chinese fears that in view of Khrushchev's pursuit of détente, including a projected state visit to the United States, the Soviets would have firmly opposed a Taiwan initiative. Yet at the same time, China did need the Soviets to deter the United States in case the Americans chose to act on Dulles' concept of massive retaliation. This evidently was the reason why Mao suddenly chose to make public Khrushchev's secret visit on July 31, 1958, that is, to sow doubt in U.S. minds about the Soviet commitment to Mao's Jinmen project. Actually, at this summit, a message was clearly conveyed to all CCP leaders that it was unlikely for the PRC to expect Soviet military support in a Taiwan war.[48] Mao was highly successful in this Sun Zi type of stratagem. Yet, it proved very costly, as it galvanized Khrushchev to retaliate against what he perceived to be Mao's adventurism in possibly dragging the SU into a war with the United States. For instance, he stopped delivery of nuclear equipment to China when these had already been loaded on a train.[49] In August 1959, the Soviets informed China that it would not provide a prototype nuclear weapon, leaving China to make the best of its verbal commitment to self-reliance.[50] In sum, learning from the Soviet Union combined with growing difficulties in the alliance relationship combined to undermine and finally end the Sino-Soviet military relationship.

Notes

1. Mao Zedong, *Mao Zedong xuanji* (disijuan) [Selected works of mao zedong, vol. 4] (hereinafter as *Mao Zedong xuanji 4*) (Beijing: Renmin chubanshe, 1991), 1481.

2. Zhongguo renmin jiefangjun junshi kexueyuan [The PLA academy of military science], *Zhongguo Renmin Jiefangjun de qishinian* [The 70 years of the PLA] (Beijing: Zhongguo renmin jiefanjun junshi kexuyuan chubanshe, 1997), 461.

3. Liu Zhiqing, "Wushi niandai xuexi Sujun de zhenglun yu jieju" [The debate and consequences of learning from the Soviet military in the 1950s], in Luan Jinghe et. al., eds., *Zhong-E guanxi de lishi yu xianshi* [The history and reality of the Sino-Russia relations] (hereinafter as *Zhong-E guanxi*) (Kaifeng: Henan renmin chubanshe, 2002), 523.

4. Lin Yunhui, Fan Shouxin and Zhang Gong, *Kaige xingjin de niandai* [The era of marching with the songs of victory] (Kaifeng: Henan renmin chubanshe, 1989), 447.

5. Mao Zedong, *Jianguo yilai Mao Zedong wengao* (disance) [Selected writings of Mao Zedong since the founding of the PRC, vol. 3] (hereinafter as *Mao wengao 3*) (Beijing: Zhongyang wenxian chubanshe, 1998), 490.

6. Liu Zhiqing, *Zhong-E guanxi*, 523.

7. Wang Jianzhu, "Zhu Guangya: bisheng jingli xiangei 'liangdan,'" [Zhu Guangya's lifelong devotion to the development of nuclear bombs and missiles], *Renwu* [Journal of Personality], no. 10 (October 2005): 9.

8. Qu Xin, "Cong zhanhou chuqi de Su-Mei dui Hua zhengce kan Zhongguo waijiao zhanlue diwei" [China's "leaning-to-one-side" policy in the background of American and Soviet China policy in the early post-World War II era], *Shiji zhijiao de Zhongguo de waijiao zhengce: huigu yu zhanwang* [China's foreign policy at the turn of the century: recollections and prospects], ed. Joseph Cheng (Hong Kong: Hong Kong University Press, 2001), 363–82.

9. Ironically, at the top and at field army levels it was one-man rule rather than the dual command (*shuangzhangzhi*) that was practiced. See You Ji, "Unraveling the Myths of PLA Political Commissars," in *Swimming in a New Sea: Civil-Military Issues in Today's China*, eds., David M. Finkelstein and Kristen Gunness (Armonk, NY: M.E. Sharpe, 2007), 146–70.

10. On the Soviet military model, see Roman Kolkowicz, *The Soviet Military and the Communist Party* (Princeton: Princeton University Press, 1967) and William Odom, *The Collapse of the Soviet Military* (New Haven, CT: Yale University Press, 1998).

11. Liu Zhiqing, *Zhong-E guanxi*, 523.

12. General Zhang Zongxun went as far as claiming that "the more one embraced the Soviet way the more seriously he was poisoned." Zhang Zongxun, *Zhang Zongxun huiyilu* [Autobiography of Zhang Zongxun] (hereinafter as *Zhang Zongxun huiyilu*) (Beijing: Zhongguo renmin jiefangjun chubanshe, 1990), 447.

13. Liu Zhiqing, *Zhong-E guanxi*, 535.

14. Sun Qimin, *Zhong-Su guanxi shimo* [History of Sino-Soviet relations] (hereinafter as *Zhong-Su guanxi shimo*) (Shanghai: Shanghai renmin chubanshe, 2002), 341.

15. Liu Miqun, "Nuer yanzhong de fuqin Liu Bocheng" [Liu Bocheng through the eyes of his daughter), *Junshi lishi* [Military history], no. 11 (2005), 28.

16. Mao Zedong, *Mao wengao 4*, 1990, 1. Also see *Mao Zedong xunji 4*, 1481, for his point that "the USSR was the best teacher that China could find."

17. During his talk with the Soviet Ambassador on 22 July 1958 Mao spent much time criticizing Stalin. He pointed to three mistakes made by Stalin during the

Chinese revolution: supporting Wang Ming, pressuring the CCP to make peace with Jiang Jieshi and creating spheres of influence in China's northeast and Xinjiang. He was particularly unhappy with the attitude displayed by Mikoyan in Xibaipo in early 1949 in treating China as a son of the USSR. Mao said that he did not like his congratulatory speech to the CCP's 8th National Congress in 1956 so he deliberately absented himself. Mao went on to say that he would write an article about the Stalin's mistreatment of the CCP before his death which would be published only in 10,000 years. Apparently Mao had tried to hide these feelings for a long time. See Yan Mingfu (the interpreter for Mao during the meeting and a member of the CCP General Secretariat in the late 1980s. He was purged after the 1989 Tiananmen incident). Yan Mingfu and Zhu Ruizhen, "Yi 1958 nian Mao Zedong yu Heluxiaofu de sici huitan" [Remembering the four meetings between Mao and Khrushchev in 1958] (hereinafter as *sici huitan*) *Zhonggong dangshi ziliao* [CCP Party History Material], no. 2 (2006), 30–31.

18. Xu Chengfang, "Mao Zedong kefu 'Sulian zhongxin zhuyi' de lilun yu shijian" [The theory and practice of Mao Zedong's effort to overcome "Soviet centralism"] in Luan Jinghe, et al., eds., *Zhong-E guanxi*, 468–78.

19. The PLA Academy of Military Science, *Junqi piaopiao—xin Zhongguo 50 nian junshi dashi shushi* [Flying the army's flag: 50 years of the great military events] (Beijing: Zhongguo remin jiefangjun chubanshe, 1997), 473.

20. For instance, in the early 1950s the Soviet advisors pressed hard to institute the one-man command system in all PLA universities. In order to prevent a direct confrontation with them, Mao asked the PLA General Political Affairs Department to appoint the presidents of these institutions with a concurrent post of political commissar. Senior general Chen Geng was an example when he was made president of the PLA Military Engineering University in Harbin.

21. Shi Dongbin, *Zhengtan miwen lu* [Untold stories about Top Leaders], www. peacehall.com (accessed October 21, 2007). See also Wang An, "Laoyibei gemingjia yu wojun tiaoling tiaolue" [PLA older generation and PLA regulations and codes], *Jiehfangjun bao* [PLA daily], April 2, 2006.

22. Zhu Kaiyin, "Lushan huiyi qian pei Peng Dehuai fang Dongou" [Accompany Peng Dehuai to visit Eastern Europe prior to the *Lushan* conference), *Bainianchao* [A tide of a hundred years], no. 11 (November 2005), 23.

23. Zheng Wenhan, *Mishu riji zhong de Penglaozong* [The image of Peng Dehuai in the diaries of his secretaries] (hereinafter as *Mishu riji*) (Beijing: Zhongguo renmin jiefangjun junshi kexueyuan chubanshe, 1998), 91.

24. *Peng Dehuai zhuan* [Biography Peng Dehuai] (Beijing: Renmin chubanshe, 1996), 546.

25. Peng particularly raised this possibility of military getting out of control after his generation of leaders passed away. Zou Aiping, "Xiao Ke zai 1958 nian junwei kuoda huiyi de qianqian houhou" [Xiao Ke in the lead-up to and aftermath of the l958 CMC enlarged conference] (hereinafter as *Junwei kuoda huiyi*) *Junshi shilu* [PLA historical events], no. 6 (June 2006): 4.

26. You Ji, "Unravelling the Myths of the PLA Political Commissars," 146–70.

27. Zou Aiping, *Junwei kuoda huiyi*, 3.

28. Zhang Zongxun, *Zhang Zongxun huiyilu*, 4.

29. Gao Liangsheng, "1958 nian Jiefangjun fan jiaotiao zhuyi chutan" [Preliminary study of the PLA's anti-dogmatism campaign in 1958] (hereinafter as *Fan jiaotiao*), *Junshi lishi* [Military history], no. 1 (1994): 9.

30. Zheng Wenhan, *Mishu riji*, 266.

31. Zou Aiping, *Junwei kuoda huiyi*, 4.

32. Zhu Yin, "Su Yu shoudao bugongping daiyu de zhenshi gushi" [The true story of Su Yu's unjust persecution], *Wenshi jinghua* [Essence of literature and history], no. 12 (2000): 4–6.

33. *Mao wengao 7*, 260–61.

34. Gao Liangsheng, *Fan jiaotiao*, no.1, (1994): 9.

35. "Resolution on Certain Questions in the History of Our Party since the Founding of the PRC," adopted by the 6th Plenum of the 11th CC (Beijing: Foreign Languages Press, 1981), 23.

36. Frederick Teiwes, *Politics and Purges in China: Rectification and the Decline of Party Norms, 1950–1965* (Armonk, NY: M. E. Sharpe, 1993), 295.

37. Yan Mingfu and Zhu Ruizhen, *sicihuitan, Zhonggong dangshi ziliao* [CCP party history materials], no. 2 (2006): 28.

38. He Min and Luo Feng, *Zhong-Su guanxi zhongda shijian shuji* [Record of major events in Sino-Soviet relations] (Beijing: Renmin chubanshe, 2007), 133.

39. Xu Yan, "On the four-sided equilibrium in the Korean War," *Zhongguo Renmin Jiefangjun guofang daxue xuebao* [Journal of the PLA National Defense University], no.12 (December 2003), 31.

40. Yan Mingfu and Zhu Ruizhen, *sicihuitan, Zhonggong dangshi ziliao* [CCP party history materials], no. 2 (2006): 60.

41. Yoichi Funabashi, ed., *Alliance Tomorrow: Security Arrangement after the Cold War* (Tokyo: The Tokyo Foundation, 2001).

42. Mao mentioned it several times later that the breakdown happened in 1958 due to the dispute over the naval cooperation. Yan Mingfu and Zhu Ruizhen, *sicihuitan, Zhonggong dangshi ziliao* [CCP party history materials], no. 2 (2006): 70.

43. Sun Qimin, *Zhong-Su guanxi shimo*, 343.

44. Su Ge, *Meiguo dui Hua zhengce yu Taiwan wenti* [Sino-U.S. relations and the Taiwan problem] (Beijing: Shijie zhishi chubanshe, 1998), 303. Shen Zhihua, "Paoji Jinmen, Zhonguo shifou gaozhi le Sulian" [Did China inform the USSR prior to the *jinmen* bombardment?" *Zhonggong dangshi yanjiu* [CCP party history research], no. 4 (April 2004).

45. Yan Mingful and Zhu Ruizhen, "1959 nian Heluxiaofu fang Hua de qianqian houhou" [Events prior to and after Khrushchev's China visit in 1959] (hereinafter as *qianqian houhou*), *Zhonggong dangshi ziliao* [CCP party history materials], no. 4 (2006): 40.

46. Author's interview of a family friend who in the 1950s took care of Soviet military experts in the PLA Air Force Academy in Beijing, July 2006.

47. Yan Mingful and Zhu Ruizhen, *qianqian houhou, Zhonggong dangshi ziliao* [CCP party history materials], no. 4 (2006): 36.

48. Yan Mingful anjd Zhu Ruizhen, *qianqian houhou, Zhonggong dangshi ziliao* [CCP party history materials], no. 4 (2006): 52.

49. Shen Zhihua, "Yuanzhu yu xianzhi: Sulian yu Zhongguo de hewuqi yanzhi" [Assistance and restrictions: the Soviet Union and China building nuclear weapons], *Lishi yanjiu* [Historical Research], no. 3 (2004). Yan Mingful and Zhu Ruizhen, "Wo liaojie de Heluxiaofu quanli dongzheng" [Khrushchev's power struggle that I know], *Yanhuan chunqiu* [Chinese History], no. 7 (2005): 5.

50. William Taubman, *Khrushchev: The Man and his Era* (New York: W.W. Norton, 2003), 393.

III

SOVIET ECONOMIC ASSISTANCE AND SOCIALIST TRANSFORMATION

6

The Transplantation and Entrenchment of the Soviet Economic Model in China

Kong Hanbing

Introduction

COMPARED WITH THE NORMAL PATTERN of international relations, those be-tween China and the USSR were more complex and more distinctive during the 43 years between October 1949 and December 1991. This was due to the fact that state-to-state relations, party-to-party relations, and the personal relations between the leaders were intertwined, together with considerations of national interests and ideology. They are hard to explain if only of one aspect of the relationship is considered.[1] For example, Sino-Soviet economic relations—trade and mutual aid—played an important role, but economic relations were conditioned by the directions taken by political developments. During the latter half of the 20th century, the Soviet model in China was first adopted, followed by a tortuous process of entrenchment, but as Sino-Soviet relations deteriorated and as Chinese society was reshaped, the application of the Soviet model became much more problematic.

The Soviet Model and Its Applicability

The Soviet model, also known as the Stalin model, refers to the socialist political, economic, cultural and diplomatic system established by the USSR in the 1930s. With regard to the economy, the Soviet model was a combination of the theory envisioned by Marx of an economy without commodity or market relations and of the Bolshevik practice of "War Communism" (1918–1920). It had the following characteristics: First, it implemented a system of unitary public ownership in the belief that the greater the degree of public ownership, the better. Second, it adopted the command system of the planned economy, which excluded regulation by the market. The so-called command economy meant that it was the government rather than the enterprises that had the right to decide what should be produced and in what quantities, to whom the products should be sold and at what price. The plans formulated by the government had the force of law while the state-owned enterprises lacked any kind of autonomy. Third, the economy was managed in a highly centralized way. Macro- as well as micro-economic decision-making, including the right to allocate and distribute human and financial resources, were all concentrated at the center. The party and the government communicated with enterprises, economic organizations and the organizations of social and economic life by issuing orders, passing resolutions, and by relying on administrative means of enforcement. Fourth, it adopted an imbalanced economic structure by giving priority to the development of heavy industry, particularly the military industries. In contrast, light industry and agriculture were neglected.

In the last ten years or more, a number of academic studies have analyzed and commented on the Soviet model.[2] The present author does not intend to discuss the merits and demerits or the rights and wrongs of the Soviet model. The author mainly examines the following points. First, to which countries could the Soviet model be applied? As noted above, the distinctive characteristic of the Soviet model was centralized control from top to bottom. This meant that countries which had a political tradition of strict centralization could more easily adopt the model. Second, during what stage of development could the Soviet model be applied? The Soviet model's superiority lay in its capacity for mobilization and centralized allocation of resources. It could therefore accomplish large undertakings in a short time by concentrating human, material and financial resources. Thus, for countries that were economically backward and eager to catch up with and surpass the advanced countries, the Soviet model was appropriate. Third, the Soviet model was also suitable for those countries that had been ravaged by war and which needed urgently to rebuild. Fourth, the suitability of the Soviet model was limited both temporally and spatially. In terms of space, in its early stages, the application of the Soviet model had more positive than negative effects. The more backward the economy of a country, the greater the attractiveness of the Soviet model, that is, of using dictatorship to overcome backwardness. Over time, however, the utility of the Soviet model declined. The greater complexity of a modernized economy and of a more complex society created pressures for decentralization, and on the political side, for democratization. In other words, the Soviet model became a victim of its success. Reforms became necessary to reverse the declining performance of socialist states. Of course, circumstances varied so that the Soviet model could endure for longer or shorter periods in different settings. But these broad patterns must be kept in mind when studying the model.

In comparative perspective, the tradition of authoritarian rule was strongest in China, followed by the USSR while it was weakest in the eastern European countries, which reflected their higher levels of economic development and modernization. In contrast, the USSR was less developed and modernized while China was at the lowest level. Therefore, the Soviet model was more applicable in China than in Eastern Europe. Therefore, the varying temporal and spatial utility of the Soviet model was also an indispensable factor that must be taken into account when studying Sino-Soviet relations, the relations between the Soviet Union and Eastern Europe, and those between China and Eastern Europe.

The Transplantation of the Soviet Model to China

While eastern European countries were forced to accept the Soviet model, China took the initiative to transplant the Soviet model. That was because of the Soviet model's high adaptability to China and China's strong desire to accept it. In China, the autocratic tradition was much longer and more deeply rooted than in Russia. Moreover, the impact of western democratic politics on pre-Communist Russia was much greater than was the case in pre-1949 China. Second, China's economy was more backward, while Chinese were extremely eager for rapid modernization. Before 1949, China had a backward agriculture-based and largely self-sufficient economy, which reduced the impact of the western market economy. China was a truly poverty-stricken country. By 1949, its economy had reached the brink of collapse. In 1949, China's total industrial output was only 14 billion current yuan. Food and agricultural production were reduced by more than a quarter compared to the peak year before 1949. Both urban and rural residents were suffering from dire poverty.[3]

At that time, China not only had to overcome its condition of backwardness as quickly as possible but also to prove the superiority of the socialist road. Scholars correctly explain the "lean-to-one-side" policy adopted by the CCP before 1949 from the perspective of diplomacy, that is, current Sino-Soviet relations and their later evolution, but this nonetheless is a shallow perspective. At a deeper level, the policy meant that the direction of China's social development became locked into the Soviet model. The reasons are as follows: First, throughout the modern period, socialism had long been the aspiration of progressive Chinese. Generations of progressive Chinese constantly thought about and ultimately chose socialism as the way to save China.

Second, the CCP was established by imitating the model of the Soviet Communist Party and by means of the direct assistance from the CPSU. Third, it was Mao Zedong's personal ideal to build a Chinese socialism like that of the USSR.[4] On June 20, 1949, Mao Zedong concluded in his famous article "On the people's democratic dictatorship," which he wrote to commemorate the 28th anniversary of the founding of the CPC, that,

> It was the Russians who assisted the Chinese people to find Marxism. Before the Russian October Revolution, the Chinese people knew neither of Lenin, Stalin, nor of Marx and Engels. It was the Russian October Revolution that sent us Marxism. The Russian October Revolution helped the whole world as well as the advanced elements in China to use the proletarian world outlook as the tool to analyze the fate of the country and to examine anew its problems. The conclusion was to follow the path of the Russians.[5]

China offered a fertile soil for the Soviet model and Chinese strongly identified with it. When it established the new government, the CPC decided to learn about all aspects of the model and to transplant it in a comprehensive way. Chairman Mao put it this way:

> We want to build a great country. The tasks before us are hard and we do not have enough experience. So we need earnestly to learn the advanced experiences of the USSR. All Party members, all those outside the Party, veteran cadres, new cadres, technical specialists, intellectuals, workers and peasants must sincerely learn from the USSR. We must not only learn the theories of Marx, Engels, Lenin and Stalin, but also learn the advanced science and technology from the USSR. We need to launch a nationwide upsurge of learning from the Soviet Union how to build our country.[6]

The various aspects of the Soviet model began to take root in China as the upsurge of learning from the USSR got underway. On the economic side, what China learned from the USSR were the modes and methods of the construction of socialism. At its core was the preparation and implementation of the first five-year plan.

The five-year plan was invented by the USSR. The first one was created in 1925 and implemented in 1928. The significance and function of the five-year plan was explained in *The Economic History of the Socialism in USSR* edited by Institute of Economic Research, Soviet Academy of Sciences, as follows:

> The grand tasks of building socialism and of economic construction can't be limited to the scope of the annual plan. We should formulate corresponding long-term plans. From these long-term plans, we can understand the growing needs and requirements of social and material life, predict the further development of these requirements and accurately understand the extent of the increas-

ing resources of the country, develop specific production plans, and determine the basic ratio among the various national economy departments and among the various regions of the country. In the five-year plans, we can quite accurately determine the direction of technological progress as well as the possibilities and economic effects for raising the level of technology in various sectors. Therefore, five-year plans became the major form of developing long-term economic plans for the USSR.[7]

By 1955, the USSR had implemented five five-year plans, and in this process, most aspects of the economic model had become deeply institutionalized.

China's first five-year plan began to be drawn up beginning in the spring of 1951 by the Central Finance and Economic Committee. Altogether there were five versions. Only in 1954, when the first five-year plan had already been in progress for more than two years, was the final version completed.[8] In August 1952, the Central Finance and Economics Committee worked out an outline for the first five-year plan, based on "a Directive for Drawing up a Draft Outline for the Five-year Plan" and on "China's Financial Circumstances and the Tasks of Five-year Construction." The latter became the title of a report by Premier Zhou Enlai. The main thrust of this plan "centered around 156 construction projects to be built with the aid of the Soviet Union, which were in addition to 694 industrial construction projects. Together they constituted a preliminary foundation for our country's socialist industrialization. With regard to agriculture and handicrafts, a preliminary industrial foundation would be created by promoting socialist transformation of agriculture and handicrafts based on collective ownership. Capitalist industry and commerce would be integrated into various forms of state capitalism, thereby establishing the basis for the socialist transformation of the private sector."[9]

The 156 projects, which constituted the main content of the first five-year plan in fact consisted of three components. The first fifty projects were constructed using the Soviet 300 million dollar loan granted in 1950. They involved the most important parts of the national economy, including the energy industries such as coal, electric power and the basic heavy industries such as steel and iron, non-ferrous metal, chemicals, as well as the defense industry.[10] The ninety-one engineering projects were to be built or rebuilt with Soviet help according to an agreement reached by the two government delegations in 1953. The last fifteen projects were added during Khrushchev's visit in 1954 in his capacity as the leader of a Soviet government delegation. The ninety-one projects were the most significant of the three components.

In order to discuss with the Soviets the concrete content of the first five-year plan, and to secure the help and support of the Soviet side, a Chinese government delegation visited the Soviet Union in August 1952 and stayed until May 1953. The delegation was led by Zhou Enlai. He was assisted by two deputies, Vice-Premier Chen Yun and Li Fuchun, the Deputy Director of the Central Finance and Economic Committee.[11] The other members of the delegation consisted mainly of the leaders responsible for key heavy industrial departments, such as energy and metallurgy, while the defense industry was represented by Su Yu, a top military leader. The delegation's composition fully reflected the fact that China attached greatest priority to the development of heavy and military industries. The delegation arrived in Moscow on August 17. Zhou Enlai met Stalin twice.[12] He returned to China on September 22 together with Chen Yun and Su Yu and others. The concrete negotiations were conducted by Li Fuchun. The talks culminated in the signing in May 1953 of "the Agreement on Assistance by the Union of Soviet Socialist Republics and allied governments to the Central Government of the PRC for the Purpose of Developing China's National Economy." According to this agreement, by 1959, the USSR would help China build and rebuild 141 large-scale projects for construction or reconstruction, including fifty projects, the building of which had been in process in the previous three years.

According to the recollections of participants and according to documents related to the 156 projects,[13] the following two aspects about this visit are worthy of special attention: First, learning about Soviet experience in drawing up of a five-year plan. In an article, Yuan Baohua, a participant in the talks, recalled that, "The goal of this visit to the Soviet Union was to discuss the projects for our first five-year plan which needed Soviet assistance. Therefore, in order to align our five-year plan with the program of the Soviet fifth five-year plan, we started to study and to discuss the Soviet plan."[14] The fifth five-year plan (1951–1955) was the Soviet Union's second postwar five-year plan. On the basis of the preceding plan (1946–1950), it aimed chiefly at completing the reconstruction and reorganization of the post-war economy, and at restoring its fixed capital stock by a means of a large-scale process of redistribution of capital and the determination anew of the speed and proportions of the national economy.[15] "By studying and discussing the draft of the Soviet Union's fifth five-year plan, we could systematically understand the formulation of the policy and content of the plan, and it helped us in enriching and improving our own five-year plan."[16]

Second, while the Chinese delegation was in the Soviet Union, its members attended a series of lectures given by Soviet specialists, and also carried out field investigations. With regards to the former, the content of the lectures were set on January 26, 1953 and the lectures began on the 30th. For nearly a month, from January 30 to February 26, 14 vice-chairmen and committee members of the Soviet Planning Committee (Gosplan) gave more than 20 lectures. Each of our ten or so delegation members took detailed notes, which afterwards were used to edit a book, *Questions about Economic Planning*, which was published by the State Planning Commission. *Lectures on the Work*

Plans of the Soviet Union, and which became an important reference when China was preparing and implementing five-year plans.

The topics on which the Soviet experts lectured included the organization of the plan and the method of planned balancing of the national economy. This included plans for industrial production, for ferrous metallurgy, for the fuel industry, for electric power, machine building, basic construction, labor allocation, cadre training and for the assignment and work of technicians. Also, lectures dealt with planning budgetary revenue and expenditure, with a plan for commodity turnover, for production expenses and one for turnover or revolving expenses. And, there were lectures on the agricultural plan, the finance plan, the plan for the supply and balancing of materials and technology, and the plans for statistical work and for new technology.[17]

With regard to site visits, delegation members who were responsible for industry investigated the Soviet Union's heavy industry even before the official negotiations began. They visited major industrial enterprises, among them the Stalin Automobile Works in Moscow, the Red Proletarian Machine Tools Enterprise, the First Ball Bearing Factory, the Transformer Factory, the Electric Motor Enterprise, the Sverdlovsk's Urals Heavy Machinery Factory, the Urals Aluminum Plant, the Synthetic Resins Factory, and a Metallurgical Plant. "By visiting these industrial and mining establishments, we acquired a personal feel for what modernized big industry looked like and we studied their management experience. Although the time spent was short, it truly enriched our knowledge."[18] This was not simply Yuan Baohua's feeling; everyone felt this way. Because they pioneered the industrialization of the new China, their personal experiences were genuinely incorporated into China's industrial development.

In June 1953, soon after the Chinese State delegation returned,

> The Party Central Committee requested the State Planning Commission to examine the opinions offered by the Soviets and with this in view to revise once again the Outline of the five-year plan. By that time, the Soviet Union had accumulated rich experiences in socialist construction, whereas we altogether lacked such experience, since we were just starting out in designing medium and long-term plans. Therefore, the opinions put forth by the Soviets were without a doubt beneficial.[19]

At that time, this probably was a very widespread view in China.

On September 3, 1953, according to Mao Zedong's instruction, Li Fuchun gave a three-part report to the Central Government on the discussions with the Soviet Government concerning aid to China. Part 1 dealt with the tasks and guiding principles for the first five-year plan; Part 2, with the results of the discussion with the Soviet Government; and Part 3, with current tasks. For the current tasks, Li Fuchun proposed that, first, in formulating our country's first five-year plan, we must take as the core the 141 enterprises which the USSR is helping China to construct and restore, and to coordinate various aspects of the national economy in accord with the principle of proportionate development. Second, we should strengthen work on infrastructure. Third, since the Soviet Union is expending much effort to design the 141 enterprises and to help us build them, and since she will send a large number of experts to China, we must therefore complete all of the preparatory construction. Fourth, we have to learn from the Soviet Union and train new talent. He said,

> economic development is a long-term, permanent undertaking, so we need a large quantity of talented technicians. We need a large number of highly trained people who have mastered advanced technology and who will serve the people's cause loyally and devotedly. If we want to foster high-level talent, we must learn from the Soviet Union, but those who are to be trained in more ordinary technical skills must also learn from the Soviet Union.[20]

During preparing the first five-year plan, China was also in accordance with the Soviet Union model and established a set of economic administrative institutions. The planned economic system had thus come into being. In the central government, the State Planning Commission was established in November 1952, and a working party which was responsible for the preparation of the draft outline of Five-Year Plan was established in April 1954. Besides, the central government also set up several specialized management agencies. In the local government, many provincial, municipal and county planning commissions and specialized management agencies were also set up, corresponding to the functional departments of the Central government. In factories, party organizations were set up. Thus, under the leadership of the party committees, production must be on the basis of the plan, and the factory directors have overall responsibility for the factory.

Sino-Soviet economic relation in the 1950s, as in the forms of economic aid, personnel support, and trade relations, actually revolved around the transplantation of the Soviet model to China. But after the Soviet and Chinese Communist Parties started to give prominence and to make public the divergences between them, an adverse current began concretely to influence Sino-Soviet economic relations. It was only then that the so-called cancellation of contracts, cessation of aid, and withdrawal of Soviet experts took place.

The Strengthening of the Soviet Model in China

Application of the Soviet model had a huge positive effect in China. In quite a short time, China established her own industrial system centered on the more than 100 heavy industry projects. For instance, in December 1953, the large-scale rolling mill, the seamless steel tubing mill, and the seventh iron-making furnace of the Anshan Iron and Steel Company began operations, symbolizing the beginning of China's socialist industrialization. In 1956, China's first automobile factory, the first aircraft factory, the first machine tool plant, and the first electronic tube factory were commissioned. Their output filled major gaps in the country's industrial system. In 1957, the Wuhan Changjiang Bridge was completed and opened to traffic.

These achievements were very exciting. They moved the people of China. Because of them, China changed its image of being poor and weak. The positive effects of the Soviet model were thus strikingly displayed. These achievements also demonstrated the superiority of the socialist system. They became symbols for Chinese of what socialism really meant. We may say that in Chinese minds the theory of the Soviet model was equivalent to genuine Marxism, and its application was real socialism. The only goal of the whole party, the country, and the people was to nurture this kind of Marxism and to achieve this kind of socialism.

In China, the Soviet model became identified with the very definition of socialism. It became increasingly institutionalized and all efforts focused on maximizing its positive effects.[21] But just during this period, after Stalin's death, the Soviet Union and the Eastern European states began to alter the Soviet model to different degrees in order to respond to what they perceived to be its negative effects. By then, the Soviet model had been practiced for almost twenty-five years in the Soviet Union, and for some eight years in the Eastern European countries. In the realm of the economy, the Soviet (Stalinist) model gave rise to a number of problems: the lack of separation between party and government, the excessive use of administrative methods in the management of the economy, one-sided emphasis on heavy industry, neglect of light industry and agriculture, excessively rapid industrialization, and collectivization of agriculture. The results were bad. The farmers lacked incentives to work. The plan for national grain purchases could not be fulfilled. Urban consumer goods were scarce, seriously affecting the living standards of urban residents.[22] Therefore, from 1953 on, the Soviet Union and the Eastern European countries started to make adjustments in the original economic system to varying degrees. In essence, this meant that the Soviet model was being "weakened."

In the Soviet Union, Malenkov implemented a "new policy" when he was the chairman of the Council of Ministers (1953–1955). He proposed to accelerate the development of light industry and the food industry, justifying this on the ground that heavy industry had by then scored great achievements. He proposed reduction in the amount of peasants' compulsory sales to the state and reduction of the agricultural tax in order to increase grain production and provide sufficient raw materials to light industry. When Khrushchev came to power, he also focused on agriculture. He reformed agricultural management, expanded the operational rights of collective and state farms, increased agricultural investments, increased the purchase prices for grain and subsidiary products, encouraged and developed household sidelines, and opened up huge wastelands to plant corn in the form of the Virgin Lands' Campaign.

With respect to industry, Khrushchev took aim at the excessively centralized system of management. He eliminated several levels of managerial authority and abolished more than half of the administrative departments during 1953 to 1956. Compared to the political weakening of the Soviet Model—he for instance, for a time put in jeopardy the rights of the central leadership to monopolize power—this economic weakening may not have amounted to much, but in fact both the political and economic model were being "weakened."

How to evaluate the "weakening" of the Soviet Model by Malenkov, Khrushchev and others? One can simply take note of this development, but what is important to note is its profound impact on China. Chinese had equated the sacred cause of socialism with the Soviet Stalinist Model, believing that it represented the material embodiment of Marxism and the truth of socialism. Tampering with the Soviet Model, therefore, had the effect of making Chinese feel that socialism itself was in jeopardy. The weakening of the Model by Khrushchev and others signified to the Chinese a betrayal of Marxism, a form of revisionism, and the restoration of capitalism. Beginning in the mid-1950s, the Chinese began to criticize revisionism, which for them meant the abandonment of the Soviet Model. At first, the Chinese Party did so internally but later it published its critiques openly. In essence the critiques were aimed at the "weakening" of the Soviet Model. Khrushchev's behavior became the object of Chinese criticism. Their evaluation of Khrushchev gave rise to the divergences between the two communist parties, which gained in intensity and finally culminated in a war of theories. At the same time, Mao Zedong, who represented the CCP, responded by continuously strengthening the Soviet Model. Politically, fighting against the personality cult was an important component of "revisionism," a term used by Chinese theorists from the 1950s to the 1970s to label reformists in Eastern Europe and the Soviet Union. At the same time, Mao simply could not accept emulation of Khrushchev's rejection of the personality cult, which was proposed at the 8th National Congress of the Chinese Communist Party in September 1956.

A year later, in October 1957, Chairman Mao proposed at the Third Session of the Eighth Central Committee of the Party "that the contradiction between the proletariat and the bourgeoisie and between the socialist road and the capitalist road were the principal contradictions in China." This was contrary to the thesis put forth a year earlier at the 8th Party Congress, namely that the contradiction between the proletariat and the bourgeoisie had largely been resolved and that the main one was between China's backward agricultural productive forces and the necessity of building an advanced industrial country. Mao's new line, combined with some other factors, had the consequence of unleashing continuous political campaigns culminating in the Cultural Revolution.[23] Economically, since any adjustment of the Soviet Model was treated as revisionist and as amounting to capitalist restoration, we developed the economy by launching the "Great Leap Forward," which entailed the "wind of communism." The result was an economy of "starvation through hunger," a "hand-to-mouth economy," and a "shortage economy." The economic adjustments in the 1960s could not solve basic problems since class struggle became more and more intense, manifested especially in the violence of the Cultural Revolution. Under the impetus of the "ultra-leftist" erroneous line, correct measures to enliven enterprises and develop the socialist commodity economy were treated as a capitalist and revisionist, condemned as the practice of "bourgeois right" and as requiring campaigns to cut off "capitalist tails." Thus, in terms of the economic structure, China did not free itself from the malpractices of the Soviet Model. Instead, there was more centralization and more rigidity. In these ways, the Soviet Model was strengthened. As a result, China experienced more than 20 years of extreme twists and turns in the development process.

Only at the end of the 1970s and especially toward the end of the century did the Reform and Opening-up policy gradually "weaken" the Soviet Model. After the "Cultural Revolution," Chinese economy came close to ruin. Without the policies of reform and opening to the outside world, socialism would be in a blind alley. So, the second generation of the collective leadership of the Party Central Committee started to seriously rethink what real socialism is and how people can build it. The conclusion Deng Xiaoping reached was that:

> What is socialism and what is Marxism? We were not quite clear about this in the past. Marxism attaches utmost importance to developing the productive forces. We have said that socialism is the primary stage of communism and that at the advanced stage the principle of from each according to his ability and to each according to his needs will be applied. This calls for highly developed productive forces and an overwhelming abundance of material wealth. Therefore, the fundamental task for the socialist stage is to develop the productive forces. The superiority of the socialist system is demonstrated, in the final analysis, by faster and greater development of those forces than under the capitalist system. As they develop, the people's material and cultural life will constantly improve.[24]

On this basis, Deng Xiaoping decided to make a change in the Soviet-style planned economy model, and introduce a market economic system. Surely, at that time he was bold. With regard to the relations between planned economy and market economy, Deng Xiaoping emphasized:

> Planning and market forces are not the essential difference between socialism and capitalism. A planned economy is not the definition of socialism, because there is planning under capitalism; the market economy happens under socialism, too. Planning and market forces are both ways of controlling economic activity.[25]

Deng Xiaoping's thesis reverses the misconceptions that planned economy is equal to socialism fundamentally, and promotes the transformation of Chinese economic development model from planned economy to market economy. This is the first step out of the Soviet Union model. But the Soviet Model began with a political mechanism, whereas it was "weakened" in China only in the realm of the management of the economy. This gave rise to the disjunction between economic and political reform. But in addition, as China began to "weaken" the Soviet Model, the relations between the two parties and states also gradually entered a stage of normalization. As the strength of the ideology attenuated, national psychology and state interests became the main features of Sino-Soviet and Sino-Russian relations.

Conclusion

The chapter discusses the transplanting of the Soviet model and its strengthening over time and suggests that the Soviet model played a major role in Sino-Soviet relations in the 1950s. That is, the fact that China and the Soviet Union were at different stages of development was a major underlying cause of the rift. The Soviet Union was in stage when it needed to modify or "weaken" its model, whereas China needed to persist in adapting it to China. Hence, each side had different attitudes toward the model, their understanding of the socialist road differed, resulting in the radical change in the relations between the two countries. At the same time the relations between the two were rich and complicated, so one shouldn't go too far in attributing the conflict entirely to the changing perceptions of the value of the Soviet (Stalinist) model. Still, this author believes that at least in the 1950s, the Soviet model was the decisive factor in the relationship. In studying the economic relations between the two countries, attention must be paid to this point.

Notes

1. Kong Hanbing, "Zhong-Su guanxishi de tedian jiqi yanjiu xianzhuang pingxi" [The characteristics of the history of the Sino-Soviet relations and the status of current research], *Eguo yanjiu* [Russian studies], no. 2 (2004): 64–68.

2. The major works had been published by (Yugoslavia) Maerkeweiai, *Commenting on Stalinist Models by Foreign Scholars* (Beijing: Zhongyang bianyi chubanshe, 1995). Li Zongyu, *Sidalin moshi yanjiu* [Studies of Stalin models] (Beijing: Zhongyang bianyi chubanshe, 1999). Chen Chongwu, *Sidalin moshi de xiandai fansi* [A reflection of the Stalinist models] (Kunming: Yunnan renmin chubanshe, 2004).

3. Chen Mingxian, *Xinzhongguo sishiwu nian yanjiu* [Studies of forty-five years of new China] (hereinafter as *Xingzhougguo*) (Beijing: Beijing keji daxue chubanshe, 1994), 70–85.

4. Kong Hanbing, "Sulian moshi zai zhongguo de queli: qianti he biaoxian" [The establishment of the Soviet model in China: its premise and manifestations], *Shanghai danshi yu dangjian* [History and construction of the CCP in Shanghai], no. 9 (2001): 33–37.

5. Mao Zedong, "Lun renmin minzhu zhuanzheng," [On the people's democratic dictatorship], *Mao Zedong xunji (hedingben)* [Selected works of Mao Zedong (consolidated edition)] (Beijing: Renmin chubanshe, 1969), 1359–1360.

6. *Xinhua baogao* [Xinhua report], no. 3 (1955).

7. Institute for Economic Research, Soviet Academy of Sciences, *Sulian shehui zhuyi jingjishi disanjuan* [The economic history of Soviet socialism, vol. 3] (Beijing: Sanlien shudian chubanshe, 1982), 9.

8. Liu Suinian, *Diyige wunian jihua shiqi de guomin jingji* [The national economy during the First Five-Year Plan] (Haerbin: Heilongjiang renmin chubanshe, 1984), 17–19.

9. Chen Mingxian, *Xinzhongguo*, 145.

10. For details of the 50 projects, see *Zhou Enlai nianpu* [Chronicles of Zhou Enlai] (Beijing: Zhongyang wenxian chubanshe, 1997), 256.

11. *Xinzhongguo waijiao fengyun (dierji)* [New China's stormy diplomacy, vol. 2] (Beijing: Shijie zhishi chubanshe, 1991), 15.

12. a.m. Ledovski, *Stalin he Zhongguo* [Stalin and China] (Beijing: Xinhua chubanshe, 2001), 179–204.

13. Yuan Baohua, "Fusu tanpan de riri yeye" [Days and nights of negotiating with the Soviet Union] (hereinafter as "Fusu tanpan de riri yeye"), *Dangdai Zhongguoshi yanjiu* [Studies of contemporary Chinese history], no. 1 (1996), 16–26. "Jianguo chuqi 156 xiang jianshe gongcheng wenxian xuanzhai" [Selected documents of the 156 project in the early years of China] (1952/9 to 1954/10). *Dangde wenxian* [Party documents], no. 5 (1999): 3–27. Su Shifang, "Guanyu wushi niandai woguo cong Sulian jinkou jishu he chengtao shebei de huigu," [Remembering the importation of complete sets of technology and equipments from the Soviet Union in the 1950s], *Dangdai Zhongguoshi yanjiu* [Studies of contemporary Chinese history], no. 5 (1998): 84, 94, 5.

14. Yuan Baohua, "Fusu tanpan de riri yeye," *Dangdai Zhongguoshi yanjiu* [Studies of contemporary Chinese history], no. 1 (1996).

15. Institute of Economic Research, Soviet Academy of Sciences, *Sulian shehui zhuyi jinjishi, diliujuan* [The economic history of Soviet socialism, vol. 6] (Beijing: Dongfang chubanshe, 1986), 283–85.

16. Yuan Baohua, "Fusu tanpan de riri yeye," *Dangdai Zhongguoshi yanjiu* [Studies of contemporary Chinese history], no. 1 (1996).

17. Yuan Baohua, "Fusu tanpan de riri yeye."

18. Yuan Baohua, "Fusu tanpan de riri yeye."

19. Liu Suinian, *Di yige wunian jihua shiqi de guomin jingji* [National economy during the First Five-Year Plan] (Haerbin: Heilongjiang renmin chubanshe, 1984), 19.

20. "Li Fuchun Guanyu yu Sulian zhengfu shangtan dui woguo yuanzhu wenti de baogao" [Li Fuchun's report on discussions concerning the Soviet governmental aid to China], *Dangde wenxian* [Party documents], no. 5 (1999): 9–18.

21. The political system, higher education system and ideology had been transplanted to China during the first five-year plan period. This chapter does not address these issues due to the limitations of space. For such discussion, see Kong Hanbing, *Zhong-Su guanxi jiqi dui zhongguo shehui de yingxiang* [The Sino-Soviet relations and its influence on China's social development] (Beijing: Zhongguo guoji guangbo chubanshe, 2004), 128–34.

22. See Zhou Shangwen, *Xinbian Sulienshi* [Newly compiled Soviet history] (Shanghai: Renmin chubanshe, 1990), 243–46, 285–90, and 498–99. Joy Schopflin, "The Practice of Stalinism in Eastern Europe," *Haiwai xuezhe lun Sulian moshi* [Overseas scholars discussing the Stalinist models] (Beijing: Zhongyang bianyi chubanshe, 1995), 195–223.

23. *Zhonggong zhongyang guanyu jianguo yilai dang de ruogan wenti de jueyi* [Resolutions of the CCP central committee concerning some questions of the CCP since the founding of the PRC] (Beijing: Renmin chubanshe, 1981), 21–22.

24. Deng Xiaoping, "Jianshe you Zhongguo tese de shehuizhuyi" [To build socialism with Chinese characteristics] *Deng Xiaoping xuanji disanjuan* [Selected works of Deng Xiaoping, vol. 3] (hereinafter as *Deng Xiaoping xuanji 3*) (Beijing: Renmin chubanshe, 1993), 63.

25. *Deng Xiaoping xuanji 3*, 373.

7

"Get Organized": The Impact of two Soviet Models on the CCP's Rural Strategy, 1949–1953[1]

Xiaojia Hou

ASSESSING SOVIET INFLUENCE ON THE PRC is a difficult task. On the one hand, it was massive, especially with regard to basic norms and perceptions, such as the faith that the development of the "productive forces" made possible by socialist "relations of production" would eventually yield a communist future as a solution for all problems "and that "socialism is the antidote to capitalism."[2] On the other hand, when it comes to specific policies and actions, Soviet input should be examined with caution, given contemporary Chinese's sensibility about sovereignty, China's fluctuating relationships with the Soviet Union, the complexity of Chinese domestic politics and ultimately the dichotomy between prescriptions and actual implementation.

This chapter examines the Soviet role in China's agricultural cooperativization movement of 1949–1953 as a case that demonstrates how Soviet ideas were conceptualized, selected and used. I argue that around the time of the founding of the PRC, Chinese had available to them two different interpretations of Lenin's "Cooperative Plan" of 1923. Mao Zedong followed Stalin's interpretation, which emphasized collective farms as the correct form of rural socialism. For Mao, this meant organizing mutual aid teams which would eventually develop into Soviet-style collective farms. Another interpretation of Lenin, elaborated by Bukharin in the mid-1920s and taken up by Zhang Wentian and Liu Shaoqi in 1948, was that socialism would be achieved through the agency of the supply and marketing cooperative (SMCs), which would link individual peasants to the urban-socialist sector. In 1949, the CCP officially adopted the latter, but soon abandoned it, instead, essentially following Stalin's collectivization model. By 1951, the route of collective farms won out over the SMCs. In the course of adopting the collectivization model, Stalin's approach to collectivization won out. Yet, paradoxically, the actual advice that Stalin gave in those years was that the Chinese should pursue a moderate course and proceed very slowly in pushing socialist transformation.

Yan'an: Learning about Stalin's Collectivization

In the early Yan'an era, the party mainly lived on the subsidy provided by the Nationalist Party.[3] Supplied by outside funds, the CCP showed little interest in peasant production or in levying taxes on peasants.[4] As the anti-Japanese war approached a stalemate in 1939, conflicts between the CCP and the Nationalist Party intensified. The CCP began extracting more resources within the base areas. The grain tax jumped from 14,000 *dan* in 1937 or 1.3 percent of output in the Shan-Gan-Ning base area to over 200,000 *dan* in 1941. Peasants were furious. Peasants revolts were reported.[5] In 1941, the Nationalist Party completely terminated the subsidy and further imposed an economic embargo against the Shan-Gan-Ning base area. The Japanese army began its "three-all" offensive against the CCP. The CCP base areas shrank and the population dropped. The economy was on the verge of collapse. CCP-peasants relations were under stress, Mao was cursed by peasants.[6] Now, for the CCP the most urgent issue was boosting agricultural production, thereby providing greater resources for the CCP and its military.[7]

Facing the enormous hardships in 1941 the CCP sent an investigation group, led by the CCP Propaganda head Zhang Wentian, to Shanxi province to "explore how to increase agricultural production and improve peasants' livelihood."[8] Spending nearly a year in Shanxi, Zhang Wentian examined rural conditions, in my view, in a much more thorough way than Mao Zedong ever did, with the sole purpose of learning how to increase agricultural output. The investigation convinced Zhang Wentian of the complexity of the rural economy. Zhang realized that lack of land was not the sole cause of rural poverty. Early during his investigation, he asserted that middle peasants were the main force of the rural economy.[9] Toward the end of his investigation, he came to learn of the key role of rich peasants in rural prosperity. He asserted that the rich peasant economy would ultimately benefit the whole society. He pointedly observed that "it is a mistake to improve people's livelihood by redistributing other people's wealth; it is better to do so by increasing production and increasing social wealth."[10] He suggested providing economic incentives to encourage new capitalism and commerce. Zhang's ideas were very congenial to the establishment of SMCs. This report, however, was suppressed and not published until 1989. Upon returning to Yan'an, Zhang Wentian became a major target of the Yan'an rectification movement. He was immediately required to participate and to criticize himself again and again. He was not given a chance to work on economic issues, despite the knowledge he had acquired during his yearlong investigation.

Mao Zedong was also thinking about agriculture. But he took a different orientation and placed more efforts on reorganizing laborers rather than offering economic incentives.[11] As the CCP raised its extraction quota, more peasants fled or simply stopped working assiduously. It was important to exert certain control over peasants. Everyone, including the elderly, women and "lazy" ones, should be participating in rural production. So Mao advocated organizing mutual aid teams in the entire base areas, through which the party would be able to "persuade" peasants to plant the kinds of crops the party was in need of. Moreover, those organizations were coordinated with wartime services.

Reorganizing peasants was not only an economic issue, but a political one.[12] Inspired by Soviet experience, Mao endowed mutual aid teams with greater meaning. Years of intense study of Soviet works in Yan'an now came to fruition.

One of the indispensable qualifications for leading a communist movement was to establish one's reputation as a Marxist theoretician. In the Long March, Mao had established his reputation as a prominent military leader, but he remained weak in Marxist theories. So after settling in Yan'an, Mao devoted himself to studying Marxist theories. A close look of his reading list reveals that Mao was obviously in favor of textbooks that introduced Marxism, most of which were published in the Soviet Union in the 1930s, rather than original Marxist classics.[13] It turned out that in terms of Marxist theories, Mao was unable to compete with his rivals, the "returned student faction" [*liusu pai*], one of whom was Zhang Wentian.[14] At this point, Stalin's *Short Course* on CPSU history, discussed in Chapter 5, provided Mao with a timely theoretical instrument.[15]

This book, it will be recalled, was published in the Soviet Union in 1938, was translated into Chinese and sent back to Yan'an in the same year. The book became a "crash-course" for teaching CCP cadres in party schools. In Yan'an Rectification Movement of 1941–1943, the book was called "the encyclopedia of Marxism" and was listed as the number 1 "must-read" text for high-level CCP cadres.[16]

Mao Zedong himself was particularly fond of this book. He used this book to criticize those comrades who "studied Marxism-Leninism not to meet the needs of revolutionary practice, but purely for the sake of study" and who were unable to "apply the viewpoint and method of Marx, Engels, Lenin and Stalin to the concrete study of China's present conditions."[17] This book provided Mao with a new model of studying Marxist theory and demonstrated to him new methods of acquiring authority. For example, inspired by the composition of *Short Course*, Mao Zedong ordered compilation of a documentary history, *From the Sixth Congress—The CCP's Internal Secretariat's Documents*, which was aimed at reconstructing the CCP's past so as to legitimize Mao's leadership as well as to lay the groundwork for Mao's role as a leading theorist.[18]

The *Short Course* served as Mao's road map for building socialism in China. Benjamin Schwartz notes that Mao had uncritically accepted the image of "socialism" as described in *Short Course*. Li Hua-yu goes further arguing that Mao had closely followed the steps outlined by Stalin in the *Short Course* and created a Stalinist economic structure after 1949.[19] What is relevant here is that in the early 1940s, when Mao was worried about the economic crisis in the base areas and searched for a method to effectively reorganize peasants, The *Short Course* taught Mao an ideal formula that could link the current mutual aid teams to a socialist future. The *Short Course* told Mao that Lenin "regarded co-operative societies in general, and agricultural cooperative societies in particular, as a means of transition—a means within the reach and understanding of the peasant millions —from small, individual farming to large-scale producing associations, or collective farms."[20] The *Short Course* also depicted the effectiveness and popularity of collective farms among Soviet peasants. Deeply impressed by this glorious Soviet history, in 1943, Mao Zedong came to portray the socialist future for Chinese peasants in his famous speech "get organized,"

> Among the peasant masses a system of individual economy has prevailed for thousands of years, with each family or household forming a productive unit. This scattered, individual form of production is the economic foundation of feudal rule and keeps the peasants in perpetual poverty. The only way to change it is gradual collectivization, and the only way to bring about collectivization, according to Lenin, is through cooperatives.[21]

Mao now came to see individual peasant farming as a backward phenomenon, regarding collective farming as signifying progress in production methods and a better way of "liberating" the productive forces. When Mao Zedong utilized the *Short Course* to establish his authority in interpreting Marxist theory, he was at the same time learning Marxist theories as interpreted by Stalin and the revolutionary language of the Bolsheviks. Evidently he absorbed the language and concepts of *Short Course* in his own work. Thus, the paragraph just quoted closely resembles the wording of the *Short Course*.[22]

Armed with Stalinist theory and Bolshevik language, Mao Zedong believed that he found an ultimate way to liberate Chinese peasants. He now would not only allocate land to poor peasants, but also teach them how to farm in groups and transform them into new laborers and lead them into a stage of socialism.

The process started with mutual aid teams, which were a traditional practice among Chinese peasants. There were many types of mutual aid teams, most of them temporary and aimed at overcoming labor or livestock shortages during the busy season. The fundamental principle was reciprocity.[23] They had nothing to do with collective ownership. But after Mao released his "Get Organized," mutual aid teams evolved into "a renovation of the production system, a revolution of relations of production among the people."[24] Even though in 1943, mutual aid teams were built on the ground of private ownership, Mao portrayed them as possessing a more progressive aspect and a necessary means in the transition to collective farms. As he said, "At present they are only of a rudimentary type and must go through several stages of development before they can become cooperatives of the Soviet type known as collective farms."[25]

Mao's speeches on mutual aid teams and collectivization were widely circulated. The slogan "get organized" was never questioned. The idea that in addition to the improvement of agricultural technology, the organization of production was a determining factor in increasing agricultural productivity was disseminated. In 1943–44, nearly all base areas launched movements to build mutual aid teams. It turns out that "get organized" was not a great success. Its effectiveness in improving productivity was rarely demonstrated, and, perhaps, the teams were even a hindrance to higher productivity.[26] Nevertheless, their influence could hardly be overestimated. Most rank and file party members knew the term "get organized," although they rarely understood its socialist implications. What they knew was that mutual aid teams were politically correct, that they came from Soviet models, had something to do with socialism and were strongly endorsed by Chairman Mao. As Mao Zedong had established his personal cult in the middle 1940s, few CCP cadres dared to question his views. So even failed mutual aid teams were repeatedly reported as successful, and the idea itself was not challenged. The party attributed the failures to bad practices, not the idea itself. Further, it was the party's responsibility to figure out how to better monitor peasants. Such kind of mentality was common and long lasting. In 1950, Zhang Wentian even used the term "mutual aid fetishism" to describe the popular belief in the myth of mutual aid teams in solving rural problems.[27]

The CCP eventually managed to overcome the financial crisis by the Great Production Campaign as the CCP claimed or through the opium trade as

Chen Yung-fa analyzes, [28] or by both. In the middle 1940s, after the anti-Japanese war and after the onset of civil war between the CCP and the Nationalist Party began, the rural economy again was marginalized. In order to mobilize peasants and to expropriate more resources for the war, from 1946 to 1948, radical land reform was carried out in north China that resulted in enormous disruptions of rural production.[29] The CCP was aware of excesses and disruptions, but for the wartime mobilization it was willing to sacrifice rural production.[30]

Supply and Marketing Cooperatives: An Alternative

In 1948, when the victory against the Nationalist Party approached, the CCP began preparing to rule the country. The Soviet model became their instant choice. CCP leaders frequently consulted with Stalin on a wide range of important issues.[31] As Soviet archives reveal, the CCP had planned to establish a socialist government, but Stalin did not support it. From Stalin's perspective, China was not yet at the stage of building socialism. He suggested that a socialist transition was premature and that the Chinese comrades should adopt a moderate and gradual course. As he cabled to Mao, "for the time being no nationalization of all land and no abolition of private ownership of land will be effected, no confiscation of the property of the commercial and industrial bourgeoisie, from the petty up to the big bourgeoisie, no confiscation of the property not only of big landowners, but also of the middle and small ones living by hired labor."[32] The CCP seemed to have accepted his suggestions. As Liu Shaoqi, secretary of Central Committee of the CCP and the number two in the hierarchy, told Mikoyan, who visited the CCP in early 1949 as Stalin's special envoy, "The transition to socialism will be lengthy in terms of time, and harsh in terms of struggle . . . we shall have to wait 10 to 15 years for the full offensive against capitalist elements in our economy."[33] The Second Plenary Session of the CCP's Seventh Central Committee in early 1949 announced new strategies of accommodating a mixed economy and the development of capitalism under the banner of "New Democracy."

In projecting the strategy of building new China, Liu Shaoqi considered China's situation in 1948 similar to that of the Soviet Union during the NEP, as he said, "Our policies are very similar to the conditions of the USSR before the capitalist uprising in 1918 and of their NEP policies, so their experience is worth thinking about."[34] Under such circumstances, Lenin's NEP was revisited and regarded as a valuable guide. Looking upon Lenin's NEP, some CCP leaders discovered another form, the Supply and Marketing Cooperatives to draw peasants into the state's orbit.

In 1923, Lenin published his far-reaching article "On Cooperation" stating that "if the whole of the peasantry were organized in cooperatives, we would be standing firmly with both feet on the soil of Socialism."[35] Lenin clearly underlined the role of cooperatives in building a socialist society, yet he died in 1924 without elaborating on it. His followers needed to figure out what kind of cooperatives should be created. In the late 1920s, heated debates arose between Bukharin and Stalin.[36] Roughly speaking, Bukharin believed that Lenin's cooperatives referred to supply and marketing cooperatives by which the state could organize small producers through commodity circulation and indirectly control them through economic regulation. In his plan a private rural economy would be allowed for a long time. Stalin, on the other hand, interpreted Lenin's cooperatives as referring to producers' cooperatives in which the state would organize small producers in collective production and directly administer them. The private sector would be eliminated. It has been generally agreed among present-day scholars that Lenin had little to say about producers' cooperatives in his article.[37] But, in the late 1920s, Bukharin was politically defeated and his theories were erased from Soviet history. Later on, the *Short Course* was compiled in which Lenin's ideas were twisted in Stalin's favor.

Disciples of the *Short Course*, such as Mao Zedong, probably believed that Lenin had originally advocated collectivization in the form of producers' cooperatives and did not know much about Bukharin's version. Plus, influenced by the Soviet economic model, many CCP leaders did not fully acknowledge the importance of commerce in production and tended to overlook commerce and commercial institutions.[38]

Nevertheless, some CCP comrades did know about Bukharin's version and were thus able to understand better the actual dynamics of the rural economy. Zhang Wentian was one of them. He studied and taught in Moscow between 1925 and 1930, years when Bukharin was still powerful. In the CCP Zhang was revered for his achievements in Marxism and Leninism. The less mentioned achievement of his is he that he was also known, at least in the leading CCP circle, for his broad knowledge of Bukharin.[39] After his year-long investigation in Shanxi, he was aware that rural economy was much more complex than implied by class struggles or mutual aid teams. In 1945, after making thorough self-criticisms that finally convinced Mao Zedong of his loyalty, Zhang Wentian was sent to take charge of Heijiang province, a province in northeast China which was later in 1949 merged into Heilongjiang province. In 1947 and 1948, radical land reform was carried out in northeast China, land was equally redistributed among peasants, followed by collective-style mutual aid teams, most of which soon collapsed, plunging the countryside in chaos. As the civil war came to an end, rural prosperity and stability became a major concern. Zhang Wentian, as a local leader, increasingly felt the economic pressure and again turned to economic issues. He knew that his CCP comrades had accumulated enough experiences to fight landlords, but they had not even begun to study the economy.[40] After a month of research on the urban and rural economy, he spoke firmly against forceful collectivization and suggested shifting the party's guideline from encouraging class struggle to encouraging rural production. Acknowledging the ultimate future of collectivization, he did not consider it was the time to start it in China. Instead, he proposed SMCs, a Soviet model that was largely omitted in the *Short Course*.

Li Hua-yu convincingly shows how Zhang Wentian was deeply influenced by Lenin's idea of the "transition from capitalism to socialism" and NEP policy.[41] I further argue here that Zhang had also incorporated Bukharin's theory, although he did not give Bukharin, known then as a traitor, any credit. As had Bukharin, Zhang asserted that one key in the transition to socialism was to organize SMCs,

> At present, SMCs in the countryside are the economic headquarters that direct the economic activities of small producers and the central linkage between agricultural production and consumption. After the land reform, they were the most important form of organization for peasants and small handicraftsmen. Without cooperatives, it would be impossible to organize economically thousands and thousands of small agricultural producers.[42]

Zhang concluded that SMCs "can not only facilitate the circulation of commodities between cities and the countryside, but also connect the state-owned economy with small producers."[43] Zhang reminded his comrades that the efforts at forced collectivization had resulted in failure and suggested securing peasants' right to private property.[44] Zhang Wentian's theory closely resembled Bukharin's project of SMCs. He then suggested including cooperatives into the major economic sectors of New Democracy.

Zhang Wentian was not the only one who discovered the form of SMC. At the same time, Liu Shaoqi also started to talk about SMCs. He planned to integrate the country's whole economy through marketing administration, and the SMC was the instrument to achieve this goal.[45] Liu pointed out that Lenin and Stalin both had emphasized the importance of cooperatives, but the CCP had not systematically worked on this matter.[46] He underscored that the alliance between cooperatives and the state-owned economy would lead China toward socialism. He particularly valued the key role of SMCs:

> Obviously, without widespread SMCs as the bridge to connect small producers and the state-owned economy, the country led by proletarians will not forcefully guide hundreds of thousands of scattered small producers; therefore, the

construction of the national economy of New Democracy will not proceed smoothly.[47]

Liu Shaoqi proposed building SMCs as the means of assuring that hundreds of thousands of peasants would produce in accordance with proletarians' demands. A close reading of Liu's works on cooperatives in this period reveals that his language was not based on the *Short Course,* but on Lenin's work during the NEP. His interpretation of Lenin's "On Cooperation" resembled Bukharin's too. Liu Shaoqi showed little interest in forming mutual aid teams and his use of the term cooperatives often did not include mutual aid teams.[48]

Liu's proposals seemed to be welcomed by the CCP leaders. Even Chairman Mao said "Comrade Liu Shaoqi did great research on this (cooperative) issue."[49] The cooperative economy was then formally included as one of the five major sectors of New Democracy economy. As part of the New Democracy policy, peasants were encouraged to work for themselves and to accumulate family wealth. Private ownership of land was protected. SMCs, not mutual aid teams, were propagandized to be established on a large scale. China was not going to launch collectivization for years to come. Liu Shaoqi told Mikoyan that "the transfer of agriculture onto socialist lines, we envisage only on condition that agriculture has been provided an industrial base."[50] In front of Mikoyan, Mao appeared to agree with Liu Shaoqi, as he told Mikoyan "we have given land to the peasants, but we have not given them the commodities they need and which we do not have. If we do not develop industry, we shall not be able to supply the peasants with commodities."[51] Mikoyan was content with both. In Liu Shaoqi's meeting with Stalin in summer 1949, this issue was not ever brought up.

Deep in Mao Zedong's heart, he was not fully convinced by the virtues of SMCs and he warned that it was wrong to let peasants take their course.[52] As early as in September 1948, he envisioned new China's economy as composed of the state economy, an agricultural economy which was developing from the private sector toward the collective economy and the economy of small artisans and capitalists.[53] Mao Zedong was not enthusiastic about SMCs. When he used the term cooperatives, in contrast to Liu Shaoqi, he mainly referred to mutual aid teams, rarely to SMCs.[54]

During his prolonged visit to the Soviet Union in the winter of 1949–1950, Mao took every opportunity to learn about economic progress in the Soviet Union.[55] On his way back to China, he managed to visit modern factories, collective farms and meet with managers. As he arrived in Shenyang in March 1950, Mao spoke with some passion to high-rank cadres in the Northeast Bureau of how much he was impressed by Soviet achievements. Mao concluded that "the history of the development of the first Socialist country has provided us the best experience. We can apply their experience."[56] Undoubtedly, this assertion reached Gao Gang, a member of the Politburo and chairman of the Northeast Bureau, and further encouraged his plan of emulating the Soviet Union in Northeast China (see next section).

Although Mao Zedong was passionate about the Soviet model, in the early 1950s, as Teiwes rightly observes, "while reserving the right to insist on his own way in matters of prime concern such as the Korean decision, Mao's general approach was to encourage broad discussion in order to reach a consensus," especially in areas where he acknowledged his inadequacies.[57] The economy was certainly one of them. Before Mao Zedong figured out a plan that could convince even himself, he decided to let his comrades to take care of the issue. He did not articulate his own views and did not challenge Liu Shaoqi's rural policy until July 1951. Challenges for Liu Shaoqi were to come from regional and provincial leaders.

Gao Gang: Playing the Ideological Card

The New Democracy policy was not unanimously supported among CCP cadres. Theoretically this policy was grounded on Lenin's NEP. But in 1949, not many CCP cadres knew about NEP, as Bo Yibo recalled.[58] Quite the contrary, many cadres were confused by it and questioned the necessity of tolerating capitalism. As Liu Shaoqi told Mikoyan, "In the party there are people who are inclined to a leftist, voluntaristic, hasty construction of socialism. This tendency reveals itself in the fact there are those who draw up unrealistic plans in which they fail to allow for our possibilities."[59] Of these leftists, Gao Gang was the most prominent. He advocated following the Stalin model as depicted in Stalin's writings of the late 1920s and realizing the socialist transformation of agriculture and industry. Being called the "king of Manchuria," he in the northeast region raised a slogan "building a model of Soviet socialism." In the summer 1949, after visiting collective farms in the Soviet Union, Gao Gang decided to aim for an agricultural breakthrough. He made a speech committing himself to bolstering the transition to collectivization by elaborating on Mao's terms "get organized" and "actively developing (agriculture) toward (modernization and) collectivization."[60] He implied that putting off collectivization with the excuse of lacking machines was a mistake of "line." On January 4, 1950, *Northeast Daily* published Gao Gang's speech that called for upgrading mutual aid teams further and promised to grant them financial incentives. It called on mutual aid teams to challenge individual farmers.[61]

Not surprisingly, Liu Shaoqi was not pleased with Gao Gang's behavior. In principle, he did not approve of an immediate transition to socialism. For rural policies, he considered that mutual aid teams in the northeast China were based on a broken and impoverished individual economy and were not a good basis for socialism. He did not believe that it was possible for mutual aid teams to develop into future collective farms and with little hesitation, he criticized Gao Gang for "leftist" errors.[62]

Gao Gang in no way accepted this charge. Unable to confront with Liu Shaoqi directly at that time, he chose to play the Soviet card. In addition to his unchallenged authority in the northeast region, he was also known for his close relationship with Soviet comrades. He had formed a particularly friendly relationship with Ivan Kovalev, Stalin's special envoy to the CCP between 1948 and 1950. Kovalev referred to Gao Gang as a "true comrade" and "an exceptional man." Andrei Ledovsky who served as Consul-General in Mukden between 1950 and 1952 also admired Gao Gang and considered him an orthodox pro-Soviet communist sympathetic to the Soviet model of economic planning.[63] Gao Gang did not waste these resources. Soon after he was criticized by Liu Shaoqi, details of this CCP internal conversation reached Stalin through Kovalev. Kovalev, by his own judgment or inspired by Gao Gang, further hinted to Stalin that divergences in different economic plans among the CCP were in essence signs of political line struggle. He claimed that pro-American and anti-Soviet sentiments were rife in the CCP. Liu Shaoqi and Bo Yibo were among these who allegedly showed their pro-American sentiment. Kovalev accused Liu Shaoqi of scheming to make a groundless attack upon Gao Gang. In this report, Kovalev's evaluations of CCP leaders, except of Gao Gang, were in general negative.[64] Stalin appeared to disapprove of this report and later even handed it to Mao Zedong. Mao's true reaction to this report and how he interpreted Stalin's motives are not known. Gao Gang's allegedly pro-Soviet sympathies and unusually close relationship with Soviet comrades might have doomed him to eventually fall, as Kovalev asserted and Ledovsky suspected.[65] But Kovalev's report must have alerted Mao of the correlation between pro-capitalist and pro-American attitudes. After all, in 1950 Stalin was highly wary of the possibility of a rapprochement between China and the United States.

Gao Gang then played the ideological card. In February 1950, he wrote to Mao Zedong claiming that Liu Shaoqi's speech in Tianjin in 1949 exposed Liu's view that China could only follow the road of capitalism, not of socialism. Gao Gang warned Mao that such kind of views had generated negative influences both in the CCP and in the international communist community. Gao Gang further reported to Mao that his Soviet comrades did not think comrade Liu Shaoqi was a true Marxist.[66] Indeed, the New Democracy policy did generate suspicion among international communists. For example, Velio Spano, a prominent Italian Communist who had traveled extensively in

China, requested to have a confidential talk with the Soviet chargé d'affaires in Beijing, P.A. Shibaev. Specifically, Spano wanted to talk with Shibaev, not as a Soviet diplomat, but as a member of the Bolshevik Communist Party. Spano declared that "blindness to the danger of capitalism is swiftly regenerating itself and the underrating of the working class was typical of the majority of top functionaries in China he had talked with."[67] Valuing their reputation in the international communist movement, for CCP leaders to be ideological deviants was of course a serious matter.

Support for an immediate transition to socialism was also common among the CCP rank and file. When Zhang Wentian strongly denounced the idea that organizing all peasants into mutual aid teams was the only way of preventing peasants from sliding to capitalism, many CCP cadres in the northeast region asked, "Since our goal is agricultural collectivization, why don't we carry it out today?"[68] *Northeast Daily* published an article claiming that the biased emphasis on peasants' own preferences was in fact worship of the spontaneity of the masses that violated Mao's assertion of not "letting peasants take their own course."[69]

Before long, in January 1950, the CC CCP appointed Zhang, without consulting with him, as a Chinese delegate to the United Nation. Zhang Wentian was astonished by this appointment and reluctantly accepted the post. He made several appeals to return to the economic sector, receiving no responses.[70] The northeast region now came under the full control of Gao Gang. Numerous mutual aid teams were built in the northeast region, quite a few incidents of forcing peasants into mutual aid teams or squeezing individual farmers were reported. Yet no punishment was imposed on Gao Gang.

Liu Shaoqi did not neglect the Soviet channel either. In the same month when Gao Gang's speech was published in the *Northeast Daily* in January 1950, Liu Shaoqi was interviewed by O.I. Chechetkina, a *Pravda* correspondent. In the interview, Liu focused on peasant issues. He told Chechetkina,

Wealthy farmers will help productivity increase and will supply towns with goods . . . The new wealthy farmers are only beginning to appear and should not be curbed . . . If we try ordering capitalism to stop, it will get us nowhere. On the contrary, we shall make things worse, because millions of peasants will turn against our regime.[71]

Chechetkina dutifully sent this report back to Moscow,[72] but we do not know the reaction from the Soviet side. On August 26, 1950, Liu Shaoqi told Soviet Ambassador N.V. Roshchin that "we are most grateful to Comrade Stalin for his timely advice about improving relations with private capital, both urban and rural, about the treatment of wealthy farmers."[73] As Meliksetov notes, the political backing by Stalin was of tremendous importance for Liu Shaoqi.[74]

Gao Gang portrayed himself as an orthodox pro-Soviet communist and justified his policy of "get organized" with the theory based on Stalin's "On Several Problems of Leninism."[75] Of course, this does not mean that the faith in Stalin's theory alone drove Gao Gang to challenge Liu Shaoqi. Gao Gang probably was more motivated by his political ambition: at the time, he was conspiring to take over Liu Shaoqi's position. The difference between Liu and Mao on New Democracy policy in general, on agricultural cooperatives in particular,[76] provided him with a chance to gain Mao's favor. At the same time, we should not overlook the impact of Soviet collectivization theory, with which CCP cadres were quite familiar, thanks to Mao's advocacy in the mid-1940s. A plan that differed from it would easily generate suspicions and confusion. In such circumstances, Gao Gang thus played his Soviet card to attack Liu Shaoqi ideologically.

Paradoxically, as mentioned earlier, at this time Stalin himself was advising the CCP to accommodate capitalism, and Liu Shaoqi was following his suggestions, whereas Gao Gang used Stalin's early work to attack Liu Shaoqi and he was supported by his Soviet comrades who should have known Stalin's current attitudes. Moreover, in the late 1920s Stalin insisted on collectivization because he was convinced that collective farms and state farms were able to turn in much higher portion of agricultural products to the state for industrialization than individual farmers. In other words, he launched collectivization to achieve "primitive socialist accumulation."

But this was not Gao Gang's line. He proposed that accumulation should mainly come from industry itself, by increasing productivity and saving more; next it should come from city taxes. Only the third source was agricultural taxes. He explicitly warned not to increase agricultural taxes and tried to lower the "scissor's price" to protect peasants. In his opinion, peasants should not be asked to make sacrifices for the sake of industrialization. If one class was to be sacrificed, it was national capitalists.[77] On what basis, then, did Gao Gang raised his proposal of transiting to collectivization? Did Gao Gang propose to transit to collectivization for the sake of collectivization? Does this mean that after years of propaganda, collectivization had become a symbol of advancement? Did it demonstrate the power of ideology?[78] Alas, documents and records available on Gao Gang are too scarce to answer those questions.

Soviet Collective Farms Emerge as the Model for China

When the Korean War broke out in June 1950 and China intervened in October, Gao Gang, as the number one leader of the northeast China that borders Korea, was deeply immersed in ongoing war logistics and much less involved in direct struggles with Liu Shaoqi, for the year to come. Between 1950 and 1951, Liu Shaoqi concentrated on the cooperative issue in order to apply his interpretation of the teaching of Lenin's "On Cooperatives."[79] He published a series of articles on it, proposing to build SMCs on a national scale. However, he then ran into another challenge from below. It was from Lai Ruoyu, the vice Secretary of the CCP Shanxi Provincial Committee who was determined that "Without collectivization, there is no modernization. . . . We now should move step by step toward this goal."[80] He proposed starting with mutual aid teams, as Mao Zedong suggested in the 1940s, followed by agricultural producers' cooperatives,[81] then move up toward collective farms. Unlike Gao Gang, Lai applied a bottom-up strategy to advance his agenda and thus played the "peasant" card.[82] A debate between Lai Ruoyu and Liu Shaoqi ensued which lasted over a year from mid-1950 to mid-1951. Liu Shaoqi took a position that adhered strictly to the doctrine of New Democracy. He introduced two principles. First, no attempt should be made to undermine private ownership in the countryside; second, mechanization was a prerequisite for full-scale collectivization. During the debate, Liu Shaoqi made his ideas increasingly clear. He did not regard mutual aid teams as a form that could pave the way for socialism since mutual aid teams or agricultural cooperatives themselves had no future. In May and June 1951, Liu Shaoqi finally got infuriated by Lai Ruoyu's stubborn stand and started to criticize Lai Ruoyu sharply and semi-publicly. Liu Shaoqi accused those who wanted to begin collectivization of pursuing "utopian socialism."

Liu seemed to have crossed the line. Mao Zedong intervened. In July 1951, Mao held a private talk with Liu Shaoqi, Bo Yibo, and Liu Lantao. He explicitly endorsed Lai Ruoyu. Mao founded his position on Stalin's prose in *The Foundations of Leninism*. Mao asserted that just as the British putting-out system had provided the foundation for a new set of production relations associated with industrialization, the Chinese mutual aid teams could perform a similar function in the creation of new production relations associated with socialism.[83] Liu Shaoqi and his followers immediately appeared to be persuaded by Mao's arguments and abandoned their viewpoint.

One reason for Liu's retreat may have been that he became convinced by the findings of rural investigations, one of which was ironically undertaken in Shanxi by Wang Qian, a subordinate of Lai Ruopyu's, namely that the SMCs had failed to provide the hoped-for commercial channel between the state and the peasants. Liu Shaoqi's cooperative plan did not work well. SMCs were established at various levels in large numbers from provinces to villages. But they were operating as ordinary commercial shops and hardly played a role in connecting peasants with urban centers, not to mention their failure to regulate the peasant economy.[84] This had also been a problem in the Soviet Union in the 1920s, where SMCs functioned as regular retail shops, at best serving the interests of the better-off peasants.[85] Mismanagement and corruption in SMCs were quite common. Peasants were left to their own devices. The majority of peasants desired to be left alone, to prosper as farmers and to dispose of their produce as they saw fit.[86]

In September 1951, Mao ordered Chen Boda, his former secretary and close colleague, to convene the First National Mutual Aid and Cooperation Conference. The keynote drafted by Liu Shaoqi for this conference was shelved. Instead, the "Resolution on Mutual Aid and Cooperativization in Agriculture (Draft)" drafted by Chen Boda, was passed. The Draft underscored peasants' aspiration for working collectively and joining mutual aid teams. It proposed a three-stage plan: starting from mutual aid teams, move up to the lower stage of agricultural producers' cooperatives modeled on Shanxi's prototypes, and end up with more advanced agricultural producers' cooperatives which should be a quasi-collective farms.[87] From then on, Liu Shaoqi ceased to actively write about the cooperatives. Indeed, at the time and in subsequent years, Liu made repeated self-criticisms for his "mistakes" on the issue of cooperatives.

In December 1951 Mao ordered the Draft sent to Party committees at various levels for trial implementation.[88] The first stage of mutual aid and cooperation movement formally unfolded.

Beyond a few remarks on the topic, detailed analysis of the first mutual aid and cooperation movement is beyond the scope of this chapter. In the first half of 1952, most party cadres above the county level were fully engaged in the "three-anti" movement and cared little about the mutual aid and cooperation movement.[89] So village cadres took control of this task. Since there were no detailed directives on the operation of producers' co-ops and few cadres knew what a socialist countryside should look like, a variety of practices were adopted. In certain old liberated areas, such as Changzhi prefecture, Shanxi, rash tendencies prevailed, that is, forcing peasants to join and socializing their means of production. But in many areas, economic factors played key roles. As a result, rich peasants took control of mutual aid teams, middle peasants only cared about making money, and poor peasants were exploited and disdained. The lack of education on collectivism was significant.

One phenomenon that particularly disturbed the Party was the lack of improvement in peasants' enthusiasm for collectivism. The Party believed that this shortcoming was rooted in the lack of socialist education carried out from above.[90] However, even Party members had wrong ideas about socialism.

They had little knowledge of collectivization, they did not know where China should go and had no faith in China's future. How to correct peasants' view of socialism and that of the vast party rank and file? How to connect mutual aid teams and agricultural producers' cooperatives with China's socialist future? How to enable cadres to guide the movement? Naturally, the CCP turned to the Soviet model for demonstration and public education.

The Visit of the Rural Delegation to the Soviet Union

In April 1952, the Ministry of Agriculture and the North China Bureau sent China's first major agricultural delegation to the Soviet Union to visit Soviet collective farms. This delegation was composed of officials, peasants, and specialists on agriculture. In September 1952, they returned to China. With their experience and observations in the Soviet Union, delegates were expected to show Chinese what a socialist country should be like, convince peasants of the bright future of collectivization, and instruct cadres on how to operate a collective farm. Upon their return, the delegates were invited to give talks and host seminars on various occasions. The media, from *People's Daily* to local newspapers, immediately focused on the visit and took this chance to carry out education on socialism. In this section I will take *Hebei Daily* as an example to highlight some key points of how Soviet collective farms were described in the media.

On September 23, 1952, a full page of *Hebei Daily* was dedicated to the interviews of the peasant delegates. The title was "the road of Soviet peasants is the road of Chinese peasants." Labor model Yu Luoshan told the reporter that he had been a member of the Sino-Soviet Friendship Association, but he knew little about socialism. He had thought that Sino-Soviet friendship meant that the Soviet Union aided China to defeat Japan and sent specialists to help build China's economy. He was not convinced that China and the Soviet Union were like brothers and he did not believe China should follow the Soviet road to socialism. During his trip, however, he learned that Soviet peasants were living in a paradise. Although working collectively, family life was maintained. One family, which Yu visited, lived in a big house with three rooms, a private yard. a storage shed, and a stockyard since it owned a horse, ten sheep, two cows and one 5-mu private plot. In 1951 it produced more than enough to supply itself with grain, milk, meat, vegetables, fruit, and sugar. Yu found out that Soviet farmers were no longer worried about food, clothing, natural disasters, and that they no longer feared having too many children. This was because agricultural productivity on the collective farms was now very high. In China it took a 5-member family more than 10 days to reap 15 mu of grain and everyone was exhausted; while in Soviet collective farms, 5 people driving one tractor and two combines could reap 900 mu of grain in one day; and at the same time everyone enjoyed sunshine riding on the tractor. What a contrast! Yu concluded that Chinese people must follow the Soviet road if they wanted to live a happy life.[91]

Yu's narrative was very typical. When it came to describing Soviet collective farms, their prosperity, material abundance, high productivity and farmers' paradise-like everyday life were emphasized. The images of every household being able to keep a large amount of private property, the miracle of tractors, and the Soviet government's subsidies for children were striking. When it came to interviewees' comments, nearly all of them emphasized how they turned from doubt to full faith in socialism. Press reports of interviews had titles such as "Collectivization and mechanization led Soviet peasants to happiness," and "We should follow the Soviet people's road."[92] Pages of photos of Soviet collective farms, farmers, and tractors were published in newspapers and exhibited publicly.

Delegates toured around to give lectures to inspire local cadres and arouse peasants' enthusiasm to build agricultural producers' cooperatives. Peasants were curious and anxious. What concerned peasants most were the details of collective farm operations. They asked, "What property was to be collectivized?" "How was the land nationalized?" "Do collective farmers own their homes?" "How do collective farmers sell their surplus products?" and "Do individual farmers exist in the USSR?" Peasants were also interested in the principles of distribution and in Soviet advanced technology. These questions indicated that peasants barely had any knowledge of Soviet collective farms, and that they were most concerned with the ownership of property. Considering that these "peasants" whom the press quoted were probably rural cadres or at least political "activists," one can appreciate how much ordinary peasants still had to learn about the Soviet model.

The effect of the Soviet model on rural cadres was striking. The CCP secretary of the fourth district of Da city, Jing Naiwen, was a member of the delegation. Before he went to the Soviet Union, he knew little about socialism and was reluctant to guide peasants. He admitted that peasants' understanding of China's socialist feature was nebulous and he himself did not have a faith in the mutual aid and cooperation movement. But after his visit to the Soviet Union, he came to know what socialism should be. He said he was now aware that Chinese peasants "were all politically backward." They did not understand the superiority of socialism and the advantage of collectivization. He was now confident that peasants would no longer be interested in becoming rich peasants once they saw the power of the collectives. Jing believed he now knew how to educate peasants and cadres of peasant origin. He told a reporter that in the future he would talk about how peasants in his district had improved their understanding of socialism (after he educated them).[93] Jing was not the only cadre who was inspired by this trip. As a matter of fact, the Party seized this chance to launch an education campaign on patriotism, on getting peasants organized and on China's socialist future. This time, the mutual aid and cooperation movement was definitely treated as an issue with significant political meaning.

In October, the Hebei provincial leaders strongly reinforced the Party's guidance on the mutual aid and cooperation movement. Party branches of each level were required to assign a cadre specifically to take charge of mutual aid and cooperative affairs. The counties investigated common people's thoughts on the movement and inspected the implementation of policies. The secretary of each county party branch was required to report every other month on his work. The secretary of each village branch had to convene village meetings regularly to educate peasants. On October 17, *Hebei Daily* published a report on how rural branches of Daming county educated peasants. In Xiaohu village, the Party members convened village conferences during holidays to educate people. They told peasants that producing more grain was not only for the benefit of the peasants themselves, but for supporting the state. They instructed peasants to make a production plan not according to peasants' needs, but according to the needs of the state. They defined this behavior as patriotism.

Taking the Soviet collective farms as the model, "get organized" became more politicized. The transition from mutual aid teams to agricultural producers' cooperatives and to collective farms was now defined as the only path to socialism. And getting organized or not was a now a line issue: one was either on Soviet road to socialism or on the road toward capitalism.[94]

The month from October 17 to November 17 of 1952 was named "Sino-Soviet Friendship Month." Newspapers published more articles on Soviet experiences, for example, with farm machinery. The SU was praised as "the most advanced country in the world"; gratitude toward the SU was voiced and the need to learn from the Soviet Union stressed. "The happy life of Soviet collective farmers" was now linked explicitly to collectivism. Soviet peasants made the country rich while at the same creating a happy life for themselves. Soviet peasants were willing to hand in more of their property to the collectives, which Chinese peasants consistently refused to do.[95] In the following months, slogans such as, "the Soviet road of collectivization is our peasants' bright future," were widely disseminated.

At the same time, the Party claimed that Stalin's last work, *Economic Problems of Socialism in the USSR*, had shown in detail how the transition from socialism to communism would be achieved. Chinese were asked to learn and master Stalin's ideas for guidance on how to construct a new life.[96] On November 10, 1952, in Beijing, the Agriculture Ministry, the Ministry of Water Resources and other central institutions invited Soviet officials and specialists to address the history of Soviet collectivization and answer questions on the operation of collective farms.[97]

Soviet models were displayed across China, education on socialism intensified, and regulations of mutual aid teams and agricultural producers' cooperatives were rigidified. Taking Soviet collective farm as the ultimate goal, the large amount of socialized assets, the advantage of large-size production and the myth of socialism, were becoming associated with China's mutual aid and cooperation movement. The media, cautiously yet firmly, justified the message that for the state's interest, sometimes individuals would have to endure some personal loss. Soviet peasants had done it; it was now Chinese peasants' turn.

Under such circumstances, the mutual aid and cooperation movement entered a new stage. Compared with the spring of 1952, economic factors were no longer the main concern. Ideology dominated. Rural cadres were no longer the leaders. Rather, they became the targets of socialist education and were pressed to serve the party rather than to protect their villagers. By the end of 1952, Soviet collective farms thus came to be regarded as the only viable future for Chinese peasants. SMCs, as an alternative, had been overshadowed.

Stalin Keeps His Distance

As noted earlier, Stalin himself had taken a cautious approach towards the early introduction of socialism into the Chinese countryside. As China plunged into this massive learning movement, Stalin provided no support and never asked about it. In October 1952, Liu Shaoqi went to meet Stalin, Mao having instructed him to consult with Stalin on the general line. Liu Shaoqi wrote to Stalin explaining the general line. Mao suggested that from now on, industry would gradually be nationalized and peasants organized into agricultural producers' cooperatives and agricultural collectives. Another question raised was the drafting of a new constitution. Four days later, Stalin commented on the letter during a meeting with Liu. He talked at length about the new constitution, but only made very brief remarks on the transition question. He said, "I think your ideas are right. When we hold the power, (we should) move, step by step, toward socialism." This was a lukewarm, if not a cold endorsement.

Liu Shaoqi now asked Stalin about another question not in his letter, namely the nationalization of private land. Mao Zedong rarely touched on this in the discussions of the general line. In 1948, Stalin had clearly opposed it. Now, Stalin reiterated his 1948 view and further discouraged eliminating rich peasants at the present stage.[98] A Russian source even recorded that Stalin urged the CCP "not to hurry with setting up of agricultural cooperatives and collective farms."[99] Stalin's attitude could hardly be read as an enthusiastic endorsement of the general line, at least not its rural economy part. It is not clear how Mao Zedong read Stalin's reply, although he claimed that Stalin had endorsed it.[100]

In accordance with Stalin's lukewarm attitude, between 1952 and 1953, when the CCP economic officials worked with Soviet comrades on drafting China's first five-year plan, agricultural cooperativization was seldom discussed. For example, Chen Yun, the CCP's leading economic official and chairman of the Financial and Economic Committee, and Li Fuchun, its vice chairman, went to Moscow in the fall 1952 to work on details of China's first five-year plan. Li Fuchun stayed in Moscow for 10 month. Both Chen Yun and Li Fuchun's biographies show that they rarely discussed rural issues with their Soviet interlocutors. During Li Fuchun's stay at Moscow, he invited quite a few Soviet specialists to teach Chinese colleagues about the industrial economy, but no rural specialists were invited. When Li Fuchun returned to China and gave report on the first five-year plan, he pointedly did not mention agricultural producers' cooperatives or collectivization at all. Instead, he emphasized commercial circulation between cities and countryside. Of course, after spending some time in Beijing, he soon modified the plan and started to talk about agricultural cooperativization.[101] This case vividly demonstrates that the Soviet side was not interested in agricultural collectivization in China, knew little about it and did not involve itself in it.

In January 1953, Zhang Wentian, who had been China's ambassador to the Soviet Union since March 1951, met the head of the Xinhua news agency, Wu Lengxi, who was visiting Moscow. Zhang Wentian asserted that it was necessary for new China to learn from the Soviet Union, but it was also important to work with China's reality. The Soviet Union had done very well in its rapid industrialization, but light industry had grown slowly, and agriculture had not done well at all. Zhang then frankly told Wu Lengxi about the weakness and downsides of Soviet collectivization system and warned that China should not simply copy the Soviet model.[102] As the head of Xinhua news agency, Wu Lengxi probably had much easier access to Mao Zedong than Zhang Wentian, and Zhang may have expected that this message reach Mao Zedong through Wu Lengxi. Whether Wu did tell Mao is not known.

Just when Zhang Wentian warned about the Soviet model in Moscow, the mutual aid and cooperation movement in China was in trouble. Rash, leftist, tendencies spread over the nation, especially in northeast China and Shanxi.

Both suffered significant drops in grain production.[103] From February to April 1953, Beijing had to issue a series of directives to rectify the rash tendency and discourage building of new agricultural producers' cooperatives. While not overtly questioning the theory of the mutual aid and cooperation movement, these directives placed substantial constraints on the movement and insisted that the peasants' mentality as small producers had to be respected.[104]

Appearing not to oppose these directives, in February 1953, Mao Zedong launched his first formal inspection trip, after 1949, to southern China to observe for himself the conditions of the country and people's attitudes toward his polices. This trip convinced him that "It is possible to achieve collectivization without mechanization, and therefore China does not have to follow the Soviet way of doing things."[105] Regardless of Stalin's cold response, and regardless of some internal worries, Mao Zedong was determined to proceed with his general line.

Starting in April, 1953, the Central Committee announced a new study program for senior and intermediate-level cadres designed specifically to teach about Soviet economic construction. The textbook was the *Short Course.*[106] Two days later, this directive appeared in *People's Daily,* sending a clear signal to the nation that Stalinism and Stalin's path to socialism were to be adopted.[107] Ideas of Stalin and Lenin were widely cited. However, as Chinese scholars have pointed out, what was reflected in Chinese media was in essence Stalin's "revolution from above," not Lenin's NEP. The party's, more precisely Mao Zedong's, understanding of Lenin's transition theory was that in the transition period, capitalism, commodity production and communism existed concurrently. The small peasant economy was rooted deeply in capitalism, upon which capitalism would survive and revive. So the fundamental feature of this transition period was the cruel struggle between dying capitalism and growing socialism. In this sense, the goal of the transition period was to eliminate capitalism, to eliminate classes, the small peasant economy, and to create a socialist society.[108] Lenin's famous statement that "small production is still very, very widespread in the world and small production engenders capitalism and the bourgeoisie continuously, daily, hourly, spontaneously and on a mass scale" was to be reiterated, extensively and intensively.

Stalin died in March 1953 and so his go-slow approach could no longer hold Mao back. Mao started to push for his agenda, first concentrating his attack on the notion of preserving the capitalist economy. It seemed that the majority of the party leaders were not wholeheartedly convinced by the general line. In addition to citing Lenin and Stalin, Mao then enlisted Gao Gang to help him to attack the leaders who disagreed with him, mainly Liu Shaoqi and Bo Yibo. Gao Gang had favored the rapid elimination of the national bourgeoisie as a class and a quick transition to socialism, close adherence to the Soviet model[109] and of course agricultural collectivization. Now with Mao's endorsement, Gao Gang took the offensive and repeatedly took ideology as his weapon. In one occasion, Gao Gang even used Stalin's attack on Bukharin's peaceful transition to criticize Bo Yibo, a close follower of Liu Shaoqi. As he said to Li Weihan, who supported Liu Shaoqi and Chen Yun, "have you ever read *On the Opposition* by Stalin? Didn't Bukharin also advocate a peaceful entry into socialism?"[110] After two months of persuasion and coercion, other CCP leaders acquiesced. In the fall 1953, Mao won acceptance of the general line from party leaders.[111]

Imposition of the Grain Monopoly

From the outset of the founding of the PRC, extracting grain from peasants had been a challenge. As early as 1951, Chen Yun, the head of the Financial and Economic Committee, proposed a policy of compulsory purchase of surplus grain (*zhenggou*). Chen Yun's proposal so vividly reminded his comrades of the Soviet Union's forced requisitioning of grain, that Chen Yun had to differentiate his approach from the Soviet one and to give it a different name. For two years, this proposal had been opposed by certain regional leaders.[112]

In 1953, a severe grain procurement crisis broke out. The sale of marketed grain plunged in every region of China. State-owned grain stores sold much more grain than they purchased. Publicly, the state blamed private traders for speculation. Internally, the state blamed peasants for hoarding their grain and consuming too much. The solution was to press peasants to sell "surplus" grain by imposition of the state monopoly on the purchase and sale of grain (*tonggou tongxiao*), thereby nationalizing the grain market.[113] As Chen Yun said, if a free market continued, the central government would have to beg peasants for grain every day, so every day would be painful. He considered nationalization of the grain market as a long-term solution.[114]

In early October 1953, an emergency meeting on the grain crisis was convened in Beijing to discuss the operation of a nationalized grain market. For the first week, the whole discussion did not touch on the general line or on cooperativization plan. Aware that the party would take away all the peasants' surplus grain from the current year plus their savings of the past,[115] the CCP leaders foresaw that peasants would resist the policy. There would be bloodshed. It was very clear to them that this was a political movement. However, to the party's dismay, the objections first came from within the party. On the provincial level, there were already complaints about abuses even before the final decision was made.[116] At county and district levels, discontent was stronger and deeper.

This was a serious matter. The cadres opposing the new policy were regarded as the backbone of the party. Li Jingquan, who took charge of the
trial introduction of the nationalized grain market in Sichuan province and
who was known for his loyalty to Mao Zedong, suggested combining the
nationalization of the grain market with the propaganda for the general line
in order to persuade those old cadres. Shifting attention to the bright future,
it would be easier to overcome the present difficulties, Li Jingquan reasoned.
Mao agreed. By adding the grain policy to the general line, it was possible that
the whole party would embrace it and implement it. In propaganda, peasants
should be told about socialism, about industrialization, and their Soviet future.[117] So in November, the propaganda for the unified purchase and sale of
the grain market was placed in the context of studying the general line. Now,
to express the discontent with the nationalization of the grain market had a
much more serious implication: "Are you questioning the Chairman's line?"

During the study of the general line, two major points were emphasized,
first, to urge peasants to sell more grain to the state; second, to draw a line
between capitalism and socialism, thereby leaving cooperativization as the
only correct path to follow. The nationalization of the grain market paved way
for cooperativization. As in the Soviet Union, the state grain monopoly was
designed to siphon off whatever surplus there was and use it for industrialization. Producers' collectives could be used to enforce the purchasing program.
Toward the end of 1953, the agricultural cooperativization movement, heading toward collectivization, was formally launched in China.

Conclusion

Without Stalin's collectivization theory, the CCP's strategy toward the peasant economy would not have been the same. However, this does not mean
that the Soviet factor dominated the policy process. Moreover, as noted,
Stalin's own attitude behavior during this period was rather detached. Stalin
never pushed the CCP to adopt his collectivization model; quite the contrary,
between 1949 and 1953 Stalin tried subtly to hold back Mao Zedong from
launching the collectivization. It is not clear to what degree Stalin's attitude
exerted some constraints on Mao. As Hua-yu Li has argued, he chose to interpret Stalin's attitude as an "endorsement" of his policies.

This essay shows the deep impact of Soviet models as well as their complexity. At times there was more than one Soviet model available; even a single
model appeared in more than one version; even one version was given different interpretations. Which model to choose and how to apply it was an issue
settled within China and not by the Soviets. Soviet models provided a kind

of filter through which assessments were made of practical situations. They provided the foundation on which domestic politics and practical pressures would play themselves out.

Notes

1. I am deeply indebted to Thomas Bernstein for his long comments and careful editing. This essay is partly inspired by insightful observations Li Hua-yu makes in her book, *Mao and the Economic Stalinization of China: 1948–1953*. I am grateful for East Asia Program Fellowship and Sicca Fellowship from Cornell University that funded my research in China and in Russia in 2005.

2. Maurice Meisner, "Stalinism in the history of the Chinese Communist Party," in *Critical Perspectives on Mao Zedong's Thought*, eds., Arif Dirlik, Paul Healy and Nick Knight (Atlantic Highlands, NJ: Humanities Press International,1997), 87. See also Stephen Kotkin, *Magnetic Mountain: Stalinism as a Civilization* (Berkeley: University of California Press, 1995), 152.

3. After the Xi'an incident in 1936, the United Front of the CCP and the National-ist Party against Japan was established. The CCP ceased to extract resources from class enemies and promised not to carry out land reform in the base areas. In return, the Nationalist Party agreed to provide subsidies which were by no means insignificant. For example, in 1939, 89.66 percent of the CCP government revenue came from the subsidy. See in Huang Zhenglin, *Shan-Gan-Ning bianqu shehui jingji shi (1937–1945)* [Social and economic history of the Shan-Gan-Ning base area (1937–1945)] (herein-after as *Shan-Gan-Ning bianqu*) (Beijing: Renmin chubanshe, 2006), 189.

4. The party's supervision over agriculture was loose and agricultural taxes, in the form of the "Grain to Save the Nation" [*jiuguo gongliang*], were very light. In 1937, the party asked for 14,000 *dan* grain which accounted for only 1.28 percent of peasants' total output. See in Huang Zhenglin, *Shan-Gan-Ning bianqu*, 197–99.

5. For example, in December 1939, Huan County was assigned a quota of 8500 *dan* by the Shan-Gan-Ning government. Local cadres were planning to collect even more. A revolt immediately occurred in January 1940. Peasants from 17 townships and 2,500 self-defense army soldiers joined the revolt. See in Huang Zhenglin, *Shan-Gan-Ning bianqu*, 185.

6. A widely circulated story was that, in a storm, a CCP cadre was "struck" by lightening and killed. Hearing the news, peasants wondered why the lightning did not strike Chairman Mao. See Jin Chongji and Chen Qun, eds., *Chen Yun zhuan* [The biography of Chen Yun] (Beijing: Zhongyang wenxian chubanshe, 2005).

7. Huang Zhenglin, *Shan-Gan-Ning bianqu*, 241.

8. Zhang Peisen, *Zhang Wentian nianpu, erce* [Zhang wentian chronicle, vol. 2] (hereinafter as *Zhang Wentian nianpu*) (Beijing: Zhongyang dangshi chubanshe, 2000), 665. Some scholars suggested that Zhang decided to take this trip because he wanted to escape from Yan'an rectification.

9. Zhang Peisen, *Zhang Wentian nianpu*, 671.

10. Zhang Peisen, *Zhang Wentian nianpu*, 693.

11. Huang Zhenglin, *Shan-Gan-Ning bianqu*, 260–61.

12. Huang Zhenglin, *Shan-Gan-Ning bianqu*, 293–300.

13. Tian Songnian "Dui jiben zhexue shuji de pizhu" [Remarks on several philosophy books] in Gong Yuzhi, Pang Xianzhi, and Shi Zhongquan, eds., *Mao Zedong de dushu shenghuo* [Mao Zedong's reading habits] (Beijing: Zhongyang wenxian chubanshe, 2003), 67–78.

14. Gao Hua, "Zai dao yu shi zhijian" [Between "tao" and "circumstances"], *Chinese Social Science Quarterly* (Hong Kong), no 5 (1993).

15. Li Hua-yu, *Mao and the Economic Stalinization of China, 1948–1953* (hereinafter as *Mao and the Economic Stalinization of China*) (Lanham, MD: Rowman & Littlefield, 2006), 96.

16. Chen Jin ed., *Mao Zedong dushu biji* [Reading notes of Mao Zedong] (Guangdong: Guangdong renmin chubanshe, 1996), 304–7.

17. Mao Zedong, "Reform Our Study," in *Selected Works of Mao Tse-tung*, vol. 3 (Beijing: Foreign Languages Press, 1965), 24.

18. Tony Saich, "Writing or Rewriting History? The Construction of the Maoist Resolution on Party History," in *New Perspectives on the Chinese Communist Revolution*, ed. Tony Saich and Hans van de Ven (Armonk, NY: M. E. Sharpe, 1994), 302.

19. Li Hua-yu, *Mao and the Economic Stalinization of China*, 95–96.

20. *Lian gong (bu) dangshi jianming jiaocheng* [History of the Communist Party of the Soviet Union (Bolsheviks)] (hereinafter as *Lian gong [bu] dangshi*) (Beijing: Shidai chubanshe, 1949), 322.

21. Mao Zedong, "Get Organized," *Selected Works of Mao Tse-Tung* (Peking: Foreign Languages Press, 1965), vol. 3, 156.

22. *Lian gong (bu) dangshi*, 365–66.

23. Chen Yung-fa, *Making Revolution—The Communist Movement in Eastern and Central China, 1937–1945* (Berkeley: University of California Press, 1986), 215–19.

24. Mao Zedong, "Lun hezuoshe" [On cooperatives], in *Jianguo yilai nongye Hezuohua Shiliao Huibian* [Collection of historical materials on agricultural cooperativization history since the founding of the PRC] (Beijing: Zhonggong dangshi chubanshe, 1992).

25. Mao Zedong, "Get Organized."

26. In 1944, severe commandism and formalism spread in the Shan-Gan-Ning base area. Quite a few rural cadres, without consulting with any peasant, sometimes even without propagating the virtues of "get organized," sat in their offices to manufacture a list by copying names. When mutual aid teams were imposed on peasants by local agents, cases of sabotage were reported; mutual aid teams easily fell apart. See in Shi Jingtang, ed., *Zhongguo nongye hezuohua yundong shiliao, yice* [Historical documents on China's agricultural cooperativization movement, vol. 1] (Beijing: Sanlian chubanshe, 1957), 264.

27. Zhang Peisen, *Zhang Wentian nianpu*, 904.

28. Chen Yung-fa, "The Blooming Poppy under the Red Sun: The Yan'an Way and the Opium Trade."

29. Old liberated regions refer to regions that were occupied by the CCP during the war against Japan. Nearly all of them were located in North China. Research on the

radical land reform in North China between 1946–48 is discussed in Huang Daoxuan, "Mengyou yihuo qianzai duishou?" [Ally or potential rivals], online article, retrieved from http://www.usc.cuhk.edu.hk/wk_wzdetails.asp?id=6520.

30. Chen Yung-fa, "Reconsidering Yan'an, Again," *Xin Shixue* [New history], Taiwan, no. 3 (1997), 146.

31. Li Hua-yu clearly discusses these issues in detail in her book *Mao and the Economic Stalinization of China*.

32. Andrei Ledovsky, "Two Cables from Correspondence between Mao Zedong and Joseph Stalin," *Far Eastern Affairs* (hereinafter as *FEA*), no. 6 (2000), 95.

33. Andrei Ledovsky, "Mikoyan's Secret Mission to China in January and February 1949," *FEA*, no. 3 (1995), 86–87.

34. Liu Shaoqi, "Guanyu xin zhongguo de jingji jianshe fangzhen" [The guideline for economic construction of new China], in *Liu Shaoqi lun xin zhongguo jingji jianshe* [Liu Shaoqi on the economic construction of the People's Republic of China] (hereinafter as *Liu Shaoqi lun xin zhongguo jingji jianshe*) (Beijing: Zhongyang wentian chubanshe, 1993), 144–49.

35. "On Co-operation," Lenin, Vladimir, *Selected Works, Volume IX,* ed., J. Feinberg (New York: International Publishers, 1937), 402–3.

36. Relationships between Stalin and Bukharin in the 1920s were quite complex. They were allies against the Trotskyite left, then they broke when Stalin turned towards forced grain collection. See Lewin Moshe, *Russian Peasants and Soviet Power—A Study of Collectivization* (New York and London: W. W. Norton & Company, 1975).

37. Li Hua-yu, *Mao and the Economic Stalinization of China*, 72.

38. Jin Chongji, ed., *Liu Shaoqi zhuan, xia* [Biography of Liu Shaoqi, vol. 2] (hereinafter as *Liu Shaoqi zhuan, xia*) (Beijing: Zhongyang wenxian chubanshe, 1998), 618.

39. In 1953, he was referred to teach Li Weihan, then the head of the United Front Department, about Bukharin. Li Weihan, *Huiyi yu Yanjiu, xiajuan* [Recollections and research, vol. 2] (Beijing: Zhonggong dangshi ziliao chubanshe, 1986), 744.

40. Zhang Peisen, *Zhang Wentian nianpu*, 836.

41. Li Hua-yu, *Mao and the Economic Stalinization of China*.

42. Zhang Wentian, *Zhang Wentian Xuanji* [Selected works of Zhang Wentian] (hereinafter as *Zhang Wentian xuanj*) (Beijing: Renmin Chubanshe, 1985), 402. Li Hua-yu, *Mao and the Economic Stalinization of China*, 73–74.

43. Zhang Wentian wenji bianjizu, ed., *Zhang Wentian wenji, sice* [Collected works of Zhang Wentian, vol. 4] (hereinafter as *Zhang Wentian wenji*, vol. 4) (Beijing: Zhonggong dangshi ziliao chubanshe, 1995), 1–5.

44. *Zhang Wentian Wenji*, vol. 4, 1–5.

45. Liu Shaoqi, "Lun xin minzhu zhuyi shiqi de jingji yu hezuoshe" [On new democratic economy and cooperatives], in *Liushaoqi lun xin zhongguo jingji jianshe*, 9–28.

46. Jin Chongji, ed., *Liu Shaoqi zhuan, xia*, 615.

47. Liu Shaoqi, "Dui 'guanyu dongbei jingji goucheng ji jingji jianshe jiben fangzhen de tigang' de ruogan xiugai" [Several amendments on the outline of the basic guidelines of economic construction and composition of economy in the northeast region], *Liu Shaoqi lun xin zhongguo jingji*, 29–43.

48. In a politburo meeting in September 1948, Liu suggested organizing cooperatives across China. He only referred to SMCs. See Liu Shaoqi, "Xin minzhu zhuyi jingji jianshe wenti" [Problems on new democratic economy construction], *Liushaoqi lun xin zhongguo jingji*, 1–8.

49. Mao Zedong, "Xianzai de xingshi he women dangqian de renwu" [Current situations and the mission of the party], *Mao Zedong wenji, wujuan* [Selected works of Mao Zedong, vol. 5] (Beijing: Remin chubanshe, 1996).

50. Andrei Ledovsky, "Mikoyan's Secret Mission to China in January and February 1949," *FEA*, no. 3 (1995), 86–87.

51. Andrei Ledovsky, "Mikoyan's Secret Mission to China in January and February 1949," 87.

52. Mao Zedong, "Zai Zhongguo gongchangdang di qi jie zhongyang weiyuan hui di er ci quan ti huiyi shang de baogao" [Report to the second plenary session of the seventh Central Committee of the Communist Party of China], *Selected works of Mao Zedong*, vol. 4.

53. Zhonggong zhongyang wenxian yanjiushi, ed., *Mao Zedong zhuzuo zhuanti zhaibian* [Selected collection of Mao Zedong's works on topics] (hereinafter as *Mao Zedong zhuzuo zhuanti zhaibian*) (Beijing: Zhongyang wenxian chubanshe, 2003), 485.

54. *Mao Zedong zhuzuo zhuanti zhaibian*, 687, 689.

55. Pang Xianzhi and Jin Chongji, eds., *Mao Zedong Zhuan* [Biography of Mao Zedong] (hereinafter as *Mao Zedong Zhuan*) (Beijing: Zhongyang wenxian chubanshe, 2003), 69.

56. Pang Xianzhi and Jin Chongji, eds., *Mao Zedong Zhuan*, 53.

57. Frederick Teiwes, *Politics at Mao's Court* (Armonk, NY: M. E. Sharpe, 1990), 17.

58. Bo Yibo, *Ruogan zhongda juece yu shijian de huigu, shang ce* [Reflections on certain major decisions and events, vol. 1] (hereinafter as *Ruogan 1*) (Beijing: Zhonggong zhongyang dangxiao chubanshe, 1991), 65.

59. Andrei Ledovsky, "Mikoyan's Secret Mission to China," 87.

60. Shi Jingtang, ed., *Zhonggong nongye hezuohua yundong shiliao*, 1020–1026.

61. Bo Yibo, *Ruogan 1*, 204.

62. Shi Dongbing, *Gao Gang hunduan zhongnanhai* [Gao Gang's failure in Zhongnanhai] (Hong Kong: Tiandi Tushu Youxian Gongsi, 1995).

63. Paul Wingrove, "Mao's Conversations with the Soviet Ambassador, 1953–55," Cold War International History Project Working Papers Series, nos. 5–6.

64. "Ivan Kovalev's Report to Stalin on Dec 24, 1949," trans. Ma Guifan, *Zhonggong dangshi yanjiu*, no. 6 (2004), 88–92.

65. In 1954, Gao Gang was labeled an antirevolutionary factionalist and committed suicide. Paul Wingrove discussed this issue in "Mao's Conversations with the Soviet Ambassador, 1953–55."

66. Shi Dongbing, *Gao Gang hunduan zhongnanhai*.

67. Arlen Meliksetov, "'New Democracy' and China's Search for Socio-Economic Development Routes (1949–1953)," *FEA*, no. 1 (1996), 80.

68. Zhang Peisen, *Zhang Wentian nianpu*, 900.

69. Bo Yibo, *Ruogan zhongda juece yu shijian de huigu.*

70. Zhang Peisen, *Zhang Wentian nianpu,* 934–35.

71. Arlen Meliksetov, "'New Democracy' and China's Search for Socio-Economic Development Routes (1949–1953)," 79–80.

72. This report is in the Foreign Policy Archives of the Russian Federation.

73. Foreign Policy Archives of the Russian Federation, folio 0100, list 43, portfolio 10, folder 302, p. 178. Quoted by Arlen Meliksetov, "'New Democracy' and China's search for socio-economic development routes (1949–1953)," 80.

74. Arlen Meliksetov, "'New Democracy' and China's search for socio-economic development routes (1949–1953)."

75. Liu Jianping, "Nongye hezuohua juece de guocheng jiqi zhengzhixue yiyi: xin zhongguo 1951" [Policy decision in the cooperative transformation of agriculture and its political implications: new China in 1951], *Kaifang shidai,* no. 2 (2003).

76. Li Hua-yu and Arlen Meliksetov have discussed this issue in their works respectively. Many Chinese scholars also have done research on this subject. One is Lu Zhenxiang. See Lu Zhenxiang, *Tansuo de guiji* [Trails of explorations] (Beijing: Zhongyang wenxian chubanshe, 2003).

77. *Remin ribao,* October 5, 1952.

78. Documents on Gao Gang are extremely scarce in Chinese given his purge. Ledovsky's biography of Gao Gang is in Russian and has not been translated into Chinese or English. A. M. Ledovsky, *Delo Gao Gana-Rao Shushi* [The Gao-Rao case] (Moscow: Institut Dal'nego Vostoka, 1990).

79. Jing Chongji eds, *Liu Shaoqi zhuan, xia* [Biography of Liu Shaoqi, vol. 2] (Beijing: Zhongyang wenxian chubanshe, 1998), 701.

80. Lai Ruoyu, "Zai shengwei kuoda huiyi shang de baogao" [Report on the provincial enlarged conference], September 1, 1949. Shanxi Provincial Archive, 00.29.1.

81. Shanxi leaders considered that agricultural producers' cooperatives combined a socialist component and a capitalist component. Individual farmers still owned the land and livestock, but the land and livestock were pooled in the cooperative as an investment. Members of the cooperative worked on the land collectively. Profits were distributed proportionally, partly according to individual labor input and partly according to individual land investment. Remuneration according to labor was considered the socialist component, thus the higher the percentage of profits distributed according to labor the more socialist and "progressive" the cooperative. The scale was moderate, usually consisting of a dozen or so families. Meanwhile, to ensure a proper "socialist" direction, setting aside communal funds and investing in communally owned goods and equipment was required of most cooperatives.

82. Xiaojia Hou, *Jumping the Gun: Local Agency and Early Experiments in the Socialist Transformation of Rural Society in Revolutionary China,* Ph.D. dissertation, Cornell University, 2006.

83. Bo Yibo, *Ruogan zhongda juece yu shijian de huigu,* 191. Translation in Li Hua-yu, *Mao and the Economic Stalinization of China,* 153.

84. "Bo Yibo's report on the first national congress of cooperative workers." July 1950. Sichuan Provincial Archive, Files on cooperation, vol. 50.

85. Lewin Moshe, *Russian Peasants and Soviet Power.*

86. Viola Lynne, *Peasants Rebels under Stalin* (New York: Oxford University Press: 1996), 15.

87. Ye Yangbing, *Zhongguo nongye hezuohua yundong yanjiu* [Research on China's agricultural cooperativization movement] (Beijing: Zhishi chanquan chubanshe, 2006), 198–99.

88. Shi Jingtang, ed., *Zhonggong nongye hezuohua yundong shiliao*, 37.

89. The "three-anti" movement was directed against three sets of vices: corruption, waste and obstructionist bureaucracy. The targeted groups were party member themselves, bureaucratic officials and the mangers of factories and other businesses. This movement was first launched in late 1951 in the northeast China, under the direction of Gao Gang, and then spread to the rest of China. Jonathan D. Spence, *The Search For Modern China* (New York: W.W. Norton, 1999), 509.

90. Xiaojia Hou, *Jumping the Gun: Local Agency and Early Experiments in the Socialist Transformation of Rural Society in Revolutionary China.*

91. *Hebei ribao*, September 23, 1952.

92. *Hebei ribao*, September 23, 1952.

93. *Hebei ribao*, September 25, 1952.

94. *Hebei ribao*, October 17, 1952.

95. *Hebei ribao*, October 30, 1952.

96. *Hebei ribao*, October 29, 1952.

97. *Hebei ribao*, November 13, 1952.

98. *Jianguo yilai Liu Shaoqi wengao* disice [Writings of Liu Shaoqi after the founding of the PRC, vol. 4] (Beijing: Zhongyang wenxian chubanshe, 2005), 525–39.

99. Arlen Meliksetov, "China's Search," *FEA*, no. 1 (1996), 80–81.

100. Li Hua-yu, *Mao and the Economic Stalinization of China*, 121–22.

101. *Li Fuchun zhuan*, 435–50.

102. Zhang Peisen, *Zhang Wentian nianpu*, 934–35.

103. In Northeast China, planned production was 44 billion catties, yet the actual production at best estimation was only 37 billion catties. Grain production in north China dropped by at least 10 percent. In Shanxi, wheat production dropped by 600 million catties. *Dangdai zhongguo liangshi gongzuo shiliao* [Historical documents on contemporary China's grain work] (Beijing: Internal circulation, 1989), 150–67.

104. On February 15, 1953, it issued the directive "Resolution on mutual aid and cooperation in agriculture." On March 16, it issued the "Directive to party committees at all levels on spring sowing and production." On March 26, *People's Daily* published an editorial entitled "The key to leading agricultural production." These three directives, titled "The Guide to Present Rural Work," were the party's fundamental guideline for leading peasants. See *Zhonghua renmin gongheguo jingji dang'an ziliao xuanbian*, 1953–57, nongye juan [Selected collection of economic archives in the People's Republic of China, 1953–57, volume on agriculture] (Beijing: Shehui kexue chubanshe, 1991), 24.

105. Li Hua-yu, *Mao and the Economic Stalinization of China*, 128.

106. Frederick Teiwes, *Politics at Mao's Court*, 49.

107. Li Hua-yu, *Mao and the Economic Stalinization of China*, 132.

108. Weng Youwei, Xi Fuqu and Zhao Jinkang, *Dangdai zhongguo zhengzhi sixiangshi* [The history of political thought in contemporary China] (Henan: Henan daxue chubanshe, 1999), 66–69.

109. Frederick Teiwes, *Politics at Mao's Court*, 36.

110. Frederick Teiwes, *Politics at Mao's Court*, 61–66.

111. Li Hua-yu, *Mao and the Economic Stalinization of China*, 121–42.

112. Details of the debates between Chen Yun and those regional leaders have not been revealed.

113. Tian Xiquan, *Ge'ming yu xiangcun* [Revolution and the countryside] (Shanghai: Shehui kexueyuan chubanshe, 2006).

114. Tian Xiquan, *Ge'ming yu xiangcun*, 25.

115. Dangdai zhongguo liangshi gongzuo shiliao [Historical documents on contemporary China's grain work] (Beijing: Internal circulation, 1989), 150–67.

116. Li Xiannian, the head of South China Bureau, briefly mentioned that Guangdong and Guangxi province both resisted the policy, Henan province was wavering, and Jiangxi vaguely opposed. Only Hunan and Hubei provincial leaders supported the policy. *Dangdai zhongguo liangshi gongzuo shiliao*.

117. *Dangdai zhongguo liangshi gongzuo shiliao*.

8

The Soviet Model and China's State Farms

Gregory Rohlf

Introduction

A T FIRST GLANCE, one might miss the influence of the Soviet model on Chinese agriculture. Village life and small scale, collectively owned, human-powered farming remained the norm in China whereas Russian agriculture over time came to be dominated by state ownership of large-scale, mechanized farms. But when we shift the analysis away from the aggregate level to a regionally differentiated view, as well as to a focus on niche products such as dairy or rubber, we see that the Soviet model was, in fact, consistently influential in the practice of Chinese state-owned agriculture through the 1980s.

But what was the "Soviet model?" What exactly was "Stalinist" about it? Hua-yu Li and others in this volume have described how the meaning and practice of Stalinism and the Soviet model changed over time. By the 1950s, for example, Josef Stalin was a cautious realist, at least in the advice that he gave to the Chinese, less committed to the ideological imperatives that had driven the horrifying purges and forced collectivization of the 1930s.[1] Moreover, Stalinism was not just a state system; the term has come to encompass cultural norms and everyday practices.[2]

With regard to state farms, in China's post-1949 agricultural history, the Soviet Union literally supplied the blueprints. The official media announced to the Chinese people and the world that China's state farms would be built following Soviet plans and methods for their *sovkhoz* farms. Russian and Eastern European advisors and technicians also prominently displayed elements of the Soviet model in the early 1950s. These farms themselves—*guoying nongchang*—would be China's most advanced and most socialist forms of agriculture. They would produce bountiful surpluses especially because they used tractors to plant and harvest long rows of grains. The images of tractor drivers and the beautiful geometry of long furrows that filled the official media were unquestionably Russian in their origins and became similarly iconic in China. Beneath the propaganda images, government documents from the time show that China's state farms were set up as "turn-key operations" based on Russian blueprints to the degree possible given China's relatively small budget for agriculture. In this, the Chinese side followed the Soviet model in the First Five-Year Plan; the lion's share of investment was channeled toward heavy industry. Agriculture received about seven percent of investment in the plan.[3]

Over time, the evidence also shows that the Soviet model in its broadest outlines remained in place in the state farm system through the 1980s. State farms chugged along the Soviet-laid tracks like other state-owned, "Stalinist" enterprises, such as the railways, steel mills, dams, and coal mines. The durability of the Soviet model of state-owned agriculture can be most clearly observed in two areas: the centralized enterprise management system and agriculture's role in national security. In the first case, state farms were run like other, socialist, state-owned enterprises, owned by all the people in the nation. State farms provided housing, schools, medical care and other social welfare benefits to employees, but were largely funded out of government coffers.[4] Although they were castigated as hopeless money-losers for most of their history, state farms were nevertheless expected to produce resources for the centrally administered national plan in much the same way as steel mills, coal mines or the electricity generating plants. Second, the Chinese state farm system is associated with national security and the domestic detention system. In fact, the Chinese Communist Party innovated on this Soviet approach by making the People's Liberation Army a large operator of state-owned farms.[5] This is perhaps the most distinctive way in which Chinese state farms were Stalinist. For Russian and Chinese citizens, being sent to remote work sites in harsh climates for exile, detention, punishment, and even sure death were similar parts of the national landscape. Qinghai province, for example, gained the moniker as "China's Siberia" because of penal institutions that were nominally state farms.[6] Two authors of a book about the prison system reported that this perception of Qinghai had percolated down to the lowest levels of society; school teachers threatened misbehaving students with the prospect of being sent to the Qinghai.[7] In this way, the Soviet Union's *gulag* and China's *laogai* system were cognates. We can see, therefore, that Stalinism and the Soviet model in agriculture indeed affected the culture and mentalities of ordinary citizens.

Overview of State Farms History

Historical Evolution through the 1980s

From the beginning of the People's Republic of China, state farms were heralded as the future of Chinese agriculture.[8] They were to be large-scale, mechanized farms run by the state with employees paid in wages rather than in a share of the harvest. Reports from the 1950s emphasized that the mechanized, state-owned farm was the highest form of socialist agricultural production; they were to contribute to a range of political, economic and even cultural goals.[9] The success of the state farms was to demonstrate the effectiveness of new socialist agriculture to family farmers whose lands had not yet been collectivized. With their higher rates of mechanization, the farms would also produce large surpluses to supply the nation with food or strategic raw materials, including grain, cotton, rubber, or dairy products. Even in the 1990s, state farms produced about 80 percent of China's rubber, about half of its fine wool, 30 percent of the nation's dairy products as well as considerable portions of its sugar, down products, cotton and farmed seafood.[10] State farms also served as vehicles for basic state-building, serving more as small "company towns" that provided housing and a range of social services to employees and their dependents. In this sense, state farms were like other large state-owned enterprises, that provided lifetime employment, as well as housing and welfare benefits to employees. Budget shortfalls for state farms—and they were immense, right from the start—were met out of provincial and national government budgets.[11] For poor farmers, leaving the collective sector in the village for a state sector job on a state farm represented a step up in status and benefits. As in other parts of the state-owned economy, employees were ranked into different wage classes based on their experience, skills and seniority, and were to be paid those wages each month in cash. For farmers accustomed to enduring hard times before the harvest, a state farm job represented a new kind of rural occupation and lifestyle.

The Chinese state-run farm was proudly modeled on the Soviet Union's experience and leadership.[12] A Ministry of Agriculture report from 1951 noted that the Soviets had helped lead the national meeting on state farms in 1950 and that they had also supplied some of the tractors to supplement those left over from a United Nations project.[13] The "Provisional Rules on the Method for Setting Up State-run Mechanized Farms" from 1952 explicitly acknowledged the importance of Soviet experiences while its elaborate and highly centralized procedures implied Soviet influence.[14] It outlined a two-year procedure for the setting up of state farms and prescribed an incremental approach to building state farms that exemplified the centralized enterprise management approach. Long and complex applications were to be submitted to the Ministry of Agriculture in which preliminary surveying, zoning, nearness to transport, water availability, soil quality, landforms, and average annual rainfall were to be described. When this had been approved, the local unit proposing the state farm would submit a more detailed plan in which the average number of frost-free days, type of agriculture practiced nearby, livestock, availability of labor, forest resources, severe weather patterns, habits and customs of locals, the amount of capital needed, forecasts for yearly production and profit, the person in charge of the proposing unit and a budget all were included. When this had been approved, a final 18-point business plan was needed. This was to include the final land-use plan, plan for enterprise development, spare-time and idle-time occupations, yearly number of tractors needed, cadres, staffers, plan for water development, yearly budgets, fuel needs and so forth.[15] The procedures—not that different from those of a grant- or loan-making institution anywhere—evoked the kind of bureaucratism that is unwieldy but hard-to-avoid in the administration of large enterprises.

The Soviet model was also the public face for state farms. The Sino-Soviet Friendship Farm established in Jixian county, Heilongjiang in 1954, was one of many set up and run with the assistance of Soviet surveyors, technicians, scientists, managers and equipment of many kinds.[16] And a 1956 speech by Wang Zhen, the Minister of State Farms and Land Reclamation, later reprinted in the *People's Daily*, offered "heartfelt thanks" to the "great" Soviet Union and Czechoslovakia for their assistance in setting up and running state farms.[17]

More broadly, Soviet expertise in agro-science was also fully and proudly embraced in the 1950s, particularly for state farms. One can see this in Chinese praise of specific Soviet agricultural scientists and Soviet agricultural science generally.[18] Certainly the spirit of "red and expert" Lysenkoist and Michurinist science was trumpeted by the Party in the 1950s (see chapter 14). Yang Minghan, a young man from rural Guangdong became nationally famous for his Michurinist agricultural research. Youth were urged to study Yang's innovative techniques of farming and grass-roots research and self-help.[19] A Ministry of Agriculture document from 1954 expressed admiration for the Soviet Michurinist advanced techniques of cultivation—close planting and deep plowing—that were being put into practice on Chinese farms.[20] In October 1955, the hundredth anniversary of Michurin's birth was celebrated with a variety of activities and events. Even the prominent intellectual Guo Moruo himself lauded Michurin as "our great scientific teacher."[21] Finally, *China Youth* serialized the novella *The Newcomer: The Manager of an MTS and the Chief Agronomist* by Galina Nikolayeva in late 1955 and urged its readers to learn from the example of Natasha who worked selflessly as an agronomist on a Machine Tractor Station.[22] In general, one can see that the Chinese followed Russian agro-science in its emphasis on practice over theory, its rejection or distrust of genetics, and in the socialist realist approach to dramatizing achievements.

State Farms and the Great Leap Forward

By the latter part of the 1950s, this heritage positioned the state farms as an easy target for Mao Zedong's hostility, particularly because of his belief that the Chinese rural-based revolution had established a new, more potent practice of Marxism. The "two-line struggle" in state farms was fought by Deng Zihui,[23] who defended conventional large-scale agriculture, or in this case, the Soviet model, against rivals such as Wang Zhen and Tan Zhenlin, who favored the Maoist solution: military-run farms, farms set up "on the fly," and the commune.[24] Tan and Wang pushed Deng out of his central role in rural policy-making for a time in the late 1950s. [25] During periods of Maoist dominance, material resources—including the quality of land, climate, the availability of machinery, quality of residences and production facilities—were regarded as of lesser significance than the subjective forces human will and energy. Moreover, the application of military campaign-style tactics and methods would also produce better economic results. In early 1958, for example, Wang Zhen claimed that the Maoist approach to housing farm workers on the highlands—using tents, sod houses or dug-outs rather than brick structures—was a way that Mao-inspired farms could become profitable faster.[26] Maoists also saw great virtue in self-sufficiency in all things. These ideas helped shape policies to both rapidly expand the amount of grain production (later known by its post-GLF slogan to "make grain the key link") and diversify production on farms.[27] For a state farm in Qinghai, for example, this meant planting significantly larger and more fields in grains such as wheat and barley. This was a Maoist innovation in that such production—growing grain in the arid, windy and cold Qinghai-Tibet plateau—was experimental and challenged conventional small farmer and agro-science expertise. The Qinghai farm also diversified its local sources of income and nutrition by expanding efforts to net more fish from Qinghai Lake, a practice that local people—primarily Tibetans—had done only rarely if at all.[28] They also began mining in the hills around the lake in order to lay the foundation for industrialization.[29] Another Maoist project on state farms was to use young, "volunteer" laborers who were, in Mao's view, uniquely capable of getting difficult and complex jobs done because of their convictions and boundless energy. In the 1950s and again in the Cultural Revolution years, the Communist Party and Youth League set up relocation schemes designed, in part, to leverage the inexpensive labor and politically correct attitudes of young people. Mao believed, too, that his communes were better than state farms as an indigenous way to both socialize agriculture and produce more food while taking advantage of China's comparative advantage of surplus labor. They would produce food on a large scale but with lower costs and more nimble local-level control.

Mao and his supporters blasted the Soviet-modeled state farms for their bureaucratism and cost. Although shrill and politically motivated, their critiques articulated a more or less accurate description of the Soviet model on state farms. It required expensive and scarce machinery and fuel to operate according to the principles of modern agricultural science. The large scale of the farms and heavy investment in many projects at once—construction of residences, canals, roads, machinery, fuel, and processing equipment—required careful recordkeeping and data analysis as well as expert management of human, land and material resources. The Soviet-inspired state farms were overseen by central government officials who had budgetary oversight over all expenditures. Finally, given the vast investment in everything from warehouses, housing, recreational facilities, canals, farm fields and machinery, state farms were slow to provide a return that approached the start-up costs.

In 1958, Wang Zhen explained how new, Maoist approaches would be more successful than the Soviet model: "We will use the great enthusiasm of the masses, courageously overcome all difficulties, resolutely struggle to set up farms from scratch (*baishou qijia*)" unlike the Soviet model, which meant "waiting until conditions are mature, to dogmatically make plans and set up farms behind closed doors, separate from the masses, be overly critical, and apply restrictions and fetters."[30] Instead of respecting science and technicians, Wang argued, one should follow the masses and their enthusiasms. His polemic was aimed mostly at the government officials and experts that his own ministry employed. To no one's surprise, as a military man, he assumed that agricultural production was a static target, not unlike a military objective during wartime. In this view, large-scale increases in agricultural output could be achieved in a burst of revolutionary action by armies of farmers sowing and reaping with nothing but the heat of their convictions to nourish and clothe them. Between 1957 and 1962, the total population on state farms grew from about 800,000 to 6 million.[31]

But by October 1960, as the colossal disaster of the Great Leap had pushed the Maoists into retreat, Deng Zihui felt confident enough in the Soviet model for state farms to speak to the land reclamation staff in the following way:

> Beginning in 1958, some said that state farms had no future and that communes had a great future. Now we can see that this view was incorrect. State farms are enterprises owned by all the people. Although at present they make up less than

five percent of the nation's cultivated area, this will increase . . . communes will in the future also become owned by all the people. In this way we can see the state farms have a bright future.[32]

In the aftermath of the Great Leap Forward, Deng regained his position and power in the government, and set about restoring central ownership and control of the resources—a fundamental tenet of the Soviet model—that had been dispersed by the Leap policies.[33] In Qinghai province, this meant shutting down all of the farms—excluding military-run farms and prison farms—that had been set up on the grasslands with laborers from outside the province.[34] In 1962, after reasserting his authority over the Maoist Tan Zhen-lin, Deng addressed the central committee and Mao himself. He claimed great accomplishments for the state farms, reaffirmed their potential superiority as producers and blamed poor management for their failures over the Leap years. Hotheaded Mao may have understood this as a direct attack.[35] Later that year, the Ministry of State Farms and Land Reclamation completed a 500 page manual with a title that only a central government official could love: *Comprehensive Land Use Planning and Design for State-Run Farms.* Published in 1963, three years into the estrangement between the People's Republic and the Soviet Union, the text was remarkably balanced in its assessment of the Soviet model for state farms:

> We must study the advanced experiences of the Soviet Union. But the historical conditions of the Soviet Union's economy, natural conditions, and land use are different from our country. So for this reason, when setting up and planning state-run farms we need to keep in mind the conditions of our country, especially the great resources and huge population.[36]

Overall, the Ministry noted in its 1986 institutional history that the Soviet model of state farms had contributed to China's state farms in many ways, particularly in the areas of surveying, planning, accounting, production management and the management of machinery.[37]

Analysis

State farms' importance in China was mainly regional, particularly along China's northern and western borders with the Soviet Union (see Map 8.1).[38] Here the Soviet Union was not so much a model as a threat. Both Russia and China had historical claims and contemporary interests along their Inner Asian and Northeast Asian borders that they hoped to consolidate in the 1950s and 1960s. Both sides tended to believe, somewhat independently of the other, that agriculture—as opposed to raising livestock, for example—was

Map 8.1. Main Areas of State Farm Development in China

intrinsic to establishing sovereignty. In border and remote areas, state farms built new towns or even constituted counties with facilities and fields spread over hundreds of square kilometers over which they had jurisdiction. In some cases, they were in areas that were lightly populated or uninhabited. In this sense, their most important product was urbanization rather than grain, meat or wool. Particularly in Xinjiang, state farms run by the *bingtuan* or Production and Construction Corps were the nucleus for many towns and cities built from the ground up after 1949.[39] Given that many of these farms were built following Soviet blueprints, one can see that the Soviet model shaped the everyday lives of millions of Chinese citizens.

Although often located in regions with low population density, the problem was not that local laborers could not be found. Rather, the development of agriculture was understood to be a cultural attribute introduced by Han Chinese who were uniquely prepared, among China's many ethnic groups, to deliver this service to the nation. Similarly, as will be described below, when

Nikita Khrushchev sent groups of young adults to the borderlands to build farms and cities, he also sent primarily ethnic Russians. Over the history of the PRC, Heilongjiang province in the far northeast, with a relatively large area of fertile, well-watered uncultivated lands, as well as a relatively small population, was a main area of state farm development. Its farms were the showplaces of the state farm system, with high rates of investment, mechanization, specialization, and surpluses, especially of grain.[40]

The boundless fields of state farms in Heilongjiang and elsewhere, cultivated by a single worker on a tractor, often a young woman, was an imported icon of the state farm. It was an image which occurred over and over again in the publications and posters of the 1950s.[41] A woman tractor driver was featured in just this way on the reverse side of the one yuan bank note introduced in 1958.[42] This and other Party-crafted images of the agricultural future depicted a version of rural life freed from the grueling manual labor, stifling parochialism and wasteful superstitions of the village. The tractor took on nearly magical qualities for villagers; with one, all things would be better.[43] State farms would be progressive places that brought the amenities of the urban life—high rise apartments, electricity, schools, movie theaters, dancing halls, medical clinics—to farmers. Just as the smoke-stacked factory and multi-story building were icons of modernity for New China, so was the tractor an icon for agricultural and rural modernity during the Mao years. In all this, the Chinese Communists followed the Soviet model closely.[44]

State farms were typically ignored in considerations of Communist Chinese agriculture, both domestically and abroad, because they have been a tiny part of the national statistical picture. In 1964, after more than fifteen years of rapid growth, China's state farms still constituted only around four percent of the national cultivated area, but produced an even smaller percentage of the nation's total agricultural output.[45] The size of the landholdings of the state farm system remained steady for decades at about four percent of China's national cultivated area. The World Bank estimated that the state farm system produced about 3 percent of the nation's total rural output in the 1990s.[46] In contrast, large state firms dominated agriculture and overall employment in the Soviet Union. Those state farms live on in the Russian Federation, where they account for 80 percent of agricultural land, have an average size of 6,000 hectares and employ an average of more than 150 workers each.[47] In contrast, state-owned enterprises of all kinds provided employment for a small minority in China, even during the peak of state socialism in the 1970s.[48]

The growth of state farms in China was limited by the basic structures of the human and physical geography of China. In the early 1950s optimistic planners believed that China's cultivated area could be doubled by using mechanized state farms in the grasslands, forests and marshes of the northern and western borders. In fact, the nation did not have much virgin land that could be cultivated profitably and sustainably. However, the broader constraint was demographic. Village agriculture—in its various iterations as co-operatives, collectives, communes, and as smallholder agriculture—employed far too many people plowing fields, harvesting and hauling who until the 1980s could not be accommodated in any other sector of the economy. Chinese policies during the Mao years therefore bound farmers to village lands and the meager surplus of the collective economy after state procurements had taken their share and through the household registration system.[49]

Nevertheless, the aggregate statistics are not inconsequential, even for a country as large as China. Nationwide, by the 1990s, there were still about 2,200 Ministry of Agriculture farms which employed and housed about 12 million people.[50] About 22 percent of farmland in Heilongjiang in the 1990s was owned by 108 state farms that were home to 1.6 million people or about 8 percent of the province's agricultural population.[51]

Beginning in the 1980s, but especially in the 1990s, state-owned farms went through a range of enterprise reforms designed to eventually make most of them independent, public corporations. Initial steps included giving farm managers more basic managerial authority in how they ran their businesses and the degree to which they could retain profits or absorb their losses.[52] State farms were also encouraged to experiment with contracting, shareholding and other kinds of enterprise reforms inspired by the Household Responsibility System, which had replaced collective farming in China's villages. State farms in one region of Heilongjiang, for example, reported in the late 1990s that most of their fields had been contracted out to employees who worked the land as their own.[53] These corporations retained partial or majority government stakes but relinquished many of their governmental and social service functions.

The dairy sector is a good example of both the niche dominance of the state farm through the 1980s as well as the enterprise reforms that began that decade. Municipal and provincial governments ran Mao-era China's largest dairies and produced the large majority of the country's dairy products consumed by city-dwellers.[54] Shanghai Bright Dairy is one such firm. Its life began in 1956 as a city government-owned enterprise. In the 1990s, Shanghai Bright began enterprise reforms and in 2002 it became a publicly traded firm that retained majority ownership by the Shanghai municipal government.[55] Beijing's Sanyuan Foods is another former municipal government-owned dairy enterprise that has been restructured into a food products conglomerate that retains state ownership.[56] Nationwide, the economic reforms of the 1980s and 1990s created a dairy sector that is dominated by family farmers, at least by volume of milk produced. But large corporate firms—that used to be state-owned firms and retain some state ownership—dominate processing and marketing of dairy products.[57]

The Soviet Model as Enterprise Management

Introduction

As the preceding section suggested, one can define the Soviet model in agriculture following the "two-line" struggle in politics. The Maoist approach was dominant during the Great Leap Forward and during the Cultural Revolution; during other periods, and up through the 1980s, the Soviet model prevailed. Throughout these decades, especially for those drawn into the vortex of "struggle," Chinese politics appeared to be a zero-sum game with factional rivalries splitting the republic from Mao's dais to the village threshing ground. Over time, however, the evidence shows that the body politic was not split into two halves. The Soviet model and Maoist methods often prescribed similar or identical solutions to complex problems. They overlapped in general ways as well. At the national level, for example, both emphasized the importance of the military and national security. At the operational level of state farms, there were many similarities, too. For example, in February 1957, Deng Zihui had argued that state farms ought to work toward self-sufficiency in grain, oils and vegetables by putting officials to work doing manual labor, building with mud bricks rather than with wood and kiln bricks, and diversifying their operations. Although he was a staunch opponent of Maoist romanticism, he supported self-sufficiency and diversification as sensible enterprise goals.[58] Or in the midst of leaping forward under Maoist fervor in 1960, Wang Zhen reaffirmed the nation's commitment to Soviet agro-science, particularly close planting.[59] And, as for that distinctively Maoist program of sending young people to border and remote regions to work on state farms; it was copied directly from the Russians' Virgin Lands program.[60]

Within the overlap of these approaches, one can see that the Soviet model was consistently influential in the state farms system. One way to document this influence is to focus on profitability and centralized decision-making as enterprise management issues. Although neither Soviet or Maoist methods had distinguished records of profit-generation, the orthodox state socialist approach emphasized that state farms as enterprises that were to be operated according to centrally determined plans and were to be evaluated based on their investment and, above all, their fulfillment of plan targets. Fulfilling plan targets meant profits flowed back to central government coffers. This places the Soviet model in contrast to both Maoist decentralization of budgetary and management authority and the enterprise reforms of China's state-owned enterprises of the past twenty years, which also devolved management and budget control to the farm level.

This is not to say that Stalinist state farms were profit-oriented; far from it. The master they served was "the plan" and central Party control of it. This is the most significant aspect of the Soviet model in enterprise management. Individual farm managers had to get approval from central government officials for every expenditure. Moreover, surpluses or profits were not theirs to keep. With no financial incentive to increase profitability, farm managers instead competed to get budget line support for housing and leisure facilities which could then be supported by the farm's production. One result was that the best equipped, most comfortable farms were the biggest money-losers. Those with more "bare bones" facilities for employees and managers were more likely to make money.[61]

The literature on Soviet management also makes clear that economic production was to serve political goals and its political master, the Communist Party, an orientation that Maoism pushed further along the "red" continuum. Although managerial expertise was touted as essential by Stalin and his successors, enterprises were still to be run by Party officials. The Soviet model also called for a variety of campaigns to reach production and other goals, a well-known feature of Chinese life during the Mao years. Soviet citizens also went to endless meetings and were constantly subject to Party-crafted messages and, above all, supervision designed to make them more loyal and more productive. In particular, Party officials in China and the Soviet Union both wielded tremendous power over their employees and citizens through the dossier system. Soviet methods in industrial management were draped in patriotism, too, and conveyed management and economic principles through the language of war and battle.[62] In all this, the influence of the Soviet model was writ large on the People's Republic at both the organizational level and in people's daily lives.

Profitability and Enterprise Management on State Farms since 1949

The focus on making state farms economically profitable enterprises that would fill state coffers rather than drain them, goes back to the earliest days of the PRC and survived the leftist phases of the Great Leap Forward and Cultural Revolution. Already in 1951, for example, a Ministry of Agriculture report on state farms articulated what were to become enduring problems and patterns of state-owned enterprises in the Mao years. [63] The problems were technical and managerial, rather than political or ideological. Since state farms were wholly state-owned from the start, no adjustments could be made to the management of farms as enterprises. Instead, wage and benefit systems were the main area of contention and reform in the operation of state farms. State farms shared this quality with other parts of the "iron rice bowl" economy.[64]

This presents an obvious contrast with the village world, where destructive political and ideological fights—sometimes no more than the settling of village feuds—were waged over the ownership and management of fields, livestock, vegetable plots, tools and other inputs as well as over the tools, output and marketing of sideline occupations. Villagers' collectively owned and run farms, for example, were believed to be undermined by hidden counter-revolutionaries or people with "bad" family backgrounds, problems that Chinese Communists saw lurking in the villages through the 1970s. The politics of land and resource ownership dogged the collective sector and undermined its productivity by alienating smallholder farmers. For Mao especially, the villages were a key battleground for socialism. Making them truly socialist was an ongoing endeavor, because of the long tradition of private landholding and management in China.[65]

In 1952, the Communist Party's highest rural policy-making group, the Rural Work Department led by Deng Zihui, addressed the management problems in its First Meeting on State Farm Work. Deng's report on state farms described the rapid growth of state farms and also offered criticisms of farm management that remained consistent over time. Officials did not use the necessary cost accounting methods, had an attitude of working carelessly without attention to profit, loss, extravagance, or waste, and believed that government subsidies to state farms were unavoidable. The organizations were overstaffed, especially with non-productive staff, leading to high levels of loss. These farms were plagued by low production and high capital investment and had to be subsidized each year, reported Deng. There were also farms with high production, and even higher capital investment which also nevertheless required increasing subsidies. The assessment included non-agricultural aspects of the farms, such as high expenditures on buildings, which "was a distortion of the advanced experiences of the Soviets." Some cadres sought to have "above all the appearance of greatness with grand buildings," which resulted in heavy investment, slow returns and drags on production. There were some farms that had been set up on poor soil or difficult topography requiring a great deal of money just to get the land into production. In general, Deng found that it was far easier to set up the farms than run them successfully.[66] In general, one can see that the metric by which farms were evaluated was sending profits or surpluses to the national plan.

Efforts were made to change the way farms were set up and run to improve their profitability. Piecework and work brigade contracting were

introduced in the mid-1950s on some farms to provide incentives, for example, or recent school graduates were recruited as laborers in part because
they were paid less than former soldiers, who otherwise constituted a large
source of labor for the system.[67] Mao-inspired policies held that setting up
and running new stand-alone farms "on the fly" with military campaign
fervor and principles of local self-sufficiency was going to be more cost effective, but it turned out to be less effective and more costly than the Soviet
model of slower growth of existing farms through centralized, bureaucratic
planning. In the late 1950s, for example, existing farms opened up new
fields haphazardly and non-agricultural enterprises started their own farms
as part of the Great Leap Forward's emphasis on grain production and self-
sufficiency. Yet, a report from the Ministry of Agricultural Reclamation in
1962, after the chaotic overexpansion of the Great Leap Forward policies
had been radically scaled back, made many of the same critiques that had
been articulated a decade earlier. Farm managers were failing to produce
surpluses, machinery suffered from poor maintenance, and advanced farming techniques were not used. Farms had high investment levels but very
low returns.[68] State farms had already gained this "bad reputation" by the
end of the 1950s.[69]

The goal of profitability as a hallmark of the Soviet model can be best seen
at the aggregate level in the rise and fall of military-run, youth-staffed state
farms in the Great Leap Forward and in the Cultural Revolution. Between
1958 and 1960, and again between 1968 and 1971, hundreds of new state
farms were set up in eighteen provinces and regions using the production
and construction corps model that had been pioneered in Xinjiang. They
became home to millions of former soldiers, their dependents, exiled Red
Guards and a range of other "misfits," the unemployed, and people relocated for dam construction.[70] The reduction in numbers in these farms in
the wake of the Great Leap Forward collapse has been alluded to already.
In the case of the Cultural Revolution, by February 1973, the national
government recommended that these new state farms be reduced in size
and numbers because of the enormous losses they were incurring. The
Lanzhou corps in western China was shut down in 1973; Guangdong, Yunnan, Guangxi and Fujian production corps followed suit in 1974. By 1975,
all corps farms were shut down.[71] Long before Maoism was repudiated, the
national government reduced its stake in state farms for primarily economic
reasons. These state farms simply lost too much money and produced too
little food or other goods.[72] Another instance in which profitability was promoted as the standard for state farm performance prior to the full embrace

of the market economy was in an influential 1977 *People's Daily* editorial. It cited the success of Hubei province's state farms as proof that the state-owned sector could produce consistent profits. In 1973, 90 percent of its farms operated at a loss. By 1976, an even greater percentage reportedly turned a profit.[73]

The most significant legacy of the Maoist policies for state farms' financial ill health was their boom in population which made it difficult to contribute large surpluses or profits to the state. The western province of Gansu, for example, reported that it placed six different kinds of laborers on state farms. This included communist officials who lost their positions as part of administrative down-sizing, "Rightist" political exiles, a variety of migrants from Shanghai, Youth League Volunteers, undocumented rural migrants from eastern China, and school graduates, orphans and the dependents of people who had already been placed on the farms.[74] Much, but not all of this population growth was linked to Maoist policies, including those of the Third Front.[75] The history of Unit 143 farm in Xinjiang is similar in its broadest outlines. In 2005, the farm had an area of 350 square km and a population of 36,000, of whom 7,200 were staff and workers.[76] It was founded in 1950 with 1,800 troops. Two years later, they had been joined by 35 men from Hunan and 410 women from Shandong. Over the next ten years, the farm gained about 3,200 recent school graduates from Shanghai, Henan, Guangdong and Jiangsu in eastern China, 400 discharged soldiers, hundreds of family members and other dependents, an undisclosed number of prisoners, as well as more than 5,100 undocumented migrants who came seeking steady meals and a paycheck. By 1964, the farm had grown to nearly 25,000 residents with an especially large increase during the Great Leap Forward.[77]

Nationwide, by 1986, the cultivated area on state farms had grown by ten times since the early 1950s, but the population on those farms grew by a factor of 29. The number of actual employees grew by nearly 14 times. These people had to be fed, housed, schooled, entertained, and provided for in retirement. The cultivated area on state farms per capita fell by more than half from the 1950s to the 1980s. (See Table 8.1)[78]

It is therefore unsurprising that state farms had difficulties making money for the national plan. In this sense they were like other state-owned enterprises, such as factories or coal mines, which also shouldered the functions of municipal governments. They did not face political pressure to make them more socialist, as was the case with village agriculture, since they were already fully owned by the state. Rather, the pressure was always to produce more for state coffers and therefore a greater return on investment.

Table 8.1.   **Per Capita Cultivated Area on State Farms, 1950s–1980s**

	Chinese mu per capita	*Hectares per capita*
1952	14.8	About 1 ha.
1962	8.4	.5 ha
1986	5.9	About .4 ha

The Soviet Model: Agriculture and National Security

The Virgins Lands and Heilongjiang, the Bei Da Huang

The most notable example of the Soviet influence on Chinese agriculture was the Virgin Lands program.[79] The Chinese side applied this model to its decades long efforts to develop the "Great Northern Wastes" (*Bei da huang*) of Heilongjiang into a grain producing region. Both countries had traditions of state-sponsored resettlement as a means to establish sovereignty. Nevertheless, it is also obvious that the Soviet plan for modern-style organized population resettlement and land reclamation was adapted and used in China.

In the 1950s, Khrushchev came to believe that the best way for the Soviet Union to solve its food crisis was through "extensification." He argued this method at Party meetings in 1953; in March 1954, the Party officially announced the plan "On Increasing Grain Production in 1954–1955 Through the Development of Virgin and Idle Lands." The Central Committee decreed that the country's effort to increase grain production should be focused on bringing empty lands in Kazakhstan, Siberia, the Urals, the Far East, and the Volga into cultivation. These dryland farms produced good harvests in several years, which encouraged expansion of the program, but drought or other severe weather caused large production drops in other years. There were many ecological problems with the scheme, including erratic weather, dust storms and soil degradation exacerbated by the rashness and grandiosity of the plan's implementation and the ecologically inappropriate farming methods used. The Virgin Lands produced generally low yields, which made the grain more expensive than grain grown in traditional agricultural areas and brought into question the usefulness of the whole endeavor. By 1963, Khrushchev admitted that Soviet Union's food problem could not be solved by extensification and that greater returns could be realized by intensification or raising the yields of existing lands.[80]

The Soviet plan was clearly a blueprint for the Chinese approach to their "virgin lands." Articles and photos published by the Russian and Chinese Communists made this link very clear in their rhetoric and imagery.[81] Youth League leader Hu Yaobang linked the Chinese youth movement in a friendly rivalry with the Soviet Union's program.[82] The evidence suggests that both Russian and Chinese youth responded vigorously to the project of building new farms in harsh conditions with like-minded peers. Elizabeth's McGuire's chapter in this book recounts the story of Chen Peixian, who had studied abroad in Moscow and subsequently volunteered to work in the Soviet Virgin Lands in 1958.[83] An editorial in the *China Youth News* asserted common knowledge of Soviet efforts among its readership and stated unequivocally that Chinese youth should emulate their Soviet Virgin Lands peers.[84]

> We all know how the "Communist Youth League City"[85] was built by Soviet youths from the staking of the first tent all the way to its construction as a beautiful city in the wastes north of Heilongjiang. All of us also know that last year more than 100,000 Soviet youth went to this new area under the slogan of "We do not seek a life of leisure," and that they have already opened up an enormous area of empty land equal to our Hebei province. This year the land will provide to the nation more than 1 billion pood [1 pood equals 16.38 kg] of grain. In China this year there are also many youth who have gone to the frontiers to work under harsh conditions. The youth who go to the frontiers to work should study the example of the Soviet youth and also study the example of the pioneering youth in our country who have mounted postings in the frontiers.[86]

Yang Hua, the leader of the first Beijing-based youth team, announced at their send-off that Soviet youths' city-building and land-pioneering was an encouraging example for the Chinese team.[87] In practice, the Chinese movement of young volunteers was also similar to the Soviet effort. The Communist Youth League in China rallied young people in patriotic meetings and promised hard-fought but glorious honor in the battle to produce more food. Russian and Han Chinese both eagerly sought to undergo the transformative "tempering" of hard work with like-minded comrades in their service to the Motherland and socialism. By December 1955, 30 teams of youth had been organized to "Attack Poverty" and "Attack the Empty Lands."[88] The first group was feted by national leaders and featured in national newspapers. Their effort was designed to model the experience for young people throughout China, but the project was in no way typical. It was extraordinarily well supported by government departments all along the way. Like Stakhanovites elsewhere in the Sino-Soviet world, the reality of model labor was far removed from the propaganda version of it.[89] Over time, many border and remote provinces and regions were home to youth volunteer reclamation team farms, but Heilongjiang bore their imprint most heavily.[90] A county in Heilongjiang commemorated its Youth League farmers in glossy photos that were typically reserved for shots of tractor factories and piles of grain and other measures of economic growth.[91]

One is struck again by the overlap of Soviet and Chinese methods. Both plans shared a naive, romantic, revolutionary approach to political and economic change that transcended the politics of state socialism in both countries, and managed to glorify both the collectivity of socialist workers as well as the accomplishments of Promethean, flag-waving individuals in both countries.

The similarities also can be observed in the ways the programs failed. Both sides realized relatively quickly that achieving cost-effective results was far more complex than the simple equations of land and labor that they relied upon. Putting food on the table in Moscow or funding industrial enterprises in Xi'an required more than good weather, rich soil, enthusiastic workers and tractors. Large-scale agri-businesses depend on capital-intensive infrastructure, and technical and managerial expertise to run smoothly and profitably. Harvesting, storing and transporting grain requires agricultural machinery, trucks, railways, fuel, spare parts and skilled personnel to use them. Deciding when to harvest and store the grain is crucial and depends on savvy local knowledge and experience that farmers accumulate over generations. In the Soviet case, transport bottlenecks, and poor or over-centralized management resulted in under-performing crops, delays in harvesting, spoilage or loss of harvested grain and neglected machinery. Khrushchev and Mao had hoped to accomplish quick agricultural growth through a great exertion of *will*. It simply was not possible to do this without great costs.[92] Nevertheless, the Chinese Party sent millions of youth to state farms in the late 1950s and again during the Cultural Revolution.[93]

Gulags, Laogai and National Security

State farms also played an important role in national security in its broadest sense—redistribution of population; the control of territory; and punishing and isolating persons considered to be a grave threat to state and society. A range of policies has been used to redress the severe imbalance of China's human and land resources. Beginning with the First Five-Year Plan (1953–1957) the government sought to redistribute the nation's human and industrial resources—the vast majority of which were located on the eastern third of the landmass—to inland provinces to achieve a more equitable and rational basis for prosperity while serving the broader goal of building national sovereignty. In this, one can see the broad application of highly centralized, national security-oriented socialism. Like Russia, China was a continental power with a proud metropolitan political and cultural core and a vast hinterland. Just as Socialism and Modernity would radiate outwards from Moscow, so did the Chinese socialist state have an unquestioned center and source at Beijing. Overall, of course, one can only conclude that the Chinese Communist Party has applied the Soviet model of territorial control with greater success, both demographically and strategically. China's administrative system of autonomous regions and the policies toward the ethnic groups that dominated them followed Stalinist cues, for example, but the Chinese side has maintained its centralized iron grip without significant interruption.

Once the household registration system was in place in the late 1950s, the Party and government were able to control where people lived and worked. Within this matrix of control, state farms were used to absorb excess labor, as has been described above. They provided jobs for soldiers released from the military, the unemployed, destitute or those displaced for the construction of roads and dams. These farms were also modern versions of the imperial strategy to reduce the cost and complexity of garrisoning troops by making them at least partially self-sufficient. State farms were also part of the nation's internal security system. Political prisoners and criminals were often sent to state farms that were run by the prison system. These farms had institutional ancestors in both imperial China's practice of internal exile and in Stalin's gulags.

In northwest China, the region most commonly associated with the prison system, most of the prisons were engaged in agricultural production or processing.[94] In the 1990s, Qinghai's prisons produced grain and vegetables as well as leather goods, bricks, tile, machine tools and hydropower machinery. Other sites had gold or copper mines.[95] Although reliable information about the prison system is difficult to find, it seems that the Chinese prison system innovated on the Soviet model in two respects. First, Mao and Maoism placed greater faith in the idea that these prisons could remold people. To this end, there was a more comprehensive system of parole and re-entry surveillance that was somewhat like being under house arrest.[96] Additionally, observers speculated that the Chinese prison system was larger both in absolute terms but also as a percentage of the total population, and has had a stronger institutional and economic foundations.[97] In these ways, state farms served the Chinese state above and beyond producing food and other agricultural products for state coffers.

This was clearly the case in the development of rubber plantations in semi-tropical Yunnan province with a conventional labor forced dominated at first by former soldiers. In Xishuang Banna (Sipsong Panna) about 1,700 soldiers set up the first rubber plantation in 1955 in an area that was dominated by the Tai ethnic group. By the end of the 1950s, 37,000 laborers from three counties in Hunan province in central China were transferred to work on state farms in southern Yunnan. When asked, they reported that they did not know exactly why they had been moved so far to work as farmers. They assumed it was because the Tai people were backward or primitive, unable to do the kinds of work required on a state farm. The state-run media popularized ideas that Han Chinese had "advanced culture" and were skilled farmers. The farms became worlds unto themselves that were linked into national government ministries, not subject to the local government's control. State farm employees' children were born in state farm hospitals, attended state farm schools, lived in state farm housing and went to state farm movie theaters. It was not until the 1980s that large numbers of local, non-Chinese laborers were hired to work for the farm. By the 1990s, Xishuang Banna state farm employees and their dependents amounted to about 145,000 people, or about 17 percent of the population.[98] Although the Yunnan region has presented less of a strategic threat historically to the nation than Heilongjiang or Xinjiang, the state farms have made permanent contributions to the state building tasks they were charged with, if only by virtue of their size and staying power.[99]

The Xinjiang Production and Construction Corps (PCC), which was founded in 1950 with former Guomindang and Communist troops illustrates even more compellingly agriculture's role in state-building. Xinjiang's state farms are the most obvious descendants of *tunken* imperial military colonization policies that had been used since at least the Han dynasty. Like state farms in Yunnan, PCC farms report directly to the central government. The corps' influence in the regional political economy of China's Far West is hard to overstate. Although shut down briefly in the 1970s, the Corps was formally re-established in 1981.[100] According to the most recent statistics, the Corps runs 174 farms and ranches on about one-third of Xinjiang's total arable land and employs about thirteen percent of Xinjiang's population. Its goals are explicitly linked with basic state building as a strategy to stabilize the Xinjiang region in the face of regional ethnic or sectarian unrest. The system has operated consistently with substantial losses, even with its wide-ranging and successful businesses, with perhaps 80 percent of its budget being funded directly by the central government in the 1990s.[101] The fact that the PCC still exists is evidence of the staying power of the Soviet model in agriculture and agribusiness.

In Qinghai province, farms were also set up in places with low populations. Their most important product has been urbanization. Delingha farm was located at the eastern end of the Chaidam basin, a desert region with tiny patches of agriculture and highland pastures. When the Communists came to power, there were a few buildings and fields at Delingha, the result of Republic of China agricultural expansion policies. The town was founded in 1954 by a group of 1,600 prisoners who were said to have built the road to Delingha as they went.[102] By 1957, a journalist who passed through wrote that the farm was already "famous" for its heroic production of grains and vegetables.[103] One laborer—a prison inmate at the time—wrote with pride in his memoirs of the various workshops they had built as well as barracks, offices and warehouses, and a guest house, in addition to the 200,000 mu of fields and kilometers of irrigation ditches. They produced a surplus of grain—one-third of the production he guessed—that was supplied to the government. In six years, they had witnessed the conversion of Delingha from wilderness into a productive farm and the growth of Wulan's county seat Baiyin into small, modern town with wide streets, electricity and new apartments.[104] Other farms like Delingha in the Chaidam basin, including the Gebi, Huantoutala, and Gahai farms were similarly staffed with a prisoner workforce—primarily Han Chinese—transferred in from outside the province. The 2000 census showed that the region now has a large majority of Han Chinese. The historically dominant Mongol population of the Chaidam basin fell to about thirteen percent of the registered population.[105]

Conclusion

In this chapter, I have documented two ways in which the state farm system was permanently imprinted with the Soviet model: in its centralized enterprise management system and through the use of state farms as parts of national security. Overall, one can also see that China's Communist Party is still committed to a degree of state ownership in industries that it considers essential to national security. The oil and automobile industries, for example, are still dominated by firms that are either wholly state owned or publicly traded corporations with majority government ownership stakes. In this, its commitment to a centralized state socialism, one can see the enduring legacy of the Soviet model.

But what about the agricultural sector? Since most state farms have also been turned into public corporations, is there any sense at all in which the Soviet model has survived? The strongest evidence supporting an enduring Soviet model is to be found in Xinjiang's PCC, an entity that mixed Stalinist state power with Maoist military production. State farms there still play the geostrategic role they were assigned in the 1950s. Although the Xinjiang farms are agricultural enterprises, they are more important to the state for their role in helping consolidate Chinese control over a region understood to be vulnerable to ethnic instability.[106] In fact, compared to the relative decline in the economic and social significance of agriculture and peasant life generally, one can see that state farms' geostrategic importance in Xinjiang in particular has remained the same or even grown.

Notes

1. Stalin advised the Chinese to be cautious in introducing socialism, but at that very same time, collectivization was harshly pursued in Eastern Europe and the Baltics, though without the upheaval of the 1930s. On the advice that Stalin gave to the Chinese Communists, see the introduction and chapter three in Hua-yu Li, *Mao and the Economic Stalinization of China, 1948–1953* (Lanham, MD: Rowman & Littlefield, 2006), 2–4, 95–116.

2. In fact, one suspects that the civilizational definition will become more important over time. There seems to be more to explain about Stalinism as a civilization, and probably more that is generalizable in the history of the twentieth century. It mixed thrilling, giddy optimism with the cruelest, most calculating demagoguery and scapegoating. It was manifested in cultural palaces, Stakhavonite heroes, and cheery music. It was scientific, martial, internationalist and yet also superstitious and isolationist. It promoted healthy leisure and yet restricted movement with internal passports. See Stephen Kotkin, *Magnetic Mountain: Stalinism as a Civilization* (Berkeley: University of California Press, 1995). Sheila Fitzpatrick, *Everyday Stalinism: Ordinary Life in Extraordinary Times* (New York: Oxford University Press, 1999). Deborah A. Kaple, *A Dream of a Red Factory: The Legacy of High Stalinism in China* (New York: Oxford University Press, 1994) and Yu Miin-ling's contribution in this volume. Stalin was a brutal tyrant who used state power to murder millions; students of the past are increasingly left only with horror at his excesses. On the "planned, logical, and 'politically correct' mass slaughter" committed by Stalin, see Stephane Courtois et al., *Black Book of Communism: Crimes, Terror, Repression*, trans. Jonathan Murphy and Mark Kramer (Cambridge: Harvard University Press, 1999), 3–9.

3. See the section on the First Five-Year Plan in Carl Riskin, *China's Political Economy: The Quest for Development since 1949* (Oxford: Oxford University Press, 1987), 53–60.

4. In this, they were like the primarily urban enterprises or "danwei" that made up the cultural and physical landscape of Chinese urban life under socialism.

5. *The Black Book of Communism* claims that the Chinese Communists built the "biggest penal system of all time," 498.

6. A popular music video in the 1990s, *Qingzang gaoyuan* [Qinghai tibet plateau] for example, as well as karaoke videos of it, mixed images of soaring peaks and flocks of animals with darks shots of people doing harsh work in heavy overcoats. The song was made famous by Li Na.

7. Richard Anderson and James D. Seymour, *New Ghosts, Old Ghosts* (Armonk, NY: M. E. Sharpe, 1998), 8.

8. A Party report from March 1949, before the People's Republic of China had even been founded, mapped out a role for "tractor farms." State farms would be mechanized first, and their tractors would help nearby farmers with their plowing and harvesting, providing farmers with an incentive to pool their land, a goal that was both ideologically socialist and economically modern. A Ministry of Agriculture report from 1952 emphasized that state-run farms used scientific methods to farm on a large scale according to careful plans. "Guoying jixie nongchang jianchang chengxu zhanxing banfa" (1952) [Provisional rules on the method for setting up state-run mechanized farms], reprinted in *Nongken gongzuo wenjian ziliao xuanbian* [Selected materials on agricultural reclamation] (Beijing: Nongye, 1983), 59–64.

9. "Zhongyang renmin zhengfu nongyebu guanyu yijiuwusan nian guoying jixie nongchang de qingkuang he jinhou gongzuo yijian" [The ministry of agriculture of the central people's government's report on mechanized state farms in 1953 and recommendations for future work], reprinted in *Nongken gongzuo wenjian ziliao xuanbian*, (1954), 107.

10. "Staff Appraisal Report China State Farms Commercialization Project," The World Bank (1998) Report no. 16004-CHA, 15. John W. Longworth and Colin G. Brown, *Agribusiness Reforms in China* (Wallingford: CAB International, 1995), 181. Since the 1990s, many of these farms have become public corporations while retaining minority or majority government stakes.

11. The government reported the following performance, based on the old yuan, in 1954. One trillion yuan had been invested in state farms over the period 1950-1953, or about 500,000 yuan per mu. Total losses over the period—understood here to mean deficits on annual operating costs—were about 100 billion yuan. "The Ministry of Agriculture of the Central People's Government's Report on Mechanized State Farms in 1953 and Recommendations for Future Work," 109. Deng Zihui, "Zhonggong zhongyang nongcun gongzuobu guanyu guoying nongchang gongzuo zuotanhui de baogao (Caogao)" (1952) [The rural work department of the central committee of the Communist Party's report at the consultative meeting on state farms (draft)], reprinted in *Nongken gongzuo wenjian ziliao xuanbian* (Beijing: Nongye, 1983), 102.

12. Parts of this section originally appeared in my doctoral dissertation, Greg Rohlf, "Agricultural Resettlement to the Sino-Tibetan Frontier, 1950–1962" (Ph.D. dissertation. University of Iowa, 1999), 354–55.

13. Wei Zhenwu, "Guanyu tuolaji nongchang gongzuo de zongjie yu yijian" (1949) [Conclusions and recommendations for the task of tractor farms], reprinted in *Nongken gongzuo wenjian ziliao xuanbian*, 20–25.

14. "Zhongyang renmin zhengfu nongye bu yi jiu wu ling nian guoying nongchang changzhang huiyi zongjie" (1951) [The concluding report from the meeting of state-run farm directors convened by the people's government ministry of agriculture], reprinted in *Nongken gongzuo wenjian ziliao xuanbia*, 29–31. "Guoying jixie nongchang jianchang chengxu zhanxing banfa" (1952) [Provisional rules on the method for setting up state-run mechanized farms], reprinted in *Nongken gongzuo wenjian ziliao xuanbia*, 59–64.

15. "Provisional rules on the method for setting up state-run mechanized farms," 59–64.

16. "Bangzhu woguo jianshe nongchang de diyi pi sulian zhuanjia dao jing" [The first group of Soviet experts to help establish farms have arrived in Beijing], *Renmin ribao*, November 3, 1954, 1. The State Council proclaimed in December that China had learned much about opening up new land and managing large-scale agricultural enterprises from the set up of the Soviet-sponsored farm. "Guanyu jianshe 'guoying youyi nongchang' de jueyi" [Resolution on the construction of the "state-run friendship farm"], *Renmin ribao*, December 27, 1954, 1.

17. Wang Zhen, "Guoying nongchang de muqian qingkuang he fazhan yuanjing" (1956) [The situation and long-term development of state farms], reprinted in *Nongken gongzuo wenjian ziliao xuanbian*, 209.

18. On the importance of studying the "politics in command" biological science of I.V. Michurin, see "Huabei quyi jiuwu san nian guoying jiexie nongchang gongzuo qingkuang yu jinhou yijian" (1953) [The situation of mechanized state-run farms in Huabei in 1953 and prospects for the future], reprinted in *Nongken gongzuo wenjian ziliao xuanbian*, 123–27. Kang Chao makes the point that the praise for and impetus to study these Soviet agro-science theories came from the Mao and the Party, rather than from agricultural scientists, most of whom were trained in North America or Europe. Kang Chao, *Agricultural Production in Communist China, 1949–1965* (Madison, WI: University of Wisconsin Press, 1970), 88. On the influence of the proletarian genetics and agricultural science of Lysenko as early as the Yan'an period, see Laurence Schneider, "Learning from Russia: Lysenkoism and the Fate of Genetics in China, 1950–1983," in *Science and Technology in Post-Mao China* ed. Denis Fred Simon and Merle Goldman (Cambridge: Council on East Asian Studies/Harvard University, 1989), 45–68. His description shows that the Lysenkoists intimidated and silenced classical geneticists but did not stop their work.

19. Liu Xiaomeng et al., *Zhongguo zhiqing shidian* [Encyclopedia of "educated youth"] (Chengdu: Sichuan renmin, chubanshe, 1995), 708–10.

20. "The Ministry of Agriculture of the Central People's Government's Report on Mechanized State Farms in 1953 and Recommendations for Future Work," 107. Ivan Vladimirovich Michurin was the most famous of Stalin's "peasant scientists." He started experimenting with hybridization of fruit in 1875. His efforts valued intuition over book-learning, folk advances over professional disciplines and practice over theory. Michurin and his results were ignored by the Russian scientific establishment but he was elevated by Stalin into a hero and policy-maker in the 1930s. He became a cult figure late in life and posthumously for his articulation of an indigenous, Bolshevik alternative to the bourgeois classical genetics of Gregor Mendel and Thomas Morgan. Books and films were devoted to him and his birth place was renamed Michurinisk in 1932. His view that environmental forces could alter the genetic code and thus be inherited was adopted and institutionalized by Trofim Denisovich Lysenko. Lysenko became a right hand man of Stalin and presided over a 16-year political reign of terror in Russian biosciences which hampered research, ruined careers and even caused the deaths of those he considered his enemies. On Michurin, see David Joravsky, *The Lysenko Affair* (Cambridge: Harvard University Press, 1970), 39–71. Also see the entry in Jeanne Vronskaya, *The Biographical Dictionary of the Former Soviet Union* (London: Bowker-Sauer, 1992), 338 and also the entry for "Biology" in *Great Soviet Encyclopedia*

(New York: Macmillan, 1973), vol. 3, 312–324. See also the romantic portrait of "I. V. Michurin in His Garden" by Alexander Gerasimov on the inside cover in *Soviet Woman*, no. 10 (October, 1955).

21. "Shoudu juxing Miqiulin baizhounian danchen jinian hui" [The capital convenes a meeting commemorating Michurin's birth], *Renmin ribao*, October 29, 1955, 1.

22. See the English translation Galina Nikolayeva, *The Newcomer: The Manager of an MTS and the Chief Agronomist* (Moscow: Foreign Languages Publishing House, 1950). The serialization began in *China Youth*, December 1, no. 17 (1955): 13.

23. Deng Zihui had headed the Rural Work Department since its founding in 1952. Deng was one of Mao's "oldest and most trusted colleagues," a Long Marcher. His position at the head of the Party's primary agricultural policy-making organization made him one of the most influential men in China during the 1950s. His advocacy of incremental moves toward rural socialism was at odds with Mao and others' calls for revolutionary leaps, decisive battles and high tides of economic and social development. Frederick Teiwes and Warren Sun, *The Politics of Agricultural Cooperativization: Mao, Deng Zihui and the "High Tide" of 1955* (Armonk, NY: M. E. Sharpe, 1993), 7.

24. "On the fly" or the (wubian) method meant that you did all things at once: Open up land, produce food, construct facilities, set aside profits and expand. *Dangdai Zhongguo de nongken shiye* [Contemporary China's land reclamation] (Beijing: Zhongguo shehui kexue, chubanshe, 1986), 121–23.

25. Deng had a long history of opposing Mao's style of "rash advance." He favored incremental, steady improvement. It was Deng that Mao had in mind when he chastised his party for tottering along on bound feet toward collectivization. Wang Zhen was a military leader that was promoted to head the Ministry of Agricultural Reclamation. Tan was an archetypical Maoist: a provincial leader who leapt on the Maoist bandwagon as a power play. On the court politics surrounding agriculture in the 1950s, see Alfred Chan, *Mao's Crusade: Politics and Policy Implementation in China's Great Leap Forward* (Oxford: Oxford University Press, 2001), 18–27, 109–14. Also see, Dali L. Yang, *Calamity and Reform in China: State, Rural Society, and Institutional Change since the Great Leap Famine* (Palo Alto, CA: Stanford University Press, 1996), 36–37. Frederick Teiwes and Warren Sun, *China's Road to Disaster: Mao, Central Politicians, and Provincial Leaders in the Unfolding of the Great Leap Forward 1955–1959* (Armonk, NY: M. E. Sharpe, 1999).

26. Wang Zheu, "Guzi geming ganjin, shixian guoying nongmu chang shengchan da yue jin" (1958) [Bolster revolutionary fervor, realize a Great Leap Forward in production on state-run farms and ranches], reprinted in *Nongken gongzuo wenjian ziliao xuanbian*, 281–87.

27. Peter Ho, "Mao's War against Nature? The Environmental Impact of the Grain-First Campaign in China," *China Journal*, no. 50 (2003), 38–39.

28. "Henan qingnian dabu huangyu," [Henan youth have caught much fish) *Gonghe bao* (July 24, 1959), 4.

29. This story also appeared in *Renmin ribao*. One cannot help but suspect that these "mines" must have been laughable holes in the ground. Zhao Huaiqing, "Qinghai Hu Pan" [On the shores of qinghai lake], in *Xinjiang Neimeng Qinghai sanji* [Scattered notes from Xinjiang, Nei Menggu and Qinghai] (Beijing: Shangwu, 1959).

30. Wang Zhen, "Guanyu kaiken huangdi fazhan quanmin suoyouzhi de guoying nongmu qiye wenti (Jielu)" (1958) [Several problems on the development of state-run agricultural and pastoral enterprises owned by the whole people by opening up new land], reprinted in *Nongken gongzuo wenjian ziliao xuanbian*, 312.

31. "Nongken bu dangzu guanyu nongken gongzuo de baogao" (1962) [The report by the party core group of the ministry of agricultural reclamation on agricultural reclamation], reprinted in *Nongken gongzuo wenjian ziliao xuanbian* (Beijing: Nongye, 1983), 312.

32. For a time in 1959–1960, Mao also advocated the conversion of communes into state-owned property. It is unlikely that he had the Soviet state farm model in mind but it does emphasize the rapidly shifting politics and policy positions of the Great Leap Forward years. Deng Zihui's speech is "Guanyu guoying nongchang jige genben zhidu de shangque" (1960) [The deliberations on several basic systems of the state farm system], reprinted in *Nongken gongzuo wenjiang ziliao xuanbian* (Beijing: Nongye, 1983), 561.

33. Deng Zihui, "Deng zihui fuzongli guanyu nanning nongchang gongzuo huiyi qingkuang de baogao" (1962) [The report of vice-premier Deng Zihui at the national agricultural reclamation meeting in Nanning] reprinted in *Nongken gongzuo wenjian ziliao xuanbian*, 500–15.

34. *Qinghai sheng zhi (shi er):nongye zhi* [Qinghai province gazetteer: vol. 12, agriculture] (Xining: Qinghai renmin, chubanshe, 1993), 15.

35. For Mao, such a mundane explanation—that technical expertise could make the farms run better—struck at the heart of his romantic, revolutionary view of political and economic change. On the other hand, we know that the temperamental Mao was also adept at compromise and outright concessions. "The report of vice-premier Deng Zihui at the national agricultural reclamation meeting in Nanning," 503–10. Deng was attacked again during the Cultural Revolution.

36. *Guoying nongchang tudi zonghe guihua sheji* [Comprehensive land-use planning and design for state-run farms] (Beijing: Nongye, 1963), 2–3.

37. *Dangdai zhongguo de nongken shiye*, [Contemporary China's land reclamation], 22–23.

38. This map originally appears in Maurice Meisner, *Mao's China and After*, 3d ed (New York: Free Press, 1999). I have altered it to emphasize several place names.

39. For an overview of Xinjiang's "peculiar institution," see James A. Millward, *Eurasian Crossroads: A History of Xinjiang* (New York: Columbia University Press, 2007), 251–54.

40. See the survey of Heilongjiang's significance in the national agricultural economy in Toshiyuki Kako and Jianping Zhang, "Problems Concerning Grain Production and Distribution in China: The Case Heilongjiang Province," *The Developing Economies*, 38, no. 1 (2000): 51–79.

41. For a superb collection of posters of these drivers, go to *Stefan Landsberger's Chinese Propaganda Poster's Page*, http://www.iisg.nl/~landsberger/index.html (accessed March 10, 2008); for Chinese woman tractor drivers in the 1950s press, see "Xinli kai le hua" [A flower blooms in my heart], *Qinghai qinzhong* [Qinghai masses], April 18, 1956, 2. Zhang Xiaoying, "Beijing yimin tan xibei yinchuan de shenghuo

qingkuang" [Beijing resettlers discuss the living conditions in Yinchuan in the northwest], *Renmin ribao* [People's daily], July 3, 1955, 6. Also see the iconic photos of State Farm 853 in 1957 and 1977, which document in dramatic fashion the transformation of marshy land into massive, tractor-cultivated fields. Chao Sung-chiao, "Transforming Wilderness into Farmland: An Evaluation of Natural Conditions for Agricultural Development in Heilongjiang Province," in *China Geographer*, ed. Clifton Pannell and Christopher Salter (Boulder, CO: Westeview Press, 1981), 48.

42. "Woman Tractor Driver Breaks New Ground," *China Daily*, (March 23, 2004). www.chinadaily.com.cn/english (accessed June 18, 2006). This first tractor driver, Liang Jun, was a well known figure featured in many posters and images. Subsequent redesigns replaced this image. The current note has an image of the Great Wall.

43. See the description, for example, in Edward Friedman et al., *Chinese Village, Socialist State* (New Haven, CT: Yale University Press, 1991), 142. "Most villagers had never heard the word [tractor]. No one had seen one. They called out for him to repeat the word *tuolaiji* and explain. What it meant, Geng told them, was the future."

44. For an overview of how the Chinese side applied Stakhanouite model laborers to a range of fields, see Miin-ling Yu's chapter in this volume.

45. As mentioned above, however, the state farms were dominant in important niches of the agricultural economy, such as dairy and rubber. Kang Chao, *Agricultural Production in Communist China, 1949–1965* (Madison, WI: University of Wisconsin, 1970), 71–72.

46. "Staff Appraisal Report on China State Farms Commercialization Project," 15.

47. The trajectory of change in the Soviet Union also differed in that the collective farms were converted in the post-Stalin era to create these state farms. On farms in the Russian Federation, see Vasili Uzun, "Large and Small Business in Russian Agriculture: Adaptation to Market," *Comparative Economic Studies*, 47 (2005). This outcome—the dominance of agribusiness over family farms in Russia—has roots in both pre-Soviet agriculture as well as in the distinctive elements of Soviet agriculture. That the longer-lived small family farm survived socialism in China, on the other hand, was an enormous boon to the economic growth of the 1980s and 1990s. Mark Selden, "Pathways from Collectivization," *Review—Fernand Braudel Center for the Study of Economies, Historical Systems, and Civilizations*, 17, no. 4 (1994): 423, 432–33.

48. Wing Thye Woo, "The Real Reasons for China's Growth," *The China Journal*, no. 41 (1999): 121.

49. This was unlike patterns and events in the Soviet Union, for example, which had a labor shortage and moved people off the land and into urban industrial positions as part of collectivization. See the comments on this in Selden, "Pathways from Collectivization."

50. "Staff Appraisal Report on China State Farms Commercialization Project," 15.

51. "Implementation Completion Project (Icr) for Heilongjiang Agricultural Development Project," ed. Heilongjiang Provincial Agriculture World Bank Loan (World Bank, 2004), 4.

52. Chung Min Pang and A. John De Boer, "Management Decentralization on China's State Farms," *Journal of American Agricultural Economics*, 65, no. 4 (1983): 665.

53. 12 of 15 state farms in one district have leased out all of their lands to farm families. Kako and Zhang, "Problems Concerning Grain Production and Distribution in China: The Case Heilongjiang Province," 64.

54. Jorgen Delman, "Cool Thinking? The Role of the State in Shaping China's Dairy Sector and Its Knowledge System," *China Information*, XLVII, no. 2 (2003): 4–5. Michael Wattiaux et al., "Agriculture and Dairy Production System in China: An Overview and Case Studies," *Babcock Institute Discussion Paper*, no. 2002–03 (2002): 21. Eduard Vermeer, "Dairy Farming in China: Organization, Feed and Fodder, Government Support and Profitability (Part I)," *China Information* 2, no. 1 (1988): 26–27.

55. France-based Danone owns about a one-quarter of the firm. Shanghai Bright is China's third-largest dairy producer. In 2006, the city government pushed the merger of Bright Dairy with three local state-owned agribusinesses to produce the new Bright Foods group. The merger is generally understood as a way to help state-owned and publicly held Chinese firms compete with multinational rivals in the Chinese marketplace. "Bright Dairy; Company's History," http://www.brightdairy.com/english/about/about.htm (accessed March 20, 2006). Mark O'Neill, "Bright Dairy Joins Food Merger," *South China Morning Post* (July 25, 2006) www.scmp.com.

56. Jamil Anderlini, "Sanyuan Foods in State-Sale Talks," *South China Morning Post* (August 3, 2006) www.scmp.com.

57. Christina Wu, "China's Dairy: Overview 2003," ed. USDA Foreign Agricultural Service GAIN Report (United States Department of Agriculture, 2003), 3. For some illuminating case studies, see Wattiaux et al., "Agriculture and Dairy Production System in China: An Overview and Case Studies."

58. Deng Zihui, "Jinian lai guoying nongmu chang de juda chengjiu he jinhou de jiben renwu" (1957) [The achievements of state-run farms and ranches in the last few years and basic tasks for the future], reprinted in *Nongken gongzuo wenjian ziliao xuanbian*, 251–58.

59. By this time, Soviet agro-science ideas had become Maoist. Wang Zhen, "Wang Zhen tongzhi zai quanguo caimao shuji huiyi shang de fayan yaodian, nongye, quanguo caimao shuji huiyi jianbao" [The important points of comrade Wang Zhen's comments at the national meeting of finance and trade party secretaries], reprinted in *Nongken gongzuo wenjian ziliao xuanbian*, 427–30. On the politics of how this came to be seen as "Maoist," see Roderick MacFarquhar, *Origins of the Cultural Revolution*, vol. 2, *The Great Leap Forward 1958–1960* (New York: Oxford University Press, 1983), 122–27.

60. This will be described in the next section on agriculture and national security.

61. Pang and De Boer, "Management Decentralization on China's State Farms," 658.

62. For more on these attributes of "High Socialism" in industrial management, see Deborah A. Kaple, *A Dream of a Red Factory: The Legacy of High Stalinism in China*, 7–9.

63. "Zhongyang renmin zhengfu nongye bu yi jiu wu ling nian guoying nongchang changzhang huiyi zongjie" (1951) [The concluding report from the meeting of state-

run farm directors convened by the people's government ministry of agriculture], reprinted in *Nongken gongzuo wenjian ziliao xuanbian*, 29–31.

64. The exemplars of the state-owned sector in this regard would be the petroleum industry, railroads or military manufacturing. Even Mao realized that his experimental policies should not undermine the effectiveness of these enterprises because of their role in national security.

65. One reason why China's rural economy boomed in the 1980s, particularly based on village and township enterprises, was that there was still a village-based economy to restore. Socialist agriculture had not obliterated the traditions, networks and mentalities of the small farmer. In contrast, the Russian socialized agriculture had mostly eliminated those things. This point is made in Selden, "Pathways from Collectivization."

66. Deng Zihui, "Zhonggong zhongyang nongcun gongzuobu guanyu guoying nongchang gongzuo zuotanhui de baogao (caogao)" (1952) [The rural work department of the central committee of the communist party's report at the consultative meeting on state farms (draft)], reprinted in *Nongken gongzuo wenjian*, 100–6.

67. On piecework, see Pang and De Boer, "Management Decentralization on China's State Farms," 659. On youth as a labor source, see Gregory Rohlf, "Dreams of Oil and Fertile Fields: The Rush to Qinghai in the 1950s," *Modern China* 29, no. 4 (2003): 472–73.

68. "Nongken bu dangzu guanyu nongken gongzuo de baogao" (1962) [The report by the party core group of the ministry of agricultural reclamation on agricultural reclamation], reprinted in *Nongken gongzuo wenjian ziliao*, 560–66.

69. Wang Zhen, who was a key figure in the build up of the state farm system in the 1950s, admitted that state farms had a bad reputation for waste. Wang Zhen, "Wang zhen buzhang zai quanguo guoying nongmu chang shehui zhuyi jianshe jiji fenzi huiyi kaimu de jiang hui (jielu)" (1958) [The remarks of minister of agricultural reclamation Wang Zhen at the opening meeting of the national meeting of activists who are establishing socialism on state-run farms and ranches (excerpt)] (Beijng: Nongye, 1983), 297–99. Zhang Linchi charged in the same year that the attacks on the state farm system's profitability were an attack by "rightist" communists of the orthodox variety on the "leftist" Maoist version.

70. See the overview in ch.1 of Shi Weiming and Feng He, *Zhiqing beiwanglu: shangshan xiaxiang yundong zhong de shengchan janshe bingtuan* [Memoires of educated youth: the production and construction corps in the up to the mountains and down to the countryside movement] (hereinafter as *Zhiqing Beiwanglu: Shangshan*) (Beijing: Zhongguo shehui kexue, 1996), 1–27.

71. It still exists. In many cases, their assets were transferred to provincial or local government, so the farms did not necessarily disappear as enterprises. Shi Weiming and Feng He, *Zhiqing Beiwanglu: Shangshan*, 21, 374–78.

72. Shi Weiming and Feng He, *Zhiqing Beiwanglu: Shangshan*. Also see Liu Xiaomeng et al., *Zhongguo zhiqing shidian* (Encyclopedia of educated youth) (Chengdu: Sichuan renmin chubanshe, 1995), 39–40.

73. The figures seem too good to be true. Nevertheless, the goal of profitability is significant. The editorial is cited in Dennis Woodward, "A New Direction for China's State Farms," *Pacific Affairs* 55, no. 2 (1982): 234.

74. *Gansusheng zhi: di shijiu juan, nongken zhi,* [Gansu province gazetteer: volume 19, agricultural reclamation] (Lanzhou: Gansu renmin, chubanshe, 1993), 57–65.

75. The Third Front policies are a superb example of the fusion of Maoism and Stalinism. Massive investment was channeled to inland provinces at the behest of the central government which had national security as its most important goal.

76. "Shihezi xingnong wang" [Shihezi net] www.shznw.com/corps/default.asp? ID=143 (accessed on October 17, 2005).

77. *Xinjiang shihezi yisisan tuan nongchang zhi,* [Gazetteer for unit 143 farm in Shihezi, Xinjiang] (Shihezi: Yisisan tuan nongchang weiyuanhui, 1988), 7–8, 28.

78. Liu Peizhi, *Guoying nongchang sishi nian* [Forty years of state farms] (Beijing: Zhongguo nongye keji, 1989), 168.

79. Parts of this section originally appeared in Gregory Rohlf, "Population Re-settlement to the Sino-Tibetan Frontier, 1950–1962," 356–58.

80. This section draws on Martin McCauley, *Khrushchev and the Development of Soviet Agriculture: The Virgin Land Programme, 1953–1964* (New York: Holmes and Meier, 1976). Martha Brill Olcott, *The Kazakhs* (Palo Alto, CA: Hoover Institution, Stanford University Press, 1987), 221–29. Frank A. Durgin Jr., "The Virgin Lands Programme 1954–1960," *Soviet Studies* 13, no. 1 (1962), 255–80. Igor Zonn, Michael H. Glantz, and Alvin Rubinstein, "The Virgin Lands Scheme in the Former Soviet Union," in *Drought Follows the Plough* ed. Michael M. Glantz (Cambridge: Cambridge University Press, 1994), 135–50. Zhores A. Medvedev, *Soviet Agriculture* (New York: W.W. Norton, 1987), 167–75.

81. See "Conquering Virgin Lands," *Soviet Union Illustrated Monthly* 61, no. 3 (March 1955), 5–7. I. Mityaev, "424 New State Farms," *Soviet Union Illustrated Monthly* 62, no. 4 (April 1955), 12–13. Y. Ilyin, "Report from Virgin Lands," *Soviet Union Illustrated* 64, no. 6 (June 1955), 9–10. Y. Belousov, "On Upturned Soil," *Soviet Union Illustrated Monthly* 65, no. 7 (July 1955), 32–33. Many Chinese-language press accounts sound the same themes. For examples, including county-level newspapers in Qinghai, see Fang Qing, "Huangyuan shang de huoju" [The torch of the empty plains], *Renmin ribao,* November 27, 1955, 2. Zhao Duonian, "Yao shi huangdi bian liangshi" [We will turn barren land into grain], *Zhongguo Qingnian bao,* November 9, 1959, appears in Union Research Service Clippings File. Zhu Jue, "Kenhuang wann-ian chunu di qingshan dui kaihuang babai sishi mu" [Plow up the ancient virgin soil; the Qingshan team opened 840 mu], *Datong bao,* October 16, 1959, 1. Wu Yanzhong, "Anmenxia gongshe jianqi yi zuo nongchang" [Anmenxia commune has built a farm], *Huzhu ribao,* February 13, 1960, 2.

82. At the send-off of the first youth team on August 31, 1955, Hu said, in effect, "if the Soviets can do it, so can we, only more and better." See his speech to the youth, Hu Yaobang, "Xiang kunnan jinjun" [Tackle difficulties], *Zhongguo qingnian bao,* September 1, 1955, 1. Also see "Shoudu qingnian jihui huansong qingnian zhiyuan kenhuang dui" [The youth of the capital gather to send off the youth volunteer recla-mation teams], *Guangming ribao,* August 31, 1955, 1.

83. Elizabeth McGuire, "Between Revolutions: Chinese Students in the Soviet Union, 1948–1966."

84. Parts of this section originally appeared in Gregory Rohlf, "Population Resettlement to the Sino-Tibetan Frontier, 1950–1962," 358–59.

85. Komsomolsk-on-Amur.

86. "Reai bianjiang jianshe bianjiang" [Warmly love the frontiers, build up the frontiers], *Zhongguo qingian bao*, April 12, 1955, 1. A piece in *Guangming Daily* in August also claimed that "we all know" about the Soviet's Virgin Lands successes. "Sulian yijing kaiken le liangqian jiubai wan gongqing huangdi" [The Soviet Union has already opened up 29 million hectares of virgin lands], *Guangming ribao*, August 17, 1955, 4. The Virgin Lands program was reported on as early as January. "Xiang xin kenqu he jianzhu ye shusong xin liliang" [Send new forces to the new reclamation districts and construction industries], *Renmin ribao*, January 9, 1955, 4.

87. "Beijing shi 5 ming qingnian faqi zuzhi qingnian zhiyuan kenhuang dui" [Five Beijing city youth begin to organize the youth volunteer land reclamation team], *Guangming ribao*, August 17, 1955, 1.

88. "Quanguo you shiliu ge shengshi qingnian zucheng zhiyuan kenhuang dui" [Sixteen provinces and cities across the nation have organized youth volunteer reclamation teams], *Renmin ribao*, December 25, 1955, 3.

89. Not only did this group get heavy press coverage at the time of its founding; its story was also the subject of a monograph published in 1989. Mei Li, ed., *Huangyuan shang de zuji: Beijing qingnian zhiyuan kenhuang dui shilu* [Footsteps on the grasslands: memoirs of the Beijing youth reclamation teams] (Beijing: Beijing shifan xueyuan chubanshe, 1989). Another group sent to De'an county in Jiangxi was visited by both Mao and Hu Yaobang. *De'an xian zhi* [De'an county gazetteer] (Shanghai: Shanghai guji chubanshe, 1991), 13.

90. On the first Youth League-sponsored movements, see Debing Li and Fang Shi, *Heilongjiang yimin gaiyao* [Migration to Heilongjiang] (Harbin: Heilongjiang, 1987), 199–203.

91. *Luobei xianzhi* [Luobei county gazetteer] (Beijing: Zhongguo renshi: 1992), plates. For another description, see Xiaomeng et al., *Zhongguo zhiqing shidian*, 244–49.

92. Parts of this section originally appeared in Gregory Rohlf, "Population Resettlement to the Sino-Tibetan Frontier, 1950–1962," 360–361. For a colorful and heroic description of the founding of one Virgin Lands farm, see Fyodor Trofimovich Morgun, *The Grain Growers* (Moscow: Novosti Press Agency, 1975) Also see Martin McCauley, *Khrushchev and the Development of Soviet Agriculture*, 176–85.

93. For an overview of China's youth farms, see the first three chapters in Xiaomeng et al., *Zhongguo zhiqing shidian*, 3–36.

94. Anderson and Seymour, *New Ghosts, Old Ghosts*, 23.

95. *Laogai Research Foundation* (accessed on July 15 2005) http://www.laogai.org/ news/newsdetail.php?id=2293.

96. See chapter six "The Aftermath: What Happens Upon Release?" in Anderson and Seymour, *New Ghosts, Old Ghosts*.

97. See the summary of a range of scholarship in the dramatically titled Courtois et al., *Black Book of Communism: Crimes, Terror, Repression*, 298–513.

98. Mette Halskov Hansen, "The Call of Mao or Money? Han Chinese Settlers on China's South-Western Borders," *China Quarterly*, no. 158 (1999): 400.

99. Two decades of Sino-Vietnamese hostility did result in border tensions and a short war in the late 1970s, so one can see a strategic rationale for Yunnan farms above and beyond the threat posed by the generally porous borders of mainland Southeast Asia.

100. James D. Seymour, "Xinjiang's Production and Construction Corps and the Sinification of Eastern Turkestan," *Inner Asia* 2, no. 2 (2000): 180–82.

101. Nicholas Becquelin, "Staged Development in Xinjiang," *China Quarterly*, no. 178 (2004): 367.

102. Xue Peng, "Delingha Qinghai guoying nongchang de yimian hongqi" [Delingha the red banner of Qinghai's state-run farms], *Renmin ribao*, November 23, 1958, 7.

103. Tianye Liu, ed., *Zai Chaidamu zhongbao pen zhong* [In the great natural riches of Chaidamu Basin] (Hong Kong: Shanghai shuju, 1957).

104. Pu Ning, *Red in Tooth and Claw* (New York: Grove Press, 1994), 175.

105. *Qinghai sheng 2000 nian renkou pucha ziliao* [Tabulation on the 2000 population census of Qinghai province], 3 vols. (Beijing: Zhongguo tongji chubanshe, 2003), 204–5.

106. The *New York Times* reported on March 10, 2008 that a terrorist attack by separatists based in the region had been thwarted. Jim Yardley and Jake Hooker, "China Says Plane and Olympic Plots Foiled," *New York Times*, March 10, 2008.

IV
SOCIETY

9

"Labor Is Glorious": Model Laborers in the People's Republic of China*

Miin-ling Yu

THE MODEL LABORER (*laodong mofan*) campaign, launched by the Chinese Communist Party beginning in 1942, was derived from Soviet Stakhanovism. The CCP imported the key features of Soviet Stakhanovism such as material and spiritual incentives, upward mobility, publicity in official media, glorification of individual achievement, and making new men, but modified them to cope with Chinese circumstances. From 1950 to 2005, the CCP held thirteen national conferences and elected 25,239 model laborers.[1] The numbers reach hundreds of thousand if model laborers down to the county level are included.

The CCP had at least two goals to promote the model laborer movement. First, it was primarily to enhance economic production in order to win wars and to become a world power. Secondly, it aimed at making a new socialist man,[2] who embodied the concept of labor as glorious, who was selflessly devoted to production and socialist construction, and eternally loyal to the party. Although the forms of propagating Stakhanovism were the same in the Soviet Union and the People's Republic of China, there were certain differences in terms of contents and emphases. These are the focus of the chapter. Its purpose is not to evaluate how much production was increased by the Chinese model workers, but to explore how the CCP created Stakhanovites, how it propagated the movement in order to mold new socialist men, and how people responded to the propaganda. As time went on the political significance of the movement increased. Moreover, it employed different propaganda strategies according to the needs of the moment. Although there were model workers in the countryside, this chapter mainly deals with the industrial ones.

Stakhanovism in the Soviet Union

A Stakhanovite as a new man can be traced back to the "positive hero" in nineteenth century Russian literature. He was an active, action-oriented, and selfless individual devoted to the common good. He stood in stark contrast to the so-called superfluous man, who sat idle all day long and only liked to talk without taking any action.[3] The positive hero was the prototype of the "new Soviet man" promoted by the Soviet authorities after the October Revolution. The earliest version of the new productive worker were the shock workers (*udarniki*), usually a group of people performing particularly laborious or urgent tasks during the Civil War. It gained new meaning in 1927–1928 when isolated groups of workers, mainly members of the Communist Youth, organized brigades to fulfill their work assignments. They worked hard, remained sober, had perfect attendance, and dedicated themselves to reducing the unit cost of every product.[4] Their work later was incorporated into socialist competitions and was also called the Izotovite movement, named after Nikita Izotov. By setting production records while also receiving privileges, they were precursors of the Stakhanovite movement.[5] The latter, however, became much more prominent in terms of propaganda and attention by top party leaders.

Due to the low productivity of the First Five-Year Plan, which did not meet official expectations, the Soviet authorities searched for various ways to rapidly increase productivity from the outset of the Second Five-Year Plan. On 30-31 August 1935, a young miner named Aleksei Stakhanov (1906–1977), working at the Irmino pit in the Donbass region, "was discovered" and lionized for his superhuman productivity. He extracted 102 tons of coal in one six-hour shift, 14 times more than the general norm. In fact, the secret of his outstanding performance reflected the division of labor. He concentrated only on extracting coal, while the rest of the work was done by auxiliary workers at the coal face. Nevertheless, all the credit went to Stakhanov alone and the authorities made him a national hero. Instantly, similar model workers appeared all over the country, even in the *gulag*, through organized socialist competitions. Thus, those who over-fulfilled production norms became known as the Stakhanovites.

In November 1935, at the First All-Union Conference of Stakhanovite Workers Stalin greatly praised the movement as the symbol of the high tide and new stage of socialist competition. Stakhanovism was closely associated with technology and thus differed from previous socialist competitions. Stalin claimed that the Stakhanovites' high productivity had proved the superiority of the socialist system over capitalism. Socialism was not to be construed as "a certain material equalization of people based on a poor man's standard of living. It required a high productivity of labor, higher than under capitalism, and in this respect, the Stakhanovite movement represented a force for the further consolidation of socialism" in the Soviet Union. Under socialism workers' material condition had improved and there was no exploitation. All lived better and merrier. These Stakhanovites were young or middle-aged workers. They mastered their own field of technique, surmounting existing technical norms and planned production capacity. They were cultured and technically trained people, models of precision and punctuality in work. They were liberated from conservatism and stagnation of certain old engineers and technicians. Stalin's speech repeatedly emphasized that the new man should possess new techniques and new culture. He hoped the workers' cultural and technical level could be brought up to the level of engineers and technicians. Only when the difference between mental and physical labor was leveled, could the communist stage be realized.[6] The authorities believed that the Stakhanovite movement paved the way for the Soviet Union to move from the socialist to the communist stage.

What Stalin meant by culture (*kul'turnost'*) was not simply literacy but also taking part in cultural activities, such as reading classic literature and going to concerts and theaters. This was highly infused with the values of the middle class.[7] Ideally Stakhanovites did not live in the factories; they had familial and cultural lives which were as important as their work. They should take advantage of the good things in life that the Soviet regime could offer. Working to exhaustion was associated not with communist zeal but with backwardness. An ideal life for Stakhanovites was someone who worked "at the factory exactly seven hours, since Soviet power does not permit anyone to work more, who regularly goes to the cinema, visits others, engages in sports and at the same time fulfills all production tasks. . . . They must not only dress beautifully and cleanly—not in the style of workers, but also speak cleanly and not swear."[8]

When Stakhanovism no longer stimulated productivity, it lost its value and was no longer vigorously promoted by the authorities. According to R. W. Davies and Oleg Khlevniuk, the movement "did not achieve a substantial change in economic performance" and "its economic significance already began to decline in 1936."[9] Since then the Stakhanovite movement was routinized as labor activism as part of socialist competition. Yet the term, "Stakhanovism," stopped being used after the Twentieth Party Congress in 1956 because it was too closely associated with the cult of personality. Due to the economic crisis in the 1980s, there were discussions again about the revival of Stakhanovism. Mikhail Gorbachev highly praised the movement on its 50th anniversary.[10] But this was only the last radiance of a setting sun. No genuine action was taken.

The Introduction of Soviet Stakhanovism to China before 1949

According to traditional Chinese culture, "only the learned rank high, all other trades are low" and "those who do mental labor rule and those who do manual labor are ruled." Therefore, people generally despised manual laborers and felt ashamed to be one. The Chinese Communists wanted to eliminate such notions. The CCP also claimed that in the "old society" the fruits of all productions were owned not by the people who labored, but by the capitalists. After the revolution, the CCP had to right the wrong by giving the fruits of production to the workers and presenting labor as sacred and glorious. Right before and after 1949 the communists published many magazine articles aimed at teenagers to explain why labor was great and pleasant. Using the theories of Darwin and Engels, these authors stated that labor was glorious because the world was created by labor and created human beings and human happiness. The pleasure of labor came from its fruit, which was owned by the laborer. In the past a laborer worked for imperialists and bureaucrat-compradors, but under communism he would work for himself and thus would need to be more devoted to work.[11] However, verbal propaganda was not sufficient to correct erroneous notions about manual labor. It was important for the CCP to use more concrete methods such as holding production competitions, appraising and electing model workers, granting them various honors and preferential treatment, and enhancing their political and social status in order to publicize the idea that manual labor was glorious.

The Chinese translation of the term, Stakhanovites (*Sitahannov yundong-zhe*), first appeared in official press in October 1936 when the CCP headquarter was located in *Baoan*.[12] But the CCP did not launch the movement until the second half of 1942. Due to the economic blockade by the Guomindang (GMD) and the lack of cadres engaged in production, the CCP was desperately struggling to survive. In order to stimulate production, the Central Committee of the CCP proposed the slogan, "ample food and clothing," and decided to launch a Great Production Campaign in all border areas. It included a campaign of emulating Zhao Zhangkui. Zhao was a worker in an agricultural tool factory. He worked hard and selflessly. He endured hardship without complaint, lived in the factory as if it were his home, and never calculated his personal losses. When the authorities went to factories to examine the production, they "discovered" Zhao Zhankui and decided to make him a production model in order to change ordinary people's attitudes toward labor as well as to enhance efficiency and productivity.[13] This would be the first Stakhanovite movement in China. However, the CCP never used "Stakhanov" directly referring to Chinese model workers probably because such a foreign term might confuse the simple folks. In an award meeting someone excitedly stated that "the Soviet Union has a Stakhanov, we have a Zhao Zhankui today. The Soviet Union has a Stakhanovite movement; we have a Zhao Zhankui movement, too."[14] The Federation of Trade Unions in Yan'an called for promoting the Zhao Zhankui campaign and emphasized its differences from the production competitions in the past. It had serious political significance. The authorities intended to use Zhao Zhankui as a model to reform workers' thought, to get rid of their selfishness, laziness, and irresponsibility and to enhance their political consciousness.[15] Here the political consciousness meant to have correct attitude toward work and value public property as the property of the revolution.

On 26 November 1943, the CCP held the First Conference of Model Laborer in Yan'an where Mao Zedong lavished praise on the Chinese Stakhanovites' high production records and glorified them as "the leaders of the people." He said the model workers' production accomplishments put the economy on the right track. This was the result of organizing the strength of the masses and could make the CCP's fight against the GMD almost self-supporting. Three days after the conference, Mao Zedong, Zhu De, Liu Shaoqi, Zhou Enlai, and so on, received 185 model workers and awarded them autographed certificates of merit. In return the model workers thanked the leadership of the CCP and the party that had enabled them "turn over" (*fanshen*, liberated from the oppressors).[16] Thereafter, promoting production campaigns and selecting Chinese Stakhanovites become a routine activity for the CCP in all border areas through the civil war period.

While propagating model laborers, the CCP put productivity as the top priority. Also, it emphasized good discipline and correct attitude toward work and devotion to the collective. Here the collective usually meant the work place, the people or even the revolution. Very rarely did the CCP mention dedication to the party or the leading role of the party, probably due to its shaky power base. This is a sharp contrast to the propaganda after 1949 when the collective increasingly referred to the party as time went on, reaching its peak during the Cultural Revolution. Under the coercive one-party state, the authorities could stress selfless devotion to the party and to the collective without worrying about resistance. Also, the Yan'an authorities emphasized that model workers, usually party members as well, get along with their co-workers.[17] This indicated that model workers not only had excellent production performance, but also the need to unite the masses and indirectly implied the CCP was popular among workers.

Selection and the Making of Chinese Model Laborers in the 1950s

In the 1950s the CCP convened three national conferences of Chinese Stakhanovite Workers. The first one was held in the fall of 1950 to encourage economic reconstruction. 464 model workers (forty-nine women) attended the first conference, including 208 from industry, 198 from agriculture, and 58 from the army.[18] The Second National Conference was held in 1956 in order to hasten industrialization and over-fulfill the First-Year Plan. In the eyes of the CCP, 1956 was the best year since 1949. The agricultural cooperative movement as well as the socialization of handicrafts, industry and commence went unexpectedly smoothly and rapidly. The official title of the Conference was not the conference of model laborers, but the Conference of Advanced Producers (*xianjin shengchanzhe*). This might have something to do with the CCP's changing policy toward intellectuals. In mid-January of 1956 Zou Enlai announced at a meeting concerning intellectuals that the majority of them had become state workers, had served socialism, and had thus become part of the working class.[19] Therefore, the term, "model laborers," which implied manual labor, seemed inappropriate for intellectuals. Although this Conference emphasized those who fulfilled the First Five-Year Plan ahead of time, it also included those with outstanding performance in the fields of education and science. Because the category of "laborer" extended to intellectuals, the total figure was the biggest one in all national conferences of model workers before and after 1956. The CCP authorities conferred the title of "National Advanced Producer" on 4,703 people.[20] In 1958 the Great Leap Forward (GLF) plunged the entire nation into the craze of smelting iron. The authorities organized and mobilized socialist competitions aiming at "competing with the advanced, learning from the advanced, and overtaking the advanced." In order to sum up the campaign experience and further increase productivity, the Third National Conference of model laborers was held in 1959. This was the last nationwide selection and commendation of model workers until the end of the Cultural Revolution.

How were model laborers selected and processed? In general, the trade unions were in charge of organizing and selecting work. A model worker had to go through different levels of elections from the workshop, factory, city, province, big administrative area, industrial sector (*chanye*), all the way to the national level. The local trade union was instructed that the nomination should come from the bottom production unit (it did not clearly state from the head of the unit or from workers) and went up level by level.[21] Such a bottom-up process was merely an ideal. That the high authorities found it necessary repeatedly to criticize top-down or arbitrary appointments, formalism, and detachment from the masses reflected the underlying reality.[22] The so-called nomination and selection process was usually all done by superiors. Very rarely was it done by low-level workers directly. And the so-called democratic discussion was mostly a mere formality. Some work units only read out the list of the candidates in the meetings or simply directly submitted the list to their higher authorities without bothering with any discussion. Therefore, it was not an exception, as occurred in Beijing Changxin Motor Plant, that no one knew that model workers had been selected.[23] In fact, since the selection process required organization and mobilization, there was great latitude for manipulation by superiors or party cadres. This had also been the case in the Soviet Union.[24]

To promote Stakhanovism both the Soviet Union and China aimed at the economic goal of increasing productivity. Compared with the Soviet Union where the key criterion of selection was record-breaking productivity, the PRC paid more attention to recycling material and to cost savings due to the dire shortage of materials. Since, as Mao Zedong pointed out, China was still a poor country, avoidance of waste and rigorously cutting expenses were long-term goals.[25] This is why Meng Tai, working in the Anshan Steel Plant, was particularly glorified by the authorities. He endured hardship to collect and store thousands of possibly usable bits of scrap, down to nails, pegs or strings of iron wire, and made his co-workers follow his example. This also indicates that the Soviet Union and the PRC were at different stages of economic construction when they each vigorously promoted Stakhanovism. Having gone through World War II and the long Civil War, the CCP simply had to scrape together everything available to restore the economy.

Moreover, the CCP was more concerned about political background which was largely ignored before 1949. In the early 1950s "to have a clean historical background" (i.e., neither the workers nor their relatives had close associations with the GMD or other reactionary organizations in the past) was not a necessary requirement. As time went on, particularly after 1957, a clean political background became a key factor for candidates. Rightists, "bad-elements" and "anti-socialists" were disqualified from the candidacy pool. The Federation of Trade Unions in Liaoning province clearly instructed its local branches that the principle of "good production, good politics and good thought" had to be upheld at all times. Often candidates were disqualified due to their bad political backgrounds.[26] The only exceptional year was 1956 when the authorities claimed that candidates need not perfectly meet all the criteria. It was unreasonable to require both an impeccable job performance and "correct" class background so that the slightest flaw of incorrect thought or behavior eliminated a potential candidate.[27] However, with the 1957 Anti-Rightist Campaign, political background checks once again became routine and strict.

One of the most serious selection problems was creating a wildly exaggerated record. There were at least two possibilities to create a fake model worker. This could occur when superiors simply chose the model worker based on their own preferences and then invented their spectacular work record afterwards. Exposure of such problems often took place during the Hundred Flowers Campaign.[28] A very different sort of fraud arose not from bad intentions as shown by an example from a Liaoning coal mine. The originally elected old worker felt that he was insufficiently literate to read the texts prepared by his work unit for the national conference. He suggested a younger, more literate co-worker to replace him at the First National Conference. His superior agreed with the suggestion. The young worker had worked hard, too, but the preferential treatment he received as a model worker made his co-workers jealous. When they accused him of misrepresentation, he lost his title of model worker.[29]

From 1950 to 1959, the three national conferences conferred the title of "national industrial model worker" on 5,286 people.[30] The large number might be good for morale, but it also posed difficulties in terms of defining the characteristics of model workers and publicizing them in a more efficient way. Therefore, it became necessary to feature some "star model workers" in order to give prominence to their outstanding features and values. In addition, those attending the First National Conference of Model Workers were a little too old[31] and most of their outstanding deeds occurred before 1949. Instead, an effort was made to find a younger model worker with achievements made under the new regime to contrast the treatment of workers under "old" and "new" China. This led to the "discovery" of a star model worker, Hao Jianxiu.

Hao Jianxiu was born into a poor worker family and had only two or three years of schooling. At 15 she began to work at the No. 6 National Cotton Factory in Qingdao. Due to the bad equipment, threads easily broke while spinning. To economize raw material, the broken thread had to be found and reconnected as fast as possible. Hao Jianxiu realized that frequent cleaning of the machine and walking in a Z-shaped circuit minimized roller waste. In the Red May Competition in 1950 she performed outstandingly with a roller-waste rate of only 0.25 percent, the average national rate being 1.5 percent. In February 1951 the authorities in Shandong province heard about Hao's performance, believed her work method should be carefully studied, disseminated to others, and publicized in the press. It was encapsulated in the slogan, "the three diligences and the three fasts" (eyes to watch diligently, fast, legs and fast hands to clean diligently and connect threads). *Qingdao Ribao* published this summary and had the practice followed in other factories. The responses were negative, especially by older workers who became exhausted by applying this method. The chairwoman of the All-China Textile Trade Union decided to invite more than 20 excellent engineers and spinners to organize a "Hao Jianxiu Work Method Study Committee." After three months' observations, tests and discussions, the committee summed up the major points of

Hao's work method: (1) maintain a correct attitude toward labor, work hard and responsibly; (2) learn modestly and be willing to enhance technical skills; (3) work with plans, manage time, prioritize; (4) never waste labor time or physical strength, reduce roller waste.[32] As a matter of fact, this summary had more to do with one's attitude toward work than with skill. Later Hao Jianxiu confessed that when the engineer summarized her work method as "making the Z-shape circuit," she had no idea what he meant.[33]

It was obvious that the authorities intentionally molded Hao Jianxiu's work method and model worker image. Hao's experience shows the deep involvement of the CCP in evaluating her performance, informing the press, studying and summing up her experience, and organizing the resulting propaganda offensive. This was similar to the party's involvement in the Soviet Union in creating the image of Aleksei Stakhanov as the model worker.[34]

Also, publicizing Hao's work method coincided with the movement for reforming the thought of intellectuals. In fact, the CCP achieved two things at one stroke by popularizing and disseminating Hao Jianxiu's work method. On the one hand, it publicized workers' creativity, demonstrating that workers were the masters of socialist society under the leadership of the CCP and enhanced workers' social status. On the other hand, it corrected intellectuals' erroneous notions of despising manual labor and workers so as to mold new socialist men with a new attitude toward labor and dedication to the collective good. One engineer from the committee publicly stated his mistakes in *Renmin Ribao* by admitting that in the beginning he subjectively looked down upon Hao's method. He "vulgarized" it and did not think there was anything special about it in terms of skill. He confessed that this was because he did not pay attention to workers' creativity and did not consider relying on workers to raise productivity. After participating in the three discussions and the struggle between new and old thought, he realized that workers had limitless wisdom and that only by closely relying on workers was good production possible.[35] Such a self-criticism matched well with the thought reform campaign among intellectuals in the early 1950s.

Propaganda and Problems of Model Laborers

In the 1950s the official press presented model workers as those who possessed a selfless zeal for work and were firmly loyal to the party in general and to Chairman Mao in particular (more radical political campaigns then reversed this order to emphasize Mao). They worked for the country and for the collective with seriousness and responsibility, were willing to use their brains to solve work problems and worked without stop if necessary, had a boundless love of labor and of the fatherland. They worked regardless of personal danger, sickness, or family crises. Ideally these were the key characteristics reflected in the "spirit of model workers" that the CCP wanted to promote. However, propaganda required more than abstract descriptions in order to attract ordinary people's attention and interest. The honor and special treatment received by the model workers, particularly the star model workers, became the most powerful means to publicize Stakhanovism.

Since the Great Production Campaign in Yan'an, the CCP had realized the importance of distributing substantial rewards to outstanding workers. During the civil war the campaign slogan, "labor is glorious, production builds up family fortunes" reflected this connection very well.[36] Rewards divided into spiritual/ritual and material categories. In a conference publicly commending the model workers, top CCP leaders received them, pinned big red flowers on their chests, and conferred medals or certificates as ways of honoring these workers. Still, the most attractive rewards for the ordinary people were material, in the form of livestock, agricultural tools and money.[37] Other material rewards were to send model workers to study at professional schools, to train them to become cadres or to award them political positions.[38]

Overall, the means of rewarding model workers had been generally set during the Yan'an period. After 1949, the scope and scale of rewards increased. The CCP used the First National Conference of Chinese Stakhanovite Workers to publicize the idea that "labor is glorious; workers have been liberated." Before the conference, a photo and graphic exhibition of model workers' achievements was organized, an accompanying pamphlet was published and a documentary film was made. During the conference, summaries of the accomplishments of 395 model workers were printed. Students, peasants, workers and soldiers were organized to visit the exhibition; while news agencies and radio stations interviewed them.[39]

In order to mold the image that the CCP put high priority on workers, the day before the conference, top CCP leaders, such as Dong Biwu, Chen Yun, Nie Rongzhen and Li Lisan, went to the Beijing train station to welcome the model workers from other provinces. The opening ceremony was held in Huairen Hall of Zhongnanhai. Mao Zedong praised them as "the model figures of the Chinese nation . . . [and as] the reliable pillars of the people's government, and as the bridge linking the People's government with the masses."[40] The representatives of the model workers spoke with one voice that the honor to attend the conference came from the wise leadership of the CCP and Chairman Mao as well as the active support of all people in the nation.[41] Their response was not entirely rhetoric. After all, under the rule of the Nanjing government, the Guomindang (GMD) never held any significant conferences to praise the accomplishments of ordinary people. The GMD only received and awarded medals to high-level officials and officers.

For many ordinary people, seeing Chairman Mao in person was like being received by the Pope, the feeling of excitement and bliss was beyond description. Many considered the reception by Chairman Mao and his personal handshake to be the highpoint of their lives. After meeting Mao Zedong, workers described how they felt more affection for him than for their own mothers. "When drinking water, we won't forget the well-driller, being liberated (*fanshen*), we won't forget Chairman Mao." Model workers claimed that when facing the toughest tasks and experiencing the greatest difficulties, thinking of Chairman Mao gave them boundless courage and confidence to overcome the challenges.[42]

During the conference all the model workers also participated in the National Day celebrations, attended parties held by the Soviet Embassy and other organizations, participated in panel discussions, visited factories and farms, and toured the Palace Museum, Summer Palace and other historical sites.[43] For most model workers who lived outside of Beijing or who never had even been to any big city, such magnificent treatment brought great honor and pride. It gave the impression that they were really the masters of the nation. When they returned to their hometowns, they proudly retold their stories about their Beijing experience to their relatives, friends and co-workers. This became one of the most forceful and efficient forms of propaganda to encourage others to strive to become model workers.

Provision of educational and upward mobility opportunities also were credible forms of propaganda. The national model workers' average educational level at the First Conference was very low. About half of them were either illiterate or had only two or three years of schooling. In order to eliminate illiteracy and promote model workers to the position of cadres, the CCP established worker-peasant crash-course middle schools in several big cities. The most famous was affiliated with Renmin University (People's University).[44] Thus, compared with the Yan'an period, the CCP now had more rewards to grant to model workers. In fact, the possibility to become a model worker offered peasants and workers one of the few opportunities for upward mobility other than joining the army. Once selected as a model worker, it was easier to become a party member. Upward mobility also included promotion to the level of cadres, managers or leaders (mostly at the level of deputy leader). One hundred industrial model workers were selected as the representatives for the First China People's Political Consultative Conference (CPPCC).[45] Among them the most extraordinary example was again Hao Jianxiu, the new model textile worker. In the fall of 1951, she went to Beijing to attend the National

Day ceremony and the First CPPCC. In 1952, she attended the International Labor Day celebration in Moscow, saw Stalin, and toured several big cities in the Soviet Union. In December 1952 she was sent to the worker-peasant school affiliated with Shandong University. In 1953 she was elected as a national textile model worker. In May 1954 she joined the CCP and studied in the high school affiliated with People's University (1954–1958), followed by four years at the Textile College in East China (1958–1962). *Renmin Ribao* covered her school life almost every year and portrayed her happy life as a model worker and a student.[46] After completing her education, Hao Jianxiu never returned to her factory as a manual worker. Instead her career rapidly advanced. Her highest professional job was vice-minister of the Textile Industry (1977–1981) and her highest political position was election as a vice-chair of the CPPCC in 2003. Her experience was very similar to the Soviet star Stakhanovite workers. Yet, in terms of political position, her advancements were even higher than her Soviet counterparts.[47]

In addition, three kinds of awards did not exist in Yan'an period, but were highly publicized after 1949, based on Soviet practices. One was sending model workers to vacation or relax in scenic resorts, such as West Lake, Lu Mountain, Qingdao, Beidaihe and so on to demonstrate that the CCP cared about workers' health. The second one was to organize some star model laborers to visit the Soviet Union to learn from their "progressive production and methods." Conversely Soviet delegations of Stakhanovites also visited China to share their production experience with Chinese workers.

The third one was the most coveted by model workers and envied by others concerned the allocation of housing. A case in point was Hao Jianxiu, for whom the authorities in her hometown built a sunny six-room house. The workers' housing had been in dire shortage. For example, in a lane of Shanghai Putuo district, 10,000 workers and their families lived in an area of only 2 square km. It was said that in 1952 the government built 217,550 dormitory units to accommodate one million workers.[48] Even if the figure was true, it was not enough to accommodate the 3 million Shanghai workers, not to mention the whole nation. In September 1951 the Shanghai authorities began to build a new worker village, Caoyang Xincun, on the west side of the city. The first batch of housing was 48 two-story townhouses for model and senior workers. The Caoyang worker village was modeled on the Soviet worker compound; it was a self-contained community, including schools, a kindergarten, a movie theater, a gym, a post office, shops, a bank, a market, a clinic, cultural facilities, and so on. Caoyang New Village became a landmark and indicator of workers' liberation. It also became a showcase and obligatory stop for foreign guests to visit. Many lessons in the anti-illiteracy campaign textbooks described the happy life of workers there.[49] This was the most practical reward and the most powerful piece of propaganda for ordinary people.

Did the Stakhanovites meet the expectation of the authorities and live happily ever after as the official press claimed? It is plausible to conclude that inspired by nationalism, by the vision of a new communist society and even by official propaganda, many model workers were indeed fully and selflessly dedicated to their work in the 1950s. They tried to set good examples by leading their co-workers to join socialist competitions and devoting themselves to production and learning, and sharing their advanced production experience. They also tried to serve as a bridge between the authorities and low-level workers, especially by working long hours and exposing their superiors' bureaucratic attitudes toward work and workers.[50] Meanwhile, they frequently complained that their supervisors ignored their proposals to improve production. They themselves or the press often attributed this to the supervisors' conservatism or to bureaucracy.[51] This was one possibility. Another could be that their proposals were simply impossible to carry out.

In theory, model workers' major activity was to continue working in their professional fields to promote higher production. In practice, many model workers, particularly the star ones, rarely returned to their former manual work positions. Instead, they occupied management or party positions and spent most of their time engaged in all kinds of social activities, such as attending various national meetings, receiving foreign delegations, giving talks on their production experience, answering the party's call for various political movements, and publicizing the CCP's new policies in the factories, armies, and schools. Certain local leaders treated model workers like "all-purpose heroes" and invited them to participate in whatever activities took place.[52] Model worker who continued in their old jobs complained that these activities caused their production to lag behind their co-workers; their credibility suffered accordingly. Another fairly common complaint was that many people required impeccable behavior from models, rather than evaluating them on a case-by-case basis. For example, for poorer model workers or those with large families to feed, the requirement to buy more government bonds than others became a serious financial burden.[53] On the other hand, some model workers soon became smug and felt superior to others. They refused to do team work and to accept criticism. They delegated important projects to their apprentices and once the products were inspected and disqualified, they would curse the inspector. Some took credit for the work of their co-workers and only thought about money. They rejected attending school or accepting less pay.[54] No wonder some people described such model workers as catchers—meaning those who only wanted to catch fame, official position, magnificent treatment, and even a wife!

In addition, Stakhanovism suffered from an internal contradiction. On the one hand, the campaign highlighted production as working for the collective good, not for individual gain. On the other hand, the presentation of model workers as individual heroes eroded the collective consciousness. This contradiction became clear in practical production work. Once the Stakhanovite campaign became routinized, the movement became a championship game for a small group of production heroes, while the rest of the workers lagged far behind. To make matters worse, some plant supervisors had the few high skilled workers concentrate on setting new production records, while the rest of workers remained idle. This resulted in lower production for the entire plant. Some workers resisted participating in such production campaigns for fear that the records set by the model workers would force them to work overtime and raise production norms. Sometimes they would sabotage model laborers' work[55] and the tension between them was strong. In the Soviet Union, the sabotage of or personal attacks on Stakhanovites took place much more frequently and with greater severity than in the PRC.[56] This was because in the PRC wages were not linked directly with productivity. Resentment against model workers was only one of the workers' responses to Stakhanovism. Ordinary people's positive views on Stakhanovism coincided mostly with the official propaganda and its expectation. Their negative opinions would not become known until the end of the Cultural Revolution when society became more open.

Propaganda Distinctions on the Adoption
of the Stakhanovite Model in China

Literal application of the Soviet model was difficult because of structural differences between the two countries, as well as the evolving preferences of Chinese leaders. Firstly, from the very beginning the Soviet authorities closely associated the movement with new technology, even when this departed from reality. Stalin claimed that the "Stakhanovite movement would be inconceivable without new and higher technology."[57] Although learning from the Soviet advanced production experience was highly publicized by the CCP until 1956, new technology did not became the key focus of the propaganda in China. In the early 1950s there were reports that the improvement of technology created a huge surplus of labor forces and factories had to pay for those workers who had nothing to do.[58] In other words, in an extremely over-populated country to use machines to replace laborers meant to increase the unemployment which ran against the CCP's great effort to reduce it and debased the legitimacy of the communist regime.

In 1954 due to the invention of a new instrument which immensely enhanced work efficiency, Wang Chonglun, nicknamed "walking ahead of time," was elected as a model worker. He and a group of model workers proposed that the All-China Federation of Trade Unions launch a national technological innovation campaign and the Union agreed. *Renmin Ribao* made some favorable reports.[59] In fact, the campaign caused many problems. Some said the innovation campaign interfered with production and planning. Many thought mechanized production in their factories could not be improved. Others stated that due to workers' low literacy and low technical skill, and limited investments, their plants lacked the necessary conditions for technical improvements. In the end the Central Committee of the CCP intervened to cancel the slogan of technological innovation.[60] Although during the Great Leap Forward the authorities greatly propagated the technological revolution, it was more a slogan, even a disaster, than the reality for many products of terribly poor quality resulted from the so-called technological revolution.

Secondly, Soviet propaganda highlighted material incentives, publicizing and emphasizing the monetary rewards as well as the magnificent treatment received by Stakhanovites for breaking production norms. The Stakhanovites were encouraged to state their material rewards in national Stakhanovite workers meetings. In their speeches they proudly told the audience how they used the money to buy a radio, a bicycle, new clothes, or perfume (very bourgeois purchases from the Maoist point of view).[61] The official star Stakhanovites' biographies did not hesitate to record such statements, "easier work, more pay," "good wages for good work," "more money means more things, additional comfort," "the more we work, the more we earn," and so on.[62] In the eyes of Maoists, these statements reflected a full-blown "economism." Maoists were not entirely wrong. For the Soviet authorities the reason for focusing on material incentives was closely linked with breaking norms and piece-rate payment. Soviet propaganda concentrated on breaking norms in order to stimulate higher productivity because Soviet workers' pay in the 1930s was based on piece-rates. Low pay gave workers little incentive to work more. The authorities intended to use Stakhanovites' record-breaking norms and their resulting high pay and prestige to stimulate production and speed up economic development.[63]

In contrast, the CCP propaganda on material incentive changed radically before and after revolution. Before 1949 the CCP press highly publicized material incentive without reservation as an expedient measure. After 1949 the official media emphasized honor and downplayed material incentive. However, the material incentive still played a major role in reality, it particularly appealing to lower level workers. In fact, many workers competed to become Stakhanovites simply because of the material incentive. Already before the turn to the left during the Great Leap Forward, the CCP criticized this tendency as the bad influence of "economism," whereas the Soviets continued to rely on monetary rewards. One reason why China did not directly link production with piece-rate payment was its backwardness. China's industrial supplies chronically suffered shortages. Using piece rates to stimulate productivity might cause workers' salaries to fall due to the sudden huge demands on raw materials and supply of tools. Also, Soviet incentive systems involved complicated administration, "required a large corps of trained labor and wages personnel to continually revise rates and calculate pay, all within the confines of a financial plan." China had ample politically reliable cadres but they were not technically well-trained.[64] And due to the demographic factor, the CCP had to adopt a low-pay policy in order to reduce the unemployment rate,[65] which was considered one of the major achievements under socialism.

Another significant factor in China that discouraged material incentives had something to do with the CCP top leaders' mentality. The authorities did not intend to link high production directly with the improvement of worker's lives. For example, in 1953 the Central Committee of the CCP instructed the Federation of Trade Unions to correct the slogan, "Production increases by 10 centimeters, welfare increases by one centimeter," because it too obviously linked the present interest of the individual to long-term collective interest.[66] Such a thought was further elaborated by Mao Zedong during the Great Leap Forward. He more explicitly stated his views after reading the *Political Economy: Textbook*, which was closely monitored by Stalin, commenting that it was not necessary to rely on material incentives every day, every month, and every year. During difficult times, as long as the Party reasoned with people, they would still work and worked well even with reduced material incentives. Mao considered it was a grave mistake in principle that the *Textbook* emphasized one-sided material incentives and did not emphasize political consciousness. The CCP ought to stress arduous struggle, the expansion of production, and the future vision of communism. The Party needed to educate people with communist ideals. It had to emphasize the subordination of personal interests to collective ones and the subordination of current interests to long-term ones. People should make national and collective interests, not personal interests, the first priority. The CCP should not follow the Communist Party of the Soviet Union, which led people to "one lover, one house, one car, one piano, and one TV, and led them to individualism, not down to the socialist road."[67] Instead of stressing material incentives, Mao Zedong relied more on mass mobilization, thought reform and other political campaigns to stimulate productivity.

The third difference between the Soviet Union and the PRC in terms of propagating the image of Stakhanovites was the cultural aspect. For Soviet Stakhanovites had to become "cultured" as Stalin expressed it in the speech in

1935—to bring themselves to the cultural level of engineers and technicians. Thus, it was not enough for them to be literate, they had to cultivate the ability to read great literature, attend concerts and theaters, and visit museums, etc. For example, the bookcases of a Soviet Stakhanovite should have the collected works of Lenin and Stalin, books written by the great Russian/Soviet writers such as Pushkin, Gogol, Chekhov, Turgenev, Tolstoy, Ilya Ehrenburg, Nikolai Ostrovsky, Mikhail Sholokhov and western writers, such as Walter Scott, Jules Verne and others—books on travel, adventure stories, descriptions of far-off countries.[68] This reflects a more wishful thinking than reality. In fact, many Stakhanovites remained illiterates and spent their free time not engaging in cultural activities but drinking. However, the propaganda projected the official expectation of workers to be cultured. Interestingly, Stalin's identification with bourgeois cultural value was in sharp contrast with Mao Zedong's preference for peasant culture. At least in their propaganda the CCP did not project the image of a model worker as in possession of the treasures of China's literary past.

Except for the period of the GLF, generally speaking, for the CCP workers,' culture meant being literate. In 1958 the Party called for technological, education and cultural revolutions. An ideal laborer was required to have both high socialist consciousness and high culture with the knowledge of science, that is, to be red and expert, to combine mental with manual labor, to combine expertise with labor, and to integrate intellectuals with workers and peasants.[69] In the beginning of the GLF the whole country plunged with zeal into carrying out campaigns to terminate illiteracy and to found peasant universities. The campaigns proved short-lived and resulted in low quality and highly inflated quantity. In theory the campaigns hoped to intellectualize workers and peasants; in practice they peasantized intellectuals. Although the slogan loudly proclaimed the goal of uniting education with labor, it turned out the authorities cared more about manual labor than mental labor. And further evidence of this is the fact that after 1958 the crash courses for peasants and workers, which were established in the early 1950s and functioned better in terms of quality education, vanished one by one.[70] Moreover, Mao constantly wanted the intellectuals to learn from peasants—at its most extreme, this took the form of the May Seventh cadre schools and sending intellectuals to the countryside to receive reeducation from the poor and middle peasants during the Cultural Revolution.

Another possible reason that the CCP cared much less about enhancing peasants' cultural level is that it gave priority to the effort to reduce the very high rates of illiteracy in the countryside. Before the communist revolutions in China and Russia, both had rural illiteracy rates of over 80 percent. According to the statistics of 1939 in the Soviet Union, in the 9–49 age group, 94 percent of the urban population and 86 percent of the rural population were literate.[71] This was twenty-two years after October revolution. Estimated by UNESCO in 2000 the total literacy rate in China was 85.2 percent.[72] This was fifty years after the revolution, and the rural literacy must have been lower than the average. Obviously due to the immense population and relative backwardness in China, the CCP in the 1950s was not able to aim too high with regard to culture.

The Discussion on Labor Models in the Reform Era

What impact CCP propaganda actually had on ordinary people was difficult to assess due to the limited sources available from the 1950s. In contrast, ordinary people were able to voice opinions on model laborers more openly in the reform era. Note should be taken of the impact of the Cultural Revolution on reform era views about model workers. Most model workers were horribly persecuted during the Cultural Revolution, because they were loyal to the party secretaries who had nominated them in the 1950s. Most of these party secretaries fell into disgrace early in the Cultural Revolution. By association, this implicated model workers who, like their party secretaries, also suffered great calamities. Many were accused of being "royalists," "fake model workers," "traitors to worker's interest," or having the "social background of a bourgeois fellow-traveler." They were criticized, denounced in public, paraded on streets, and jailed. Many died or become handicapped.[73] On the other hand, a few model workers such as Hao Jianxiu, Wang Jingxi, Yu Fengying, and Li Suwen became members of the Revolutionary Committees set up in 1968, seemingly holding high positions during the Cultural Revolution. However, they were actually just pawns of factional political infighting.[74] They merely served a decorative function for the proletarian dictatorship and did not hold any real power at all. Their power evaporated with the fall of the Gang of the Four.

The havoc of the Cultural Revolution disillusioned many people with the CCP and the ideals of communism. Influenced by the market economy, people expressed negative attitudes toward model laborers more explicitly and visibly starting in the early 1980s. The negative views were fully exposed in a novel, *A Life in the World* (*Rensheng Zaishi*). The protagonist of the novel, Chen Aizhen, was a textile model worker from 1950s. Her only focus and joy in life was work. But people in early 1980s tended not to believe that happiness or a sense of self-worth could be found in labor. Chen was cold shouldered not only by her co-workers but also by her own children when she focused on correcting factory shortcomings and enhancing productivity.

They mocked her ossified thinking, considering it to be unrealistic. A young worker even retorted, "Being a model worker . . . so what? During the Cultural Revolution you were persecuted, too." Some considered her to be "an evil member of the herd." Her hard work and devotion to her job had forced everyone else to work more. After the collapse of the Gang of Four, Chen Aizhen was never reelected. Another young worker bluntly told her that it was easier to be a model worker simply by bribery than by working hard. The novel, however, ends with the triumph of Chen's commitment to the value of labor.[75] This reflected not the views of the majority but the author's (or the Communist Party's) wishful thinking. However, there were still some positive views of the model laborers. Some model workers were hired by private companies to advertise new products because they were considered to be symbols of honesty and reliability. Many did well at their new jobs.[76] Their success in advertising also reflected the positive views many ordinary people still held of the model workers of the 1950s.

After a twenty-year interval the national selection of industrial model workers was resumed in 1979. Meanwhile, in order to search for new avenues of reform and to denounce the claims promoted by the Gang of Four that distribution according to labor was equal to material incentives, the merits of Stakhanovism were again discussed in the official press in the late 1970s.[77] During the 1980s and more intensively in the 1990s, public attention turned to the value of model workers and the importance of material incentives in light of the miserable situation of many old model workers and the impact of the market economy. Increasingly more people were urged not to expect perfection from model workers who were doing the most difficult jobs while denying themselves fame or profit. Some stated that poverty should not become the hallmark of model workers or of socialism. Their glorious hard-work should not come at the expense of their health. Model workers should be allowed to have personal enjoyment and entertainment. And they had the right to choose work, rather than have to accept work appointed from above.[78] The relatively open market brought a greater humanism and individualism to people's thinking concerning model workers. In general, in the 1950s model workers were expected fully to devote themselves to the collective without any consideration of their own benefit. In the reform era, they were allowed to seek personal rewards and enjoy life. Honor and collective good were no longer the only legitimate considerations.

Although the CCP tried to improve the living condition of those model workers who languished in poverty, they also knew that the efforts were far from sufficient. In order to respond to the challenges of the market economy, the authorities proposed to transform model workers. They maintained that model workers should emphasize professional skills over simple hard work and creativity over mere experience. They also praised enterprises paying model workers high salaries to advertise new products, because this enabled them to serve as the leaders of market competition.[79] When the CCP encouraged old model workers to work for big private enterprises, to a certain degree this suggested that the workers served the capitalists. In a sense, this is a great leap backward in terms of communist ideology. Some old model workers probably became confused by the rejection of the old ideology and questioned the purpose of their many sacrifices of the 1950s to construct a "beautiful communist society."

In April 2005, the 13th National Conference of Model Workers in Beijing selected 2,969 national model workers. Four features marked this conference and attracted national attention. (1) For the first time, twenty-one migrant workers from the countryside were selected for their contribution to urban construction. Without objection all highly applauded this selection. (2) Famous athletes, such as Yao Ming and Liu Xiang, became model workers. Some questioned whether selecting model workers should reflect the "celebrity effect." Others argued that these outstanding athletes' success mainly came from their innate physical talent which could not be obtained simply by emulating them. (3) Most controversially, many managers and senior officials were elected and questions arose whether the selection was for labor models or for leading cadres. They argued that the contributions of many senior government or party officials relied on the power of their positions, not their own labor. This was particularly unfair to the peasants, workers, and teachers.[80] (4) Equally controversially, thirty-three private entrepreneurs were elected, including Liu Yonghao, ranked as one of the top ten billionaires in China by *Forbes* magazine. Many argued that they were capitalists. How could they be considered as laborers? A sociology professor objected on the grounds of social justice. He maintained that the term, laborer, had been expanded erroneously to encompass all fields. Model workers had become, in principle, the outstanding people in all professions and trades.[81] The official response to such criticisms was "the criteria for selecting model workers have to evolve with the times. . . . Whoever creates a fortune for the society becomes a laborer and thus is qualified for selection."[82] Whether rich private entrepreneurs were entitled to be model workers was not a question the authorities could directly answer, now that capitalists were allowed to join the Communist Party. This is a kind of dilemma the CCP cannot solve up to the present. Also, when the definition of "model worker," like the definition of "communism" "has to evolve with the times" and has become so broad, the term actually becomes meaningless.

Conclusion

Stakhanovism was a product of communist ideology. The Communist Party primarily had two aims in promoting it: economically to increase productivity with greater devotion to work and politically to raise correct consciousness of devotion to the collective good in order to mold a new man. The CCP adopted the Soviet practice of selecting model workers which was coordinated with mass mobilization, organization and propaganda. Although the forms of propaganda between the two countries were similar, the contents had different emphases due to the structural constraints which included China's relative backwardness, over-population, and low literacy. Another crucial distinction is that Mao paid far more attention to political consciousness than Stalin. Also, he preferred peasant culture while Stalin preferred a bourgeois one.

There is a good example to illustrate the significance of political consciousness on selecting model workers. In the early 1950s a worker in Dalian always went to the factory earlier to make all necessary preparations before his work time began. Because of his professional attitude toward work, many suggested he should be elected as a model laborer. He replied, "It is nothing. I have been doing it this way since the Japanese came to Manchuria." This reply instantly disqualified him as a model laborer for having low political consciousness.[83] Before 1949 he could be selected as a model laborer for his devotion to work. However, after 1949 the CCP would not settle only for this, political correctness, which included acknowledging the leadership of the party, became increasingly important.

In the 1950s some model workers competed for selection for material reasons and appreciated the CCP's role in enhancing their social status, others also identified with the ideal of communism. Many model laborers considered themselves liberated by the communist regime. In return, they bravely took the toughest jobs, worked devotedly for socialist construction, and loyally followed party policies, right or wrong. This was exactly the spirit of the new socialist man, which the authorities wanted to promote. However, the market economy has destroyed a large number of socialist values which were highly publicized by the CCP in Mao's era. For ordinary workers the fame and material rewards which under Mao could be gained mainly by becoming a model worker came through other channels in the reform era. Today the title of model worker has degenerated into a decorative symbol for top officials, party cadres and millionaires. Even though the CCP claims Mainland China is still a socialist country, the economic and social structures have gone through tremendous changes or even metamorphoses. In reality, the criteria for electing the model workers run into some absurd contradictions just as the CCP is trying to integrate China into the capitalist system.

Notes

* The author would like to thank the National Science Council for funding this project (NSC95-2411-H-001-055). She would also like to express gratitude for comments made by Professors Thomas Bernstein, Yong-fa Chen, Don Filtzer, Hua-yu Li, Gilbert Rozman, and Marilyn Young and help provided by Mr. Jan Adamczyk from Slavic and East European Library, University of Illinois at Urbana- Champaign.

1. The figures before 2000 come from the All-China Federation of Trade Unions website, http:acftu.people.com.cn/BIG5?67589/4612353.html, (accessed on 23 November 2007). In 2005 there were 2,969 model laborers.

2. The term "*xinren*" in Chinese has no gender. In translation I use "man" instead of "person" for I fully agree with Jochen Hellbeck's view that new Soviet or socialist man had distinctly male features. See Jochen Hellbeck, *Revolution on My Mind: Writing a Diary Under Stalin* (Cambridge: Harvard University Press, 2006), 366(8).

3. Rufus W. Mathewson, Jr., *The Positive Hero in Russian Literature* (Palo Alto, CA: Stanford University Press, 1975).

4. Lewis H. Siegelbaum, *Stakhanovism and the Politics of Productivity in the USSR, 1935–1941* (New York: Cambridge University Press, 1988), 40, 54.

5. Nikita Izotov also became a Stakhanovite in the mid-1930s. Semen Gerberg, *Stakhanov i Stakhanovtsy* [Stakhanov and stakhanovites] (Moskva: Politizdat, 1985), 39.

6. "Rech' na pervom vsesoiuznom soveshchanii Stakhanovtsev (17 noiabria 1935 g.)" [Speech at the first all-union conference of stakhanovite workers, 17 november 1935], *I. V. Stalin: Sochineniia* [I. v. stalin: works], ed. Robert H. McNeal (Palo Alto, CA: Hoover Institution, Stanford University Press, 1967) vol. 1 [XIV], 79–101.

7. For the most illuminating and detailed account of middle class values in Stalin's era see Vera S. Dunham, *In Stalin's Time: Middle Class Values in Soviet Fiction* (Durham and London: Duke University Press, 1990).

8. Sheila Fitzpatrick, *Everyday Stalinism: Ordinary Life in Extraordinary Times* (New York: Oxford University Press, 1999), 233–44.

9. R. W. Davies and Oleg Khlevnyuk, "Stakhanovism and the Soviet Economy," *Europe-Asia Studies* 54, no. 6 (2002), 397–98. Lewis H. Siegelbaum, *Stakhanovism*, 306–7.

10. "Nesmerknushchie traditsii trudovogo podviga, Rech' M. S. Gorbacheva" [Immortal tradition of labor feats, speech of M. S. Gorbachev], *Pravda*, 21 September 1985, 1–2.

11. Yu Guangyuan, "Laodong chuangzao shijie (1)(2)(3)" [Labor creates the world], *Zhongguo qingnian*, no. 11–13, July-August 1949, 11, 14, 13–14. Yuan Bing, "Weishenmo laodong shi weida he yukuai de?" [Why is labor great and pleasant?], *Jinbu Qingnian* [Progress youth], no. 219 (Jan. 1950), 12–13. Zhang Bi,"Laodong chuangzao shijie" [Labor creates the world], *Jinbu qingnian*, no. 222 (April 1950), 9–12.

12. "Shehuizhuyi jianshe shenglide Sulian gongren zhuangkuang" [Soviet workers' condition in socialist construction victory], *Hongse zhonghua* [Red china], 15 October 1936, 3(N).

13. Xie Anbang, "Zhao Zhankui yundong de zuoyong jiqi jingyan" [The function and experience of zhao zhankui campaign], in *Zhongguo gongren yundongshi yanjiu wenji* [Collected research works on the history of chinese labor movement], ed. Cao Yanping (Beijing: Zhongguo gongren chubanshe, 2000), 156–62.

14. "Nongju gongchang jiangli mofan gongren Zhao Zhankui" [Agricultural tool factory awarded to the model laborer, zhao zhankui], *Jiefang ribao*, 29 September 1942, 2(N).

15. "Zonggonghui haozhao kaizhan Zhao Zhankui yundong" [Federation of trade unions calls to launch Zhao Zhankui campaign], *Jiefang ribao*, 12 October 1942, 2 (N). Gao Changjiu, "Jixu zhankai Zhao Zhankui yundong" [Carry on promoting Zhao Zhankui campaign], *Jiefang ribao*, 22 December 1942, 1–2(N).

16. Mao Zedong, "Zuzhi qilai" [Get organized] *Mao Zedong Xuanji* (Beijing: Renmin chubanshe, 1953), vol.3, 928–36; "Sishi niandai Yan'an dashengchan yundong" [The great production campaign in yan'an in the 1940s], http://www.globalview.cn/ReadNews.asp?NewsID=2206 (accessed on 25 December 2007). "Shan-gan-ning bianqu diyijie lao-dong yingxiong daibiao dahui xuanyan" [The declaration of the first representative conference of labor heroes in the border areas of Shanxi, Gansu and Ningxia], *Jiefang ribao*, 17 December 1943, 1(N).

17. *Renmin ribao*, 18 November 1948, 1; 16 September 1949, 4(N).

18. *Renmin ribao*, 23 September 1950, 1(N). For the gender issue of model workers, please see Yu Miinling, "Woman Holds the Plow?—Female Tractor Driver in the PRC," in *Parting Ways: Politics and Economics across Taiwan Strait Since 1949*, ed. Chen Yongfa (Taipei: Institute of Modern History, Academia Sinica, 2006), 171–206.

19. Zhou Enlai, "Zhengzhi baogao, (zhier)" [Political report, part II], *Renmin ribao*, 31 January 1956, 2(N).

20. Among them were more than 100 scientists and professors, 250 people in the arts and literature, and 31 athletes. Xinhuashe, "Yingjie quanguo xianjin shengchanzhe daibiao huiyi" [Welcome national representative conference of advanced productive laborers], *Renmin ribao*, 28 April 1956, 1(N). "Yipi wenhua yishu gongzuozhe, yundongyuan he tiyu jiji fenzi jiangchuxi quanguo xianjin shengchanzhe daibiao huiyi" [A batch of cultural and art workers, athletes and sport activists will attend the national representative conference of advanced productive laborers], *Renmin ribao*, 29 April 1956, 3(N). Later during the Hundred Flowers Campaign, some presidents of universities called for reevaluating the appropriateness of including professors at higher education as advanced producers. See "Chuxi quanguo rendaihui huiyi bufen daibiao zuotan gaodeng jiaoyu gongzuo wenti" [Attending national people's congress a number of representatives discussing the problems of higher education works], *Renmin ribao*, 4 July 1956, 7(N).

21. "Shanghaishi 1950 niandu laodong mofan yundong chubu zongjie (xiuzheng gao)" [A preliminary summary on the model laborer campaign of 1951 in shanghai, revised version] Shanghai Archives, C1-2-197, 21–23.

22. Jiangsu Archives, 3008/Changqi/6/3–4, 8 September 1950; 3003/Changqi/40/35, 4 December 1952.

23. "Changxindian jiche xiulichang xuanchu qici laoda daibiao hou, gongren hai bu zhidao" [Changxindian locomotive repair plant had selected the 7th model laborer conference representatives, but the workers still did not know about it], *Neibu Cankao* [Internal reference] (hereinafter as *NC*), 21 April 1958, 447. "Beijingshi zai pingxuan laomo zhong suo faxian de wenti" [Discovering problems in the process of appraising and selecting model laborer in beijing], 2 March 1956, 354–55.

24. Lewis H. Siegelbaum, *Stakhanovism*, 170.

25. Mao Zedong, "Guanyu zhengque chuli renmin neibu maodunde wenti" [On correctly handling problems of people's internal contradictions], *Renmin ribao*, 19 June 1957, 1(N).

26. During the "Three Antis Campaign" (1950–1952) those who were penalized were not allowed to be in the candidacy pool. Jiangsu Archives, 3008/Changqi/6, 3003/Changqi/40, 4 December 1952, 36, Shanghai Archives, 3 February 1955, C1-2-1625, 76; B1-2-112,13, 19; A45-1-138, 2-5; Liaoning Archives, DE22/Yongjiu/165, 11, 94.

27. Xu Yao, "Dangzuzhi yao jiaoyu ganbu zhengque di zhangwo xianjin shengchan-zhe de biaozhun" [Party organization must educate cadres in order to correctly master the criteria of the advanced productive laborers], *Renmin ribao*, 8 April 1956, 3(N).

28. Zhou Jingyu, "Shangmianyao, xiamianzao" [Whatever the higher authorities want, the lower level makes it]. Ji Wan, "Jingren de 'chuangzao'" [Astonishing "creation"], *Renmin ribao*, 29 November 1956, 2(N).

29. Liaoning Archives, DE22/Yongjiu/6, 2-6; DE22/Yongjiu/164, 93.

30. The statistics are based on *Zhongguo zhigong laomo dazidian* [Dictionary of china model laborers], ed. Li Yongan (Beijing: Zhongguo gongren chubanshe, 1995).

31. The average age was 35.5 years old; the oldest 61, the youngest 17. The statistics comes from calculation based on *Zhongguo zhigong laomo dazidian*.

32. *Renmin ribao*, 21 August 1951, 2(N); Men Hong, "Hao Jianxiu gongzuofa shi zenyang zongjie chulai de?" [How was hao jianxiu's work method summarized?] *Renmin ribao*, 3 September 1951, 2(N). "Fulu yi: hao jianxiu gongzuofa de chansheng jiqi yingxiang" [Appendix 1: The making and impact of hao jianixu's work method], in *Qingdao shizhi: fangzhi gongyezhi* (Gazetteer of qingdao city textile industry) (Beijing: Xinhua chubanshe, 1999), 230–37.

33. Hao Jianxiu, "Wo zai xuexiao li" [I am in school], *Renmin ribao*, 26 September 1954, 5(N).

34. Donald Filtzer, *Soviet Workers and Stalinist Industrialization* (London: Pluto Press, 1986), 181–82.

35. Wang Erxiang, "Women jishu renyuan yao dapo baoshou sixiang, zhongshi gongren qunzhong de zhihui he chuangzaoli" [We, technical personnel, must smash the conservative thought and pay attention to the wisdom and creativity of the labor mass], *Renmin ribao*, 3 September 1951, 2(N).

36. *Renmin ribao*, 12 April 1947, 2(N).

37. *Renmin ribao*, 17 June 1948, 1; 23 December 1948, 2; 18 March 1949, 2(N).

38. *Renmin ribao*, 22 August 1947, 2; 23 July 1948, 2; 28 September 1949, 6(N).

39. "Zhengwu yuan fabu: Guanyu zhaokai zhandou yingxiong daibiao huiyi he gongnongbing daibiao huiyi de jueding" [The Administration Yuan announces: decision on convening representative conference of combat heroes, workers, peasants and soldiers], 21 July 1950, Shanghai Archives, C1-2-197, 6. "Zhou Enlai zongli mingling gongbu guanyu quanguo gongnongbing laodong mofan daibiao huiyi de zongjie baogao" [Prime minister Zhou Enlai orders the publication of the summary report of the national representative conference of worker-peasant-soldier model laborer], *Renmin ribao*, 19 December 1950, 2(N).

40. "Mao Zedong zhuxi daibiao zhonggong zhongyang zai quanguo zhandou yingxiong he quanguo gongnongbing laodong mofan daibiao huiyishang de zhici" [Chairman Mao Zedong represents the Central Committee of the CCP to make a speech in the national representative conference of the combat heroes and worker-peasant-soldier labor models], 25 September 1950, in *Jiangguo yilai zhonggong zhongyang guanyu gongren yundong wenjian xuanbian* [Selected documents of the Central committee on the labor movement since the founding of the PRC), ed. Zhonghua quanguo zonggonghui bangongting (Beijing: Zhongguo gongren chubanshe, 1989), vol. 1, 10.

41. *Renmin ribao*, 23 September 1950, 1(N).

42. *Renmin ribao*, 29 September 1950, 2; 2 October 1950, 2; 5 October 1950, 3; 21 October 1950, 2; 28 March 1959, 2; 21 October 1959, 2(N).

43. "Zhou Enlai zongli mingling gongbu guanyu quanguo gongnongbing laodong mofan daibiao huiyi de zongjie baogao," *Renmin ribao*, 19 December 1950, 2(N).

44. Hu Chaozhi, "Sannian lai de zhongguo renmin daxue fushe gongnong sucheng zhongxue" [The affiliated worker-peasant intensive-course of middle school of the People's University in the past three years], *Renmin ribao*, 28 December 1953, 3(N).

45. "Shuzi he shishi" [Numbers and facts], *Renmin ribao*, 1 May 1955, 2(N).

46. Hao Jianxiu, "Baowei women heping de xingfu de shenghuo" [To protect our peaceful and happy life], *Renmin ribao*, 7 September 1952, 4(N); Hao Jianxiu, "Wozai xuexiao li," 26 September 1954, 5(N).

47. Aleksei Stakhanov's highest political position was deputy to the Supreme Soviet. Among Soviet Stakhanovites, only Nikolai Smetanin was appointed to the highest professional position, that of Minister of Light Industry. Lewis H. Siegelbaum, *Stakhanovism*, 274.

48. "Quanzong dangzu guanyu jiejue gongren juzhu wenti de baogao" [The party core group of All-China Federation of Trade Unions' (hereinafter as AFTU) report on solving workers' housing problems], in *Jianguo yilai zhonggong zhongyang*, vol. 1, 32. "Shuzi he shishi," *Renmin ribao*, 1 May 1955, 2(N).

49. Zhuang Zhiling, "Shanghai diyi ge gongren xincun—Caoyang xincun" [The first workers' new village in Shanghai—Caoyang new village], http://www.archives.sh.cn/shcbq/shzhjs/200301160189.htm (accessed on 25 December 2007). Zhang Zhongqing ed., *Meili de Caoyang Xincun* [Beautiful Caoyang new village] (Shanghai: Shanghai jiaoyu chubanshe, 1960). Zhu Zonglin et al., *Caoyang xincun haofengguang* [A wonderful sight of Caoyang new village] (Shanghai: Laodong chubanshe, 1953), 1–3.

50. *Renmin ribao*, 15 May 1952, 2; 22, 28 July 1952, 2; 24 September 1952, 6(N).

51. *Renmin ribao*, 18 July 1951, 6; 21 April 1953, 2; 6 November 1954, 3(N); 17, 20 September 1955, 2; 5 March 1956, 6(N).

52. "Guanxin laodong mofan" [To show concerns for model laborers], *Renmin ribao*, 25 February 1955, 3(N).

53. "Siming laomo xinli de hua" [Four model laborers' words from their hearts], Liaoning Archives, DE22/Yongjiu/101, 30–36.

54. "Angang laomo zizhang le bijiao yanzhong de jiaoau qingxu he jingji zhuyi sixiang" [Model laborers in Angang seriously grew more proud sentiments and economicist thoughts], 25 November 1954, 326–27.

55. *Renmin ribao*, 31 July 1952, 2; 29 March 1956, 2; 30 March 1956, 1(N). "Shanghaishi 1950 niandu laodong mofan yundong chubu zongjie (xiuzhenggao)" [Initial summary of model-labor campaign in shanghai in 1950], Shanghai Archives, C1-2-197, 21–23.

56. Donald Filtzer, *Soviet Workers*, 192–97, 210–15. Lewis H. Siegelbaum, *Stakhanovism*, 196–99, 290–92.

57. "Rech' na pervom vsesoiuznom soveshchanii Stakhanovtsev (17 noiabria 1935 g.)," *I. V. Stalin: Sochineniia*, vol. 1 [XIV], 80.

58. "Quanzong dangzu guanyu aiguo zengchan yundong de zonghe baogao" [The summary report from the party group of AFTU on the patriotic campaign of increasing production], in *Jianguoyilai zhonggong zhongyang*, vol. 1, 42.

59. "Quanguo gedi jishu gexin yundong zhubu zhankai" [Throughout the country the technological innovation campaign develops step by step], *Renmin ribao*, 17 July 1954, 2(N).

60. Zhonghua Quanguo Zonggonghui ed., *Zhonghua quanguo zonggonghui qishi nian* [Seventy years of AFTU] (Beijing: Zhongguo gongren chubanshe, 1995), 334–35.

61. Sheila Fitzpatrick and Yuri Slezkine ed., *In the Shadow of Revolution* (Princeton: Princeton University Press, 2000), 331–41.

62. Joshua Kunitz, *Along Came Stakhanov* (Moscow: Co-Operative Publishing Society of Foreign Workers in the USSR, 1936). G. Griedrich, *"Miss U.S.S.R." The Story of Dusya Vinogradova* (Moscow: Co-Operative Publishing Society of Foreign Workers in the USSR, 1936).

63. Donald Filtzer, *Soviet Workers*, 180–92.

64. Andrew G. Walder, *Communist Neo-Traditionalism: Work and Authority in Chinese Industry* (Berkeley: University of California Press, 1986), 117–18. For the change of the wage system in China, see Yang Zhancheng, "Woguo gongzi zhidu de fazhan bianqian" [The development and transformation of the wage system in our country], http://news.sohu.com/20060208/n241732611.shtml, (accessed on 2 May 2007).

65. Zhou Enlai called it, "the rice for three people was shared by five." "Zhou Enlai tongzhi guanyu laodong gongzi he laobao fuli wenti de baogao" [Comrade Zhou Enlai's report on the problems of labor wage and labor welfare], *Jianguoyilai zhonggong zhogyang*, vol. 1, 614–15.

66. "Zhonggong zhongyang dui quanguo zonggonghui dangzu guanyu, 'Shengchan zhang yicun, fuli zhang yifen' kouhao wenti de qingshi de pishi" [The written instruc-

tion of the CCP to the requesting instruction on the slogan problem of "production increases 10cm, welfare increases 1cm"], *Jianguoyilai zhonggong zhongyang*, vol. 1, 169–71.

67. Mao Zedong, *Du Shehuizhuyi Zhengzhijingjixue pizhu he tanhua* [Comments and talks on the socialist political economy] (Beijing: Zhonghua renmin gongheguo guoshi xuehui, 1998), 428, 807.

68. G. Griedrich, *"Miss U.S.S.R.,"* 24. Ivan Gudov, *Put' Stakhanovtsa: Rasskaz o moei zhizni* (The Journey of a Stakhanovite: Story of My Life) (Moskva: Gos. Sotsial'no-Ekonomicheskoe izdatel'stvo, 1938), 130.

69. Editorial, "Dao laodongzhe de hongqi xia jihe" [To assemble under laborer's red flag], *Renmin ribao*, 25 September 1958, 7(N).

70. Chen Xuewei, "Zhishifenzi de Mao Zedong yu Zhongguo de zhishifenzi" [Mao zedong as an intellectual and china's intellectuals] in *Shuobujin de Mao Zedong* [Endless talk about MAO], ed. Zhang Suhua et al. (Shenyang: Liaoning renmin chubanshe, 1993), vol. 1, 283.

71. Sheila Fitzpatrick, *Education and Social Mobility in the Soviet Union, 1921–1934* (New York: Cambridge University Press, 1979), 137–38.

72. "National Literacy Policies/China," http://www.accu.or.jp/litdbase/policy/chn/index.htm, (accessed on 11 September 2007).

73. For example, according to some incomplete statistics from six cities in Heilongjiang, there were 338 national model workers and 2837 provincial and city level model workers before the Cultural Revolution. During the Cultural Revolution about 28% of them were persecuted: 870 were criticized and denounced at public meetings and 21 underwent investigation. Among them, 8 were wrongly sentenced on the charge of being a "spy" or "counter revolutionary," while 13 were persecuted to death. By the first half of 1980, most model workers had been rehabilitated. *Zhonghua Quanguo Zonggonghui qishinian*, 411–12.

74. Wang Sumei, "Yu Fengying, yushuo dangnian haokunhuo" [Yu Fengying, talking about those years felt puzzled], *Laonianren* [Elderly], no. 2 (1999), 10–12. "Li Suwen: Daqi daluo hou zhaohui laomo de ganjue" [Li suwen, after the big rise and big fall eventually found the feeling of being a model laborer], *Baolin*, no. 2 (2004): 37–38.

75. Hu Wanchun, "Rensheng zaishi" [A life in the world], *Hu Wanchun zhongpian xiaoshuoji* [Hu wanchun's novella collection] (Harbin: Heilongjiang renmin chubanshe, 1983), 1–70.

76. Genfu, "Bulao de aixin" [Love is forever young], *Dangzheng Luntan* [Party Forum], no. 4 (2005), 46. Shun Dayun, "Laomo zai shichang jingji zhong shengzhi" [Model laborer's value increases in the market economy], *Zhongguo rencai* [Talents of china], no. 11 (1996), 22.

77. Feng Ruilan and Su Shaozhi, "Bixu guanxin laodongzhe de wuzhi liyi" [Must care for laborer's material interest], *Shehuikexue zhanxian*, no. 3 (1978), 73–76. Wang Shouhai, "Sulian sanshi niandai de Sidahannuofu yundong" [Stakhanovite movement in the soviet Union in the 1930s], *Shehuikexue zhanxian*, no. 1 (1980), 82–89. Zhou Shangwen, "Chongping Sidahannuofu yundong" [Reassess stakhanovite movement], *Shanghai Shiyuan xuebao* [Shanghai normal college bulletin], no. 2 (1980), 22–27.

78. Zhong Yongwei, "Dajia doulai guanxin aihu laomo" [All together to show concern and care for model laborers], *Huagong Guanli* [Chemical engineering management], no. 8 (1996), 43. Wang Tusheng, "Shige laomo bage bing" [Among ten model laborers eight got ill], *Weishi*, no. 5 (1998), 68. Zhang Yi and Ji Yao, "'Nv'laomo' guanghuanxia yanshixia de buxing hunyin" [The unfortunate marriage disguised under the halo of "female model laborer"], *Sanyuefeng* [March wind], no. 1 (2002), 7–10. Zheng Dongliang, "Laomo biaozhun de bian yu bubian" [The changing or unchanging standard for model laborers]. Liu Huanjie, "Hu laomo de qu shenghuo" [Model laborer HU's interesting life], *Huabei dianye*, no. 1 (2004), 76–77.

79. Shen Dayun, "Laomo zai shichang jingji zhong shengzhi," *Zhongguo Rencai*, no. 11 (1996), 22–23. "'Laomo' yeshi 'wuxing zichan'" ["Model laborer" is also an "invisible asset"], *Liaowang xinwen zhoukan* [Outlook news weekly], no. 12 (March 1999), 51. Su Bei, "Xin shidai laomo de jiazhi he neihan" [Model laborer's value and internal quality in the new epoch], *Sixiang zhengzhi gongzuo yanjiu* [Studies on thought and political work], no. 5 (2004), 21.

80. Huijie and Zhimin, "Laodong yu chuangzao chengjiu rencai—cong 2005 nian quanguo laomo pingxuan biaozhang kan kexue rencai guan de xin shijian" [Labor and making a competent person—from selecting and commending model laborers in 2005 to see the new experience of viewing of the scientific and competent person], *Zhongguo Rencai*, no. 9 (2005), 18–19. Sima Tingfeng, "Quanguo laomo de xin miankong" [New faces of national model laborers], *Wangxiang* [Panorama], no. 14 (2005), 4. Yongyuan, "Laomo guanduo minshao de sikao" [Thoughts on many officials and few ordinary people among model laborers], *Shidaichao* [Current of the era], no. 9 (2005), 5. "Laomo pingxuan yinfa san da zhengyi" [Selection of model laborers leads to three big controversies], *Nanfang zhoumo* [Southern weekend], http://news.runsky.com/homepage/n/rec/userorbjectlai547979.html, (accessed on 11 August 2006).

81. Sun Liping, "Laomo pingxuan de ganga" [The embarrassments of selecting model laborers], *Zhongguo gaige* [China reform], no. 6 (2005), 52–53.

82. Zhang Xuemin, "Jinnian quanguo laomo pingxuan de xin bianhua" [New changes of selecting national model laborers this year], *Zhongguo shihua* [China petrochemical], no. 7 (2005), 82. Wang Beiping (Vice Chair of Federation of Trade Unions in Beijing), "Hongyang laomo jingshen, zunzhong laomo jiazhi" [To promote model laborer's spirit, respect model laborer's value], *Gonghui bolan* [Trade union survey], no. 9 (2005), 4–6.

83. Told by Lan Yingnian in Beijing, 25 May 2007.

10

The Soviet Impact on "Gender Equality" in China in the 1950s*

Jian Zang

THE SOVIET IMPACT ON GENDER equality in China was profound, especially in the 1950s when the Chinese Communist Party (CCP) started emulating many practices of the Soviet Union. Of the various facets of Soviet gender equality, the one that had the greatest influence in China was equality of job opportunities for women. An entire generation of women in China benefited from this Soviet influence not only in their way of thinking, but also in the way they lived their lives.[1]

Most of the studies of gender equality in China in the 1950s, first published in the 1970s and 1980s, were written by Western scholars.[2] Mechthild Leutner, a German scholar and an authority on women's studies in China, argues that the majority of Western literature on gender equality in China has emphasized the socialist character of China, thereby distinguishing the Chinese concept of gender equality from the Western concept of "women's liberation." Western scholars who have a positive view of the "socialist liberation" of women stress the benefits that the CCP has bestowed upon Chinese women. By contrast, scholars who focus on the negative consequences of "socialist liberation" argue that the totalitarian nature of Chinese socialism has prevented the true liberation of women. From this negative perspective, Chinese women not only lost their femininity during the process, they were also prevented from achieving real liberty.[3]

In more recent literature, most Western scholars interested in gender issues have turned their attention to the study of the changing status of women in China. These scholars argue that since the liberation of women has often been subordinated to the larger goals of class struggle and revolution, no real

gender equality has been achieved in China. In fact, they argue, many traditional ideas and practices with regard to women continue to persist in China
today.

Most Chinese scholars, beginning in the late 1990s, have focused their studies on rural women or on the impact of the 1953 marriage law on Chinese
women.[4] This chapter introduces some new perspectives about an under-
studied yet extremely important subject: the Soviet influence on gender
equality in China in the 1950s.

Equality between Men and Women in China: The Soviet Impact

After seizing power in 1949, the CCP confronted many challenges concerning
women's issues: how to mobilize Chinese women so that they could contribute to the socialist construction of the country, how to define the notion of
women's liberation under socialism, and how to show the world that Chinese
women were indeed achieving equality with men under the leadership of the
CCP. As China had done in the 1950s with regard to the economy—that is,
emulated the Soviet road to socialism—the CCP also sought during this period to learn from the Soviet Union about how to achieve the socialist liberation of women.

In 1949, the first national magazine on women's issues, *Women of New
China*, was published. The CCP and the Chinese government sought to use
the magazine as a propaganda vehicle to educate Chinese women about how
women lived and worked in the Soviet Union and in so doing to inspire Chinese women to follow the Soviet example. Between 1949 and 1955, *Women
of New China* included many articles that portrayed the life of Soviet women.
Special efforts were made to show how women in the Soviet Union, like their
male counterparts, actively participated in production and in many types of
social activities, and how society showed the same respect for women as it
did for men. In 1956, the title of the magazine changed from *Women of New
China* to *Women of China*, and with the worsening of relations between the
two countries in the late 1950s, fewer and fewer articles were published about
women in the Soviet Union.

Women of New China was published by the All-China Women's Federation (ACWF), a government organization that played an important role in
organizing and mobilizing Chinese women. Similar to other organizations
in China, it had a top-down structure, and it had the ability to exercise its
influence in the most remote corners of Chinese society. The ACWF and
its magazine had a profound impact on Chinese women during the 1950s.
Women of New China was particularly effective in providing Chinese women

with information in two areas: Stalin's views concerning women, and the everyday lives of Soviet women.

Publicizing Stalin's Views on Women

As in most of its propaganda, the CCP publicized the views of party leaders on a particular topic before dealing with the topic itself. Accordingly, in order to introduce the life of women in the Soviet Union, *Women of New China*, in its inaugural issue, published an article written by Stalin and entitled "On Working Women." In this article, Stalin made three points: first, working women are among the most oppressed group in society; second, working women and farmers are the great reserves for the proletarian class; and third, the most important task for any communist party is to liberate working women and farmers from the exploitative influences of the bourgeois class.[5]

In homage to Stalin at the time of his death in 1953, *Women of New China* published a special issue that included three articles by Stalin. In addition to Stalin's "On Working Women." One was the text of a speech Stalin delivered to a gathering that was celebrating the fifth anniversary of the First Conference for the Representatives of Working Women and Female Farmers. In his speech, Stalin not only refuted widely held views that education was wasted on women, he also emphasized the importance of educating women, making three arguments to support his position. First, he maintained that if women were uneducated and ignorant, they could not work side by side with men, and they might even undermine the country's economic construction. Second, if women were uneducated and ignorant, they could possibly be harmful to Soviet society and the cooperatives. Third, women are mothers and educators of the next generation. For the sake of the next generation and the future of the Soviet Union, he recognized how important it was that women in the Soviet Union should be educated in socialist ideology to raise the next generation of socialists. At the same time, Soviet women should be taught to reject priests, kulaks, and the capitalist class.[6]

Stalin believed that working women were uneducated and ignorant and that it would be essential to educate them. In 1953, the three arguments Stalin made in his speech were accepted without question by Chinese women. At that time, the opinions expressed by party leaders were treated as if they were the words of the gods, in contrast to the situation in China today, where such a description of working women would be treated as an egregious example of sexism and male chauvinism. In any case, around the time of Stalin's death, Chinese women were asked to read Stalin's articles and they were expected to accept his ideas. The third article included in the special issue was entitled

"Stalin on the Liberation of Women through Collective Farms." In this article Stalin emphasized the important role to be played by female cooperative workers in the building of socialist farms.[7]

After a careful examination of all of Stalin's writings, the editorial board of *Women of New China* could only find three articles for the special issue concerning Stalin's views on women. None of the articles was a full-length study; they were all speeches that he delivered at various meetings. Compared to Mao Zedong and other CCP leaders, it could be concluded that Stalin gave less attention to women's issues than did the CCP leaders.

Follow the Good Example of Soviet Women

While making known to Chinese women Stalin's views on women's liberation, education, and their role in building socialist cooperative farms, *Women of New China* also described, in plain and easy language, the life that Soviet women were leading. The magazine articles portrayed an ideal world for Chinese women to dream about: women in the Soviet Union seemed to be the happiest people in the world. Since the establishment of the Soviet socialist system, the articles maintained, all unequal systems had been eliminated, including gender inequality. The articles said that women in the Soviet Union were enjoying equal opportunity in jobs, education, vacations, and pay. The happy life of Soviet women was the result, according to the articles, of their active participation in the country's economic social activities in response to calls from the Soviet government.

Between 1950 and 1955, certain columns of *Women of New China* were used to publicize the life of Soviet women. Two columns were most notable at the time: "Follow the Good Example of Soviet Women," and "The Soviet Union's Today Is Our Tomorrow." The ideas presented in the columns were repeated time after time, and these ideas eventually took deep root in the thinking of many Chinese women.

One interesting aspect of the magazine's propaganda was the parity that was maintained between the number of Soviet examples and the number of Chinese examples concerning the equality of women. For example, examples of success in the Soviet Union were matched by corresponding Chinese examples. In this way, it was made clear to the readers that although China had followed the Soviet Union, it had also achieved its own successes. The CCP was highly sensitive about China's position relative to the Soviet Union and did not want to leave the readers with the impression that China was still far behind the Soviet Union in liberating its women.

One example of the magazine's efforts to show that China was as successful as the Soviet Union can be seen in its treatment of women's participation in political leadership roles. In 1949, *Women of New China* reprinted an editorial from *Izvestia* that described the progress women had made in the Soviet Union in economic and political life as well as the genuine freedom that they enjoyed in pursuing their life goals. The editorial particularly emphasized the leadership roles that Soviet women occupied. According to the editorial, close to five hundred thousand women representatives were elected to the local Soviets, about seventeen hundred women were elected to Soviets at the republic level, and about two hundred and seventy-seven were elected to the National Congress of Soviets. All of this high level of political participation by women, according to the editorial, was brought about by the success of the revolution and socialism.[8]

To show that Chinese women had achieved successes comparable to that of Soviet women in terms of ascending to leadership positions, an article appeared in *Women of New China* in that same year that talked about the leadership roles of Chinese women in the newly established Chinese People's Political Consultative Conference (CPPCC), an organization for non-communist party leaders and prominent societal figures. It not only identified the number of women representatives in the organization, it also indicated their professions.[9]

In 1953, the situation in China changed dramatically. What were portrayed as "local elections" took place nationwide that year and Chinese women not only participated in elections, but were also elected to local representative bodies. According to an article that appeared in *Women of New China* in 1954, during the 1953 local elections, 34.01% of registered women voters voted, and women accounted for 17.31 percent of all representatives elected. In Beijing, 106 women were elected to Beijing municipal representative bodies, meaning that 18.8 percent of the representatives in the Beijing were women. Such data were used to show that Chinese women not only had rights to participate in elections, they also had the ability to enter leadership positions.[10]

In the early 1950s, numerous stories appeared in *Women of New China* that showed the parity of successes of women in China and the Soviet Union. In its July 1952 issue, the magazine presented the story of Maria Roriniva, a Soviet textile worker who worked as hard as her male co-workers in building socialism.[11] In the same issue of *Women of New China*, the story of Hao Jianxiu, a Chinese textile model worker, was also told.[12]

In the January 1952 issue of the magazine, stories were presented showing the important contributions made by Soviet rural women in building socialist collective farms, and it was reported that more than 200,000 women held leadership positions at these farms. Some women headed collective farms, while others led production teams. Prominent among these accomplished women was a model tractor driver who had won the Stalin Award.[13] In the same January issue, to show how far Chinese women had come since their original liberation, two Chinese female tractor drivers, Liang Jun and Dong Lisheng, were presented as models for rural Chinese women to follow.[14]

Women of New China also introduced its readers to Soviet women who had successfully entered competitive fields that thus far had been dominated by men. In the April 1952 issue, readers learned about female pilots in the Soviet Union and came to know the story of Pasko, one particular female pilot.[15] In 1952, China did not have any female pilots, and so no comparable stories could be told about Chinese women. The magazine, nevertheless, featured Chinese female ground crew members who belonged to the Chinese air force.[16]

By the early 1950s, many women in the Soviet Union were entering higher education and were graduating from colleges and universities. In China, however, the majority of women, especially working women and rural women, had just begun to learn how to read and write. To show the progress of Chinese women in higher education and to demonstrate that women had the same educational rights as men did, the magazine showcased a female exchange student, Li Wenxun, who was attending Moscow State University in 1954. On the cover page of the October 1954 issue, *Women of New China* printed a photo of Li Wenxun and one of her Soviet classmates looking happily at a map of China. The photo on the cover page of the magazine sent a strong message to the world that Chinese women, like women in other advanced countries, enjoyed educational opportunities equal to those of men.[17]

For equality in employment to occur, it was essential that a reliable childcare system be established so that women could join the labor force with ease. By the 1950s, the Soviet Union, according to the magazine, had not only established such a system, but had also produced excellent experts on childcare. The most prominent Soviet figure in the field was Galina.[18] China was still lagging behind the Soviet Union in producing experts similar to Galina, but China had found its own ways of caring for children while their mothers were at work. In the August 1952 issue of *Women of New China*, feature stories and photos were published that showed the unique features of China's childcare solutions in both rural and urban settings.[19]

In addition to publicizing model examples of the Soviet Union, *Women of New China* also presented information in a variety of areas to Chinese women. For example, the magazine published a large number of reports written by Chinese visitors to the Soviet Union. The visitors wrote about their wonderful impressions of the Soviet Union and the good things they saw there.[20] In 1955, the magazine, for the first time, discussed birth control in the Soviet Union.[21] The magazine also provided information to Chinese women so that they could learn how to make Soviet-style dresses.[22]

For most Chinese in the 1950s, the highest honor imaginable was to have the opportunity to either visit or study in the Soviet Union. For most Chinese women, however, it was impossible to do either. The closest they could come to either was to imitate the fashion styles of Soviet women. For many Chinese working women, the most fashionable clothing was a Lenin-style jacket. In the beginning, the Lenin-style jacket was for men, but somehow it became popular among Chinese women. In the process, the Lenin-style jacket evolved into a revolutionary-style type of clothing equal to the commonly known *Zhongshan*-style (Sun Yat-sen-style) of clothing. At that time, the height of fashion for a revolutionary Chinese woman was to wear a Lenin-style jacket with a short haircut.[23]

Many young Chinese women also loved Soviet-style dresses. One particular type was called a *bulaji* in Chinese; if fact, it was simply a one-piece dress. Over time, more and more young Chinese women came to prefer the *bulaji*, and fewer and fewer opted for the traditional Chinese *chipao*. In 1956, when the magazine changed its title to *Women of China*, a feature article addressed the changes in fashion in China.[24]

Understanding the Meaning of Gender Equality in the 1950s

Due to differences in history, culture, and economy between China and the Soviet Union, Chinese propaganda about Soviet women's way of life had to take into account the special circumstances of Chinese society. To do so, the CCP focused on the issues that were most important for Chinese women at the time: illiteracy among women, marriage, and participation in the labor force.

Beginning in the early 1950s, the CCP set about bringing women into the work force. Under slogans such as "Times have changed!" "Women can do what men do!" and "Men and women are equal!" Chinese society entered a new phase of development. Within a short span of time, a large number of women changed from being home-makers to becoming working women and professional women in society. Such a drastic change in the status of women was unprecedented in Chinese history. It was the result of a policy introduced by the CCP and implemented by the central government; it was the first time in Chinese history that such a policy had been instituted.

The introduction of the new concept that women should be treated as the equals of men and the new practice of equal pay for women had a dramatic impact on the life of Chinese women. The position of women in the family had also begun to change. As women joined the labor force, their relationships with their husbands began to change. Many husbands began to share household chores with their wives: doing laundry, shopping for food, cooking meals for the family, and taking care of the children. Since working women were contributing to family income, they gradually began to take charge of family finances.

In the 1950s, it became popular for young women to find their own mates rather than to have their families choose marriage partners for them. The introduction of a new marriage law undoubtedly facilitated this change, but working in society put many young women in a much stronger position to find their ideal marriage partners. At the time, some husbands did not want their wives to work outside of the homes. As a result of rapidly changing attitudes in society, such husbands were frequently criticized and sometimes even condemned by relatives, neighbors, and society at large for their conservative and traditional ways of thinking.

The widespread participation of Chinese women in the labor force beginning in the early 1950s produced two major changes: first, it created the conditions for equality between men and women at a societal level; and second, it provided the economic foundations for equality between men and women in daily life. During the thirty years from 1949, when the CCP seized power, to 1979, when Deng Xiaoping launched the economic reforms, China achieved great improvements in the position of women in society. There was a remarkable narrowing of the gap between men and women in the areas of job opportunity, education, social position, and position within the family.

As a result of the changes taking place in Chinese society from the early 1950s, the concept of equality between men and women based on equal opportunity in jobs and pay continued to gain in strength in the minds of millions of Chinese people. The central role played by the CCP and the Chinese government in these changes cannot be overlooked, for they fostered and nurtured acceptance of this concept and enforced the associated practices continuously. The success of the government's dissemination of these ideas, ironically, goes a long way toward explaining why Chinese women had such a hard time accepting forced early retirement or job loss during the reform era.

Some scholars have criticized the changes in gender roles that began in the 1950s, saying that these changes went too far in erasing the differences between men and women and in de-feminizing Chinese women in the process.[25] It is important to note, however, that although China emulated Soviet policy and practice concerning gender equality, the de-feminization of Chinese women had little to do with the emulation of Soviet practices. Soviet women continued to dress in a feminine way as they entered the work force. The de-feminization of Chinese women, to the extent that it occurred, can be traced more directly to the excesses of the Cultural Revolution. The militaristic ideals of female fashion and behavior arising from the practice of young women wearing military uniforms during the Cultural Revolution contributed more to the de-feminization of Chinese women than did their entry in the work force beginning in the early 1950s.

The CCP's promotion of gender equality took place within the context of the construction of a socialist planned economy in China, and, as with socialist economic construction, gender equality was advanced through a top-down process. While the party could bring about massive changes at the level of cultural understandings and national institutions with regard to gender equality, these changes were far more dramatic in urban areas than in poor rural areas, where harsher economic conditions, lower literacy levels, and more resistance to social and cultural change posed major obstacles to the spread of gender equality.

The economic reforms that began in the late 1970s generated drastic changes in the structure of China's economy. The growth of market forces in the economy undermined the role of central planning in the economy and challenged many economic practices from the past. Gender equality, which was promoted under the auspices of China's planned economy, also suffered challenges. During the reform era, Chinese women faced great difficulties in finding and keeping jobs. The situation was even more serious in big cities such as Beijing and Shanghai and in the cities in the Northeast where many industrial complexes were eliminating jobs to respond to market forces. Women turned to the party for help, and they became increasingly nostalgic for the time when they were guaranteed jobs and equal pay.

Economic reform in China effectively destroyed the Soviet model of gender equality, and decision-makers in China often found themselves caught in a difficult balancing act. On the one hand, they had to protect gender equality, but, on the other, they had to strive for economic efficiency so that enterprises could survive and prosper and China could develop. How could China promote both priorities at the same time? It appears that the CCP is still struggling to find the right balance between these two competing goals.[26]

Gender Equality: Conceptual Differences between China and the West

Conceptual developments concerning gender equality followed different evolutionary processes in China and the West, except for the early days of this process in China. After the 1911 revolution led by Sun Yat-sen, the quest for democracy and individual rights dominated reform efforts in China, many social and political movements emerged in pursuit of these objectives. Among these movements were ones dedicated to establishing rights for women in politics, economy, and education. During the post-1911 era, many Chinese, especially intellectuals, adopted Western concepts concerning gender equality.

New concepts began to emerge after the establishment of the CCP in 1921. The CCP had made the liberation of women an important objective in its larger struggle for national sovereignty and national liberation, thereby subordinating the attainment of women's rights to its larger revolutionary goals. During this period, gradual and subtle changes began to take place in the way that Western concepts concerning gender equality and the liberation of women were translated and applied in China. After the establishment of the People's Republic of China (PRC), further changes in concepts and practices occurred. The CCP began to produce slogans to spread its ideas about gender equality and the liberation of women including: "The times have changed, and women and men are equal!" and "Women can shoulder half of the sky!"

Since the 1950s, Chinese concepts concerning gender equality and the liberation of women began to diverge from Western concepts. These Chinese concepts began to take root in the Chinese psyche. The Western emphasis upon male supremacy as the major obstacle to gender equality, most powerfully represented by the feminist commitment to toppling the "white male club" and the male-dominated power structure, had little or no influence in China until the reform era. For Chinese women, the focus of attention has been on the struggle against the oppression of traditional gender roles. The Chinese concept concerning gender equality from the early 1950s on held that men and women are equal and that women can do whatever men can do. This approach sought to reduce the gap between women and men in many areas. The Chinese concept further emphasizes the benefit of gender equality for society as a whole in addition to the benefit for individual women, while the Western approach attaches more importance to the rights of women as individuals. Even with the drastic changes in recent years, it is still hard for Chinese women to accept Western feminist ideas that emphasize individual rights and attacks on male chauvinism as guiding principles. Chinese women have, in fact, achieved a great deal of gender equality during the last sixty years under the CCP, but they are still striving for greater equality of treatment.[27]

Conclusion

China's emulation of Soviet gender policies, especially in the priority they gave to full employment for women, had a profound impact in China. Although the period of intensive emulation of Soviet policies lasted only about seven years, 1949 to 1956, the enduring influence of these polices upon Chinese society has been enormous. There have been conflicting views among the scholars about the extent to which China achieved gender equality in the 1950s; there have also been debates about the merits of instituting almost full employment for women during that time. Regardless of the differences among scholars on a range of issues, one thing is clear, however: as a result of China's emulation of Soviet gender policies, the principles of equal job opportunity and of equal pay for men and women have continued to be nurtured in China, even surviving the collapse of relations between the Soviet Union and China in 1960. For Chinese women and for the Chinese people more generally, those ideas became bedrock principles in Chinese society, at least until the unleashing of market forces during the period of economic reforms.

For many Chinese women, Western feminist ideas are not only foreign, but also uninteresting. Chinese women cling instead to familiar ideas about equal job opportunity and equal pay that were learned in the 1950s. These ideas have permeated the thinking of Chinese people ever since. For Chinese women today, the most urgent issues are those that are closely related to their own lives. For them, at a personal level, what is the meaning of gender equality? Should women become homemakers again rather than stay in the workplace? What role should women play in the workplace? And finally, have the economic reforms since the late 1970s provided real opportunities for Chinese women? While an examination of the Soviet impact on Chinese women might be viewed by some as merely an academic exercise concerning insignificant matters from the past and therefore without relevance for women in China today, it is, in fact, necessary to understand the influences of the Soviet Union on China's approach to gender issues in order to comprehend post-1949 developments concerning women in China.

Most Chinese scholars believe that women can be liberated by following a distinctively Chinese socialist path, different from the Western feminist concept of women's liberation.[28] In order to understand the Chinese approach, these scholars recognize the need for additional research to establish the historical connections between Stalinist ideas about the liberation of women, Mao's ideas in this area, and the current policies and practices in China relating to the liberation of women.[29]

Notes

ˈI would like to thank Professors Thomas P. Bernstein and Hua-yu Li for their constructive comments and Dr. Jim McLendon for his editorial assistance.

1. In writing this chapter, I mainly drew information from one journal, *Zhonguo funu* [Women of China]. Renamed in 1956, the journal was originally called *Xin Zhonguo fun* [Women of the New China]. Between 1949, when the People's Republic of China was established, and 1978, when the economic reforms began, this was the only national journal published in China that provided comprehensive coverage of women's issues. As a result, scholars studying women's issues at the national level during the 1950s, 1960s, and 1970s have come to rely heavily on this journal as a research source. Two regional monthly journals dealing with women's issues did exist in the early 1950s. One of them was *Guangzhou fun* [Women of Guangzhou], and the other was *Xi'nan funu* [Women of the Southwest]. Both of these journals, however, were short-lived. There were no newspapers dedicated to women issues between 1949 and 1984. The first national newspaper that covered women's issues, *Zhongguo fun bao* [Women of China], did not appear until October 1984. For detailed information about journals published in China concerning women's issues, please see, Wang Shu-Hwai et al., *Hai neiwai tushuguan shoucang youguan funu yanjiu zhongwen qikan lianhe mulu* [International union list of Chinese journals relating to women], Institute of Modern History, Academia Sinica, Taiwan, 1995.

2. Marilyn B. Young, *Women in China: Studies in Social Change and Feminism* (Ann Arbor: Center for Chinese Studies, University of Michigan Press, 1973). Kay Ann Johnson, *Women, the Family, and Peasant Revolution in China* (Chicago: University of Chicago Press, 1983). Judith Stacey, *Patriarchy and Socialist Revolution in China* (Berkeley: University of California Press, 1983). Margery Wolf, *Revolution Postponed: Women in Contemporary China* (Palo Alto, CA: Stanford University Press, 1985). Elisabeth Croll, *Feminism and Socialism in China* (London and Boston: Routledge & K. Paul, 1978). *The Women's Movement in China: A Selection of Readings, 1949–1973* (London: Anglo-Chinese Educational Institute, 1974).

3. Mechthild Leutner, "Ouzhou ren de zhongguo funu guan: cong Marco Polo dao jintian" [European perceptions of Chinese women: from Marco Polo to the present], *Funu yanjiu luncong* [Theoretical research on women], no. 1 (2000): 7–10.

4. Dong Miaoling, "Zhongguo gongchandang yu xin zhongguo de funu canzheng" [The Chinese Communist Party and the political participation of women in the new china], *Zhonggong dangshi yanjiu* [CCP party history research], no. 3 (2000), 61–63. Li Qiaoning, "1950 niandai zhongguo dui nongcun funv de shehui dongyuan" [The social mobilization of rural women in China in the 1950s], *Shehui kexue jia* [Social scientists], no. 6 (2004): 146–48. Gao Xiaoxian, "'Yinhua sai,' 20 shiji 50 niandai nongcun funu de xingbie fengong ["Yinhua contest": the gender-based division of labor among rural women in the 1950s], *Shehui xue yanjiu* [Sociological research], no. 4 (2005): 153–71. Tang Haidi, "Xin zhongguo chuqi nuxing wenhua yanjiu shulue" [A brief introduction to research on women's culture in the early days of the new China], *Shoudu shifan daxue xuebao* [Journal of Capital Normal University], supplement issue (2004), 19–25. Zhang Zhiyong, "Jianguo chuqi huabei nongcun hunyin zhidu de gaige" [Marriage reform in rural north China after the founding of the PRC], *Dang-dai zhongguo shi yanjiu* [Contemporary history of China], vol. 9, no. 5 (2002): 71–79. Guo Yuhua, "Xinling de jiti hua: Shanbei jicun nongye hezuohua de nvxing jiyi" [The psychology of collectivization: women's memory of agricultural cooperativization in

ji village, northern Shanxi], *Zhongguo shehui kexue* [Social science in China], no. 4 (2003), 48–61.

5. "Stalin lun laodong funv" [Stalin on working women], *Xin zhongguo funv* [Women of new China] (hereinafter as *XZF*), no. 1 (1949): 6–7.

6. Stalin, "Yingjie di yijie nugong nongfu daibiao dahui wu zhounian de jianghua" [Speech at the celebration of the fifth anniversary of the first conference of representatives of working women and female farmers], *XZF*, no. 4 (1953): 6.

7. Stalin, "Jiti nongzhuang dui funv jiefang de zuoyong yu yiyi" [The liberation of women through collective farms], *XZF*, no. 4 (1953): 7–8.

8. "Sulian xiaoxibao shelun: dadan di tiba funu danren Suweiai de gongzuo" [The editorial of the Soviet *izvestia:* boldly promoting women to work for the Soviet Union], *XZF*, no. 5 (1949): 7–8.

9. "Renmin zhengxie nu daibiao chengfen he zhiye tongji" [Statistics on family backgrounds and professions of female representatives of the CPPCC], *XZF*, no. 4 (1949): 39.

10. Li Qiyang, "Xianfa caoan guanchuan zhe nannu pingdeng de jingshen" [The draft constitution reflects the spirit of equality between men and women], *XZF*, no. 7 (1954): 4–5.

11. "Women you zhaodao le xin qiaomen" [We again found new "tricks"], *XZF*, no. 7 (1952): 33–34.

12. Hao Jianxiu, "Wo kandao de Sulian" [The Soviet Union I saw], no. 7 (1952): 20–22.

13. "Wo ruhe zai jiti gongzuo gangwei shang zhandou zhe: Sulian diyige nu tuolaji shou Angulina" [Working hard at my workplace: story of the first Soviet female tractor driver], *XZF*, no. 1 (1952): 24–25.

14. Liu Lumin, "Tuolaji shou Dong Lisheng" [Tractor driver Dong Lisheng], *XZF*, no. 1 (1952): 22.

15. Ivanov, trans. He Si, "Sulian yingxiong Pasko" [Pasko, the Soviet hero], *XZF*, no. 4 (1952): 24–25.

16. "Tamen shi xin zhongguo funu de guangrong: ji diyipi nu kongdiqin renyuan qifei dianli" [They are the pride of women in new China: story of the first group of female ground crew members of the Chinese air force], *XZF*, no. 4 (1952): 14–15.

17. *XZF*, no. 10 (1954), cover page.

18. *XZF*, no. 11 (1952), cover page.

19. Chen Jiayong and Lu Yi, "Ziyuan liangli banhao bao wawa zu" [Voluntary, mutually beneficial baby-sitting teams], *XZF*, no. 8 (1952): 22–23.

20. Li Fenglian, "Wo kandao Sulian funu jiji canjia le laodong shengchan" [I saw Soviet women enthusiastically participating in production]; Xu Keli, "Funu shi jianshe zhong de juda liliang: Sulian Dong'ou canguan yinxiang" [Women are a great force in construction: impressions from visits to the Soviet Union and Eastern Europe], *XZF*, no. 8 (1950): 22–23.

21. "Zenyang renshi biyun wenti" [Questions concerning contraception], *XZF*, no. 4 (1955): 27.

22. Yang Cangyi, "Jizhong qunzi de fengzhi fangfa" [Methods for making Soviet-style dresses], *XZF*, no. 4 (1955): 26.

23. *XZF*, no. 10 (1950) and no. 18 (1951), cover pages.

24. Xiao Ling, "Yijian hua qipao yinqi de fengbo" [A stir over a flowery *chipao*], *Zhongguo funu* [Women of China], no. 4 (1956): 18–19.

25. Li Yinhe, "Zhongguo feixing hua yu funu diwei" [The de-feminization and societal position of Chinese women], Women's Studies Center of Peking University, ed., *Beijing daxue funu wenti shoujie guoji yantaohui lunwen ji* [Collection of papers presented at the first international seminar on women's issue at Peking University], unpublished, 1992.

26. "1988—Nuren de chulu: gan wen lu zai hefang?" [1988—women's way out: dare to ask which way to go], *Zhongguo funu* [Women of China], no. 1 (1988): 4–5.

27. Zang Jian, "Dui 80 niandai zhongqi zhongguo funvshi yanjiu de fansi" [Reflections on the history of women in China in the mid-1980s], *Zhonghua nvzi xueyuan xuebao* [Journal of the institute for Chinese women], supplement (1999), 62–65.

28. Li Xiaojiang, "Nuxing? zhuyi—wenhua chongtu yu shenfen rentong" [Female? ism?—culture conflicts and the identity], "Guanyu qimeng: yu Professor Chris Gilmartin de duihua" [A dialogue with Professor Chris Gilmartin about "enlightenment"] (Jiangsu: Jiangsu renmin chubanshe, 2000), 242–55.

29. Shan Shilian, "1956 nian yu Mao Zedong de wenhua sixiang jiegou" [1956 and the structure of Mao Zedong's cultural thoughts], *Bolan qunshu* [Chinese book review monthly], no. 6 (2004): 16–23.

V

SOVIET INFLUENCE ON
SCIENCE AND EDUCATION

11

Soviet-Chinese Academic Interactions in the 1950s: Questioning the "Impact-Response" Approach

Izabella Goikhman

INTERNATIONAL ACADEMIC INTERACTIONS HAVE THREE main dimensions: po-litical, implementational, and discursive. Analyzing processes within those dimensions and the interdependencies between them provides the most comprehensive understanding of different modes of interactions and their consequences in the political and academic realms. Numerous studies deal with the Soviet impact at the discursive level by analyzing Soviet influences on the Chinese educational system in general[1] and specific institutions[2] or particular Chinese academic discourses.[3] The recent works of Chinese scholar Shen Zhihua provide valuable insights into the framework of policies which regulated the engagement of foreign assistance.[4] But the political background that made possible and desirable the science and knowledge transfer through international academic interactions with socialist states, first and foremost the Soviet Union, as well as the implementation of those interactions have not been as yet researched. Two main questions need to be answered: Why were China and the Soviet Union interested in academic interactions in the first place? How was the knowledge transfer implemented?

The absence of those research questions in past and contemporary studies is due to the still very strong legacy of the so-called impact-response approach, often in its derived form—the "influence model"—in the fields where re-search on Chinese academia is conducted. The "impact-response" approach, which is usually associated with John King Fairbank, dominated the Western studies on China from the 1950s until the 1980s. Within this paradigm China was shown as a passive object merely reacting to foreign influence. The rise of the so-called China-centered approach[5] since the late 1980s has changed the view of China by underlining its own interests and agency. However, this shift had almost no influence either in the research on Sino-Soviet relations in the 1950s, the Chinese educational system or, as a few historians of science have noted, the history of Chinese science and humanities in the 20th century.[6]

The "impact-response" paradigm implies an opposition or a conflict between China and the West, which usually includes Russia and the Soviet Union. For this reason and because of its major impact on international security, the Sino-Soviet schism is probably the most often researched aspect of the Sino-Soviet relationship. But while concentrating on conflicts, only seldom have Western scholars focused on interactions and cooperation.[7] Unlike their Western colleagues, Chinese and Soviet (Russian) scholars paid particular attention to Soviet aid in the 1950s,[8] but even in doing so they followed the "impact-response" paradigm by presenting the Soviet Union as the active subject of the relations, while China was considered as a passive object or a receiving part.[9] This is just as true for research that evaluates Soviet help to China positively—like the works of Soviet, Russian,[10] and, more recently, Chinese scholars[11]—as it is for works which tend to portray Soviet aid as a tool of influence and refer to Soviet policy as "social imperialism"—as it was done for a long time in Chinese historiography.[12] In analyzing the Chinese educational system the only action that the Chinese side is given credit for is the creative application of the Soviet model.[13] Moreover, the Sino-Soviet knowledge transfer is not analyzed at all.[14]

The legacy of the "impact-response" paradigm is not only apparent in the constructed dichotomies of China vs. West and/or passive vs. active. The search for foreign impact and influence forces scholars to concentrate on micro-histories of disciplines and institutions and prevents them from looking at the larger context. This can be observed first in the lack of the integration of the history of the interstate relations before the period studied: the relations between the Chinese Communist Party and the Comintern or the Soviet Union are not taken into account in the works on Sino-Soviet relations in the 1950s, and, second, in not considering contemporary political and social contexts: Although several studies have been published on the Soviet impact on the Chinese educational system as well as on particular Chinese academic discourses,[15] to this day the literature on Sino-Soviet cooperation and Soviet advisors in China in the educational and academic fields basically fails to focus on Chinese interests in foreign expertise.[16]

The concept of intercultural transfer can prove fruitful in overcoming the legacy of the "impact-response" approach for Sino-Soviet relations in the academic realm. Analyzing the intercultural transfer helps to identify its actors, mechanisms of diffusion, and strategic utilization of knowledge, as well as to integrate the transfer processes into the broader social and political context.[17] This approach emphasizes the interactions between the different cultures or states instead of influences,[18] thus providing insights not only on intercultural conflicts, but also on cooperation and negotiation processes.

Following this approach I will analyze in this chapter the Chinese policy behind the science and technology transfer and the implementation of Soviet-Chinese academic interactions[19] in the 1950s and demonstrate that the Chinese side was an active subject in this field of relations and thus challenge the problematic "impact-response" approach.[20]

On September 12, 1961, F. Klejmenov—an advisor for scientific and technological cooperation at the Soviet embassy in the People's Republic of China—expressed his view on Chinese policy behind the scientific and academic cooperation with Soviet Union: China had tried to shape the co-operation as one-sidedly as possible and to be only the receiving part, thus establishing a foundation for future development in science and development on her own [*sobstvennymi silami*].[21] Such a statement is not at all unusual for the rhetoric of mutual accusations, which was adopted by the Soviet Union and the PRC in the beginning of the 1960s. Yet, this statement was not made publicly and therefore did not have an immediate propaganda value. Could Klejmenov's remarks on the nature of scientific and technological coopera-tion between Beijing and Moscow thus prove true after all? While documents of the Communist Party of China (CCP) dealing explicitly with this question remain to be found at this point, I will use various publications and a broad range of available archival materials[22] to support my view, that close academic cooperation with the Soviet Union as part of the so-called lean to one side-policy served as a means to provide a reasonable academic foundation for China's policy of self-reliance.

In the first part of my chapter I will deal with the political dimensions of Sino-Soviet academic interactions by outlining the situation before 1949 and analyzing the relationship between the "lean to one side" policy as the main foreign policy strategy and "self-reliance" as an important concept in domestic policy and locating the role of science and technology transfer within those concepts. In the second part of this chapter I will concentrate on the implementational level of the interactions in the academic realm during the 1950s and finally provide an explanation of how the implementation of those interactions can be understood in the broader context of long-term self-reliance strategies.

The Political Dimension of Sino-Soviet Academic Interactions:
The Decision to "Lean to One Side," Self-Reliance and Science Transfer

The Sino-Japanese War (1937–1945), followed by the Civil War (1946–1949) had ruined the Chinese economy. The communist leaders recognized that the reconstruction of China's economy could not succeed without foreign aid. Giving foreign aid the first priority was "absolutely necessary" under those "objective conditions," Mao explained in 1962.[23] The Communist leaders perceived the neighboring Soviet Union as the only major country from which they could hope to get the badly needed assistance.[24] The majority of research literature on this subject confirms this view: The Soviet Union was the only source that could and was willing to provide China with the assistance needed.[25]

The "lean to one"—that is, the Soviet—"side" policy (*yibiandao*) was first enunciated in Mao's article "On the People's Democratic Dictatorship," published on July 1st, 1949, in *Renmin ribao* (People's Daily). However, already in the fall of 1947 Chinese leaders had started to look for a better and a closer relationship with the Soviet Union. The relations between the CCP and the Soviet Union (and Comintern) had been complicated since the 1920s.[26] Not only Mao, but also other Chinese leaders disagreed with Comintern directives and were dissatisfied with the China policy of the Soviet Union. The failures of Stalin's and the Comintern's policies were formulated by Mao in his talk with Soviet ambassador Yudin in 1956: Stalin had overvalued the revolutionary potential of the Guomindang (GMD) and forced the Chinese communists into a united front, which resulted in enormous losses on the Communist side. After the end of World War II, Stalin was still not convinced that the CCP could win a domestic civil war and insisted on the signing of a peace agreement with the GMD and consequently the establishment of a "democratic republic." Even in 1947, when Communist forces were already winning in China, he continued to do so.[27] The Soviet Union was as unhappy about Mao's repeated rejection of Stalin's requests to tie up the Japanese forces during the war and the Rectification Campaign as Mao was about Stalin's policy.[28]

Against this background, the alliance with the Soviet Union does not appear all too natural. Scholars provide different reasons for Mao's decision to lean on the Soviet side: ideological reasons such as communist internationalism, according to which Chinese Communists saw themselves as a part of World Communism and in direct opposition to the imperialist countries; and strategic reasons such as the perceived threat posed by the United States and the American pro-GMD-policy along with the view that the Soviet Union was the only possible source of needed assistance.[29] Probably both ideological and pragmatic reasons played a decisive role. In the following section I will try to elaborate on the relations between the "lean to one side" policy and the concept of self-reliance as well as the relevance of science and technology for these policies.

According to Liu Shaoqi the proclamation of the "lean to one side" policy was the first public statement on the importance of Soviet aid for the Chinese revolution: Before, Mao had always emphasized that the Chinese communists should not rely on foreign help, but only on themselves.[30] Liu's statement can be considered as an effort to influence the Soviets in their decision to provide aid to China, but the Maoist concept of self-reliance[31] had never excluded foreign expertise. On the contrary, it was always seen as a political instrument to achieve self-reliance.

This concept was developed in the late 1930s and 1940s, when local autonomy—economic and military—became a strategy for survival.[32] From the very beginning, self-reliance did not mean autarky and did not preclude international exchanges and foreign assistance—as long as China maintained the ultimate initiative. Mao Zedong[33] highlighted the importance of foreign assistance almost each time he mentioned self-reliance.[34] Foreigners were to be welcomed in China, so that the Chinese could learn from their advanced experience.[35] Yet Mao made a clear distinction between a dependency-relationship to the donor-countries and foreign aid based on a self-reliance policy of the receiver[36] and warned of "mechanical absorption of foreign material." Chinese communists should treat foreign material as they do their food: "first chewing it, then submitting it to the working of the stomach and intestines with their juices and secretions, and separating it into nutriment to be absorbed and waste matter to be discarded—before it can nourish us."[37]

Hence, the decision to "lean to one side" did not contradict the principle of self-reliance. Nevertheless, notions of self-reliance as the main domestic policy disappeared from the media after the "lean to one side" policy was proclaimed. New slogans were used instead now, such as "independence" and "sovereignty." This lets various scholars conclude that the principle of self-reliance was abandoned from 1949 to 1958.[38] But in fact, it was more a rhetorical change than a new policy.[39] Not mentioning self-reliance publicly had two motives: In the international realm it was better tactically not to mention it, since after all China needed Soviet assistance and had to dispose of Stalin's suspicions about Mao being a "Chinese Tito."[40] In China, the politics of "leaning to the Soviet side" had to be promoted both within the CCP itself and also in the public sphere in general: While the majority of the Chinese population had little understanding of the Soviet Union, most intellectuals and urban residents had a rather unfavorable impression of the Northern neighbor, because of imperialist policies of Tsarist Russia, Stalin's post-war China policy, and the problematic practice of Soviet troops in Manchuria.[41]

There are some indications that the doctrine of self-reliance did not disappear from discussions within the CCP. Just twenty days after the official proclamation of the "lean to one side" policy, Deng Xiaoping informed the comrades of the East China Bureau of the CPC Central Committee, reiterating Mao's instruction:

> the sooner we carry out our foreign policy of leaning to one side, the more favourable it will be for us. . . . As regards our domestic policy, we must stress the need for *conscientiously relying on our own efforts;* we should not just call for it but should earnestly set about doing it (*Chairman Mao says it is even more important for us to adopt this policy from the perspective of the long-term building of a new democracy*).[42] By doing so, that is, by occupying the whole of China, leaning to one side and relying on ourselves, we can not only lay a solid foundation for ourselves, but also compel the imperialists to yield to us.[43]

During the summer of 1949 other communist leaders postulated self-reliance as the main goal of the economic reconstruction of China.[44]

In December of the same year Zhou Enlai elaborated in detail on the relations between foreign assistance and self-reliance. According to him, China needed foreign aid and welcomed sincere help of friendly nations, but China should mainly be self-reliant. Again, speaking about domestic and foreign relations, Zhou emphasized that between foreign help and self-reliance the priority should always be given to self-reliance—both in the economic and in the political realm. Later he added that honest aid of friendly nations helped China to reach self-reliance.[45]

Thus, foreign assistance was viewed as an instrument to achieve self-reliance from a long-term perspective. But what was the role of science and technology transfer within this strategy?

The development of science and technology was seen by the CCP as essential for the building of new democracy. Based on Marxist theories and traditions which had always regarded science and technology as the foundation of economic and social change,[46] it was in the 1920s and 1930s when Chinese communist leaders supported the use of science in order to build a new China and undermine the old system.[47] In 1940 Mao made a statement on the immediate importance of science for socialist production: "Natural science is one of man's weapons in his fight for freedom. For the purpose of attaining freedom in society man must use social science to understand and change society and carry out social revolution."[48] With almost no basis for indigenous development and within the framework of this particular understanding of science, transfer of advanced scientific knowledge and technology from abroad became indispensable for the revolutionary transformation of society.[49]

The Soviet Union was for several reasons the most convenient source of knowledge transfer. First of all, the Soviet Union was the only country which already had succeeded in developing a socialist science which served economic needs. Soviet scientists and scholars could therefore not only provide the Chinese with advanced scientific knowledge, but this knowledge would also be rooted in Marxist-Leninist ideology. Since knowledge transfer is especially difficult in cross-cultural settings, the Marxist values as a shared cultural context could contribute to better translatability and convertibility of knowledge provided by the Soviet Union.[50]

Secondly, Soviet experts who were to help China would be much less dangerous politically and not as difficult to control as experts from other countries, who potentially did not share as many ideological values with the CCP: They would be—in Mao's later words— "both red and expert."[51] And, finally, because of the difficult relations in the past, Chinese communists had already developed their own patterns of interactions with Soviet experts during the 1920s and the 1930s and had learned how to obtain the maximum autonomy in dealing with them.[52] For Mao, who had been suspicious about close and uncontrolled relations with any foreign country,[53] those considerations might have been quite important, although—as mentioned above—explicit statements are yet to be found.

The Soviet Union was willing to provide China with assistance for several reasons: the internationalist basis of Soviet help which was highlighted by Soviet and Russian scholars was important not only because it was proclaimed to be the basic principle of Soviet foreign policy. In the particular situation of ideological bipolarity of the post-war system, the USSR had to act according to this principle. National image building was extremely important, since "the most important aspect of an actor's reputation in world politics is the belief of others that it will keep its future commitments even when a particular situation . . . makes it appear disadvantageous to do so."[54] Helping China despite of its still very difficult economic situation helped the Soviet Union to increase its prestige in the international arena. Even in the beginning of the 1960s after the sudden withdrawal of the Soviet specialists from China, the Soviet general line was to fulfill the commitments stipulated in the newly formulated agreements, so that the Chinese side wouldn't be able to accuse the Soviet Union publicly of not being interested in cooperation[55].

The Soviet specialists helped China to rapidly develop its science and economy, but they also could channel the development in a specific direction. It was a matter of Soviet security that China become strong, but it was also a matter of Soviet security that China should become only as strong as the USSR wanted it to be. Controlling the flow of knowledge was a first priority under the direct supervision of the Central Committee.

Another important aspect is often forgotten by the scholars of Sino-Soviet relations: the increase in knowledge that the USSR gained from the exchanges.[56] The Soviet scholars and especially scientists had to inform the Soviet leadership about the newest Chinese scientific developments. Especially in the second half of the 1950s, the demand for parity in the academic exchanges became more and more pronounced). Furthermore, the Soviet Union needed Chinese cooperation for the realization of important large-scale projects, such as the exploitation of the Amur River basin.[57]

Considering the partly contradictory motives of the PRC and the Soviet Union and to what extent China had to rely on Soviet help in various areas, the real challenge for the Chinese leaders was to find a balance between obtaining the assistance and avoiding total economic and political dependence on the Soviet Union.[58] Science transfer was crucial for this objective. Unlike technology transfer which involves import of foreign equipment and acquisition of technological processes as they were being utilized, science transfer enables the "nationalization"—in this case "sinification"—of foreign knowledge and technology, which implies that the receiving party achieves the required scientific level and is able to improve the transferred technology or knowledge through innovation of its own.[59]

If self-reliance was the goal of the Chinese communists and knowledge transfer within the "lean to one side" policy was an instrument to achieve ultimate national independence, it must have influenced patterns of Sino-Soviet academic interactions.

Implementing Policies: Sino-Soviet Academic Interactions in the 1950s within the Framework of the Long-Term Self-Reliance Strategy

Soviet-Chinese science and technology transfer in the 1950s is considered to be one of the most remarkable in modern history.[60] While before 1953 exchanges of publications were the main channel for the transfer of academic knowledge, after 1953 the academic cooperation was further institutionalized and personnel exchanges became increasingly important.[61]

Although the exact number of Soviet advisors and experts who worked in China is not clear, because there was no explicit definition of who was an "expert" and the available statistics are mostly fragmentary, probably around 10,000 non-military advisors served in China between 1949 and 1960.[62] Combining Russian and Chinese archival sources, Shen Zhihua claims an even higher number of over 12,000 experts.[63] The Chinese Academy of Science (CAS) alone engaged more than 60 Soviet consultants and invited over 820 Soviet scholars to visit the Academy.[64] More than 20,000

Chinese students,[65] technicians, and scholars studied in or visited the Soviet Union.[66] There also were Soviet students—mostly sinologists—who studied in China, but the exact number is unclear.[67] The exchange of publications, research materials, the translation of books, and a broad range of joint research projects and expeditions were also important modes of knowledge transfer.

Sino-Soviet academic interactions were part of a broader science and technology transfer and involved knowledge transfer on different levels: between academicians and professors, scholars in the Soviet and Chinese Academies of Sciences, but also between workers in research institutes and students. Some of the Soviet advisors and visitors in China were well-known scientists and occupied important positions in the Soviet Academy of Science (Akademiia Nauk SSSR [AN SSSR]) as for example, B. R. Lazarenko, the vice secretary general of the Division of Technical Sciences of the Soviet Academy of Sciences, who served as a consultant to the president of the Chinese Academy of Sciences for two years (1955–1957), or Soviet experts in education, who usually were at least associate professors.[68] Chinese delegations on the highest level often consisted of famous scholars and scientists: In 1953, for example, Guo Moruo (the president of the CAS at time) visited the Soviet Union[69] and Qian Sanqiang (director of the Institute for modern physics at the CAS) headed a delegation of Chinese scholars.[70] There also were contacts between research institutes and academic organizations at the lower level,[71] which involved less well known scholars. Those contacts are not as well documented as the ones on the higher level.

However, the activities of "high-ranking" delegations and experts were not limited to the one institution to which they were invited. The already mentioned Chinese delegation headed by Qian Sanqiang visited around 100 scientific institutions of the Soviet Academy of Sciences, various ministries, universities, and institutes. They also went to academies of sciences and research institutions in different Soviet republics.[72] The same is true for Soviet specialists in China: they not only worked on specific topics to which they had been assigned, but also gave lectures to broader audiences, including scholars of other disciplines and other academic institutions, who came from different cities, technicians, laboratory assistants, graduate, and post-graduate students. They also travelled to different research institutes as consultants and gave lectures there.[73] Furthermore, between 500 and 1,000 copies of the translated texts of their lectures were printed and sent to various academic institutions, libraries, and enterprises all over China.[74] So the scope of the manpower involved in the academic interactions and participating in the knowledge transfer was much higher than any statistics on visiting scholars would let us assume.

According to the importance that science and technology occupied in the Chinese view on independent development, the Chinese side took the initiative and brought up the topic of Sino-Soviet cooperation in science and technology already in negotiations before the founding of the PRC. In February 1949, when Mikoyan was in Xibaipo, Soviet assistance was mostly wanted in military, industrial, and economic spheres.[75] Yet, the Chinese delegation headed by Liu Shaoqi, which was in the Soviet Union from June to August of the same year, also concentrated on technology, science, and culture. The request to send Soviet teachers to China to lecture and, the other way around, to welcome Chinese delegations to the Soviet Union for information and study as well as admitting Chinese students for study in the Soviet Union was answered positively.[76]

Together with a Chinese delegation, a group of 220 Soviet specialists went to China in August 1949. Officially, they were going to help the newly established communist regime in Manchuria.[77] The first public result of the agreements on academic and cultural cooperation reached in Moscow was a visit of a delegation of forty-three Soviet scholars and artists, which came to China in September 1949 to take part in the celebrations of the founding of the PRC.[78] Thereafter, Mao repeatedly emphasized to the Soviet experts that Chinese communists had to rely on themselves both in the war against Japan and during the civil war[79] and that the Chinese side was not willing to blindly follow Soviet advice: The Soviet advisors had just come to China and were not too familiar with the particular circumstances in the country and therefore should consult their Chinese colleagues.[80] When Soviet specialists come to China, they have to learn about Chinese specific features, Mao stressed again in 1950.[81] Mao made it clear: The Chinese side was interested in cooperation, not in commands.

In the months after the founding of the PRC, Chinese leaders repeatedly contacted Soviet ambassador Roshchin to describe the existing difficulties and to ask for more help. Guo Moruo, for example, told him that most of the devices and materials of the Chinese Academy of Science had been taken to Taiwan by the GMD.[82] Soviet experts were sent to China when they were requested by the Chinese part.[83] For Shen Zhihua this constituted the difference between China and Eastern Europe. According to him, Soviet advisors were sent to Eastern Europe to control the newly established socialist states, but they came to China because they were invited by the Chinese leadership to help to consolidate the new regime and to advance China's economic and scientific development.[84] Although the Soviet Union had also its own interests in mind when helping China, Shen Zhihua makes an important point that challenges the "impact-response" approach: Obviously, the Chinese side was an active subject of this cooperation.

During the years 1950–1951 three agreements were signed concerning the work conditions of Soviet specialists in China.[85] These agreements were considered important breakthroughs by the Chinese side. The Chinese Ambassador in the Soviet Union, Wang Jiaxiang, who was negotiating with A. A. Gromyko, the deputy foreign minister, about the first agreement, expressed the will of Chinese leadership to publish the agreement and a communiqué. The Soviet side refused to do so, pointing out that agreements on Soviet specialists which were signed with other socialist states had not been published before.[86] Of course, other topics were subject to negotiation. Some of them concerned phrasing,[87] others addressed more sensitive topics, such as the funding of specialists. While the Chinese side succeeded in reducing some salaries, they could not convince the Soviets to bear the expenses for the pre-term recall of the specialists with no regard to the length of their stay in China.[88] The Soviet side insisted that they would only accept the costs for recalling specialists who had worked in China for less than six months.

Although three agreements dealt with all kinds of specialists, no special agreement was made to promote academic relations. After Stalin's death in 1953, the scientific and technological cooperation became institutionalized and much more intensive than before. In October 1954, "The Convention on Science and Technology Cooperation" was signed, which further stipulated the establishment of a Science and Technology Cooperation Commission, which—beginning in 1955—held approximately two annual sessions alternating between Peking and Moscow.[89] This Commission was responsible for relations in the fields of natural sciences. The cooperation in social sciences and humanities was planned and carried out solely by the Soviet and the Chinese Academies of Sciences, which signed respective cooperation agreements. Important decisions concerning the Chinese development, such as developing the Chinese "Long-Term Program for Developing National Sciences and Technology between 1956 and 1967," involved complex processes of negotiations between Chinese and Soviet experts.[90]

Chinese were not only active in making general political decisions, but they also could actively influence their ultimate implementation, whereas Soviet authorities could not. One reason for this was lack of supervision: Although the nomination of specialists was a complicated process always involving the CC of the CPSU, Soviet authorities failed to adequately supervise their expatriate workers in China, just as it had been when Comintern advisors worked in China in the 1920s and 1930s. The director of the Foreign Department of the Presidium of the Soviet Academy of Sciences[91] complained about the bad connection with Soviet experts, who did not report everything about their life and work in China as they should have, which made supervising their work impossible.[92] Even to the Chinese the Soviet leaders admitted of not being able to control every single specialist working in China.[93]

There is some evidences that the Soviet embassy had to rely on Chinese sources to obtain information about the activities of Soviet citizens working in China. V. P. Fedotov, who worked as a translator in the Soviet embassy in Beijing, writes that the bulletins of the Foreign Experts Bureau (*Waiguo zhuanjia gongzuo ju*) were so important that almost everybody in the embassy who knew Chinese was engaged in their translation. Those bulletins were kept in the embassy only for a day.[94]

Interviews with former Soviet advisors and experts let Deborah Kaple to come to the conclusion that "much of the work associated with the programs depended on Soviet specialists, teachers, and advisors" and not on the institutions that sent them to work in China.[95] There are also some indications that the working plan of Soviet specialists was prepared by the inviting institutions, sometimes including a detailed program not only by month, but also by day and hour,[96] which was then discussed when the experts arrived.[97]

The lack of Soviet control is also well-illustrated in Mikhail Klochko's account on his work in China.[98] Klochko's case also emphasizes that the Chinese side could ask for a specific individual as a specialist and could—at least to some extent—influence the period of his or her stay in China,[99] although after 1953 both states agreed that the Chinese should consult the Soviet Embassy on matters of invitation and hiring of experts.[100] Other scholars reported on extensions of their working period in China after requests from Chinese institutions to which they were assigned.[101]

The evaluation of the specific Soviet scholar by Chinese institutions seems to have been more important than the opinion of Soviet chief advisors, as the following case demonstrates: In May 1957 G. P. Serdyuchenko, who was at that time the advisor of the president of the Chinese Academy of Sciences, Guo Moruo, tried to reduce the duration of E. M. Tenishev's[102] stay in China by claiming to the supervisor of the Culture and Science Division of the Soviet embassy, N. G. Sudarikov, that the Chinese side was dissatisfied with Tenishev's work. As it became clear that Serdyuchenko had only expressed his own opinion, Tenishev was not called back and his stay was later even prolonged.[103]

The increasing institutionalization of science and technology transfer and the rapidly growing number of Soviet experts in China since 1954, together with problems with some Soviet advisors and mismanagement on both Chinese and Soviet sides, provoked a renewed accentuation of "self-reliance" in China and a tendency to reduce the number of experts. Already in January 1956—even before Khrushchev's secret speech at the Twentieth Party Congress of the CPSU in February 1956 which is often seen by scholars as the turning point in Sino-Soviet relations—Zhou Enlai warned the intellectuals not to seek solutions from the Soviet Union for every single question, because this would result in dependency. However, he also stated that Soviet help was still needed on many technical questions.[104]

In October 1956, under the influence of the Twentieth Party Congress of the CPSU and the events of the Polish October the Soviet authorities issued the "Declaration on the Further Strengthening of Foundations of Friendship and Cooperation between the Soviet Union and other Socialist Countries," which included a willingness to call back Soviet specialists working abroad.[105] However, the Chinese side still needed Soviet assistance and promoted close academic ties with the Soviets as well as the further institutionalization of academic exchanges, which made the knowledge transfer more effective. Yet, they also needed to avert the possibility of dependency, the import of unwanted ideas and of Soviet influence in domestic political affairs.[106]

In December of the same year the Central Committee of the CCP approved the "Outline for the Long Term Development of Science and Technology for 1956–1967," which formulated the basic principles of future academic cooperation: striving for self-reliance, but using the assistance of the fraternal states, learning from the achievements of foreign countries, but combining them with particular Chinese experience. Establishing a basis for self-reliance in science and technology was proclaimed as the main goal for everyone working in scientific fields.[107]

Concrete changes of the policy of engaging Soviet specialists followed. In February 1957 at the meeting of the State Council Chen Yun criticized some departments which employed too many Soviet specialists. Thereupon the State Council issued a notice, which formulated the new principles of hiring Soviet experts: reducing the numbers of experts and engaging them only when they were really needed. In the notice by the State Council brought out in August, this principle was called "fewer but better" (*shao er jing*),[108] probably after Lenin's famous article published on March 4, 1923, which postulated the priority of quality over quantity.

According to the new policy, the number of Soviet specialists in China decreased starting in 1957. However, in some academic fields the number of Soviet experts actually continued to increase:[109] not only in the field of new technologies such as computers[110] and nuclear research,[111] but also in other academic fields like ethnography, where the first direct contacts between scholars had only started in 1956.[112]

In September of 1958, the CC of the CPSU suggested again that the number of Soviet specialists in China should be reduced. The reason—as it was explained to the Chinese side—was the possibility that the presence of Soviet experts could hinder the activities of Chinese personnel and prevent their further development.[113] During the meeting of the Soviet Politburo two months earlier there was no discussion of what the rationale was. The resolution about the Soviet experts in China was very short: "We want to get rid [of them]."[114] Reducing the number of Soviet specialists was seen as "politically and economically justified."[115]

While the Soviet side did not hide its intention to lower the number of Soviet specialists working in China, the Chinese side did not reveal their policy. Even in 1959, when the tendency was already clear and the Soviet representatives were talking about the structural change in Soviet-Chinese exchanges according to the Chinese cultural and economic development, the Chinese officials explained that the relatively small number of planned delegations and events was due to the celebrations of the 10th anniversary of the PRC.[116]

Although the changes in the policy on academic exchanges have to be seen within the context of the gradually deteriorating Sino-Soviet relationship, the importance of the state of science and technology for these relations should by no means be underestimated either: The 1958 decision "to make self-reliance . . . [the] major policy and striving for foreign aid a secondary aim"[117] was only possible because of the level of scientific and technological development which China had already reached with Soviet help.

At that time, most of the Soviet scholars who visited China reported on "well equipped" scientific facilities and well educated Chinese scholars.[118] In contrast to earlier reports, which had emphasized the impact of Soviet help, Soviet scientists made it clear in their reports that they themselves had gained new knowledge during their stay in China, which could ultimately prove beneficial for Soviet science too.[119] Although statements like these have to be understood within the Soviet political context—the scientific cooperation had to be declared as something beneficial to both sides—this change must clearly be taken into account.

There were already problems with the transfer of knowledge from China to the Soviet Union in the preceding years. Soviet experts had complained about not being informed enough about Chinese conditions,[120] and it was the Soviet side that made efforts to make Sino-Soviet knowledge transfer possible by setting up a special group of scholars in order to provide Soviet scholars with information on the most important Chinese publications in natural science and the humanities.[121] But despite the enormous developments mentioned by Soviet visitors, it was in the years after 1956 that the Chinese started to take their commitments to carry out the various cooperation agreements between China and Soviet Union less seriously: they delivered fewer books and technical materials than had been stipulated in agreements.[122]

The Soviet side started to get worried about the inequality of the academic relations in 1957. While summarizing the characteristics of Soviet-Chinese relations in the academic realm, Lazarenko, at that time the major Soviet advisor at the CAS, pointed out that the major problem was the passivity of the Soviet side due to ignorance of the actual academic level in China. Some of the Chinese academic fields were already highly developed and should be studied by Soviet scholars and scientists. According to his advice, the Soviet side should stop only helping China, and let a "normal" cooperation begin.[123] One year later the same arguments appear in the report about the contemporary state of the relations between the Academies of Sciences.[124] The plans for cultural and scientific cooperation reflected the wish to form a more equal cooperation: the Chinese side complained about their Soviet comrades being too concerned about the parity of the exchanges.[125]

In the reports to the Soviet Foreign Ministry this topic was not brought up. On the contrary, the obvious inequality in the commitments was excused as normal because of the leading role of the Soviet Union in economics and science. But the inequality was questioned by the staff of the Far Eastern Section of the Soviet Foreign Ministry. The notes made on the margins state: "Should not this discrepancy be questioned? This can be explained far better with lack of knowledge of China and with the inability of the Soviet organizations to carry out proper measures to learn from Chinese achievements."[126]

Although the criticisms were appropriate—the Soviet side failed to organize the transfer of knowledge from China—it was also China that was not interested in equal partnership. In May 1960, the advisor for scientific and technical cooperation of the Chinese Embassy in Moscow, Huang Yizhang, did not hesitate to speak out in conversation with the head of the Division for States of People's Democracies at the SAS, S. I. Prasolov. While talking about difficulties in the implementation of the cooperation plan for 1960, Prasolov brought up the issue of equivalent exchanges, which were part of the agreement. According to this agreement the Soviet part had already sent scientists and scholars to China, while China had not sent a single one to the Soviet Union. Huang had a simple explanation for this situation: For him as a representative of the Chinese side, the exchange was not about money or equivalence; it was about the most effective way to raise the level of Chinese science. Prasolov had to make clear that the equivalent exchange served Soviet needs by sending Soviet experts to China.[127]

It is also striking that most of the Sino-Soviet knowledge transfer that benefited the Soviet Union took place between Chinese scholars of Chinese history and Soviet sinologists.[128] Chinese scholars who were involved in disciplines with higher priority—natural science and technology—usually visited the Soviet Union or studied there in order to gain new knowledge and not to transfer their own knowledge to their Soviet colleagues. That was the background that led Klejmenov to conclude in 1961, that China had only had its own development in mind from the very beginning.[129]

Conclusion

The knowledge transfer from the Soviet Union was not always beneficial for Chinese academics: Examples are the shutting down of certain disciplines like sociology[130] or the dissemination of theories later proved false, like "Lysenkoism" in genetics,[131] which were also direct results of the close academic interactions. But the Chinese strategy to use Soviet assistance to establish a reasonable foundation for the future independence of China's academic system, thereby promoting economic and social development, proved successful. Not only was China able to further its own development after the Sino-Soviet split, China had also become an important source of knowledge transfer, herself providing quite a number of developing countries with aid. Sino-Soviet academic interactions played an important role in avoiding total dependence on the Soviet Union, because it provided theoretical and applied knowledge that could be used later.

Notes

1. See, for example, Stewart Fraser, "China's International, Cultural, and Educational Relations: With Selected Bibliography," *Comparative Education Review* 13, no. 1 (1969), 60–87. Ronald F. Price, "Convergence or Copying: China and the Soviet Union," in *China's Education and the Industrialized World. Studies in Cultural Transfer*, ed. Ruth Hayhoe and Marianne Bastid (Armonk, NY: M. E. Sharpe, 1987), 158–83, 316–22. Suzanne Pepper, *Radicalism and Education Reform in 20-th Century China. The Search for an Ideal Development Model* (Cambridge: Cambridge University Press, 1996), 157–255. Li Tao, "Jianguo chuqi qian Sulian jiaoyu zhuanjia lai Hua de lishi kaocha" [The impact of the former Soviet educational experts on chinese education in the 1950s and 1960s], *Shanxi daxue xuebao (zhexue shehui kexue ban)* [Journal of shanxi university (philosophy and social science edition)] 29, no. 1 (2006), 135–40. Wang Gang, "Woguo gaodi jiaoyu xuexi Sulian jingyan yanjiu zongshu," *Ningbo daxue xuebao (jiaoyu kexue bao)* [A comprehensive study of china's higher education learned from the Soviet Union] 28, no. 2 (2006), 84–88.

2. See, for example, Douglas A. Stiffler, *Building Socialism at Chinese People's University: Chinese Cadres and Soviet Experts in the People's Republic of China, 1949–1957* (Ph.D. dissertation, University of California, San Diego, 2002). Wang Wen, "Zhongguo daxue xuexi Sulian jiaoyu jingyan kaizhan jiaoxue gaige de lishi huigu – yi Qinghua daxue wei anli" [Historical retrospect of teaching reforms in tsinghua university with the educational experience of the soviet union], *Qinghua daxue jiaoyu yanjiu*

[Qinghua university education research] 24, no. 6 (2003), 79–85. Peng Zeping and Yao Lin, "Chongqing gaojiao xuexi qian Sulian jiaoyu jingyan de lishi yu fansi" [Reflections on colleges' and universities' borrowing of the former soviet education experiences in chongqing in the 1950s], *Chongqing youdian xueyuan yuabao (shehui kexue ban)* [Chongqing college of posts and telecommunications monthly (social science edition)] 54, no. 2 (2003), 93–97. Zhang Jiuchun and Zhang Baichun, "Founding of the Chinese Academy of Sciences' Institute of Computing Technology," *IEEE Annals of the History of Computing* 29, no. 1 (2007), 16–33.

3. See, for example, A. M. Reshetov and Khe Goan', "Sovetskaya Etnografiya v Kitae" [Soviet ethnography in China], *Sovetskaya Etnografiya* [Soviet ethnography] 4 (1990), 76–93. Gregory Eliyu Guldin, *The Saga of Anthropology in China: From Malinowski to Moscow to Mao* (Armonk, NY: M. E. Sharpe, 1994), 111–30. Q. Edward Wang, "Between Marxism and Nationalism: Chinese Historiography and the Soviet Influence, 1949–1963," *Journal of Contemporary China* 9, no. 23 (2000), 95–111. Cheng Huanwen, "The Effect of the Cold War on Librarianship in China," *Libraries & Culture* 36, no. 1 (2001), 40–50. Laurence Schneider, *Biology and Revolution in Twentieth-Century China* (Lanham, MD: Rowman & Littlefield Publishers, 2003). Ou Bao, "Teoriya rezonansa v 1950-kh gg. v Kitae" [The resonance theory in China in the 1950s], in *Rossiisko-kitaiskie nauchnye svyazi: problemy stanovleniya i razvitiya* [Russian-Chinese scientific relations: problems of formation and development] (Sankt-Peterburg: Nestor-Istoriya, 2005), 170–85. Hu Danian, "The Reception of Relativity in China," *ISIS* 98 (2007), 539–57.

4. Shen Zhihua, "Dui zai Hua Sulian zhuanjia wenti de lishi kaocha: jiben zhuangkang ji zhengce bianhua" [A historical investigation of Soviet experts in China: circumstances and policy changes], *Dangdai Zhongguo shi yanjiu* [Contemporary chinese history] 9, no. 1 (2002), 24–37. *Sulian zhuanjia zai Zhongguo* [Soviet experts in china] (Beijing: Zhongguo guoji guangbo chubanshe, 2003). *A Historical Examination of the Issue of Soviet Experts in China: Basic Situation and Policy Changes,* http://www.shenzhihua.net/zsgx/000133.htm, (accessed on 11 May 2007).

5. Paul A. Cohen, *Discovering History in China. American Historical Writing on the Recent Chinese Past* (New York: Columbia University Press, 1984).

6. Grace Shen, "Murky Waters. Thoughts on Desire, Utility, and the 'Sea of Modern Science,'" *ISIS* 98 (2007), 585. Wang Zuoyue calls for the "transnational turn" in the study of history of science in China, which would emphasize the transnational nature of the science in modern China. Wang Zuoyue, "Science and the State in Modern China," *ISIS* 98 (2007), 567–69.

7. Lowell Dittmer, *Sino-Soviet Normalization and Its International Implications, 1945–1990* (Seattle and London: University of Washington Press, 1992), 10. William C. Kirby, "China's Internationalization in the Early People's Republic: Dreams of a Socialist World Economy," *China Quarterly* 188 (2006), 872.

8. Alexei D. Voskressenski summarizes the different approaches: "The significance and the appraisal of Soviet help to the PRC is interpreted differently—Soviet and Russian researches trying to overestimate it, Chinese to underestimate, and Westerners to neglect it." Alexei D. Voskressenski, *Russia and China. A Theory of Inter-State Relations* (London and New York: RoutledgeCurzon, 2003), 19.

9. The "impact-response" model is also predominant in current research on the relations between the CCP and the CPSU and the Comintern. For questioning this approach and the necessity to analyze these relations as interactive, see Mechthild Leutner, "The Communist Party of China (CCP) and the Communist Party of the Soviet Union (CPSU) and the Comintern (CI) in the 1920s and early 1930s: Interactions between Cooperation and Defense," in *Global Conjectures: China in Transnational Perspective* (Berliner China-Hefte/Chinese History and Society 30), eds. William C. Kirby, Mechthild Leutner and Klaus Mühlhahn (Berlin: Lit Verlag, 2006), 41–55.

10. See, for example, L. V. Filatov, *Ekonomicheskaya otsenka nauchno-tekhnicheskoy pomoshchi Sovetskogo Soiuza Kitaiu 1949–1966* [Economic evaluation of the soviet scientific-technological assistance to China, 1949–1966] (Moscow: Nauka, 1980). *Rossiysko-kitayskie nauchnye svyazi: problemy stanovleniya i razvitiya* [Russian-Chinese scientific relations: problems of formation and development] (Sankt-Peterburg: Nestor-Istoriya, 2005). Yu. M. Galenovich, *Rossiia-Kitai-Amerika: Ot sopernichestva k garmonii interesov?* Russia-China-American: From rivalry to harmony of interests? [Moscow: Russkaia Panorama, 200b].

11. See, for example, Shen, *Sulian zhuanjia.* Zhang Baichun, Zhang Jiuchun, and Yao Fang, "Sulian jishu xiang Zhongguo zhuanyi de tedian jiqi yinxiang" [The characteristics and influence of the technology transfer from the soviet union to the P. R. china during the 1950s], *Kexue xue yanjiu* [Science and research] 22, no. 3 (2004), 279–83. Jiang Long, "Beijing hangkong xueyuan de jianli yu Sulian de yuanzhu" [The establishment of the Beijing college of Aeronautics and the aid of the soviet union], *Zhongguo keji shiliao* [Historical materials of china's science and technology] 25, no. 1 (2004), 54–80.

12. On the impact of Soviet aid on Chinese perceptions of "social imperialism," see Dennis M. Ray, "Chinese Perceptions of Social Imperialism and Economic Dependency: The Impact of Soviet Aid," in *China's Changing Role in the World Economy*, ed. Bryant G. Garth (New York: Praeger Publishers, 1975), 36–82. Yu Fai Law, *Chinese Foreign Aid: A Study of Its Nature and Goals with Particular Reference to the Foreign Policy and World View of the People's Republic of China, 1950–1982* (Saarbrücken and Fort Lauderdale: Breitenbach Publishers, 1984).

13. See, for example, Price, "Convergence or Copying." Suzanne Pepper, *Radicalism*, 157–255.

14. Although the dimensions of Sino-Soviet knowledge transfer were much smaller than the Soviet-Chinese transfer, it did take place in some fields like Chinese history and Chinese medicine. *Vestnik Akademii Nauk (AN) SSSR* [News of the societ academy of scienes] 23, no. 7 (1953), 59; 25, no. 6 (1955), 56–57; 26, no. 7 (1956), 78–79; 28, no. 9 (1958), 108; 29, no. 3 (1959), 104. Irina Strazheva, *Tam techet Yantszy. Vospominaniya* [The Yangzi River flows there, memoirs] (Moscow: Nauka, 1986), 16. N. N. Osipova, "Etapy razvitiya refleksoterapii v strane" [The stages of the development of reflexology in (our) country] *Perspektivy traditsionnoi meditsiny* 1 (2003), 9–10.

15. See notes 1–4.

16. This is also true for the history of Chinese science in general, Shen, "Murky Waters," 586. The already mentioned recent works of Shen Zhihua on Soviet advisors

in China are an important exception, because they highlight that the CCP was the decisive force in hiring Soviet advisors. However, Shen Zhihua mostly concentrates on military and economic advisors and does not use the broad empirical data provided in his studies to analyze the role of the Chinese on the implementational level. Shen Zhihua, "Yuanzhu yu xianzhi: Sulian yu Zhongguo de hewuqi yanzhi (1949–1960)" [Aid and restriction: The USSR and the development of atomic weapons in China (1949-1960)], *Lishi yanjiu* [Historical studies] 3 (2004), 110–31. Shen, "Dui zai Hua." Especially Shen, *Sulian zhuanjia.*

17. Johannes Paulmann, "Internationaler Vergleich und interkultureller Transfer. Zwei Forschungsansätze zur europäischen Geschichte des 18. bis 20. Jahrhunderts" [International comparison and intercultural transfer. Two research approaches to European history of the 18th until the 20th centuries], *Historische Zeitschrift* 267 (1998), 649–85.

18. Johannes Paulmann, "Grenzüberschreitungen und Grenzräume. Überlegungen zur Geschichte transnationaler Beziehungen von der Mitte des 19. Jahrhunderts bis in die Zeitgeschichte" [Frontier crossing and frontier spaces. thoughts on the history of translational relations since the mid-19th century until contemporary history], in *Geschichte der internationalen Beziehungen. Erneuerung und Erweiterung einer historischen Disziplin* [The history of international relations. Renewel and expension of a historical discipline], eds. Eckart Conze, Ulrich Lappenküper and Guido Müller (Köln: Böhlau Verlag, 2004), 169–96.

19. By academic interactions I mean the various contacts between institutions and individuals involved in academics (scholars, students, and research workers), which made the transfer of academic knowledge possible. The impact of those interactions on particular discourses is not discussed in this chapter.

20. This chapter presents preliminary results of the research for my dissertation project "Soviet-Chinese academic relations in the 1950s."

21. Rossiiskiy Gosudartvennyi Arkhiv Noveishei Istorii [Russian government archive of contemporary history] (RGANI), f. 5, op. 35, d. 185, ll. 15–16.

22. The research in Russian archives was supported by a grant from the German Academic Exchange Service (DAAD).

23. Mao Zedong, "Talk at an Enlarged Working Conference Convened by the Central Committee of the Communist Party of China, January 30, 1962," http://www.marxists.org/reference/archive/mao/selected-works/volume-8/mswv8_62.htm (accessed on 10 May 2007).

24. Bo Yibo, ct. in Dieter Heinzig, *Die Sowjetunion und das kommunistische China, 1945–1950. Der beschwerliche Weg zum Bündnis* [The Soviet Union and Communist China, 1945-1950: the arduous road to the alliance] (Baden-Baden: Nomos, 1998), 196. Mao Zedong, "Lun renmin minzhu zhuanzheng (30.06.1949)" [On the People's Democratic Dictorship], in *Mao Zedong xuanji* [Selected works of Mao Zedong], vol. 4 (Beijing: Renmin chubanshe, 1968), 1362–63.

25. In the 1970s and 1980s a theory of America's "lost chance" in China was prevalent among American scholars. Since the 1990s, this view has been challenged by scholars and new archival documents. For details see, Chen Jian, *Mao's China & the Cold War* (Chapel Hill and London: University of North Carolina Press, 2001), 38–48.

26. See, for example, Mechthild Leutner, "The Communist Party." For extensive collection of former secret archival documents on the relations between the Chinese Communist Party and the Comintern see, M. L. Titarenko et al., *VKP(b), Komintern i Kitai: Dokumenty* [VKP(b), the Comintern, and China: Documents] (Moscow: ROSSPEN, 5 vols., 1994–2007).

27. P. F. Yudin, "Zapis' besedy s tovarishchem Mao" [Protocol of the conversation with comrade Mao], *Problemy Dal'nego Vostoka* 5 (1994), 103–5.

28. Li Hua-yu writes on the importance of Mao's refusal: "Even today, some Russian scholars are still bitter about Mao's refusal to help the Soviet Union on these occasions." Li Hua-yu, *Mao and the Economic Stalinization of China, 1948–1953* (Lanham, MD: Rowman & Littlefield Publishers, 2006), 23.

29. For the discussion of the "lean to one side" approach see, for example, Friedrich W. Y. Wu, "From Self-Reliance to Interdependence? Developmental Strategy and Foreign Economic Policy in Post-Mao China," in *Modern China* 7, no. 4 (1981), 459. Yu Fai Law, *Chinese Foreign Aid*, 103. Steven M. Goldstein, "Nationalism and Internationalism: Sino-Soviet Relations," in *Chinese Foreign Policy. Theory and Practice*, eds. Thomas W. Robinson and David Shambaugh (Oxford: Oxford University Press, 1994), 231–32. Heinzig, *Die Sowjetunion*, 196. Chen Jian, *Mao's China*, 50. Zhang Yuhui, "Xiang Sulian 'yibain dao' waijiao jueze zhong de yishi xingtai yinsu" [The ideological elements in the Soviet 'predominate' diplomatic decision], *Xiboliya yanjiu* [Siberian studies] 33, no. 3 (2006), 80–81.

30. Arkhiv vneshney politiki Rossiyskoy Federatsii [Archive of the foreign policy of the ʀussian ʀederation] (AVPRF), f. 0100, op. 43, p. 302, d. 10, l. 27, ct. in Heinzig, *Die Sowjetunion*, 302–303.

31. I use the term self-reliance as an umbrella term both for *zili gengsheng* and *duli zizhi* (maintain independence and hold initiative).

32. Friedrich W. Y. Wu, "From Self-Reliance to Interdependence," 454–455. Steven M. Goldstein, "Nationalism and Internationalism," 228–229. Li Guilan, "Lüelun Mao Zedong de zili gengsheng sixiang" [A brief discussion of ᴍao ᴢedong's thought on self-reliance], *Tianzhong xuekan* [Journal of ᴛianzhong] 16, no. 3 (2001), 12. Qin Xiaobo and Tian Hong, "Kangzhan shiqi Mao Zedong de waijiao sixiang jiqi qishi" [Mao Zedong's diplomatic thoughts during the war of resistance against Japan and their enlightenment], *Shenyang shifan daxue xuebao (Shehui kexue ban)* [Shengyang teachers college monthly (social science edition)] 29, no. 6 (2005), 75–78.

33. Some of the texts were edited by CCP bodies, so they not only represent Mao's views, but also the prevailing views within the CCP. Stuart R. Schram, *Das Mao-System. Die Schriften von Mao Tse-tung. Analyse und Entwicklung* [original title: ᴛhe political thought of ᴍao ᴛse-tung] (München: Carl Hanser Verlag, 1972), 129–130.

34. Mao Zedong, "Lun fandui Riben diguozhuyi de celüe (27.12.1935)" [On tactics against Japanese imperialism], in *Mao Zedong xuanji* [Selected works of Mao Zedong], vol. 1 (Beijing: Renmin chubanshe, 1968), 147. Mao Zedong, *The Question of Independence and Initiative within the United Front (November 5, 1938)*, http://www.marxists.org/reference/archive/mao/selected-works/volume-2/mswv2_11.htm, (accessed on 10 May 2007). Mao Zedong, "Lun zhengce (25.12.1940)" [On policy], in *Mao Zedong xuanji* [Selected works of ᴍao ᴢedong], vol. 2 (Beijing: Renmin chuban-

she, 1968), 723. Mao Zedong, "Bixu xuehui zuo jingji gongzuo (10.01.1940)" [We must learn to do economic work], in *Mao Zedong xuanji* [Selected works of Mao Zedong], vol. 3 (Beijing: Renmin chubanshe, 1968), 917. Mao Zedong, "Kang Ri zhanzheng shengli hou de shiju he women de fangzhen (13.08.1945)" [The situation and our policy after the victory in the war of resistance against Japan], in *Mao Zedong xuanji* [Selected works of MAO zedong], vol. 4 (Beijing: Renmin chubanshe, 1968), 1030. Mao Zedong, *Lun xin jieduan* 1938 [On the new stages], ct. in Qin Xiaobo and Tian Hong, "Kangzhan," 76.

35. Mao Zedong, *CCPCC order on diplomatic work (18.08.1944)*, ct. in Shuguang Zhang, "Sino-Soviet Economic Cooperation," in *Brothers in Arms: The Rise and Fall of the Sino-Soviet Alliance, 1945–1963*, ed. Odd Arne Westad (Palo Alto, CA: Stanford University Press, 1998), 192–93. The idea of gaining access to knowledge and expertise through foreigners was not new—there has been a long tradition of foreign advisors serving Chinese modernization both in Qing- and Republican China. William C. Kirby, "Traditions of Centrality, Authority, and Management in Modern China's Foreign Relations," in *Chinese Foreign Policy. Theory and Practice*, eds. Thomas W. Robinson and David Shambaugh (Oxford: Oxford University Press, 1994), 24–26. Jonathan Spence, *The China Helpers: Western Advisers in China 1620–1960* (London: The Bodley Head, 1969). William C. Kirby sees the Sino-Soviet exchange as a "logical extension of earlier approaches." William C. Kirby, "Traditions of Centrality," 28.

36. Mao Zedong, "Bixu xuehui," 917. Although Mao used this perspective to describe China's relations with the imperialist states, one can clearly find its signs also in the relations with the USSR and the Comintern, where Chinese leaders tried to remain as autonomous as possible, particularly during the Yan'an period. See Mechthild Leutner, "The Communist Party." Michael H. Hunt, *The Genesis of Chinese Communist Foreign Policy* (New York: Columbia University Press, 1996), 125–58.

37. Mao Zedong, "Xin minzhuzhuyi lun (January, 1940)" [On new democracy], in *Mao Zedong xuanji* [Selected works of MAO zedong], vol. 2 (Beijing: Renmin chubanshe, 1968), 667. Mao's metaphor describes exactly the modes of knowledge transfer as they are described in recent studies on knowledge sharing: socialization, externalization, combination and internalization, cp. Nigel J. Holden, and Harald F. O. von Kortzfleisch, "Why Cross-Cultural Knowledge Transfer is a Form of Translation in More Ways Than You Think," *Knowledge and Process Management* 11, no. 2 (2004), 134.

38. Friedrich W. Y. Wu, "From Self-Reliance to Interdependence," 453. Kenneth Lieberthal, *Governing China: From Revolution through Reform* (New York and London: W. W. Norton, 1995), 76. David Kerr, "Has China Abandoned Self-Reliance?" *Review of International Political Economy* 14, no. 1 (2007), 80.

39. However, this does not imply that the concept of self-reliance remain the same through the years. Some features changed, but some basic assumptions which are relevant to this chapter remained: the will to keep the initiative and the use of foreign expertise to achieve self-reliance. For the development of the concept of self-reliance see Friedrich W. Y. Wu, "From Self-Reliance to Interdependence." Li Guilan, "Lüelun Mao Zedong." Kerr, "Has China Abandoned Self-Reliance?"

40. I. V. Kovalev, "Dialog Stalina a Mao Tszedunom (2)" [Stalin's dialog with MAO zedong (2)], *Problemy Dal'nego Vostoka* 1–3 (1992), 86. Zhang Yuhui, "Xiang Sulian," 81–82.

41. Yu Minling, "Learning from the Soviet Union: CPC Propaganda and Its Effects. A Study Centred on the Sino-Soviet Friendship Association," *Social Sciences in China* 26, no. 2 (2005), 101. Especially scientists and scholars seem to have been sceptical about the USSR as a role model. Chen Yun complained to Soviet ambassador Roshchin in October 1949 about pro-American feelings among Chinese scholars and experts. N. B. Roshchin, "1949g., oktyabrya 28. Zapis' besedy posla SSSR v KNR N. B. Roshchina s zamestitelem prem'er-ministra i predsedatelem finansovo-ekonomicheskogo komiteta Chen' Yunem o finansovo-ekonomicheskom polozhenii, podgotovke skhematicheskogo plana vosstanovleniya proizvodstvennykh moshchnostei na 1950 g. i o sovetsko-kitaiskikh otnosheniyakh" [28. 10. 1949. Protocol of the conversation of the ambassador of the USSR in the PRC, N. B. Roshchin, with the vice prime minister and chairman of the financial-economic committee, Chen Yun, about the financial-economic situation, the preparation of a schematic plan of reconstruction of production capacities for 1950 and about the state of the soviet-chinese relations], in *Sovetsko-Kitayskie otnosheniya* [Soviet-chinese relations], vol. 5, book 2, eds. A. M. Ledovskiy, R. A. Mirovitskaya, and V. S. Myasnikov (Moscow: Pamyatniki istoricheskoy mysli, 2005), 205 (ll. 30–31). According to Zeng Zhaolun, deputy minister of education, university personnel refused to learn from the Soviet Union and opposed reorganization before thought reform in the years 1951–1952, maintaining that American-style education was superior. Pepper, *Radicalism*, 173. In order to convince Western-trained scientists to accept Soviet ideas of science and learning, a special resolution of the Chinese Academy of Science was issued in 1952: "The Decision of CAS on Strengthening the Learning and Introducing Soviet Advanced Science." Zhang Baichun, Zhang Jiuchun, and Yao Fang, "Technology Transfer from the Soviet Union to the People's Republic of China 1949–1996," *Comparative Technology Transfer and Society* 4, no. 2 (2006), 122. For an account on resistance to Sovietization of universities and the reorganization of higher education in China after the founding of the PRC, see, Douglas A. Stiffler "Der Widerstand gegen die Sowjetisierung der Universitäten und die Umstrukturierung der Hochschulen in China (1949–1952)" [The resistance against the sovietization of universities and reorganization of institutions of higher education in china (1949-1952)], in *Zwischen Autonomie und Anpassung: Universitäten in den Diktaturen des 20. Jahrhunderts* [Between autonomy and adaptation: universities under dictatorships in the 20th century], eds. John Conelly and Michael Grüttner (Paderborn: Ferdinand Schöningh, 2003), 199–227.

42. Italics mine.

43. Deng Xiaoping, *Break the Blockade Imposed by the Imperialists (July 19, 1949)*, http://english.peopledaily.com.cn/dengxp/vol1/text/a1150.html, (accessed on 10 May 2007). Chinese original document: "Dapo diguozhuyi fengsuo zhi dao," in *Zhongguo Gongchandang wenxian xinxi* [Database of the communist party of china], http://data. people.com.cn/directLogin.do?target=cpc, (accessed on 10 May 2007).

44. See, for example, Zhou Enlai, "Huifu shengchan, jianshe Zhongguo (23.07.1949)" [Restore productivity, build China], in *Zhongguo Gongchandang wenxian xinxi* [Database of the communist party of china], http://data.people.com. cn/directLogin.do?target=cpc, (accessed on 11 Oct. 2007). Chen Yun, "Gongren jieji yao tigao zhengzhi juewu (25.08.1949)" [The working class must improve its political

consciousness], in *Zhongguo Gongchandang wenxian xinxi* [Database of the Communist Party of China], http://data.people.com.cn/directLogin.do?target=cpc, (accessed on 11 October 2007).

45. Zhou Enlai, "Dangqian caijing xingshi he xin Zhongguo jingji de ji zhong guanxi (22–23.12.1949)" [A few matters of the present economic situation and the economy of New China], in *Zhongguo Gongchandang wenxian xinxi* [Database of the Communist Party of China], http://data.people.com.cn/directLogin.do?target=cpc, (accessed on 11 October 2007).

46. Yeu-Farn Wang, *China's Science and Technology Policy, 1949–1989* (Stockholm: University of Stockholm Press, 1991), 36.

47. Richard P. Suttmeier, "Party Views of Science: The Record form the First Decade," *China Quarterly* 44 (1970), 147. On the importance of science in China in the first half of 20th century see, D. W. Y. Kwok, *Scientism in Chinese Thought, 1900–1950* (New Haven, CT: Yale University Press, 1965).

48. Mao Zedong, "Speech at the Inaugural Meeting of the Natural Science Research Society of the Border Region (February 5, 1940)," in *Quotations from Mao Tse-Tung*, ch. 22, "Methods of Thinking and Methods of Work," http://www.marxists.org/reference/archive/mao/works/red-book/index.htm, (accessed on 10 May 2007).

49. On the role of Mao's "continuous revolution" in shaping Chinese foreign policy, see Chen Jian, "Mao's China" 2001.

50. On problems in cross-cultural knowledge sharing see, for example, Holden and von Kortzfleisch, "Cross-Cultural Knowledge Transfer."

51. The term "both red and expert" (you hong you zhuan) was used by Mao for the first time in the document "Sixty Articles of Working Methods (draft)" presented to the PCC on 31 January 1958. "Both red and expert" became a slogan embodying the CCP's expectations for specialists.

52. See note 26.

53. William C. Kirby, "Traditions of Centrality," 14.

54. Robert Keohane, *After Hegemony: Cooperation and Discord in the World Political Economy* (Princeton, NJ: Princeton University Press, 1984), 116.

55. RGANI, f. 5, op. 35, d. 185, ll. 18-20. The archival sources show that the Soviets were very surprised about the Chinese side declaring the Soviet commitments void in 1961 as well as about the uncooperativeness of the Chinese representatives during the eleventh session of the Science and Technology Cooperation Commission (ibid. 11. 1, 10–15). The withdrawal of the specialists in l960 was not even mentioned as a possible explanation.

56. The only study mentioning this aspect is T. G. Zazerskaya, *Sovetskie spetsialisty i formirovanie voenno-promyshlennogo kompleksa Kitaya (1949–1960 gg.)* [Soviet specialists and the formation of the Chinese military-industrial complex (1949–1960)] (Sankt-Peterburg: NII Chimii, 2000).

57. In 1954 the Soviet Council for Research on Productive Forces (Sovet po izucheniyu proizvodstvennykh sil) started to conduct research in the Amur River basin. Soon it became obvious that the ultimate aim—economic utilization of the region and water regulation—could not be achieved without research on the Chinese side of the river. Rossiiskii Gosudarstvennyi Arkhiv Ekonomiki [Russian state archive

of economy] (RGAE), f. 399, op. 1, d. 567, ll. 15, 21, 44. The agreement about the Sino-Soviet joint research in the Amur River basin for the years 1956–1960 was signed in 1956, *SSSR-KNR (1949-1983): Dokumenty i materialy* [USSR-PRC (1949-1983): documents and materials] (Moscow: MID SSSR, 1985), 174–78.

58. On the contradiction between nationalistic goals and the necessity to obtain foreign resources and technology for domestic economic development see, Zhu Tianbiao, "Nationalism and Chinese Foreign Policy," *China Review* 1, no. 1 (2001), 1–27.

59. A. G. Ivanchikov, *Teoreticheskie i prakticheskie aspekty privlecheniya inostrannoi tekhnologii v KNR* [Theoretical and practical aspects of attracting foreign technology to the PRC] (Moscow: Nauka, 1991), 26.

60. Yeu-Farn Wang, *China's science*, 42. Zhang, Zhang, and Yao, "Technology Transfer," 150.

61. A. A. Antipovskiy, N. E. Borevskaya, and N. V. Franchuk, *Politika v oblasti nauki i obrazovaniya v KNR 1949–1979* [Science and education policy in the PRC, 1949-1979] (Moscow: Nauka, 1980), 201. Shen Zhihua, "Dui zai Hua," 30. Shen Zhihua, *Sulian Zhuanjia*, 193–95. The engagement of numerous Soviet experts in Renmin Daxue (People's university, Renda) in the years before 1953 is an exception. Renda was to become the model university of New China, hence various developments including academic exchanges with the Soviet Union took place there earlier than in other academic institutions. See Douglas A. Stiffler's chapter in this book.

62. Deborah A. Kaple, "Soviet Advisors in China in the 1950s," in *Brothers in Arms: The Rise and Fall of the Sino-Soviet Alliance, 1945–1963*, ed. Odd Arne Westad (Palo Alto, CA: Stanford University Press, 1998), 120. Zhang, Zhang, and Yao, "Technology Transfer," 141–142. According to Soviet sources approximately 20 percent of all the experts sent to China were involved in cultural spheres, which included academics. A. S. Tsvetko, *Sovetsko-Kitaiskie kul'turnye svyazi* [Soviet-chinese cultural relations] (Moscow: Mysl', 1974), 33.

63. The highest number of Soviet experts in China was recorded in 1956. The total number reached over 3,000, approx. 400 experts worked in cultural and scientific fields. Shen Zhihua, *A Historical Examination of the Issue of Soviet Experts in China: Basic Situation and Policy Changes*, http://www.shenzhihua.net/zsgx/000133.htm, (accessed on 11 May 2007).

64. Zhang, Zhang, and Yao, "Technology Transfer," 142.

65. Between 1952 and 1963, 318 Chinese students studied in the Soviet Academy of Sciences, 206 of them finished their studies with doctoral or candidate degree. The vast majority studied natural sciences: physics, chemistry, mathematics, biology, but some of them also studied history and philosophy, Filatov, *Ekonomicheskaya otsenka*, 151.

66. Yu Fai Law, *Chinese Foreign Aid*, 79. Zhang, Zhang, and Yao, "Technology Transfer," 138–40. It is difficult to separate the numbers of those, who were involved in technology transfer and those involved in academic interactions, since there are no special statistics.

67. Reshetov and Khe list names of some Soviet students. Reshetov and Khe, "Sovetskaya Etnografiya," 95. While students from other socialist states started to study in China in the beginning of the 1950s, Soviet students did not arrive until 1956, with the

exception of a small group of aspirants in the Foreign Service, who came in 1952. Barna Tálas, "China in the early 1950s," in *Communist China in Retrospect: East European Sinologists Remember the First Fifteen Years of the PRC*, ed. Marie-Luise Näth (Frankfurt am Main: Peter Lang, 1995), 38. Jan Rowinski, "China in the Crisis of Marxism-Leninism," *Communist China in Retrospect: East European Sinologists Remember the First Fifteen Years of the PRC*, ed. Marie-Luise Näth (Frankfurt am Main: Peter Lang, 1995), 65, 68. Those aspirants, however, lived in the Soviet embassy and had Chinese classes there. Later they studied at the Department of Foreign Relations at the Renda. V. P. Fedotov, *Polveka vmeste s Kitaem: Vospominaniya, Zapisi, Razmyshleniya* [Half of a century with China: memories, notes, thoughts] (Moscow: ROSSPEN, 2005), 62.

68. Zhang, Zhang, and Yao, "Technology Transfer," 143.

69. *Vestnik AN SSSR* 23, no. 7 (1953), 59.

70. *Vestnik AN SSSR* 23, no. 6 (1953), 50–52. 23, no. 11 (1953), 87–89.

71. Zhang, Zhang, and Yao, "Technology Transfer," 125.

72. *Vestnik AN SSSR* 23, no. 6 (1953), 50–51.

73. Mikhail A. Klochko, *Soviet Scientist in Red China* (New York: Praeger, 1964). Strazheva, *Tam techet Yantszy*, 24.

74. Strazheva, *Tam techet Yantszy*, 24.

75. Ren Bishi asked, for example, for "not less than 500" specialists in national economy. "1949 g., fevralya 2. Zapis' bedesy A. I. Mikoyana s chlenami politbiuro TsK KPK Zhen' Bishi i Chzhu De po voprosam ekonomiki" [02.02.1949. protocol of A. I. Mikoyan's conversation with members of the Politbureau of the CC CCP, Ren Bishi and Zhu De, about economic questions] (AVPRF, f. 39, op. 1, d. 39, l. 31–38), in *Sovetsko-Kitayskie otnosheniya* [Soviet-Chinese relations], vol. 5, book 2, eds. A. M. Ledovskiy, R. A. Mirovitskaya, and V. S. Myasnikov (Moscow: Pamyatniki istoricheskoi mysli, 2005), 56 (l. 37). The question of sending a group of Chinese specialists to Moscow to study the soviet banking system was also discussed. "1949 g., fevralya 6. Zapis' besedy A. I. Mikoyana s Mao Tszedunom po aktual'nym voprosam politiki KPK" [06.02.1949. protocol of A. I. Mikoyan's conversation with Mao zedong on current questions of CPC politics] (Arkhiv Prezidenta Rossiykoy Federatsii [APRF]) [Archive of the President of the Russian Federation], f. 39, op. 1, d. 39, l. 78–88, in *Sovetsko-Kitayskie otnosheniya* [Soviet-Chinese relations], vol. 5, book 2, eds. A. M. Ledovskiy, R. A. Mirovitskaya, and V. S. Myasnikov (Moscow: Pamyatniki istoricheskoi mysli, 2005), 86 (l. 86).

76. A. Ledovskiy, "Vizit v Moskvu delegatsii Kommunisticheskoi partii Kitaya v iyune-avguste 1949 g. (I)" [The Moscow visit of a delegation of the Communist Party of China from June to August 1949 (I)], *Problemy Dal'nego Vostoka* 4 (1996), 81–82. The founding of a "model university" was discussed too. For a discussion of Renmin Daxue as a model university in the PRC, see Douglas A. Stiffler, *Building Socialism*.

77. Heinzig, *Die Sowjetunion*, 375–76.

78. Shi Zhe, *Zai lishi junren shengbian. Shi Zhe huiyilu* [At the side of history's giants: memoirs of Shi Zhe] (Beijing: Zhongyang wenxian chubanshe, 1991), 426–28, ct. in Heinzig, *Die Sowjetunion*, 372.

79. Shi Zhe, *Zai lishi*, 428–29, ct. in Heinzig, *Die Sowjetunion*, 372–73.

80. Li Yueran, *Waijiao wutai shang de xin Zhongguo lingxiu* [New china's leaders in the diplomatic arena] (Beijing: Jiefangjun chubanshe, 1989), 15, ct. in Heinzig,

Die Sowjetunion, 378. Already in the 1930s some of Mao's statements pointed out that foreigners —also Russians—could not understand the situation in China as well as the Chinese themselves could. Donald S. Zagoria, "Mao's Role in the Sino-Soviet Conflict," *Pacific Affairs* 47, no. 2 (1974), 141.

81. Arkhiv Vneshney Politiki Rossiyskoy Federatsii (AVPRF), f. 0100, op. 43, pap. 317, d. 166, l. 5.

82. AVPRF, f. 0100, op. 42, p. 288, d. 19, l. 63–65, ct. Shen Zhihua, *Sulian Zhuanjia*, 104.

83. On the procedure see Klochko, *Soviet Scientist*, 117–19. Strazheva, *Tam techet Yantszy*, 9. B. A. Belen'kiy, *I povtorit' sebya v uchenikakh* [And to replicate oneself in one's students] (Kishinev: Shtiinca, 1988), 130. E. R. Tenishev, *U tiurkskikh narodov v Kitae* [Among Turkic peoples in China] (Moscow: Nasledie, 1995), 5.

84. Shen Zhihua, *Sulian Zhuanjia*, 93.

85. The agreements were signed on 27.3.1950, 25.10.1950 and 06.12.51. For the first agreement, see Rossiikii Gosudastvennyi Arkhiv Sotsial'no-Politicheskoy Istorii [Russian state archive of socio-political history] (RGASPI), f. 82, op. 2, d. 1253, ll. 27–30. The text of the second agreement is still classified. For details on the third agreement, see Zazerskaja, *Sovetskie specialisty*, 46.

86. RGASPI, f. 82, op. 2, d. 1252, ll. 2–3.

87. RGASPI, f. 82, op. 2, d. 1252, ll. 1, 3, 105–6, 116–17.

88. RGASPI, f. 82, op. 2, d. 1252, ll. 2, 9, 105, 116.

89. For the protocols of the sessions during the 1950s, see: RGAE, f. 9493, op. 1, d. 910, 914, 919, 927, 935, 941, 953, 1006, 1016, 1022.

90. Zhang, Zhang, and Yao, "Technology Transfer," 126–128. Klochko, *Soviet Scientist*, 6. Antipovskiy, Borevskaya, and Franchuk, *Politika v oblasti nauki*, 190–91. Belen'kiy, *I povtorit'*, 133–34.

91. The director's name and the year when the document was issued are not given in the source.

92. Arkhiv Rossiiskoi Akademii Nauk [Archive of russian academy of science] (ARAN), f. 579, op. 1, d. 140, ct. in E. S. Levina, "Istoriya i problemy sovetsko-kitayskogo sotrudnichestva v 1950-kh—nachale 1960-kh gg." [History and problems of soviet-chinese cooperation in the 1950s and in the beginning of the 1960s], in *Rossiysko-kitayskie nauchnye svyazi: problemy stanovleniya i razvitiya* [Russian-chinese scientific relations: problems of formation and development] (Sankt-Peterburg: Nestor-Istoriya, 2005), 99.

93. *SSSR-KNR*, 225.

94. Fedotov, *Polveka*, 100. Fedotov does not mention if the bulletins were provided by the Foreign Experts Bureau according to certain agreements or were obtained through other channels.

95. Deborah A. Kaple, "Soviet Advisors," 117.

96. Strazheva, *Tam techet Yantszy*, 15, 21.

97. Strazheva, *Tam techet Yantszy*, 38. Tenishev, *U tiurkskikh narodov*, 230.

98. Klochko, *Soviet Scientist*, 64–65, 119.

99. Klochko, *Soviet Scientist*, 22, 117–19.

100. Shen Zhihua, *Sulian Zhuanjia*, 160–161.

101. Tenishev, *U tiurkskikh narodov*, 132, 199, 203. G. G. Stratanovich, "Poezdka v Kitaiskuiu Narodnuiu Respubliku" [A trip to the People's Republic of China], *Sovetskaya Etnografiya* 2 (1958), 106.

102. E. M. Tenishev was a Turkic languages specialist from the Institute of Linguistics at the AN SSSR who was sent to China in 1956 to help the CAS explore Turkic languages.

103. Tenishev, *U tyurkskikh narodov*, 161–62.

104. Zhou Enlai, "Guanyu zhishifenzi wenti (14. 01. 1956)" [On the question of intellectuals], in *Zhongguo Gongchandang wenxian xinxi* [Database of the communist party of china], http://data.people.com.cn/directLogin.do?target=cpc, (accessed on 11 October 2007).

105. *SSSR-KNR*, 182.

106. Steven M. Goldstein, "Nationalism and Internationalism," 240. As to the danger of uncritical copying of Soviet models, see Mao Zedong, *Talks at the Chengtu Conference, March 1958*, http://www.marxists.org/reference/archive/mao/selectedworks/volume-8/mswv8_06.htm, (accessed on 10 May 2007).

107. "1956-1967 nian kexue jishu fazhan yuanjing guihua gangyao (xiuzheng cao'an) 1956" [An outline for the long term development of science and technology for 1956-1967 (draft)], in *Zhongguo Gongchandang wenxian xinxi* [Database of the Communist Party of China], http://data.people.com.cn/directLogin.do?target=cpc, (accessed on 11 October, 2007)

108. Shen Zhihua, "Dui zai Hua," 32–33. Shen Zhihua, *Sulian Zhuanjia*, 277, 307–9. As Shen Zhihua correctly notes, this decision also had economic background: to reduce the immense expenditures involved in hiring Soviet specialists. Shen Zhihua, "Dui zai Hua," 32.

109. Shen Zhihua, *Sulian Zhuanjia*, 307–9.

110. Zhang, Zhang, and Yao, "Technology Transfer."

111. Shen Zhihua, "Yuanzhu yu xianzhi."

112. Reshetov and Khe, "Sovetskaya Etnografiya," 79f.

113. *SSSR-KNR*, 225.

114. Rossiiskaya Akademiya Nauk, ed., *Prezidium TsK KPSS 1954–1964, vol. 1: Chernovye protokol'nye zapisi zasedanii. Stenogrammy* [The presidium of the CC CPSU. Drafts of session's notes. shorthand notes] (Moscow: ROSSPEN, 2004), 326.

115. Gosudarstvennyi Arkhiv Rossiiskoi Federatsii [State archive of Russian federation] (GARF), f. 9576, op. 19, d. 30, t. 1, l. 367.

116. GARF, f. 9576, op. 19, d. 30, t. 1, l. 17.

117. Mao Zedong, "Talk at an Enlarged Working Conference."

118. Klochko, *Soviet Scientist*, 96. Strazheva, *Tam techet Yantszy*, 17. E. M. Murzaev, *Puteshestviya bez prikliucheniy i fantastiki. Zapiski geografa* [Journeys without adventures and fantasies. Notes of a geographer] (Moscow: Geografgiz, 1962), 20. *Vestnik AN SSSR* 25, no. 2 (1955), 63; 26, no. 3 (1956), 128; 27, no. 1 (1957), 77.

119. *Vestnik AN SSSR* 26, no. 2 (1956), 84; 27, no. 1 (1957), 74; 28, no. 2 (1958), 105; 28, no. 5 (1958), 106–8; 29, no. 11 (1959), 78; 29, no. 9 (1959), 52; 30, no. 2 (1960), 76.

120. Douglas A. Stiffler, *Building Socialism*, 331.

121. *Vestnik AN SSSR* 22, no. 11 (1952), 116.

122. Filatov, *Ekonomicheskaya otsenka*, 139. Levina, "Istoriya i problemy," 101, 108–9.

123. ARAN, f. 579, op. 2, d. 98, ll. 77–78.

124. ARAN, f. 463, op. 16, d. 17, ll. 45–56.

125. GARF, f. 9576, op. 19, d. 30, t. 1, l. 19.

126. AVPRF, f. 100, op. 46, pap. 193, d. 64, ll. 18, 29.

127. AVPRF, f. 100, op. 47, pap. 198, d. 51, l. 21.

128. *Vestnik AN SSSR* 23, no. 7 (1953), 59; 25, no. 6 (1955), 56–57; 26, no. 7 (1956), 78–79; 28, no. 9 (1958), 108; 29, no. 3 (1959), 104. Stratanovich, "Poezdka," 107.

129. RGANI, f. 5, op. 35, d. 185, ll. 15–17.

130. On the impact of Soviet-Chinese knowledge transfer on Chinese sociology, see, for example, Bettina Gransow, *Geschichte der chinesischen Soziologie* [The history of chinese sociology] (Frankfurt and New York: Campus Verlag, 1992), 135–155.

131. On the impact of Soviet-Chinese knowledge transfer on Chinese genetics, see, for example, Schneider, *Biology and Revolution*.

12

"Three Blows of the Shoulder Pole": Soviet Experts at Chinese People's University, 1950–1957

Douglas Stiffler

Introduction

IN OCTOBER 1951, AT THE FIRST ANNIVERSARY of the founding of Chinese People's University [*Zhongguo renmin daxue*, hereinafter: "Renda"], the chief Soviet advisor to the university's administration, Kudriavtsev, summed up his view of the role of the Soviet experts. Noting that the school in its first year had already graduated some thousand cadres from its Specialized Intensive Courses, Kudriavtsev proclaimed proudly that, in the near future, Renda's cadres would be making their contributions in work units all over China. Kudriavtsev praised the Chinese Communist Party and government for its foresight in this, and then pointed directly to the role of Soviet knowledge:

> The secrets of your success are your powerful adoption of the Bolshevik way of doing things, your revolutionary spirit. . . . Your successes are also due to your frequent and insistent mastery of Soviet experience combined with Chinese experience. This will shorten the course of your development from the most basic level to the most advanced level.[1]

Soviet experts would draw on their own experiences in revolutionary industrialization in the Soviet Union as they became participants in China's struggle to make the leap to modernity:

> We Soviet advisers do not feel like guests or onlookers, but like participants in this process. To this end, we are willing to contribute all the experience and knowledge we have gained in 34 years of building socialism.[2]

Kudriavtsev put into eloquent terms the sense of mission that seemed to animate the Soviet teachers at Renda in the closing years of Stalin's rule, and the beginning of the rule of Mao.

The years of Sino-Soviet cooperation at Chinese People's University, as in China as a whole, would not be perfectly smooth, however. The People's Republic of China and the Soviet Union were societies at very different stages in their revolutionary transformations, and the 1950s were to be watershed years for both regimes. During the years 1950–53, the Chinese teachers and students at Renda bent all their efforts to assimilating the new Soviet knowledge as rapidly as possible. This often meant a rather one-sided and uncritical approach to that knowledge. The death of Stalin was a critical turning point for both Soviets and Chinese. While the Soviet teachers at Renda before 1953 had seemed like uncomplaining supermen (and –women), after 1953 they were more willing to complain about their working conditions. For their part, after 1953, the Chinese began to take a much more critical approach to the new Soviet knowledge, such that by 1956–57 they were rejecting some aspects of this knowledge outright.

In the case of one Soviet expert, Perikl Petrovich Ionidi, a teacher of Marxist dialectical materialism, this criticism became public in the spring of 1957, during the Hundred Flowers' campaign. The Soviet embassy's involvement, and the public criticism, shows how greatly the Soviet-Chinese relationship had changed between 1950 and 1957. While in 1950–53, it had been the Chinese bending over backwards to accommodate the Soviets, in spring 1957 the roles were reversed: the Soviets went all-out to mollify the prickly Chinese.

This chapter will trace the contours of these changes in the Sino-Soviet relationship at the grassroots level, in working relationships between Chinese and Soviets at Chinese People's University. What explains the nature of the changes in the Sino-Soviet relationship at Renda from 1950–57? Change in the Sino-Soviet relationship at Renda was, I believe, driven by two other processes: first, change in the domestic political atmosphere in each country, e.g., the post-Stalin "Thaw" in the Soviet Union and the increased top-level skepticism toward the Soviet Union in China; and second, the Chinese tradition of "cyclical" borrowing from the West, that is, a stage of wholesale importation succeeded by one of greater skepticism and selective rejection.[3] We will see both of these at work in the changing Sino-Soviet relationship at Chinese People's University in the 1950s.

Soviet Experts and Chinese People's University

During the 1950s, approximately eleven thousand "Soviet experts"—advisors, teachers, and technical specialists of various sorts—participated in a massive effort to build China's modern infrastructure at breakneck pace.[4] Higher education was one area in which Soviet influence was particularly strong during the 1950s. Soviet experts in the Ministry of Higher Education played important roles in the Sovietization of Chinese higher educational institutions in the early 1950s, and continued to work in the Ministry until 1959. In addition to these Soviet advisors at the top of the hierarchy, the Chinese employed hundreds of Soviet teachers at higher educational institutions in the 1950s. A total of 861 Soviet experts worked in Chinese higher education institutions from 1949 to 1959.[5]

Chinese People's University was the brainchild of Liu Shaoqi, an orthodox, Soviet-trained Chinese Communist, and the number two man in the Chinese Communist hierarchy. Liu travelled to Moscow in the summer of 1949 and suggested, among other things, that the Soviets establish an institution "similar to the former Chinese Workers' University" of the 1920s to train Chinese cadres to run a Soviet-style state and economy. Stalin declined to establish the university in the Soviet Union, but agreed to send Soviet teachers to China to establish such an institution. Liu had suggested that the Soviets send as many as 200 Soviet experts, but the number was eventually whittled down to approximately fifty. Chinese People's University was formally inaugurated in October 1950, with Liu Shaoqi calling for the university to take the leading role in adapting "advanced Soviet experience" to Chinese conditions.[6]

Chinese People's University thus played a pioneering role in the employment of Soviet experts in higher education institutions. In 1950, the Soviet advisor Fillipov reported that of forty-nine Soviet teachers in the higher educational institutions of Beijing, thirty-seven taught at Chinese People's University.[7] Indeed, the Soviet experts [*Sulian zhuanjia*], advisors and teachers who began arriving in numbers at Chinese People's University in the summer of 1950, were the largest single group of Soviet experts at any educational institution in China in the 1950s.[8]

Approximately seventy to eighty Soviet teachers taught at Renda from 1949 to 1957, in all of the faculties and departments of the new, Soviet-style university. The majority of these helped to establish the foundation of Renda during its first three years, from 1950 to 1953. The plan had been for a contingent of fifty Soviet teachers to establish the new Soviet-style university, but the actual numbers of Soviet experts for the first three years had fallen somewhat short of this: forty-one in 1950–51, forty-eight in 1951–52, the year the contingent was closest to full strength, and forty-two in 1952–53. Many of the Soviet teachers departed for home in the summer of 1953, however, leaving just twenty-one during the 1953–54 academic year. The numbers of Soviet experts dropped gradually in subsequent years, until there were just seven left in 1956–57, the final year that Soviets taught at Renda.[9]

In order to understand the role that Soviet experts played, it is necessary to review briefly the academic structure of Chinese People's University at its creation. The university design, originally drawn up by Soviet advisors in the winter of 1949–50, came within the course of the year to comprise eight core departments [R. *faku'ltety*]: Economic Planning, Finance and Credit, Factory Management, Cooperatives, Trade, Law, Diplomacy, and Russian. The departments all had Chinese directors and vice-directors, as well as Party committees. Most academic work at the university, however, was carried on in forty-one sub-departmental *jiaoxue yanjiu zu* [teaching-research groups], or *jiaoyanshi*, for short [lit. "teaching-research offices,"or "teaching-research groups"]. This academic structure, unfamiliar in the West, was based on the Soviet structure of *faku'ltety* [faculties, or departments] and their subordinate *kafedra*, which Vice-Rector Cheng Fangwu at Renda translated as *jiaoyanshi*.[10] The Chinese teaching-research group, like the Soviet *kafedra*, was organized around specific courses or groups of courses within a field, and as its name suggests, was the basic academic group for both teaching and research in a particular sub-field. Teaching personnel in this system identified themselves with their teaching-research group (rather than faculty/department), which suggests something of the tendency in the Soviet system for narrow specialization. The *jiaoyanshi*, a Soviet academic structure first translated into Chinese terms at Renda in 1950, is still widely in use in Chinese education today.[11]

There were forty-one teaching-research groups at Renda in the fall of 1950. Eight of these teaching-research groups were non-departmental, that is, they were directly under the Academic Affairs department. Several of these taught courses which were requirements for students in all or multiple departments, and thus were part of what may be considered Renda's core curriculum. These teaching-research groups were: Fundamentals of Marxism-Leninism, Political Economy, History of the Chinese Revolution, Russian Language, Physical Education, Pedagogy, Chinese Language, and Mathematics.

The Soviet experts in 1950–51 were distributed among all of the departments and in the key required courses at Renda, with very few exceptions. The largest single contingent of 11 Soviet teachers were members of the Russian department, many of whom were from Harbin and who arrived early, in the fall of 1949.[12] The departments which taught the new Stalinist economic disciplines had the greatest concentration of Soviet experts. The Finance and Credit Department led the way with six experts, including two each in Financial Administration and two in Accounting. The Factory Management department boasted three experts, and both the Cooperatives and Trade departments had two experts each. Outside these economic fields, the Law department had a substantial contingent of four Soviet experts, and the Diplomacy department had one. The Soviet experts who had the greatest impact school-wide, however, were those in the required courses: Fundamentals of Marxism-Leninism, with a contingent of four Soviets (soon to grow to six in the spring of 1951), and Political Economy, with two (to grow to three in the spring of 1951). The only required courses that were under the direction of Chinese exclusively were History of the Chinese Revolution and Physical Education.[13]

Students at Chinese People's University in its early years were largely Chinese Communist cadres recruited from the six large military-administrative regions, with an admixture of "ideological retrainees." There existed a serious divide in the early years between younger cadres with relatively high levels of education (middle school or some college) and older cadres who sometimes possessed only elementary-school-level educations. This considerably complicated Renda's mission of training Chinese Communist cadres in the new Soviet knowledge.[14]

During its first several years, Chinese People's University focused on training cadres in Stalinist economic-managerial specialties as well as ideology. After 1953, however, economic-managerial training was subordinated as Renda, at the direction of the Ministry of Higher Education, which assumed overall leadership in the Sovietized ideological-social sciences—especially in the training of political theory teachers—and in certain functional administrative specialties closely tied to government Ministries (e.g., archives). Regional higher education institutions looked to Chinese People's University, and especially to the teachers it trained, to remake Chinese higher education and its academic fields, in the Soviet style.[15] Soviet experts played critical roles in this effort during the whole period they served at the university, from 1950 until 1957.

1950–1953: Three Blows of the Shoulder-Pole if You Disagree with the Soviet Expert!

Internal reports produced in 1950–53 on the work of the Soviet experts reveal Renda's Soviet experts policy to have been extremely accommodating. A November 11, 1952 report entitled "Report on Work of Experts at Chinese People's University" presents the contributions made by the experts in creating Renda, especially stressing the experts' role in training a large cadre of instructors. In the "problems" section of the report, difficulties at Renda are *not* attributed to the experts but to those Chinese who "adopt an arrogant attitude" and are unwilling to learn from the Soviet instructors, to insufficient Chinese efforts to acquaint the Soviet experts with Chinese conditions, and to difficulties with the Chinese translators.[16] Thus, in each case, responsibility for making the relationship work seemed to be a matter for the Chinese side guided by the principle that the Soviet experts could "do no wrong."

This, in fact, was the explicit policy for work with the Soviet experts in the early years, as remembered by interviewees. The interviewees summed up the policy of "no disagreement with the Soviet experts" in an oft-repeated aphorism of the time: *you li san bian dan, wu li bian dan san*, which means that, if one objects to something and the objection is "reasonable, then three blows of the shoulder pole [will be given], if unreasonable, then [you will be struck] by the shoulder-pole three times." Thus, anyone with the audacity to challenge the Soviet experts, whether right or wrong, would be punished. This was the explicit policy toward the Soviet experts until the death of Stalin.[17]

A supplement to the above report, dated December 1952, refers more specifically to problems with the Soviet experts. The purpose of the supplement is to argue that "in only two or three years . . . [Renda] has thoroughly studied the system and methods of Soviet higher education," has trained over 500 instructors, and so can be shown to have made effective use of the Soviet experts. Problems, again, seem on the surface to come from the Chinese side:

> In the past two years there have also been some small problems. These are mainly caused by the arrogance of a few of our instructors and graduate students, [which results in] impolite behavior toward the experts, or by the improper work style of some of our leader-comrades, or [we] are sluggish/negligent in our work, failing to complete tasks according to plan, and this leads to the experts' dissatisfaction.[18]

There were some situations, however, in which the experts themselves may have been partially to blame, and here, Renda recommended patience and persuasion:

> There are some Soviet comrades who have very strong personalities, and when they encounter questions where they are convinced that [we] have no theoretical basis [for our positions] they insist on their own opinions and are hard to reason with. In this circumstance, it is best not to continue the debate, but rather give them some time to become acquainted with conditions, and then later try to come up with ways to settle the issue. If there is no resolution to the issue, it could [negatively] influence our cooperation.[19]

Overall, these documents from late 1952 reveal a very accommodating official attitude toward the Soviet experts, an attitude typical of the period of Sino-Soviet cooperation before Stalin's death.

To smooth relations, the Chinese translators were blamed for sometimes "playing tricks" on the experts in deliberately failing to translate or mistranslating, which resulted in misunderstandings which angered the experts. This became an occupational hazard for the translators, as the main channel for linguistic and cultural communication. The Chinese side made the translators responsible for smoothing relations between the Soviet experts and Chinese personnel at Renda. In cases where Chinese asked impolite questions of the Soviet experts which amounted to an "interrogation," the Renda administration instructed the translators not to translate the questions. In cases where the Soviet experts used abusive language, the translators also were instructed not to translate. However, the translators were also blamed by both sides for "playing tricks" in cases where they refused to translate or did not translate accurately. The Renda administration put the Chinese translators—linguistic and cultural intermediaries for the Chinese and Soviets—in a very difficult position.[20]

While the November 11, 1952 document was written to emphasize the lengths to which the Chinese should go to work with the Soviets, there is a clearly identifiable tone to parts of it which suggests just how hard the Soviets could be for the Chinese to understand, and to get along with. The Chinese noted the extreme seriousness with which the Soviet experts approached their work:

> [One] can see that the experts have a considerable spirit of socialist competition, and that having the success of their work in the unit affirmed within a definite period of time is their greatest happiness, and indeed can fire their enthusiasm. At the same time, they are very serious about criticism. If there is any criticism of them, then they will not eat and will not sleep, but will want to make up for the shortcomings in their work. Therefore, when we express criticism of their work, we should be very careful.[21]

The Chinese also noted their rigid insistence on carrying out plans "to the letter":

> If we finalize a plan, then it must be completed according to schedule, regardless of whether the work is relatively important or unimportant (in the case of special circumstances, changes can of course be made). Consequently, we must have appropriate foresight, and must be careful in drawing up plans, because once they are created (it will be expected) that the plans will be strictly carried out. What gives the Soviet experts the greatest headaches is when we make too many changes and when we procrastinate.[22]

What on the surface seems to be praise of the Soviet experts' diligence and strict regard for work discipline often seems to carry a note of exasperation, as in the above excerpt, in which the Soviet experts are said to demand that all items of the plan be carried out "whether the work is relatively important or unimportant." Nonetheless, the Chinese at Renda in the 1950–53 period had orders to work with the Soviet experts humbly, avoiding all conflicts.

1953–1957: Reassessment, Disillusion, and Friction

By 1954, a new policy had taken effect at the Ministry of Higher Education. The policy was designed to restore balance in relations with the experts—neither rejecting Soviet advice (an attitude criticized as "conservatism" or "empiricism")—nor becoming overly dependent on it ("dependency" in this period, soon to be called "dogmatism").[23] Specifically, the Ministry of Higher Education now required that universities employing Soviet experts demonstrate that they were being used effectively.[24] The Renda administration, therefore, began to ask the teaching-research sections for detailed accountings of the academic activities of the Soviet experts; these were then turned into reports that were submitted to the Ministry of Higher Education on a biannual basis. During the 1955–56 and 1956–57 academic years, this more critical approach to the work of the Soviet experts continued and intensified, growing finally into a suspicion of Soviet experts working in certain ideologically sensitive areas.

Documents from 1954–55 show a number of changes in attitudes at Renda toward the Soviet experts. By May 1954 the period of "half-study/half-teach" in learning from the Soviet experts—which meant a rather mechanical struggle to comprehend and then transmit the material: with no time for attention to Chinese conditions—had been declared over. Reliance on Soviet experts, stated the Renda administrators, should gradually be reduced, with experts retained only for teaching of the numerous instructors and graduate students in the political instructor training program, and for new courses of study.[25] This new course was affirmed in communications with the Ministry of Higher Education during 1954–55, in which Renda stated that experts would only be needed in certain specialized areas in the future, and then only for short periods of time.[26] The plan was to substitute trained and competent Chinese instructors for the Soviet experts as soon as possible.[27] In the meantime, however, more forthright Chinese criticism of the Soviet experts was now possible, as part of the general post-Stalin trend of a more discriminating approach to Soviet knowledge. And even as the Chinese in the post-Stalin period were changing, so were the Soviet experts themselves.

Some of the evaluations of experts were unabashedly positive, such as that of the Archives expert Seleznev (at Renda 1952–55), who is given credit for single-handedly creating this course of study at Renda, and whose negative points, the Department stated, were not worth mentioning.[28] The Criminology Teaching-Research Section of the Law Department credited the Soviet expert Ke-er-jin (at Renda 1954–56) with delivering lively and well-received lectures in criminology, with leaving a very valuable collection of 24 lectures on the subject, and with making a real effort to incorporate Chinese materials into his teachings (such as using real cases from Beijing and Tianjin).[29] The evaluators of Bogdanovich, the Industrial Economics expert (at Renda from 1952–55), wrote that he taught better than the previous two experts in the Teaching-Research section, Volkov (at Renda 1950–51) and Filatov (at Renda 1951–52), and that during this expert's tenure, teaching quality had risen every year.[30]

Negative evaluations, however, became increasingly common. The Russian Department, in a December 1955 report, claimed that the Soviet teachers of Russian were weaker than in the past, less willing to work hard, and that "the experts never acted like this before."[31] While the Soviet experts in the 1950–53 period were publicly celebrated as paragons of self-sacrificing work and struggle, the internal evaluations of 1954–55 show Soviet experts who seem unwilling to work as hard (and uncomplainingly) as they had in the past. A May 1954 report noted that some of the experts were in poor health and objected to the heavy workloads, complaining that: "There is too much work. Man is not a machine. There is always a limit to man's spirit/energy."[32]

The growing friction with the Soviet experts involved a number of basic issues: 1) onerous work requirements; 2) experts' disagreements with Chinese social and political practices; 3) failures in communications, some resulting from a tendency to give experts less and less information; 4) experts' lack of knowledge of China, leading to disagreements on politically significant issues; and 5) deeper ideological disagreements, first becoming acute in 1956–57. If the internal reports on the Soviet experts at Renda in 1954–55 are to be believed, the Soviet experts were not the uncomplaining supermen that they seemed to have been in the 1950–53 period. Now some Soviet experts were complaining bitterly about the Chinese demands for ever more teaching and writing of instructional materials. Some Renda administrators responded sympathetically:

The Soviet expert needs from 30-40 hours a week to prepare his lectures, is not able to fully rest on Sundays as he is occupied with preparing classes. This is already very hard work, but we have also asked the expert to expend a lot of energy in directing scientific research work, preparing and delivering specialized reports, [work] which the expert has not been able to do because, in fact, it is not possible. So, in making these kinds of requests, we have just been paying attention to making use of the expert and have not been considering the degree [to which this increases] the Soviet expert's overall work burden.[33]

It appears, then, that at least some of the Renda administrators at the departmental and teaching-research section level, were aware that too much was being asked of the Soviet experts. The fact remained, however, that pressures from the Rectorate and, in turn, from the Ministry of Higher Education, continued to dictate that Soviet experts be used to the fullest.

The Chinese Communists had a tradition, dating from Yan'an egalitarianism, of involving students in evaluation of their instructors in a format basically the same as that of the group criticism/self-criticism meeting. High Stalinist academic culture, on the other hand, was basically authoritarian and hierarchical, and here the Chinese and Soviets lacked common ground. In a July 1955 evaluation of the Industrial Economics' expert Bogdanovich's work, Chinese Teaching-Research Section administrators reported that Bogdanovich had complained about the practice of students openly criticizing instructors in student-run evaluation meetings. Bogdanovich felt that instructors should be evaluated by department chairs who would visit the instructors' classes, a proposal which would maintain the sense of academic hierarchy that the Soviets stressed.[34]

Failures in communication were probably among the most frequent causes of disputes between the Soviet experts and their Chinese hosts. The aforementioned Soviet archives expert complained in 1954 of the Chinese failure to inform him in advance of a meeting called "to criticize bourgeois science."[35] During the 1954–55 academic year, the Statistics Department wanted the Soviet statistics expert to give a talk on statistical study in the Soviet Union, but the expert misunderstood the Chinese translation: he thought that the Chinese wanted him to "change his point of view."[36] These cases from 1954–55 may have been rather innocent miscommunications, but by late 1956 the evidence suggests that the information provided to Soviet experts was being more carefully controlled and limited. In late 1956, the Soviet experts in Fundamentals of Marxism-Leninism expressed unhappiness that they were being excluded from the examination of Chinese graduate students.[37]

Perhaps most damning, in the eyes of the Chinese at Renda, were the many incidents in which they perceived the Soviet experts failing to understand the Chinese situation and yet insisting on the Soviet point of view. They offended the strong Chinese sense of national pride and independence, and probably were a factor in later Chinese charges of Soviet "great-power chauvinism" and "hegemonism."

In reports and evaluations, the Chinese administrators at Renda referred to the Soviet experts as having little or no knowledge of China, and urged sporadically that the Soviet experts be provided information on China, in Russian translation, information that was extremely scarce in the early and mid-1950s. In June 1955, it was reported that the Soviet Marxism-Leninism expert Pavlov had made two incorrect assertions: that China in 1949 had achieved a socialist revolution, and that Chinese peasants did not have an "ownership" mentality in regards to land. In their report, the Teaching-Research section administrators recommended that, in the future, a knowledgeable Chinese instructor be assigned to each Soviet expert to provide necessary information on China. Further, the administrators pointed out that "this point should stimulate our desire to work independently, and not be dependent."[38] The next year, departmental administrators also judged the Marxism-Leninism expert Bei-si-te-lei-he's knowledge of China to be insufficient.[39]

There is much evidence that many of the Soviet experts themselves were aware of their lack of knowledge of China, and further, despite endless rhetoric on the necessity "to combine advanced Soviet experience and Chinese conditions," were disturbed by the near complete focus at Renda on acquiring Soviet knowledge to the evident detriment of the "Chinese conditions" part of the formula. In 1954–55, a chorus of voices from the ranks of the Soviet experts complained of their Teaching-Research sections' failure to conduct relevant research on the Chinese situation, to integrate heretofore entirely separate course sections dealing with the Soviet Union and China, and to create new, China-based courses of study. Blame for these failures implicitly rested not with the Soviet experts but with the Chinese side, which had failed to provide the Soviet experts with the information, in Russian translation, that the experts needed to "combine Soviet experience and Chinese conditions" and hence to aid in the creation of new China-based instructional materials and courses of study.

Numerous Soviet experts repeated such criticisms in the years 1954 to 1956. In December 1954, the Soviet archives expert Seleznev suggested hiring a Chinese to teach the history of Chinese archives, but the Teaching-Research section reported that this would be difficult.[40] The same month, Birman complained that the Finance course was completely USSR-based and needed the addition of China-based content.[41] Birman repeated his criticism in the June 1955 discussion meeting of Soviet experts, which suggests that little or no progress been made on this score in the intervening months.[42] In the 1955–56 academic year, however, Birman was reported to have finally done away with separate sections on finance in the Soviet Union and finance in China, and amalgamated the two.[43]

Teaching Chinese law or Chinese statistics alongside the Soviet courses appears to have been a preliminary step to the more through integration of Soviet theory and Chinese practice, but several Soviet experts in Law and Statistics complained that there had been no further progress in integrating the Soviet and the Chinese. That these departments had courses with Chinese content at all, however, seems to have been an accomplishment. Other Soviet

experts complained of the preponderance of Soviet examples and comparative neglect of Chinese content in courses offered in their fields. In an opin-
ion-survey meeting of Soviet experts held at the end of 1954–55, one Soviet
Law expert reported that, in the International Relations Department, courses
in diplomacy and international law were almost entirely based on Soviet examples.[44] In his evaluation of July 1955, Bogdanovich was reported to have
urged the use of more Chinese and fewer Soviet examples.[45] The law expert
Valiakhiietov urged that a China-based course of study in law be created.[46]
The Agricultural Economics expert Dubinov reported that he had urged the
Materials' Center in his Department to collect more Chinese materials, but
the Center had been slow to act on this advice.[47]

Why were the Soviet experts complaining of the lack of Chinese content in
their courses of study in these years? Soviet experts probably spoke up on this
issue, first, because they were asked by the Chinese to do so (hence the end-
of-the-year opinion meeting) and second, because, as academics, they really
did feel a desire to learn more about China and to include this knowledge
in their teaching and writing. A number of the experts, for example, actively
conducted research in China related to their fields of study, and published
academic works on their Chinese research after they returned to the Soviet
Union. So it is certainly understandable why they would have wanted more
access to Chinese materials for incorporation into their teaching and writing.
The Chinese, for their part, may have been none-too-eager to put the combination of "Soviet experience" and "Chinese conditions" into hands other
than their own.

While Renda repeatedly told the Ministry of Higher Education in these
years that Soviet experts at Renda would be phased out, the school did continue to request experts in certain areas, complained about lack of satisfactory
responses, and rejected some of the Ministry's suggestions in regard to the
type of expert to be employed. By the mid-1950s, the school had new programs in Agricultural Economics and so continued to request Soviet experts
in this area. The same holds true for the archives program, which had gotten
a strong start with the Soviet archives expert Seleznev. The school sought a
Soviet specialist in the area of newspaper journalism, but ended up instead, to
the school's dissatisfaction, with an expert on the history of the soviet press.[48]
Soviet experts on 19th-century Marxist ideology continued to be in demand.
The Marxism-Leninism Teaching-Research Section asked the experts to give
specialized lectures on 19th-century Marxism and on Leninism before the
Bolsheviks came to power in the Soviet Union.[49] At the end of the 1955–56
academic year, the Philosophy Department wanted a new Soviet expert to
continue the training of graduate students and instructors, and asked especially that a specialist in logic be employed.

Thus, Renda continued to request experts in specialized areas in 1956–57, which parallels the situation of employment of Soviet experts in China as a whole, that is, Soviet experts after 1956 were only supposed to be employed in highly specialized, "cutting-edge" fields.[50] For the years 1957–59, the Ministry of Higher Education informed Renda that two Soviet experts could be sent, one in philosophy and one in political economy.[51] The school replied that an expert in political economy would not be needed, but that Renda could use an expert in the history of economic theory.[52] This is an interesting statement on Renda's position vis-à-vis Stalinism, on the eve of the Great Leap. Political economy meant the Stalinist five-year plan version, which had been taught at Renda since 1950 by experts such as Breev in national economic Planning and V.A. Zhamin. By February 1957, however, the Renda administration knew that the political winds had shifted and Stalinist economics were out of favor in China; hence, an expert in history of economic theory would be someone who could provide perspectives and perhaps alternatives as the "Stalinist economic sciences" were abandoned.

Despite these exchanges with the Ministry about possible employment of experts in 1957–59, there were to be no new Soviet experts at Renda after the 1956–57 academic year. The atmosphere of the Sino-Soviet relationship had worsened considerably in the year since the CPSU 20th Party Congress and the events of 1956. This was not obvious in the propaganda of the time, which continued to stress undying Sino-Soviet friendship and the unshakeable solidarity of the socialist bloc, but in relations between the leaderships, and at the operational level of Sino-Soviet contacts, changes were obvious.

The Case of Perikl Petrovich Ionidi: How to Teach Dialectical Materialism?

At Chinese People's University in 1956–57, new frictions broke out between the Chinese and the few Soviet experts remaining, frictions which had been carefully controlled, usually by Chinese restraint, in the past. The Soviets, for their part, appear to have bent over backwards to solve the problems, but to no avail, as the Chinese decided to discontinue the hiring of Soviet experts. Ionidi had come to Renda in September 1956 to teach dialectical and historical materialism, a post now in the Philosophy Department that had been held the previous year by the aesthetics expert Skarzhenskaia and in 1952–55 by the energetic young Moscow University instructor Vladislav Kelle. Just as Skarzhenskaia's teaching focused on the esoteric subject of Marxist aesthetics, so Ionidi's specialty was also esoteric: the philosophical bases of science, and in particular, the "materialist" and "dialectical" bases of the work of the 19th-century Russian chemist D. Mendeleev. Ionidi's background was in the natural sciences. He had a candidate's degree in Chemistry and later earned a second degree in Philosophy.

Ionidi's enthusiastic lectures, delivered as late as 1957, on Mendeleev's purported dialectical materialism continued a theme that originated in late (High) Stalinist academic culture. D. Mendeleev was a 19th-century Russian scientist who won fame at home and abroad for his invention of the Periodic Table of the Elements, as well as other discoveries. The Soviets treated Mendeleev as an approved "founding father" of his discipline, and in accordance with Stalinist academic proclivities, tried to attribute to Mendeleev a proto-"dialectical materialist" worldview appropriate to such a long-dead scientist of international stature: a homegrown scientist to whom Soviet scientists could pay homage.[53]

Some of Ionidi's colleagues in the Philosophy Department, evidently emboldened by the Hundred Flowers policy, decided to take Ionidi to task—publicly—for what seemed like a far-fetched claim that Mendeleev was a dialectical materialist. At a February 1957 public convocation to commemorate Mendeleev's contribution to science, and chaired by Renda's Vice-Rector and Party boss, Hu Xikui, one faculty member from Philosophy stood up and voiced objections to Ionidi's talk, which was entitled "The scientific and philosophical significance of Mendeleev's Periodic Table of the Elements." The faculty member stated that Mendeleev could not have been a dialectical materialist. In response, Ionidi conceded that Mendeleev was a "materialist" and a "dialectician," but not necessarily a dialectical materialist in the full Marxist-Leninist sense of the word. This incident, reported on the front page of the *Renda Weekly*, could only have been seen as a serious blow to the authority of the Soviet experts, and shows that there was definitely pent-up sentiment among teaching staff, on the eve of the full flowering of the Hundred Flowers campaign, to challenge the Soviet experts.[54]

While the above challenge to Ionidi was taking place publicly, another challenge to the Soviet expert was developing behind the scenes. At Renda, Ionidi was called upon to teach basic courses in dialectical and historical materialism, courses which touched upon issues of Marxist-Leninist dialectics then in open dispute in both the Soviet Union and China. Unable to identify an "orthodox" position on these dialectical questions, and possibly lacking sufficient training in these areas, it appears that Ionidi chose a safer and easier route. Rather than taking a possibly dangerous position on disputed questions, he instead chose to teach the various opinions on questions of dialectics then current in both Soviet and Chinese philosophical journals. This solution satisfied nobody, however. The Soviet cultural attaché at the Embassy was somehow informed of the problems with Ionidi's teaching, and contacted Renda directly to ask for a meeting with Renda's administration.[55]

The Soviet cultural attaché, Sudalikov, visited Renda on the morning of April 13, 1957, along with the Party Secretary from the Soviet Embassy in charge of cultural affairs, the First Secretary and a translator. They were received by the Vice-Rector and school Party boss Hu Xikui, as well as He Sijing, Xu Bin, and Fang Hua of the Philosophy Department. The secretary Ge Ping was also present. Sudalikov, speaking first, referred to the Chinese penchant to not criticize the Soviet experts directly:

> Our point-of-view of the Chinese comrades is that [they] do not directly refer to the shortcomings of the Soviet comrades, [but you] must understand that among good things, there will be those which are unsatisfactory to varying degrees or which are bad. There may be the type of expert whose levels are not high, and if you do not criticize their shortcomings, they will not advance—they may spend two or three years in China and make no progress at all. [You] can raise the issue of their shortcomings with us, and also can raise the issue directly with them.[56]

The head of the Dialectical and Historical Materialism Teaching-Research Section, Xu Bin, then gave a careful summary of the work of Ionidi, emphasizing that his main work was tutoring graduate students and instructors in "objects [*duixiang*] of dialectical and historical materialism, the negation of the negation, and categories of dialectical materialism," and revising teaching outlines in light of the 20th Congress of the CPSU.[57]

In evaluating Ionidi, Xu Bin first carefully noted that the expert had worked hard to satisfy the Chinese side, and had provided materials regarding "disputes in academic circles"—presumably those in the Soviet Union. Further, the expert had also paid attention to disputes in Chinese academic circles. After he was given a March 1956 article in Russian translation from the Chinese periodical *Research in Philosophy* [*Zhexue yanjiu*] on the "negation of the negation," Xu Bin noted that he had referred to this article in his lectures, but had pointed out what, in his view, were its incorrect points. Further, Xu Bin stated that graduate students were dissatisfied with Ionidi's lack of specificity in his teaching, his tendency to read reports in which he referred to questions in dialectics broadly but with no clear central point. Finally, Xu Bin complained that Ionidi's lectures on Mendeleev were difficult to follow, as few if any of his audience had a natural science background.

In response to this criticism, the Soviet cultural attaché Sudalikov then gave the Soviet side's appraisal of Ionidi. Sudalikov stated that Ionidi's work on the philosophical bases of Mendeleev's work had been so specialized that Ionidi was poorly qualified to teach basic philosophical issues. But Ionidi's mistakes, in Sudalikov's eyes, went beyond lack of qualifications:

> We think he has made mistakes in his [writing of instructional materials] for the dialectical and historical materialism course of study. [We think] that he should forthrightly admit to [you] Chinese comrades that he himself is unable to take

the responsibility for the specialized dialectical materialism course of study, which he does not understand. If he were to take this responsibility, he would have to study for a semester the "negation of the negation," "categories of dialectical materialism," etc., issues which are in dispute in the Soviet Union.[58]

Sudalikov continued to lambaste Ionidi by revealing that the Soviet side had assigned five people to examine Ionidi's eight-hundred pages of lecture drafts. While no "mistakes in principle" had been found, Ionidi had referred to the points of view of many different people, "many of whom were not representative of the [mainstream] factions in the philosophical community." Ionidi's lecture drafts quoted others extensively, but lacked analysis and differentiation, something essential, considering that the lectures are for students. Sudalikov pointed out that Ionidi's presentation of a sampling of opinions, without proper analysis, was not befitting of an expert, and that the same knowledge could be better obtained by subscribing to some academic journals.[59]

For their part, the Chinese side agreed with Sudalikov's criticisms, but seemed a bit surprised by the Soviet's vehemence regarding Ionidi's mistakes. Xu Bin stated that the Soviet expert's presentation of a variety of different viewpoints was actually not unrelated to the requests of Ionidi made by the Chinese side, in accordance with the "Hundred Flowers" policy. The Chinese agreed with Sudalikov's suggestion that Ionidi's work be examined further, and that in the future, more care be taken to assure that the Soviet experts' were competent in the specific areas desired.[60]

That the Soviet side should be particularly careful in issues regarding dialectics is no surprise. The Soviet ambassador, Pavel Yudin, who was informed of the above dispute and who approved the investigation of Ionidi, was himself a philosophy expert and member of the Soviet Academy of Sciences. Yudin had originally been sent to China by Stalin in 1950, at Mao's request, to aid in the compilation and translation into Russian of the first volume of Mao's *Selected Works.* Yudin served as ambassador in China in the mid-1950s, and saw Mao frequently: the two engaged in lengthy discussion of Marxist-Leninist philosophy.[61]

The Soviet side thus perceived quite early that Mao, aspiring to a leadership position in the socialist world, sought the necessary qualification as a first-rate theorist, a creative developer of Marxism-Leninism. Stalin indulged Mao in this regard, and it was the policy of Stalin's successors to show respect for Mao as a theorist (despite what they may have felt privately on this score). So any disputes regarding Marxist-Leninist dialectics had to be handled very carefully. Further, 1956–57 had been a year of power shifts in the socialist camp. Mao had given the important speech "On Contradiction Among the People" in February 1957. Coming on the heels of this, a Soviet expert at a university speaking out on political-philosophical issues embarrassingly in dispute in the Soviet Union could prove to be a significant irritant in already strained Sino-Soviet relations. From the Soviet perspective, the problem had to be nipped in the bud.

On April 15, 1957, two days after the visit of Sudalikov, the Renda administration informed the Ministry of Higher Education that Renda would not be needing any more Soviet experts in the future. The Renda administration reported favorably on the Soviet cultural attaché's visit, and reported that the following measures would be taken:

> 1. [We intend to] organize the core teaching personnel of the Philosophy Department to discuss Ionidi's lectures, and then make arrangements to conduct a discussion among all the teachers so as to reach a common understanding, to rectify our academic and cultural style [*xuefeng, wenfeng*] and to exert great efforts to make progress in the writing of lectures.
> 2. In the very near future [we will] organize a meeting of all of the heads of departments and teaching-research centers where there are experts in order to examine the experts' teaching and issues of cooperative relations.
> 3. [We intend to] reexamine the plan for the hiring of experts for the coming academic year, and, in general, do not plan to hire any more.[62]

The speed with which the Renda administration informed the Ministry of its plans —only two days after Sudalikov's visit—suggests that the Renda administration may have been looking for a pretext to discontinue the employment of Soviet experts, and found it in Ionidi's difficulties in teaching in the rapidly changing field of dialectical and historical materialism. Though the Ministry of Higher Education had planned to assign two Soviet experts to Renda for 1957–59, these plans were evidently shelved. When Ionidi and the other five remaining Soviet experts departed in June 1957, they brought to a close the era of direct Sino-Soviet cooperation at Chinese People's University.

Conclusion

What explains the changes that took place in the relationship between Soviet experts and Chinese cadres at Renda in the two period 1950–53 and 1953–57? In brief, I would argue: the different revolutionary "stages" of the two societies and the larger political events in the Sino-Soviet relationship together conditioned the atmosphere in which the Soviets and Chinese worked. In addition, the Chinese had a tradition of cyclical adoption and rejection/backlash in imports of foreign ideas and systems, and the import of Soviet educational ideas and systems in the 1950s can be seen as another episode in this ongoing process of creating Sino-foreign syntheses.[63]

Chinese Communist cadres in 1950–53 were at the height of enthusiasm for their new regime, and determined to transform their country as the Soviet Union had transformed theirs. Stalin was the undisputed leader of the socialist camp, and the Chinese—from Mao on down—were determined to follow his example in order to create a powerful, modern, industrialized, socialist state. The Soviet experts, for their part, had been brought up in the Stalinist academic system and felt considerable pride in their own and their country's accomplishments.

The death of Stalin in March 1953, as well as China's successful "standing up" to the United States in the Korean War, changed the dynamic of the relationship. With Stalin gone, Mao and the Chinese leadership were on a par with Stalin's successors as leaders in the socialist world: there was no more need to kowtow. Reassessment of the 1950–53 period in learning from the Soviet Union began soon after Stalin's death, and resulted in a more critical and selective approach to "combining advanced Soviet experience and Chinese conditions." The Chinese, and the Soviets, would call for more attention to the "Chinese conditions" part of the equation. The Secret Speech and de-Stalinization in 1956 accelerated trends already in evidence since 1953.

Finally, China's educational borrowing from Western countries had been underway for about a century, and had been characterized by rather abrupt shifts from wholehearted enthusiasm to partial rejection, a process which resulted in new Sino-foreign syntheses in ideas and institutions. This had certainly been the case in the May Fourth Period of the 1910s and 1920s when Chinese intellectuals rejected China's cultural traditions *in toto*, only to tack back to cultural conservatism in the 1930s. Viewed in this context, Chinese People's University was a success: By 1957, having utilized the Soviet experts successfully, the university enforced a Sovietized ideological and institutional orthodoxy in regional academic institutions nationwide. Some aspects of the Soviet academic regimen—and Soviet experts themselves—were no longer necessary.

Notes

1. "Enthusiastically celebrating the first-year anniversary, our school holds a grand commemoration meeting," *Renmin daxue zhoubao* 32 [People's University weekly] (hereinafter as "Enthusiastically celebrating the first-year") (October 14, 1951), 1.

2. "Enthusiastically Celebrating the First-Year," 1.

3. On this theme, see Suzanne Pepper, *Radicalism and Education Reform in 20th-century China: The Search for an Ideal Development Model* (New York: Cambridge University Press, 1996). See also Ruth Hayhoe, *Chinese Universities, 1895–1995: A Century of Cultural Conflict* (New York: Garland Publishing, 1996).

4. Shen Zhihua, *Sulian zhuanjia zai Zhongguo* 1948–1960 [Soviet experts in china 1948–1960] (Beijing: Zhongguo guoji guangbo chubanshe, 2003).

5. Mao Lirui and Shen Guangqun, eds., *Zhongguo jiaoyu tongshi* [A comprehensive history of Chinese higher education], vol. 5 (Beijing: Jiaoyu kexue chubanshe, 1988), 88.

6. For Sino-Soviet negotiations on the creation of the new university, see Douglas A. Stiffler, "Creating 'New China's First New-Style Regular University,' 1949–50," in Paul Pickowicz, ed., *Dilemmas of Victory: The 1950s in the People's Republic of China* (Cambridge: Harvard University Press, 2007).

7. V. Fillipov, "Doklad o rabote gruppi Sovetskikh prepodavatelei v vysshikh uchebnykh zavedenii g. Pekina" [Report on the work of soviet teachers in the higher educational institutions of the city of beijing], December 18, 1950, Rossiskii Tsentr Khraneniia i Izuchenia Dokumentov Noveishei Istorii [Russian center for the preservation and study of the documents of modern history] (hereinafter as zx RTsKh-IDNI), Fond 17, opis 137, delo 723, 2.

8. Soviet military advisors and personnel were present in China in large numbers during the Korean War years. A large civilian contingent of 1,500 Soviets worked on the jointly managed Chinese Changchun railway in the early 1950s. See Luo Shixu, *You miyue dao fanmu: Sulian zhuanjia zai Zhongguo* [From honeymoon to estrangement: soviet experts in china] (Beijing: Shijie zhishi, 1999), vol. I, 329.

9. See Appendices B and C in Douglas A. Stiffler, *Building Socialism at Chinese People's University: Chinese Cadres and Soviet Experts in the People's Republic of China, 1949–57* (Ph.D. dissertation, University of California, San Diego, 2002).

10. Xu Bin interview, Beijing, October 17, 2000. Xu Bin was the translator for the chief Soviet advisors in the Rector's office in the 1950s.

11. Suzanne Pepper, *Radicalism and Education Reform in 20th-century China*, 174–75.

12. There was a large Russian community in Harbin, some of whom were descendants of White Russian émigrés who came to China after the Bolshevik revolution. Other Russians had come to Harbin to work on the Russian (and then Soviet-owned) Chinese Eastern Railway. On this history of the Russian community in Harbin, see: David Wolff, *To the Harbin Station: The Liberal Alternative in Russian Manchuria, 1898–1914* (Palo Alto, CA: Stanford University Press, 1999). James H. Carter, *Creating a Chinese Harbin: Nationalism in an International City, 1916–1932* (Ithaca, NY: Cornell University Press, 2002).

13. The non-departmental Russian teaching-research group was distinct from the Russian Department in that it taught the Russian courses required school-wide. Mathematics and Chinese language were both remedial, and required in some departments. Pedagogy had originally been a department in the spring of 1950, and was transferred to Beijing Normal University in 1952 along with the Soviet expert, Popov.

14. Douglas A. Stiffler, "Creating 'New China's First New-Style Regular University,' 1949–50."

15. Ruth Hayhoe, "Chinese Universities and the Social Sciences," *Minerva* 31, no. 4 (1993), 478–503.

16. "Zhongguo renmin daxue guanyu pinyong Sulian zhuanjia gongzuo qingkuang jiandan baogao" [Summary report of the work conditions and employment of soviet experts at Chinese People's University] (November 11, 1952), Renda Archives 62A, 1–3.

17. Gao Fang interview, December 17, 1998.

18. "Zhongguo renmin daxue guanyu pinyong Sulian zhuanjia gongzuo qingkuang jiancha buchong baogao" [Supplementary investigation report concerning Chinese People's University's employment of soviet experts and the conditions of their work] (draft; 1952) (hereinafter as "Zhongguo renmin daxue"), Renda Archives 62A, 13–14.

19. "Zhongguo renmin daxue," 13–14

20. "Fujian 2, Zhongguo renmin daxue xi, jiaoyanshi zhuanjia gongzuo zhidu zhanxing guiding (cao an)" [Attachment 2 (draft) temporary regulations for the work system of experts in the departments and teaching-research sections of Chinese People's University] (May 12, 1954), Renda Archives 112A, 18. "Zhongguo renmin daxue guanyu pinyong Sulian zhuanjia gongzuo qingkuang jiancha buchong baogao" [Supplementary investigation report concerning Chinese People's University's employment of Soviet experts and the conditions of their work] (draft, 1952) Renda Archives 62A, 10–15.

21. "Zhongguo renmin daxue," 14.

22. "Zhongguo renmin daxue," 14.

23. Suzanne Pepper, *Radicalism and Education Reform in 20th-century China*, 188. Zhang Jian, "Luetan gaodeng xuexiao xuexi Sulian xianjin jingyan de chengjiu he wenti" [A brief discussion of the accomplishments and problems of higher education institutions in learning from the advanced experience of the Soviet Union], *Renmin Jiaoyu* [People's education] (February 1955), 12–15.

24. On October 5, 1954 the Ministry of Higher Education issued a directive entitled "Guanyu zhongdian gaodeng xuexiao he zhuanjia gongzuo fanwei de jueyi," [Decision concerning key higher education institutions and the scope of the work of experts]. The directive established the following as "keypoint" universities: Chinese People's University, Beijing University, Qinghua University, Harbin Polytechnical University, Beijing Agicultural University, and the Beijing Medical Insitute. In addition, the directive defined "main responsibilities and scope of work" for Soviet experts in higher education institutions all over the country. JYDSJ, 114.

25. "Zhongguo renmin daxue Sulian zhuanjia gongzuo jiancha baogao (chugao)" [(Draft) investigation report on the work of Soviet experts at Chinese People's University] (May 1954), Renda Archives 112A, 14–15.

26. "Zhongguo renmin daxue ben xueqi lai Sulian zhuanjia gongzuo jiancha baogao," [Investigation report on the work of soviet experts during the past semester] (January 10, 1955), Renda Archives 112A, 22. See also "Gongye jingji zhuanjia Bo-ge-da-nuo-wei-ai tongzhi zaixiao gongzuo de gongzuo zongjie" [Summing-up of the

work at the school of the industrial economics expert comrade Bogdanovich] (July 1955), Renda Archives 153A, 162.

27. "Gaojiaobu zonghedaxue si Sulian guwen Ge-li-si-qin-ke jiancha xuexiao gongzuo jiyao" [Main-points summary of the work of examination of the school by the Soviet advisor Gerasichenko of the Ministry of Higher Education, Comprehensive Universities department] (March 10, 1955), Renda Archives 141A, 3.

28. "Dang'an zhuanjia M. S. Xie-lie-zi-nie-fu tongzhi zaixiao gongzuo de zongjie baogao" [Summing-up report on the work at the school of the archives expert, comrade M. S. Seleznov] (July 1955), Renda Archives 153A, 216.

29. "Zhongguo renmin daxue falu xi xingfa jiaoyanshi Ke-er-jin zhuanjia gong-zuo de zongjie" [Summing-up of the work of expert Ke-er-jin in the Criminal Law Teaching-research section of the law department of Chinese People's University] (July 1956), Renda Archives 166A, 15–20.

30. "Gongye jingji zhuanjia Bo-ge-da-nuo-wei-ai tongzhi zaixiao gongzuo de gongzuo zongjie" [Summing-up of the work at the school of the industrial economics expert comrade Bogdanovich] (July 1955), Renda Archives 153A, 154.

31. "Ewen xi diyi, er Ewen jiaoyanshi 1955.12.14 zhuanjia gongzuo jiancha baogao" [December 14, 1955 investigation report of the work of experts in the numbers one and two teaching-research sections of the Russian department] (December 14, 1955), Renda Archives 153A, 84.

32. "Zhongguo renmin daxue Sulian zhuanjia gongzuo jiancha baogao (chugao)" [(Draft) investigation report on the work of soviet experts at chinese people's university] (May, 1954), Renda Archives 112A, 14.

33. "Jingji tongji zhuanjia Ji-mi-te-li-ye-fu tongzhi zaixiao gongzuode zongjie baogao" [Summing-up report on the work at the school of the economic statistics expert Dmitriiev] (July 1955), Renda Archives 153A, 185.

34. "Gongye jingji zhuanjia Bo-ge-da-nuo-wei-ai tongzhi zaixiao gongzuo de gongzuo zongjie" [Summing-up of the work at the school of the industrial economics expert comrade Bogdanovich] (July 1955), Renda Archives 153A, 156.

35. "Zhongguo renmin daxue Sulian zhuanjia gongzuo jiancha baogao (chugao)" [(Draft) investigation report on the work of soviet experts at Chinese People's University] (May 1954), Renda Archives 112A, 14.

36. "Jingji tongji zhuanjia Ji-mi-te-li-ye-fu tongzhi zaixiao gongzuode zongjie baogao" [Summing-up report on the work at the school of the economic statistics expert Dmitriiev] (July 1955), Renda Archives 153A, 185.

37. "Zhongguo renmin daxue 1956 nian nianzhong zhuanjia gongzuo baogao" [1956 mid-year report on the work of experts at chinese people's university], Renda Archives 167A, 21.

38. "Zhongguo renmin daxue Ma-Lie zhuyi jichu jiaoyanshi Ba-fu-luo-fu zhuanjia gongzuo de zongjie" [Summing-up of the work of the expert Pavlov of the Chinese People's University fundamentals of Marxism-Leninism teaching-research section], Renda Archives 166A, 2.

39. "Zhongguo renmin daxue Ma-Lie zhuyi jichu jiaoyanshi Bei-si-te-lei-he zhuanjia gongzuo de zongjie" [Summing-up of the work of the expert bei-si-te-lei-he

of the Chinese People's university fundamentals of Marxism-Leninism teaching-research section], Renda Archives 166A, 9–10.

40. "Dang'an zhuanxiuke Sulian zhuanjia Xie-lie-zi-nie-fu tongzhi zi 1952 nian dao 1955 nian 5 yue gong tichu zhongda jianyi shijiu xiang" [The archives short course Soviet expert, comrade Seleznev's nineteen important suggestions made from 1952 through may 1955] (1955) Renda Archives 143A, 9.

41. "Caizheng xinyong xi Sulian zhuanjia A. M. Bi-er-man tongzhi zi 1954 nian 12 yue daoxiao hou qian jin gong tichu zhongda jianyi qi xiang" [The credit and finance Department Soviet expert, comrade A. M. Birman's 7 important suggestions made after his arrival at the school in December 1954 to the present] (1955), Renda Archives 143A, 22–24.

42. "1954–55 xuenian mo juxing Sulian zhuanjia zuotanhui jilu zhengli" [Edited record of the 1954–55 end-of-year discussion meeting of Soviet experts] (June 28, 1955), Renda Archives 152A, 43.

43. "Zhongguo renmin daxue caizheng xi Bi-er-man zhuanjia gongzuo de zongjie" [Summing-up of the work of the Chinese People's University, finance department expert birman] (July 1956), Renda Archives 166A, 44.

44. "1954–55 xuenian mo juxing Sulian zhuanjia zuotanhui jilu zhengli" [Edited record of the 1954–55 end-of-year discussion meeting of soviet experts] (June 28, 1955), Renda Archives 152A, 45.

45. "Gongye jingji zhuanjia Bo-ge-da-nuo-wei-ai tongzhi zaixiao gongzuo de gongzuo zongjie" [Summing-up of the work at the school of the industrial economics expert comrade bogdanovich] (July 1955), Renda Archives 153A, 156.

46. "Zhongguo renmin daxue guojia yu faquan lishi jiaoyanshi zhuanjia G. M. Wa-li-he-mi-tuo-fu tongzhi de zaixiao gongzuo zongjie baogao" [Summing-up report of the work at the school of the expert, comrade Valiakhiietov of the Chinese People's university history of national sovereignty law teaching-research section], Renda Archives 166A, 162.

47. "Nongye jingji zhuanjia Du-bin-nuo-fu tongzhi zaixiao gongzuo de zongjie baogao" [Summing-up report of the work at the school of the agricultural economics expert, comrade Dubinov] (July 1955), Renda Archives 153A, 207.

48. "Zhongguo renmin daxue 1956 nian nianzhong zhuanjia gongzuo baogao" [Chinese People's University 1956 mid-year report on the work of experts], Renda Archives 167A, 21.

49. "Zhongguo renmin daxue ben xueqi lai Sulian zhuanjia gongzuo jiancha baogao" [Examination report of the work of soviet experts at chinese people's university during the past semester] (January 1955), Renda Archives 112A, 19.

50. Mao Lirui and Shen Guangqun, eds., *Zhongguo jiaoyu tongshi* [Comprehensive history of chinese higher education], vol. 5 (Beijing: Jiaoyu kexue chubanshe, 1988), 105.

51. Attachment to "Zhonghua renmin gongheguo gaodeng jiaoyubu qing zai shencha nixiao pinqing zhuanjia jihua ji jinxing zhunbei gongzuo" [The people's republic of china ministry of higher education requests that your school again examine your plan for the employment of experts and the carrying-out of preparatory work], Renda Archives 174A, 3–5.

52. Letter to the Ministry of Higher Education from Chinese People's University (March 7, 1957), Renda Archives 174A, 9–10.

53. Nikolai Krementsov, *Stalinist Science* (Princeton: Princeton University Press, 1997), 50–51.

54. "Jinian Men-de-lie-ye-fu shishi 50 zhou nian—Xiao xueshu weiyuanhui juxing kexue baogao hui" [Commemorating the 50th anniversary of Mendeleev's death—school's Academic Committee holds a scientific report meeting] (February 23, 1957), *Renda Weekly* 134, 1.

55. "Sulian Dashiguan wenhua canzan Su-da-li-ke-fu lai xiao fangwen jilu" [Record of the Soviet Embassy Cultural Attache Sudalikov's visit to the school] (hereinafter as "Sulian Dashiguan wenhua canzan"), Renda Archives 174A, 12–14.

56. "Sulian Dashiguan wenhua canzan," 12.

57. "Sulian Dashiguan wenhua canzan," 12.

58. "Sulian Dashiguan wenhua canzan," 13.

59. "Sulian Dashiguan wenhua canzan," 13.

60. "Sulian Dashiguan wenhua canzan," 10.

61. See the chapter on Yudin in Luo Shishu, *You miyue dao fanmu: Sulian zhuanjia zai Zhongguo* [From honeymoon to estrangement: soviet experts in china], vol. 1 (Beijing: Shijie zhishi, 1999), 146–89.

62. Letter to Minister Yang and Vice-Minister Huang of the Ministry of Higher Education from Chinese People's University (April 15, 1957), Renda Archives 174A, 11.

63. On this theme, see Suzanne Pepper, *Radicalism and Education Reform in 20th-century China.* See also Ruth Hayhoe, *Chinese Universities, 1895–1995: A Century of Cultural Conflict* (New York: Garland Publishing, 1996).

13

Lysenkoism and the Suppression of Genetics in the PRC, 1949–1956

Laurence Schneider

"In the new China, Morgan is not desired; Michurin is."

—*Peoples' Daily*, 29 June 1952

"[It is] . . . wrong . . . to say that 'Michurin's theory is socialist,' or that 'Mendel's and Morgan's principles of heredity are capitalist.' We must not believe such stuff."

—Lu Dingyi, 26 May 1956

B Y THE END OF 1949, Lysenkoist biology began to be proselytized in China under the aegis of the CCP's comprehensive pro-Soviet policy. Passionate Chinese advocates of Lysenkoist biology, aided by its Soviet missionaries, tirelessly campaigned to establish it as the exclusive approach to biology in China and to banish classical genetics from teaching, research, and publication. Due to the significant presence of Western-trained geneticists in China, however, it was by no means a simple matter to get Lysenko's doctrines accepted there, even during the period of blind emulation of the Soviet Union. For this reason, in 1952, the CCP formally espoused Lysenkoist biology and banned Western biology related to genetics. Though muted, resistance did continue, but the ban became quite effective over the next five years, the period of the first Five-Year Plan.

At this time, the CCP adamantly promoted Lysenkoist biology not simply to emulate the orthodoxies of the Soviet Union. More to the point, it did so because it was apparently necessitated by the "Stalinist model" of economic development the CCP chose to follow. That model focused on capital inten-sive, urban heavy and military industries, and that is where the Soviet Union directed its aid to China. China's agriculture was expected to provide a sub-stantial portion of the necessary capital. And Lysenkoist biology was expected (because of Soviet claims) to provide cheap, quick, easy to implement means of raising agriculture's output exponentially. Incredibly, not until the end of China's first Five-Year plan did the Chinese begin to learn the truth about Soviet agriculture and Lysenkoism: that the former was pretty much a disas-ter and the latter pretty much bad science. While the Soviets had restricted China's access to accurate information about its economy, the Chinese un-critically and naively (by their own later admission) wanted to believe in the power of the Soviet example.

From the time of its arrival in China, Lysenkoism was dictatorial and dog-matic. It was both a reflection and source of divisive tensions between the CCP and Chinese intellectuals. It politicized the science community, and it was an early source of a growing displeasure with the role of the Soviet Union in China. By the end of 1956, Lysenkoism had lost its Party-endorsed mo-nopoly, and the ban on "bourgeois" biology was revoked. These resounding reversals—Mao described them as "doing somersaults"[1] —were less a result of dissent from the Chinese science community than from telling attacks on Lysenkoism within the Soviet Union and Eastern Europe. Additionally, they came from the CCP's complex—and eventually, quite public—concern that China was borrowing indiscriminately from the Soviet Union and had be-come overly dependent on Soviet expertise. The "genetics question," as the CCP delicately labeled it, may well have been an extreme and hence unique case. Touching upon and illustrating so many sensitive issues, however, ge-netics became an exemplar for a host of other problems the CCP sought to resolve on the eve of the second Five-Year Plan.

What Is Lysenkoism?[2]

In the *Communist Manifesto*, Marx encouraged his readers to abandon phi-losophy which saw itself merely as a means of understanding the world and replace it with a philosophy which saw itself as a means of changing the world. Echoing Marx, Lysenkoist biology relentlessly reminded its new audience in China that the goal of biology should be to change and control nature, not merely to understand it. Lysenkoist biology was premised on a transformist belief that all of organic nature was infinitely malleable and subject to human manipulation. At the heart of this belief were two principles that clashed most violently with classical genetics.[3]

The first principle was that the effective source of all organic change and development—including evolution and new species—was the environment, that is, forces outside of organisms, not within them (like chromosomes or genes). Second was the corollary that humans could fundamentally reshape organisms (especially food plants) to their own benefit solely through the manipulation of the organism's environment. These Lysenkoist principles were necessarily extended to the realm of heredity, which, in effect, was defined as "internalized environmental conditions."[4] Lysenkoism asserts that acquired characters can be inherited, and so, cumulative changes in an organism caused by the environment are the substance of its "hereditary nature" and the legacy its progeny will inherit.

Lysenkoism was built on claims that, following these principles, food plants could be improved so that they would grow in previously hostile environments, or grow more abundantly in native settings. Lysenkoism's self-styled "agrobiology" consisted of a set of transformist techniques to exploit what it called the phasic or stagelike development of plants. By manipulating the temperature or available light at the appropriate time of a plant's development, it could be changed in a desired direction, and even changed in its "hereditary nature." For example, particular characters of a food grain could be changed so that those originally requiring a moderate climate could be made to grow in harsh northern climates.

T. D. Lysenko (1898–1976), who gave these ideas his name, was trained in the provinces as an agronomist during the 1920s. Throughout the 1930s, he was a most ambitious careerist, climbing with ruthless energy and Machiavellian acumen to the pinnacle of the Soviet science bureaucracy. In 1938, with the support of Stalin, Lysenko became the president of the Lenin Academy of Agricultural Science. A decade later, at the infamous July–August 1948 meeting of that academy, Lysenko and his followers completed the imposition of the hegemony of their approach to biology, banning classical genetics altogether.[5]

By this time, Lysenko had expanded his basic set of biological ideas in two directions. He took guidance respectively from I. I. Prezent (1902–1970?), an influential ideologue with pretensions of expertise in dialectical materialism, and I. V. Michurin (1855–1935), a homegrown horticulturist turned into an icon by Lenin. The "Lysenkoism" that was brought to China in 1949 was an amalgam of their ideas and those of T. D. Lysenko.

Lysenko found Michurin valuable for his nativist and populist image as well as his alleged role as an earlier practitioner of Lysenko's biological principles. Working with the fruits and vegetables of his locale, Michurin had reputedly bred scores of new varieties that were exceptionally hardy and prolific. His much-quoted motto was co-opted by Lysenko to set the tone for the new biology: "Don't wait for favors from nature; we must triumph over nature." Lysenko went so far as to designate Michurin as the true successor to Darwin, based on Michurin's understanding of the environmental sources of evolution and on his aggressive intervention in the evolutionary process by way of creating (supposed) new species with his breeding techniques. Never at a loss for a catchy label, Lysenko designated Michurin's (and his own) school of evolutionary thought "Creative Darwinism."

Michurin used intuitive, trial-and-error techniques that he said were successful because of his intimate familiarity with his local environment and his personal, hands-on involvement in the selection and breeding process. Moreover, Michurin pooh-poohed formal agricultural science taught in big cities and in universities where no one got their hands dirty, no one was involved directly in production, and everyone was caught up in fancy theories, mathematical techniques, and statistics that bore no relationship to reality. Lysenko approvingly echoed Michurin's anti-intellectualism and mockery of establishment biology, and he used Michurin to legitimize his own famous lack of experimental rigor. By the time Lysenkoism was introduced to China, Michurin had become its patron saint and chief exemplar. Lysenko and his missionaries introduced their work to China under the name of "Michurinism" (Mi-chu-lin-zhuyi), a name that stuck throughout the entire period of Lysenkoist dominance there.

I. I. Prezent was a graduate of Leningrad State University's Faculty of Social Sciences in 1926, and soon specialized in the philosophy of the life sciences. He aided Lysenko's rise to dominance in Soviet biology and provided him with the trappings of ideological legitimacy—a dialectical materialist and properly socialist rationale for attacking and rejecting classical genetics. Lysenko took from Prezent the argument that science inevitably has a class nature: If Marxism is correct, then how could science developed within bourgeois-capitalist society be appropriate for a revolutionary socialist one? Science produced by and practiced in a bourgeois-capitalist society could only be idealist, formalistic, metaphysical. Only science that evolved out of a socialist society, like Lysenko's biology, was valid.[6]

This class approach to science judged classical genetics with particular harshness. Geneticists were decried for the isolation of their laboratories from nature and production. Their concept of the gene was condemned as a mere figment of bourgeois idealism. Lysenkoism saw hostility to dialectics and to transformist principles where classical geneticists claimed the basic material of heredity to have a fixed structure, function, and location. Lysenko summarized all of these ideas in his 31 July 1948, opening speech to a session of the Lenin Academy of Agricultural Sciences. This speech became the point of departure for the teachings of Chinese Lysenkoites and their Russian mentors. It was translated many times into Chinese and was used endlessly as a template for explanations of Michurin biology and for arguments against classical genetics and against Darwin's approach to evolution.

Lysenko's speech (along with others delivered at the academy session) was an indictment of biologists who practiced the "old biology" and/or criticized Lysenko's new biology. Some of those thus indicted had already suffered ill consequences; others would meet severe punishments ranging from the loss of positions at universities and the academy, to jail and death. Stalin had not only approved of Lysenko's hegemony and edited his 1948 speech, he obviously also served Lysenko as a political role model.[7] Lysenko's enmity, however, was not limited to Soviet scientists: He was making a grandiose declaration of revolutionary war against all practitioners of the "old biology" and classical genetics from Weismann, to Mendel, to the contemporary biologist T. H. Morgan. And just as Lenin's Comintern had brought its design for revolution to China in the 1920s, Lysenko determined to bring his biological revolution there a generation later.

It should be noted here that there never was reliable evidence that Lysenkoism/Michurin biology ever supported its claims to the creation of new plant species or notable and sustained improvements in plant production. It is true that Michurin and some of his followers did breed new *varieties* of plants. The techniques they used, however, were familiar from local custom to horticulturalists, plant selectors, and farmers throughout the world. Inherent in the Lysenko/Michurin project were some fatal problems, the most egregious among them being the express abandonment of common rules of scientific evidence. There was no way to evaluate its claims because controls and statistical study were not practiced as a matter of principle. "Evidence"—as presented in a flood of Chinese periodical literature—was purely anecdotal. Additionally, the project created from whole cloth a set of "theories" to explain the qualitative or quantitative claims. These theories simply ignored the previous century or more of biological science and followed a strained logic invented on the spot.

On the other hand, there is considerable and solid evidence that the application of Lysenko/Michurin theory and technique could have disastrous consequences. For example, the Soviet's implementation of Lysenko's "close planting" theory resulted in the ruination of vast areas of newly planted forest.[8] And a central claim, having to do with grafting plants, was utterly demolished in the mid-1950s when East European scientists tried to reproduce results brashly touted by the Lysenko/Michurin establishment.[9] As we shall see, this latter debacle soon contributed to the fall of Lysenko and Lysenkoism's loss of its monopoly in China.

Lysenkoism in China

In 1949, few Chinese biologists were familiar with Lysenko's work before it
was incorporated into a full-blown ideology. Thus, the Chinese science community in general was quite unprepared to deal with the militant promotion
of Michurin biology by Chinese and then Russian Lysenkoites within months
of the CCP's formal accession to power on October 1, 1949.

Chinese Lysenkoites used the new agricultural schools of northeast China as
their earliest base of operations. By the autumn of 1951, they had spread their
influence throughout the country via major agricultural schools and research
institutes as well as small, local agricultural colleges, extension programs, and
research stations. All of these were controlled until the mid-1950s by a new
Ministry of Agriculture, quite sympathetic to Lysenkoism and active in its
promotion.[10] The ministry created in the Beijing area what soon became the
country's largest and leading agricultural science institution, Beijing Agricultural University. It was also intended to be the institutional base and guiding
light for a national campaign to make Lysenkoism immediately the exclusive
orthodoxy of agricultural biology, and eventually of all biological science. To
implement this ambitious plan, the Party appointed Luo Tianyu (1900–1986),
a Party veteran who spent the war years in Yan'an as a science educator. In the
early 1940s, he sponsored education reforms that conscientiously embodied
Mao's populist Rectification (*zheng feng*) campaign. For this, he was rewarded
with the chairmanship of Yan'an university's Department of Agriculture, followed by the deanship of the new agricultural university.[11]

When Luo assumed control of Beijing Agricultural University, its faculty
had already been assigned Party cadre to implement policy and to organize
and lead mandatory study cells for CCP policy and Marxism. To these, Luo
added mandatory study of Michurin biology. Furthermore, he required that
all faculty formally renounce classical genetics and embrace Michurinism.
The university's three distinguished program heads, however, refused to follow this requirement and openly engaged in critical debates with proponents
of Michurin biology. Not only did they challenge Luo's authority, they also
denied him distinguished converts who could serve as models for the rest
of the faculty and the forthcoming national pro-Soviet campaign to "learn
from the advanced experience of the Soviet Union." The fate of these three is
instructive.[12]

Li Jingzhun (C. C. Li), a 1940 Cornell Ph.D. in plant genetics and a specialist in biostatistics was co-director of the school's agronomy program. Luo
removed him from his administrative position and forbade him to teach
genetics and biometry courses. Li became so intimidated by Luo that he and
his family soon fled China and found sanctuary in the United States. Li's co-

director was Tang Peisong, a 1930 Johns Hopkins Ph.D. in plant physiology. After Luo removed him from his co-directorship, he subjected Tang to a humiliating public "thought remolding" session before the entire school as well as representatives from other Beijing universities. Tang was then ostracized from the school for criticizing and resisting the Party's policy of learning from the Soviets. And finally, there was Wu Zhongxian, director of the animal science program. He was a 1937 Edinburgh Ph.D. in animal genetics and biostatistics. He protected himself by not expressing his dissent publicly and by shifting his teaching and research out of genetics and into animal nutrition when his courses in bio-statistics were abolished.[13]

In just a short time then, Luo Tianyu had brought turmoil to his university, alienated some of its star faculty, and, only by force, converted the curriculum to Michurin biology. Elsewhere he displayed rather more entrepreneurial skill and political savoir faire. For example, in late 1948, at the inception of four other major agricultural research organizations in the Beijing area, he had managed to pack them with zealous Michurinists.[14] The work of these four organizations along with Beijing Agricultural University was constantly cited in national publications to illustrate the accomplishments of Michurin biology.[15] The research of virtually all other plant biologists was ignored.

Another organization important to Luo Tianyu's campaign was the China Michurin Study Society, which was devoted to spreading Michurin biology to the masses. With Luo as its national president, the society celebrated hero workers and peasants who were reputed to have accomplished amazing quantitative and qualitative production results using Michurinist techniques. For revolutionary China the Michurin Study Society, according to Luo, was a new kind of organization wherein all social elements worked together and followed Mao's "mass line."[16] By the end of 1951 the Michurin Society claimed to have fifty branch societies spread all over China.[17] It now advertised itself and spread the good news about Michurin biology through its official journal which was filled with translations from Soviet reports on the results of using Michurin's and Lysenko's techniques with wheat, cotton, and livestock. There were also simple descriptions of Russian agronomists and reports on Michurinist curricula in secondary education.[18]

Within the larger community of biological scientists, Luo Tianyu used every available venue to promote Michurin biology and to assert its control. In 1950, for example, among the prominent organizations he targeted was the Beijing Biological Studies Society whose members came from the Chinese Academy of Science (CAS) as well as the universities. At its annual conference, Luo commandeered an entire day of panels for the explication and discussion of Michurin biology.[19] Earlier that year, in Nanjing, Michurin advocates used the lecture hall of the venerable Science Society of China to stage a more confrontational "symposium" on "Michurin Theory and Morgan Theory." Founded in 1915, the Science Society published the longest-lived and most sophisticated science journal in China. At this 1950 symposium, only Michurin biologists presented papers and the occasion clearly signaled that the Science Society had been taken over by Luo's people.[20]

Soviet-Chinese Tensions over Lysenkoism

In 1950, the eminent embryologist Zhu Xi was a member of the CAS Experimental Biology Institute; he became its director three years later.[21] Apparently, his research field and this position put him out of the political reach of Luo Tianyu. Consequently, Zhu Xi engaged in sardonic criticism of Michurin biology and Lysenko; and continued doing so until Lysenkoism lost its monopoly. The CCP responded to Zhu Xi the way they did with other senior scientists—by letting the Soviets deal with him. For example, he led a 1953 zoologists' delegation sent to the Soviet Union to see how biology was done there. In spite of the Lysenkoite proselytizing, he reported that he had got the Soviets to agree with him that it was inappropriate to apply Michurin biology indiscriminately in China, where concrete conditions often differed from the Soviet Union.[22]

That same year, Zhu Xi became one of the first Chinese biologists directly criticized by a Soviet Lysenkoite. In response to his recently published article on variation in the evolutionary process, Zhu was paid a visit by I. E. Glushchenko, who was one of a legion of Soviet "experts" lecturing and consulting in China.[23] Glushchenko, the director of the Soviet Academy of Sciences Institute of Genetics, took offense at the "Morganist" implications in the piece, which he had read in translation. Zhu Xi's published summary of their talk is laced with irony, and he makes the Soviet biologist appear patronizing, preachy, and trite. For example, Glushchenko faulted Zhu for failing to express an awareness of Michurin fundamentals, and warned him that no matter how good Chinese experimental technique might be, conclusions would continue to be lacking unless Chinese studied the dialectical materialism of Engels, Stalin, and Chairman Mao (especially Mao's essay "On Contradiction"). Zhu Xi expressed his gratitude for the personal attention and "friendly criticism" from his Soviet colleague.[24] This is among the earliest examples of an emerging form of dissent—lightly veiled criticism of Soviet arrogance and the CCP's "learn from the Soviets" policy.[25]

Other senior Chinese scientists were proselytized by Soviet Lysenkoites invited to tour China and help with the teaching of Michurin biology. The earliest visitor was V. N. Stoletov, Soviet minister of higher education and chair of the Department of Genetics at Moscow University. He is described in David Joravsky's classic study of Lysenkoism as "one of the original and most virulent Lysenkoites."[26] Stoletov lectured at Beijing Agricultural University in December 1949.[27]

Close on Stoletov's heels came N. I. Nuzhdin, a specialist in genetics and evolutionary theory on the staff of the Genetics Institute of the Soviet Academy of Sciences.[28] He stayed for a lengthy lecture tour of the country and also proselytized key scientists like Tan Jiazhen.[29] Tan, a 1935 Caltech Ph.D. was among China's most eminent representatives of Morganism (evolutionary and population genetics were his specialty). He reports that when Nuzhdin's tour took him south, he visited Zhejiang University, specifically to convince Tan of the merits of Michurin biology and to ask Tan to convert. At this time, Luo Tianyu's campaign was largely confined to the northeast and to agricultural science institutions. Zhejiang was not as yet troubled by Lysenkoism, and Tan was teaching classical genetics without interference. He was therefore quite comfortable telling Nuzhdin politely to go make his pitch elsewhere.[30] When Tan moved to his new position at Shanghai's Fudan University in 1952, Lysenkoism had moved into the south and was there to greet him with a vengeance. Meanwhile, Nuzhdin's lectures were translated into Chinese, anthologized, and distributed widely, making this one of the earliest textbooks on Michurin biology. Many more Lysenkoite visitors would follow him, and many more such textbooks would be published.

Disseminating Michurin Biology

During its first years in China, Michurinism created a strong demand for science technical writers and translators with some biology training. One of the most prolific translators and elegant writers working for Luo Tianyu was Mi Jingjiu, whose career from 1950 to 1956 is instructive. He was an interpreter for visiting Russian biology experts, a translator of Russian language texts, and a publicist of Michurin biology through publications and public lectures.[31]

In 1950, Mi Jingjiu was a twenty-five-year-old graduate student in plant breeding and genetics at Beijing Agricultural University. Up to that time, he had received a first rate education in biology, including graduate training from Li Jingzhun and Tang Peisong. He decided to drop out of the graduate program because the advent of Michurin biology in China seemed to foreclose a career in the areas of his training. On the other hand, he saw immediate opportunities to use his knowledge of Russian in combination with his knowledge of Chinese biological science terminology. Mi felt compelled to join the Lysenkoites because of the pressures being applied on all students and faculty at the university.

Publication outlets were needed for the flood of literature that followed the relentless translations and Michurin propaganda literature promoted by Luo Tianyu and his associates. In contrast to Mi Jingjiu, Huang Zongzhen[32] influenced Michurin biology in the early 1950s through his position as an editor at Science Press (*Kexue chuban she*). He joined the press when it was taking over the publications of the Chinese Academy of Sciences and becoming the central clearinghouse for most of the country's science periodical literature.[33] Like Mi, Huang was trained in plant physiology but he managed to finish a degree and win an appointment to the CAS Institute of Experimental Biology. In 1949, Huang became a believer in Michurin biology and joined the CCP. The Party chose him for the Science Press because he was a Michurinist. He was assigned to the editorial staff of *Biology* (*Shengwuxue tongbao*) and *Botany* (*Zhiwuxue bao*), serious CAS journals with a large audience among scientists and lay readers. These publications were distributed nationally and were consulted for institutional and educational information as well as for the latest in research news.

Huang had the authority himself to determine what was published in these journals, and he determined that a steady stream of Michurinist articles appear and that no "Morganist" material be published, especially from the United States. As soon as this policy was implemented, he began to be lobbied, ever so discreetly, by some of his former professors and others who asked him not to promote the expansion of Michurin biology. Huang was forced to concede that they sometimes correctly pointed out the "low level" of Michurinist scholarship; but he would not relent and, like Mi Jingjiu, continued to play an active role in the promotion of Michurin biology throughout the 1950s.

Michurin Biology Agitprop

The prolific work of Lysenkoites like Mi and Huang was directed at the natural science community, higher education, and Party cadre. Even though the practice of biological science in China was soon swamped by the literature they produced, Luo Tianyu and his associates branched out further, bringing their promotion of Michurin biology into two, linked, Party-designed campaigns: one to sell the PRC's increasingly more intimate relationship with the Soviets, and another to bring science to the people. Ad infinitum, something like the following mantra acted as the rationale for carrying out these campaigns in dozens of magazines, periodicals, newspapers, pamphlets, and elementary school textbooks: Science is good because it is necessary for accomplishing what China needs to become prosperous and powerful; the Soviet Union is the world's leader in science and will help China become scientific by learning from the Soviet Union. Luo Tianyu's group saw to it that these publications were fed with a steady stream of material that addressed the superiority of Soviet science using illustrations from Lysenkoist lore.

One can see the Lysenkoites taking full advantage of the two national campaigns in children's magazines like *Science for the People* (*Kexue dazhong*) and *Popular Science Monthly* (*Kexue huabao*) and, for barely literate farmers, in *People's Agriculture* (*Dazhong nongye*). With simple texts and attractive illustrations and photos, science and agriculture were introduced with examples from the Soviet Union and from the experience of Chinese farmers using Michurin biology. The underlying messages were clear: science must displace mass superstition and ignorance, the people must be able to use science to reach the CCP's ambitious goals for economic construction; and Michurin biology could increase agricultural production on the cheap, with virtually no investment of the precious capital needed for forthcoming industrial development in China. The promotion of Michurin biology seldom even mentioned the western biology and agricultural science it was fighting to displace. In passing, it did so in literature illustrating the fabulous results of its "easy to understand, easy to use" cultivation techniques. On these occasions, it made the point that Michurinism worked in practice while the other biology was bogged down in useless, esoteric theory.[34]

Luo Tianyu and his colleagues were also responsible for a small but powerfully confrontational body of literature whose purposes clearly were to embarrass China's geneticists and their colleagues, put them on the defensive, and undermine any support they might have within the CAS or the Party. In this literature, the "fact" that the geneticists were bourgeois and for the most part educated in the United States led to the conclusion that they were therefore disloyal to the Chinese Communist revolution and should be treated as counterrevolutionaries. Anti-American propaganda during the Korean War must surely have contributed to this invective. And, more broadly, the campaign to remold intellectuals was explicitly aimed at destroying their pro-American views. Vituperation expanded to accuse the classical geneticists, because of their belief in the "immutable gene," of creating the belief in a hierarchy of races with immutable human qualities. American genetics was found guilty by association with the very worst of the world's racism. Morgan's laboratory and gene theory are somehow related to fascist racism, and to American anti-black racism, slavery, and anti-miscegenation laws. For good measure, the "Mendel genetics community" of America is accused of sympathy with Hitler. By extension then, all geneticists were fascists, racists, and enemies of the working class because geneticists were directly or indirectly responsible for the development and criminal application of eugenics.[35]

Attacking Luo Tianyu, Defending Michurin Biology

By 1952, Luo's nationwide media campaigns for Michurin biology were apparently quite successful. Whatever credit with the CCP this may have brought him, however, was eventually erased by his inflammatory verbal attacks on the geneticists, as well as his heavy-handed treatment of their professional careers. In late 1951, the CCP began scrutinizing Luo's embrace of Michurin biology and arrived at the conclusions that not only cost Luo his job, but also required him to be subjected to excoriating criticism and "thought reform" before a national audience.

Complaints about Luo's tough management style were being lodged with the CCP from early 1950, after he had bullied Li Jingzhun out of the university and out of China. This made for very bad press at a time when the CCP was trying to recruit scientists into the Party and encourage the return of Chinese scientists still overseas.[36] Prominent biologists soon began using their personal connections with the CCP to lobby against Lysenkoism in general and Luo Tianyu in particular.[37]

One account of Luo's loss of party confidence claims that mounting criticism forced him to defend himself in a letter to Liu Shaoqi in the summer of 1950. That letter was forwarded to Chairman Mao, who was so concerned with Luo's bad management and flawed thinking that he called for a thorough investigation and appropriate action. By the end of the year, a Party Central Committee investigation concluded that Luo must vacate his administrative post by March 1952.[38]

Firing Luo Tianyu, however, did not end the Party's problems with anti-Lysenkoist lobbying. For example, Tan Jiazhen spoke out against the spread of Michurin biology in May of 1952, at a conference on reform of higher education, sponsored by the Ministry of Education and the Ministry of Agriculture. The former ministry displayed some support for Tan, while the latter continued its support for Lysenkoism.[39]

By this time, the CCP concluded that the conflict between Michurin biology and "Mendel-Morgan" genetics had to be formally settled, under Party auspices, once and for all. This was the year before China's First Five-Year Plan was to be launched and the conflict was a potential source of trouble in a number of areas. First, the Party continued to campaign for membership from the scientific community and to recruit the support of that community for the plan. Additionally, since the plan was dependent on a massive amount of Soviet aid and expertise, the CCP could not permit the further expansion of anti-Soviet sentiment that the imposition of Michurin biology had produced.

Importantly, the CCP also wanted to resolve the conflict within the biological sciences because the Party had convinced itself that Michurin biology did work and that it could increase agricultural production significantly. This was vital because Soviet aid for economic development was concentrated in heavy and arms industries, not agriculture. This impelled China's anticipated Five-Year Plan to follow a Stalinist model that accordingly concentrated development on the urban, heavy industrial sector and expected to pay for this development largely out of "surplus" agricultural production.

The Party thought it best to resolve the conflict in biology through well practiced techniques. It began by scapegoating Luo Tianyu. Making a spectacle of his "errors" while giving Michurin biology the imprimatur of party policy, the CCP made itself look decisive, in control, and not at all responsible for the conflict. The Central Committee worked all this out first through a "criticism meeting of Luo Tianyu's many mistakes" in April 1952; and then in a "Symposium on Work within the Biological Sciences" held from April to June of 1952. The detailed conclusions reached by these two meetings monopolized the front page of *People's Daily*, on 29 June 1952.[40]

The Case against Luo Tianyu

High on the *People's Daily* list of Luo Tianyu's transgressions was "sectarianism," which refers to cadre who use their Party status to create factions or to create divisiveness between the Party and non-Party intellectuals, thereby shutting out the very scientists the Party wished to reform. Luo was found guilty of paying too much attention to "the backward masses," becoming a demagogue, and being incapable of rallying together non-Party scientists.

Further, Luo was found guilty of alienating non-Party scientists by acts of libel. He was admonished that since a good Marxist-Leninist takes different approaches to politics and to science, it is therefore thoroughly inappropriate to generalize and say that all of the "old biology" is idealist, reactionary, in service to the bourgeoisie, or fascist. Instead, "we ought to say that the struggles between Morganism and Michurinism are expressions in science of two world views. If some parts of the old biology are demonstrated to be false science, [however, and] if some conclusions of the old genetics are based on fascist principles . . . then these must be reformed." The Party drew two conclusions from this: First, "if one says that the old genetics is reactionary, it does not follow that the practitioners of the old genetics are ipso facto members of the politically reactionary element." And second, the CCP would oppose any further use of Michurinism as a weapon in a sectarian battle.

The second set of findings against Luo Tianyu addressed his scientific limitations, his "empiricism" and "dogmatism," and his consequent failure to understand Michurin biology. These transgressions are evident, it was charged, in Luo's narrow focus on the minutiae of practical productive experience and his subsequent neglect of systematic agronomic theory and laboratory work. The Party expressed profound concern that "if one separates rational from empirical knowledge, and sets them in opposition—stressing one over the other—then both will be wrong." The Party determined that Luo Tianyu's limited and naïve understanding of science in general made it impossible for him to grasp the essentials of Michurin biology. It followed, then, that he had not been in a position to show the Mendel-Morganists the limitations of the "old biology" and the superiority of the new. A proper presentation of Michurin biology and a proper understanding of its accomplishments would surely make believers out of biologists who had thus far resisted.

Alongside its *People's Daily* criticism of Luo Tianyu, the Party declared, in no uncertain terms, its rejection of Morganism and its complete support of Michurin biology: The "proven accomplishments" of Michurin, Lysenko, and Soviet agriculture put to shame the Morganists and their useless experiments, statistics, and obscure theoretical issues. Only Michurin biology recognizes and has been able to exploit the central truth of the biological world—the unity of organism and environment.

There is no evidence that any Chinese party officials, Morganist scientists, or Lysenkoists had an inkling about the disastrous state of agriculture under Stalin. If they had, it is not too much to imagine that such information would have raised serious doubts at this time about the efficacy of Michurin biology for Soviet agriculture and its potential efficacy for China.

The New Rules of the Game

What then were the new rules for biologists that the Party promulgated on the front page of *People's Daily?* In retrospect, it is clear that party cadre and the scientific community understood that "Mendel-Morganism" was completely banned from research, publication, and education. It was likewise understood that a biologist could not be penalized for refusing to acknowledge the validity of Michurin biology or avoiding it in her/his work. One could be sanctioned, however, for violating the ban or challenging Michurinism; but only the Party itself could judge a violation of the policy and impose sanctions.

The Party was making an offer that the scientific community could not refuse. It acknowledged the legitimacy of professional scientists, and the validity of formal science education, research, and theory. And, crucially, scientists were not to be accused of political crimes because of their scientific beliefs.

In return, the scientific community would accept the imposition of Michurin biology without any further dissent.

In July 1952 Tan Jiazhen, now a prominent figure in the biology community, was required to publish a response to the *People's Daily* policy statements in the form of a "self-criticsm" statement for the widely circulated CAS journal, *Science (Kexue tongbao)*.[41] His statement acknowledges the new policy and, implicitly, agrees to comply with it. Intent on making his true feelings known, however, his "confession" is blatantly ironic: He avows that he no longer believes that Lysenko is a renegade against science," a "crackpot," or a "half-baked scientist who used science to make political capital." He now disavows his "blind worship of the false principles of academic freedom and the separation of science from politics." And finally, he now sees that it was just capitalistic propaganda that made it appear that there was no longer any academic freedom in the Soviet Union, and that geneticists were actually imprisoned there. Now he knows that "no one is jailed in an independent people's nation just because his ideas differ."[42] This irony in Tan's self criticism was followed by a standard Lysenkoist checklist of the faults of Morgan genetics, seasoned with many of the appropriate clichés. Nevertheless, when it came to his personal scientific beliefs, he used the license provided by the new Party guidelines and straightforwardly refused to deny the validity of gene theory, and refused to concede that the environment is the basic force in heredity.

The 1952 policy arrangement governed the biological sciences successfully until 1956. Biologists like Tan Jiazhen, who refused to convert to Michurinism, found themselves doing no research at all and teaching general biology courses in which sensitive topics were simply avoided. If they continued to lobby against the arrangement, they did so with great caution, through their patrons in the higher echelons of the Party's science bureaucracy. Tan Jiazhen, for example, worked through Zhu Kozhen, a Party member, university president, and head of the CAS Planning Bureau. Zhu was "quite unsympathetic to Lysenkoism." And Tan found further support within the Ministry of Education.[43] Tang Peisong was able to use his famous father's connections to convey his dissent and even to overcome the 1950 loss of his position from Beijing Agricultural University. A follower of Tang's father occupied a post "higher up in the CCP hierarchy" and used it to void the charges made against Tang and then to find a permanent position for him in the CAS Institute of Biology.[44]

Lysenkoism and Michurin Biology at Flood Tide, 1952–1955

Under protection of the 1952 Party policy, Michurin biology continued to spread to every corner of China, to every level of education, obliterating what was left of the teaching and practice of the "old biology." It had no trouble recruiting new promoters, including Western-educated converts with training in genetics. Visiting Soviet experts, nevertheless, continued to tour the China circuit and command large, compliant audiences; and translations of Soviet biology texts continued to dominate. The CCP tried to keep Michurin biology in the national spotlight by sponsoring an endless series of ceremonial conferences and celebrations, like the Michurin centenary in 1955. It was also kept in the spotlight as a result of Party-approved public criticism and censorship of scientists accused of deviating from Lysenkoist doctrine, or who appeared to criticize a Chinese or Soviet Michurinist. All of this was dramatically at play in the literature on Darwin and evolutionary theory.

Lysenko's 1948 Lenin Academy speech outlines the approach to Darwin that Michurin biologists followed closely in China;[45] hence, the literature that was nominally written about evolution was not at all interested in illuminating Darwinian evolutionary theory. Instead, its purpose was to rehash the fundamentals of Michurin biology. It is actually about Michurin's self-styled "Creative Darwinism," which claimed to embody the only valid understanding of evolution. Its scant discussion of Darwin is all dedicated to his deviations from Lysenko's doctrine. For example, Michurin biology acknowledges that competition and struggle do occur *between* species, but concludes that Darwin was dead wrong when he suggested that there was struggle within a species or that such struggle could contribute to natural selection and then to evolution. For Michurinists, the environment of course remains the sole force that drives organic change and evolution.

Darwin is also decried for his insistence that evolution occurs gradually, through the accumulation of small changes over very long periods of time. Michurin biology, again, attributes Darwin's confusion here to his failure to grasp fully the fundamental role of environment and the heredity mechanism which reshapes organisms in response to the environment. This error of Darwin is further related to his passive, observational attitude toward nature. Had he thought more like an interventionist and been concerned with practical changes of nature, he might have recognized the potential power of humans to alter nature and even to create new species quickly—as Lysenko claimed he had himself done.

Between 1950 and 1952, the earliest full-scale assaults on Darwinism by Chinese Lysenkoites came from a variety of sources: There was a nationally mandated college-level textbook, poorly cobbled together from Soviet texts.[46] Soon there followed well crafted middle-school texts, lucidly written by Fang Zongxi, who received a 1949 Ph.D. in genetics from J. B. S. Haldane at University College, London. When Fang returned to China, he immediately accepted a position as biology editor (that is, Michurin biology) for People's Education Press [*Renmin jiaoyu chubanshe*]. Soon, he became China's most prolific author/editor of Michurin biology textbooks that were uniformly lucid and sufficiently abreast of doctrine to avoid criticism and calumny.[47]

Pei Wenzhong, the accomplished paleontologist who unearthed "Peking Man" in 1926, made a well publicized conversion to Engels' dialectical materialism in 1950 and then he too joined the ranks of Michurin biology. His initial contribution to it was a secondary school primer that acted as the first Chinese endorsement and outline of Michurin biology's treatment of human evolution.[48] Lysenkoist doctrine considered the speculations of Engels to be the only correct analysis of the subject. In a fifteen page, unfinished essay from 1876, Engels argued that in the course of evolution the characteristic fundamentally differentiating a hominid (ape) from a homo sapien (human) is "labor"; and indeed, he said, eventually "labor creates man." Engels outlines a dialectical process that begins with erect-standing apes freeing their hands to grasp and use "tools" with which to alter and control nature. This behavior in turn stimulates the development of more adept hands, a larger brain, communication through language, and complex social organization—all required for more efficient labor. Engels's provocative argument hinges on the Lamarckian premise that life forms evolve in the direction of their "needs" (like bigger brains needed for more sophisticated forms of labor). Pei Wenzhong publicly expressed his support for Engels' argument.[49]

Not everyone, however, was as compliant and risk averse as Pei and Fang; and the CCP and the CAS were especially sensitive to doctrinal lapses in the area of human evolution and the interpretation of Engels. Between 1952 and 1956, repeatedly and with increasing bellicosity, biologists, anthropologists, and science journalists were pilloried in the press for their criticism of an approved textbook or for raising a question about Engels' theory of human evolution.[50] There were punishments that persisted for over four years, comprising vehement reviews in science periodicals and national newspapers, proscription of the miscreant's books, and—in at least one high-profile case—self-criticism sessions before CAS and university audiences.[51] It seemed not to matter at all that those punished were apparently all devout Marxists and students of dialectical materialism and never Mendel-Morgan geneticists. Nor did it seem to matter that, in fact, Michurin biology and "Creative Evolution" had successfully established their hegemony in China. In any case, it was obviously felt that the limits of controversy must be repeatedly indicated, and any hint of dissent dramatically preempted.

Undermining the Legitimacy of Michurin Biology

In 1955, the centenary of Michurin was celebrated in China with gaudy publications and high-profile speechifying events. Michurin biology's claims to extraordinary accomplishments were enumerated and the success of its campaign was flaunted. Nevertheless, a cloud hung over the hype and self-congratulation. It had been recently revealed in China that, since 1952, Lysenko's ideas on the evolution of species had been under steady attack from a formidable alliance of some of the Soviet Union's most distinguished biologists.[52] In China, knowledge of this was repressed for two years, then in late 1954, the ongoing "speciation debates" finally began to be translated and published.[53] At China's Michurin centenary celebration, a prominent public speech was given to allay concern about the Soviet developments and to assure that they would have no effect on the stability of Michurin biology.[54]

The speciation debates, however, were just the first of a series of seismic events that did profoundly undermine the legitimacy of Lysenkoism in the Soviet Union and the PRC: In late 1955 came public revelations by the biologist, Hans Stubbe, president of the East German Academy of Agricultural Science. At Beijing Agricultural University, he presented the results of his comprehensive research on a central tenet of Lysenko's agricultural science ("vegetative hybridization"): He concluded that there was no scientific foundation for its claims—none whatsoever.[55]

The next event was also of immediate relevance for the application of Lysenkoist doctrine to agriculture. In February 1956, Chairman Khrushchev held an all-Soviet conference on the production of hybrid corn seed. Up to this time, Lysenko, for characteristically obscure reasons, had condemned the use of hybrid techniques in spite of their productive results in North America. Up to 1952 or so, he had successfully banned hybridization; the ban was then quietly lifted in the Soviet Union but it remained in effect in China. The Soviet conference completely abjured Lysenko's position and established a national program for the production of hybrid corn. Chinese Morganists saw this, like the speciation debates, as more Soviet-based leverage against Lysenkoism.[56]

And finally, there was Lysenko's loss of the Academy of Agricultural Sciences presidency. In April, he was forced to step down in response to vociferous opposition.[57] The news of that event was conveyed to the Chinese quickly and in person by N. V. Tsitsin, a Soviet biologist who had been invited to help China plan a twelve-year science development program. He shocked his Chinese colleagues with his sharp and unprecedented public criticism of Lysenko.[58]

Preparations for the Second Five-Year Plan and the Retreat of Lysenkoism

By this time, the genetics question in China had become enmeshed in many of the policy discussions undertaken in connection with the approaching second Five-Year Plan. The process of resolving the genetics question—and potential results of doing so—resonated with other Party-designated problem areas such as the intellectuals, science, and relations with the Soviet Union. The degree to which the genetics question had become freighted with global issues is already evident in Chairman Mao's strong reaction to the critique of Lysenkoism by the East German biologist months before the fall of Lysenko. He instructed Lu Dingyi's Central Propaganda Department to research the question of Lysenkoism and genetics with the aid of the CAS and all other relevant government agencies and persons.[59] Shortly thereafter, Zhou Enlai led the national meeting devoted to "the question of the intellectuals" where he mandated Lu's department to form two committees: one to develop a twelve-year science plan and another to concentrate on finding a means of resolving the genetics question.[60] In turn, Lu appointed Yu Guangyuan, who worked in the department's Science Division, to assist with the twelve-year science plan and to manage the genetics question.[61] Immediately following the January conference on intellectuals, Yu Guangyuan was given the additional responsibility for holding before year's end a large, lengthy, and definitive symposium, hopefully to mark the end of the genetics question.[62] Yu later became vice-president of CASS and an economic reform theorist in the 1980s.

This flurry of Party activity was punctuated with grand policy speeches that suggested, more or less, how the key problem areas, including the genetics question, should be understood and resolved. In Zhou Enlai's keynote speech at the meeting on intellectuals he alluded to the genetics question in his criticism of Party sectarianism and indiscriminate emulation of the Soviet Union.[63] Regarding the latter, he said clearly that China could not indefinitely rely on Soviet experts and that "there had been such defects as undue haste, arbitrary learning, and mechanical application. Some comrades even arbitrarily rejected the achievements of the capitalist countries in science and technique. These defects should henceforth be avoided."[64]

In his April 1956 speech "On the Ten Major Relationships" Mao commented on some of the same themes, especially dependency on the Soviets. He said that "We mustn't copy everything indiscriminately and transplant mechanically. Naturally, we mustn't pick up their shortcomings and weak points." China had adopted weaknesses from the Soviet Union, Mao said, and "while [Chinese] were swelling with pride over what they had picked up [from socialist countries and the Soviets], it was already being discarded in those countries; as a result, [the Chinese] had to do a somersault."[65]

The following month, it was in Lu Dingyi's Double Hundred address that the tribulations brought about by Lysenkoism were most explicit and given their most focused attention. He began by uncoupling the natural sciences from social class, thus rejecting a premise of Lysenkoism. He said

[The natural sciences] have their own laws of development. The only way they tie up with social institutions is that under a bad social system they make rather slow progress, and under a better one they progress fairly rapidly. . . . It is, therefore, wrong to label a particular theory in medicine, biology or any other branch of natural science "feudal," "capitalist," "socialist," "proletarian," or "bourgeois."[66]

Lu concludes from this that it is "therefore wrong, for instance, to say that 'Michurin's theory is socialist,' or that 'Mendel's and Morgan's principles of heredity are capitalist.' We must not believe such stuff." He then connects this kind of error with the questions of Party/scientist and Soviet/Chinese relations: "Some people make this sort of mistake because they are sectarian. Others do it unconsciously by trying to emphasize, but not in the proper way, that one ought to learn from the latest scientific achievements in the Soviet Union."[67] And lastly, he repeats Zhou Enlai's call for better Party-intellectuals relations. While he expresses an understanding that mutual efforts are necessary here, nevertheless he expects the initiative to be taken by the Party. Indeed, he accuses the Party's treatment of scientists and other intellectuals to be corrupted by arrogance, hostility, and a doctrinaire approach to scientific research as well as artistic and literary endeavor. Lu expects to see free and open discussion among intellectuals and between them and the Party- without the recourse to any special administrative measures.

Well before Lu Dingyi's speech was delivered, Party cadre had already been charged to solicit intellectuals to air their concerns, criticisms, and suggestions, but there was resistance on the part of some party leaders to carry this out. For different reasons, there was some reluctance on the part of some intellectuals to go public. Nevertheless, from the beginning of 1956, scientists and literary intellectuals had begun to criticize in personal terms the kinds of issues that Zhou Enlai, Mao, and Lu Dingyi spoke about abstractly.[68]

For example, in the May 1 issue of the *Guangming Daily*, Tan Jiazhen and Liu Xian, both from Fudan University in Shanghai, wrote candidly about their problems. Liu wrote a stunning exposé of his ordeals since the publication of his book on human evolution. Tan, who had been discreetly silent since his 1952 "self-criticism," wrote as chair of his biology department that

> many top class intellectuals are tied down with administrative duties and very few of them are actually doing any research. This is an enormous waste. . . . Here I think it is necessary to repeat: there is a difference between science and politics. A scientist should not separate himself from politics; but sciences themselves—particularly the natural sciences are classless.[69]

Many other general complaints were published at this time about mechanically copying the Soviets, the overwhelming presence of Soviet textbooks, and the proscription of American science and culture.[70] By the end of May, scientists were speaking out directly to the issue of Lysenkoism. For example, a Beijing Agricultural University professor with a doctorate from Cornell wrote of his support for the new openness policy because of his fearful experience with Lysenkoism. In the Beijing *Guangming Daily*, he wrote that those faculty who were critical of Lysenko had not spoken out before for fear of reprisal and being charged with undermining confidence in Soviet science.[71]

In August of 1956, personal testimony for the Hundred Schools policy had spread from the national papers to the science journals. *Science* (the main journal of the CAS) began an extensive series of published forums for which dozens of scientists wrote paragraph- to page-length statements on what was good about the policy and what problems it would help to solve. Among the most common sources of outrage was the Soviet Union's direct or indirect interference with the heretofore commonly accepted scientific techniques for determining facts and laws, and its arbitrary and dogmatic imposition of alleged scientific truths. For this forum, an editor of the Science Press condemned the role that the press was forced to play in Soviet dominance of science in China. He wrote that since its 1950 inception to mid-1956, Science Press had published 330 science monograph titles, but only 11 came from outside of the Communist bloc. He said the press had to smuggle translations of European or American publications into China under the camouflage of phony Russian title pages. He revealed how Science Press was censored and tightly controlled where the Soviet speciation debates were concerned; as a result, the press was permitted to translate nothing that was critical of the Lysenkoites. This editor was convinced that general deference to Soviet science in combination specifically with Lysenkoism was responsible for a chilling effect throughout China's scientific community. His local remedies were to enlarge the editorial independence of Science Press; expand its scope beyond the current "one field, one school" approach; and begin providing China's science community with translations from all schools of Soviet science, as well as from Europe and America.[72]

These cascades of Party policy and public criticism formed a backdrop to the subtle but persistent efforts of Lu Dingyi and Yu Guangyuan to disaggregate the Party's 1952 policy on genetics, abrogate its problematic elements, and then establish a new set of principles that were in keeping with the Double Hundred policy. Lu invested this effort with particular importance because it concerned the first area of science affected by the Double Hundred policy. He felt that, being first, it should be a model for developing and implementing the policy.[73]

In the spring and summer of 1956, Lu and Yu had hammered out their new set of principles in corridors and backrooms (according to Yu) where they talked with and twisted arms of biologists from both camps. Before they completed this work, however, they informed the genetics community that the Party had reached a decision to abrogate the 1952 policy. Lu was so confident about the decision that he encouraged them "to return to their work" in education and research in the early summer of 1956. The Morganists met to consider this welcome development; however, many agreed that it would be a mistake to resume their work without a specific and clearly articulated statement from the highest party level that all of the new principles would become formal Party policy. Lu Dingyi eventually brought back assurances from Zhou Enlai that all of the principles would reliably be in place when the geneticists resumed their work—presumably after the genetics symposium, scheduled for August.[74]

The following are the broad principles they determined to be appropriate:

- Science orthodoxies and monopolies are impermissible: The CCP will not do what the Soviet Communist Party had done when it "created the Lysenko faction and gave it its privileged place." The CCP would not make rulings on scientific controversies (but rather would leave the settlement up to the science community); and the ideas of minorities would be protected.
- Political attacks disguised as philosophical labels must cease.
- Only scientists should decide if and when philosophy (e.g., Dialectical Materialism) is of any aid to science.[75]

Not on this occasion, nor on any other did the Party forthrightly acknowledge that its 1952 policy on Michurin biology was the source of the problems that Lu and Yu were trying to fix; or that the CCP had indeed already done what the CPSU did when it "created the Lysenko faction." Nevertheless, these new principles fundamentally resolved the key problems caused by the 1952 party endorsement of a monopoly for Michurin biology and a ban on Morgan genetics. Before the genetics symposium began, the principles had become formal party policy. Lysenkoites came to the symposium knowing that their privileged position was gone and their hegemony was over; Morganists came with the knowledge that they could resume their teaching and research according to their own lights, and that doing so could no longer be grounds for libelous attack and Party repression.

The Genetics Symposium[76]

Even though Lu Dingyi's announcement of these principles and his apparent resolution of the genetics question preceded the August 1956 Genetics Symposium, the event was no mere ritual. It turned out to be a tense, emotional two week confrontation between representatives of what was now called "the two schools" of genetics—Morganism and Michurinism. Each school presented state of the science summaries of its various fields; then open discussion followed, usually eventuating in excoriating criticism of Michurin biology by the Morganists. Detailed proceedings show the Morganist presentations brimming with belatedly acquired information about recent developments in the West's genetics revolution, like the nature and role of DNA and RNA revealed by molecular biology, bio-chemistry, and bio-physics. Morganist speakers lamented that Chinese scientists had been arbitrarily denied any access to knowledge about these developments which validated the premises of "Morganism" but left China's biology cut off from the mainstream.

Michurinist presentations were straightforward rehashes of the very same material that had filled their journals over the previous five years. In open discussion, Michurinists were obviously unaccustomed to challenges and the need to explain and justify their claims. They were quickly put on the defensive and remained so throughout the symposium. For example, they spoke with uncharacteristic civility about the possibility of a synthesis between the two schools (a casual notion earlier suggested by Lu Dingyi).[77] They implored the Morganists not to "lump together Academician Lysenko and Michurin"; nor should Lysenko's mistakes "be taken as the mistakes of the entire Michurin school."[78] And at the nadir of their defense, the Michurinists sought to justify themselves as a legitimate "school" by arguing that Morganists misunderstood Michurinism only because of a "difference of scientific language." Once each school learned the other's language, they argued, it would come to acknowledge the other's legitimacy and appreciate its contributions.[79]

Alternating between expressions of outrage, ridicule, and bewilderment, the Morganists unequivocally rejected the notion that Michurinism had anything to offer for a "synthesis." And it is precisely the point, they responded, that natural science is a *universal* language—the same for all scientists in the West, the Soviet Union, and in China.

Morganists were exhilarated and emboldened by the restitution of their legitimacy and by Lu Dingyi's admonition to engage freely in "the clash of ideas."[80] Michurinists, unfamiliar with a level playing field, were cowed. Throughout the onslaught from the Morganists they remained decorous, and obsequiously expressed their unswerving allegiance to the principles of the Hundred Schools policy.

Conclusion: "Somersaults"

Where to begin explaining the CCP's enablement (and disablement) of Lysenkoism in China? Certainly the CCP's disconnect from the science community is an important place to start. Lacking a significant number of scientists in its membership, the Party was seriously challenged when it came time to evaluate a research proposal, let alone an entire field like plant biology. Surely an important reason for the Party's half-hearted recruitment of scientists (in spite of its expressed desire to do so) was its inability to come to terms with the scientific community's need for independent authority over its own work. Lu Dingyi's "principles" are especially striking where they leave the settlement of scientific controversies up to scientists. (This is soon undermined, however, during the Great Leap Forward and then again in the Cultural Revolution.) I know of no evidence that the CCP consulted with any of China's accomplished plant biologists before giving carte blanche to Lysenkoism. The latter's authority was seen to derive from the CPSU and the CCP. Therefore, when any aspect of Michurin Biology was challenged, the authority of the Party was challenged. And Lysenkoism's unrelenting insistence on the class-based authority of science was welcomed by the CCP precisely because it appeared to provide dialectical-materialist muscle to the argument for Party control of science and scientists.

The CCP was thus quite vulnerable to Lysenkoism's artful fraud. The PRC's development plans were based on a wishful fantasy of agricultural productivity guaranteed by an unexamined, untested Michurin Biology. It is said that an experienced confidence man does not force himself on a victim, but rather arranges for the victim, who is motivated by the prospect of easy gain, to invite him to carry out his fraud. The CCP, looking for a cheap, quick fix for development was the perfect mark for Lysenkoism's agriculture growth scam.

Of course, for the CCP, Lysenkoism's initial claim to legitimacy was its origin and (presumably successful) practice in the USSR. Scientific validity was not an issue. Independent testing was unnecessary (and perhaps a slight to Soviet generosity). In retrospect, one can see how the CCP, facing immense problems with agriculture, should by all means have given consideration to Michurin Biology; but surely the Party should have felt obliged routinely to examine, test, and evaluate its techniques and theories. In any case, nothing forced the CCP to make its naïve, irresponsible surrender to Lysenkoist flim flam. Throughout the 1950s, Chinese scientists condemned the PRC's obsequious and uncritical adoption of many aspects of Soviet science and culture. They argued that China had freed itself from Western imperialism only to subject itself to Soviet imperialism; and that Lysenkoism was just "colonial science." Conversely, at the August 1956 genetics symposium, there was apparently unanimous agreement that the CCP had disassociated itself from Lysenkoism only because the USSR had done so first; that the CCP was still aping the CPSU and still unwilling to trust the advice of its own science community.[81]

While the latter cynicism is understandable, a more accurate interpretation would probably be that the changing position of Lysenkoism in the Soviet Union enabled spokespersons for the Chinese science community to get a hearing in higher echelons of the Party. Moreover, the CCP policy toward genetics—in retrospect at least—clearly was part of a much more comprehensive evaluation of Chinese-Soviet relations, an ongoing evaluation that was increasingly more concerned about China's dependence, and increasingly disappointed with the benefits of the relationship. Party leaders, before the genetics symposium, did repeatedly question and criticize borrowing uncritically from the USSR.

Ultimately, imitation of the USSR is an incomplete explanation of the initiation and termination of the CCP's support of Lysenkoism. In the light of the CCP's future relationships with the science community, it becomes apparent that some of the most egregious attitudes of Lysenkoism toward science and scientists were renewed and implemented when the CCP was in an anti-Soviet mood, and when Lysenkoism was fading from significance or altogether marginalized in China. That is to say, these were occasions when the CCP's science policy could not be explained as slavish imitation of the Soviet Union: for example, the harsh treatment of science during the Great Leap Forward (1958–1959) and the Cultural Revolution (1966–1976). Both of these campaigns reiterated some of Lysenkoism's most provocative principles, such as the class nature of science, the invalidity of "ivory-tower" science education and research, and the sovereignty of "people's science."

Yet neither of these campaigns provided Lysenkoists any opportunity to enhance their declining status or make special gains. In the case of the Great Leap, the Lysenkoists believed that they shared an ideological position with the campaign and hence an advantage over the Morganists, whom they therefore tried to intimidate back into passivity and silence.[82] This came to naught, however, because the Great Leap embodied an argument that China's science and technology could neither be entrusted to forces outside China, like the USSR, nor to forces inside China, like science and technical experts. Science could only be entrusted to the People, guided by the Party. Professional, specialized scientists and their institutions, it was argued, were dangerously inclined to self aggrandizement, at the expense of the nation and the people. And further, the Great Leap promoted the idea that all of the inventiveness and creativity required for national welfare derives from the masses. Unfortunately for the Lysenkoists, their own efforts had made themselves, in important ways, indistinguishable from all the other scientists: they were solidly based in professional research and teaching institutions, and their theories and methods had to be taught to the masses rather than being derived from them. And finally, there was no way of disguising Lysenkoism's Soviet ties at a time when the Soviets were rapidly losing their appeal to the CCP.[83]

For similar reasons, during the Cultural Revolution the Lysenkoists were in no better a situation. Virtually the entire teaching and research community was shut down on the grounds that it harbored and practiced corrupt bourgeois (or revisionist) values.[84] Tan Jiazhen was fond of saying that "there was only one good thing about the Cultural Revolution: the Lysenkoists finally got a taste of their own medicine."[85]

The immediate legacies of Lysenkoism in China are plain to see. In addition to the fear and anguish it engendered, there were opportunity costs to science that the PRC could ill afford. For nearly six years, the science community was almost completely cut off from the revolutionary developments within the bio-sciences, including the successful exploration of the structure and functions of genes. Chasing after and rebuilding this crucial field was a monumental task. And during these same years, because the practice of the bio-sciences was so restricted, the potential improvement of some vital crops was precluded. For example, how much more corn might have been produced during this period if just the old, well tested use of hybrid techniques had been allowed?[86]

Post-1956, the fate of Lysenkoism and Michurin biology in China was a rapid, thorough, and quiet retreat. By the early 1960s, they had been marginalized. No longer a subject of controversy, they soon disappeared from public discourse. Lysenkoist influence was reduced from the national scale to only two significant institutions: the Beijing Agricultural University, and the new CAS Genetics Institute. From early 1961, as the Double Hundred policies were revived, the entire bio-sciences community (excluding Michurin biologists) began a multi-year effort to reeducate China about genetics. With complete access to all print media, step by step, Lysenkoist misinformation was corrected with dignity, eloquence, and an ocean of scientific data. Then, up-to-date information was provided respectively for school textbooks, for lay readers, and for scientists. Biologists contributing to this effort no longer engaged in polemics with or about Lysenkoism; typically it was not mentioned at all. Under the leadership of Tan Jiazhen, Fudan University's new Genetics Research Institute took the responsibility of coordinating national efforts to revive China's genetics research community and restore its relations with international science. In the short run, these efforts were quite effective; but it was only possible to pursue their fulfillment after the Cultural Revolution.[87]

Notes

This essay is a condensation of chapters four and five in my *Biology and Revolution in Twentieth Century China* (Lanham, MD: Rowman & Littlefield, 2003).

1. See Mao's "On the Ten Major Relationships," 25 April 1956, in *Selected Works of Mao Zedong*, vol. 5 (Beijing: Foreign Languages Press, 1977), 303.

2. This sketch of Lysenkoism is based on T. D. Lysenko's "The Situation in Biological Sciences," his 31 July 1948, opening speech to the Lenin Academy of Agricultural Sciences, in *The Situation in Biological Science: Proceedings of the Lenin Academy of Agricultural Sciences of the USSR* (Moscow: Foreign Languages Publishing House, 1949), 11–50. It also draws on major standard analyses: David Joravsky, *The Lysenko Affair* (Cambridge: Harvard University Press, 1970), 202–9. Loren R. Graham, *Science and Philosophy in the Soviet Union* (New York: Knopf, 1971), 219–37.

3. For the historical context of the transformist tradition, see Douglas R. Weiner, "The Roots of 'Michurinism': Transformist Biology and Acclimatization as Currents in the Russian Life Sciences," *Annals of Science* 41 (1985), 243–60.

4. See Lysenko, "The Situation in Biological Sciences," 41; and Graham's discussion in *Science and Philosophy*, 223.

5. The term "genetics" itself was not outlawed. Chinese Lysenkoites attempted to co-opt the term and distinguished between "socialist" Michurin genetics and "bourgeois" Mendel-Morgan genetics. This persisted even after Lysenkoism lost its CCP-mandated monopoly in the late 1950s, for example, when a number of Lynsenkoite research centers were consolidated into the CAS Institute of Genetics, publisher of the journal *Genetics*. These were among the last bastions of Lysenkoism in China. The term "genetics" was reclaimed by the latter-day practitioners of Mendel-Morgan biology in the 1960s, before the Cultural Revolution. Its center of gravity was Tan Jiazhen's Genetics Institute at Fudan University.

6. Loren R. Graham, *Science and Philosophy*, 209. And see the chilling description of Prezent's career and ideas in Douglas R. Weiner, *Models of Nature: Ecology, Conservation, and Cultural Revolution in Soviet Russia* (Pittsburgh: University of Pittsburgh Press, 1988) and Weiner's *Little Corner of Freedom: Russian Nature Protection from Stalin to Gorbachev* (Berkeley: University of California Press, 1999).

7. For Stalin's editing, see Kirill O. Rossianov, "Stalin As Lysenko's Editor: Reshaping Political Discourse in Soviet Science," *Russian History*, no. 1 (1994), 49–63.

8. See Laurence A. Schneider, *Biology and Revolution in Twentieth Century China*, 201, 210n69.

9. See discussion below in this essay.

10. Agricultural education and research network: See Chen Fengtong, *Ziran kexueh* [Natural science], no. 1 (October 1951), 388–89. Li Jingzhun (C.C. Li) interview University of Pittsburgh, 9–10 January 1985.

11. For Luo Tianyu, see my *Biology and Revolution*, 104–8.

12. Li Jingzhun interviews, January 1985. Tang Peisong, interview, Beijing, 19 May 1986. Wu Zhongxian interview, Beijing, 31 May 1986.

13. Interviews with Li Jingzhun; Tang Peisong; Wu Zhongxian.

14. All of these zealots were trained in Chinese or Japanese agriculture schools; only a few had graduate training; none studied in Europe or North America. All were CCP members: some were recent recruits, some Yan'an veterans like Luo. I have found no information about when and how they—or Luo—were introduced to Michurin biology. See *Biology and Revolution* 124, 136n21.

15. For example, see the post-1949 progress reports by Zu Deming, "Liangnian lai Huabei nongyeh kexue di jinchan" [The advance of agricultural science in north china during the past two years], *Ziran kexue yuekan* [Natural science monthly], no. 6 (November 1951), 483–85. Liang Zhenglan, "Michulin xueshuo zai Zhongguo di tuiguang" [Popularization of Michurin theory in China], *Kexue dazhong* [Science for the masses], no. 12 (1954), 445–46. Zu and Liang inherited Luo Tianyu's leadership in 1952.

16. See description of the society's inauguration, *Kexue tongbao* [Science] (hereafter as KXTB), no. 1 (May 1950), 32.

17. *Michulin xuehui huikan*, no. 3 (15 September 1951), 106–107. See note 18 for this journal. This membership information suggests approximately five thousand members. There is no way to corroborate this. Whenever and wherever possible, the society advertised its existence and growth: see announcements of a new Shanghai branch with 100 members, in *Jiefang ribao* [Liberation daily] reprinted in KXTB, no. 3 (1950), 194; and Zhejiang University branch of more than 300 members in *Zhejiang ribao* [Zhejiang daily], reprinted in KXTB, no. 5 (1950), 343.

18. The *Michulin xuehui huikan* was probably initiated at the beginning of 1951. I have only found issue no. 3 (15 September 1951), in the Hoover Institution Chinese collection. This 108-page issue was published in Beijing by the CAS Institute of Genetics and Plant Cultivation. Luo Tianyu is prominently listed as editor and as president of the society.

19. This Society was founded in 1946 according to the 1950 conference program reported in KXTB, no. 5 (1950), 339–41.

20. "Michulin xueshuo yu Morgan xueshuo. Zuotanhui jilu" [Michurin theory and Morgan theory. Symposium record], *Kexue* [Science], no. 3 (1950), 69–78.

21. Zhu Xi (Yu-wen), 1899–1962. He held a 1932 doctorate from Montpellier University. See *Zhongguo dangdai kexuejia zhuan* [Biographies of contemporary Chinese scientists] (Beijing, 1983), 76–90.

22. See Zhu Xi's trip report in KXTB, no. 10 (1953): 23–30, and comments on the trip in *Guangming ribao*, 25 May 1956.

23. David Joravsky describes Glushchenko as the chief international salesman for Lysenkoism. His specialty was "vegetative hybridization," that is, grafting. See *The Lysenko Affair*, 224–26.

24. Zhu Xi, "Ji yu Glushchenko jiaoshou di tanhua" [Record of a talk with professor Glushchenko], KXTB, no. 1 (1953), 80–81.

25. Corroboration of Zhu Xi's attitude and tactic comes in 1956, when he directly criticizes CCP "indiscriminate use of Soviet science" and advises the Chinese and the Soviets to use Anglo-American science. See *Guangming ribao*, 25 May 1956.

26. David Joravsky, *The Lysenko Affair*, 159.

27. See report on practical results of Michurin biology in its first year, KXTB, no. 11 (1951), 195–97.

28. David Joravsky, *The Lysenko Affair*, 221n, and passim.

29. Nuzhdin lecture tour: see Li Jige, KXTB, no. 3 (1951), 145–49; KXTB, no. 11 (1951), 195–97; and survey article dated 31 December 1955, in *Beijing nongyedaxue xuebao* [Journal of Beijing Agricultural University], no. 1 (1956).

30. Tan Jiazhen, interview, Fudan University, Shanghai, 16 August 1984. But compare Tan's 1952 "self-criticism" wherein he says that during his visit with Nuzhdin, they talked and argued; and the Soviet biologist helped him to greater understanding not by pitching Michurin biology, but by revealing the faults of the old genetics. See "Pipan wo dui Michulin shengwu kexue di zuowu kanfa" [Criticizing my mistaken attitude about Michurin biology], KXTB, no. 8 (1952), 562–63.

31. Biographical information comes from Mi Jingjiu, interview, Beijing, 12 June 1986.

32. Biographical sketch of Huang is principally based on Huang Zongzhen, interview, Beijing, 26 May 1986. (Co-conducted with Dr. William Haas.)

33. For sketches of its aggressive expansion and general history, see *Kexue chubanshe sanshi nian* [Thirty years of the science press] (Beijing: Kexue chuanshe, 1984).

34. For example: see KXTB, no. 5 (1950): 344. KXTB, no. 6 (1951): 631–34; and Shen Yencheng, ed., *Michulin xueshuo zai chumu jie yingyong* [Application of Michurin theory in livestock] (Nanjing: n.p., 1951).

35. For example: see Chu Qi, *Yichuanxue di Michulin luxian* [The Michurin line on genetics] (Shanghai, May 1950; 4th ed., September 1952; 4 printing, January 1954); and anthology of translated Soviet texts *Michulin xueshuo jieshao* [Introduction to Michurin theory], edited by Northeast Agricultural Science Research Institute (Beijing, April 1950).

36. Tan Jiazhen; Tang Peisong interviews. Both Tan and Tang agree that the Li Jingzhun affair had strong repercussions on Luo's power. This evaluation is supported by Li Peishan et al., eds., *Baijia zhengming—fazhan kexue de biyou zhilu: 1956 Qingdao yichuanxue zuotanhui jishi* [Let a hundred schools contend, develop the road which science must follow: proceedings of the Qingdao genetics symposium] (Beijing: Commercial Press, 1985), 6–7.

37. Tan Jiazhen; Tang Peisong, interviews.

38. Jiang Shihe, "'Michulin xueshuo' zai Zhongguo 1949–1956: Sulian di yingxiang" [Michurinism in China: Soviet influence], *Ziran bianzhengfa tongxun* [Dialectics of nature] (hereafter as ZBT), no. 1 (1990), 20.

39. Tan Jiazhen, interview; also see, Tan Jiazhen, "Pipan wo dui Michulin."

40. Organizations participating in the symposium were Zhu Kezhen's CAS Planning Bureau, and analogous bureaus in education-and-culture, and in public health. The criticism meeting was reported by Liang Xi, "Wo duiyu Luo Tianyu tongzhi suo fancuowu di ganxiang" [My impressions of the errors of luo]; and the symposium was reported in "Wei jianchi shengwu kexue di Michulin fangxiang er douzheng" [Carry on the struggle in biology for the Michurin line]. Both in *Renmin ribao*, 29 June 1952, 1. This summary is drawn from both pieces.

41. Tan Jiazhen, "Pipan wo dui Michulin."

42. Tan Jiazhen, "Pipan wo dui Michulin."

43. Tan Jiazhen interview. And see *Biology and Revolution*, 142.

44. Tang's father, Tang Hualong (1874–1918) had a long and distinguished political career which included prominence in anti-Manchu revolutionary politics before 1911 and parliamentary politics thereafter. In his interview with me, Tang Peisong chose not to divulge the name of his father's follower. *Biology and Revolution*, 124, 136n20.

45. All of the titles discussed in this section follow this format very closely. The format also reflects the lectures of Mi Jingjiu's Soviet instructor, A. V. Dubrovina. See her *Darwin zhuyi* [Darwinism], ed., trans. Mi Jingjiu (Shanghai: CAS, 1953).

46. *Darwin zhuyi jiben yuanli* [Basic principles of Darwinism], ed. CAS Genetics and Seed Selection Research Bureau and Beijing Agricultural University (Shanghai: Commercial Press, 1952; 2d ed. 1953; 3d ed. 1954).

47. For example, Fang's 1952 textbook: *Darwin zhuyi jichu* [Foundations of darwinism], based on a 1942 Soviet textbook translated by the PRC's Ministry of Education under the title of *Darwin zhuyi jichu guoben*; and see *Zhongguo xiandai shengwuxue jiachuan* [Biographies of contemporary Chinese biologists], ed., Tan Jiazhen (Changsha: Hunan Science and Technology Press, 1986), vol. 1, 453–60.

48. Pei Wenzhong, *Ziran fazhan jianshi* [The evolution of life] (Beijing, 1950). "Afterword" dated December 1949.

49. See Frederick Engels "The Part Played by Labor in the Transition from Ape to Man," in *Dialectics of Nature* (Moscow: Progress Press, 1972), 170–83. And Pei, *Ziran fazhan*, preface.

50. For example, the case of Zhang Congping who criticized the CAS Darwinism textbook: His review essay was in *Shiwuxue tongbao* [Zoology], no. 3 (1953). For blistering criticism of Zhang, see multiple authors in *Shiwuxue tongbao*, no. 10 (1953), 390–97; and Song Zhenneng, KXTB, no. 1 (1954) 72–75; Huang Zuojieh, "Zai ping Zhang Congping 'Darwin xueshuo jichu,'" *Yichuanxue jikan* [Genetics quarterly], no. 1 (1956), 92.

51. For example, the case of Liu Xian, who tried too hard to make sense of Engels. Criticism begins in *Renmin ribao*, 17 June 1951. For overview of his case and sample criticisms, see KXTB, no. 4 (1955), 74–81, and no. 11 (1955), 101–102. For the CAS symposium on his errors, see *Shiwuxue tongbao*, no. 11 (1955), 5. Also see Liu's exposé of his ordeal, discussed in Roderick MacFarquhar, *The Hundred Flowers* (New York: Columbia University Press, 1960), 90–91.

52. For Soviet speciation debates, see Loren R. Graham, *Science and Philosophy*, 239–41.

53. The CAS translation series was *Sulian Guanyu wuzhong yu wuzhong xingcheng wenti di taolun* [Soviet debate on species and their origin] (Beijing: Science Press), vol. 1 (October 1954) to vol. 21 (June 1957). And see KXTB, n. 12 (1954), 26–37 on initiating periodical discussion.

54. See Tong Dizhou, 28 October 1955, centenary speech, KXTB, no. 11 (1955), 21–23. And Mi Jingjiu, "Guanyu wuzhong ji wuzhong xingcheng wenti di taolun" [On the speciation debates], *Yichuanxue jikan*, no. 1 (1956), 54–70.

55. For Stubbe's visit to Beijing Agricultural University, see Wu Zhongxian, interview. For Stubbe's work, see L. I. Blacher, *The Problem of the Inheritance of Acquired Characters*, ed., trans. F. B. Churchill (Washington, DC: Smithsonian Institution and National Science Foundation, 1982), 237–38.

56. Hybrid corn: See Joravsky, *Lysenko Affair*, Chapter 9; and Graham, *Science and Philosophy*, 243. And see Chinese evaluation in Laurence Schneider, ed., *Lysenkoism in China: Proceedings of the 1956 Qingdao Genetics Symposium*, trans. Laurence Schneider and Qin Shihzhen (Armonk, NY: M. E. Sharpe, 1986), 16.

57. See description in Graham, *Science and Philosophy*, 240–41.

58. Tsitsin; see Joravsky, *Lysenko Affair*, 81–83, 160, 400. Also see Blacher, *Problem of the Inheritance of Acquired Characters*, 237. For the Chinese response: see Li Peishan, et al., "The Qingdao Conference of 1956 on Genetics," in Fan Dainian and Robert S. Cohen, eds, *Chinese Studies in the History and Philosophy of Science and Technology*, (London: Kulwer, 1996), 45–46; and Schneider, *Lysenkoism in China*, passim.

59. Gong Yuzhi, "Fazhan kexueh di biyu zhi lu" [Develop the necessary road for science], *Guangming ribao*, 28 December 1983, 2.

60. The most extensive discussion of the twelve-year science plan is in Xu Liang-ying and Fan Dainian, *Science and Socialist Construction* (Armonk, NY: M. E. Sharpe, 1982). This is a translation of *Kexue he woguo shehuizhuyi jianshe* (Beijing: Renmin, 1957). The discussion also has much to say about the genetics question and the Double Hundred policy. And also see Gong Yuzhi, "Fazhan kexue."

61. Yu Guangyuan (b. 1915) was educated at Qinghua University during the 1930s, and received a strong foundation in social theory as well as mathematics and the philosophy of science. After 1949, he was a prolific contributor to *Xuexi* [Study] the major party intellectual journal that later was called *Hongqi* [Red flag]. He was a sophisticated student of dialectical materialism and a translator of Engels' *Dialectics of Nature*. He also wrote knowledgeably on probability theory and statistics in natural science research, and was discreetly critical of Lysenko's attitude toward these subjects.

62. Genetics symposium: See Gong Yuzhi, "Fazhan kexueh;" and also see Tong Dizhou, opening speech at Qingdao Genetics Symposium, August 1956, in Schneider, *Lysenkoism in China*, 1.

63. Zhou Enlai, "On the Question of the Intellectuals," 14 January 1956, in *Communist China, 1955–1959: Policy Documents with Analysis*, ed., trans. R. R. Bowie and John K. Fairbank (Cambridge: Harvard University Press, 1962), 129.

64. Zhou Enlai, 136–38.

65. "On the Ten Major Relationships," 25 April 1956, in *Selected Works of Mao Zedong*, vol. 5 (Beijing: Foreign Languages Press, 1977), 303.

66. Lu Dingyi, *Let a Hundred Flowers Blossom, Let a Hundred Schools of Thought Contend* (Beijing: Foreign Languages Press, 1958). I am following the annotated presentation in Bowie and Fairbank, *Communist China*, 153, 156–57.

67. Bowie and Fairbank, *Communist China*, 157.

68. For the early outpouring of criticism by intellectuals, see Roderick MacFarquhar, *The Origins of the Cultural Revolution* (New York: Columbia University Press, 1974-1997), vol. 1, 33–34.

69. Tan, cited in Roderick MacFarquhar, *The Hundred Flowers Campaign and the Chinese Intellectuals* (New York: Columbia University Press, 1960), 91, and for similar examples, 112.

70. Roderick MacFarquhar, *The Hundred Flowers*, 80, 91, 110–11, 128.

71. See Professor Lin Chuanguang, Vegetation Protection Department, Beijing Agricultural University, *Guangming ribao*, 25 May 1956.

72. Zhao Zhongzhi, "Kexue chuban gongzuo yu 'Baijia zhengming'" [The work of science press and the hundred schools), KXTB, no. 11 (1956): 48–50.

73. Undated letter from Lu Dingyi to Yu Guangyuan, cited in Yu Guangyuan, "Zai 1956 Qingdao Yichuanxue zuotanhui shang di jianghua" [Unofficial materials on the Qingdao genetics symposium], ZBT, no. 5 (1960), 13. Yu Guangyuan, interview, Beijing, 20 May 1986 (co-conducted with Dr. William Haas).

74. Wu Zhongxian, interview.

75. Yu Guangyuan, "Zai 1956 Qingdao Yichuanxue zuotan hui," 5–13.

76. The symposium was held in Qingdao, August 10–25, 1956. Its proceedings were originally published as *Yichuanxue zuotanhui jilu* [CAS and a Ministry of Higher Education] (Beijing: Kexue chubanshe, 1957), 283. The progress of the symposium was followed in national newspapers and science journals. When it ended, there was such a strong demand for copies of the proceedings that the unusual step was taken to print up a new batch for national distribution (see preface of April 1957 printing of proceedings). It was republished for the thirtieth anniversary of the Hundred Schools by Li Peishan et al., eds., *Baijia zhengming—fazhan kexue de biyou zhi lu: 1956 Qingdao yichuanxue zuotanhui jishi* (Beijing: Commercial Press, 1985). Portions of the proceedings were translated in Schneider, *Lysenkoism in China.*

77. Yu Guangyuan, "Zai 1956 Qingdao yichuanxue zuotanhui," 5–13.

78. Laurence A. Schneider, *Biology and Revolution*, 172–73.

79. Laurence A. Schneider, *Biology and Revolution*, 175–76.

80. Laurence A. Schneider, *Biology and Revolution*, 171.

81. See Laurence A. Schneider, *Lysenkoism in China*, passim.

82. Tan Jiazhen, interview. Bao Wenkui, (plant geneticist) interview, Beijing Agricultural University, 3 June 1986. Liu Zedong (medical genetics), interviews, Institute of Genetics, Fudan University, 15 September 1984, 20 June, 1986.

83. Laurence A. Schneider, *Biology and Revolution*, 177–81.

84. Interviews: with Hu Han, former Michurinist and Deputy Director, CAS Institute of Genetics, Beijing, 8 August 1984; Shao Qichuan, CAS Institute of Genetics Academician, Beijing, 11 August 1984, 23 May 1986; Mi Jingjiu, former Michurinist and faculty member, Beijing Agricultural University, Beijing, 12 June 1986. At the time of the CR, Beijing Agricultural University and the CAS Institute of Genetics (among a few other institutions) were known as Lysenkoist havens. The CR visited the same severe fate on them as virtually all other teaching and research institutions; but my interviews with people who had first-hand experience did not reveal whether CR operatives actually bothered to distinguish between an institution with Lysenkoist ties and others. Perhaps a university was simply a university and by definition should be closed.

85. Tan Jiazhen, interview.

86. Laurence A. Schneider, *Biology and Revolution*, 199–202.

87. For post-CR developments in China's biology, see *Biology and Revolution*, part III.

14

Between Revolutions: Chinese Students in Soviet Institutes, 1948–1966

Elizabeth McGuire

Introduction: Goals and Challenges, Literal and Symbolic

CHINESE STUDENTS IN THE SOVIET UNION in the 1950s and 1960s were highly visible representatives of "New China" in direct interaction with the ordinary people, institutions, and landscapes of "Soviet socialism." In literal terms, their task was to master Soviet technologies critical to China's economic and military development. But they also had an equally important symbolic function: it was their job to act out Sino-Soviet "friendship" on an individual level. Despite the fact that the 1950s were the golden age of the Sino-Soviet alliance, it wasn't easy.

For one, while the 1950s may have been the beginning of the state-to-state USSR-PRC relationship, in human terms they were a continuation of three decades of intimate and tempestuous CPSU-CCP relations. Many of the Chinese in charge of the educational exchange in the 1950s had been students in the Soviet Union themselves in the 1920s, and their memories enabled, structured and limited the experiences of the younger generation. They made sure that Chinese students were selected with extreme care, and their attention ensured that the students enjoyed high status both inside China and in the Soviet Union. In turn, Soviet authorities were eager to show the Soviet Union in the best possible light. And yet their management of foreign students was far less centralized and high-level than on the Chinese side, which meant that Chinese experiences of Soviet socialism were varied and uneven. Some Chinese students felt they had not seen enough of Soviet reality—others, that they had perhaps seen a bit too much.

While the leadership on both sides complicated both the pragmatic and symbolic goals that had been set for the educational exchange, Chinese students found themselves facing challenges posed by history itself. However deeply entangled Chinese revolutionaries historically had been with the Soviet Union, the two revolutions still had separate chronologies of development: Soviet communism as a political and economic system was three decades older than the Chinese variant. The Sino-Soviet educational initiative assumed that this "age difference" was an opportunity, rather than an obstacle. Even in their more trivial actions—kissing a girl, cramming for an exam, spending a summer in the country—Chinese students pulled the two revolutions together, often consciously. Their difficulties (as well as those of the authorities who attempted to regulate them) highlight just how problematic separate revolutionary chronologies were for the pragmatic operations of international socialism—and for the success of a Chinese revolution in line with *contemporary* Soviet socialism. In fact, one might argue that the Chinese students in the Soviet Union experienced both the pragmatic and the symbolic tensions inherent in the Sino-Soviet alliances, tensions that would ultimately manifest themselves in the split that finally ended the educational initiative for good.

When the Chinese students began to return home in the late 1950s and early 1960s, they found their technical skills quickly sidelined by the Cultural Revolution. And yet, many still went on to fill positions both in technical management and the political leadership, areas in which Russian returned students were overrepresented in terms of their percentage of China's educated population as a whole. Today, most are retired, left in peace to contemplate—with pride, ambivalence and nostalgia—the role they played in China's development and the history of international socialism.

Defining the terms: Sino-Soviet technology transfer.

In 1946, a 20-year-old Chinese boy named Ren Xiang unexpectedly found himself running a textile factory in Harbin.[1] Ren's father was a Hunanese named Ren Zuomin, a cousin of Ren Bishi who had traveled to the Soviet Union in the very first group of Chinese students to study in Moscow in 1921. As a teenager in Yan'an, Ren dreamed of going to the Soviet Union to study like his father, and like some other lucky Yan'an children. Instead, Ren attended the Academy of Physical Science in Yan'an.[2] The rudimentary training he would have received there was the best science education the CCP had to offer, and it fell far short of what Ren needed to run a textile factory in 1946. Ren had to rely on the expertise of his subordinates to do his job; he felt terribly young and stupid.[3] Ren perceived the shortcoming as his personal one, but lack of technical education was an increasingly critical problem for the Chinese Communist Party as a whole.

In desperation Ren wrote to Li Fuchun and Chen Yun in the Northeast Bureau of the secretariat of the Central Committee, asking to go back to school. To his surprise, a replacement for him in the textile factory was dispatched immediately and Ren himself was sent to Harbin, where the party gave him a new western suit of clothes and a pair of shoes, and told him he'd be going to the USSR for technical training. He took off his uniform, turned in his gun and began to worry about his inability to speak Russian.[4]

In September 1948, Ren Xiang and 20 other young Chinese sons and daughters of high-ranking CCP officials left Harbin for the USSR—the first group of Chinese communists to go to the Soviet Union for education since before the war, and the first group ever to seek technical rather than ideological or military training.[5]

* * *

Between 1948 and 1963 China sent about 8,000 students to the Soviet Union to study in institutes of higher education—nearly 80 percent of all Chinese students abroad during this time.[6] In the late 1950s, Chinese students made up close to half of the Soviet Union's foreign student population.[7] About two-third studied science and engineering; military, political, arts and humanities students were comparatively few.[8] This massive, expensive[9] initiative was one element of a serious bilateral effort at technical transfer that was based on the assumption that China's revolution could and would fall in line with the Soviet Union's post-war development toward socialist technocracy. It was one of the more tangible manifestations of Sino-Soviet "friendship," the companion piece to the more-studied policy of sending Soviet experts to China.[10]

And yet the challenges and possibilities for Chinese students in the Soviet Union were quite different from those of Soviet experts in China. The experts could have an immediate impact, whereas it would take years to see results from the Soviet education of Chinese students, who had to learn Russian and math before they could master basic engineering, much less advanced technology. Another difference between the experts and the students (and between the students and other visitors to the Soviet Union such as diplomats, politicians, or members of delegations) was that the students were going to the Soviet Union to get an education—to have their minds developed and shaped in some way. Both the Soviets and the Chinese were determined to control the influence the Soviet Union would have on China through the students.

That the education should be technical was one element upon which both sides agreed. The subjects the students studied indicated assumptions about the proper nature of Soviet influence on China. Evenly dispersing students across disciplines would have revealed a generalized emphasis on Soviet epistemology, and perhaps a notion that any discipline at all might be revolutionized and that the Soviet version was therefore necessarily superior to the Chinese one. On the other hand, careful selection of only key disciplines that were critical for Chinese economic development and could not be learned in China would have suggested a more pragmatic agenda.

The reality was a mix of the two: although there was a decided focus on science and technology, Chinese students still studied everything from livestock management to filmmaking.[11] In 1956, Li Fuchun blasted choices like nutrition, hygiene, pedagogy, and library sciences and demanded that students abandon majors that could be studied in Chinese schools or with the help of Soviet experts in China.[12] As time went on, requirements that the subjects chosen be those that could not be studied in China became more insistent.[13]

Another barometer of Chinese intentions was the average age of students sent. In the beginning, high school graduates formed a large proportion of students sent abroad, but the number of college graduates eventually increased, until graduate students were the majority. The explicit idea was that China's educational infrastructure and human resources should have developed so quickly that sending young people abroad for college was no longer necessary. The assumption was that a one-time Soviet-Chinese technical transfer (a great leap whose failure preceded the Great Leap) could be accomplished quickly and efficiently.[14]

Despite the pragmatism of the agenda, both sides were nevertheless preoccupied with controlling the symbolic, representational elements of the exchange—and were frustrated by the difficulty of doing so. Unlike other travelers to the Soviet Union, the students stayed for a long period of time and were broadly dispersed in regular Soviet schools. No matter how hard authorities tried to mediate and script their experiences, unanticipated circumstances forced the students into creative enactments and spontaneous reinterpretations of the Sino-Soviet relationship.

One way to measure the historical significance of the students is to examine what they did _after_ they went home. For the most part, as we shall see, they embarked on careers in research and academia (interrupted by the Cultural Revolution) and ultimately figured disproportionately in the country's political and economic elite. But the educational exchange was not only a (Russian) cause whose (Chinese) effect should be measured in its aftermath, but also a series of simulacra of the larger Sino-Soviet relationship, whose most significant meanings rest in the moments of their occurrence.

Precedents and memories: Russian returned students from the 1920s and the educational initiative of the 1950s:

In the summer of 1952, Liu Shaoqi gave a speech at the special school in Beijing that had been founded to prepare Chinese students to go to the Soviet Union. Liu didn't mince words: he said each student cost China the equivalent of 25 village *families' annual incomes, and encouraged them to study as hard as possible. But he also shared some of his own experiences with them: he had studied briefly in Moscow in 1921, and had vivid memories of his time there. He advised the students to observe the Soviet Union very carefully. "There are lots of things worth studying there," he supposedly said, "but there are also things you can't bear to see, like women wearing necklaces and rings with precious stones. Not everything in the Soviet Union is good; they also have beggars, thieves, and drunkards."*[15]

* * *

Liu had been in the very first group of idealistic young Chinese radicals to travel to the Soviet Union, and he studied there for six months under very difficult conditions. The Chinese students in this pioneering group had to sneak into the Soviet Union; once there they hardly had anything to eat; their clothes were leftover Red Army coats and boots; their classes were rudimentary and hindered by a lack of translators; their relations with Soviet and other foreign students were practically nonexistent if not downright hostile; and their experience of the Russian Revolution was shaped by the contradictions of the early NEP period, when black markets and prostitution were rampant. No wonder Liu warned the students against utopian visions.[16]

Liu also had another point of reference for Chinese experiences in Russia: his son and daughter, Yunbin and Aiqin, had grown up in a special, privileged Soviet school for the children of international socialists, and had gone on to attend Soviet institutes of higher education after the war, where they had fallen in love, gotten married, and had children. Liu ordered his son and daughter back to China and forbade them to bring their spouses (one a Russian, the other a Spaniard) with them, drawing a boundary between the Soviet and Chinese revolutions at once national and intimate.[17]

In their youth in the 1920s, many future leaders of the Chinese Communist Party had been educated in the Soviet Union, including about 7 percent of all Central Committee members up to 1987. Even more notable is the fact this 7 percent represents almost 40 percent of college-educated CC members during this time.[18] Equally striking in symbolic terms was the decision by top Chinese communists like Mao Zedong, Liu Shaoqi, Zhu De, and many others to send their biological children to the Soviet Union in the 1930s and 1940s.

Now that the early CCP leaders were the fathers of a nation, they began sending its children to the Soviet Union as well.[19] Like all parents attempting to ensure that their children are both better cared for and better behaved than they themselves ever were, the Chinese leadership lavished considerable attention on the educational initiative. There was a three-person commission created in 1950 to manage Chinese students abroad at the highest level: its members were Nie Rongzhen, Li Fuchun, and Lu Dingyi, all of whom had studied in the Soviet Union in the late 1920s, and they reported directly to Zhou Enlai, who sometimes addressed departing students himself.[20] Liu Shaoqi was also deeply involved, speaking with students on many occasions and weighing in on minute decisions: one handwritten letter from the Ministry of Education archives shows him deliberating whether or not the test scores of two Chinese students were high enough to go to Russia.[21]

Beyond the high-level personal attention, the students became the focus of vast and expensive bureaucratic efforts at the local and national level. There was a special school founded in Beijing to teach students Russian and otherwise prepare them for their journeys. [22] Conditions at this school were excellent by contemporary Chinese standards; one student from a poor provincial family recalls putting the two steamed buns he got for breakfast on his first day at the school in his pocket for later; it never occurred to him that he would be fed three meals a day![23] But the expenditure came with serious oversight: the Ministry of Education and the Foreign Ministry cooperated to generate a flood of regulations for the selection and preparation of the students down to the most intimate detail. In turn, city governments and provincial capitals created bureaucratic committees to implement them. By 1955 Shanghai alone had 103 fulltime and 68 part-time employees devoted to recruiting students to go abroad.[24]

The result was that the experiences of students in the 1950s were quite different from those of the older generation in the 1920s. Whereas Liu himself had had to sneak across the border with a couple of friends, students from the 1950s went in large groups, filling entire train compartments and even trains that sometimes arrived in Moscow with great public fanfare to the tune of "Moscow-Beijing," the new anthem of Sino-Soviet friendship.[25] If Liu had had to make do with Red Army clothes, some of the students of the 1950s were given five years' worth of clothing before they left, along with everything else they might have needed right down to toothpaste.[26] If Liu and his classmates had been too hungry to study, the 1950s students sometimes chose not to eat because they didn't like the food, or to save their money for other things.[27] Just like students from other Peoples' Democracies, Chinese undergraduates in the Soviet Union received a monthly stipend of 500 rubles and graduates got 900; students in the elite Komsomol school received 1200 rubles, more than Mao's official salary at the time, and had so much money left over they could buy things like cameras.[28] In case the students were unaware of their good fortune, former students from the 1920s like Liu Bocheng visited Moscow and reminded them how much tougher Soviet life had been way back when.[29]

Another key difference that Liu was unlikely to have mentioned was in the political status of the students in the 1950s. Whereas the students of the 1920s had been ardent internationalists for whom the Bolshevik Party was all-powerful both theoretically and pragmatically, the students of the 1950s, while encouraged to respect Soviet rules, were clearly managed by the Chinese government. In the 1920s, Chinese students in the Soviet Union had been subject to the whims of the Bolshevik Party and had even been drawn into its factional disputes, sometimes with tragic consequences. When they ran into trouble, they had no sovereign authority to which they could appeal. Now, things were to be different. After some initial difficulties (the first group of 21 Chinese students to arrive in the Soviet Union in 1948 were kept out of Moscow for fear of angering the GMD) the Chinese government signed an official agreement with the Soviet Union, just like other countries, that regulated the terms of student exchange, and the Soviet Union billed China for half the cost of its students.[30] Like other socialist countries, China had a special, official section in its Moscow embassy for the management of the students.[31]

Moreover, the Chinese students were supplied with Chinese newspapers and journals and gathered frequently for political meetings, and as time went on were even returned home periodically for political study.[32] Under these conditions, it would have been inconceivable for Chinese students in the 1950s to do what some of their fathers had done: form a pro-Soviet faction. At the same time, Soviet political conditions had changed, too. When Chinese students made public anti-Soviet statements in the 1960s, Soviet authorities monitored such developments at the highest level, but it never occurred to them to punish Chinese students individually, as the Soviet government had done in the 1920s and 1930s when it exiled or shot Chinese Trotskyists.[33]

And yet, while the Chinese students of the 1950s were safer than those of the 1920s, they were also less free. The Chinese leadership was uncommonly eager to control the personal behavior of the students, and again the result was an experience very different from their own. The promiscuity of student life in Moscow in the 1920s was the stuff of legends back in China; extramarital affairs and liaisons with Russian women had been common, resulting in dozens of illegitimate children, many of whom were left in Moscow when their revolutionary parents returned to China. The 1920s romances of Chinese students in the Soviet Union unfolded in the context of a more general romanticization of the Russian Revolution by young Chinese radicals.[34]

Now that the revolutionaries of the 1920s were all grown up with a state of their own, they limited the emotional exposure of China's youth in the Soviet Union: they banned love, from the very beginning. Although such prohibitions were common in the socialist camp, the Chinese seemed particularly explicit and strict. When the first group of 21 students departed in 1948, they were told in no uncertain terms by elders who knew of what they spoke, "No making love until your studies are over."[35] And each set of formally articulated rules contained some iteration of this restriction: "It's best not to fall in love or get married while studying," ran a mild version.[36] "In order to concentrate your energies on completing your studies," another one read, "in regards to love you should restrain yourself, deal with it correctly, it's not permitted to marry during your time of study."[37] Whatever the language, all the students understood the rule. Lest there was any doubt, Liu Shaoqi, as we have seen, made an example of his own two children.

Of course, not all Chinese students in the 1950s followed the rule all the time. Actually, some married other Chinese students even while they were in the Soviet Union, obtaining Soviet marriage certificates and meeting no trouble from the Chinese authorities, especially if they waited until near the end of their studies.[38] But relationships with foreigners were more problematic. Chinese men found Russian and Jewish women (the younger the better, some college-age Chinese chased high school girls) particularly beautiful—"like dolls," and they believed that Soviet women were attracted to them because they were more loyal, diligent, and sober than the average Russian man.[39]

Ren Xiang, the 1948 student whose acquaintance we made in the beginning, still remembers the Russian sweetheart he left behind when he returned to China. "I almost got married," he recalled. "A Russian girl, she really loved me, it's too bad I didn't dare bring her home [to China] . . . she was so good to me, not just in an ordinary way . . . she said she loved me, and I told her I loved her too, I just didn't have a way. She said what do you mean no way . . . later she went to my cousin's, and she cried, 'I love him, why doesn't he care about me?' And she [my cousin] explained it wasn't that I didn't care about her, it was that we Chinese had a rule, we couldn't . . . in the end when it came time for me to graduate, she came to see me often, she held me, she kissed me, I wanted to move and I couldn't, I said no, I can't, don't . . ."[40]

Ren Xiang was able to resist the charms of the Russian woman, but others were not, and their stories are legend amongst sixty-something Russian-educated Chinese men today. One Beijing University history professor had a colleague who married a Soviet woman and brought her back to China; her life there became so unbearable during the Cultural Revolution that she left him, returned to the Soviet Union, and remarried. In the 1980s this man traveled to the Soviet Union, but refused to go to Leningrad where he had studied and met his former wife. He still had deep feelings for her and asked his friend to bring her a letter, but he was afraid to go see her himself, out of consideration for her new life with her soldier husband.[41] In a similar instance of marital separation via geopolitical split, a Russian woman left her Chinese (former student) husband and their son and went back to Moscow at the outbreak of the Cultural Revolution. They thought they'd be reunited within a few years, but only ten years later did they even establish contact, and by then, the husband had gone blind.[42] In another case, a man who married a Russian woman in the 1950s decided not to return to China, and got the help of Soviet authorities to stay, but the Chinese were determined to capture him; he was subsequently killed in a suspicious train accident.[43]

Star-crossed lovers caught in the vortex of the Sino-Soviet affair were so symbolic that they attracted high-level attention. In August 1961 a note from the KGB to the Soviet Central Committee described the situation of a young male Russian student at Leningrad State University who had met and fallen in love there with a Chinese girl in 1956. The case was unusual because it was a Russian boy and a Chinese girl. This romance came up for Central Committee review because the boy had been picked up in the border town of Khailar; the girl was waiting on the other side and had sent word to him through passengers on the Beijing-Moscow train that she would cross the border illegally. When their plan was discovered, the boy threatened they would both kill themselves if they could not be reunited. Having related this tale, the KGB suggested to the Central Committee that if the boy could get PRC permission to enter China, the USSR should allow him to depart.[44]

These particular lovers' ultimate fate is unknown, but given that even Liu Shaoqi's children weren't allowed their foreign spouses, it seems unlikely that they succeeded in convincing the Chinese government. However much Chinese were encouraged to make friends with Soviet citizens, or to consider them brothers, no matter what they weren't to do as their parents had done, and consider them lovers.

High-profile, high-pressure: the Soviet Union hosts China's new elite

On November 17, 1957 Mao Zedong paid a visit to Moscow State University, where he addressed a huge crowd of Chinese students who had been waiting all day for the privilege. He came with an entourage that included Deng Xiaoping, Peng Dehuai and several others, but it was Mao they had come to see, the uniformed military students in the front rows of the MGU auditorium and some disappointed spillovers in a smaller side room who were promised that Mao would come and greet them too. They waited for hours and were told he might not come.

When Mao finally made it to the auditorium, he wanted to sit down, but the students just wouldn't let him. They had heard he sometimes talked for two or three hours at a time, and they were hoping for a grand performance, but Mao spoke for just a half-hour. "The world is yours," he said, mispronouncing the word "world" so badly in his Hunan-inflected Chinese that he had to resort to English, and when some students didn't understand that, to ask the Chinese ambassador for the Russian word for world. "We're placing our hopes on you." Later, he told the students they should be brave and modest, that he wished them good health, that they should study well and work hard, and "unite intimately" with Soviet friends. When he finished, he said, "I'm done." The students couldn't believe that was it and tried to get him to stay. A girl student called up, "How about a smoke?" and so Mao smoked and joked with the students in the front rows. "Do you have heads?" he asked the crowd at some point. "Yes." "How many?" "One." The socialist camp, he said, should have just one head, the Soviet Union. "Did you read Dream of the Red Chamber *or not?" he asked. "It's not the west wind that prevails over the east, it's the east wind that will definitely prevail over the west."*

Afterwards, he decided to make an impromptu visit to a dorm where some Chinese students were living. The students hurried back to the dorm to tidy up. As he entered, one of the girl students threw open her door and he went in. Mao also visited the student section at the Chinese embassy twice during his stay. On his second visit, there was dancing, and all the girls wanted a turn, so they devised a system whereby each would dance for two minutes and then Mao would switch partners, all the while using his left hand to count the beat of the music. "You," he said, smiling, to one of his partners, "seem like a foreign girl."[45]

* * *

The very process by which students were chosen to go to the Soviet Union marked them as members of a new post-revolutionary elite. There was a saying that what was good enough for the party wasn't necessarily good enough to study abroad.[46] The students were supposed to be the cream of the crop, with impeccable class backgrounds, excellent grades, good Russian, and, if they were older, solid work experience. They passed through a screening process that became ever more complex as time went on, a multi-level vetting that began in their school or workplace, proceeded through testing in their subject and multiple health exams, and continued through their six-month or one-year preparation period at the special school in Beijing.[47]

It hardly mattered *where* the students were preparing to go, the increasingly elaborate selection process in and of itself served as a barometer for status in New China. And the arguments that ensued—one student recalls heated debates over whether individual students should or shouldn't be allowed to go based on their class background and pre-revolutionary experience—were really about where to draw the line between talent and politics in the definition of a new super-elite, part of a much larger dilemma that all socialist countries faced about elite formation.[48] Even the enormous Shanghai bureaucracy despaired of gathering accurate information about potential foreign exchange students and lamented the difficulty of deciding who could go to revolutionized Russia when China itself had not yet been revolutionized.[49] In turn, Soviet authorities complained about the low quality of students that foreign countries sent to them, and specifically requested that the Chinese do a better job of selecting workers to go to the Soviet Union.[50]

No matter how carefully they chose, the Chinese government could not prevent individual students from failing in their studies, getting sick, lacking enthusiasm—or in the worst cases abandoning their studies altogether or committing crimes. In 1952, for example, a Chinese student was sent home for alleged theft.[51] The KGB reported to the Soviet Central Committee that one Chinese music student in Novosibirsk had cast his studies aside and begun to roam the Soviet Union at random, showing up in Moscow, where he twice visited the English embassy, and later in Kharkov, where he threatened passport authorities that he would return to China and tattle about his poor treatment in the Soviet Union. The KGB suggested reporting him to the Chinese embassy.[52] Sometimes, word of a student's failure to complete his studies would reach the Soviet Central Committee, which was asked to intercede with the Chinese embassy to resolve the matter.[53]

But mostly, the students received positive attention. As students breathlessly recalled even years later, their journey to the Soviet Union brought them dazzlingly close to the upper echelons of the Chinese Communist Party. Before they left, many were addressed by one leader or another, and while they were in Russia they attended speeches by whomever happened to come to town.[54] If they were lucky enough to be in Moscow, they could boast of spending Sunday afternoons at the embassy for movies.[55] Even if they didn't enjoy any direct contact with the Chinese leadership and spent the entire time far from Moscow, they still had a sense of greater proximity to power during their time in the Soviet Union, if only because they knew that their behavior would be reported upon and that they always had a chance to distinguish themselves.[56]

Chinese students enjoyed extraordinary symbolic status not only in the Chinese context, but also in their new Soviet environment. Students up to the late-1950s, before popular awareness of trouble at the top (and even after) remember being treated quite well by average Soviet people, who went out of their way to cook for them, to teach them Russian, to get them theater tickets and all other manner of special privileges.[57] And Chinese students were often overcome by the beauty of Moscow and the friendliness and openness of their Russian classmates.[58] Despite all the pressure to perform, many Chinese students still remember their time in the Soviet Union as a happy flow of fun, "roller skating (?), ice skating, dancing, movies, opera, museums . . . making nature sketches with Soviet classmates, going to a sanatorium by the sea . . . visiting classmates' dachas . . . to Leningrad, Kiev . . . being taken in private cars to see the sights . . ."[59] Whereas Chinese students in the 1920s faced some harassment with clear racial overtones, the Soviet people really do seem to have put their best foot forward with the Chinese in the 1950s.[60] One former student remembered that he and his Chinese friends used to joke that they could stay out as late as they wanted with no worries of safety—even the hooligans were polite to the Chinese![61]

Just as the Chinese authorities went to great lengths to ensure that the students representing their revolution were top-notch, so also the Soviet Union worried a good deal about foreign students' exposure to real socialism. One Komsomol report explicitly noted that foreign students become a key source of information about the Soviet Union once they return home and are viewed as experts on Soviet life, and that therefore special efforts should be made to ensure that each student goes home "a convinced supporter of . . . our way of life."[62] And yet, to become an advocate for the Soviet way of life, students needed to know what that way of life was, and this presented a problem. Soviet authorities had two, not necessarily contradictory impulses: to segregate the students and carefully circumscribe their access to the "Soviet way of life," and to inundate them with systematic, almost encyclopedic information.[63]

There was endless hand wringing, for example, over where foreign students should live. One option, and the one initially embraced, was for them to live in dorms with Soviet roommates.[64] But post-war conditions in Soviet dorms were not good, and the Komsomol and the Party Central Committee fielded numerous complaints about poor living situations for foreigners, including lousy cafeteria food.[65] And although most Soviet students were friendly and curious, not all liked living with foreigners either, and the Komsomol reported that for some students, especially those who were the only Russians in a room full of Chinese, living with foreigners felt like an "exile," while another said that he stopped going to the cafeteria after the arrival of black students in his school because he found it unpleasant to sit at the same table with them.[66] And so, as a result of various problems, an opposite idea emerged: that special, better dorms should be built where only foreign students lived as well as special cafeterias where only foreign students ate and where they would be served their own national dishes on a regular basis.[67] And in fact, there was a special Chinese dining hall at Moscow Energy Institute where Chinese from schools closeby would also eat.[68]

Along the same lines, a constant suggestion was to limit the number of cities where foreign students could study to a few major urban centers where conditions were better and where they could be managed in a more centralized fashion.[69] Yet even these urban centers weren't necessarily uniform in the exposure and impression they gave. Students at Leningrad University's history department recall being surprised when they got back to China and talked with their counterparts from Moscow. The Leningrad students had had a Soviet advisor who had been purged in the 1930s and shared information about the dark side of Soviet history, whereas the Moscow students knew nothing at all of the terror.[70]

It was precisely this kind of uneven experience that worried Soviet authorities, and their ambivalence about the extent and nature of foreign student exposure to Soviet political life was profound. The Komsomol noted that local party officials tended to have one of two reactions to foreign students: extreme caution and excessive rule-making, or indifference on the grounds that foreign students should be equal to Soviet students and therefore no special measures should be taken for them.[71] Uncertain local officials inundated the Komsomol with questions: could foreign students participate in military training, attend Komsomol meetings, participate in social organizations like the Red Cross or sports clubs, go on excursions to other cities, have their own newspapers, help with dorm construction projects? Could foreign students be criticized along with Soviet students, or be awarded prizes?[72] These questions were often answered unsystematically by local officials on the ground.[73]

Whereas the Chinese had a special, high-level commission to deal with its students abroad, the Soviet Union had no such organization to manage foreign students in the Soviet Union. The result was that key issues were left unresolved throughout the 1950s; for example, even the politically important question of the organization of foreign students into *zemliachestva*, or national groups, took over a decade to resolve: temporary regulations regarding the *zemliachestva* were passed in 1947 but they provided insufficient guidance. Numerous drafts of new regulations circulated throughout the 1950s, but the Central Committee only approved the Ministry of Education's final draft in 1961.[74] In 1952 the Komsomol suggested that the Ministry of Education create a special, centralized department to deal with foreign students, but this does not appear to have been done, at least in 1958 the Komsomol still complained it had not been done.[75] In 1959 the Central Committee was considering a proposal to organize a permanent commission on work with foreign students with representatives from all relevant bodies —which means no such commission existed at that point. It seems that the Ministry of Education's department of external relations handled foreign student affairs but the archival records for this department are spotty at best.[76] Documents from the Chinese Foreign Ministry Archive, dated 1950–1955, show that when the Chinese had a question regarding their students, they addressed it to the Soviet Foreign Ministry's Far Eastern division, which in turn relayed the question to the Ministry of Education. Only in the late 1950s does it seem that the education ministries talked directly to each other.[77]

Given the Soviet authorities' unambiguous desire for control but tenuous bureaucratic grasp, perhaps no policy seems more contradictory than the one that allowed foreign students to travel throughout the Soviet Union during the summer, and even participate in summer labor activities alongside Soviet students.[78] Whereas daily life in the big cities was more or less consistent with the idea of an ever-progressing Soviet Union, once students got out into remote villages, as many Chinese did, Soviet socialism lost its shine. Students remember arriving in small villages in Kazakhstan to help with the harvest, which the government had ordered to be collected in ten days, only to discover there was wheat from the previous year that had never been harvested.[79] The vast difference between the rhetoric and reality of state socialism became clear, at a time when many young Chinese were in the first throes of enthusiasm for "New China."

Chinese Students Bridging the Gaps between the Russian and Chinese Revolutions

As the summer of 1958 approached, Chen Peixian and his three Chinese classmates at the Moscow Railway School got wind of a Moscow city education department plan to send college students to participate in the Virgin Lands campaign in a village in Kazakhstan just over 100 miles from Xinjiang. Chen and his friends got excited about this chance to deepen their knowledge of the Soviet Union. After obtaining permission from the section of the Chinese embassy in charge of managing the students, they signed up.

Any rosy visions they'd had of summer in the countryside were quickly dispelled by the reality of Kazakhstan. They used up their bug repellant almost immediately and were left defenseless against the legendary swarms of Kazakh mosquitoes. Competing with the mosquitoes were the flies, huge ones with green heads that dive-bombed the soup the minute it appeared. But by far the worst trial was the effect of the unrefridgerated, spoiled meat (that the cafeteria had no choice but to use) on their digestive systems. Years later, Chen recalled this aspect of his Kazakh experience in graphic terms.

It was in this weakened physical state that the Chinese faced an unexpected, nerve-racking dilemma. Their Soviet classmates—who, unlike the Chinese, were supposed to be paid for their work and were not, it seems, in Kazakhstan on a completely volunteer basis—were livid about the conditions. In a strange echo of the famous conflict on the Battleship Potemkin, the spoiled meat was a particular sticking point. The obstinacy of the village leader in charge of the students (the Chinese called it "bureaucratism") escalated the conflict. The Soviet students went on strike, creating a huge problem for the Chinese.

Chen recalled years later, "As far as the Soviet officials were concerned, since we had volunteered to go for labor training . . . naturally we shouldn't strike; as far as the Soviet students were concerned, since we wanted to be friends with them, we couldn't let them misunderstand us, to think that the Chinese students didn't support and sympathize with their battle to oppose bureaucratism. We four deeply understood that this matter had strong policy ramifications, dealing with it well could advance Sino-Soviet friendship, dealing with it poorly not only

would influence our relations with our Soviet classmates, it would even under-
mine the image of Chinese students."

The four Chinese wracked their brains and came up with a solution: they would
offer to do ALL the work—their own work plus that of the Soviet students—and
thereby maintain good relations with both sides. From a policy angle it worked
but physically, it was hell. The students were stationed at a delivery point where
wheat was brought to dry in the sun. Their job was to unload wheat from trucks
whenever it was delivered and turn it out to dry. They worked so hard they almost
couldn't eat, each awful meal interrupted by multiple trips to unload trucks, and
to the restroom. The labor and the digestive issues brought them near physical
collapse . . . but they survived and were nominated by the local government for a
Virgin Lands gold medal, a keepsake that Chen treasures to this day.[80]

* * *

The Chinese students in the Soviet Union were positioned exactly at the
human interface of the Sino-Soviet relationship. They were to be the Soviet
Union's number one students and best friends, all the pressure of the hopes
and fears of both sides bearing down on their daily lives. In a larger sense, one
might almost see the experiences of students like Chen as precariously bridg-
ing the gaps between the Russian and Chinese revolutions—in time, in space,
in culture, in ethos—gaps that the project to bring a contemporary Soviet-
style revolution to China audaciously assumed away.

So overwhelming was the students' sense of duty that their experience in
the Soviet Union seems, at least from their memoirs and recollections, to
have been permeated with public symbolism and stripped of private resonance. Whereas memoirs and fictionalized accounts of Chinese students in
the Soviet Union from the 1920s through the 1940s take a multitude of forms
and represent a riot of perspectives and interpretations, there appear to be no
published 1950s accounts beyond the official, collective memoir published
by the *Ou Mei Tongxue Hui* and another collective memoir by the alumni
of the Soviet Komsomol School.[81] In these memoirs as in interviews, former
students tell little stories like Chen's Virgin Lands adventure that are saturated
with a dual sense of serving and representing country and revolution.

Once in the Soviet Union, the students found themselves in all sorts
of symbolic relationships and situations. Most directly, students were
expected to perform in friendship rituals—one student recalls that so
frequent were the requests that he and his classmates participate in and
speak at community events in order to "propagandize Sino-Soviet friendship" that they often didn't get home until one or two am and had
to ask school officials to intervene.[82] If they refused, as did one of the
twenty-one students who came in 1948 and attended an agriculture institute, they were written up by the Soviet Komsomol—Komsomol archives

quote this student as saying he didn't want to speak in public about his experiences in the USSR because none of them were good.[83] He was the exception to the rule—records at the time and later reminiscences show the Chinese as cooperative symbols.[84] Some students even recall being taken in by elderly Soviet women who had lost their families in the war—one encouraged the Chinese to call her "mother," while another woman told the Chinese that she was hoping to marry her daughter to a Chinese, and that she put pictures of Chinese boys all over her house to convince the girl.[85]

Under all this public pressure, the Chinese did their best to rise to the occasion. Institutes from all over the Soviet Union sent reports to the Komsomol in Moscow on the performance of foreign students, right down to naming individuals who had performed very well or very poorly.[86] Whereas Eastern European students skipped class, got drunk, and made anti-Soviet statements with alarming frequency,[87] the Chinese seem to have always gotten good grades, or at least to always have worked as hard as humanly possible to overcome the language barrier and eventually excel.[88] After a time, Chinese performance became a self-fulfilling prophecy: one student remembers that when he didn't do his homework, his Soviet teacher asked: "Did you come from China or not?" In another case, the Komsomol discovered that a Chinese who could not speak two words of Russian was given top scores by his Russian teacher—apparently just being Chinese was enough.[89]

So eager were the Chinese students to excel that their public performance took on a somewhat dubious cast: they were goody-two-shoes. The Komsomol reported that Chinese students complained about Soviet students listening to the radio late into the night or getting drunk and bringing home boyfriends and girlfriends and carrying on with them right in front of their roommates.[90] One Chinese student at Moscow Energy publicly stated that the behavior of certain Soviet students disqualified them as examples for the Chinese, with their bad grades, their cheating, their poor discipline and truancy. Another Chinese, also at Moscow Energy, announced that Mao had instructed them to learn three values from Soviet youth: internationalism, hard work, and collectivism, but that of the three, Soviet students really only exhibited internationalism.[91] Despite warnings from the top against displaying "great power chauvinism,"[92] some Chinese students in the Soviet Union seemed to revel in their preeminent position, shading symbolic pretensions of leadership in the socialist camp into their own individual performances.

At times the fervor of the Chinese students became a cause for alarm—especially when it led to illness. One institute noted a "not entirely normal" situation with the Chinese students, whose group had "instituted draconian rules." "They don't allow them to amuse themselves even a little bit or be distracted from their studies and they are punished for even the least infraction." One Chinese student whose grades were suffering from his enthusiasm for the guitar was punished by the group. The Chinese at this institute didn't participate in sports and disbanded the choir they themselves had set up.[93] In some cases students worked so hard they became sick, and Chinese instructions to the students came to routinely include warnings about maintaining their health, and even suggestions that grades weren't so important after all.[94] But this could hardly reduce the pressure so many students felt inside and outside the classroom.[95]

Part of the problem was that the Chinese were being asked to meet educational objectives that would have been difficult under any circumstances, while operating in the grey zone between two revolutions. They knew they were supposed to "become one with" their Soviet classmates, but their Soviet classmates were busy listening to jazz, making love, and cheating on tests. Even though the Chinese students in the Soviet Union did far less political study than their counterparts in China (and in retrospect felt blessed to have been shielded from difficult 1950s movements like the Anti-Rightist Campaign), they still looked like diehards in the Soviet context.[96] Once, a Chinese student asked a Russian friend why the Soviet students didn't do more political study, and the friend replied that as far as he knew, the USSR had gone through a similarly intense period just after the Russian Revolution but then had relaxed, and that the same thing would happen eventually in China. The Chinese student took offense, but years later came to believe his Russian friend had been right.[97]

This casual conversation about differences in the behavior of young Chinese and Russians brought these two students to one of the most central questions of the Sino-Soviet relationship in the 1950s. The reason young Chinese had trouble fitting into the social environment of postwar Soviet institutes wasn't timeless cultural difference: in the 1920s, Chinese students had proven themselves every bit as capable of making love, skipping class, and fomenting opposition as any Soviet student of the 1950s, and then some. It was instead the very historically specific fact that while Russian and Chinese students were the same age, the revolutions they represented were not. Regardless of whether the Chinese were simply at an earlier moment on a universal chronology of revolutionary development (as the Russian student suggested and the Chinese student came to believe later on) or whether China was charting a unique revolutionary order as it moved through time (as the Chinese student believed in his youth), Russia's socialist state was three decades older than China's, already in middle age.[98]

In this light, the experiences of students like Chen in the Virgin Lands are particularly curious. Whereas the first twenty years of Bolshevik rule were marked by unprecedented social upheaval, in the postwar years, if the Soviet Union was going to continue to define "revolution" for the world, the definition was going to have to change—to encompass the very scientific, economic, and cultural achievement that is anathema to the violent social change that the Soviet Union itself had laid down as the first phase of socialism. But the Soviet state had an uneasy relationship with its own life cycle; initiatives like Khrushchev's Virgin Lands seemed to suggest that the Soviet revolution was timeless, still compatible with and relevant to younger revolutions of the postwar era.

Khrushchev's Virgin Lands campaign, begun in 1954, was a flagship program that resettled thousands of Russians and other Soviet ethnic groups in Kazakhstan, where they put vast tracts of land under cultivation for the first time in order to increase Soviet production of wheat. Although not nearly as coercive or destructive as Stalin's collectivization had been, the sheer scope of the transformative vision of the Virgin Lands was reminiscent of an earlier, maximalist phase of the Soviet revolution in its resettlement of people and reshaping of Soviet geography, not to mention its production of propaganda and creation of heroes.[99] In retrospect, we can see that it also presaged increasingly radical revolutions in Asia. The Virgin Lands, however, was part of a quixotic revolutionary revival, even perhaps a mid-life crisis, whereas the impending Great Leap Forward would be China's first foray into the maximalist policies of a young revolutionary state. Their proximity in time, then, was almost an accident. And yet it was the closest the two revolutions ever got.

The Virgin Lands gave Chinese students in Moscow an opportunity to personally and consciously merge the Soviet and Chinese revolutions—just as they moved closer geographically to the Soviet-Chinese border, so also they moved into a rarefied metaphorical space where the revolutions mingled in spirit. But, as Chen's experience so graphically suggests, one could occupy that zone only at great personal cost—it was a peripheral, unhealthy place. Moreover, what Chen saw in the Virgin Lands was the failure of Khrushchev's policy and the rejection of revolutionary sacrifice on the part of Soviet youth. Chen glosses over this by referring to the universally pejorative "bureaucratism" as the cause of the problem, and he focuses on his own successful resolution of the conflict posed by asynchronous revolutions writ small.

When China sent thousands of students to the Soviet Union to study engineering, physics, economics, and film, it was almost as if China were falling into step with current Soviet history, as if world revolution were to have a single, Soviet chronology. In reality, the technocratic revolution that the Sino-Soviet educational exchange had been geared to produce only began after China's maximalist phase ran its course, with the accession to power of Deng Xiaoping—the (French and Soviet-educated) great champion of Chinese international exposure and involvement. If such a revolution had somehow occurred in the 1950s, it would have collapsed China's revolutionary chronology and absorbed it into the Russian one, permanently changing the meaning and significance of "socialist internationalism"—just as the Russian Revolution had supposedly drawn minority ethnic groups into Russia's developmental timeline and transformed "national liberation movements" within Soviet borders.

The Sino-Soviet Split and the Educational Initiative

In 1955 23-year-old Zhang Yanlin entered Moscow's famous Bauman Institute. At first the whole thing was difficult for him—language, life, studies. But the school's Komsomol came to the rescue, assigning two people to help him. They asked if he was a member of the Komsomol back in China. When he told them that no, actually, he was a member of the Party and a veteran of the war, their attitude toward him adjusted a bit—they were able to place him in terms of Soviet society. "We have a few students like that here," they noted. Zhang took the opportunity to tell them that music late at night bothered him. They were surprised—going to sleep to music, they told him, is one of life's greatest pleasures. From this point on Zhang had a much easier time, working hard and making friends with his classmates just as he was supposed to do.

Student life still had its stressful moments. Once, when he turned in sloppy calculations for an individual project, his teacher scolded him and told him he was going to report to Mao that Chinese engineers are careless. Another time, he volunteered for the Virgin Lands but got so sick he ended up in the hospital.

By 1960, though, his five years of study were drawing to a close, he had finally passed all thirty tests required for graduation, and he was eagerly awaiting the high point of his studies, a chance to do practical training in the rocket division, to operate "the real thing." But one day a junior professor informed him abruptly, with no explanation, that he wasn't going to be able to complete his practical training. Why, Zhang asked? The teacher was annoyed. "There is no why, because it's a national secret!" Zhang looked at the teacher uncomprehendingly, and the teacher lost patience. "Zhang, how come you don't get it? You going to see our rocket launching base really won't do!"

However aware Zhang had been of the geopolitical importance of his studies, they were still his studies, the occupation of a man who had overcome many obstacles to achieve an objective that was now within his reach. Zhang was just young enough to forget that something, anything, even the imperatives of geopolitics, might trump his personal ambitions and interfere in his individual fate. "In an instant," he later wrote, "I grew up a lot."[100]

* * *

Conflicts over technology transfer were at the heart of the Sino-Soviet split. China demanded that the Soviet Union share its most sensitive nuclear technology; the Soviet Union demanded that China accept its help in building long-wave radio stations on Chinese territory that would nevertheless be Soviet-owned.[101] Both sides, then, sought to call the bluff on the Sino-Soviet relationship, to force the other to take high-stakes national security actions that would decisively define the Soviet Union and China as two parts of one whole—as brothers. But the Soviet Union and China weren't really brothers. Extreme demands pushed the alliance too far, and its failure fundamentally affected the students.

The Sino-Soviet relationship fell apart at a critical moment in the educational effort. The process of educating Chinese students in Soviet institutes did have its own internal chronology, somewhat beyond the control of either government. The story of Zhang Yanling's training at the famous Bauman Institute is a case in point. The exchange began in the early 1950s when trust between the two sides was at its peak, but little could be accomplished immediately. When the Chinese students first arrived in the early 1950s, whatever the wishes at the top, they had to spend most of their time learning Russian and basic science. The very first decent-sized crop of students finished the typical five-year technical training program only in 1958 or later. It was 1960 before Zhang was prepared to play with rockets. By the time the Chinese students were ready to be the agents of high stakes technology transfer, the relationship had already fallen apart. In order for students like Zhang to have continued on in their studies, observing and mastering the most sensitive Soviet technology, trust would have had to have increased—and instead it had declined.

Between 1956 and 1957 China radically reduced the number of students it sent.[102] Yet awareness of tension at the top dawned on students in the Soviet Union very slowly. Like Zhang, they were totally focused on doing what they had been told by Mao himself as late as 1957 to do, study and be friendly to Soviet students. So they were often surprised to discover that the geopolitical relationship that had so profoundly shaped their lives was shifting. And their ignorance seems to have been somewhat deliberately prolonged. Chinese students learned about Khrushchev's Secret Speech only slowly; one Leningrad history student recalls the Chinese Party and Komsomol branches in his university didn't breathe a word to the students about it.[103]

Just as "friendship" had generated a wide array of curiously historical personal experiences, so also did "split." China was still sending handfuls of students to the Soviet Union right up to the outbreak of the Cultural Revolution. In 1965, for example, 24 advanced Russian students were sent to Moscow to improve their pronunciation; the Sino-Soviet education had been reduced to training people to communicate well enough to quarrel. In a reprise of the experiences of the first 21 students sent in 1948 (the 4821), when they arrived in Moscow they were told by Russian authorities they could not stay in the capital. Whereas the 4821 had been sent to Ivanovo, six hours outside Moscow and still in the very heart of revolutionary Russia, in 1964 the 24 students had to return to Irkutsk. One of the 24, named Li, remembers that the leader of the group of Chinese didn't know why; they speculated it was because Chinese students had made trouble in recent years with their demonstrations during public parades and events in the capital.[104]

The 24 students attended university in Irkutsk, where their lives were filled with uneasy moments. They lived in a dorm, two Chinese and two Soviet students per room. The Soviet "students," Li recalls, were all highly vetted military men and either Komsomol or Party members. Whenever the Chinese went out on the street, which was rare, they were conspicuously followed by men they believed to be KGB agents. Despite their basic sense of trust in the people of Irkutsk, they still somehow feared for their physical safety (unlike the students in Moscow in the 1950s) and made a rule that no one should go out alone. Generally speaking, their casual relations with ordinary Russians were limited to basic interactions on the street or in the market, and the occasional dinner at a teacher's house.[105]

For their part, the Chinese had two student organizations—one open, official one for interacting with the Russian authorities—and the other unofficial and secret. Once, a Chinese student went out dancing with a Soviet girl, and was severely chastised by the group. All the students met every night at 9 pm to listen to the 7 pm evening news from Beijing. At the time, Li recalls, he and the other students believed that China was 100% correct in its dispute with the Soviet Union, and admits that they made various provocative gestures, like putting up incendiary wall newspapers on China's national day and physically barricading the area to prevent the posters from being taken down.[106]

How, one wonders, in this delicate climate, could the students have the sort of conversations and interactions that would allow them to fulfill their mission—to improve their pronunciation? "Debate," Li answers. These students improved their pronunciation through endless arguments over ideological issues with their Soviet counterparts.

Back in China

Although numbers of Chinese students in the Soviet Union had been dwindling since the early 1960s, it wasn't until January 1967 that the Chinese Ministries of Education and Foreign Affairs issued a formal order bringing all students home from abroad.[107] Back in China, many returned students had only a few years to pursue their careers before the onset of the Cultural Revolution, which curtailed their immediate influence on the Chinese economic, cultural and political scene.

In the 1960s when students returned home they were subject to a period of education and thoughtwork, and a committee to organize such work was formed.[108] One student who experienced it recalled that they were told not to ask questions about what they didn't understand and not to express their own viewpoints. The returned students had absorbed a deep-seated Soviet belief in the economic and cultural development of ethnically or economically disadvantaged peoples through education. In fact the students embodied this idea, so contrary to the emerging Maoist faith in egalitarian mass movements, and on some level, so offensive to national pride. Only through brainwashing, recalls this student, could the returned students be rid of their Soviet-style thinking.[109]

And, beginning in the late 1950s, there was an implicit ceiling on their careers. Students who returned in the mid-1950s, up to 1956, enjoyed high status and high salaries, but as Sino-Soviet relations worsened at the top, returnees came to be seen as people who could be useful only after substantial thought work. One Beijing university history professor who returned in 1959 remembers that his colleague who returned in 1956 had a salary three times as high as his own.[110] It wasn't that later returnees were prevented from working or even working in high status places like Beijing University; it was just that they were considered unlikely to rise high in their organizations. Only in the 1980s, backed by Deng Xiaoping could they take what they had learned in the Soviet Union and use it in their jobs.[111]

In certain, highly critical areas, however, Russian returned students played a role out of proportion to their tiny numbers or possibly incomplete educations and regardless of their political status. When Mao decided in 1955 to focus on developing China's nuclear capabilities and asked Chen Yun and Nie Rongzhen to gather the cadres to do it, they tapped Russian returned students.[112] Another striking example was the leadership role one of China's most gifted students played in the development of guided submarine missile technology.[113] Another military student sat out the Cultural Revolution in China's Vietnamese embassy, analyzing U.S. military strategy there.[114] Russian military expertise never went out of style in China.

Even students with less critical knowledge ultimately were able to pursue careers in line with their educations. In general, the Cultural Revolution seems to have hit returned students a bit harder than other intellectuals, not so much because of their Soviet experience in and of itself, but because their foreign education gave those who wished to have it a pretext for persecuting them.[115] And yet, the Cultural Revolution did not permanently eliminate the influence of Russian returned students in China. Perhaps most striking is the fact that, by my calculations, 90 percent of the participants in the Ou Mei memoir report careers that appear roughly in line with their educational specializations; despite the Cultural Revolution, these students were not forever yanked from their areas of expertise.[116] When students are asked how, exactly, their Soviet training affected their later careers, they answer as all people who received excellent higher education do: it taught them not information, but the means to evaluate it; not theory, but ways of applying it. Like all good education and regardless of the intentions of the Soviet government, Soviet education was a gift without strings attached, to be used by the students in all their endeavors—even for theoretical attacks on the Soviet Union itself.[117]

A rough survey of the level of professional achievement of this sample of students shows that a full 45 percent became researchers and professors; a further 13 percent who were researchers and professors rose to become administrators or managers in their institutions, and another 4 percent achieved the highly prestigious *yuanshi*, Academician designation, either in China or the Soviet Union (a member of the Russian Academy of Science). Chinese researchers spent months compiling a list of all the Chinese *yuanshi* who had studied in the Soviet Union, and discovered 109 of them, about 1 percent of all Soviet returned students. About 11 percent of the students in the memoir had military careers, mostly in military training and education (i.e., they could be counted as professors or researchers as well); 5 percent became cultural or political workers; 5 percent went to work in embassies or doing other foreign relations work; the rest were distributed amongst miscellaneous careers in industry, medicine, or local government.[118]

While the paradigmatic outstanding 1950s student studied engineering and returned home to head an institute, there were some who went to the Soviet Union explicitly to gain leadership skills and subsequently pursued political careers. Between 1951 and 1957 China sent 138 students to the Soviet Central Komsomol School[119] (less than 2 percent of all students sent), whose graduates included a future Minister of Foreign Affairs, Qian Qichen; a vice-director of Beijing University; a head of the Central Committee's International Bureau; a vice-chair of party work in the Ministry of Foreign Affairs, a vice-minister of propaganda, a vice-secretary of Heilongjiang province, and others.[120] It's worth noting however, that the returned students who rose highest in the political hierarchy, Jiang Zemin and Li Peng, were both engineers.

A true estimate of the overall political clout of the returned students would require a detailed investigation of China's post-1949 factional politics, but a few proxies are readily available. Perhaps the most obvious is the percentage of Politburo members who studied in the Soviet Union. Between 1928 and 1987 about 15 percent of all Chinese Politburo members had been educated in the USSR. Returned students from the 1950s did not make it into the Politburo until 1987 (the ones appointed at the 13th Party Congress), when 3 of 17 Politburo members were Soviet returned students. The three were Jiang

Zemin, Li Peng—and Yang Shangkun, who was much older and had studied in the Soviet Union in the 1920s. In 1992 the number was 4 of 20, all from the 1950s. In 1997 it fell to 3 of 22. In 2002 and 2007 there was not a single one.[121] Measured in this way, it would seem that the political power of the Russian returned students "peaked" in the late 1980s and early 1990s.

One specialist in the study of the Chinese leadership has made a detailed analysis of China's so-called third generation leaders, defined more variously and carefully than my simple calculation of Politburo membership: those late 1980s/early 1990s successors to Deng Xiaoping led by Jiang Zemin who have now been succeeded by a "fourth generation" led by Hu Jintao. His research shows less significance for Russian education than the Politburo figures. About 14 percent of 224 of China's most rarefied "third generation" elite had been educated abroad; of these, 60 percent had studied in the Soviet Union, 10 percent in other eastern bloc countries, and the remaining 30 percent had been in the U.S., Europe, and Japan.[122]

Since Russian returned students represented about one-half of one percent of all college graduates in the years between 1953 and 1966 it seems clear by any indicator that they are overrepresented both in technical management positions and the political leadership.[123]

* * *

Now that the prominence of the Russian returned students has finally waned, what remains of the Chinese Soviet experience is nostalgia. Interviews and memoirs of former students suggest that they are engaged in (and sometimes actively resisting) the complicated task of retroactively disentangling their personal lives from the life of their country and the fate of world socialism. It's hard, and they are deeply ambivalent about it.

Their efforts are also assisted and complicated by continuing official involvement. From the Russian side, large institutes such as Moscow State University and Moscow Energy Institute coordinate events and publications for foreign alumni, and the Chinese figure prominently among participants.[124] In China, a formal association of Russian returned students was founded in 1989 as part of the larger European American Student Association, whose headquarters are right near Tiananmen Square. Notwithstanding the collapse of the Soviet Union, the organization grew in official membership (to about 3600 in 2004) and prestige in the mid-1990s, after the students began to retire and move out of the leadership.[125]

Students recall that unofficial gatherings of students and commemorative events began even earlier, and that the first meetings and celebrations of the association were exciting, after years of suppression of normal schoolmate gatherings. In 1994 the Russian branch organized its first Chinese New Year's celebration, a tradition that has continued in the 2000s, and put out a CD-rom and accompanying book of students' favorite Russian songs, in Russian and Chinese translation.[126] Some say that today, the meetings have grown a bit stale. As it gathers them for holidays, publishes their memoirs, and puts them in touch with historians, this association generates memories and publicly structures their significance.

And so, even after all these years, there is still, sometimes, something a bit hesitant, perhaps a bit stilted, about some students' descriptions of their personal experiences. It is as if history had requisitioned this part of their lives, and is giving it back to them only in pieces.

Notes

1. Zhu Xun, ed. *Xiwang jituo zai nimen de shen shang: huiyi Su suiyue* [We're placing our hopes on you: Remembering the Soviet years] (hereinafter as *Xiwang jituo*) (Beijing: Zhongguo qingnian chubanshe, 1997), 290. This book is a two-volume collection of short memoirs of about 200 Chinese students in the Soviet Union in the 1950s and 1960s.

2. Interview with Ren Xiang, Beijing, October 22, 2004.

3. Ren Xiang interview.

4. Zhu Xun, *Xiwang jituo*, 290.

5. Du Weihua and Wang Yiqiu, *Zai Sulian zhangda de hongse houdai* [Red generation: growing up in the Soviet Union] (Beijing: Shi jie zhi shi chubanshe, 2000), 642–43, 653–54.

6. Li Tao, ed., *Zhonghua liuxue jiaoyu shilu 1949 yihou* [A historical record of Chinese education abroad after 1949] (hereinafter as *Zhonghua*), vol. 1 (Beijing: Gaodeng jiaoyu chubanshe, 2000), 220. This is a two-volume collection of official documents regarding Chinese students abroad after 1949. In addition to the 8,000 students in institutions of higher education, an additional 7,500 or so did fieldwork in various Soviet institutions and organizations. Zhu Xun, ed., *Xiwang jituo zai nimen de sheng shang (jixu): nan wang de zhengrong suiyue* [We're placing our hopes on you (continued): an extraordinary, unforgettable time] (Beijing: Zhongguo qingnian chubanshe, 1997), 441.

7. Rossiiskii Gosudarstvennyi Arkhiv Noveishei Istorii (RGANI) 535/58/9; Rossiiskii Gosudarstvennyi Arkhiv Sotsial'no-politicheskoi Istorii (RGASPI) (Komsomol) 1/46/248/11.

8. Zhu Xun, *Xiwang jituo (jixu)*, 441.

9. Calculating the total cost is difficult but some idea of the magnitude can be gleaned from a Soviet account of the total expenditures on foreign students in the first six months of 1959: over 26 million rubles, of which 17 million went to Chinese students for education and maintenance, a sum that did not include stipends, and only covered undergraduates. Gosudarstvennyi Arkhiv Rossiiskoi Federatsii (GARF) A650/1/226/1–7.

10. For example, Shen Zhihua, *Sulian zhuanjia zai zhongguo, 1948-1960* [Soviet experts in china, 1948–1960] (Beijing: Zhongguo guoji guangbo chubanshe, 2003). I am deeply grateful to Shen Zhihua for his assistance and encouragement for my research in Beijing.

11. For an excellent idea of the range of majors from operatic conducting and oil painting to nuclear physics, peruse the Zhu Xun volumes.

12. Li Tao, *Zhonghua*, 148.

13. Li Tao, *Zhonghua*, 148–51.

14. On increasing the age of Chinese students see Li Tao, *Zhonghua*, 148–50, 152–53, 163–65, 220–27. Actually, the Soviet Union itself noted in 1961 that socialist countries were sending more graduate students and fewer undergraduates, and chalked it up to the success of Soviet educational assistance. RGANI 5/35/180/188.

15. Zhu Xun, *Xiwang jituo, 15* and *Xiwang jituo (jixu)*, 421.

16. The fourth chapter of my forthcoming UC Berkeley dissertation, "The Sino-Soviet Romance," describes in detail based on Soviet archives and Chinese memoirs the experiences of China's very first group of students to go to the Soviet Union in 1921. It also tells the stories of the children of top Chinese leaders in the Soviet Union in the 1920s and 1930s, again based on archives, interviews, and memoirs. Excellent sources of information about Chinese students in the Soviet Union in the 1920s and 1930s include Yu Miin-Ling, *Sun Yat-sen University in Moscow, 1925–1930*, Ph.D. dissertation, New York University, 1995, and Alexander Pantsov, *The Bolsheviks and the Chinese Revolution, 1919-1927* (Richmond, Surrey: Curzon Press, 2000).

17. For an account of Liu Yunbin and Aiqin's experiences, see Du and Wang, 109–149. Liu Shaoqi made his pregnant daughter come home without her husband; he was a bit more lenient with his son.

18. Wolfgang Bartke, *Biographical Dictionary and Analysis of China's Party Leadership, 1922–1988* (Menchen: K. G. Saur, 1990), 383–93. I arrived at the 40% figure by dividing the number of CC members listed as having studied in the Soviet Union (90) by the total number of members listed as having some higher education beyond middle school (215) but excluding 25 graduates of the Soviet-organized and funded Whampoa Military Academy, some of whom also studied in the Soviet Union.

19. There was also some overlap between the "biological" and "national children." For example, besides Liu Shaoqi's children and Zhou Enlai's adopted son Li Peng, Central Committee member Ye Jianying, who had studied in the Soviet Union in 1928–1930 and also at Whampoa Military Academy, and sent his daughter to the Soviet Union in the 1950s; his letters encouraging her in her studies became general knowledge. Zhu Xun, *Xiwang jituo (jixu)*, 416.

20. Zhu Xun, *Xiwang jituo (jixu)*, 417, 426.

21. I received a copy of this document from the Ministry of Education archives from a team of researchers at Huadong Shifan Daxue's Russian Research Center. Liu Shaoqi to Li Fuchun, September 18, 1952. The Huadong group was created by the Chinese Ministry of Education in December 2006 to research the history of Chinese students in the Soviet Union in the 1950s and 1960s. It is led by Huadong senior professor Zhou Wen and includes one doctoral student, Li Peng whose dissertation is due to be completed in 2008, as well as two masters' degree students. Shen Zhihua

put me in touch with this group for two days of talks and information exchange in December 2007.

22. Zhu Xun, *Xiwang jituo (jixu)*, 419.

23. See the two-part special from a Hong Kong Phoenix TV series called *China Town* that focuses on experiences of Chinese abroad. "Returning to Moscow: Stories of Chinese Students in the Soviet Union," is available for viewing online, though the access is sporadic, http://v.youku.com/v_show/id_co00XMTMxOTA1NTI=.html.

24. Shanghai City Archive, "Yi jiu wuwu niandu Shanghai bu xuanba liu Su yubei sheng gongzuo zongjie." This archive has a computerized search mechanism; this document can be located by its title.

25. Zhu Xun, *Xiwang jituo*, 18–19.

26. Zhu Xun, *Xiwang jituo*, 15.

27. Zhu Xun, *Xiwang jietuo*, 18. Zheng Yifan interviews, Beijing, August–September 2004.

28. Li Ziping interview, Beijing, October 21, 2004. The Chinese government actually made a special request that its graduate students' stipend be only 700 rubles per month, 200 rubles less than the Soviet standard for foreign students. RGANI 5/35/58/10. And later in 1958 the Chinese tried to reduce students' stipends further, to 480 rubles for undergraduates and 600 rubles for graduates, and tried to convince the Soviets to let the Chinese pay 100% of the costs instead of 50% as stipulated by the original agreement. GARF 9396/19/31/207. See Chinese Foreign Ministry Archive (CFMA) 109-345-02, 36-36; 109-240-02, 95 on accounting difficulties.

29. Zhu Xun, *Xiwang jituo (jixu)*, 428.

30. Li Tao, *Zhonghua*, 83–84. Zhu, *Xiwang jituo (jixu)*, 421. Chinese Foreign Ministry Archive 109-240-01, 23–25.

31. The special embassy section was created in 1951, Zhu Xun, *Xiwang jituo (jixu)*, 418, and exists to this day.

32. Li Tao, 169–72, 233–34. Zhu Xun, *Xiwang jituo*, 125–28, Zhu Xun, *Xiwang jituo (jixu)*, 435. For a description of Soviet repression of Chinese Trotskyists, see Alexander Pantsov, 189–208.

33. RGANI 5/30 r 4653/456/74–76.

34. See Yu Miin-ling's and my own forthcoming dissertation.

35. Du and Wang, 647.

36. Li Tao, *Zhonghua*, 244.

37. Li Tao, *Zhonghua*, 237.

38. Zheng Yifan interviews; Zheng himself married a fellow Chinese student and has the wedding certificate to prove it.

39. Zheng Yifan interviews. Xu interview (name has been abbreviated to protect anonymity of the interviewee), September 12, 2004, Beijing. Ren Xiang interview.

40. Ren Xiang interview.

41. Xu interview.

42. See the above-cited Hong Kong documentary. He eventually remarried a Chinese woman, but moved to Moscow in 1990, where he has been ever since.

43. Zheng Yifan interview.

44. RGANI 5/30/369/106.

45. This account of Mao's visit is culled from the numerous reminiscences in Zhu Xun, *Xiwang jituo (jixu)*, 9–74. See particularly 20–22, 26, 29–32, 41, 57, 68.

46. Li Tao, 101–4. Zhu Xun, *Xiwang jituo (jixu)*, 14.

47. The majority of the Li Tao documents are related to standards of selection, 71-267. Zhu Xun, *Xiwang jituo (jixu)*, 425.

48. Zhu Xun, *Xiwang jituo (jixu)*, 14.

49. Shanghai City Archive, "Yi jiu wu wu niandu Shanghai bu xuanba liu Su yubei sheng gongzuo zongjie."

50. Komsomol (RGASPI) 1/46/152/64–69. Zhu, *Xiwang jituo (jixu)*, 423. They asked for skilled workers or experts with worker backgrounds.

51. Chinese Foreign Ministry Archive, 109-00239-01, 100–1.

52. RGANI 5/30/369/55–56.

53. RGANI 5/35/221/190–92.

54. Zhu Xun, *Xiwang jituo (jixu)*, 427–28, describes one such visit and chat between Peng Dehuai and three students when he was visiting Moscow in 1954. Li Fuchun met with students in 1956. Zhu Xun, 435. Zhou Enlai, Deng Xiaoping, and Mao also visited.

55. Zhu Xun, *Xiwang jituo*, 76.

56. When students won prizes or honors in the Soviet Union news often reached Beijing. See for example Zhu Xun, *Xiwang jituo (jixu)*, 186–90.

57. Zhu Xun, Xiwang jituo, 217.

58. See the Hong Kong television documentary, cited above. Also Zhu Xun, *Xiwang jituo*, 129–33.

59. This is a quotation from a sample survey provided to me by the Huadong Shifan Daxue research group. The group sent out five hundred surveys to former students, and received over 100 back. They are currently tabulating the responses, which will presumably be published later on.

60. There were cases of harassment of Chinese in the 1950s, too, however, such as the beating of a Chinese girl by "hooligans" on the street in Tashkent in 1957. RGASPI Komsomol 1/46/208/29–36.

61. Xu interview.

62. Komsomol (RGASPI) 1/46/208/65–76.

63. For a particularly good example of these two impulses together see Komsomol (RGASPI) 1/46/135/26–30.

64. Komsomol (RGASPI) 1/46/135/10, 16, 55. And some Chinese explicitly requested to be split up and placed with Soviet students. Komsomol (RGASPI) 1/46/164/87–94.

65. Komsomol (RGASPI) 1/46/41/47–48, 1/46/135/47, 1/46/293/25. RGANI 5/35/58/13.

66. Komsomol (RGASPI) 1/46/247/26; RGANI 5/35/202/50–51. In another case, three Soviet students "boycotted" a Bulgarian student for her uncleanliness. RGASPI (Komsomol) 1/46/135/39.

67. Komsomol (RGASPI) 1/46/184/24–25, 35–38, 1/46/293/168/25.

68. Komsomol (RGASPI) 1/46/247/54–55.

69. Komsomol (RGASPI) 1/46/164/20–33, 37–39.

70. Xu interview.

71. Komsomol (RGASPI) 1/46/184/98–99.

72. Komsomol (RGASPI) 1/46/152/10, 64–69, 72–76, 1/46/164/7–13, 37–40.

73. Komsomol (RGASPI) 1/46/135/3–6, 1/46/208/10–36.

74. RGASPI 1/46/135/3–4, RGANI 5/35/147/183–90.

75. Komsomol (RGASPI) 1/46/152/74–76, Komsomol (RGASPI) 1/46/232/25–27.

76. RGANI 5/35/122/43–51. GARF 9396/19/45.

77. See Chinese Foreign Ministry Archive documents such as 109-00345-01, 34–37, 48–50; 109-00345-03, 1–3; or 109-00346-01, 40–41, on the early 1950s. See GARF 9396/19/31 on the late 1950s. Unfortunately, such records are hard to find in any archive.

78. Soviet arrangements for foreigners' summers are commonly found in the archives, see for example RGANI 5/35/202/58–53, 68.

79. Xu interview. Zhu Xun, *Xiwang jituo,* 134–53, are all reminiscences about the Virgin Lands, including selections from one student's diary of her time in the Soviet countryside. GARF 9396/19/26 and 9396/19/45 contain reports about Chinese and other foreign student participation in summer labor campaigns including the Virgin Lands.

80. This story is a summary from a short memoir in Zhu Xun, *Xiwang jituo,* 134–37.

81. The Ou Mei memoir is the collection already cited many times, edited by Zhu Xun. The other is Gong qing tuan zhongyang qingyun shi gongzuo zhidao weiyuanhui, Zhongguo qingshao nian yanjiu zhongxin, eds., *Liuxue suiyue: Sulian zhongyang tuanxiao Zhongguo ban xueyuan huyilu* [Years studying abroad: memoirs of the chinese student group at the Soviet Central Committee комsomol school] (Beijing: Zhongguo qingnian chubanshe, 2003). This is a collective memoir of 27 of the 138 Chinese students at the Soviet Central Komsomol School. For a variety of accounts of the early 1920s at Communist University for the Toilers of the East, see, for example, the account of an anarchist, Bao Pu, *Chi E youji* [Travel notes on red Russia] (Shanghai: Bei xin shuju, 1927), versus the account of Trotskyist Peng Shuzhi, Claude Cadart and Cheng Yingxiang, *Memoires de Peng Shuzhi: l'envi du communisme en Chine* (Paris: Gallimard, 1983), versus the unpublished memoir of his future wife, Chen Bilan, at the Hoover archive, versus the straight party-line account in Xiao Jingguang, "Fu Su xuexi qianhou" [Going to the Soviet Union to study], *Geming shi ziliao* [Materials on party history], no. 3 (1981).

82. Zhu, *Xiwang jituo (jixu),* 103–6. For examples of symbolic "friendship" see Zhu, *Xiwang jituo (jixu),* 138–41, 150–55.

83. Komsomol (RGASPI) 1/46/135/39.

84. Zhu Xun, Zhu Xun, 88–91.

85. *Xiwang jituo,* 68, 96–99, 142–49.

86. Komsomol (RGASPI) 1/46/152/39–40 is an example of a report to the central Komsomol with individual student grades from an Odessa institute. Other reports list names more casually.

87. On Eastern European behavior see RGANI 5/35/58/13, Komsomol (RGASPI) 1/46/125/12–15, 24–26, 1/46/208/87–103, 1/46/247/30.

88. Komsomol (RGASPI) 1/46/135/48, 1/46/164/20–33, 87–94. Komsomol (RGASPI) 1/46/184/109–16, 1/46/208/43–56. The single Chinese reported for playing cards and fighting was the exception that proved the rule. Komsomol (RGASPI) 1/46/176/109–13.

89. Zhu Xun, *Xiwang jituo*, 156, 1/46/247/22–25.

90. Komsomol (RGASPI) 1/46/208/43–56.

91. Komsomol (RGASPI) 1/46/184/47–50, 65–66.

92. Li Tao, *Zhonghua*, 236–37, 243–45.

93. Komsomol (RGASPI) 1/46/208/43–56.

94. Li Tao, *Zhonghua*, 238–39. Ma (name has been abbreviated) interview, October 1, 2004, Beijing Ou Mei Tongxue Hui headquarters.

95. Not all students remember their time in the Soviet Union as one of overwhelming pressure and tension. Zheng Yifan, Zi Pingli interviews.

96. Zheng Yifan interview.

97. Zhu Xun, *Xiwang jituo*, 125–28.

98. Lorenz Luthi notes that Maoist radicalism had its origins in what he calls "revolutionary Stalinism," which preceded the "bureaucratic Stalinism." Lorenz Luthi, *The Sino-Soviet Split, 1956–1966*, (Ph.D. dissertation, Yale University, 2003).

99. Michaela Pohl, "The Virgin Lands between Memory and Forgetting: People and Transformation in the Soviet Union, 1954–1960," (Ph.D. dissertation, Indiana University, 1999). I thank Eleonor Gilburd for bringing this dissertation to my attention, and for her comments on this chapter.

100. Zhu Xun, *Xiwang jituo*, 92–95. For their part, the Soviet institutes that hosted the Chinese students and had to refuse them opportunities to do practical work in sensitive areas felt uncomfortable; the famous Mendeleev Chemistry Institute in Moscow, which had to refuse to allow Chinese students to participate in training related to the peaceful use of atomic energy in 1962, appealed to the Ministry of Higher Education to either allow such students to participate in the appropriate practical training, or else not to ask the institute to accept foreign students who would not be allowed to really complete their educations. RGANI 5/35/2002/65.

101. "The Emerging Disputes Between Beijing and Moscow: Ten Newly Available Chinese Documents, 1956–1958," www.wilsoncenter.org/topics/pubs/ACF1AA.pdf.

102. Li Tao, *Zhonghua*, 221–22.

103. Zheng Yifan interview.

104. Li (name has been abbreviated to protect anonymity of interviewee), August 30, 2005, Beijing.

105. Li interview.

106. Li interview.

107. Li Tao, *Zhonghua*, 266–67.

108. Zhu Xun, *Xiwang jituo (jixu)*, 445.

109. Xu interview.

110. Xu interview.

111. Xu interview. Deng actually advocated the promotion of foreign-educated students as early as 1961, Zhu, *Xiwang jituo (jixu)*, 448.

112. Zhu Xun, *Xiwang jituo (jixu)*, 431.

113. Zhu Xun, *Xiwang jituo (jixu)*, 434–35.

114. Even during the Cultural Revolution: one student, for example, who completed his undergraduate degree at the Gagarin Institute in Moscow was stationed in Hanoi during the Vietnam War, and used his Soviet military education to analyze American war strategy there. Ma (name has been abbreviated) interview.

115. Xu interview. Incidentally, the Cultural Revolution was a travesty not only in the professional and personal lives of the returned students, but also to the historical record. Many students burned all their personal documents from their time in the Soviet Union, leaving only the most innocuous scraps of paper, and even these could turn out to be problematic. One student recalls keeping some pictures of Russian cultural sights, and being told that these were suspect because they contained "nudity," presumably sculptures or paintings.

116. I obtained these statistics and others by creating an Excel database with an entry for each participant in the memoir that listed their majors, their Soviet school, their jobs upon returning home and highest noted career achievement. It's possible that students who participated in the memoir were those whose subsequent biographies were most connected to their time in the Soviet Union; still, 90 percent is a striking number. Another good source of similar information will be the survey conducted by the Huadong Shifan Daxue researchers. If the Ou Mei Tongxue Hui has such statistics for all its 3,600 members, it hasn't made them available to researchers.

117. An interview with a former student in the October 4, 2002 *Beijing Qingnian Bao* emphasizes these themes, as did many of my interviewees. I thank Li Peng for providing me with this article.

118. Again these statistics are based on my own tabulation from the Ou Mei volume.

119. *Liuxue suiyue*, 2003.

120. Zhu Xun, *Xiwang jituo (jixu)*, 418.

121. This information results from crossing Politburo lists with information available in the previously cited *Biographical Dictionary and Analysis* by Bartke.

122. Li Cheng, *China's Leaders: The New Generation* (Lanham, MD: Rowman & Littlefield Publishers, 2001).

123. I calculated their percentage using figures from Leo A. Orleans, "Graduates of Chinese Universities: Adjusting the Total," *China Quarterly*, no. 111 (September 1987), 447.

124. See *Nam—50!* [We're 50!] (Moscow: Moskovskii Energeticheskii Institut, Upravleniia Vneshnikh Sviazei, 2003). I also visited MEI and spoke with its head of alumni relations in late 2003. The Hong Kong documentary cited above followed some Chinese students back to their reunion at Moscow State University.

125. Pamphlet provided by the organization summarizing its history since 1989, "Ou Mei tongxue hui liu Su fenhui," (no date or publisher).

126. *Nanwang de xuanlu* [Unforgettable melodies] (Beijing: Ou Mei tongxue hui liu Su fenhui, 1999).

VI

LITERATURE AND FILM

15

Coming of Age in the Brave New World: The Changing Reception of *How the Steel Was Tempered* in the People's Republic of China[1]

Donghui He

My young ones, why not work at learning the *Poems?* By the *Poems* you can stir, by them you can observe, by them you can have fellowship, by them you can express reproach. Close to home they let you serve your father; farther away, they let you serve your lord.

—Confucius[2]

You have to have this education if you are going to be happy; for happiness consists in making the most of yourself. You have to have this education if you are going to be a member of the community; for membership in the community implies the ability to communicate with others.[3]

— Robert Hutchins

An education in great literature, Robert M. Hutchins and his fellow educational entrepreneurs asserted, enables an individual to develop personally and fully integrate into society. In America this idea was manifest in the publication of Britannica *Great Books of the Western World* (1952), a set of 54 volumes the editorial board of Encyclopedia Britannica selected from ancient and modern classics to represent the European canon of humanities, from Homer to Freud.[4] In the spirit of Mathew Arnold's notion of culture as "the best that has been known and said in the world," the *Great Books of the Western World* were marketed to the general public as the ultimate source of socio-cultural literacy and personal well-being in post-war America.[5] Indeed, it could be observed that many cultures try to establish or reestablish themselves by enforcing a selection of canonical works with the intent to provide public inspiration, give perspective and create community identity. Almost simultaneous with the publication of the Great Books in the United States, a much more aggressive campaign to inject the right socio-cultural literacy into the young generation swept the People's Republic of China—officially and popularly called the new China—as part of a top-down rejection of both the western canon with its emphasis on a liberal education and the traditional Chinese canon with its endorsement of established socio-political hierarchy.[6]

The equivalent of the "great books" that defined Chinese society and individuals' roles in it in the second half of the twentieth century was borrowed from the Soviet Union. *How the Steel Was Tempered* (1934), in particular, served as an important link in a socio-cultural project, binding the making of the socialist new person to the symbolic building of the new socialist state. Written by Soviet Civil War veteran Nikolai Alekseevich Ostrovsky (1904–1936), *How the Steel Was Tempered* tells the compelling story of how a young Ukrainian from a worker's family grew into a mature Bolshevik and, like the writer himself, wrote his life into a book while bed-ridden with bone tuberculosis. The novel was deliberately popularized as the "textbook for life" in China.[7] As the archetype of the dedicated "socialist new persons," who were to construct the new socialist China—thereby giving purpose to their own lives—the protagonist Pavel Korchagin was used as the yardstick with which an individual's growth could be conveniently measured in the PRC.[8] The reading of the book became a formative experience for young Chinese readers until the reform period in the late 1970s.

A correspondent of *The People's Daily* provided this overview of the impact of this Soviet hero in China over the second half of the twentieth-century:

> People born in the 1940s say: "We are nostalgic for Pavel's time."
> People born in the 1950s say: "Pavel's actions have deeply influenced ours."
> People born in the 1960s say: "Pavel's spirit has long stimulated our thought."
> People born in the 1970s say: "We are constantly reminded of Pavel's story."[9]

Even setting aside the credibility of such a consistent reader response across a span of generations, the fact that a Soviet novel of marginal aesthetic merits sustained focused public attention throughout decades of radical social changes and policy shifts is remarkable. As Russian cultural critic Lev Gudkov suggests, "Patterns of mass reading are contingent on the institutional structure of a given society and uniquely reflect or mediate shifts in values or mindsets occurring in that society."[10] While state publishers and schools played an essential role in shaping public culture and mass reading habits in China from the early 1950s to the mid-1970s, the operation of this system, nonetheless, changed in subtle but significant ways after the Sino-Soviet official split. More specifically, the publication of the unabridged edition of the novel was suspended for ten years when the publication system was completely commandeered by the Cultural Revolution and ceased to produce readable literature. A typically overlooked issue in the study of the Chinese reception of the novel is how it was read across generations despite or because of social upheaval and continuous cultural reconstruction. Any discussion of the influence, impact, and reception of Soviet literature in China will remain elusively vague as long as it ignores structural factors such as these.

This chapter asks how the material conditions and institutional framework in which the book was read affected the readers' reception of the Soviet hero and their own relation with the Chinese Communist Party-state. To what extent was agency expressed or restricted in the reading and interpretation of the book? The focus of this discussion will be readings of *How the Steel Was Tempered* by pre-teen to college-aged readers from the 1950s to the late 1970s—the typical readers of the novel during the period when the novel was read en masse in China. Treating the reading of *How the Steel Was Tempered* as a culturally connective action that bound Chinese readers to the state as well as to the Soviet archetype, my discussion highlights three specific periods that roughly corresponded with the coming of age of two generations of Chinese readers as well as the rise and fall of Sino-Soviet relations. The first part focuses on the early years of the PRC, with a special emphasis on the reading of the novel as a unifying activity prompted by visions of Soviet grandiosity and oriented toward the present and future greatness of China; the second part concentrates on the Cultural Revolution after the Sino-Soviet split when institutional failure opened the novel to readers' own discretionary interpretation and toward more personal conceptions of the Soviet Union; the third part of the discussion directs attention to the end of the intensive collective reading of Soviet literature, after the normalization of Sino-Soviet relationships and the advent of new international partnerships. Together they show how the Soviet archetype was used both as an institutionally reinforced model and as a resource for dissident criticism.

The materials used for this discussion are drawn from statistics, prescriptive prefaces and post-scripts provided by publishers, and memoirs of readers that alternately confirm or deny other sources. Memoirs were admittedly written retrospectively instead of at the time of reading, but the fact that the now middle-aged writers frequently use their experience with *How the Steel Was Tempered* as an important component of their generational identity signifies both the lasting effect of the novel and the evolution of its reception in China. Readers' memoirs are additionally important given the fact that library records and other archive materials on the readers are either unavailable or inadequate for the period when the book was not published and not supposed to be circulated. My hypothesis is that the ever-transforming ways in which readers experienced *How the Steel Was Tempered* illuminate the changing complexities of cultural communication through Soviet literature in post-1949 China.

Bringing Home the Revolutionary Prodigal: The Making of the Obedient Public Reader

The socialist new person was a recent addition to the genealogy of the new people in twentieth-century China. Since the turn of the twentieth century, the young people and the new nation had already often been imagined as metaphors for each other in socio-political discourse. In 1900, socio-political reformers like Liang Qichao already envisioned the rise of an "adolescent China" (*shaonian Zhongguo*) in counterdisposition to the hegemonic vision of old China. Liang argued:

> The fate of China rests on the shoulders of the young. The nation will be strong if the young are; the nation will be wise if the young are; the nation will prosper if the young do; the nation will stand on its own if the young can; the nation will be free if the young are; the nation will make progress if the young do; China will be stronger than Europe if its young are; China will reach the summit of the world if its young can.[11]

The coming of age of this "new youth" who were trusted with the task of national rebuilding, was popularly represented in terms of a newly acquired sexual awareness and justified as a spontaneous, anti-establishment individualism. From Yu Dafu's *Sinking* (1921), Ding Ling's *Miss Sophie's Dairy* (1928), to Guo Moruo's *Ye Luoti's Grave* (1924), nearly all major Chinese writers of the 1920s proclaimed in public their ecstasy or agony of coming of age. Literary historian Leo-fan Lee describes those who explored this youth-centered atmosphere of the early twentieth-century as the "romantic generation," emphasizing their assimilation of Western romanticism.[12] In this context, romanticism was not simply identified with the dramatic ascendance of sexuality in public representation but also with the fact that love becomes unprecedentedly purposeful. Indeed, the idea of love as a progressive mobilizer was collectively invested and reflected in the works of both popular and literary writers, as well as of social theorists. Popular sociologists and scientists tried to persuade the public that free love constituted the "scientific" basis for Chinese eugenics theory and the reconstruction of the Chinese nation;[13] literary work targeted at urban intellectuals and even popular drama aimed at traditional audiences participated in popularizing the idea that an individual's desire for love can be expected to challenge and break down confining social structures. As Mao Dun put it succinctly, "love *was* revolution."[14] Love was revolution because it prioritizes individuals over institutionally imposed social roles. In the Chinese context, love-cum-revolution climaxed in the metaphor of leaving home in its literal and symbolic defiance of the Confucian emphasis on the family and state hierarchy. In Ba Jin's *Family* (*Jia*, 1931), a novel that encapsulated all the popular ingredients of the Chinese story of coming of age in the 1930s, the birth of the new youth is realized in the protagonist's stepping out of the family compound.[15]

Nonetheless, when the "socialist new person" became the call of Chinese modernity after 1949, the revolutionary prodigals became reminders of a problematic past. The socialist new person was expected to be completely free from the "feudal remnants" of the distant past and the "colonial residue" of the Republican period (1911–1949), including that of the old "new youth." This ideal was embodied in the idea of "growing up with the PRC" (*gongheguo de tongling ren*).[16] Two months before the founding of the PRC, the soon-to-be president of the Chinese Writers' Association, Mao Dun declared: "A majority of progressive writers in Guomindang ruled areas are petty bourgeois intellectuals. Their worldview leans toward the Euro-American bourgeois cultural tradition, making it impossible for them to achieve a comprehensive and in-depth understanding of history and reality."[17] The CCP's leading literary theorist He Qifang further specified that the "new youth" had outlived their purpose:

> An overwhelming majority of the new literature born after the May Fourth movement is devoted to depicting petty bourgeois intellectuals. Even the cream of it is limited to democratic revolution as understood by the petty bourgeois. Although they probably played a positive role in helping intellectuals and young students more closely identify themselves with revolution in the past, they are inadequate in educating today's intellectuals and young students.[18]

In other words, no existing literary works by domestic writers were good enough for the young. A new model of more progressive culture had to be imported—in this case, from the Soviet Union—for the cultural reconstruction of the new China and for correcting the petty individualism instilled by the revolutionary prodigals of the Republic period.

This need for a more restrictive formula was supplied by *How the Steel Was Tempered*. As a manual for the making of the "socialist new person," the Soviet novel was to replace the unruly coming of the age novel targeted at the Republican period.

Katherina Clark classifies *How the Steel Was Tempered* as a "politicized variant of a *Bildungsroman*,"[19] wherein the protagonist "mastered his willful self, became disciplined, and attained an extrapersonal identity."[20] Differently put, a politicized *Bildungsroman* differs from a classical *Bildungsroman*—"education novel" or "formation novel"—in its reconceptualization of maturity.[21] The classic *Bildungsroman*, as exemplified by Goethe's *Meister Wilhelm* or Henry Fielding's *Tom Jones*, is traditionally about a young man who grows through many adventures and finally becomes an adult, typically affirming the entry of the hero into bourgeois respectability.[22] However, only the beginning of *How the Steel Was Tempered* seems to follow the bourgeois convention; like the protagonist in *Tom Jones*, Pavel Korchagin comes from a humble background. He grows up in a small town in the Ukraine, where he finds himself restricted by poverty and class oppression. Also like Tom Jones, his development from adolescence to adulthood begins with a chance encounter with the opposite sex; in Pavel's case, it is Tonia Tumanova, the daughter of a forest warden. Tonia opens up to him a world of learned gentility, alluring and enigmatic but far beyond Pavel's social and cultural experience. Nonetheless, unlike *Tom Jones* and other classical *Bildungsromane*, *How the Steel Was Tempered* refuses to accept socio-economic success as the measure of maturity.[23] Pavel Korchagin turns his back on Tonia after a brief flirtation. Instead of embracing her world of gentility, a word that has the derogatory connotation of "petty bourgeois" in the context of the socialist new culture, Korchagin pursues a more ambitious goal—one in which his personal development is meant to converge with the grand course of proletarian revolution. Korchagin breaks up with Tonia when he finds it impossible to reconcile her trivial personal concerns and his faith in the epoch-making Bolshevik revolution. He leaves his hometown first to join the army and later to participate in the construction of the Soviet state. Once he decides on his role in Soviet society, Pavel Korchagin perseveres to "stay in the ranks" despite his deteriorating health. In the process, Korchagin finds exalting love in his female comrade—commissar Rita Ustinovich—though he eventually marries Daya Kyutsamaya who helps with the writing of his autobiography. In sum, Pavel Korchagin leads what he considers a meaningful, as opposed to a "pointless" and selfish life. Here a meaningful life is measured by his Marxist vision of history as an impersonal force that would inevitably move beyond capitalism toward communism. His previous fascination with Tonia must be overcome in order to become completely politically self-actualized.

While "extrapersonal identity" seems like a new development in twentieth-century Chinese literature, the expectation for an individual's total servitude to a political cause is ironically resonant with the Confucian emphasis on the individual's subordination to a higher cause—family or state. If the new anti-establishment culture at the turn of the twentieth-century was articulated in terms of the spontaneous pursuit of sexuality as opposed to Confucian self-discipline, the new socialist culture was one that reprioritized discipline. The growth of the socialist new person is ultimately measured by his ideological conformity to the communist cause. As many literary critics have pointed out, *How the Steel Was Tempered* also has a longer and denser genealogy than the *Bildungsroman* in Russia. It takes its roots in the tradition of orthodox Christian hagiography: an essential element of the state *Bildungsroman* is the hero's path to martyrdom and immortality in the memory of the future generations. It has numerous parallelisms within spiritual texts of *The Lives of the Saints*.[24] It is interesting, however, that in the appropriation of the national tradition for the making of a new socialist state culture, both China and Russia turned to its own national roots. Thus in China Pavel Korchagin's undying spirit was imagined in secular terms, a kind of Confucian immortality through posterity reinvented in terms of the perpetuity of the socialist state.

It should be noted that although communism is now widely dismissed as utopian and as Régine Robin puts it "an impossible aesthetic,"[25] it was, nonetheless, a utopia built out of concrete infrastructures and tangible material culture in the China of the 1950s and the early 1960s thanks to its predecessor the Soviet Union. The vision encapsulated in the slogan "the Soviet Union today is our tomorrow" suggested its accessibility and imminence while demanding new political systems, artifacts, and a new kind of people with a shared vision of "tomorrow." In 1952, the deputy head of the Propaganda Department of the CCP, Zhou Yang, argued: "Soviet literature is embedded in a social system that is the most advanced, glorious, and blessed in human history. It exemplifies to us the noblest personality and loftiest morality."[26] Soviet literature as such was officially recommended as a model to enable a similar reality in China. Zhou Yang further explained:

> [Literature] should present real life images of characters representing the new forces in their struggle against the old. Its characters should be actively and aggressively engaged in changing the life surrounding themselves. Literary work can only educate the masses in the socialist spirit with the presence of these new people. Our own writers are accustomed to writing about old people and times but are inept in creating the new person. The new people born out of their pen are frequently superficial, all sharing an identical political profile with an absence of distinctive character or psychological depth . . . Soviet literature has successfully created full-fleshed images of the new people, new people committed to the construction of communism. Soviet literature has set up an example for us.[27]

In 1954, the Chinese Writers' Association issued a list of books in literary and Marxist classics for the intellectual and political elite. Its recommendation for young readers as an impressionable and therefore specially protected group was that they were "free to choose Soviet literature."[28]

This "recommendation" was not open-ended. The choice was predetermined by the newly reconstructed publishing industry and a prophetic vision of the future of the state. Soon after the founding of the PRC, the center of publishing and the distribution network were relocated from Shanghai to Beijing. This move was accomplished through the nationalization of the publishing industry, including the overnight takeover of the KMT's state organs, the gradual annexation of privately owned prestigious presses, and the subjection of minor publishers to "natural death" in the First Five-Year Plan by excluding them from the state distribution system and cutting their normal supply of printing paper.[29] By the time socialist reform was accomplished in China in 1956, a centralized publishing industry had emerged. This meant a dramatic reduction in the popular magazines and entertainment papers (*xiaobao*) that had flourished in Shanghai foreign concessions since the turn of the century. Although some new periodicals were also established and a portion of old ones revamped, still, few foreign literature titles were published after 1949 that had not been previously published. Public attention was strategically directed to fewer titles, select magazines, and official "big" newspapers instead of more diverse publications.

This restructuring of Chinese cultural production led to the relocation of public attention to a new, narrower literary canon. It represented a shift to socialist new culture imported from or modeled after the Soviet Union. The area most affected by this change was the popular canon directed at young readers. Soviet *Bildungsroman* were prioritized over other genres in "cultivating the socialist new person" (*zuo shehui zhuyi xinren*) in China. *How the Steel Was Tempered* was reintroduced to this effect. Although the novel was first introduced to China in the 1930s, the framework in which it was read was differently structured after 1949.[30] Instead of being a marginal literary work as in the Republic period, the novel was endorsed by the communist party state as *the* sourcebook of socio-political literacy for all citizens of China, especially the young and ambitious. The standard post-1949 Chinese translation of *How the Steel Was Tempered* was published by the newly established and most prestigious publisher in literature in PRC—the People's Literature Publishing House (PLPH). PLPH specialized in the publication of obvious classics in Russian and Soviet literature—the mainstay of canonic literature in the 1950s while a greatly reduced number of titles from West Europe and America were continuously published by its Shanghai subdivision. PLPH used Mei Yi's translation as the standard Chinese translation of *How the Steel Was Tempered*. This translation was initially commissioned by the Communist Party in 1938, an earlier version was published in Shanghai by Xinzhi

Publishing House in 1942, reprinted in the communist bases in the late 1940s, and widely circulated among the military.

French literary critic Gerard Genette refers to prefaces and postscripts as the "threshold of interpretation" in the sense that they connect the time the text was written with the time it is read.[31] The 1942 edition *How the Steel Was Tempered* was accompanied by a two-page translator's postscript. In it, Mei Yi singled out the significance of the novel to the military in the midst of the Sino-Japanese war. Since 1949 marked the beginning of new China and China's official integration with international communism, new prefaces were required to relate the text to the new development in China and to supply an updated guide to the reader. The first PLPH edition of *How the Steel Was Tempered* is equipped with an unusually large amount of preface materials addressed to the readers of the new China. "The Translator's Postscript to the New Edition" only fills half a page, acknowledging in checklist fashion the source of the text (*The Making of a Hero* by Alec Brown, New York: International Publishers, 1937); the illustrator (A. Reznichenko); and the letter from the author's widow Raisa Ostrovskaia.[32]

The two prescriptive prefaces for the 1952 edition came directly from the Soviet Union: one in the form of Raisa Ostrovskaia's letter ("In Lieu of a Preface") and the second being Grigory Petrovsky's preface. Ostrovskaia's letter, titled "To the Youth of Democratic China," takes the perspective of someone intimately acquainted with the author and one who looked up to the author as a blend of author and hero. The letter underlines the heroic efforts that the paralyzed Nikolai Ostrovsky made to undertake the project, the satisfaction he reaped from working ("returning to the fighting ranks"), and the recognition he received from both the state (he received the Order of Lenin) and general readers. The keynote of her letter can be boiled down to "joining Korchagin." According to Ostrovskaia, as a communist with an international vision, Nikolai Ostrovsky had a deep and broad interest in what took place in China. If it were not for health reasons, "he would have galloped to your support, as he said, 'to be with my own brothers.'" Since his soldierly impulses could not be realized due to his health condition, Ostrovskaia offers some practical examples and advice to Chinese readers of how "to be with Ostrovsky," including "reciting *How the Steel Was Tempered* with the collective" and "reminding ourselves of the way Pavel Korchagin overcame difficulties."[33]

To further motivate Chinese reader to be with Pavel Korchagin/Nikolai Ostrovsky, Raisa Ostrovskaia's letter incarnates the spirit of the Soviet hero in the form of an uplifting image of Soviet Russian-style globalization, identified with "world record work, world record achievement, tremendous cultural development, and great thirst for knowledge."[34] This image of the first socialist

country depicted in light of material modernization was widely popularized
in China through Soviet film and women's magazines among other artifacts.
For example, the Soviet musical *The Cossacks of Kuban* imagines that collective farms competed with each other to buy pianos at the agricultural fair and
automobiles, which were said to be common household commodities among
kolkhoz members. Women's magazines cast Soviet women in high fashion
outsmarting Hollywood film icons. In short, the Soviet Union supplied mate-
rialistic imagination for more than one social groups in China.[35] This worldly
vision of international communism made the spirit of Pavel Korchagin concrete and accessible. This concrete connection between Pavel's spirit and an
advanced socialist modern society made it feasible for the Chinese to aspire
for a membership in the communist camp. The indisputable reputation of
this worldly prospect of the Soviet Union in the 1950s largely supported the
readers' desire to identify with the Soviet hero.

Ostrovskaia's electrifying letter is complemented by a formal preface, written in the 1930s by the chair of USSR Central Executive Committee, Grigory
Petrovsky for Young Guard Publishers. Petrovsky presents himself as one
who is authorized to critique the text and the development of the hero. His
concept of growth is one taken by "the new man of socialist era" who acts in
the best interest of the community. This entails showing "loyalty to our socialist motherland"; "purging the remains of the old life"; and "plunging oneself
into the building of a new [communal] home."[36]

In his preface, Petrovsky emphasizes the importance of self-discipline
for personal development. He rates Korchagin's relationship with Tonia as
debasing, holding: "A mistake that Pavel Korchagin has made and then corrected was his involvement with a young woman who had not renounced her
non-proletarian family and social connections." Pavel Korchagin's growth
is measured by the fact that he "ultimately denounced his feelings for her.
Though he was still in love with her, he dedicated himself wholeheartedly
to socialist construction."[37] Korchagin's path to maturity is identified with
overcoming his individuality and merging his life into the collective cause of
communism.[38] It is a path toward revolution and away from personal love.

The officially sanctioned readings as suggested in prefaces were institutionally reinforced in China the 1950s. Excerpts from the novel were included in
textbooks aimed at grade school students and taught in the classroom setting accompanied by guidance provided by instructors. It is suggested in the
directions on classroom instruction provided by the Ministry of Education
that students be assigned passages "to recite so as to remember." Additionally, the novel as a whole was assigned as mandatory "extracurricular reading
of classical foreign literary works for grade 9 students" in the *1955 Grade 7–9
Literature Instruction Program* issued by the Ministry of Education. The book

was also shortlisted as required reading for university students.[39] The passage most often recited, memorized, and incorporated into real life situations was Pavel Korchagin's conclusive observations of a meaningful life:

> One only lives once, and he must live it so as to feel no tortured regrets about wasted years and never know the burning shame of a mean and petty past; to live so that in dying he might say: "all my life, all my strength, were given to the finest cause in all the world—the fight for the Liberation of Mankind."[40]

Recollections from the 1950s frequently associate that time with public readings and recitations of Soviet novels. A typical example can be found in Wang Meng's description of the discussion of *How the Steel Was Tempered* organized by the Youth League of Elementary School Teachers in Beijing in 1951. As usual, the discussion focuses on "Pavel Korchagin and love." Although it is referred to as a discussion, there is no discussion at all—not even a rhetorical "devil's advocate" approach. Questions such as "Why should Pavel Korchagin break up with Tonia?" are directly answered in Pavel Korchagin's voice—his decision to choose revolution over love. Consequently, "the closer people looked into the issue, the more understanding they had of Pavel's greatness, self-discipline, and sacrifice! At last all present recited in a chorus Pavel's aphorism 'one only lives once . . .' which brought tears to everyone's eyes."[41] Speaking in his voice, the participants imagined themselves merging with Pavel Korchagin. Rejection of Tonia in chorus served as the ligament binding the collective.

To assume such uniformity was a spontaneous response to the book in the 1950s, however, would be erroneous. Indeed, Korchagin's relationship with Tonia constituted one of the most sensitive areas in which readers' political consciousness was tested. While attending a creative writing workshop in 1954, apprentice writer Chen Chong was reprimanded for saying that "Tonia is vividly portrayed."[42] His superior took the remark as evidence that Chen "still holds on to a bourgeoisie world."[43] Chen Chong quickly realized that he was not supposed to approach the episode from the perspective of creative writing. He consulted many reading guides on the novel until he could recite the correct interpretation: "Pavel's brief relationship with Tonia was a mistake, a sidetrack on his way to becoming a true communist."[44]

In 1958, in a public speech given at Beijing No. 65 Secondary School, Raisa Ostrovskaia revealed that the prototype of Tonia was still alive, now a respected school teacher. The fictional Tonia—the epitome of bourgeoisie value—was fabricated to underscore Korchagin's growth. This revelation was extremely important to the audience. According to writer Liu Xinwu, then a student in the audience, "the faculty and students lived in the ecstasy and excitement brought by this revelation for a long time."[45] The audience obviously cared about Tonia more than they wanted to admit.

The reading of the novel was so closely monitored that tampering with the standard quotations was cause for trouble. Stories of the prevention of such tampering and the rectification of the perpetrators were abundant. In one such story, a university student was immediately deemed in need of communal help when he copied the first sentence of Pavel's maxim in his diary but left out the rest of the passage because he was reluctant to dismiss as "waste" and "petty" the life led by his farmer parents and everybody he knew outside of the university. In his opinion, "one does not contribute much to the society for about twenty years combining childhood and old age. Even in the prime of life, one is subject to mundane everyday obligations, such as courtship and family life." He therefore concluded that he could not possibly "devote all [his] strength and life" to the revolutionary cause as Pavel Korchagin did.[46]

This student received generous "help" from the Youth League and Student Union in correcting his divergence from the collective norm. Indeed, students from the entire university rushed to his rescue. At first, such "help" took the form of "fine breeze and drizzle" (*hefeng xiyu*), that is, a mild reorientation. Soon, the "help" turned into a type of organized harassment. Wherever he went—classrooms, lecture halls, cafeterias, his dormitory, the library—a crowd tailed him for discussion. Each and every fellow student gave him a "helping" hand until he eventually gave up and stopped resisting.[47]

Attention, trust, and obedience to official instructions are generally attributed to the age group educated in the 1950s. Nonetheless, beneath their devoted collectivism was discipline through institutionalized guidance, peer pressure, and internalized self-censorship. Moreover, the official image of Soviet Union which young people popularly aspired to emulate was of a prosperous, successful, and most importantly, credible model. In other words, although Pavel Kochargin was officially supposed to be admired for his abstract qualities, the popularization of the Soviet saint in China was more corporeal than spiritual from the beginning. As the editor-in-chief of *How the Steel Was Tempered*, Zhang Fusheng, rightly points out, "a novel cannot produce such impact by itself."[48]

Home Alone? Underground Reading during the Cultural Revolution

A dramatic change in readers' interactions with the novel came during the Cultural Revolution. Writer Wang Xiaoying's reflection described the experiences of many ambitious young "elite" members in their late teens and early twenties by the time the Cultural Revolution broke out. Wang maintains:

> I might have continued to follow Pavel Korchagin's footsteps if it were not for
> the Cultural Revolution. The movement destroyed the beautiful dream we had

conceived. We consequently experienced a painful, profound, and complex change in our worldview.[49]

The changed reception of the Soviet novel was attributive to the drastic shift of social and institutional framework within which the book was read. Changes in the Sino-Soviet relationship were an important factor. Nonetheless, its impact on the reader was subtle and gradual instead of dramatic and immediate. At first the changed official attitude toward the Soviet Union did not create more than a minor de-emphasis on the novel. Public recitations of the Soviet novel established in the early 1950s discontinued in the late 1950s. *How the Steel Was Tempered* was slightly elbowed aside from the public when 10 new novels by domestic writers—later known as "red classics"—were published in 1959 and publicly endorsed at the expense of earlier literature.[50] Nonetheless, the publication of *How the Steel Was Tempered* continued in large editions until the Cultural Revolution. In fact, after the general public had been informed of the Sino-Soviet break-up, the CCP began to offer China as the new home for Pavel Korchagin. From 1964 to 1966, *The People's Daily* carried numerous articles, accusing the Soviets of abandoning the Soviet hero even though Pavel Korchagin remained the officially promoted youth icon in the Soviet Union.[51]

The reception of the novel was far more heavily impacted by institutional changes that took place during the ten years of the Cultural Revolution. The Soviet Cultural Revolution, as Sheila Fitzpatrick defines it, was "an aggressive movement of the young, proletariat and communists against the cultural establishment."[52] The Cultural Revolution in China similarly started from the cultural front but was not limited to it. Institutional instability affected habits of mass reading in two significant ways: 1) the school system central to the structured reading of the novel was paralyzed; and 2) public access to novels was blocked beginning in 1966. For example, *How the Steel Was Tempered* not only lost its status as the "textbook for life" but was withdrawn from public circulation, as all novels except Hao Ran's *Bright Sunny Skies* were banned.

Intensified censorship during the Cultural Revolution gave rise to what may be described with some irony as a booming publishing industry. The period from the summer of 1966 to 1972 witnessed a prodigious production of "correct" ideas and images—monographs, collections, and edited volumes of Mao's work; and posters of Mao's quotations; Mao poems, and portraits.[53] However, the boom in the printing industry was one dimensional. Until 1970, new titles were largely restricted to scripts or the musical scores of revolutionary model operas. Of the 3,300 new titles published, 1,778 were in political reading, mostly collections of newspaper editorials, 340 titles in children's books (including 178 titles of picture books based on model operas) and popular science readings. The only memorable event in the publishing history of the Cultural Revolution was the reissue of *The Concise Chinese Dictionary* (*Xinhua zidian*) in 1971, with 34, 530,000 copies issued nation-wide.[54] According to writer Lin Da's not completely anecdotal impression, books on the shelves of bookstores during the Cultural Revolution comprised: "60% Mao, 30% Marx, Engels, Lenin, and Stalin, and 10% reference materials for political criticism."[55] This meant no novels or readable books were officially supposed to be available for the public.

Since few books that were actually read were officially available to the public, reading in general became an underground activity. The shortfall in readable books from the state distribution system also compelled readers to rely on alternative, mostly private, resources for reading materials. Lin Da recalls: "I had not read books in public nor bought the books I read in public areas for ten years. The books I read were all smuggled in clandestinely. I had no idea where they came from or where they went next."[56]

Wang Anyi admitted:

Most of books I read were obtained [stolen] from libraries that had abolished routine management. Some books drifted to us from the recycling stations, which were filled with books thrown out as left-over from the past. All of these books came to me from someone or other who in their turn had borrowed them from some other people.[57]

Although some readers could obtain unexpected titles from unexpected sources, the book that was more available than others in any collection, public or private, was *How the Steel Was Tempered*. Owing to its special status in China, *How the Steel Was Tempered* was the most printed title by any foreign author after 1949. From 1952 (except 1960) until the Cultural Revolution, the novel was continuously in print. During the peak of Sino-Soviet fraternity in the 1950s, it was generally printed more than once a year. For example, in 1952 it went to 6 printings; 8 in 1954, and 9 printings in 1955; in 1958 the book was printed once but with a print run of 600,000 copies. Even the official breakup between the two communist parties did not interrupt the publication of the book. In July 1965, the last printing before the Cultural Revolution still reached 65,020 copies.[58] In 13 years, the book was printed 25 times and a total of more than 1,000,000 copies were published and distributed by PLPH alone. (Earlier editions by other publishers, abridged and children's editions by China's Youth Publishing House and China's Children's Publishing House are not counted.)[59] Admittedly, the novel's actual availability remained speculative during the Cultural Revolution when the book was not published.

The ambiguous status of *How the Steel Was Tempered* during the Cultural Revolution further contributed to its relatively easier access. In fact, the novel was never officially censored. By contrast, "red classics"—the ten new novels by domestic writers published in 1959 which shared the limelight with the Soviet novel for about six years until 1965—were all blacklisted either as bad or very bad during the Cultural Revolution due to their connection with sections of the CCP that fell from grace during the Cultural Revolution. *How the Steel Was Tempered* remained intact, even though it disappeared from the public along with banned books. This ambiguity made a significant difference in terms of getting around parental censorship. Parents would generally not hesitate to release the book to their children. While some families threw away, destroyed, or locked up banned books and sensitive titles to protect their children from "bad influence" and possible trouble, *How the Steel Was Tempered* was generally exempt from such parental censorship.[60] In writer Liu Xiaofeng's case, his mother reminded him when he was eleven that it was time for him to read the regular version of the novel instead of the abridged edition.[61] "Everyone read *How the Steel Was Tempered* before the end of the Cultural Revolution."[62] Writer Ha Jin's observation represents experiences typically gleaned from my interviews with academics and artists who were pre-teens or teenagers during the years of the Cultural Revolution.[63]

However, this did not mean that the reading of *How the Steel Was Tempered* continued unchanged in the 1960s. Like banned books, this book also became material for private reading. It could no longer be read in public libraries or recited in public gatherings. In addition, it was not officially assigned to any age group. In the 1950s, *How the Steel Was Tempered* was formally assigned to students of grade nine and above. During the Cultural Revolution such age specification no longer applied. A younger group of readers identified themselves as typical mass readers of the novel from the mid-1960s to the mid-1970s.

A special contribution these young readers made to the reading of the novel was "partial" reading. Unlike readers "growing up with the PRC," the younger readers were not particularly inspired by the futurist vision ascribed to the novel. Instead of looking for a role model for their own development, they focused on fragments of the novel. For example, Korchagin's childhood experiences appeared more relevant to their own experiences than his political maturity. Literary critic Dai Xun's response to the novel at age 9 was typical: "Pavel Korchagin started as a boy about my age. Like me, he got into fights with other kids. He also liked to read, but had no access to books. He was a lot like myself on many levels. This kind of closeness I could not find in works by Chinese writers."[64] Indeed, even the politicized *Bildungsroman* was discontinued during the Cultural Revolution. In compliance with the official emphasis on perfect revolutionary heroes, character flaws, ambiguous sentiment, or any room for development was eliminated from the new Cultural Revolution literature that began appearing after 1972.[65] That means all the characters sprang fully formed from the author's head as mature communists without defect, leaving no room for the naive attraction to deviant ideas that forms the backbone of character development in the traditional *Bildungsroman*. Even a teenaged protagonist such as Hong Yu in *The Making of a Doctor* (Hong Yu) appears as an adult. In Dai Xun's words, the Cultural Revolution heroes were "red inside out"—that is, utterly public, devoid of ambiguities and perfect revolutionaries. By contrast, Korchagin's adolescent pre-Bolshevik moments appealed to adolescent readers as something they could relate to and identify with.

Nonetheless, "revolution versus love" was likewise used as a reference for growth in underground reading, but revolution no longer served as the unquestionable measure of maturity. Instead Korchagin's "mistake" became the major attraction for the adolescent readers. Their discovery in the novel began with Korchagin's "debasing" love relationship with Tonia. The character of Tonia Tumanova impressed the adolescent readers as a being from a different world almost in the same way she impressed Pavel Korchagin. During the Cultural Revolution, femininity was equated with the bourgeois and was minimized in public representation. For many young boys, Tonia thus represented their first acquaintance with the opposite sex in literature. Liu Xiaofeng recalled in his memoir 20 years later that Tonia was his "first concrete image of a beauty"; he subsequently "conceptualized beauty in the form of Tonia."[66] Literary critic Ding Fan admitted: "*How the Steel Was Tempered* was the first novel of my adolescent reading. Strangely, the love relationship between Pavel and Tonia, particularly descriptions of the adolescent fantasies of a romantic kind, impressed me deeply." Literary critic Li Jingze confesses that "Regardless whether Tonia was good or bad, there is something special about her. She is beautiful. Her sailor's blouse, short skirt, her agile movements, and sunny laugh left an enduring impression on a Chinese boy in the early 1970s."[67] It is impossible to tell whether Tonia awoke adolescent dreams of heterosexual love or whether the adolescent readers read their dreams into Tonia. In either case, unlike Korchagin, they did not grow disenchanted with Tonia; and unlike readers of the 1950s, they were not obliged to overcome or repress this sentiment.

However, the absence of immediate mediation by instructors and the framing of texts did not mean these young readers were completely free from the influence of structured reading. Li Jingze recalls that "the copy of *How the Steel Was Tempered* I read was old . . . Many people who had read it left their marks on it. What they considered as maxims and purple passages were underlined in red ink. I would reread the underlined parts, admiring their rhythm and beauty."[68]

For Liu Xiaofeng, the shadow of orthodox reading at first overpowered the lure of femininity. By the age of nine, he had already internalized a healthy dose of vigilance against the bourgeois and was able to exercise some kind of self-censorship. In his first reading of the novel, Liu Xiaofeng tried to reconcile Pavel Korchagin with Tonia as he would revolution and love. Though he was fond of Tonia, at this stage he had no doubt about Pavel Korchagin's course: "I cared for Tonia's position in revolution. I cared very much indeed because I could (dared) not love her if she excluded or was excluded by revolution."[69] He wished that Tonia could join the revolution so that she and Korchagin could marry and spend the rest of their lives together.[70] In his novel of growing up during the Cultural Revolution, Wang Shuo's autobiographical persona admits that he is fascinated by "the episodes in which the revolutionaries are romantically involved with bourgeois ladies . . . He felt pity for Pavel when he lost Tonia."[71] That sense of pity showed a timid desire to revise the story and give it a more satisfactory conclusion.

Tonia acquired a positive ethical dimension when the readers became disenchanted with revolution. According to Liu Xiaofeng, he realized when reading the novel a second time in the early 1970s: "The three girlfriends Pavel has had in his life are no more than evidence of his devotion to revolution, proof of his will power to discipline himself and disregard of individual existence."[72] The urge to be fair to Tonia, to reclaim apolitical and underrepresented individualism eventually overcame the wish to be loyal to Pavel and the revolution he represented. "[If you wish my love to return] you must be with us. And I would be a poor husband to you if you expect me to put you before the Party. For I shall always put the Party first, and you and my other loved ones second,"[73] Pavel's parting words to Tonya, once a passage in the essential repertoire for public recital, appeared arrogant and illogical to readers who felt the need to address its injustice to Tonya and her love.

Individualism—"cheap individualism" in the words of Pavel Korchagin, gained a place in these private readings in part because it was cheapened, condemned, and suppressed in public representation. Tonya, the incarnation of individualism and personal love, also wins admiration as the one who has a deeper understanding of life than the Bolsheviks. "What right do you have to speak to me like that? I don't ask you who your friends are and who comes to see you"[74]—Tonia's independence, which had been overlooked in public readings, won respect in private readings. She was applauded for being the one who knows without preaching: "How gracious! She would not accept any conditions attached to love, even if imposed by the man she loved. She loved Pavel as 'the man.' Once Pavel lost his self, her love for him dissolved."[75] Private readings eventually subverted the official reading.

The concept of collective memories of private readings may appear oxymoronic. However, if private reading was a shared experience for readers of literary works during the Culture Revolution, for pre-teen and teenaged readers, limited resources made *How the Steel Was Tempered* the focus of collective attention in private sphere. Dai Xun admits that he did all his reading "in a grimy apartment room while outside the window the whole society was boiling in turmoil . . . However, what I believed to be unique to myself in the 1960s, turned out to be a shared experience."[76] These young readers not only shared the experience of reading *How the Steel Was Tempered* repeatedly and intensively but they also revised the state *Bildungsroman* to show that they had outgrown it and refused to grow up into revolutionary fighters. Private reading clearly put the novel to new purposes at odds with the ultra-revolutionary fanaticism of the Cultural Revolution. The novel therefore not only served as a sourcebook of growth for the obedient public readers in the 1950s but, due in large part to its popularity and the lack of alternative sources, it still supplied the building blocks for the rebellious private readers of the Cultural Revolution to imagine and describe their development.

Despite its revisionist reading by adolescent readers, *How the Steel Was Tempered* was fundamentally resonant with the Chinese Communist Party state's expectation for ideological education even during the Cultural Revolution. Attempts to reuse it were made once the storm and stress period of the movement of was over. In 1972, six years into the Cultural Revolution, the Propaganda Department permitted the reprinting of Maxim Gorky's *Mother* and Nikolai Ostrovsky's *How the Steel Was Tempered*, in an attempt to revive the book industry, alleviate the shortage of readable books, and restore institutional control over cultural circulation.

The People's Fine Art Press released its reprint of abridged pictorial edition (*xiaoren shu*) immediately in 1972. The pictorial edition of *How the Steel Was Tempered* came in two palm-sized, thin volumes. The small book is framed by a heavy-handed prescriptive reading of the history of socialist revolution, replete with authoritative statements by communist leaders. Its epigraph is a quotation from Lenin: "The autocracy cannot be abolished without the revolutionary action of class-conscious millions, without a great surge of mass heroism, readiness and ability on their part to 'storm heaven,' as Marx put it when speaking of the Paris workers at the time of the commune."[77] This militant beginning sets the tone for the introduction that follows on the next three pages. The goal of these beginning materials is to reinstate the image of "the first socialist country in the world built by Lenin" as opposed to the post-Stalinist Soviet Union, referred to as "socialist imperialists and social Fascists." The introduction specifies: "the pictorial edition of *How the Steel*

Was Tempered enables us to see that the great Soviet people would not allow such betrayal."[78]

The unabridged edition by PLPH, nonetheless, took another four years to appear in bookstores. Mei Yi was undergoing reform through labor in 1972 as a well-placed cultural bureaucrat before the Cultural Revolution. The publisher was compelled to abandon his translation because of Mei's problematic status at that time. A collective—the translation group of the Russian Language Department of Heilongjiang University and worker-peasant-soldier students admitted to the program in 1972—led by a faculty member, Huang Shunan (his name unacknowledged), were commissioned to providing a new Cultural Revolution translation of *How the Steel Was Tempered* for PLPH.[79]

PLPH's Cultural Revolution edition of *How the Steel Was Tempered* that appeared in 1976 was produced in the same spirit as the 1972 pictorial edition. The preface was written in the name of a larger collective—"workers from the third Section of Daqing Oil Field, worker-peasant-soldier students of the 1973 class, and revolutionary teachers of the Chinese Department coauthored the preface after consultations and discussions."[80] It emphasizes: "Soviet revisionists have trampled on the red flag that Pavel Korchagin defended with his life." China, on the other hand, is represented as the true heir of Lenin, Stalin, and directly related to Pavel Korchagin as the representative of orthodox Marxism: "we [Chinese] are upholding the red banner of Marxism, Leninism, and Mao Zedong thought while braving our way to communism."[81] In other words, the Soviet Union no longer deserved Pavel Korchagin once it turned its back on Lenin and Stalin. Instead the CCP was in a position to claim the Soviet hero.

In the 1976 preface, orthodox Marxism and revisionism are presented as being embodied in two polar different readings of *How the Steel Was Tempered*. It alerts the reader to a Soviet revisionist reading which is to believe that "the source of Pavel's extraordinary perseverance lies in his humanism. Humanism is key to the magnetism of his character."[82] It then goes on to criticize this humanized reading as a distortion of Pavel Korchagin, "the proletarian soldier" and "undermining the combat spirit of the people."[83] The orthodox reading it offers echoes Petrovsky's conceptualization of the socialist new man, by now an essential ingredient of China's own discourse of revolution: "love cannot be separated from class consciousness. Pavel condemned Tonia's bourgeois mentality and broke with her once he merged his destination and ideas with the proletariat." It probes into "the deficiencies of the novel" in the form of "an excessive elaboration of Pavel and Tonia's acquaintance and erotic relationship" and the "despair Pavel expressed as his health deteriorated and before his work was published."[84] The last appears to allude to new touches added to public representations of the Soviet hero, epitomized, for example, by the 1975 Russian film adaptation of the novel. The film starts with Pavel Korchagin's suicide attempt, giving Pavel Korchagin a human face and some psychological depth. One may tend to agree that such treatment gives more spotlight on his will-power but Chinese readers were supposed to remain securely enclosed within the framework initially provided by politicians like Petrovsky.

The PLPH preface offers little that had not been officially pronounced. Condemnation of Soviet revisionism as "bourgeois humanism" was in the newspapers, textbooks, and in daily broadcasting throughout the Cultural Revolution.[85] The CCP's attitude was clear but its vision of reconstruction and development was vague against a background of economic and cultural stagnation. Although the development of the protagonist was recommended to readers as the model for their socialization and self-fashioning, it required a picture of substantial socio-economic development for the novel to be persuasive. In the 1950s the breathtaking picture of Soviet modernity, in which overt materialism was seamlessly blended with communist ideology, beckoned the Chinese reader to join the spirit of Korchagin. With the Sino-Soviet split, this visually impressive picture was officially abandoned in China. An equally enticing replacement was not yet available.

The abandoned picture of the Soviet Union, by contrast, acquired the allure of what it might have been for the Chinese, a tangible and perhaps the only familiar model of personal and socio-economic development. Dai Xun, for example, imagined participating in the world represented by the elegantly dressed Russian boys with sleek hair that he found in a poster "The Young Soviet Navy Fleet" in his neighbor's apartment. It highlights his own material and spiritual deprivation. Comparing himself to a young Gorky who cherished lofty ideals while living in poverty, he was particularly impressed by Tonia's "aristocratic gracefulness."[86]

To many others, the historical, social, and personal development projected in the early years of the PRC were hard to imagine from the perspective of the young readers during the Cultural Revolution. Even if they wanted to believe, material conditions suggested the opposite—that China had regressed when compared with the 1950s when the country was pursuing Soviet-style global communism. As Joseph R. Levenson observed: "the Cultural Revolution had a provincial cultural spirit."[87] It was blocking the prospect of material modernization. For adolescent readers, that provincializing revolution only meant more restraints and isolation. The Soviet "revisionism" which was officially identified with capitalism received a new orientation as "petty bourgeoisie" in a positive sense of the word in underground reading. In her fictional autobiography of growing up during the Cultural Revolution, the president of Chinese Writers' Association Tie Ning revealed a scene in the early 1970s when three teenage girls locked themselves up in a bedroom to peruse "western fashion" found in a copy of old, slightly tattered *Soviet Women* (*Sulian funü*) from in the 1950s.[88] The magazine which was supposed to represent the new international fashion of the working class, was being used as a window to the fashion of Rome and London. The return of the "petty bourgeoisie" owed its success to the crusades against it.

Revisionist readings of *How the Steel Was Tempered* constituted a form of rewriting or what Tzvetan Todorov refers to as "construction."[89] Not necessarily materialized in print, it provided the embryo of post-socialist literature.

Like post-modernist writing in general, it was derived from a master narrative but simultaneously undercut that narrative. It represents a shift from a utopia which is thoroughly public, desexualized, and militant to a construct of private, re-sexualized, domestic everydayness primarily imagined in terms of femininity, fantasies that constituted the mainstream of post-socialist literature.

Putting Old Wine into New Bottles? Rehabilitating the Soviet Hero

In 1980, the Soviet hero was officially rehabilitated and rescued from his previous official application during the Cultural Revolution. PLPH resumed the publication of Mei Yi's translation of *How the Steel Was Tempered* in 1980. Mei Yi emphasizes that "in the early 1970s, PLPH repeatedly asked for permission to reprint *How the Steel Was Tempered*. Each time, the "Gang of Four," intervened by demonizing the translator."[90] The fact that the Gang of Four ordered the publication of the novel during the Cultural Revolution was wisely left unsaid. The reappearance of Mei Yi's translation connoted the rehabilitation of the translator and the restoration of the cultural establishment.

"Rehabilitation" (*pingfan*) could apply to nearly all literary works published before 1966 because most were banned during the Cultural Revolution. However, the word was often used specifically to refer to the restoration of a revolutionary tradition that was allegedly interrupted, if not advanced too far for its own good during the Cultural Revolution. For example, "red classics" by domestic writers, such as *Red Cliff, The Song of Youth, Tracks in the Snowy Forest*, were the first to appear in bookstores as the reputation of their authors was rehabilitated. It therefore comes as no surprise that in "The Translator's Postscript" Mei Yi reiterates an allegedly Marxist vision of socio-cultural hierarchy (namely, socialist culture is superior to that of capitalism). The translator insists: "objective restrictions obliged Pavel to draw his inspiration from *Gadfly, Giuseppe Garibaldi, Spartacus, The Iron Heel* and the like by bourgeois writers from Britain, Italy, and America." By this comparison, he leads the reader to view themselves as "fortunate to receive guidance directly from works such as *How the Steel Was Tempered.*"[91]

However, after the "book famine" (*shuhuang*) of the Cultural Revolution, readers readily gave up their "privileged" access to correct reading in exchange for a diversity of "problematic" readings such as those to which Pavel Korchagin was exposed before 1917. The 1980s saw a continuity in avid reading, but the sources of reading material multiplied. Repeated intensive reading of a single Soviet novel due to the restricted availability of books was replaced by extensive reading in "rediscovered" works both at home and abroad. As the gate was gradually lifted for the publication of a backlog of Western and Chinese works, aspiring readers had a lot of catch-up reading to do in classics, high modernism, and popular literature. As Yu Hua put it, he anxiously looked for a new mentor "in order to survive and get ahead in an avalanche of books."[92]

Socialist new literature that fell between pure literature (classics and modern classics) and light entertainment was largely unread. Mei Yi predicted that Pavel Korchagin "will be with us" in the era of economic reform,[93] however, the market response in the 1980s suggested otherwise. In the early 1980s when memories of the "book famine" of the Cultural Revolution were still acute, books were sold out the moment they appeared on bookstands: 500,000 sets of *Arabian Nights* were sold out within months; 400,000 copies of *Death on the Nile* disappeared from the bookstore in two weeks; Freud's *Interpretation of Dreams* was forever out of stock no matter how much and how frequently bookstores ordered the book. However, the 260,000 copies of the post-Cultural Revolution edition of *How the Steel Was Tempered* remained on the shelves till the next year.

The 1980s was the logical end of the repeat-intensive reading of *How the Steel Was Tempered* in China. It was materially possible and intellectually feasible for readers to advance their education beyond the official *Bildungsroman*. As such it served as a necessary interval between reading and remembering, between the experiences of reading and reflecting/reappropriating of such experiences.

Conclusion

The intensive mass reading of *How the Steel Was Tempered* in China had its beginning and end. This history may be compared to a well-known story in the history of reading—the reading revolution that occurred in Europe in the late 18th century. Until the end of the 18th century, according to Leah Price, "people of all social classes owned a few books that they read 'intensively': slowly, repeatedly, and reverently. The classical example of repeat-intensive reading was the Bible, a book read year after year, never outdated."[94] The end of this period was generally attributed to the proliferation of new publications such as magazines, newspapers, and novels at the turn of the 19th century. If the transition from intensive to extensive reading in this classic case was made possible by the participation of commercial publications, the beginning *and* end of intensive reading of a socialist canonical work in China was contained within the evolving structure of a state cultural establishment that temporarily and deliberately suspended the commercial market. While censorship was no doubt an important factor shaping this history, the list of canonical works and available books shrank for over a decade until only one or two items remained. Ironically, the books that survived accumulated increasingly varied interpretations of the very kind of ambiguity that the state set out to abolish in the first place.

However, like the "revisionist" Soviet Union, the CCP continues to try to inculcate revolutionary ideals into the young. In the year of 2007, 2,600,000 copies of *How the Steel Was Tempered* were printed by the PLPH and presented as a gift to high school students in impoverished remote rural regions. If the "Soviet tomorrow" is becoming more of a founding myth than a future vision even for the government, it is not as a "textbook for life" but an archive of coming of age stories for two generations of Chinese readers that the novel has been repeatedly adapted to stage, film and television since the 1990s. Each adaptation represents a generational reading of the novel, a snapshot of life under changing circumstances in communist China. Like the family Bible in eighteenth-century Europe which is inscribed with the births, baptisms, marriages, and deaths in the family the changing reception of *How the Steel Was Tempered* chronicles the coming of age for generations of Chinese readers as well as the marriage, estrangement and reconciliation of communist China and Soviet Russia.

Notes

1. I would like to thank Thomas Bernstein, Sean Deitrick, Erika Evasdottir, Elizabeth McGuire, Yuri Slezkine, and Steven Taubeneck for reading drafts of this chapter and for their constructive comments, to Zhang Fusheng, the current editor of *How the Steel Was Tempered,* for kindly responding to many specific inquiries. My colleague Natalie Pervukhin graciously helped with the Russian translation despite her preference

not to be troubled by "Soviet trash." Individuals who shared their experiences of *How the Steel Was Tempered* are acknowledged as they arise in the chapter.

2. Confucius, *Analects* XVII, 9, in *An Anthology of Chinese Literature*, ed. and trans. Stephen Owen (New York: W. W. Norton, 1996), 58.

3. Robert M. Hutchins, Preface, in *A General Introduction to the Great Books and to a Liberal Education*, eds. Mortimer J. Adler and Peter Wolff (Chicago: Encyclopedia Britannica, 1959), v–viii, v–vi.

4. For the evolution of the "great books" from a university curriculum to its publication in encyclopedia forms for the general public see Tim Lacy, *Making of a Democratic Culture: The Great Books Idea, Mortimer J. Adler and Twentieth-century America*, (Ph.D. dissertation, Loyola University, 2006), 1–219. For the marketing and popular reception of the *Great Books* see Joan Shelley Rubin, *The Making of Middle Brow Culture* (Chapel Hill: University of North Carolina Press, 1992), 148–97.

5. Matthew Arnold *Literature and Dogma* (New York: AMS Press, 1970), xi.

6. There are two Chinese terms for "New China," with slightly different orientations. The adjective *xinhua* had been already in use before 1949 such as in *New China Daily* [Xinhua ribao] and New China News Agency. This term was used with a specific reference to the Chinese Communist Party in counterdistinction to the National Party. "*Xin Zhongguo*," on the other hand, came into wide circulation after 1949 as a synonym for the People's Republic of China in popular as well as official contexts. The Secretary-General of the Central People's Government of China defined this "new China" in terms of a "*genuine* People's Republic of China" as opposed to the Republic China which was "against the will of the people." "Double Tenth Is no Longer China's National Day," *North China Daily News* (October 10, 1949), 2.

7. "Gangtie shi zenyang liancheng de: lixiang de qizhi yu rensheng de jiaokeshu" [*How the Steel was Tempered*: The banner of idealism and the textbook for life] in *Yuwen cankeshu for Grade 8* [Reference book for grade 8 chinese] (Beijing: renmin jiaoyu chubanshe, 2007), 246–47. The novel was recommended for grade 9 students in the 1950s.

8. The concept of the "socialist new person" in China was largely a derivative of the "new Soviet man," even though it could be regarded as a variant of the "new people" (xinmin), which in its turn could be traced back to the turn of the twentieth-century. For changing conceptions of the "socialist new person" in Mao and Deng's period respectively see Mao Zedong, *Lun jiaoyu geming* [On educational revolution] (Beijing: Renmin jiaoyu chubanshe, 1967). Deng Xiaoping, *Deng Xiaoping lun wen yi* [Deng Xiaoping on art and literature] (Beijing: Renmin wenxue chubanshe, 1989).

9. Liu Qiong, "Wei lixiang fendou de ren—'lianghui' daibiao weiyuan dan dian-shiju *Gangtieshi zanyang lian cheng de*" [People who fight for their ideal: representatives of the PEOPLE's congress discussing HOW THE STEEL WAS TEMPERED), *Renmin ribao*, March 12, 2000, 4.

10. Lev Gudkov, "The Institutional Framework of Reading," *Russian Studies in Literature* 40, no. 1 (Winter 2003–4), 33–54.

11. Liang Qichao, "On Adolescent China," in Qiu Sang, ed. *Shaonian zhongguo shuo* [On adolescent China] (Beijing: Dongfang chubanshe, 1998), 66–71, 66.

12. Leo Ou-fan Lee, *The Romantic Generation of Modern Chinese Writers* (Cambridge: Harvard University Press, 1973), ix.

13. Hiroko Sakamoto, "The Cult of 'Love and Eugenics' in May Fourth Movement Discourse," *Positions* 12, no. 2 (2004), 329–76, especially 351.

14. Quoted in Jianmei Liu, *Revolution plus Love* (Honolulu: University of Hawaii Press, 2003), 53, emphasis mine.

15. A well known socio-economic critique of the revolutionary prodigal first came from such seasoned writers like Lu Xun. See Lu Xun, "Nala zuohou zanyang?" [What happens to Nora after the door slams behind her?], in *Lu xun quanji* [Complete works of Lu Xun] (Beijing: renmin wenxue chubanshe, 1998), vol. 1, 158–65.

16. *Shengyu 50 niandai* [Born in the 1950s], CCTV, 2006.

17. Mao Dun, "Zai fandongpai yapo xia douzheng he fazhan de gemin wenyi" [The struggle and development of revolutionary art and literature despite the oppression of anti-revolutionaries], in Wu Di, ed., *Zhongguo dianying yanjiu ziliao* [Source materials of Chinese film studies] (Beijing: wenhua yishu chuabanshe), vol. 1, 15–24, 18.

18. He Qifang, "Yige wenyi chuangzuo wenti de zhenglun" [A debate on literary and artistic creation], in Wu Di, 51–57, 55.

19. Katerina Clark, *The Soviet Novel: History as Ritual* (Chicago: University of Chicago Press, 1981), 16–17.

20. Clark, 16.

21. Examples include Sun Jing "Zhongguo xiandai 'chengzhang xiaoshuo' de xushixue yanjiu," [Narratology of the modern Chinese *bildungsroman*], M.A. thesis (Qingdao University, 2002). Fan Guobin, *Zhuti de shengcheng: 50 nian chengzhang xiaoshuo yanjiu* [The formation of the subject: a study of the 50 years of *bildungsroman*] (Beijing: Zhongguo xiju chubanshe, 2003).

22. Jerome Hamilton Buckle, *Season of Youth: The Bildungsroman from Dickens to Golding* (Cambridge: Harvard University Press, 1974), 17. Although it is almost an academic consensus to use Goethe's *Meister Wilhelm* as the classic example of the genre, *Tom Jones* had a much larger general audience, making it more appropriate for my study of mass reading.

23. Franco Moretti, *The Way of the World: The Bildungsroman in European Culture* (London: Verso, 1987), 229 n1.

24. During the general religious revival in Russia after perestroika the narrative of Koirchagin's life was reinterpreted as the celebration of the religious devotion over secular convictions. See Clark 47–48, 151–52. Alyssa W. Dinega, "Bearing the Standard: Transformative Ritual in Gorky's *Mother* and the Legacy of Tolstoy," *The Slavic and East European Journal*, vol. 42, no. 1 (Spring, 1998): 76–101.

25. Régine Robin, *Socialist Realism* (Palo Alto, CA: Stanford University Press, 1992), 41.

26. Zhou Yang, "*Shehuizhuyi xianshi zhuyi: zhongguo wenxue qianjin de daolu*" [Socialist realism: the direction for Chinese literature], in Hong Zicheng, ed., *Zhongguo dangdai wenxueshi: shiliao xuan 1945–1999* [Selected documents of modern chinese literary history: 1945–1999] (Wuhan: Changjiang wenyi chubanshe, 2002), 220–27, 220.

27. Zhou Yang, 226.

28. Hong Zhicheng, 228.

29. For dissucsion of cultural institutional reconstruction see Sun Xiaozhong, *Jianguo chuqi Shanghai chubanwu de shoubian he gezao* [The takeover and reform of publishers in Shanghai in the early years of the PRC], forthcoming by Shanghai jiaoyu chubanshe.

30. For the publication of *How the Steel Was Tempered* in China before 1949, see Wang Jiezhi and Chen Jianhua, *Youyuan de huixiang* [Enduring echoes] (Xining: Ningxia renmin chubanshe, 2002), 384–85.

31. Gérard Genette, *Paratexts: Thresholds of interpretation*, trans. by Jane E. Lewin (Cambridge: Cambridge University Press, 1997), 1.

32. Mei Yi, "Zaiban houji" (Postscript for the reprint of the 1942 edition), in *Gangtie shi zenyang liancheng de* [How the Steel was Tempered], Nikolai Ostrovsky, trans. Mei Yi (Shanghai: Sanlian, 1946), 453–54. Mei Yi, "Xinban houji" (Postscript to the new edition), in Nikolai Ostrovsky, *Gangtie shi zenyang liancheng de*, trans. Mei Yi (Beijing: People's Literature Press, 1952), 628.

33. R. Ostrovskaia, "*Zhi minzhu zhongguo de qingnian*" [To the youth in democratic China], in Nikolai Ostrovsky, 1952, i–vii, iv, vi.

34. R. Ostrovskaia, vi–vii.

35. For reception of *The Cossacks of Kuban* in the rural areas, see Tina Mai Chen, "Internationalism and Cultural Experience: Soviet Films and Popular Chinese Understandings of the Future in the 1950s," *Cultural Critique* 58 (Fall 2004): 82–114.

36. Petrovsky, "Xu" (Preface), in Nikolai Ostrovsky, 1952, 1–7, 4, 5.

37. Petrovsky, 5.

38. For the elevation of subjectivity at the expense of the body in Korchagin's maturity see Lilya Kagnosvky, "How the Soviet Man Was (Un)Made," *Slavic Review* 3 (2004), 577–96.

39. *1955 nian chuji zhongxue wenxue jiaoxue dagang* [Literary instruction outline for grade 7–9, 1955] (Beijing: renmin jiaoyu chubanshe, 1955), 12. Also see Jiang Dai. "*Bao'er: duoyuan wenhua chanshi beihou de lishi dongyin*" [Pavel: The historical incentive behind multi-cultural interpretation], *Eluosi wenyi* [Russian literature and art], no. 3 (2002): 63–65, 64.

40. Nikolai Ostrovsky, *How the Steel Was Tempered*, trans. R. Prokofieva (Moscow: Progressive Publishers, 1976a), 271.

41. Wang Meng, *Lian'ai de shijie* [The season for love] (Beijing: renmin wenxue chubanshe, 1993), 9.

42. Chen Chong, "Bushi wo bumingbai" [It is not that I do not understand] (hereinafter as "Bushi wo bumingbai"), *Wenxue ziyou tan* [Chat on literature], 3 (2000): 56–60, 57.

43. Chen Chong, "Bushi wo bumingbai," 56–60, 57.

44. Chen Chong, "Bushi wo bumingbai," 56–60, 57.

45. Liu Xinwu, "Chongdu Gangtie shi zenyang lian cheng de" [Rereading *How the steel was Tempered*], *Wenxue ziyou tan* [Chat on literature], 5 (1997): 17–21, 19.

46. Liang Xiaosheng, *Chongsu bao'er kechajin* [The reconstruction of Pavel Kochargin] (hereinafter as *Chongsu bao'er kechajin*) (Beijing: Tongxin chubanshe, 2000), 14, 15.

47. Liang Xiaosheng, *Chongsu bao'er kechajin*, 15.

48. Zhang Fusheng, interviewed by the author, October 12, 2005.

49. Wang Xiaoying, "Cong Chuanduan kangcheng dao Tuo'ersitai—waiguo wenxue yu wo" [From Yasunari Kawabata to Tolstoy—foreign literature and I], *Wai-guo wenxue pinglun* [Forum of foreign literature], 4 (91), 126–28, 126.

50. See Chen Chong, 56–57.

51. For a more detailed discussion of these articles see Miin-ling Yu, "A Soviet Hero, Pavel Korchagin, Comes to China," *Russian History* 29, nos. 2–4 (Summer–Winter 2002), 329–55, 343.

52. Sheila Fitzpatrick, 34.

53. Liu Gao, and Shi Feng, eds., *Xin zhongguo chuban wushinian jishi* [A chronology of publications in China from 1949–1999] (Beijing: Xinhua chubanshe, 1999), 99, 102.

54. Liu Gao, 136.

55. Lin Da, *Dai yiben shu qu Bali* [Taking a book to Paris] (Beijing: sanlian, 2002), 12.

56. Lin Da, 15.

57. Wang Anyi, *Wodu wokan* [I read, I see] (Shanghai: Shanghai renmin chubanshe, 2001), 5.

58. Archive material of PLPH.

59. For earlier Chinese translations and reprints of Mei Yi's translation by other publishers see Chen Jianhua, *Yaoyuan de huixiang: eluosi zuojia yu Zhongguo wenhua* [Distant and enduring echo: Russian writers and Chinese culture] (Yinchuan: ningxia renmin chubanshe, 2002), 384–85.

60. For censorship imposed by parents see *Wang Xiaobo wenji* [Collected works of wang xiaobo] (Beijing: Zhongguo qingnian chubanshe, 1999), vol. 4, 310.

61. Liu Xiaofeng, "Jilian dongniya" [Still enamored with Tonia], *Dushu* [Reading], no. 6 (1994): 84–92, 84.

62. Ha Jin interviewed by the author, 10 November 2004.

63. Interviewed by author included Dai Xun, Ha Jin, Liu Dong, Liu Xipu, Luo Dajun, Song Yongyi, and Zhang Yiwu.

64. Interviewed by author June 1, 2006.

65. For an analysis of literary works produced in the early 1970s see Bonnie S. Mc-Dougall and Kam Louie, *The Literature of China in the Twentieth-century* (London: Hurst & Company, 1997), 368.

66. Liu Xiaofeng, 85.

67. Li Jingze, "*Zuichu dude naxie shu*" [The books I read as a child], *Guowai wenxue* 2 [Foreign literature] (2000), 24–26, 25.

68. Li Jingze, 24.

69. Liu Xiaofeng, 85. Ding Fan, "How to Establish an Historical and Aesthetic Axis: Rereading *How the Steel Was Tempered*," *Contention in Literature and Art* 5 (2000), 76–78, 78.

70. Liu Xiaofeng, 89.

71. Wang Shuo, *Dongwu xiongmeng* [Fierce animal] (Beijing: Taihai chubanshe, 2000), 15.

72. Liu Xiaofeng, 90.

73. Ostrovsky, 1976, 210.

74. Ostrovsky, 1976, 108.

75. Liu Xiaofeng, 91.

76. Dai Xun, "Shuo bu jin de huati: qiansulian yu zhongguo" [An inexhaustible subject: The former soviet union and china], *Wenxue pinglun* 3 [Literary critique] (1999), 86–88, 86.

77. Nikolai Ostrovsky, *Gangtie shi zenyang liancheng de*, abbrev. Wang Su, illustr. Yi Jin (Beijing: renmin meishu chubanshe, 1972), vol. 1 and 2. English translation in *V. I. Lenin: Collected Works* (Moscow: Foreign Language Publishing House, 1963), vol. 15, 178.

78. Wang Su, Introduction, in Nikolai Ostrovsky, 1972.

79. Worker-peasant-soldier students refer to those who studied at Chinese universities from 1971 to 1977. In this period, working experiences instead of academic preparation was an essential criterion for university admission. Grassroots cadres and "revolutionary masses" played a decisive role in selecting students for universities.

80. *Renmin wenxue chubanshe bianjibu* [Editorial department of people's literature press], *Chuban shuoming* [Publisher's notes], in Nikolai Ostrovsky, 1976b.

81. Preface, in Nikolai Ostrovsky, 1976b, 9, 12.

82. Preface, in Nikolai Ostrovsky, 1976b, 10.

83. Preface, in Nikolai Ostrovsky, 1976b, 10.

84. Preface, in Nikolai Ostrovsky, 1976b, 8, 9.

85. *Shanghai wenyi chubanshe, Suxiu wenyi pipan ji* [Critical essays on soviet revisionist literature and art] (Shanghai: Shanghai wenyi chubanshe, 1975), 158, 169, 295.

86. Interview by author.

87. Joseph R. Levenson, *Revolution and Cosmopolitanism* (Berkeley: University of California Press, 1971), 47.

88. Tie Ning, *Da yunü* [The big bathers] (Shenyang: Chunfeng wenyi chubanshe, 2000), 103.

89. Tzvetan Todorov, "Reading as Construction" In Susan R. Suleiman and Inge Crosman, eds., *Reader in the Text* (Princeton: Princeton University Press, 1980), 67–82, 78.

90. Mei Yi, "Yihou ji" [Postscript], in *Gangtie shi zenyang liancheng de* [How the steel was Tempered], Nikolai Ostrovsky (Beijing: Renmin wenxue chubanshe, 1980), 495. For Mei Yi's experience during the Cultural Revolution see Yang Zhaolin, ed., 45–46, 211–13.

91. Mei Yi, 1980, 496.

92. Yu Hua, *Meiyou yitiao daolu shi chongfu de* [Every path is unique] (Shanghai: Shanghai wenyi chubanshe, 2004), 119.

93. Mei Yi, 1980, 498.

94. Leah Price, "Reading: The State of the Discipline," *Book History* 7 (2004) 303–20, 317.

16

Film and Gender in Sino-Soviet Cultural Exchange, 1949–1969[1]

Tina Mai Chen

"THE SOVIET UNION IS OUR TOMORROW" was a common phrase of 1950s China that, in its simple grammatical structure, linked the subjectivity of the Chinese people ("our") to specific geopolitical frameworks and revolutionary temporalities. The relationship this slogan laid out between geopolitics and Chinese subjectivity during the Maoist period invites us to inquire into the range of meanings encapsulated through visual and textual references that configured the Soviet Union in the 1950s as China's future, and in the 1960s and 1970s as China's antithesis. In this chapter, I am interested in exploring the cultural dimensions of geopolitics as one means through which the Soviet Union as discursive signifier and powerful nation-state became integrated into the everyday experiences and self-understanding of Chinese at all levels of society. By looking at Sino-Soviet cultural exchange, and film in particular, we can better understand the importance of internationalist and transnational culture in the politics of Mao's China; while also opening up spaces for consideration of the gendered aspects of Chinese subjectivity and its geopolitical reference points.

Between 1949 and 1953, the People's Republic of China (PRC) imported 234 full-length films. Those films with the largest audiences and number of screenings were films imported from the Soviet Union. Through these films, visual culture emerged as an important medium for giving meaning to the Soviet Union within China. Even though Chinese national film distribution networks were in a nascent stage in the first few years of the PRC, by 1953 five Soviet films were screened between 15,600 to 37,600 times, with audiences ranging from approximately 15 million to over 32 million. These films were

Kuban Cossacks (USSR 1949; PRC 1951), *Tractor Drivers* (USSR 1939; PRC 1952), *Unforgettable 1919* (USSR 1952; PRC 1952), *She Defends the Motherland* (USSR 1943; PRC 1952) and *Fall of Berlin* (USSR 1949; PRC 1950).[2] The films showcased either the success of socialist collectives or military struggle and were produced during a period in Soviet film when the film industry functioned to reinforce the legitimacy of the Soviet state. The films all participated to some extent in propagating the cult of Stalin.[3] But the films also featured female protagonists who captured the attention of Chinese audiences for their patriotism and partisanship, as well as their appearance. Through Sino-Soviet film exchange, Soviet actresses such as Marina Ladynina (*Kuban Cossacks* and *Tractor Drivers*), Vera Maretskaia (*She Defends the Motherland*), and Marina Kovaleva (*Fall of Berlin*) became recognizable and politically sanctioned faces of socialism in the PRC. The meaning of these women and their on-screen personas thereby became part of shifting state and popular articulations of socialism in 1950s and 1960s China.

Analysis of the debates occasioned by these films when initially released in the PRC in the early 1950s, as well as the discussions linked to screenings in the late 1950s and 1960s, provides us with a viewpoint from which to examine relations between the Soviet Union and China. By looking at the place of these films and their female protagonists in Maoist China, this chapter takes on a threefold purpose. First, it outlines the importance of Soviet film for Sino-Soviet cultural exchange and Sino-Soviet relations more generally. Second, the chapter examines representations of gender in Soviet films popular in China and considers how particular Soviet female films stars participated in the articulation of female subjectivities in the PRC. Third, the chapter concludes by arguing that gender and culture are key elements through which the Soviet Union and the PRC produced socialist visions, reinforced the legitimacy of their socialism vis-à-vis each other, and envisaged foreign policy.

Soviet Film in China, 1949–1976

In the introduction to his book on Soviet experts in China, Shen Zhihua remarks that the masses learned about the Soviet Union through Soviet films and Soviet specialists who were sent to China.[4] Along with the chapters in this volume by Elizabeth McGuire, Douglas Stiffler, and Izabella Goikhman, Shen highlights the importance of Soviet experts and exchange programs for the unfolding of Chinese socialism. I take up the other half of his claim, that of Soviet film, and ask what we can learn about politics and their gendered dimensions within China and across the Sino-Soviet border if we are to focus on films and the film industry.

In the early years of the Maoist period, import of Soviet film was based on a series of agreements and practices that had been developed in Northeast China (Manchuria) between 1945 and 1949. Namely, the All-Union Corporation for Export and Import of Films, usually referred to as Sovexportfilm, was responsible for the international circulation of Soviet films. To this end, Sovexportfilm established offices in Harbin and Dalian in 1945 and 1946 respectively and bought, rented, or controlled a number of theaters in the major cities of the region.[5] In these areas, Sovexportfilm and the Sino-Soviet Friendship Association (SSFA) functioned as the key institutions for organizing screenings and disseminating programs featuring Soviet film.[6] By the end of 1948, Soviet films were also well integrated into the Chinese educational system. *Dalian ribao* reported on 14 September 1948 that almost all Harbin schools saw and discussed the Soviet films *A Village Schoolteacher*, *The Red Scarf*, *The Young Guard*, and *Tales of a Siberian Land*.[7] In addition to distributing films, Soviet initiatives to provide equipment for film distribution in China included the manufacture of film projectors for mobile projection teams. In this capacity Zenith, a company managed by the Harbin Sovexportfilm office, produced forty film projectors in 1948 for film projection units in Manchuria.[8]

Even in the areas under firmer GMD control and in which the combined activities of SSFA and CCP activities prior to 1949 were less central to the cultural landscape than Dalian, Soviet film still occupied an important position. Sovexportfilm's Shanghai office was established in 1946 and built upon pre-existing relations with Asia Films of China that dated to 1934 and concerned distribution of Soviet films within Guomindang China. While the number of spectators was more limited than in Manchuria (with 1,354,865 spectators in 1947 and 1,501,334 in 1948), the stock was still quite substantial. In 1949 the Shanghai office held approximately 200 prints of fiction, documentary, and scientific films.[9] The distribution of these prints took place according to a July 1948 three-year agreement. This agreement licensed films to Asia Films of China for distribution everywhere in China except Manchuria, Xinjiang, and Hong Kong and divided net earnings according to a 60/40 formula between the company and Sovexportfilm.[10] With the liquidation of Asia Films of China in 1948, a similar agreement was signed with the new Chinese company, East China Films, and film rights in Manchuria given to the North China Distribution Board.[11]

Both Sovexportfilm and the USSR Ministry of Cinematography recognized that the military successes of the CCP and People's Liberation Army in 1948 and 1949 created new opportunities for distribution of Soviet film. With the imminent change in government and the anticipated nationalization of Chinese studios a new agreement was worked out. The 1949 agreement stipulated that Soviet film distribution would be conducted in China by four representative offices: the head office in Beijing and the branch offices in Harbin, Dalian, and Shanghai.[12] The terms of distribution and screening provided that the Central Cinematography Board of the PRC would oversee distribution while fifty percent of gross earnings went to Sovexportfilm. This agreement was put in place for a one-year period and through annual renewals provided the basic framework until the Agreement of 1954.

Exchange agreements between the Soviet Union and China from 1954 reflected the restructuring of the Chinese film industry under the CCP. By 1954, the Chinese film industry was less dependent on Soviet films, expertise, and technology because China's own studios were producing more films, had the capacity to dub approximately 40 films per year, and China actively imported films from other countries besides the Soviet Union.[13] The relative strength of the Chinese film industry can be seen in the new agreements put in place in 1954. These insisted on more equality in the financial terms of exchange and distribution as films moved from the Soviet Union to China, and vice versa. The new agreement stipulated that the Chinese purchase licenses for films and all future profits would then be fully controlled by the Chinese.[14] These new conditions promised greater revenue for China from Soviet film, and meant that Soviet films in China circulated on the same terms as did Chinese films in the Soviet Union.

Nineteen fifty-four thus marked a turning point in what we can consider the geopolitical nexus of the exchange agreements. Prior to 1954 China was the recipient of Soviet film and film technology, and exchange agreements reinforced the relative strength of the Soviet Union and its film industry over China. The year 1954 can be seen as a moment of equalization and in the subsequent years China asserted itself as the center of socialist film exchanges. This can be seen in the decreased Soviet share of the Chinese cinema market from approximately 90 percent from 1949–1952, to 42.58 percent in 1952, 36.15 percent in 1953, and 30.77 percent in 1954. The decreased share is only one part of the larger picture, however; the number of people within China who had access to film increased to such an extent that even with the decreased share of the market, the number of viewers of Soviet film often increased.[15] Another point to consider is that the Soviet Union provided almost all scientific films imported to China through 1957. This reinforced the association between the Soviet Union, film, and advanced technology. At the same time, however, the orientation toward an increasingly independent China following the end of the Korean War (1953) and the Bandung Conference (1955) meant a greater focus on China at the center of Third World anti-imperialism.

As China and the Soviet Union moved in different directions with respect to theories and practices of socialism, the process of negotiation for exchange became increasingly complicated. China refused to purchase films it deemed

Table 16.1. Import Statistics of Soviet Films, 1949–1957

Year	Feature Films		Documentary		Science Films		Other Films		Totals	
	USSR	All	USSR	All	USSR	All	USSR	All	USSR	All
1949	3	3	0	0	0	0	0	0	3	3
1950	65	65	4	4	11	11	6	6	86	86
1951	25	29	3	3	8	8	25	26	61	66
1952	14	48	20	21	3	3	17	22	54	94
1953	18	44	12	17	24	32	24	37	78	130
1954	24	48	10	15	34	36	22	30	90	129
1955	26	67	10	12	34	40	11	33	81	152
1956	49	128	9	10	59	78	12	34	129	250
1957	27	94	6	9	28	32	17	44	78	179
Total	251	526	74	91	210	240	134	232	660	1089

Notes: Czechoslovakia was the country that supplied the second largest number of imported films with total films in all categories ranging from eight to seventeen per year from 1952 to 1957.
Data from *Zhongguo dianying faxing fangying tongji ziliao jiangbian (1949–1957)* [Handbook of statistical data on China film circulation and screening) (Beijing: Zhongguo dianying faxing fangying gongxi, 1958), 157–161.

revisionist and often preferred films from other socialist countries rather than
Soviet films of "The Thaw" period.[16] The decline in Sino-Soviet import and
export of film in the late 1950s led to another restructuring of the exchange
process by the Soviet Union. By October 1959, the Soviet Trade Mission
began the practical management of commercial distribution of Soviet film.
The closing of Sovexportfilm offices in China in 1960 ensued and Mezhkniga
(*Mezhdunarodnaia Kniga* [International Books]) assumed Soviet cinema
interests in China.[17] Over the next five years the number of Soviet films accepted by the Chinese Cinematography Board for exhibition in China declined significantly. This was due to the economic crisis and currency control
that followed the Great Leap Forward, as well as to the political estrangement
between the two nations. Observations by the Soviet Trade Mission on Soviet
films in China confirmed that Soviet films purchased in the early 1950s were
shown regularly in Chinese cities but that few new films were introduced or
discussed in the press. The 1963 Chinese campaign against Soviet art and
"new wave cinema" as an expression of revisionism further compounded
these developments. By 1965 each side was committed to only minimal exchange; China agreed to premiere one Soviet film and vice versa. In the years
prior to the Great Proletarian Cultural Revolution, the initiative for Sino-
Soviet film exchange largely came from the Soviet Union and by 1966 film
exchange basically ceased.[18]

Even as the Chinese press stopped reporting on Soviet films and very few
new Soviet films entered into China, old Soviet films were shown in major
cities and in the countryside. Films such as *Lenin in October, Lenin in 1918,*
and *The Battle of Stalingrad* continued to be popular; as were some of those
mentioned above whose female heroines had gained a following such as Marina Kovaleva in *The Fall of Berlin,* Vera Maretskaia in *A Village Schoolteacher,*
and Galina Vodyanitskaia in *Zoya.* These films and almost all other Soviet
films shown in the 1960s and during the Cultural Revolution were purchased
by China before 1956. Despite the continuity in terms of their availability to
Chinese audiences, the screening of these films both before and after the Sino-
Soviet split was accompanied by complex shifts in the framing of the films in
propaganda and press materials. I now turn our attention to the discussion
of specific films imported from the Soviet Union in the 1950s and 1960s
in order to analyze film exchange as a component of Sino-Soviet relations
and its gendered dimensions. Examination of specific Soviet films in China
demonstrates that Mao's understanding of class struggle and historical stages
was articulated for the masses, in part, through visual and textual references
to the Soviet Union, as well as Soviet female film stars and their on-screen
characters.

Engendering Analysis of Sino-Soviet Film Exchange

Soviet women who came to the People's Republic of China in official capacities tended not to be the Soviet experts responsible for training Chinese in different aspects of technical production and industrial development. Rather the women were Soviet film stars who appeared as part of delegations to promote Sino-Soviet friendship or they were women who came on short-term exchanges generally related to healthcare or education.[19] Clearly, there is a gendered politics of expertise at work here that privileges the male body as the international conduit of knowledge.[20] In this paper, however, I am interested in analyzing how gender was used to legitimate or de-legitimate particular socialist visions, and the ways in which the Chinese state promoted specific understandings of sexuality and gender as part of the articulation of Mao's theory of class struggle and continuous revolution, as well as the critique Soviet revisionism.

Sino-Soviet negotiations concerning the specific films that would be imported, where they would be screened, what types of promotional materials would be used, and who would participate in cross-border film delegations took place within the context of Sino-Soviet Friendship and the deterioration of this relationship. By the mid-1950s Mao Zedong set policies that allowed for two potentially contradictory constructions of socialist womanhood to circulate and that were directly related to his analysis of socialism in the Soviet Union. First, through campaigns such as the Dress Reform Movement, the notion of a post-revolutionary socialist woman who enjoyed material benefits because of the success of socialism was, albeit briefly, part of politically ratified praxis.[21] Second, Mao Zedong became increasingly vocal in his critique of systems of material rewards within socialism. For Mao, this was a crucial aspect of class struggle in post-revolutionary socialist society.[22] I argue in this paper that debate over the appropriateness of material rewards and what I have termed "fun-loving post-revolutionary" subjectivities in the building of socialism took place through gendered language and characterizations where the class enemy (whether an individual, collective, or nation-state) was feminized and sexualized.[23]

Scholars of Sino-Soviet relations are familiar with Mao's scathing critiques of the use of material incentives as well as his emphasis that socialist transformation must apply to all social relations including relations between production and the superstructure, and the relations between different sectors including economy, politics, ideology, culture, and so on.[24] Rarely, however, are these comments connected to gender politics and cultural relations. Yet, Mao's critique of the Soviet use of material incentives and its more strident articulation following Khrushchev's de-Stalinization was part of a renewed focus on what Mao understood to be the current stage of China's revolution and the danger of bourgeois remnants and new sprouts. This was a framework that often mobilized gendered discourse and visual imagery. Specifically, those men and women whose bodies and actions seemed to celebrate individual desire, consumer practices, and ambiguous class consciousness were seen as contrary to the Chinese revolution, and accordingly their bodies and actions were discredited through visual and textual references to improper sexuality or gender roles. One of the best known examples from the Cultural Revolution period of discrediting individuals through sexualized appearance as symptomatic of incorrect politics was the April 1967 forced donning for a criticism session of ping-pong ball "pearl" necklace and qipao by Wang Guangmei, Liu Shaoqi's wife. The Red Guard actions sought to de-legitimate Wang, Liu, and Soviet revisionism through visual reminders of Wang's performance of incorrect socialism and sexuality in her visit to Indonesia in 1963 and interactions in China with Sukharno.

The fates of Soviet female film stars in China often were embroiled in these interlocked debates over correct socialism and sexuality. Soviet female film stars occupied an important position in the everyday experiences of Maoism because photographs, films, and other visual materials frequently accompanied newspaper reports and campaigns promoting the activities of model women and men in the Soviet Union. Moreover, few Chinese men or women had opportunities for direct contact with these Soviet models so the connections they forged with their Soviet counterparts were through representational bodies. The exception to this was Chinese students studying in the USSR and the relatively small number of Chinese national model workers who traveled to Moscow as part of official Chinese delegations. Chinese women in these delegations had opportunities for direct contact with Soviet men and women; but even their experiences were mediated through visual and print propaganda for the majority of Chinese. For example, Liang Jun, who was officially recognized as China's first female tractor driver, was a woman well known to Chinese because her story was featured in the national Chinese press on numerous occasions. Liang Jun incorporated into her well-rehearsed and officially sanctioned life narrative the inspiration she received from watching the Soviet film *Tractor Drivers* and from specific Soviet female characters like Dasha who drove a tank against the German invaders after her family was killed in the film *She Defends the Motherland*.[25]

Liang Jun's life story reinforced the central tenet of early 1950s propaganda campaigns to "Learn from the Soviet Union" and from Soviet models. These campaigns held up Soviet women as progressive examples for Chinese women and men. The lifestyles and struggles of Soviet models were seen as prefiguring the struggles that Chinese were undertaking; moreover identification with Soviet model women as part of an international socialist struggle was encouraged. But what forms of identification occurred? And how did these forms of identification change as part of a Maoist reconfiguring of the geopolitical frameworks and revolutionary temporality of socialist struggle?

We can begin to answer these questions about the relationship between gendered subjectivities, revolutionary ideologies, and geopolitical frameworks that either forged connections—or reinforced distinctions—between Soviet and Chinese socialism by analyzing the role of certain prominent Soviet female film stars in Maoist China. These film stars include Marina Ladynina, Vera Maretskaia, and Marina Kovaleva, each of whom starred in numerous

Marina Ladynina

Soviet-era films. I have singled them out because both Ladynina and Marets-kaia visited China as part of the delegations, in 1952 and 1956 respectively, and because the films that they starred in were extremely popular in China upon their initial release in the 1950s but had different fates after the Sino-Soviet split in the 1960s.

Marina Ladynina

Let me begin by considering Marina Ladynina and her role in the making of Chinese socialism. Marina Ladynina starred in a number of Soviet films that were immensely popular in China, including *Tractor-Drivers* (1939; PRC 1951), *Kuban Cossacks* (1949; PRC 1950), and *Tales of the Siberian Land* (1947; PRC 1951). Two of these films in particular—*Tractor Drivers* and *Kuban Cossacks*—were staples of rural film projection units, thereby ensuring that those in China who had access to mobile or permanent film exhibition likely saw these films. Notably, audience numbers for *Tractor Drivers* and *Kuban Cossacks* exceeded 17 million each in their first two years of circulation, a time when the number of rural film projection units was still relatively small. Moreover, Ladynina traveled to China as part of a Soviet delegation for the 1952 November Film Festival that included actors Boris Chirkov (Maxim in *The Gorky Trilogy*) and Nikolai Cherkasov (Professor Polezhaev in *The Baltic Deputy*).[26] As part of the delegation Ladynina met with Mao Zedong as well as workers, peasants, and youth and she spoke to audiences before screenings of films. For this 1952 Soviet delegation, the actors were particularly sought after, and the crowds called out to the actors by the names of the characters they played on screen.[27] Chinese who had contact with the delegation also sang songs from the Soviet films, particularly those from *Kuban Cossacks* and *Tractor Drivers*, thereby further reinforcing identification of Ladynina with the characters she played on screen.[28]

Tractor Drivers and *Kuban Cossacks* are both light-hearted musicals directed by Ivan Pyriev in which Ladynina plays characters who are cheerfully successful within the socialist agricultural collective. These films celebrate prosperity and happiness on the collective farm and hyperbolize the success. Film historians have noted that these films were produced in the Soviet Union precisely when agriculture was undergoing a severe crisis in the late 1930s;[29] however, in the Chinese context their initial circulation in 1950 and 1951 corresponded with the period of economic restructuring after eight years of war against the Japanese and four years of civil war. Moreover, because the films were always located in the Chinese future—as a promise of what was to come—characters such as Dasha (played by Klara Luchko) and Galina (played by Ladynina) embodied a specific aspect of socialist liberation: a fun-loving post-revolutionary female agency. This fun-loving post-revolutionary womanhood was premised upon an agency that was clearly located in the agricultural cooperative but that allowed for carefree expressions (and fulfillment of) consumer desires and flirtatious sexuality.[30] The dance scenes and songs in *Tractor Drivers*, and the scenes at the fair in *Kuban Cossacks*, are about the good life.

Elsewhere, I have analyzed the power of the "good life" imagery in China and its association with the Soviet Union as China's future.[31] I have argued that from its inception the Chinese Communist Party (CCP) viewed love and sexuality as important aspects of society that needed to be redefined within a socialist framework. Here it is the temporal frameworks of internationalism and women's liberation that interest me because they shed light on how particular embodiments of female agency can simultaneously be part of—and displaced from—a Maoist ideology of gender and revolutionary geopolitics. In the case of Marina Ladynina and the roles she played for 1950s Chinese audiences, the CCP chose to provide guidelines for interpretation. The editor of *Dazhong Dianying* responded to a query regarding the portrayal of Soviet citizens as fun-loving by stating: "Soviet people are determined but this does not mean that they don't have feelings."[32] She clarified by stating that once the Soviet Union evolved into a happy and prosperous society the people could express their love at various levels—for each other, for their culture, and for the collective farm—*because* of the new society. In other responses to reader queries in the film, the editor made clear that love as shown on screen in these films was part of China's future, not the Chinese present. For women working in newly formed Chinese cooperatives, therefore, they were called upon to identify with Marina Ladynina *and* to see her characters' lives as just beyond the horizon. Thus, positive desire and sexuality, as embodied by Ladynina, was a component of the political culture of the 1950s, even if its realization was projected into the Chinese future.

Another point to remember is that in the context of the initial circulation of these films—and the rapid and promising development of socialism in China—identification by urban (as opposed to rural) women with Ladynina would be marked by campaigns such as the 1956 "Dress Reform Campaign."[33] This campaign came out of an early assessment by Mao Zedong and the CCP that confident and mature socialist societies would have socialist women who dressed nicely. Post-revolutionary women could develop practices of beauty and fashion that were socialist rather than capitalist or feudal—and they might even wear pretty clothes *for* the socialist nation.[34] When coupled with Soviet women as objects of Chinese desire, post-revolutionary womanhood thus was located not only in the Chinese socialist nation but the global socialist future. This type of international identification, that allowed for the possibility of a female socialist subjectivity based in a post-revolutionary moment, was short lived, however. It could not survive the change in Sino–Soviet relations that came with Khrushchev's de-Stalinization, Mao's critique of Soviet revisionism, and the renewed focus within China on class struggle that began with the Great Leap Forward and became more pronounced in the 1960s and with the Cultural Revolution. As a result, the films featuring Marina Ladynina were shown less often. Other Soviet films, also released in China in the early 1950s, became staples of film projection units through the 1960s. These films included *Fall of Berlin* (1949; PRC 1950), with female lead played by Marina Kovaleva; as well as *A Village Schoolteacher* (1947; PRC 1950), *She Defends the Motherland* (1943; PRC 1951), and *Mother* (1955; PRC 1955)—all of which had Vera Maretskaia as the female lead.

Village Schoolteacher and *She Defends the Motherland* were among the first films to be imported into the PRC and dubbed in Chinese in 1950, but Vera Maretskaia did not travel to the PRC until 1956. At this time she was part of a delegation sent to celebrate the November Soviet Film Festival, which featured the films *Mother, Unfinished Tale, Alien Kin*, and *Soldier Ivan Brovkin*.[35] The 1956 delegation was made up of six members, in addition to Maretskaia, including director Leonid Lukov (*Different Destinies* [1956], *Private Alexander Matrosov* [1947], *Mother* [1941]), and actor Sergei Bondarchuk (*Young Guard* [1948] and *Unfinished Tale* [1955]). Over the course of their stay they visited Beijing, Nanjing, Shanghai, Hangzhou, and Canton for a total of 18 meetings with 25,000 audience members.

In contrast to Marina Ladynina, whose sometimes comic and always fun-loving characters seemed best suited to a post-revolutionary future, Vera Maretskaia embodied a female subjectivity rooted in struggle and resistance rather than fulfillment. In this role she was deemed relevant to China both before and after the Sino–Soviet split. The films with her as the female lead continued to be shown from the early 1950s and throughout the Cultural Revolution period and to receive official sanction as appropriate representations of socialist womanhood across the various political campaigns. Maretskaia's characters both before and after the Sino-Soviet split embodied a form of socialist womanhood that met the needs of campaigns that highlighted "the present" and ongoing nature of revolutionary struggle.

The form of socialist womanhood represented by Maretskaia was summed up in a 1952 article that encouraged the Chinese to learn from Maretskaia and her character in *Member of Government*. The article emphasized her commitment to the Communist Party and her embodiment of great strength.[36] This characterization of Maretskaia's characters was reinforced in another article of the same year that discussed the unforgettable female characters of Soviet films. In this case, the article praised the characters played by both

Maretskaia and Ladynina; the former for her patriotism and commitment to the Party and the latter for her proximity to rural life and her leadership role in this capacity as seen in *Kuban Cossacks*.[37] Already at this moment in the early 1950s a tension was evident, however, in the relative importance of the women and their characters for Chinese socialism. The text sandwiched references to Ladynina between much more substantial paragraphs discussing Maretskaia in *Member of Government, She Protects the Motherland*, and *A Village Schoolteacher*; whereas the visual layout prominently featured a film still from *Kuban Cossacks* of Ladynina smiling at the camera, albeit placed among photographs of other women. The combined visual and textual interplay in 1952 between these two forms of socialist womanhood as part of socialist China's past, present, and future pointed to the tensions between a female socialist subjectivity rooted in struggle that linked past and present, but haunted by the promise of a more glamorous future post-revolutionary womanhood. This article highlighted the geopolitical frameworks and revolutionary temporalities gave meaning for Chinese film to the Soviet Union, historically contingent configurations of Sino-Soviet relations, and China's socialist revolution.

Vera Maretskaia as Varenka in *A Village Schoolteacher* (1947).

Vera Maretskaia as Pasha (aka Comrade P) in *She Defends the Motherland* (1943). Placard reads: "I am a partisan. I killed German soldiers."

The tensions between a fun-loving post-revolutionary subjectivity rooted in the rural collective versus a female subjectivity contingent on militarized, patriotic and partisan struggle against class and national enemies were, on one hand, about different ideas about the appropriate roles for women in socialist society. On the other hand, the different visions of female subjectivity can also be understood in relation to questions of revolutionary temporality, historical periodization, and Maoist political praxis as related to the identification of antagonistic and non-antagonistic contradictions. That is, discussion of these female Soviet film stars participated in defining the meaning, nature, and form of Chinese and global socialist revolution as envisioned by Mao in the 1950s and 1960s.

In 1950s China, Maoist discourse located China within a history of socialism that began with the October Revolution and then followed the course of history laid out by the Soviet Union.[38] In the 1960s, with the Sino–Soviet split and contesting interpretations of socialism, Maoist revolutionary discourse identified China as the only nation upholding the legacy of the October Revolution, proclaimed China the centre of a Third World-focused global struggle, and highlighted the ongoing class struggle even within socialist nation-states.[39] Maretskaia's female roles found a place in both moments of the Chinese revolutionary struggle because of the focus on determined, principled, and unwavering support for the Communist Party and socialism. Moreover, the Maoist focus on continuous revolution and class struggle meant that in the 1960s the female roles of Maretskaia could be loosed from Soviet history and co-opted for a socialist history where the enemy was ever-present.

The characters Maretskaia played on screen proved important and relevant to the fervent reminders of the dangers of revisionism and global attempts to undermine socialist China that characterized Maoist praxis from the late 1950s, and which contributed to the ideological basis of criticism of the Soviet Union. The roles played by Maretskaia are marked by several common characteristics: one, the women are left alone either by the death or political arrest of their husbands/lovers and she then takes up a militant defense of nation or promotion of socialism; two, the characters find fulfillment in the CPSU and socialism rather than personal love relations; three, the characters are not always young and attractive—but showcase strength and determination as they undergo a desexualization over the course of the film; four, the characters themselves always occupy and defend domestic/national space whereas the male characters in the film often take up duties in international space.

These characteristics, while linked to support of the CPSU when originally screened in both the USSR and PRC, could be reinterpreted in the altered historical context of the late 1950s and 1960s as values that enabled critique of revisionism within, and embodied by, Soviet leadership (and their purported Chinese puppets). The desired traits ascribed to Maretskaia were distanced from the revisionist Soviet state and praised as the essential elements of a revolutionary people, whether in the Soviet Union or China. This was accomplished, in part, by a rhetorical strategy deployed in national media accounts about Soviet revisionism and those Soviet films still available in China that differentiated between the revolutionary Soviet people and the revisionist Soviet state and leadership. As such, the 'motherland' that Vera Maretskaia worked to defend against fascism/capitalism/revisionism became the broader space of socialism (now associated with China not the USSR). The fate of the Chinese and global socialist revolution then depended upon producing socialist citizens who embraced a subjectivity forged through class struggle and loyalty to the Party, as embodied by Maretskaia and her Chinese counterparts such as Xi'er in *White-Haired Girl*, Liu Hulan, and Zhao Yiman.[40]

Mao's preoccupation with revisionist elements within the Chinese and global socialist revolutions meant it was no longer appropriate that women celebrate a (future) socialist femininity or be portrayed primarily as the embodiment of nationhood. The roots of capitalism and feudalism, Mao emphasized, still existed in China thus making it difficult to imagine male and female subjectivity in which people were liberated from the constraints of feudalism, patriarchy, and capitalism and thereby freed to embrace gender-specific styles as socialist citizens. Instead, Mao's interpretation of the state of socialist revolution in the 1960s demanded that ideal socialist men and women were those actively engaged in struggle against local and global anti-revolutionary forces and their substantiation at the individual level. Thus as Mao targeted Soviet revisionism, U.S. imperialism, and launched campaigns within China to "Never forget Class Struggle" and "Learn from Lei Feng," transnational and national cultural products emphasized a revolutionary heritage of military and class struggle rather than post-revolutionary lifestyles. In this context, and in the politics of Sino-Soviet film exchange, Stalinist classics and their film stars dominated in China.

In terms of nation-wide screenings and access to Soviet female film stars, by 1963, with the increasingly difficult conditions in China for showing Soviet film, films selected by the CCP for purchase and/or screening were dominated by historical films and those that depicted the life of the Soviet people before the 20th Party Congress of 1956.[41] Within this context, available Soviet films included those that featured Maretskaia such as *A Village Schoolteacher* and *She Defends the Motherland,* as well as *Fall of Berlin* and the re-release of *Zoya*. The film *Zoya* (dir. Lev Arnshtram, 1944) perhaps most clearly exemplifies the importance for Mao's China of internationalist cultural representations of woman with total dedication to struggle. *Zoya* is based on a the story Zoya Kosmodemyanskaya (played by Galina Vodianitskaya in the film), an 18-year-old Moscow girl captured as a guerilla fighter behind Nazi lines. The movie uses flashback scenes to show Zoya's childhood that are set against torture footage by the Nazis. In this way she simultaneously embodied the female soldier as well as innocent childhood. Her martyrdom in the mist of the collective struggle mean that she is distanced from any expression of a future post-revolutionary sexuality, and the tensions it created in revolutionary temporal schemas as well as female socialist subjectivity. Notably, Zoya had a Chinese counterpart in Zhao Yiman, a Chinese guerilla fighter who died a martyr when she refused to give names of CCP members to the Japanese. Importantly, the filmed version of *Zhao Yiman* circulated in China alongside both the original release of *Zoya* in the early 1950s and its re-release in the 1960s.[42] The contemporaneous circulation of the two films, featuring young female soldier-heroines, points to the internationalist aspects of Maoist visual culture, as well as the ways in which this culture consolidated particularly inflected geopolitical frameworks and revolutionary temporal schemas that increasingly questioned and removed particular associations of Soviet womanhood and "the future" as relevant to the Maoist revolutionary present.

In 1960s China, one of the major concerns in terms of female subjectivity as expressed and promoted through Sino-Soviet cultural linkages was circulation of characters whose resolve and loyalty was uncompromised. Zoya and Zhao Yiman, with their choice of death over betrayal of the Party and socialism, embodied a socialist subjectivity bounded by the "now-ness" of class struggle and a totalizing commitment to this struggle.[43] The Chinese held that post-1956 Soviet films lacked this revolutionary resolve and reflected a backward impulse that went against the desired historical progression of socialist revolution. In the post-1956 period, then, Soviet films that failed to express unequivocally a form of subjectivity that did not uphold the Maoist maxim "do not fear hardship do not fear death" were declined for import. For example, the Central Film Bureau in China rejected the Soviet film *Immortal Garrison* (1956), even though the main plot of *Immortal Garrison* follows Soviet servicemen overcoming their desire to return to wives and loved ones and instead putting their energies into the siege at Brest. But it was not the actions of the male soldiers that concerned the Chinese authorities. Rather they were concerned about the lack of iron resolve by the women soldiers and the isolation of the garrison from the actions of the Soviet armed forced. The problem, as far as Chinese authorities were concerned, was that the women soldiers surrendered and that even though the male soldiers acted admirably, their

Natasha (Marina Kovaleva) and Alesha (Boris Andreyev), *The Fall of Berlin.*

actions were beyond the immediate reach of the Party and therefore were dangerous and (potentially) counterrevolutionary models for emulation.[44]

But we should not jump to easy conclusions that the internationalist imagery of Maoist socialism and geopolitics fully resolved the tensions between appropriate forms of female subjectivity in favor of a militarized partisan focused on uninterrupted struggle. Even those films that were considered the safest expressions of revolutionary culture and virtue in the USSR, like the paean to Stalin in *Fall of Berlin*, had moments in which alternate emotional commitments and subjectivity linked to sexualized bodies could not be ignored. Here we can consider the final scenes of *Fall of Berlin* during which the protagonists Alesha and Natasha engage in a passionate kiss in front of Stalin as part of the fictionalized mass crowd scene of Stalin's arrival in Berlin at the moment of the city's liberation. Given that Chinese-produced films in this period are marked by a complete absence of kissing, even between couples legitimated by the state, there must have been some interest in China in this close-up kiss between Alesha and Natasha, even if this kiss visually reinforces the triangulation of legitimate love in which love is rendered legitimate when refracted through the prism of the Communist Party and its leaders. Still, in *Fall of Berlin*, the kiss stands out because it is the climax to a personalized relationship that runs through the film and it lends an erotic moment to the appropriation of individual love for patriotism, Stalin, and the Party.

In addition, the attractive face of Marina Kovaleva with slightly upturned chin featured prominently in press materials for the film in the 1950s and 1960s. Notably, Soviet officials praised these press materials for their high quality and ability to appeal to the Chinese masses.[45] Yet when we consider the advertisement below, the eye moves from Stalin to Andreyev to Kovaleva in such a way that the love story interwoven with that of the anti-Fascist struggle and socialist fortitude is not overridden by its relationship to Stalinist iconography. The gaze of Andreyev and Kovaleva appears to settle on the same point, whereas Stalin is set apart from this gaze (in the advertisement if not in the film itself). In addition, Kovaleva's upturned chin and arched neck suggest the expected defiance against fascism and commitment to socialism, while also introducing a moment of yearning that could be read as yearning for Stalin, the socialist future, or her lover. This photograph of Natasha (Marina Kovaleva) at the bottom left was frequently used in Chinese media materials.

In urban areas we may speculate that viewers were not likely to hold their breath for the kiss between Alesha and Natasha in front of Stalin because they had limited access to other Soviet films that had been at the center of controversy in Sino-Soviet film exchange. These films, including *Forty-First* and *Cranes are Flying*, provided access to more diverse expressions of female subjectivity and to a visual aesthetics associated with personal emotions.[46] But it

Poster listing new movies.

is not just the visual impact of an on-screen kiss that was significant. Perhaps more important is the suggestion in the conclusion of *Fall of Berlin* that the end of war might bring resumption of carefree love between the two model workers. In this moment, the film re-introduced the socialist future into the visual narrative and thereby reopened the temporal focus of revolution beyond struggle and the present. To point to the future also meant the return of consideration of post-revolutionary socialist womanhood and multiple forms of (future) female subjectivity. Because the concluding scenes also remind the viewer of the opening scenes in which Alesha and Natasha playfully frolic in the fields, the ideological separation between China and the Soviet Union, the "present" of class struggle and the "future" of a post-revolutionary subjectivity—a separation that was at the crux of the Sino-Soviet conflicts as well as Maoist Theory as related to continuous revolution and Third Worldism—was blurred. Even as Marina Kovaleva's character was located within a Maoist framework that emphasized continuous revolution and struggle against revisionism, the final scene of Fall of Berlin moved the focus from the "now-ness" of struggle to thinking about what the socialist future might hold. But given that in the 1960s the framing context of screenings of Fall of Berlin linked the October Revolution to China and Mao—and distanced it from the Soviet state—this future was no longer Soviet; it was refracted through a Chinese and Maoist prism.

Conclusion

Through these examples of the filmic representation of socialist womanhood embodied by Soviet female film stars—and their place in diplomatic, cultural, and ideological aspects of Sino-Soviet relations—we become more aware of the intertwined nature of ideological debates, cultural products, gendered subjectivity, and geopolitical contests over the relative positioning of the Soviet Union and China in the global history of socialist revolution. Recognition of gender and culture as key elements in Sino-Soviet relations deepens our understanding of the ways in which the debates over socialist form, the legitimacy of material rewards, and the place of class struggle within socialist societies became part of the lived experiences of Chinese in urban and rural areas. This was, by no means, a homogeneous lived experience—nor was film equally influential across groups and regions. Yet, as I have argued in this chapter, study of Soviet film in China provides us with an alternative starting point to consider patterns of continuity and change in Sino-Soviet relations during the Maoist period; and to appreciate internationalist and transnational identifications that gave meaning to the shifting relations. By looking at Soviet film in

China, with a particular focus on Soviet female film stars, we can gain a more nuanced understanding of the multiple meanings associated with the "Soviet Union" as discursive signifier and nation-state before and after the Sino-Soviet split. What we can see is that Soviet film was a key component in the complex and interlocked politics of: one, defining and enacting revolutionary temporal schemas ("now-ness" and "the future"); two, producing and policing appropriate forms of female socialist subjectivity; and, three, establishing and defending specific geopolitical formulations of global socialism. For this reason, whether conceived as "China's future" or China's antithesis, the Soviet Union, its films and female film stars, were important points of reference in the shifting frameworks and historical contradictions that informed Maoist cultural politics and the international political cultures of socialist revolution.

Notes

1. Research for this project was supported by the Social Sciences and Humanities Research Council of Canada. I would like to thank Sergei Kapterev for his excellent work as a research assistant and Lasha Tchantouridze and Oleh Gerus for assistance with Russian sources. Thanks are also due to Hua-yu Li and Thomas Bernstein for inviting me to participate in the conference and to all conference participants for comments on an earlier draft. Sections of this chapter have been previously published in Tina Mai Chen, "Socialism, Aestheticized Bodies, and International Circuits of Gender: Soviet Female Film Stars in the People's Republic of China, 1949–1969," *Online Journal of the Canadian Historical Association* 18, no. 2 (2007), 53–80.

2. Figures from *Dianying faxing tongxun* [Film circulation newsletter], April 1954, n.p. The only other imported film from a socialist country with similar distribution and audiences was the Korean film *Youth Swimteam* with 22,372 screenings and an audience of 17,995,540. The 5 top Chinese films for this period had audiences of between 20 million (*New Heroes and Heroines*, 1951) and 73 million (*White Haired Girl*, 1951).

3. On the use of film for the Cult of Stalin see Evgeny Dobrenko, "Creation Myth and Myth Creation in Stalinist Cinema," *Studies in Russian and Soviet Cinema* 1, no. 3 (August 2007): 239–64.

4. Shen Zhihua, *Sulian zhuanjia zai Zhongguo, 1948–1960* [Soviet experts in China, 1948–1960] (Beijing: Zhongguo guoji guangbao chubanshe, 2003).

5. "Upoln. SEF v Man'chzhurii N. Putintsev zamministru kinematografii SSSR Kolotozovu, 23 dekabria 1947 g. Otvet na telegrafnyi zapros ot 18 dekabria 1947 g." [Letter from sovexportfilm representative in Manchuria N. Putintsev to the USSR deputy ministry of cinematography kalatozov, December 1947], Russian State Archives of Literature and Art (hereinafter as RGALI), f.2918, op. 2, d. 64, l. 35–36.

6. The Chinese-Soviet Friendship Society worked in conjunction with VOKS and Sovexportfilm.

7. Quoted in Shen Zhihua, *Sulian zhuanjia zai Zhongguo* [Soviet experts in China, 1948–1960] (Beijing: Zhongguo guoji guangbao chubanshe, 2003), 121.

8. "Spravka ob organizatsii prokata sovetskikh fil'mov v Kitae. Pis'mo Ministru Kinematografii SSSR tov. Bol'shakovu, I.G. ot Zam. Upravliayushchego V/Kinematografii SSSR Soveksportfil'm tov. Moskovskogo" [Report on the organization of Soviet films' distribution in China]. A secret report by Deputy Manager of Sovexportfilm Moskovskii to USSR Minister of Cinematography Ivan Bolshakov. 9 June 1949. RGALI, f. 2456, op. 4, d.204, l.124.

9. This figure did not include the stock of Asia Films of China or that of Southern Films which distributed Soviet film in the region referred to as the South Seas Countries.

10. Southern Films Corporation (Hong Kong) oversaw distribution in Hong Kong, as well as in Guangdong, Guangxi, and Fujian after 1948. Sovexportfilm established relations with Southern Films Corporation in 1948. "Zametky po dokladu tov. Lytkina. 15 fevralya 1950 g." [Lytkin's report, February 15, 1950], RGALI, f. 2918, op. 2, d. 126, l. 81–82.

11. "Zametki po dokladu tov. Lytkina. 15 fevralya 1950 g. (Lytkin's Report, February 15, 1950)," RGALI, f. 2918, op. 2, d. 126, ll. 81–82; "Nekotorye voprosy prokata v Kitae (kratkaia spravka)" [Short note on some issues of film distribution in China] (undated, probably 1950), RGALI, f. 2918, op. 2, d. 131, l. 59.

12. "Spravka ob organizatsii prokata sovetskykh fil'mov v Kitae. Pis'mo Ministru Kinematografii SSSR tov. Bol'shakovy, I.G. ot Zam. Upravliayushchego V/Kinoobedineniyem Soveksportfil'm tov. Moskovskogo" [Report on the organization of Soviet films' distribution in China]. A secret report by Deputy Manager of Sovexportfilm Moskovskii to USSR Minister of Cinematography Ivan Bolshakov, 9 June 1949, RGALI f. 2456, op. 4, d. 204, ll. 120–124.

13. On Chinese film production, see Paul Clark, *Chinese Cinema: Culture and Politics since 1949* (Cambridge: Cambridge University Press, 1987). In 1949 and 1950, all imported films came from the Soviet Union; between 1952 and 1957 the countries from which China imported more than 10 films were Czechoslovakia (40), Poland (22), Hungary (34), German Democratic Republic (28), Hong Kong (17), Japan (17), Romania (12), Bulgaria (14), Korea (13), France (10), Italy (10). *Zhongguo dianying faxing fangying tongji ziliao jiangbian (1949–1957)* [Handbook of statistical data on China film circulation and screening] (Beijing: Zhongguo dianying faxing fangying gongxi, 1958), 157–58.

14. "Obiasnitel'naya Zapiska k godovomu balansu Predstavitel'stva SEF za 1955 g. 18 ianvaria 1956" [Required memorandum on the annual balance of the representative of SEF for 1955, January 18, 1956] (Sovexportfilm's annual report for 1955), RGALI, f. 2918, op. 2, d. 238, l. 3.

15. There was a 26% increase in the number of viewers from 1952 to 1953. "Prokat sovfil'mov v strane v 1953–1954 g." [Report on the distribution of Soviet films in 1953–1954], RGALI, f. 2918, op. 3, d. 148, l. 17; "Spravka o prokate sovfil'mov v KNR (1956 g.)," [Information on Soviet films' distribution in 1956], RGALI f. 2918, op. 3, d. 150, l. 56.

16. On Thaw era film and the ideological frameworks, particularly as related to the intelligentsia, see Sergei Kapterev, *Post-Stalinist Cinema and the Russian Intelligentsia, 1953–1960: Strategies of Self-Representation, de-Stalinization, and the National Cultural Tradition*, (Ph.D. dissertation, New York University, 2005).

17. "O prokate sovfil'mov v Kitaye—Komitet po vneshneekonom. sviaziam, torgpredstvo, Mezhkniga, MVT, drugie organizatii, 1959–1960" [On Soviet film distribution in China—the committee for foreign economic relations, the trade mission, Mezhkniga, the ministry of foreign trade, other organizations, 1959–1960], RGALI, f. 2918, op. 5, d. 39, l. 3.

18. "From Kazennov to Davydov, 15 November 1963," RGALI f. 2918, op. 5, d. 262, l. 2; "Otchot ob eksporte-importe v 1963 g. Davidovu ot Sladkovs'kogo (sostavil Kazennov), 20 dekabria 1963 g." [(Secret) report on export and import for 1963 from sladkovskii to davydov; compiled by kazennov], 20 December 1963, RGALI, f. 2918, op. 5, d. 262, l. 2.

19. This point is based on anecdotal evidence and my impression from scattered stories on Chinese women or Soviet women in exchanges since I have not been able to find a breakdown by sex of Soviet experts or of Chinese sent for training in the USSR.

20. Tina Mai Chen, "Female Icons, Feminist Iconography? Socialist Rhetoric and Women's Agency in 1950s China," *Gender & History* 15, no. 2 (August 2003): 268–95.

21. Antonia Finnane, *Changing Clothing in China: Fashion, Nation, History* (New York: Columbia University Press, 2007).

22. On the components of Mao's thought that were brought together by 1967 as the "theory of continuing revolution under the dictatorship of the proletariat," see Graham Young, Mao Zedong and the Class Struggle in Socialist Society," *Australian Journal of Chinese Affairs*, no. 16 (July 1986), 41–80. Also see Michael Dutton, *Policing Chinese Politics* (Durham, NC: Duke University Press, 2005) on the shifting application of the "friend/enemy" dyad and its implications.

23. Rosemary Roberts, "Feminising the Counter-revolution: An Analysis of Negative Characters in the Revolutionary Model Works of the Chinese Cultural Revolution," in Robert Cribb, ed., *Asia Examined: Proceedings of the 15th Biennial Conference of the ASAA* (Canberra: ASAA conference proceedings, 2004).

24. Editorial Department of *Renmin ribao* [People's daily] and *Hongqi* [Red flag], "Comment on the Open Letter of the Central Committee of the CPSU (IX)," 14 July 1964 (Beijing: Foreign Languages Press).

25. This appeared in accounts authored by Liang Jun and others in the 1950s. She told me a similar story in an interview conducted in 1996 and as recently as 2003 in a Taiwanese newspaper story on Liang Jun, she made the same comments about Soviet films and her career choice to become a tractor driver.

26. RGALI, f. 2918, op. 1, d. 119, l. 56, "Pis'mo o mesiachnike kitaisko-sovetskoi druzhby Ivanu Gregoryevichu Bol'shakovu ot A. Fedorova" [A. Fedorov's letter to Ivan Grigorievich Bolshakov regarding Sino–Soviet friendship month film festival] (hereinafter as "Pis'mo o mesiachnike"), 21 November 1952.

27. "Pis'mo o mesiachnike."

28. The power of the songs as a source of cultural identification was reinforced for me when one interviewee in 2002 joyfully sang one of the main songs from *Kuban Cossacks* in response to my questions about what she remembered of Soviet films in the 1950s. Chengdu, interview by author, 2002.

29. Richard Taylor makes this point and also analyzes how the kolkhoz musical was an act of faith in which audiences were willing to collaborate despite—or because of —its futuristic promises divorced from daily realities. Richard Taylor, "Singing on the Steppes for Stalin: Ivan Pyr'ev and the Kolkhoz Musical in Soviet Cinema," *Slavic Review* 58, no. 1 (Spring 1999), 143–59.

30. Importantly, the female characters in *Kuban Cossacks* are not beset with the class ambiguities of the male protagonist. Ex-Cossack Gordei (played by Sergei Luklanov) was critiqued in the Chinese press because of his proclivities for bourgeois life and for moments of weakness when he focuses on himself as individual rather than the collective. Galina has none of these ambiguous characteristics and her strength of character is what enables Gordei and others to embrace a proper socialist identity.

31. See chapter four in my manuscript in progress, Tina Mai Chen, *Electric Shadows and Everyday Internationalism: Soviet Film and the Making of Maoist China.*

32. Mei Liang, "Rang women jinyibu de liaojie Sulian renmin de shenghuo" [Explaining Soviet lifestyle to allow us to progress], *Dazhong dianying* [Popular cinema] (1951), 14–16.

33. The Dress Reform campaign was promoted in newspapers such as *Zhongguo qingnianbao* [China youth] and others that targeted youth and promoted urban leisure, in sections such as *Zhoumo* [Weekend]. While these papers were technically national papers certain sections took urban youth to be their primary readers.

34. See Finnane, *Changing Clothing in China: Fashion, Nation, History*; also Antonia Finnane, "Yu Feng and the 1950s Dress Reform Campaign: Global Hegemony and Local Agency In the Art of Fashion," in *Wusheng zhi sheng: jindai Zhongguo funü yu wenhua, 1650–1950* [Silent voices: women and modern Chinese culture, 1650–1950], ed., Yu Chien Ming (Taipei: Academia Sinica, 2003), II, 235–68.

35. RGALI, f. 2918, op. 3, d. 150, l. 77, "Otchet o provedenii festivalia sovfil'mov v KNR, posviashchennyi 39-oi godovshchine VOS revoliutsii. Za podpisu upolnomochennogo SEF v KNR A.P. Zakharevicha, 12 dekabria 1956 g." [Report on the Soviet film festival in PRC dedicated to the 39th anniversary of the great october socialist revolution]. Signed by A. P. Zakharevich, the representative of Soviet Export Film in PRC, 12 December 1956.

36. Chuang Yuan, "Bixu lianyong funü de chenda liliang, 'wo kan zhengfuyuan'" [We must follow the great strength of women, I saw "member of government"], *Dazhong dianying* [Popular cinema], no. 3 (1953): 18.

37. No title, *Dazhong dianying*, no. 4 (1953): 8–9.

38. Tina Mai Chen, "Socialist Geographies, Internationalist Temporalities, and Traveling Film Technologies: Sino-Soviet Film Exchange in the 1950s and 1960s" in *Time Signatures: Technologies and Temporalities in Chinese Screen Cultures*, eds., Olivia Khoo and Sean Metzger (Briston, UK: Intellect, 2009).

39. On Mao's Three World Theory [Sange shijie lilun], see Tang Tsou and Morton Halperin, "Mao Tse-tung's Revolutionary Strategy and Peking's International Be-

havior," *American Political Science Review* 59 (1965), 80–99. Also William E. Ratliff, "Chinese Communist Cultural Diplomacy toward Latin America, 1949–1960," *The Hispanic American Historical Review* 49, no. 1 (February 1969), 53–79.

40. Discussion in the press in 1961 of the song *Liu Hulan* exemplifies how the military aesthetic associated with women soldiers of the 1940s produced a female subjectivity in the 1960s in which the female soldier was a metonymic representation of socialist revolutionary dreams coming to fruition, rather than national liberation more narrowly defined. Wen Jie, "Hongzhuang suguo—Mantan 'Liu Hulan' geci de yuyan he biaoxian shoufa" [Red and white—thoughts on the language and expressive techniques of the song "Liu Hulan"], *Renmin ribao*, 20 April 1961, 7.

41. RGALI, f. 2918, op. 5, d. 205, l. 10, "Ot Kazennova-Davidovu 15 noiabra 1963 g." [Letter from Kazennov to Davydov], 15 November 1963.

42. *Zoya* was one of the Stalinist classics, along with *The Battle of Stalingrad* and *Fall of Berlin*, selected by the Chinese for the 1965 Soviet Film Festival.

43. On Maoism and revolutionary time, see Rebecca Karl, "Mao Zedong, The Cold War, and Global Revolution," paper delivered at the University of Manitoba, Winnipeg, Manitoba, 28 September 2007.

44. RGALI, f. 2329, op. 8, d. 519, l. 36-37, "Spravka o khode vypolnenniia plana meropriyatii po kul'tsotrudnichestvu mezhdu SSSR i KNR na 1957 g." [Report on the implementation of the plan for cultural cooperation between the USSR and PRC for 1957], 21 November 1957.

45. RGALI, f. 2918, op. 2, d. 126, l. 67, "Iz otcheta tov. Loseva po rabote v Shankhae za fevral' ot 28 marta 1959 g." [From comrade Losev's report for February on the work in Shanghai], 28 March 1950.

46. The CCP deemed *Cranes are Flying* inappropriate for national circulation and it only circulated in limited screenings in urban areas, primarily viewed by students and urban film workers. Similarly, *Forty-First*, which literally depicted love for the class enemy as the Bolshevik female soldier and her White Russian prisoner develop a sexual relationship, was only shown to limited urban audiences. For analysis of these films in relation to female sexuality and Sino-Soviet relations, see Tina Mai Chen, "Socialism, Aestheticized Bodies, and International Circuits of Gender: Soviet Female Film Stars in the People's Republic of China, 1949–1969," *Online Journal of the Canadian Historical Association* 18, no. 2 (2007): 53–80.

VII

THE ERA OF REFORM AND THE
IMPACT OF THE SOVIET COLLAPSE

17

China's Concurrent Debate about the Gorbachev Era

Gilbert Rozman

THE GORBACHEV ERA REMAINS A SUBJECT of intense debate. Russians look back on how reform degenerated into collapse and stagnation in the 1990s amidst conflicting views of the abandonment of socialism. Americans seek lessons for how they won the cold war even if the Putin era casts doubt on prior conclusions. Of all the debates, however, China's may carry the most significance. Its leaders are still preoccupied with preserving communist party control and even interpreting the history of international communism in ways conducive to the legitimacy of their domestic and global strategy. In contrast to recent debates in Russia and the United States, Chinese concentrate on the very themes that fascinated them when Gorbachev was still in power. Rather than focus on the lessons they drew in later years, which has been ably done elsewhere,[1] this chapter takes us back to the pivotal juncture in history when the Chinese were reacting to ongoing developments. In this way, we can assess how their interpretations reflected emerging thinking about comparative socialism and international relations, including the evolution of Sino-Russian ties, and we can conclude with how China's debate contributed to the dual theories still ascendant of socialist transformation and great power geometry.

The Chinese debate on the Soviet Union in 1985–91 was markedly different from the debates of 1978–1985 and 1992–2007. In the earlier period China was launching reforms after two decades of Maoist radicalism culminating in the disorienting spectacle of the Cultural Revolution. Experts and officials alike were anxious to reassess what were the historical experience of socialism and its prospects in the competition with capitalism. Their prime objective was to draw lessons for setting the direction for China's reforms.[2] From the 1990s lessons of a different sort were at the top of the agenda. The search was under way for why the Soviet system had failed in order to fortify China's communist rule against a similar outcome.[3] In contrast, the Gorbachev era was a time of energetic pursuit of normalization just as far-reaching reforms in both countries were compared with potential for spillover from one country to the other. Distinct from the lethargic Soviet interest in lessons from China,[4] the Chinese closely followed events in the Soviet Union. Public interest may have been driven by different motivations, as seen in the massive demonstrations on Tiananmen Square that coincided with Gorbachev's May 1989 visit, but it echoed the intense scrutiny in official circles of what was unfolding in the USSR. This was a time of peak parallelism between countries absorbed in what Chinese labeled "reform socialism."

From early 1981 when the flagship journal in the field started publication, the terms "reform" (*gaige*), reserved initially mainly for economic change, and "orthodoxy" (*zhengtong*) were contrasted. The guiding instructions of the senior figure Liu Keming made clear that a principal objective was to draw lessons from Soviet experience—its great achievements as well as its serious troubles—to steer China forward on the path of socialism.[5] Increasingly, the focus turned to how the Soviet Union was reconceptualizing socialism, engaging in shared pursuit of socialist reform.[6] The winding down of the cold war also brought intense concern about the global balance of power and its ideological worldview.

At stake in assessments of the Soviet Union were fundamental questions about: 1) the future of that country, recognized as more important for China's history since 1945 than any other; 2) the future of socialism, the crux of China's political and social system vital to the legitimacy of its leadership; 3) the outlook for global great power relations or regional relations in Northeast Asia, of prime importance in international relations; and 4) the prospects for China's rise in comprehensive national power by maximizing access to essential inputs from other countries and mobilizing internal resources and will. Naturally, the communist leadership of China and the analysts working under its direction were not disinterested observers. Their "approved" outcome tightly shaped coverage even if some striking differences in preferences can be clearly detected in the writings of this period.

Official China preferred a Soviet Union not of middle class, humanist values nor of long-demeaned Tsarist chauvinist ones, but with a statist, power-enhancing worldview tempered by a moderating awareness of the need for integration into the world economy. It approved of the rejection of traditional socialism, at least as an economic system, while welcoming the Soviet leadership's embrace of reform socialism as a gradual, controlled process of borrowing from the capitalist system without unhinging the political order and the thinking of either ordinary people or the educated elite. Conscious of stages in the building of socialism and then in the transformation away from the traditional model, the Chinese were inclined to see their country as well behind their mentors in constructing an advanced socialist system but now setting the pace in transforming it.[7] This created great potential for mutual learning and appreciation, as what some may now have envisioned as the "co-leaders" of international socialism joined in reviving a shared heritage, but not in any kind of alliance or polarized global strategy. Of great significance to official China was the replacement of an ideological foreign policy for maintaining supremacy over a bloc of countries denied the right to experiment with their own reforms or own advantageous foreign dealings with a narrowly realist approach for maximizing national power in a world of multiple poles and diverse states free to pursue their own economic interests. It followed that Russia should upgrade relations with China in order to balance recent U.S. power gains in the strategic triangle, while cautiously improving ties with the United States, Japan, and the capitalist states of Europe in order to achieve the stability and global economic ties needed for domestic transformation. Writings did not, however, only evaluate how closely changes in the Soviet Union conformed to this script. In uncertain times they clashed over the script, leaving behind a discordant record.

Under guidance of regularly updated instructions to experts in the field but often split between clashing agendas, the debate unfolded in two main stages—1985–89 and 1989–91. Prior to June 4, 1989 the focus was comparative socialism, although by early 1987 censorship silenced the bold champions of this field. After June 4, it proved easier to discuss the Soviet Union in the context of international relations. Only in early 1992 after the collapse of the Soviet Union threatened to produce a conservative backlash that could call into question what Deng Xiaoping had been trying to accomplish did Deng's interpretation (what I label the theory of socialist transformation) bring some closure. By tracing the debate across these two stages and through its lasting impact, we are able to assess what became the final influence of the Soviet Union on China's development path.

Changing Instructions to the Field of Soviet Observers

I start by contrasting the instructions in 1986 and early 1988 with those in 1991 to the Chinese Association of Soviet and East European Studies, representing the specialists. Early in 1986 a presentation by senior leader Wu Xiuchuan strongly endorsed this field's importance for understanding the fundamental Marxist-Leninist principles, developing scientific socialist theory and practice based on almost seventy years of experience, and serving the construction of both a material and a spiritual culture for moderniza-tion. Wu asserted that now with change under way in these countries there are more questions to study. Eschewing mention of any clash of views in the leadership about how to respond to the Gorbachev challenge, he called for in-tensifying research, avoiding the dogmatic, simplistic, one-sided approaches of the past, and meeting the need for freer and more creative work. If careful to remind specialists in the field that they must strictly observe party and state policies and discipline, Wu's speech left no doubt of top-down support for a pro-reform agenda.[8] This mattered since at the start of 1984 the anti-spiritual pollution campaign had cast a shadow on efforts to write about ideological and political issues, and still in 1985, when barriers were falling, confusion remained over how openly topics related to the comparative history of social-ism could be addressed even in internal circulation sources, such as the one that reported his remarks.[9]

Already in the last part of 1984, a journal had reported that a group of specialists on the Soviet Union and East Europe in Beijing had proposed a forward step for research, following new standpoints, contents, and methods. They called for comparing those states where reform was going relatively well with capitalist states, even if the results would show the socialist cases well behind. This would make it possible to explain what policies were mistaken. In the process concentrating on reform of the economic system would not suffice; multidirectional research is needed, linking to the political system as well.[10] This bold appeal goes beyond the instructions handed down to the field as a whole, exposing the impatience to delve deeper and the eagerness of specialists to take advantage of a momentary opportunity when controls had slackened to pursue more serious scholarship.

After the purge of Chinese Communist Party leader Hu Yaobang and the ouster from the Party of some of the most free-thinking analysts of compara-tive socialism, the Thirteenth Party Congress in the fall of 1987 offered fresh encouragement for reform-oriented exploration of many long-ignored issues in the Soviet past. Zhao Ziyang's advocacy of the theory that China is only at the initial stage of socialism provided the impetus, recognizing that China borrows from the theory and practice of others and they have many things in common, including similar problems. Zhao had called for the urgent de-velopment of grand theory, which was interpreted to mean new concepts and new boundaries, while breaking away from dogmatism, traditional views, and stagnant or erroneous thought. This unabashed post-congress appeal to spe-cialists to follow closely the Soviet changes—party-state relations, democrati-zation, social justice, and the law were mentioned as topics of Chinese study in order to deepen reform—gave a big boost to far-reaching scholarship.[11] Compared to early 1986 and also early 1987, bold analysis became easier.

Again the pendulum swung sharply back from June 1989, when Zhao was purged and the Tiananmen demonstrators were condemned along with many who had written about ideology, including comparative socialism, as advocates of bourgeois spiritual pollution or worse, as counterrevolutionaries. For a time conservatives tightly controlled writings on sensitive subjects, such as the Soviet Union's history and its ongoing reforms. In the report at the July 19, 1991 Association meeting, we learn that it had achieved rich results in serving the direction set by the 1978 Third Plenum, but now there were new demands from the center's leading comrades, and the conference speaker pledged that the field would not disappoint them. He made clear that they would fulfill their historical responsibility of supporting and using a Marxist position, a Marxist viewpoint, and Marxist methods to advance their field. Their priorities included strengthening research into socialist theory, providing a deep summary of the lessons of the Soviet experience in building socialism, and tracing and studying changes in the current political and economic situation.[12] This was a recipe for narrowly reinforcing the thinking handed down from above. Yet, even when the debate about Soviet socialism had become tightly controlled, divergent views on its international impact continued to be aired.

In 1992 the post-June 4 restrictions were somewhat loosened as economic reforms were reinvigorated and Deng took exception to rigidly narrow interpretations of the collapse of the Soviet Union, but the field never recovered its earlier liveliness.[13] After the apogee of wide-ranging debate in 1985–89 and the nadir of censorship in 1989–91, the year 1992 is important not only for ushering in a new period in China and in Sino-Russian relations, but also for the theoretical synthesis that has held to today.[14] It marked the culmination of China's liveliest debate about the Soviet Union since 1949.

The Debate over Gorbachev's Changes: 1985–1989

In explaining their rival's deviation from the supposedly normal course of history, Chinese, unlike their Soviet counterparts, did not spend a lot of energy during the years of the schism tracing the roots in intellectual, social, and political history.[15] They did posit, however, a heritage of Tsarist imperialism, in which official thinking marked with feelings of superiority and driven by leaders prone to forcefully expand their power set a bad precedent that lingered after socialism was established. A worldview rooted in a disturbing past drew criticism for distorting the course of socialism into revisionism and great power chauvinism. Yet, in 1979–80 Deng Xiaoping decided to drop these labels that stood in the way of comparisons;[16] soon a literature arose on how reform socialism was emerging in many countries and would have to become the Soviet choice as well. With China and the Soviet Union both now understood to have fallen off course, it was time to point to the positive efforts in the Soviet Union too to get back on track, to "reform."[17] Having spent little effort on explaining what had gone wrong apart from formulaic condemnations, the Chinese quickly adopted a new approach.

While global attention concentrated on Deng's empirical approach to reforms based on what worked in practice, theory remained a focal point: in the prolonged 1979 conference on theory that concluded when Deng imposed the four cardinal principles; in 1981 in the resolution assessing Mao's place in history; in early 1984 when the campaign against spiritual pollution concentrated on reform theorists who were testing the limits by reinterpreting sensitive Marxist themes such as humanism and alienation; and from the end of 1984 when new license was given to "theorists" of socialism, soon coinciding with Gorbachev's theoretical renaissance and feeding off its intensity. Having under Deng approached theory modestly, in contrast to Leonid Brezhnev's bombastic claims, Chinese humbly put their country at the initial stage of socialism in need of massive borrowing.[18] Yet, this did not mean that leaders and censors were adverse to claims of superiority: socialism would prove successful against capitalism,[19] as lessons from socialist experiences elsewhere would enable China to accelerate its development. Writings on the Soviet Union were essential to make their case. Past Soviet theoretical errors served as evidence of what had gone wrong and needed to be corrected, and even tentative signs of shifting course drew praise as proof that success was in reach.

In the era of normalization China was intent on removing ideological barriers that had plagued relations, first showing that it considered the Soviet Union along with each Eastern European country a socialist state, then essentially normalizing ties with the five states of Eastern Europe which had been treated as hostile and indicating that foreign policy rather than ideology was critical to normalization with the Soviet Union too, and quickly restoring multi-dimensional cooperation with each of them with the momentum considered favorable for a breakthrough with Moscow too. After Beijing signaled in June 1981 its shift to a self-reliant foreign policy, standing separate from the West as well as the Soviets, prospects grew for finding common ground with Moscow. Voting behavior at the United Nations on Third World issues drew the two closer. China's opposition to the Solidarity Movement in Poland and to other attempts to diminish communist party authoritarianism became clearer. By September 1982 a policy of equidistance between the two superpowers emerged, as talks to normalize relations began with Moscow. With Soviet interest growing in the wake of new tensions with the United States, leaders had reason to expect new emphasis on balancing the strategic triangle that would give China scope to maneuver. Unlike a few years earlier, the United States was now in the position of urging China to sustain its anti-Soviet thrust rather than the other way around. Sending Deputy Premier Li Peng to Chernenko's funeral in 1985, Beijing showed the importance it placed on this relationship. The term "comrade," was revived, suggesting that party-to-party ties could advance, and the fact that Gorbachev met Li alone indicated that normalization of relations was now possible. But it was only in mid-1986 with the removal of the Soviet officials who had led in demonizing China and Gorbachev's Vladivostok speech that Moscow showed seriousness about bilateral ties, and this was neutralized, to some degree, by haste to improve relations with the United States, indicating that the triangle would not become balanced as China desired.[20]

China's leaders had encouraged hopeful assessments of Soviet transformation in the first half of the 1980s, albeit with abstract reasoning about what was needed as well as wishful thinking on how Yuri Andropov's policies could begin an era of reform. For a time translated articles led the way in exploring forbidden topics,[21] but they became less common by 1985. When Gorbachev took office, the tone became more upbeat and specific. Observers responded with new optimism toward Soviet reforms as the 27th Party Congress in early 1986 appeared to be a turning point with many positive effects: recognizing contradictions in the current stage of development as China had done; noting the need for far-reaching reforms, again in line with China's earlier switch and showing interest in what China's reforms had accomplished; approving changes in foreign policy to support the new domestic line with positive implications for China's foreign policy; offering more scope for China in the international communist movement; and digging into the errors of past leaders that for a time seemed to parallel efforts in China, as in the summer of 1986 when there was intensified coverage of Stalin's political and intellectual mistakes.[22] Long after China dropped the terms "revisionism" and "social imperialism," the Soviets declared in 1987 that no party has a monopoly in defining socialism and that there is room for both a Soviet and a Chinese path of development. Indeed, recognizing commonalities in the reform track, they translated Deng Xiaoping's work.[23] Awareness was growing of shared requirements for socialist reform. The debates over socialism in the two countries were becoming intertwined, despite the dangers that this could pose for keeping control from above on how far these debates should be permitted go.

Tracing Chinese coverage of the Soviet Union in internal journals in 1986–88 reveals great attentiveness to what was transpiring. Just accurately and vividly conveying the ongoing criticisms by Soviet leaders made a compelling case for how dysfunctional the jointly inherited system was. Early 1986 commentators faulted Gorbachev for being too timid, as in the argument that theory is the most important problem in reform and he has yet to touch it or that resistance by officials with privileges is intense without much evidence that the struggle will vigorously target them.[24] A roundtable discussion of the 27th Party Congress was laudatory, stressing the rejection of Brezhnev's notion of "developed socialism" in favor of a more modest outlook that saw stagnation as the problem and recognized diverse approaches to socialist construction.[25] Veteran Chinese experts such as Liu Keming warned that the outcome was still in doubt, depending on the intensity of the struggle against inertia, dogmatism, and conservatism,[26] or that the sickness of the political system is that it did not separate the party from the government and the former takes over.[27] Yet, we find through much of 1987 signs of drawing the line, for instance remarks that the theory of Lenin was correct and even that Stalin was a great Marxist.[28]

Blocked from expressing many of their criticisms or forthright comparisons, bold thinkers searched for less-controlled themes to channel their comparative and historical arguments. For example, they drew the conclusion that both countries are focused on a redistribution of power, sometimes along the same lines but with different early priorities as they face similar resistance. We read also that China starts with the economy, and the Soviet Union with the leadership. China moves from rural to urban, and the Soviet Union from top to bottom. As China separates ownership and management, the Soviets defend workers' democratic rights. Such analysis suggests that both sides need to learn from the other and that comparisons offer rich promise.[29] In 1987 some articles lionized Gorbachev, as Chinese censorship was relaxed again and Soviet bold moves drew renewed attention, or suggested that Gorbachev had achieved a breakthrough in the theory of socialism, including pointing to social justice as the critical stimulus for social progress. Capturing the new mood, another article concluded that the more socialism is advanced, the more democracy is advanced, a realization that possibly will lead to a rejuvenation of socialism in the world.[30] Highly praising Gorbachev as sticking to socialism while accusing Brezhnev of having damaged it, the author implied that China should follow the new reform example.

Despite these signs of boldness, the field of comparative socialism had suffered a sharp setback in the first part of 1987. In 1986 it appeared to be leaping ahead as a basis for far-reaching theory after developing cautiously in the previous period as a means to draw limited lessons for China's reforms. It had started along specific lines: comparative agriculture, comparative education, comparative urban planning, etc. Gorbachev's early interest in perestroika appeared consistent with this limited coverage, offering many tempting targets of research on rather narrowly based reforms. Yet, when Gorbachev in 1986 added *glasnost'* and "new thinking" on subjects deemed sensitive by the Chinese leadership, the scope for comparative study was widened with the possibility of pointing directly at sensitive issues that leaders would be most nervous about raising. One line of bold thinking insisted that China lacks experience and needs to learn from the Soviet Union, given the fact that what happened in the latter also had happened in the former to a considerable degree. It stressed that Soviet history demonstrates that the most serious problems resulted from leftist mistakes, which cannot be narrowly blamed on specific leaders, and must be traced to flaws in the theory and failure to consider real conditions.[31]

If in May 1986 Chinese still assessed Gorbachev as pointing to mistakes in the past as a means to launch primarily economic reforms and as struggling with doubtful prospects to improve ties with the United States in order to limit the costly arms race,[32] as the year proceeded they recognized a leader struggling with the fundamental transformation of the socialist system. By March 1987 Chinese argued that reform had moved beyond its initial stage into a new stage in which the political system as well as the economic system would be the target, adding that this was bringing some positive changes to society as well as the economy and it was winning support from cadres as well as workers.[33] Even as controls tightened inside China for a time in 1987 during the short-lived campaign against bourgeois liberalization, Gorbachev was providing fertile material for deeper exploration into the recesses of a socialist system.

Discussions of Soviet democracy reached their peak in 1987. One reason was to provide information on what was happening in a country where moves toward democracy were then in the ascendancy but not yet as suspect as they would become. Another was to make use of the label "socialist democracy," to explain the benefits of a different style of governance for economic management and socio-cultural life, raising the efficiency of society. As long as authors made clear that it would proceed under party control, it was acceptable to conclude that socialist democracy would progress, but quotations from Lenin often proved more permissible than those from Gorbachev.[34] A balancing act was required in coverage of this theme. On the one hand, it was obligatory to defend the denial of direct democracy in favor of a high degree of centralization, as if this were a response to special conditions and did not really signify abandoning the principle of democracy and the basic interests of laboring people. On the other, observers were expected to echo the Soviet line that insufficient democracy after circumstances had changed put a brake on development. To reconcile these themes, they had to insist that leadership must change to permit more democracy inside and outside the Party, arguing that Nikita Khrushchev did not go far enough in reforming the excesses of the Stalin model, while adding that Party leadership remains essential in bringing forth manifestations of democracy such as openness and autonomy. Such balancing often proceeded without acknowledging the fundamentals of democracy, which increasingly were being recognized in the Soviet public debate.[35] Yet, bold advocates explained that the measures taken by Gorbachev were a prelude to more substantial political reform even if hopes should not be high because of the fierce resistance by officials. They stressed that reform of a political system is difficult, especially one with such serious drawbacks, pointing to the psychological legacy and the need for a new political logic.[36]

When we look back at the rise and fall of comparative studies of socialism, we cannot overlook the role of Su Shaozhi, director of the Institute of Marxism-Leninism and Mao Zedong Thought, who accelerated the critique of Stalinism and strove for a full and honest appraisal of the entire history of socialism through comparisons. Emboldened at times of relaxed control over the debate on the Soviet Union, he directly challenged Hu Qiaomu and Deng Liqun, who had led the anti spiritual pollution campaign in 1984 and in 1987 gained renewed leadership over propaganda after Hu Yaobang's fall. In 1985–86 Su launched a grand project for the comparative study of socialism, describing its wide-ranging scope in *Guangming ribao* in October 1985: not only economic organization but national customs and networks of social relations, traditions of political administration, the background of cultural concepts, and even the path and type of revolution. As this project was advancing quickly in the second half of 1986, Su unreservedly expressed the goals of his research. A draft of his article was pulled from publication in *Marxist Studies*, No. 1, 1987, and in August 1987 he was "requested" to resign from the Chinese Communist Party for having advocated bourgeois liberalization.

Another person expelled from the Party at that time was Li Honglin, who later reported on how on November 1, 1986 Hu Yaobang met with organizers of the Planning Conference for the Social Sciences for the period of the Seventh Five-Year Plan (1986-1990), criticizing the leadership of the very party that he headed for interfering with scholarship and promising that the Central Committee would "never hit with sticks again."[37] With Hu purged, theoretical work was set back by the anti-bourgeois liberalism campaign of early 1987. A crackdown on Hu's associates, such as Su and Li, signified a decision to curtail the emergent comparative study of socialism. Nonetheless, given the high priority on following what Gorbachev was doing and the replacement of Hu by Zhao Ziyang, those allowed to continue found it possible to air similar views. Without reviving the term comparative socialism, studies continued.

Even as the need for coverage of ongoing Soviet developments provided an opportunity to present specifics about democracy and about past failings of centralization that served to stimulate discussion of political reforms in China, wariness was spreading as some Chinese leaders reacted suspiciously to Gorbachev's endorsement of ever more far-reaching democratic changes, and they tightened censorship. In 1986 discussion of the importance of political reform had sharply intensified in China. It was possible to echo Gorbachev's appeal to expose the internal problems of the centralized system and to limit the Party's excesses, such as raising the banner of strengthening its leadership while aiming to serve narrow private interests.[38] Couched in terms of continuing the October Revolution and showing the superiority of socialism over capitalism, arguments could be presented by year end that called for reforming the socialist model to realize the full potential of this system and respond to the reform currents in other socialist countries.[39] Even after controls tightened over comparative socialism,[40] the field regained some momentum under Zhao, resorting to indirect expression of comparative judgments.

In 1988 the focus was squarely on reform of the political system, again amidst talk of entering a new stage of reform, but with new warnings of the difficulties ahead, including talk of mounting problems in China's own economic reforms and awareness that Soviet economic reforms were running into severe difficulty. Coverage was not hostile to Soviet intentions in combining different types of reform, even if it was skeptical of the results.[41] A common theme was the need for synchronization of various types of reform. Some Chinese pointed to Gorbachev's struggles to argue that reform must not be limited to economics: if cultural, social, and political reforms are constrained, economic reforms will fail.[42] Just as the struggle within China over how to proceed with reforms was intensifying, Gorbachev's bold moves were riveting the attention of those charged with drawing a blueprint for change and theorizing about the future.

Deng Xiaoping was no doubt uncomfortable with "rightist" attempts to hijack the criticisms of the Soviet theme in a way that would accelerate China's convergence with the West. After all, Chinese ideological errors long exceeded Soviet ones and could also become the subject of relentless criticism should the door be opened wide to negating Stalin and Stalinism. Thus, tolerance for criticisms of Soviet history, which had become prominent in the previous period of drawing lessons for China's reform of socialism, was slow to evolve into approval for sustained investigation into mistakes or deviations from some idealized historical path. Whatever the errors in building socialism, none were to be treated as so egregious as to stand in the way of a properly conceived strategy of reform. China's leaders showed more restraint than Gorbachev in criticizing Soviet excesses.

Two lines of argument called into question this forward-looking approach with little blame placed on the past. One was the tendency of serious political reform advocates to find in the distinctive course of Soviet history reasons why the country's development became derailed, making the case that only far-reaching political reforms now could put it back on track. Soviet arguments about a lack of democratic traditions which could easily be transposed to China, however, faced recurrent censorship. The other was the inclination to place personal blame on a succession of Soviet leaders, suggesting a track record of abuse of unchecked power and poor judgment that could recur. Long accustomed to demonizing Khrushchev and Brezhnev, some Chinese did not need much prodding to find fault with Gorbachev. By the second half of 1988 as one side took the view that the difficulties in Soviet reforms could be addressed only through vigorous political reform—a position with parallels in China as the leadership split and public dissatisfaction was growing at a time of inflation—the other warned that Gorbachev had turned in a dangerous direction. After June 4, 1989 the issue was settled. Gorbachev had become a threat to socialism.

The Debate over the Late Gorbachev Policies

By July 1989 censorship tightened over publications dealing with Gorbachev, as China's leaders accused him of encouraging "bourgeois liberalization," and before long, of also condoning the collapse of socialism in Eastern Europe. Some leaders pressed for a clear repudiation of him; others pointed to Boris Yeltsin as an even greater danger. For two years China continued to work with Gorbachev and to keep up the pretense that his policies were socialist, while saying as little as possible about them and stifling coverage even in internal publications. There was somewhat of a siege mentality, combining fear of disorder and isolation at home with concern over the contagion of Gorbachev abroad. Hardliners gained more power, trumpeting conspiratorial theories.[43] They felt that the Soviet Union was not a foreign entity and insisted that they knew it well enough to explain what had happened, often in the direst terms and with the most stringent warnings against continuation of the reform agenda inside China.[44] While Deng may have discouraged this kind of debate as a waste of time with the added danger that a "single truth" would obscure seeking truth from facts, the conservatives had free rein for a time to impose their simplistic answers and deny any open exploration by others.

Chinese have a history of treating ideas as the prime moving force of history and have put the country's guiding thought (zhidao sixiang) on a par with the status of the communist party as a determining factor in transformation. While taking note of ethnic conflict and the poor economic situation in the Soviet Union, the thrust of much criticism centered on betrayal of fundamental principles of socialist thought. Similar criticism had been leveled at Khrushchev's approval for the insidious "thaw" literature with its abstract humanist themes as well as his delegitimizing verdict on Stalin, arguing that the result had been confusion of thought.[45] Viewing failure at reform as testimony to misdirected theorizing about socialist transformation under Gorbachev, analysts stressed the significance of getting the theory right. This justified a new theoretical orthodoxy, although in 1989–91 it left open how the fate of the Soviet Union would be treated and faltered in explaining Deng's reform legacy.

While coverage faded of Soviet domestic developments, foreign affairs still drew much attention. Chinese publications had long left little doubt of their preoccupation with the relative power of the Soviet Union and the United States, the two competitors seeking global hegemony.[46] Comparing their power, Chinese could steer their own realist foreign policy toward maximum advantage. At first, it was not just a matter of power but also of who was on the offense, leading to further stress on pressing the Soviets to retreat. Even as Deng Xiaoping had praised the first-year accomplishments of Gorbachev, he had left no doubt of the need to resolve the three fundamental obstacles in order to normalize bilateral relations. The Vladivostok speech introduced new ideas for improving relations, such as reconsidering the Soviet position on how to settle the border dispute while making the border a zone of friendship. In 1986 Gorbachev also began to act on the three obstacles, removing troops from Mongolia and indicating plans for a pull back from Afghanistan. Stressing the removal of Vietnamese troops from Cambodia, Deng insisted on more.[47] Yet, as Gorbachev relaxed cold war tensions and also met Deng's demands for normalizing relations, Chinese viewed the response as mixed due to Gorbachev's excessive trust in the international community and loss of focus on national power. Above all, his priority on improving ties with the United States in a way that could only make his country dependent defied the logic of balancing U.S. power by reaffirming an independent stance and turning elsewhere for partners. In 1987–88 as Moscow resolved the three obstacles one-by-one, it was assumed that a realist course would have been to solidify the Moscow-Beijing dyad to provide leverage within the strategic triangle. In an environment where the European powers and Japan were tightly linked to the United States, it was primarily China that could have offered some room for maneuver. The fact that it did not receive the appropriate priority was a problem, but even more so was the response after June 4, 1989 when Moscow did nothing to counter the sanctions by the West imposed on China and proceeded only hesitantly to build on the new foundation of normalized relations.

Even if Soviet leaders neglected a balance of great powers, it was still possible after June 4 to approve of improving Sino-Soviet relations. After all, Deng had praised Gorbachev's new thinking in May 1989, even comparing it to his own worldview. This legitimated further positive assessments. Even if criticisms of Gorbachev turned to his biography, his faulty reasoning, and even his suspect motives to explain why he was so enamored of the West, they did not negate the value of the gains achieved in bilateral ties. Jiang Zemin's visit to Moscow in the spring of 1991 was seen as an opportunity to move back onto the track of a strategic triangle. Gorbachev had pulled back from his repeated concessions toward the United States, and even some reformers in Moscow were arguing, "In the coming age of a new world order the balancing of interests between our two great powers will remain as important as before . . . it is important to have a strong rear to rely on. For China, the Soviet Union is such a rear, and vice versa."[48] Thus, an element of hope was kept, especially when contacts with Soviet hardliners in the military and elsewhere suggested that Gorbachev's hold on power was uncertain and others were already eyeing China as an alternative to one-sided partnership with the West.

As Chinese affirmed that their country was a socialist developing great power that must avoid dependence on any other country or international group even as it participated in the international division of labor, they argued that the Soviet Union as another great power would likewise accept a new division of labor, including opening the treasure house of Siberia. There was even some optimism that new strategizing in Moscow or growing decentralization would bring the two states closer economically and overcome political confusion in that country.[49] Thus, even if Gorbachev kept leaning to the West, there were some grounds for hope.

Generally, Chinese analysis takes for granted that liberal thought and bourgeois development of a society without strong statist leadership brings dependence on the West. To allow an internationalized elite to spread its emerging worldview or, worse, to gain control over the reins of power is tantamount to abandoning one's national identity and interests. At stake in China in the Tiananmen showdown and simultaneously in the Soviet Union as Gorbachev's "new thinking" spread trust in the West and neglected the goal of maintaining a balance of power was loss of all that had been achieved in building a strong, independent state as a force to block the United States' designs for global hegemonism, which, in turn, are heir to centuries of imperialist expansion through military or peaceful means in pursuit of control and domination. While explanations of the 1989 collapse of East European socialist regimes and three years later of the Soviet Union focused on international causes linked to a strategy of "peaceful evolution" (*heping yanbian*), it was argued that the strategy would fail as countries resumed the realist pursuit of great power gains that would lead to multipolarity.[50] Already the theme of multipolarity had arisen as a response to a "new world order."

In this environment, it appeared that China's existing goal of reducing tensions and stabilizing the environment for its economic development would be more difficult.[51] Yet, Deng rejected this conclusion, taking an upbeat approach in 1992 that China's market economy under new reforms would flourish and the situation would be stable while great power relations sorted themselves out to no great detriment to China. Deng took care to keep the reaction in China to events in the Soviet Union calm. When the Soviet bloc collapsed, when the communist party lost its monopoly, and when the Soviet Union fell, after frantic debate each time, Deng quieted and redirected the discussion. He rejected those who would have boldly asserted China's leadership of the remaining communist movement. He also kept faith in Russia as a great power that would reassert its nationalistic identity and respond to China in pursuit of mutual benefit as powers in the global system. The message spread that the new era would provide stability and an opportunity for China's economic development and rise.

After the disappointment of the failure of the coup against Gorbachev in August 1991, some conservative leaders proposed drastic measures. Not only had reform of socialism failed in the Soviet Union, they judged that it could well be failing in China too and required policy reversals and even renewed class struggle to be saved.[52] If these differences reflected a profound challenge to Deng Xiaoping's legacy, they were kept largely beyond the reach of academic writings. With the comeback of Deng in early 1992 to lead a new wave of economic reform and consolidate a theoretical response aimed at the left more than the right, China's course shifted. Gorbachev's image became fixed as a villain no longer subject to any redemption, but, in a narrower sense, reform socialism regained its priority as China's development strategy backed by a theory no longer subject to serious debate over its fundamental tenets.

The United States had connived to break up the Soviet Union and now it plotted to control the country, but its plans would fail, Chinese argued in 1992. Tsarist Russian traditions would reemerge supplemented by the legacy of decades of superpower glory.[53] They contended that the breakup of the Soviet Union was desired by the United States as part of its hegemonic ambitions, and a similar objective was sought for China. Connecting June 1989 and December 1991, this approach combined accusations against geopolitical ambitions with warnings about the goal of creating one global civilization under Western values.[54] Reliance on economic assistance without sufficient vigilance can draw a country further into the Western orbit with dangerous implications, but Deng made clear that global economic integration would go forward and need not be a threat.

Initial coverage of the reasons for the fall of Soviet communism attributed the tragedy to imperialist interference as part of a strategy of peaceful evolution. Along these lines, treatment of internal factors emphasized theoretical mistakes that echoed the theory of peaceful evolution and brought destruction in the name of reform. In addition, reports in 1992 made clear that Chinese were debating Gorbachev's motives for encouraging such theorizing, with some saying that he started with this theory with the aim of destroying communism and others arguing that the theory evolved in stages.[55] Whatever the turning point on the path to destruction, analysts stressed theoretical errors that contributed to it: Loss of organizational control enabling anti-communist groups to spread like mushrooms in 1988, glasnost without limits causing people to lose their belief in communist party leadership, abstract humanism putting man at the center and insisting on humanizing international relations, and finally eliminating the party monopoly on power and opening the floodgates to full Westernization in 1990–91.[56] A link was often drawn between naive calls for "serving the interests of all mankind," abandoning any image of an enemy, and giving the United States an opening to advance its strategy of "peaceful evolution," thus inducing the collapse of the Soviet Union.[57] Although explanations for this collapse became more varied, many kept blaming gullibility toward the West.

By the 1990s, the Chinese debate on the causes of a calamitous outcome in their alter-ego, the Soviet Union, was paralleling the Soviet debate two decades earlier on the calamitous loss of their strongest partner in the socialist camp. In both cases the search into the causes of socialism going awry produced an approved orthodoxy with censors alert to prevent heretical challenges, but this proved hard to enforce as a far-reaching search for diverse causes allowed some disguised conflicting opinions to slip into the public arena. With parallels between the two cases obvious, censors limited the debates. Since the Chinese image of extreme authoritarianism reminded people of the Stalinist past, it was easy to project a negative image in the 1970s in the Soviet Union. Likewise, because the Russian image in the 1990s of chaos and a society in deep trouble reminded Chinese of their Cultural Revolution, the image was easy to convey too.

With conservatives clearly asserting the upper hand after June 4, the debate on Gorbachev slipped from sight. When it resumed on a much lower key from 1992 in the search for what brought down the Soviet Union and the communist system, the failure of the transition in Russia amid fear of ideology causing economic chaos, such as occurred in the Cultural Revolution, played into the hands of the conservatives. Even past Chinese sympathizers with Gorbachev concluded that his impact and even more that of Yeltsin, who never won a following, led Russia down the wrong road for China. Few saw gains from democracy by 1993–94; instead, they observed privatization favoring bureaucrats who used their power to seize state assets as their own. Yet, remarks to that effect could not be published, arising only in interviews. The intense differences from 1989, resurfacing as conflicting views of why the communist bloc collapsed and then the Soviet Union did too, narrowed as Russian conditions gave more credibility to Deng's theoretical shift. In early 1992 Deng refocused the discussion on what had happened. Criticism of the Soviet way was necessary to prove that China had been correct in its crackdown on June 4, but a line had to be drawn if Deng were to revitalize his reform program and leave a legacy conducive to continued rapid economic development.

China's leaders had set three missions for their country, which leaders in Moscow were failing to accomplish: to develop the economy and avoid shocks that could send it reeling; to realize national unification and not lose territory; and to oppose hegemonism and not accommodate it. Moscow's failure on all three goals left it a sorry example, since even Chinese reformers, for the most part, shared these objectives. Nationalist appeals in the 1990s made effective use of the negative Soviet example for spreading interrelated theories on how to transform a socialist state and how to achieve global multipolarity.

Toward Theories of Socialist Transformation and Great Power Geometry

From 1985 to 1992 China experienced a process of theoretical flux, marked by sharp challenges to previous dogma and vague answers at a time of pragmatic economic reform that some have interpreted as suggesting the irrelevance of theory. Yet, theory was being taken seriously. It was evolving, and, arguably, by the end of the period, the leaders of China had found a revised understanding of socialism that offered a roadmap to further reforms. Responding to the Soviet intellectual challenge, China under Deng Xiaoping refined a theory of competition between socialism and capitalism and of what is needed for socialism, however defined, to maintain control and stand firm against foreign pressure for democratization. This theory produced the framework for a worldview that has endured for the past 15 years, buttressed by the contrast drawn with the Soviet Union.

Censorship made serious criticisms of Mao Zedong, the full truth about the Cultural Revolution, and acknowledgment of the fundamental structure present in China unacceptable in approved Chinese publications, but debate about the Soviet Union in search of lessons for China became a priority for internal circulation writings for about a decade. Furthermore, over most of the first four years of Gorbachev's tenure, Hu Yaobang or Zhao Ziyang welcomed the search for reform ideas extending to politics and found positive evaluations of Gorbachev helpful. The study of the history of socialism approved in the first half of the 1980s, although at times restricted for going too far, became a vehicle to prove the need for Gorbachev and what he was attempting. Bold writings went further in clarifying Stalin's real crimes, the importance of Khrushchev's reforms, and the continued failure to implement a system of checks and balances. For Chinese intellectuals and some officials as well, hopes were raised for overcoming arbitrary authoritarianism and shedding clear light on the excesses of a system that had proven very costly to the Chinese people and still denied their initiative. Early in 1984 in the campaign against spiritual pollution censorship tightened against such transgressions as treating the early Marx differently from the late Marx and briefly three years later there was again an effort to curb debate over Khrushchev's humanism and glasnost after Hu Yaobang fell. Yet, in 1988 and early 1989 the struggle intensified, centering specifically on Gorbachev. He was not to be the subject of open invectives in this period of rapidly normalizing ties, but in contrast to the indirect praise for his contribution to comparative socialism there was also rising anxiety about his potential to destroy socialism. In opposition to the theoretical aspirations of those who embraced Gorbachev as a stimulus for China's convergence with the West, a theoretical approach that rejected his approach to socialism persisted and after June 4, 1989 became the nucleus of a new framework on the socialist transformation.

Chinese went from direct, if narrow, comparisons in the first half of the 1980s, to sharp direct comparisons for a time in 1986, to indirect but still trenchant comparisons in 1987–89, to silence in 1989–91, to insistence on sharp differences that supposedly negated the value of making comparisons from 1992. Yet, one basic comparison increasingly resonated to the concern of the leadership: losing control from the top, as Russia did, does not free the vitality of democratic forces, as many Westerners argued, but brings disorder in a vast country accustomed to communist centralization. This simple message negated the need for other comparisons. Writings ignored scholarly themes identified just a few years earlier by comparative socialism in favor of simple, theory-supporting contrasts.

The Soviet experience lent support to the following arguments: 1) socialist revolution provided the only way in China's and Russia's circumstances to raise the country from its backwardness; 2) even if it did not, whatever mistakes were committed after the revolutions, advances under socialism were greater than they would have been under capitalism; 3) even if this was not true, to abandon socialism now would slow development, throwing the country into decline and even anarchy; and 4) continuity now in political leadership and political system was the preferred way to borrow heavily from capitalist countries and, ironically, to realize the potential of socialism. In the Soviet case leaders made a mistake in interpreting the ideology, threatening the legitimacy of the political order. They allowed views subversive of the basic ideology of socialism to permeate public discussion, taking a wrong turn especially at the 19th Party Conference in June 1988, where humanistic and convergence-oriented ideals prevailed and the Soviets dropped their guard against the threat of capitalism. Bad theory led the way to collapse. In contrast, China's development of good theory, beginning with Deng Xiaoping's moves in 1979 and culminating with the implicit framework of 1992 leads to rejuvenation. For that a country needs continuity with its past and pride in itself in facing the future.

When China loomed as a negative example in Moscow in the 1970s, reformers fought an indirect struggle under tight censorship to use its negative image to hint at parallels with Soviet shortcomings and make the case for reform at home. Yet, with the Soviet Union serving as a negative example in China in the 1990s, reformers in Beijing and Shanghai were even less successful in arguing for guilt by association and boosting reform prospects. The main reason was the success of the Chinese leadership in coopting the reform agenda and in convincing the Chinese people that they had taken a different path from Moscow. The lingering image of the Cultural Revolution as a time of ruinous disorder and of the Soviet reforms as having provoked disorder, also, found a receptive audience. Chinese leaders managed to develop a theory of socialist transformation to fit the mood of the times. It rejected the past as a guide to the future, but it did not repudiate past decisions as, on the whole, destructive for moving forward. The socialist system could be retained in the abstract. It accepted elements of modernization theory while rejecting convergence as the outcome. Reform could proceed without inducing a shift to the model in the West. It embraced globalization economically even as it insisted on strengthening state power within a global balance of power to limit the spread of a new world order based on Western values and U.S. hegemony. These dualities applied not as a formalized claim for the indefinite future, but as a framework for a transition that would last for decades.

The debate over the Soviet Union helped Chinese leaders backed by academic subordinates to articulate a revised version of modernization theory distinct in important respects from theories once popular in the West.[58] As it emphasized borrowing and experimentation in local areas to find the best results to show the country the way, it also stressed state direction and control as the key to success. This debate also led to a kind of civilizational approach stressing the danger of pollution from the outside without questioning the need to open the door to knowledge of what was happening outside the country. China's communists identified themselves as battling not only for socialism but also for Chinese civilization. Finally, China also refined a kind of theory of the world order. Accordingly, they stressed a stable, global equilibrium allowing room for rapid economic growth, but balanced enough to inhibit serious interference in a country's internal affairs; a stratified world where political great powers coexist and wield disproportionate influence; and an emerging regional order with great scope for expanding a rising state's influence.[59]

Official Chinese thinking suggests that state legitimacy comes more from economic results and consumer satisfaction than democratic elections and that state capacity is more important than checks on state power. Theory is dominated by a state-centered approach, denigrating an individual-centered one. The socialist transformation may unleash individual incentives and offer ample rewards, but the state represents the force that ensures stability, provides theoretical clarity, and maximizes power in a dangerous world. If this theory never became a formal doctrine with a clear designation, unless one is content with the vague concepts of "socialism with Chinese characteristics" or the oxymoron of a "socialist market economy," it has, nonetheless, guided China from 1992 and seemed to be vindicated by both the failure of Russia in the 1990s and its revival along lines favored by China thereafter. In 1985–89 the theory of socialism could not be divorced from the shadow of Soviet rethinking, and in 1989–91 it acquired a different cast under the dual shadow of the June 4 shock and the Soviet heresy. By 1992 we find a resurgent theory that has largely remained to today.

Conclusion

Whether the focus was on the fate of the Soviet Union, the socialist system, or the international system, Chinese leaders were anxious to determine where the Soviet Union was heading. It mattered greatly for internal analysis on where China was heading and what policies might lead in a more promising direction. In one response, the Soviet Union loomed as a more developed socialist country ready to enter a new stage of socialism that would likely show the way for China. It was converging with the United States based on its high level of urbanization, industrialization, and education, and an expanding elite was challenging the narrow political elite that had monopolized power. Those who framed this perspective, however indirectly, they were compelled to make their arguments, saw political reform as the natural next step for a socialist country that had achieved a high level of development, noting that the past Soviet development path had been unbalanced. Had political reform been undertaken earlier, it could have done better. In this way, they put socialist democratization at the center of reform socialism. Their view was essentially supportive of convergence with the West. After June 4, 1989 they became casualties of tightened censorship as authoritarianism was reaffirmed as key to China's transformation.

From 1986 to 1991 official China grew increasingly nervous about Gorbachev's impact. In late 1986 and the first part of 1987 it was linked to the purge of Hu Yaobang and Chinese Communist Party reform intellectuals. From June 1989 it meant recognition of parallels between the demonstrations in China that had been repressed and the forces unleashed by Gorbachev and then alarm over the collapse of socialist regimes and the international communist bloc. And in 1991 it was marked by shock over the collapse of the Soviet Communist Party monopoly and then of the Soviet Union itself. While there were interludes of hope—early Gorbachev when Hu Yaobang orchestrated a positive response and mid-1987 to early 1989 when Zhao Ziyang reinvigorated debate in the face of many negative evaluations—the overall trend was disappointment in a leader who was turning his country away from the domestic and international role desired in China.

In 1985 there was enthusiasm for Gorbachev but doubt that he would be bold enough in his reform and foreign policy moves. In 1986–87 a mixture arose of positive evaluations and mounting skepticism, as China's leaders were divided, their struggles reverberated in assessments of Gorbachev, and the Soviet scene kept shifting. By 1988 and the first months of 1989 views had become polarized, as the critics intensified their warnings about the damage he was doing and his backers grew more enthusiastic and found more ways to advocate the causes he was championing. The June 4 massacre of demonstrators and comprehensive crackdown made it clear that praise of Gorbachev's reform had become unacceptable. As long as China's leaders were encouraging some political reform, such as separation of the party and government and replacement of older and less competent cadres, and were focused on overcoming leftist opposition to reforms, positive coverage of Gorbachev's reforms served their interest since the Soviet Union served as a mirror for China. Yet, when leaders grew anxious about ideological challenges or the potential for instability, they took measures to block contagion from their neighbor.

Images of Russia in the 1990s confirmed a theoretical outlook that had only been nascent in the 1980s. To abandon the path of socialism is to halt national development, to fall prey to dependency on the United States and its allies who will ignore your national interests, and to bring chaos and even despair to your people. While many Chinese analyses still focused on the causes of the collapse, others turned to the consequences of collapse with lessons not only for China but for reassessing what Soviet leaders had done incorrectly under Gorbachev. Their economic mistakes were most obvious. Social errors aroused the least interest and did not become major sources of controversy. Political errors could not easily be denied, but there was room for different slants with important implications. Of all issues, international policies could elicit some of the liveliest divergences as China weighed alternative responses to U.S. power and multilateral cooperation.

The basic message is that the Stalin model was flawed but not irredeemable and that the Soviet Union had a chance to reform if it delivered needed benefits to the people with little delay and kept tight control at the top. After all, the Soviets had better material conditions than China and had a long record of such control. Errors by Gorbachev led to overall failure. Official China insisted on the need for centralization, by which the system could be repaired. It came to view Gorbachev as taking the wrong path, either because of foolish choices or, as many leaders suspected, malicious intent. While a few bold voices appeared to argue that the Soviet system had to be destroyed and could not be reformed, this message angered officials. Two decades after Gorbachev had launched his signature reforms, Chinese were still under instructions to repudiate his approach and approve of socialism as a viable system of organizing a society that could have been reformed in the Soviet Union as it was in China.

In the fall of 1992 Chinese leaders were celebrating Deng Xiaoping's success in advancing and uniting the guiding thought of China as his greatest historical contribution. While most observers found little theoretical clarity or depth to these tributes on the eve of the Fourteenth Party Congress,[60] Chinese boosters praised Deng's theory for liberating thought, seeking truth from facts, and illuminating socialism with Chinese characteristics. In fact, Deng had differentiated his views from those of Gorbachev with regard to how a socialist system should be transformed. The debate over the Soviet Union provided a window on how the struggle over theory unfolded and on what became the essential elements of Deng's framework in the wake of the Soviet collapse and China's isolation, left virtually alone as the standard bearer of socialism. Scornful of Gorbachev's alleged alternative theory combining "convergence," "shock therapy," and "democratization," China's leaders anticipated a test between the new Russia and their own state over the coming years over which would gain the advantage in domestic development and international status in the emerging world order.

Looking back in 2008, most observers would conclude that China prevailed in this test. Russian domestic policy has broken with its tendencies of the 1990s, rebuilding a strong, central political authority. Russian national identity has disavowed the goal of becoming part of a single world community, distancing itself sharply from such ideals with suspicious overtones reminiscent of Soviet times. And Russian foreign policy has returned to realist objectives of expanding state power and extending state influence. In each of these respects Russia has narrowed the distance with China and vindicated the reasoning in that country that these steps would best serve Russia's national interest. Having emerged supreme over "rightist" efforts to develop the field of comparative socialism, the Chinese theory of socialist transformation has so far stood the test of time as the virtually uncontested guide to why China succeeded and the Soviet Union did not, and why Russia would revert to many Soviet features and regret the transition it followed.

For more than a decade many argued that such reversions in Russia also serve China's national interest. When Yeltsin catered to anti-Americanism, turned toward multipolarity, and searched for the "Russian idea" as distinct from universal values, these moves were treated as a sober awakening. As Putin rebuilt a centralized order focused on asserting state interests, China's leaders took satisfaction in a Russian leader who met their long-expressed expectations. He was setting Russia on a transition that, in critical respects, mirrored the socialist transition articulated in China's theory that emerged as the Soviet system collapsed. Moreover, his foreign policy relied heavily on the strategic dyad with China, addressing U.S. power in what Moscow increasingly regarded to be a strategic triangle. Yet, we may question whether these developments are really in China's lasting interest. More vigorous Russian support for state control over the economy and local government leaves in doubt Chinese pursuit of economic integration across open borders. More nationalist expression of state goals along with xenophobic attitudes among many Russians makes China a possible target, second only to the United States, but perhaps one day in the forefront. Finally, more emphasis on making Russia a pole in a multipolar world, even amidst claims that the strategic partnership is the backbone of foreign policy, could backfire on China as Russia looks to Northeast and Central Asia as arenas under threat from China's growing clout. The theory of socialist transformation may have resonated well in 1992 and never been subject to serious questioning over the following fifteen years, but its application could be doubted in an era of China's growing regional ascendancy and Russia's growing assertiveness on the fringes of the global system. Just as in the 1950s the two countries found it hard to proceed along the same track because national interests diverged, in the 2010s the two may face renewed tensions after again achieving long-desired goals for synchronizing domestic and foreign affairs policies but not reducing the potential for conflicting power objectives.

Sino-Russian agreement on security thinking about great power relations occurred in stages, largely as a result of Russia converging with China. By June 2002 Putin said that U.S.-Russia-China ties should form a "stable arch," while Chinese recognized that many of his views were the same or similar to China's new security concepts. (Xia, 2006, p. 22) If in 1989–91 Chinese accusations against alleged plots for world dominance by the United States were much more strident than Soviet views, from the late 1990s and especially under Putin Russia's tone in opposing hegemony and even globalization has grown harsher than China's. A consensus on realist, great power balancing was reached by 1996 and then advanced to the level China had been seeking from Gorbachev in 1986. Yet, this obvious success could carry the seeds of new tensions with an emboldened Russia. Just as the theory of socialist transformation may leave China ill-equipped for solving cascading domestic problems in the coming era, the theory of multipolarity may leave it opposite an assertive Russia ready to cause more instability than a globalizing China may find comfortable. The lessons learned from the Russian experience satisfied China's leaders in the short run, but they could haunt a rising and more responsible China.

Notes

1. David Shambaugh, "The Chinese Discourse on Communist Party-States," *China's Communist Party: Atrophy and Adaptation* (herein after as *China's Communist Party*) (Berkeley: University of California Press, 2008), 41–86. Also see the chapter in this volume by Guan Guihai.

2. Gilbert Rozman, *The Chinese Debate about Soviet Socialism, 1978–1985* (hereinafter as *The Chinese Debate about Soviet Socialism*) (Princeton, NJ: Princeton University Press, 1987). Yan Sun, *The Chinese Reassessment of Socialism, 1976–1992* (Princeton, NJ: Princeton University Press, 1995). N. P. Riabchenko, *KNR-SSSR: Gody konfrontatsii (1969–1982)* (Vladivostok: Dal'nauka, 2006).

3. David Shambaugh, *China's Communist Party.*

4. Gilbert Rozman, "Chinese Studies in Russia and their Impact, 1985–1992," *Asian Research Trends*, no. 4 (1994), 143–60.

5. Liu Keming, "Fakanci" [Foreword], *Sulian Dongou wenti* [Problems of the Soviet Union and Eastern Europe] (hereinafter as *Sulian Dongou wenti*), no. 1 (1981): 1.

6. Xiandai guoji guanxi yanjiusuo, Sulian Dongou yanjiushi, ed., *Sulian dui shehuizhuyi de zairenshi* [The Soviet Union's reevaluation of socialism] (Beijing: Shishi chubanshe, 1988).

7. Gilbert Rozman, "Stages in the Reform and Dismantling of Communism in China and the Soviet Union," in *Dismantling Communism: Common Causes and Regional Variations*, ed. Gilbert Rozman (Baltimore, MD: Johns Hopkins University Press, 1992), 15–58.

8. "Yao jiaqiang Sulian Dongou guojia lishi he xianzhuang de yanjiu" [The need to strengthen the study of the history and current conditions of the soviet union and

East European countries], *Sulian lishi wenti* [Questions concerning Soviet history] (hereinafter as *Sulian lishi wenti*), no. 2 (1986), 1.

9. Internal (*neibu*) sources provide the bulk of material on which this paper is based. They were not meant to be sent out of the country and were not readily shared with foreigners, although they often were accessible in academic environments within China. The debates under review served for discussions among academics and for guidance of officials.

10. Xu Shi, "Bai dui Sulian Dongou yanjiu xiangqian tuijin yibu" [To advance forward a step the study of the Soviet Union and Eastern Europe], *Shijie jingji yu zhengzhi* [World economy and politics] (hereinafter as *Shijie jingji yu zhengzhi*), no. 11 (1984), 1–2.

11. "Shenke linghui shisanda de jingshen, jinyibu jiaqiang dui Sulian he Dongou guojia de yanjiu" [Deeply grasp the 13th party congress' spirit: strengthen the study of the Soviet Union and East European countries], *Sulian Dongou wenti*, no. 1 (1988), 1–2.

12. "Zhongguo Sulian Dongou xuehui zhaokai disanjie nianhui" [The Chinese Association of Soviet and East European Studies opens its third annual meeting], *Sulian Dongou wenti*, no. 2 (1991), 87–91.

13. Gilbert Rozman, "Sino-Russian Mutual Assessments," in *Rapprochement or Rivalry? Russia-China Relations in a Changing Asia*, ed. Sherman Garnett (Armonk, NY: M. E. Sharpe, 2000), 147–74.

14. Many internal journals became open (*gongkai*) publications from 1992–93, dropping the feature of instructions to the field and operating clearly under the new consensus about theory. It became easier to follow academic analysis, but harder to detect differences of view on critical issues related to the development of the Soviet Union and socialism.

15. Gilbert Rozman, "Soviet Reinterpretations of Chinese Social History," *Journal of Asian Studies*, (November 1974), 49–72.

16. Gilbert Rozman, *The Chinese Debate about Soviet Socialism.*

17. Jin Hui, "Sulian de jingji zhanlue he jingji gaige," [The Soviet economic strategy and economic reform] *Sulian Dongou wenti*, no. 1 (1983), 1–9. Zhang Zhanzhong, "Sulian de shangye gaige" [The Soviet commercial reform], *Sulian Dongou wenti*, no. 6 (1983), 45–52.

18. Gilbert Rozman, *The Chinese Debate about Soviet Socialism.*

19. This mantra of socialism's superiority to capitalism was widely repeated; even some of the boldest views paid obeisance to this formulaic and, at times, obligatory claim.

20. Raymond L. Garthoff, *The Great Transition: American-Soviet Relations and the End of the Cold War* (Washington, DC: Brookings Institution Press, 1994), 81–89. Elizabeth Wishnick, *Mending Fences: The Evolution of Moscow's China Policy from Brezhnev to Yeltsin* (Seattle: University of Washington Press, 2001). Alexander Lukin, *The Bear Watches the Dragon: Russia's Perceptions of China and the Evolution of Russian-Chinese Relations since the Eighteenth Century* (Armonk, NY: M. E. Sharpe, 2003).

21. A bibliography of articles on the Soviet Union for the period May–June 1982 listed almost 200, of which the vast majority were translations. Under the first heading

of politics and law the first items covered long taboo subjects—four on Bukharin, four on Stalin, and two on Trotsky. "Sulian Dongou yanjiu ziliao suoyin" [Bibliography of materials for the study of the Soviet Union and Eastern Europe], *Jinri Sulian Dongou*, [Today's Soviet Union and Eastern Europe], no. 6 (1982): 65–71.

22. "Chinese Views of Soviet Reforms," *Foreign Broadcast Information Service, Analysis Report*, April 8, 1987, 1–30.

23. Sun Hanbing, *Zhongsu guanxi jiqi dui Zhongguo shehui fazhan de yingxiang* [Sino-Soviet relations and their influence on the development of Chinese society] (Beijing: Zhongguo guoji guangbo chubanshe, 2002), 533–42.

24. *Sulian Dongou wenti*, no. 2, 1986.

25. "Beijing bufen zhuanjia xuezhe tan Sugong ershiqida" [Some ʙᴇɪjing specialist scholars discuss the sovieT communist party's 27th congress], *Sulian Dongou wenti*, no. 2 (1986), 1–14, 52.

26. *Sulian Dongou wenti*, no. 6, 1986.

27. *Sulian Dongou wenti*, no. 1, 1987.

28. *Sulian Dongou wenti*, no. 4, 1987.

29. *Sulian shehuikexue yanjiu*, no. 7, 1987.

30. *Sulian shehuikexue yanjiu*, no. 10, 1987.

31. Mei Wenbin, "Sulian shehuizhuyi jianshezhong de zuoqing wenti" [The problem of left deviation in the construction of Soviet socialism], *Sulian shehuizhuyi de yanjiu* [Studies of sovieT socialism], no. 1 (1987), 12–18.

32. Tang Xiushan, "Geerbaqiaofu mianlin shuangchong tiaozhan" [Gorbachev faces a dual challenge], *Liaowang* [Outlook], no. 10 (March 5, 1986), 29–30.

33. Wang Conglie, "Sulian gaige jincheng" [The course of Soviet reform], *Liaowang*, no. 10 (March 9, 1987), 26–27.

34. Zhou Biwen, "Bashiniandai yilai Sulian guanyu minzu wenti de ruogan lunxu" [Some discourse concerning nationality questions in the Soviet Union since the 1980s], *Sulian shehuikexue*, no. 3 (1987), 11–17.

35. Wang Qi, "Sulian shehui minzhuhua: quzhe er manchang de licheng" [Soviet social democratization: complications and their tortuous course], *Sulian Dongou wenti*, no. 6 (1987), 19–25, 86.

36. Jin Hui, "Sulian de zhengzhi tizhi jiqi gaige de dongxiang" [Soviet political system reform trends], *Sulian Dongou wenti*, no. 2 (1987), 1–7, 80.

37. Li Honglin, "'Right' and 'Left' in Communist China: A Self-Account by a Theoretician in the Chinese Communist Party," *The Journal of Contemporary China*, no. 6 (Summer 1994), 24.

38. Wu Yaohui, "Sulian Dongou guojia zhengzhi tizhi gaige de lishi kaocha" [Historical investigation of the political system reforms in the Soviet Union and East ᴇuropean countries], *Shehui kexue* [Social science], no. 8 (1987), 11–16.

39. Wu Renzhang, "Shiyue geming yu Sulian moshi de gaige" [The October Revolution and reform of the Soviet model], *Sulian Dongou wenti*, no. 6 (1987), 26–32.

40. Gilbert Rozman, "The Comparative Study of Socialism in China: The Social Sciences at a Crossroads," *Social Research* 54, no. 4 (Winter 1987), 631–61.

41. Zhao Longkang, "Sulian zhengzhi tizhi gaige de congti gouxiang" [The overall concept of reform of the Soviet political system], *Liaowang*, no. 25 (June 20, 1988).

42. "Sulian Dongou xingqi gaige langchao" [The wave of reform upsurge in the Soviet Union and Eastern Europe], *Liaowang*, no. 43 (October 27, 1986), 31.

43. Jeanne L. Wilson, "The Impact of the Demise of State Socialism in China," in *The Transformation of State Socialism: System Change, Capitalism or Something Else?* ed. David Lane (New York: Palgrave, 2007), 269–85.

44. Interviews in China over the following fifteen years produced many remarks about lingering views among officials of Gorbachev conspiring to bring down socialism, even working conspiratorially in league with the United States to achieve this outcome.

45. Li Shufan, "Lun Lianmeng de jieti" [Discussing the breakup of the Union], *Waiguo wenti yanjiu* [Studies of foreign questions] (hereinafter as *Waiguo wenti yanjiu*) no. 2 (1992), 3–4.

46. Zhang Jingling, "Shilun yu dangqian fanba youguan de jige renshi wenti" [Trial discussion of some questions of consciousness regarding current anti-hegemonism], *Sulian Dongou wenti*, no. 6 (1982), 1–5.

47. Sun Hanbing, *Zhongsu guanxi jiqi dui Zhongguo shehui fazhan de yingxiang* [The Sino-Soviet relations and its impact on the social development of China] (Beijing: Zhongguo guoji guangbo chubanshe, 2002), 538.

48. Alexander Bovin, "We Need Better Relations with China," *Moscow News*, no. 20 (1991), 3.

49. Qu Yifeng, "Dongbeiya hezuo qianjing ji woguo zhanlue duice de sikao" [Prospects for Northeast Asian cooperation and our country's counter strategy thinking], *Xiboliya yanjiu* [Siberian studies], no. 5 (1991), 1–8.

50. Luo Zhaohong, "Shijie jingji yu zhengzhi xingshi de huigu he zhanwang" [Reflections and outlook for the world economic and political situation], *Shijie jingji yu zhengzhi*, no. 2 (1992), 1–4.

51. Chen Qiyou, "Guanyu zai Yatai diqu jianli zhengzhi xinzhixu de tansuo" [Exploration concerning establishing a new political order in the Asia-Pacific region] (hereinafter as *Yatai diqu*), *Guoji wenti yanjiu* [Studies of international issues], no. 1 (1992), 3.

52. Jeanne L. Wilson, "The Impact of the Demise of State Socialism in China," 269–85.

53. Xu Zhixin, "Yuan Sulian diqu de weiji yu xifang de yuanzhu" [Discussing the crisis in the Soviet Union and western assistance], *Dongou Zhongya yanjiu* [Studies of East Europe and Central Asia], no. 3 (1992), 37–41.

54. Ma Shufang, "Guanyu Xifang yuanzhu Eluosi xin wenti de sikao" [Thinking about new questions related to western assistance to Russia], *Eluosi yanjiu* [Russian studies], no. 1 (1995), 14–20.

55. Yu Hanxi, "Geerbaqiaofu de rendaode, minzhude shehuizhuyi yu Sulian de yanbian" [Gorbachev's humanistic, democratic socialism and Soviet transformation], *Sulian wenti yanjiu ziliao* [Materials for the study of Soviet questions] (hereinafter as *Sulian wenti yanjiu ziliao*), no. 3 (1992), 1–6.

56. Xu Wence, "Sulian jieti yu rendaode minzhude shehuizhuyi pochan" [The breakup of the Soviet Union and the bankruptcy of humanistic, democratic socialism] *Sulian wenti yanjiu ziliao*, no. 4 (1992), 6–8.

57. Li Xiumin, "Geerbaqiaofu shidai Sulian you kuozhang dao shousu de duiwai zhengce" [The foreign policy of the Gorbachev era Soviet Union from expansion to contraction], *Waiguo wenti yanjiu*, no. 2 (1992), 20–25.

58. Luo Rongju, *Cong Xihua dao xiandaihua* [From westernization to modernization] (Beijing: Beijing daxue chubanshe, 1991). Luo Rongju, "An Initial Concept of a Marxist theory of modernization," *Social Sciences in China*, no. 2 (1988), 63.

59. Wang Jiafu, "Lun Dongbeiya shichang de zhanlue jiegou" [Discussing the strategic structure of the Northeast Asian market], *Longjiang shehuikexue* [Amur social sciences], no. 4 (1992), 35–41. Chen Qimao, *Yatai diqu*, 1–8.

60. *Renmin ribao*, October 12, 1992, 3. *Liaoning ribao*, October 19, 1992, 1.

18

The Fate of the Soviet Model of Multinational State-Building in the People's Republic of China[1]

Minglang Zhou

Introduction

IMPERIAL CHINA EVOLVED INTO A HUGE EMPIRE by employing strategies of assimilation and of accommodation.[2] Successive imperial courts generally adopted an assimilationist approach in southern and southwestern China where, with military conquests and/or deterrence, imperial bureaucracies were established to implement imperial rules while schools were built to "civilize" the local population. Meanwhile, the courts usually embraced an accommodationist approach in northern and northwestern China where, with military deterrence and/or royal marriages, favorable trade privileges and military cooperation were negotiated. Under a grand scheme of "divide and rule," the imperial courts' skillful deployment of these two strategies worked well to maintain the political and territorial integrity of the empire until the Qing Dynasty lost the Opium War and signed the Anglo-Chinese Treaty of Nanking in 1842.[3] From then on the Qing faced Western powers' encroachment on what was still internationally recognized as sovereign China.[4] The British extended their influence to western China, including Tibet and Xinjiang, while Russia expanded southward to the Qing's northern sphere. Consequently the Qing Dynasty lost territories to Russia and met strong secessionist challenges in Mongolia, Xinjiang and Tibet, eventually losing control of Outer Mongolia in the early 20th century.

Thus, modern China has been perceived, at least by the Chinese, to have inherited compromised and fragmented borders from the Qing Dynasty, whose great role in expanding and consolidating the territories of the empire in the 17th and 18th centuries is, however, now celebrated in the People's Republic. To guard against Western encroachment and to protect territorial integrity, different political forces within China tried to find means from the West to build a stronger modern China. Among these forces was the young Chinese Communist Party (CCP), which considered Western encroachment as a form of Western colonialism within the theoretical frame of Marxism and Leninism, and promoted the Soviet style of federalism for a multinational state in 1922.[5] The CCP's federalist approach eventually evolved into regional autonomy within a unified China when the People's Republic of China (PRC) was founded in 1949. The Soviet model of multinational state-building, however, was still considered the blueprint for the PRC for handling the national question.[6] The PRC adopted the Soviet model by constitutionally endorsing three basic doctrines: equality of all national minorities; regional autonomy for minorities; and equality of all minority/national languages and cultures. Concretely, this meant equal treatment for minorities and the Han majority as PRC citizens and CCP members, a system of regional autonomous administrations, and freedom of minority language use and cultural development.

However, after the disintegration of the Soviet Union in 1991, continued practice of the failed Soviet model obviously became questionable in China, apart from the fact that the PRC had started to abandon the Stalinist model of the economy a decade earlier.[7] Thus, China has quietly replaced the Soviet model with its "one-nation-with-diversity" model (*duoyuan yiti*). This new model assumes an inclusive Chinese nation (*zhonghua minzu*) consisting of various ethnic groups—a two-level conceptual structure (instead of the Soviet's one level within a state) that seems to allow more room for identity negotiation and reconciliation. The adoption of this model is seen in a series of policy changes, including amendments to existing laws and enactments of new ones since the late 1990s. The new model still endorses the three basic doctrines, but it appears to downgrade minorities' political equality within the CCP, to moderate the political rights associated with regional autonomy while increasing economic rights, and to allow freedom of minority-language use and cultural development within shrinking domains.

In this chapter I first examine the CCP's adoption of the Soviet model before and after the founding of the PRC and show specific Soviet assistance in China's practice of the Soviet model of multinational state-building in the 1950s. Second, I discuss China's replacement of the Soviet model with a Chinese model and examine its impact on China's minorities. I evaluate, preliminarily, the new Chinese model's strengths and weaknesses in comparison to the Soviet model and the American model of "one nation with diversity"—the "melting pot" model.

China's Adoption of the Soviet Model of Multinational State-Building

The blueprint that the Soviet model of multinational state-building provided for the CCP had three theoretical components, namely aspects of Marxist-Leninist and Stalinist theories; they became the guiding principles for the CCP in its management of the national question. Practically, I look at how the CCP institutionalized and implemented these principles following the Soviet Union together with the role of Soviet advisors who facilitated China's implementation of the Soviet model in the 1950s.

The CCP's Adoption of the Theory of the Soviet Model

Two fundamental views from Marxism-Leninism, and Stalinism have theoretically guided the CCP's approach to the national question. First, as early as 1922 during its Second National Congress, the CCP acknowledged Lenin's view that "different nations are advancing in the same historical direction, but by very different zigzags and bypaths," and that there are more cultured/advanced nations and less cultured/advanced ones.[8] According to this view, being culturally and economically different, China's minorities had the right to be politically different, that is, to have the right to self-determination during the Republican period and have the right to regional autonomy during the PRC, so that they could eventually catch up with the "advanced" Han in economic and cultural development. Moreover, this view also underpins the Han's big-brother-style assistance to minorities in their economic and cultural development and the affirmative-action policies in the PRC.[9]

Second, also during the 1922 congress, the CCP adopted the Leninist categorization of nations into the oppressors and the oppressed and advocated struggle against the oppressors with the goal of winning true equality among nations as an integral part of the overall communist revolution.[10] However, not until 1923, at its Third National Congress, did the CCP explicitly put forward the principle of national equality in China.[11] This principle was enshrined in the PRC's provisional constitution of 1949, the Common Program (General Principles), and the 1954 Constitution (General Principles) and its later versions.

Third, while acknowledging early on Lenin's view on the historical development of nations, the CCP did not emphasize until the 1950s the Stalinist view that a "nation" is a historical category and that nations undergo three stages—formation, conflict, and convergence.[12] This view assumes that nations formed during capitalism, come into conflict during the later stage of capitalism or imperialism, but will converge during communist rule in the

Soviet Union, China and elsewhere. In short, these three essential Marxist, Leninist, and Stalinist views together underlined the CCP's theoretical considerations of the national question in China and were the foundations for the CCP's policies and PRC's laws until the 1990s.

Adapting the Soviet Model to China: A Federal or Unitary System?

The process of copying and implementing the Soviet model involved two interwoven key issues—models of the state and scope of minority rights. The first issue was whether the CCP should strive to build a multinational state based on Soviet-style federalism in which minority communities joined as republics or built a unified, multinational state, within which minority communities gained regional autonomy. The second issue boiled down to the choice of two principles: self-determination or regional autonomy for minorities. Obviously inseparable, these two issues have always dominated the CCP's struggle with the national question in China.

As early as 1922 at its Second National Congress, the CCP first proposed, following the Soviet Union, that a true democratic republic be established for China proper and autonomous republics be established for the Mongolian, Tibetan and Muslim Turkic areas and that all these four republics form the Chinese Federal Republic on a voluntary basis.[13] This Soviet-style federalism was promoted as the sole approach to the national question until 1931, when the Chinese Soviet passed its constitution at its First National Congress. With federalism as a choice, this Chinese Soviet Constitution allowed three options for minority governments: independent minority republics, federal minority republics of the Chinese Soviet, and regional autonomy within a unified China.[14] Clearly modeled after the 1918 Russian Soviet Constitution,[15] the Chinese Soviet Constitution stipulated that, regardless of their nationalities, all members of the working class had the right to vote for and be elected to government offices, had freedom of religion, and had the right to self-determination or autonomy. The essence of these stipulations is found in the 1918 Constitution of the Russian Soviet Federated Socialist Republic which contained the rights to self-determination (chapters 3 and 4), freedom of religion (chapter 5), and to voting and election (chapter 13).[16]

The CCP began to downplay Soviet-style federalism and minority independence when Japan expanded its invasion of China by attempting to set up puppet governments in minority communities as "independent" states, such as Manchukuo. In 1936, when it published an open letter to Muslim communities, the CCP offered them only regional autonomy, though it still recognized self-determination as the principle for the national question.[17] This approach was reaffirmed in the CCP's "Ten Guidelines to Fight the Japanese

Invasion and to Save China" published in 1937.[18] It was an attempt to pre-empt Japanese efforts to set puppet governments in Mongolian and Muslim communities, as Liu Shaoqi explicitly spelled out in the same year.[19] This approach was eventually accommodated in the CCP and Mao Zedong's vision of China as a multinational state, which would be a unified new democratic republic.[20] As it evolved, the principle of self-determination was gradually overtaken by the principle of equality upon which minority autonomy was based.

This approach to autonomy appears to have been finalized at the Sixth Plenum of the CCP's Sixth Central Committee in October 1938, at which Zhang Wentian and Mao Zedong, the old and new CCP leaders, both stressed autonomy on the principle of equality.[21] It was not only the basis for the CCP's solutions to the Muslim and Mongolian issues but also became part of the governing guidelines for the CCP-ruled areas.[22] The approach was, in fact, implemented in some of the CCP-ruled areas during the Anti-Japanese war of 1937–1945. In the CCP's *Shaan-Gan-Ning* Border Region, autonomous governments were established for concentrated Muslim and Mongolian communities, minority affairs committees were set up for minorities scattered in Han-dominant communities, and quotas were given to minority communities to elect legislators to local governing bodies,[23] a pattern that was to be repeated during the PRC. However, the CCP did not give up Soviet-style federalism as its ultimate goal. The Party Constitution revised and passed at the CCP's Seventh National Congress in 1945 still claimed to be striving to build a new democratic federal republic of China.[24]

By 1945, the CCP was left with two options—federal minority republics and regional autonomy—having abandoned the idea of independent minority republics. Between 1945 and 1949, the practice of regional autonomy expanded from the *xiang* (township) and county levels in Shaan-Gan-Ning to the provincial level in Inner Mongolia when the latter set up an autonomous government in 1947. However, evidence suggests that the CCP did not make a final decision between the two options until 1948 or 1949 when it faced the challenge of building a new China. In 1949 the PRC leadership and the Soviet leadership had direct communication on minority rights in the CCP-ruled new China. In early 1949, when A. I. Mikoyan visited Mao Zedong and the CCP headquarters in Xibaipo near Beijing, he conveyed Stalin's suggestion that China encourage Han migration to Xinjiang to reinforce its control.[25] According to Andrei M. Ledovskii,[26] Mikoyan and Stalin suggested that the CCP should not be so generous as to allow minorities independence and reduce the territory of CCP-ruled China, but only give minorities autonomy. This does not mean that the concept of regional autonomy was a Soviet idea nor does it mean that the CCP simply followed Moscow's advice. Liu Chun, vice chairman of the PRC State Commission on Nationality Affairs during the 1950s and 1960s, claimed that China's concept of regional autonomy could be traced back to Mao Zedong's speech at the Sixth Plenum of the Sixth CCP Central Committee in 1938.[27] In that speech, Mao stated that "under the principle of uniting against the Japanese invasion, the Mongolian, Hui, Tibetan, Miao, Yao, Yi, Fan, and all nationalities should be given equal rights as the Han, enjoy the right to manage their own affairs by themselves, and build a unified country with the Han."[28] This self-management concept is cited as the original theoretical foundation of the PRC's regional autonomy.[29] In addition, the CCP might have already made a decision on regional autonomy before Mikoyan's visit. In October 1948, Li Weihan, then director of the CCP United Front Department, supervised the draft of the first version of the Common Program of the Chinese People's Political Consultative Congress (CPPCC), then known as the Draft of the Chinese People's Democratic Revolutionary Principles, which included national equality and regional autonomy, but did not mention republics.[30] Gong Yuzhi reported that during the drafting process Mao Zedong asked Li Weihan whether the new China should adopt Soviet-style federalism or regional autonomy within a unified state for minorities, and Li advised Mao that the latter should be adopted.[31] This first draft served as the basis for the second version of the draft titled the New Democratic Common Program in July and August 1949 and the final version of the Common Program in September 1949. However, some accounts seem to suggest that Mao Zedong and Li Weihan made the decision for regional autonomy during preparations for the CPPCC in 1949 after Mikoyan's visit.[32] If this was the case, then the Soviet proposal on regional autonomy might have had more influence on the CCP's decision.

In any case, at the First Plenum of the CPPCC, Zhou Enlai explained to minority representatives why the Party proposed regional autonomy within a unified China instead of republics within a federal China.[33] He gave two reasons: Western imperialists' attempt to sabotage China's unification and the successful experience with Inner Mongolia's regional autonomy. Still conceding explicitly that any nation had the right to self-determination, Zhou asked the minority representatives to support the CCP's proposal on regional autonomy, which the representatives did. As it was passed at the CPPCC, the Common Program contained four articles endorsing equality of all nationalities, regional autonomy for minorities, the right to join/organize armed forces, and freedom to use minority languages and enjoy minority cultures. Immediately after the passage of the Common Program, on October 5, 1949, the CCP Central Committee instructed its regional bureaus and field-army CCP committees that the term "self-determination" should no longer be used in its minorities policy, because it might be employed by imperialists and minority reactionaries to sabotage the unification of China.[34]

In drafting the 1954 Constitution, the PRC incorporated the same four rights for minorities while working in close consultation with the Soviet Union.[35] Actually Mao Zedong and the CCP were heavily pressured by Stalin to hold the National People's Congress and pass a constitution within five years after seizing power.[36] During the drafting process, the drafting committee and the CCP Politburo consulted several versions of the Soviet Constitution, particularly the 1936 version and Stalin's report on it, East European constitutions, all earlier Chinese constitutions and the main Western constitutions.[37] After the first draft was completed in late March 1954, Peng Zhen asked the Soviet advisors working for the CCP Political and Legal Committee to read the draft and make editorial suggestions. The advisors passed their suggestions to the Soviet ambassador and the Soviet advisor general who conveyed them to the CCP.[38] In his conversations Mao Zedong confirmed that some of their suggestions were adopted in the revised draft. As soon as the draft was revised and passed by the Central People's Government Council for national discussion on April 14, 1954, it was sent to Moscow for the post-Stalin CPSU Central Committee's review and comment. Stalin had been known as a heavy-handed editor of foreign constitutions, since he made extensive amendments to the draft of the Polish Constitution in 1951, including changes in grammar, terminology, and rights.[39] However, had he still been alive by the time the final draft of the Chinese Constitution was sent to Moscow, he would probably have been more diplomatic since his relationship with Mao was different from that between him and the Polish leadership. Of course only further Soviet archival research and the availability of the PRC archive can reveal what comments or suggestions were made by the post-Stalin CPSU regarding the final draft. A comparison of the Common Program and the 1954 Chinese Constitution finds the essence of the CPSU Central Committee's 1949 proposal in Article 3 of the Constitution, which states that regions with national autonomy are inseparable parts of the PRC. Whatever impact the Soviet Union had on the 1954 Chinese Constitution did not change the Common Program's four basic principles on national equality, regional autonomy, the rights of the military forces, and the rights and freedoms related to minority languages and cultures.

The Soviet Model and the Language Issue in China

China seems to have wanted to confine Soviet expertise to more technical areas while excluding Soviet interference on policy making. For example, the

PRC State Commission on Nationalities' Affairs was apparently one of only two ministries (the other being Foreign Affairs)[40] that had no Soviet advisors working at the ministry headquarters. The State Commission did, however, approve the appointment of two Soviet ethnologists as technical advisors to the Central University for Nationalities. One was N. N. Cheboksarov, who came to Beijing in July 1956 when works by Soviet ethnologists had already changed the study of Chinese ethnology. As advisor to the president of the Central University for Nationalities, Cheboksarov taught graduate courses, gave a series of lectures on ethnology, and helped the university with its research plans for the 1956–1957 and 1957–1958 academic years.[41] Trying to survey the State Commission's minority policy-making process, Cheboksarov prepared a questionnaire with a few dozen questions for the commission to answer. However, without responding, the Commission passed the questionnaire onto to its chairman, Ulanfu, also vice premier of the PRC, who ordered that it be "ignored."[42]

The other ethnologist, G. P. Serdyuchenko had arrived in Beijing already in October 1954 along with several other Soviet linguists.[43] He served as the linguistic advisor to the Central University for Nationalities as well as of the Institute of Minority Languages of the Chinese Academy of Sciences, where he taught graduate courses. While much of Serdyuchenko's work focused on the technical issue of standardizing writing systems for minority languages, his technical work did have significant and broad policy implication for Sino-Soviet relations and for China's implementation of the Soviet model of multinational state-building. Serdyuchenko's early work in China, however, had focused more on the reform of the Chinese writing system than on minority languages, which probably reflected both his political agenda as well as Chinese debates then under way.

In the early 1950s debates on the reform of the Chinese writing system were unfolding nationally over whether China should adopt a kana-style, Roman or Cyrillic script to replace the Chinese characters. Serdyuchenko appears to have been well aware of China's dilemmas in selecting a script. He knew that China was not very willing to accept the Cyrillic alphabet to replace the Chinese script, even after some Soviet leaders personally promoted it to the Chinese leadership.[44] He was sure, however, that China was planning some sort of alphabetization, since Mao Zedong had made it clear in 1951 that "the Chinese script must be reformed along the common orientation, alphabetization, of world writing systems."[45] Therefore, Serdyuchenko walked a fine line in promoting the Cyrillic alphabet for use by the Chinese.

At the first national conference on the reform of the Chinese script in Beijing in 1955, Serdyuchenko suggested that a kana-oriented script (*zhuyin fuhao*) could not reach the ultimate goal of phonetization of Chinese, since this script was not completely phonetic and could be very complicated.[46] A kana-like writing system would be much more difficult to learn than an alphabetic writing system and therefore very impractical. He believed that Romanization was better, and the roman-based Latinxua designed by Qu Qiubai and Soviet linguists was a reasonable system, though it might need some improvement. Cyrillization was best of all, as Serdyuchenko clearly implied in the last two of his four criteria for choosing a script. First, the alphabet should fully represent all phonemes in Chinese. Second, the alphabet should be easy to read and write. Third, the alphabet should have a material and technological base—supplies of typewriters and printing technology and equipment. And fourth the alphabet should promote the intended political development—the victory of socialism all over the world. It was obvious to the audience that only the Soviet Union could supply China with printing and communications technology and equipment. Moreover, the Soviet Union was the political and military ally of China in the 1950s and the leader of the socialist world. Serdyuchenko suggested that the Cyrillic script was both linguistically and politically superior to the other two alternatives.

If he was somewhat cautious in promoting the Cyrillic script for Chinese, he was more aggressive in promoting an "alliance of writing systems across Sino-Soviet borders,"[47] ideally throughout the whole of China and at least throughout the Altaic language communities, either of which would have given the Soviets more influence in China.[48] Originally, writing reforms for minority languages in northern China had not been on the Chinese government's priority list. There was neither a plan to survey minority languages in northern China, nor a plan to engage in any major writing reforms there in the 1950s because those languages already had functional writing systems.[49] After learning about this situation, Serdyuchenko asked the State Commission on Nationalities Affairs to do a comprehensive survey of all minority languages in China. In a then classified report submitted to the State Commission on Nationalities Affairs and Institute of Linguistics in 1955,[50] Serdyuchenko specifically proposed the Cyrillic alphabet for all Altaic languages spoken in China, since those communities neighbored the Soviet Union. China in fact adopted Serdyuchenko's advice. But in the following few years, some students in Altaic language communities were using Soviet textbooks which read, "Our motherland is the Soviet Union. Our capital is Moscow." This was not what the CCP expected to see. The alliance of writing systems across Sino-Soviet borders was rejected along with other Soviet influences in 1958, as China was making a distinction between Soviet influence and Soviet experience. Mao Zedong and the CCP would not tolerate excessive Soviet influence though they wanted to take advantage of Soviet experience.

While Serdyuchenko did not succeed in promoting the Cyrillic alphabet, he did exert much influence in the realm of China's minority languages. In his graduate courses, speeches at relevant conferences, and advice on specific projects for minority languages,[51] he promoted what he called the "Soviet experience," which he summarized in a speech to China's first national conference on minority languages in December 1955.[52] Serdyuchenko elaborated five aspects of the relationship between writing and standard languages for minority communities, aspects that constituted the Soviet model of minority language maintenance and development for the building of a multinational state.

First, a standard language developed from oral languages should include both standard written and oral forms. Standard language differed from local dialects in that it is planned and codified. It is much richer and more commonly used than any local dialect, so it can serve all social, political, administrative, scientific and cultural needs of the people and serve socialist construction. Thus, the establishment of a standard language takes time and effort. In return, it changes, enriches and develops the vocabulary, phonology and grammar of a minority language. The development of a standard language is closely associated with political, economic, and cultural development. Language changes with the society that it serves. The standardization of pronunciation, vocabulary, grammar and orthography of a language can lead to a language turning into a national or common language for a nation. Clearly, the establishment of a standard language is an important form of social and cultural codification, a conscious plan that limits the scope of the language's internal development so that it serves the unity of the nation. With the correct implementation of the CPSU's minority policy, languages of the Soviet nations developed into national standard languages or minority community standard languages.

Second, the presence of a standard language facilitates national and linguistic convergence. Many minority languages in the Soviet Union developed from clan languages to tribal languages, and then to national languages. When the various nations entered the Soviet era from the old Russian Empire, many of them were merely tribes and tribal alliances, not nations strictly speaking, because of uneven social and economic development. During the Soviet period, many tribes and tribal alliances rapidly converged into socialist nations, so that some languages and newly created writing systems lost their independent existence. For example, the Altai used to be comprised of more than ten different tribes, but became one nation. In its minority language policy, the Soviet Union did not promote forced assimilation, but allowed for the natural development of socialist nations.

Third, in the process of creating unified writing systems, the base dialect for the standard language must be selected first, so that its grammar and vocabulary could become the basis for the development of the standard national language. In the Soviet Union, usually the most prestigious and popular dialect was selected as the base dialect, because the general development for that language could be found within it. The standard pronunciation was usually based on the most prestigious but not necessarily the most popular dialect that was used in the political, economic and cultural center of the minority community in question.

Fourth, the standardization of terminology was an essential part of the development of standard languages for minority communities. The vocabulary of Soviet minority languages developed in three ways: semantic change in old terms, loss of some outdated terms, and enrichment with new terms. The new terms came from two major sources, Russian and the minority languages themselves.

Finally, loanwords from the majority language could contribute to the development of national languages. Russian loanwords saw two different stages of development in minority languages. In the first, Russian loanwords underwent phonological changes in accordance with the phonology of the borrowing languages. Russian *kommunist* (communist) became *kemyvnis* in a minority language, or Russian *telefon* (telephone) became *tilipun*, depending on the phonology of the borrowing language. In the second stage, Russian loanwords kept their original phonology and grammar so that they enriched the phonology and grammar of the borrowing minority languages. For example, *kommunist* and *telefon* became the common forms in all minority languages in the Soviet Union.

At the conference Serdyuchenko asked China to take maximum advantage of the Soviet experience. Both his speech and the lessons drawn from the Soviet experience were warmly received by the conference and its participants. Indeed this report, together with his earlier classified report, directly shaped the formation of China's model for the maintenance and development of minority languages. Corresponding to the model of multinational state-building, this linguistic model advanced a standard dialect based on a minority political and economic center, developed a writing system on it, and standardized native and borrowed terminology in consolidating the relationship between a standard language and a nation. This allowed one language to be developed for each nation and the mainstream language to connect to each minority language by loaning common terms to them. This model was extensively applied in the development and maintenance of minority languages in China in the 1950s and partially readopted in the 1980s.[53]

In short, in building a multinational state, the CCP accepted Marxist-Leninist and Stalinist principles, adopted Soviet-type legislation on minority rights, and employed the Soviet linguistic model for cultural accommodation. In this multinational model all national groups are equal within a state and are supposed to integrate into a single people in the communist stage. However, the relationship between the integration and the state is not obvious from those borrowed principles. It seems that the state should facilitate the integration as the policies in the Soviet and China suggested, though in 1958 Mao Zedong commented that class would be eliminated first, then the state would dissolve, and finally nationalities would converge.[54] The issue of the state's role in facilitating this integration was very contentious, and its mishandling may have been the last straw in the collapse of the Soviet Union. It also caused lasting damage to ethnic relations in China, where minorities have essentially lost confidence in the true equality promised by the CCP.

China's Replacement of the Soviet Model: One Nation with Diversity

When the Soviet Union disintegrated at the end of 1991, the CCP leadership was devastated since it had barely emerged from its own crisis over the student demonstration in Tiananmen in 1989. It was probably disoriented until Deng Xiaoping reaffirmed the continuation of the economic reform during his tour of south China a few months later in the spring of 1992. Subsequently China concluded that the Soviet model of multinational state-building had played a major role in the Soviet fall. China then sought to replace the management of China's national question as the Soviet Union went from a role model to a lesson of failure in the eyes of the CCP.

Negative Learning from the Failure of the Soviet Union

The role that ethnic relations played in the fall of the former Soviet Union and the Eastern Bloc shocked the CCP leaders, particularly when they found that the Soviet Union had endured over 2,100 demonstrations and riots involving over 10 million minority participants in 1988 alone and bloody ethnic clashes in 14 of the 15 Union Republics between 1989 and 1990.[55] The Chinese government sponsored a series of studies of the collapse, which found that ethnic relations were the most important factor. China appears to have drawn four key lessons regarding minorities policies from the Soviet failure.[56]

First, the Soviet federal system gave the republics too much power, enabling them to legitimately separate from the Union when conflicts arose.[57] Constitutionally the Soviet federal system recognized the sovereignty of the republics, while in practice the CPSU consolidated all power into the Party and government center in Moscow. However, the Soviet Constitution was not updated in a timely way so as to legitimize the centralized control that actually existed, hence failing to prevent the legitimate secession of the republics that claimed their sovereignty as independent states. The consequence was that the Baltic Republics broke away, starting the domino effect that led to the dissolution of the Soviet Union. This demonstrated to the CCP the importance of ruling by law in state-building.[58]

Second, the Soviet nativization (*minzuhua* in Chinese or *korenizatsiia* in Russian) process promoted too many minority officials locally, which led to the minority dominance of both the government organs and party apparatuses in the republics.[59] It was particularly dangerous, and contrary to Leninist principles, when the Soviet Union nativized the party apparatuses in the non-Russian republics. For example, at one point as many as 96 percent of the provincial-level CPSU leaders in Ukraine were non-Russians.[60] Once the local communist party apparatus was disproportionately filled with minority officials who were nationalists instead of communists, Moscow lost control of the national question. In addition, the nativization process created what John H. Miller calls "diarchy."[61] In the republics the first secretary of the Party was usually a minority member from the local community who claimed all the public attention and authority as the leader, while the second secretary was usually a Russian who might have more weight in decision-making behind the scene but was less visible in public. From March 1954 to March 1976, of the 259 the republic party secretaries appointed, 125 were Russians and 134 non-Russians. The diarchy seems to have worked well when the CPSU was in full control, but the second party secretary had no public authority in times of crisis. To make matters worse, attempted changes in the diarchy directly led to ethnic riots, as exemplified by the replacement of Dinmukhamed Kunaev with Gennadii Kolbin as the first secretary of the Kazakh Party organization, when Mikhail Gorbachev tried to push Russianization by the CPSU Central Committee on the party apparatuses in the republics in the mid-1980s.[62] The Soviet practice suggested to the CCP that it should be a candidate's commitment to the communist party, not his/her nationality, that really matters when selecting party officials, and that party officials from a local community and working there may have undesirably strong national sentiments.

Third, the Soviet Union failed to fully develop its economy and frequently allowed huge economic disparities to develop that separated the republics rather than united them.[63] These problems were first caused by the struggle between centralized and decentralized economic management. The republics were not motivated nor given room to play their roles when there was too much centralization, but they fought only for their own interests while ignoring the Union's interests when there was too much decentralization. The second major cause of the problem was the effort to confine republics to specializing in one major branch of the economy, in which they presumably had a comparative advantage. The result was that those republics primarily engaged in industry, such as Russia, Estonia, and Latvia, were much richer than those engaged mainly in agriculture, such as Tajikistan, Kyrgyzstan, and Uzbekistan. When the Union's overall wealth index was 100, Tajikistan, Kyrgyzstan, and Uzbekistan's indexes were below 50, but Russia, Estonia, and Latvia's were as high as 140. Such inequality did not contribute to the Union's unity. The CCP's response to this Soviet lesson has been its effort to give autonomous regions sufficient economic power and to facilitate diversified economic development in minority communities in order to eliminate potentially disruptive economic gaps between minority areas and Han areas.

Fourth, the political reform initiated by Mikhail Gorbachev was directly responsible for the collapse of the Soviet Union.[64] Gorbachev's policies of *glasnost* and *perestroika* are considered to have done great damage not only with regard to Stalin's theories and practices but also against most of Soviet history.[65] They provided legitimate political cover, for example, for the Baltic Republics to question the legitimacy of the Soviet acquisition of these republics and eventually to break away from the Union. These policies also started a political process of diversification that weakened the leadership of the CPSU and shifted power to the Soviet congresses of the republics. The change allowed nationalist forces to take over the congresses of the Non-Russian Soviet Republics in elections, leading to their declarations of independence. This lesson has shown the CCP the danger of political diversity and the crucial role of the legislature when a symbolic power is turned into a real one.

These four lessons have compelled the CCP to take actions to correct similar problems in handling the national question in order to prevent any Soviet-style failure in China before it is too late.

A Chinese Nation with Diversity

China actually started its exploration of a new approach to the national question before the collapse of the Soviet Union. The incident mentioned above, namely the replacement of the native Kazakh, Dinmukhamed Kunaev with a Russian, resulting in riots, caught China's attention. China saw this event as a sign of danger brought about by liberal political reforms and later as the beginning of the fall of the Soviet Union.[66] However, the CCP probably did not feel pressured to act immediately in the late 1980s. But already during this period, in 1989, Fei Xiaotong, the best-known Chinese anthropologist, delivered a speech entitled "The Pattern of Diversity in Unity of the Chinese

Nation" at Hong Kong Chinese University. He put forth three concepts: the Chinese nation (*zhonghua minzu*), the process of the formation of the Chinese nation, and diversity in unity of the Chinese nation, which he claimed had been forming in his mind since the 1950s.[67] The Chinese nation includes the 56 nationalities as its basis, but it is not just a collection of the 56 nationalities; it is a national entity that has developed from a common emotion and desire for a shared destiny of opportunities and successes. This concept entails two levels of identity representation: a lower level of ethnic identities for each of the 56 nationalities, of which the Han is one, and a higher level of Chinese national identity for all Chinese citizens. In the process of the formation of the Chinese nation, it is said that the Han played the core role of integrating various national elements into the Chinese nation—a nation that has surpassed the Han to embrace the diversity. The concept of "the diversity in unity of the Chinese nation" assumes that the two levels of identities neither replace nor contradict each other, but coexist and co-develop with linguistic and cultural diversity. This is best known as "one nation with diversity" (*duoyuan yiti*).

Fei's theory of "one nation with diversity" soon drew the attention of the PRC government, which was in urgent need for a solution to the national question—a solution that could augment or replace the Soviet model of multinational state-building. The State Commission on Nationalities Affairs sponsored a symposium on Fei's theory in May 1990 supplemented with studies on various aspects of ethnic relations in China.[68] In September of the same year, Jiang Zemin, then President of the PRC and General Secretary of the CCP, adopted this theory in a speech to local leaders in Xinjiang.[69] Jiang told the audience that the Chinese nation is made of 56 ethnic groups and, in this big family of the motherland, the ethnic groups enjoy a new socialist ethnic relationship: the Han cannot do without the minorities, the minorities cannot do without the Han, and the minorities cannot do without each other. Since then the three "cannots" have formed the CCP's basic views on the national question.[70] At the CCP 16th National Congress in 2003 it was further stressed that China should constantly increase the Chinese nation's cohesiveness (*ningjuli*), which Hu Jintao defined as "common prosperity and common economic development for every ethnic group within China."[71] At the CCP's 2005 working conference on minority work, Hu Jintao officially adopted the terminology of the Chinese nation with diversity (*zhonghua minzu duoyuan yiti*) in defining ethnicity in the PRC.[72]

The rectification of names has been both a philosophical issue and a practical issue in Chinese culture and politics since the time of Confucius. This proved to be no exception for the CCP and the PRC government. With the Soviet model being phased out and the Chinese model of "one nation with diversity" being adopted, the term *minzu* in Chinese is now given a new meaning, since the official English translation as "nation" and as "nationality" suffered from its association with Stalin's formulation. In Beijing in 1997, the State Commission on Nationalities Affairs held a forum on whether "minzu" should be officially translated into "nation/nationality" or "ethnic group."[73] The participating experts unanimously agreed on the term "ethnic group" for "minzu" because the new English term can better represent the spirit of China's new orientation in its minorities policy, an orientation that departs from Stalin's concept of the national question. In the following year, the State Commission on Nationalities Affairs officially changed its English name into "the State Commission on Ethnic Affairs." The rectification of the English translation is undoubtedly intended to justify China's reform of its management of its ethnic affairs to the international community. The rectification of the English term may result in changing domestic terminology, but at present I don't see any eagerness to change the Chinese term *minzu* in the state's discourse. To be sure, *zuqun* (ethnic group) is sometimes used in scholarly discourse to refer to ethnic groups and in state discourse to refer to minority communities before the PRC.

The replacement of the Soviet model with the new Chinese model has had direct impact on China's minorities policies. To address the four major lessons from the fall of the Soviet Union, China began to reformulate its strategy in dealing with its ethnic question and to revise its law on autonomy for minority areas. The new strategy is "to speed up economic development but to downplay the national question" (*Jiakuai jingji fazhan, danhua minzu wenti*). The first clause of the policy statement has been seen frequently in China's newspapers and public documents, but the second part was communicated only orally among various levels of CCP and government officials in the 1990s. This strategy treats rapid economic development in minority communities as the focus of China's minorities policy, because the gap between the rapidly developing eastern coastal regions, where the Han mostly live, and the economically underdeveloped western regions, where minorities generally live, is considered the cause of ethnic conflicts in present-day China.[74] Therefore, at the CCP's 1999 conference on minority work, Jiang Zhemin announced the "Great Western Development Project" (*xibu da kaifa*) which aims at economically integrating relatively underdeveloped western China with relatively advanced coastal China. The State Council officially launched this project in 2000. If it is successful, this project will eliminate or reduce the economic disparity between developed Han communities in the coastal provinces and developing minority communities in the inland provinces. It will also increase the mobility between people in Han communities and those in minority communities. This project is supposed to lead to greater ethnic, economic, geographic, and linguistic integration between the Han and the minorities as well as integrations among the minorities themselves.

To curtail the political power of minority groups and to prevent any chance of minority groups seizing legal power in autonomous regions, as minorities did in the former Soviet Union, work had started in the early 1990s to examine problems in the PRC's Law on Minority Regional Autonomy, passed in 1984, and to explore a possible revision of the laws. In July 1991, the CCP United Front Department started a series of discussions of the issues connected with the local implementation of the 1984 laws with various ministries of the State Council and subcommittees of the National People's Congress. Their discussions identified two major problems in the 1984 law, problems that were very similar to those that had led to the failure of the former Soviet Union and the Eastern Bloc.[75]

First, in drawing up local legislation for autonomy, minority regions tried to obtain from the central government more power to control local economies, more power than the PRC Constitution and Law on Autonomy would explicitly allow. They wanted to specify in local legislation and laws how much of the products and profits produced by central-government-controlled businesses should go to the autonomous governments of the regions where these businesses were physically located. For example, in a draft of its local autonomy legislation, the Inner Mongolian Autonomous Regions tried to stipulate that 15 percent of the total iron and steel products produced locally would be for local use. Autonomous regions also wanted to legislate the amount of financial support that they would receive from the central government. For example, in the draft of its local autonomy legislation, the Guangxi Zhuang Autonomous Region even attempted to set aside its own revenue and tax base for the central government as well as the amount of funding to be received from the central government. Guangxi also tried to arrogate to itself in its local legislation more control over foreign trade and foreign currency. All these attempts by Inner Mongolia and Guangxi were perceived to have infringed upon the central government's power, but they did not necessarily violate the 1984 law on autonomy, which failed to address these issues comprehensively.

Secondly and more seriously, autonomous regions wanted to gain more local political power than allowed by the PRC Constitution and Law on Autonomy, using the local people's congresses to pass laws for this purpose. Some autonomous regions tried to legislate the minimum percentage of minority officials in the local governments as well as in the local legislature. For example, Article 20 of the draft of the Inner Mongolian Autonomy legislation stipulated that the Standing Committee of the regional People's Congress and the Regional Autonomous Government should have no fewer than a membership of 40 percent Mongols, and that both the chairman of the regional People's Congress and the Governor of the regional Government be Mongolians. Articles 13 and 16 of Yanbian Korean Autonomous Prefecture's Autonomy Legislation proposed an even higher degree of required local representation, stipulating that over 50 percent of those in the local legislature and government be Koreans. The same situation was found in autonomous prefectures and counties in Yunnan as well. In addition, Article 77 of the draft of the Inner Mongolian Autonomy Legislation required that the President of the regional Superior Court and the regional Attorney General must be Mongolians. But neither the PRC Constitution (Articles 113 and 114) nor the PRC Law on Autonomy (Article 16) allow the designation of a specific percentage of minority representatives in the local people's congresses or on the standing committees of those congresses. And, constitutionally, the courts and prosecutorial organs are not part of the autonomous governments. Clearly, the central authorities considered these local legislative initiatives as unconstitutional and as representing a dangerous development.

Some autonomous regions wanted more economic power, and some wanted more political power, while many desired both. These demands for economic and political power seriously challenged the central government's authority. Drawing on lessons from the Soviet failure, the PRC realized that these problems must be satisfactorily resolved before they could spin out of control. Based on the lessons of the Soviet collapse, the CCP leaders concluded that the central government should not relinquish political power and should not allow minority dominance of local party apparatuses, or even of the local legislatures in autonomous regions. At the same time, they realized that the autonomous regions should have more economic control in a "socialist" market economy.[76]

More than nine years after the fall of the Soviet Union, on February 28, 2001, the National People's Congress passed the revised PRC Law on Autonomy for Minority Regions.[77] The revision included rewriting of 20 articles of the 1984 Law, deleting two old ones, and adding nine new ones. The majority of the revised articles deal with social and economic development; others with the Central Government's responsibilities; and still others with the proportion of minority officials in autonomous governments. Three cover language use. Generally speaking, the revised Law on Autonomy gives local governments more power or responsibility in social and economic development, but takes away some political power.

For example, Articles 17 and 18 of the 1984 version of the Law on Autonomy stipulated that an autonomous government and its organs should be staffed with as many minority officials as possible. But the 2001 version of these articles require only the staffing of a reasonable number of minority officials in an autonomous government and its organs. The term "reasonable" (heli) can be understood to mean in proportion to the minority population in an autonomous region. Currently, with the exception of the Tibetans in Tibet, no single minority group has a dominant (50 percent or more) population in an autonomous region.[78] For example, the Mongolians amount to only 17.1 percent of the total population in Inner Mongolia. Clearly, the revision of Articles 17 and 18 is a legal step aimed at the prevention of any possible runaway situations like those that happened in the Soviet republics. On the other hand, Articles 31, 32, 34, 55, and 57, give autonomous regions more rights in foreign trade, local taxes, local budgets and local finance, all of which are consistent with China's economic reform and marketization.

Articles 37 of the 2001 version of the Law on Autonomy, together with the PRC's 2001 National Commonly Used Language and Script Law,[79] has also downplayed the role of minority languages and cultures while promoting *putonghua* (Mandarin) as the super language in a structured linguistic order.[80] For example, the teaching of Chinese is now required to start in the early or later years in elementary schools, instead of the later years of elementary schools or in middle schools (Article 37). Minority officials are now required to learn to use both standard oral Chinese and standard written Chinese (Article 49). These measures may be considered as a representation of the demotion of "nationalities" to "ethnic groups" in the new model of "one nation with diversity," where *putonghua* as the common language is to dominate. On the other hand, the revision of Article 47 suggests that more attention is paid to individual citizen rights in minority communities because the revised clause calls for bilingual staffing of courts of law and prosecutorial organs in autonomous regions.

In summary, China's change of the Soviet model of multinational statebuilding to the Chinese model of "one nation with diversity" has three direct effects on minorities and minority communities. First, politically and legally the PRC treats minorities and Hans equally as PRC citizens and autonomous regions equally as a regular province with less special consideration. For example, at the 17th CCP National Congress in 2007, Hu Jintao, the general secretary, did not devote a special section of his report to ethnic issues, but integrated these issues into relevant sections addressing the nation as a whole. Second, the PRC gives more attention and priority to socioeconomic issues related to minorities and their communities, as demonstrated by the unfolding Great Western Development Project and the State Council's recent programs to reduce financial burdens on minority students and on schools in minority communities. Third, in the political realm, the CCP scrutinizes more closely its minority members' loyalty to the Chinese nation and less often entrusts them with the authority to rule the regions that include their own ethnic communities. For example, the CCP has not appointed any minority members as the (first) secretary of the party apparatus in an autonomous region since the late 1980s, as it had in the cases of Ulanfu in the 1950s and of Azizi Seypidin in the 1960s–1970s. All these political, legal and socioeconomic practices deviate significantly from the PRC's practices between the 1950s and the 1980s' and, of course, from Soviet practices.

Preliminary Evaluation of the Chinese Model of State-Building

Will the Chinese model help China solve its ethnic question in the 21st century? There are no simple answers. I briefly examine the issue in relation to three other models: China's traditional cultural universalistic model, the Soviet model, and the American model of one nation with diversity—the melting pot model.

First of all, neither China's traditional cultural universalistic model nor the Soviet model assumes a close relationship between a nation and a state. In both models, without the underlying concept of the nation-state, ethnicity may be reconciled within the state as multi-ethnic or multinational and eventually beyond the state as one people under heaven or under communism. In the culturally universalistic model, ethnicity may be negotiated between the locals and the state, imposed by the state, asserted by the locals or it may transcend the state, all depending on how much Confucianism and the Chinese language are embraced.[81] The imperial court might categorize minorities into raw/barbarian, cooked/sinicized, or regular Chinese while the local communities might have completely different perceptions. For example, during the Qing before the 20th century, were the Manchus or the various minority communities in south and southwestern China perceived to be more Chinese? The measurement of Chineseness was eventually the degree to which Confucianism and the Chinese language were embraced as the sources of authority. The Manchus of the Qing were perceived to be more Chinese and more authoritative when they adopted Confucianism as the state ideology and used Chinese as one of the imperial court languages. Regardless of their ethnicity, by accepting the Confucian way and speaking Chinese, individuals might advance with little barrier via the imperial examination system, while ethnic groups might legitimately replace one Chinese state with another, as the Manchu did, within the perceived scope of the Chinese civilization. Neither ethnicity nor state mattered within the breadth of the Chinese civilization.

In the Soviet model, nationality is similarly constructed within the context of socialism and communism, and nationality may transcend the state in the utopia of communism. If they believed in communism and practiced it, individuals might advance though the bureaucratic system to the top of their localities or the top of a multinational state, regardless of their nationalities. In the former Soviet Union, Stalin himself was an example, being a non-Russian. In China, as noted above, several first party secretaries of autonomous regions were natives as well as Politburo members. In these two models the state is only a tool to maintain a certain order or way where equality exists, theoretically, and mostly practically, among communists or among Confucians who are confined neither by ethnicity nor by race.

Finally I bring the American melting pot model into the discussion because on the surface, at least, there are surprising similarities in terms of diversity and cohesion between the Chinese and American models of one nation with diversity, though neither Fei Xiaotong nor the PRC has explicitly made this connection. Regarding the relationship between ethnicity and the state, neither the Chinese nor the American model appears to allow any ethnic transcendence beyond the state, which is a nation-state. These two models require the reconciliation of ethnicity within the state, a reconciliation that defines the essential identity as Americanness in the American model or as Chineseness in the Chinese model.

How is this accomplished? The American model creates a democracy through which its citizens, regardless of their ethnicity, are promised freedom and equal opportunity to pursue their American dreams. This model has a broad appeal to all ethnic groups in America, though it does not work perfectly in practice and the "melting-pot" metaphor is now being challenged.[82] The Chinese model is supposed to reconcile ethnicity also within the state through what is called the Chinese nation's cohesiveness (*zhonghua minzu ningjuli*).[83] It is not clear presently how well the Chinese state can instill the sense of cohesiveness in its citizens regardless of their ethnicity. In other words, how does this model pave the way for Chinese citizens, regardless of their ethnicity, to perceive that they have the freedom and equal opportunity to pursue their "Chinese dreams"? In the last few years the PRC appears to have combined the imperial approach of promoting Confucianism nationally and the Chinese language throughout minority regions with a strong drive for equal socioeconomic development. This approach may work if the pursuit of equal socioeconomic development is sufficiently guaranteed for every ethnic group. A study by Jian Zhang[84] has convincingly shown that when they are doing well socioeconomically, minorities are ready to identify with Chineseness politically, though not genealogically. Minorities who live in cities and receive more education are more likely to identify themselves first as Chinese and then as ethnic minorities. In this sense, the PRC's strategies—"to speed up economic development and to downplay the national question" and to strive for "common prosperity and common economic development for

every ethnic group" – may be on the right track to building a Chinese nation
with diversity.

Conclusion

The fall of the Soviet Union and China's construction of a socialist state with
Chinese characteristics has prompted China to replace the Soviet model of
multinational state-building with the Chinese model of "one nation with
diversity." The change has both theoretical and practical implications for
China's management of what is now considered the ethnic question instead
of the national question. It has political, legal, social and socioeconomic implications for China's minority communities. However, the Chinese model of
"one nation with diversity" still needs to develop an effective vehicle or way
for creating and maintaining "cohesiveness", in the CCP's term, to reconcile
ethnicity within the state, the Chinese nation-state. Whether the Chinese
model of "one nation with diversity" can successfully solve its ethnic question
depends largely on the successful creation and deployment of such a vehicle,
probably also via some "democracy," a term that is said to have been one of
the most frequently used terms in Hu Jintao's report at the 17th CCP National
Congress in 2007.

Notes

1. An early version of this chapter was presented at the 2007 AAS annual conference in Boston, MA. I appreciate Dr. Thomas Bernstein and Dr. Hua-yu Li's critical
and constructive comments on the draft of this chapter. I am solely responsible for
any errors.

2. Minglang Zhou, *Multilingualism in China: The Politics of Writing Reforms for
Minority Languages 1949–2002* (hereinafter as *Multilingualism in China*) (Berlin and
New York: Mouton de Gruyter, 2003), 2–8.

3. Colin Mackerras, *China's Minorities: Integration and Modernization in the Twentieth Century* (Hong Kong: Oxford University Press, 1994), 44–45.

4. June Teufel Dreyer, *China's Forty Millions* (Cambridge: Harvard University
Press, 1976), 9–14.

5. *Dang de minzu zhengce wenxian ziliao xuanbian* [Selected documents on the
CCP's minorities policies] (hereinafter as *Minzu zhengce*) (Beijing: Zhongguo shehui
kexueyuan minzu yanjiu suo, 1981).

6. For discussions of the Soviet model as the blueprint for China, see Walker
Connor, *The National Question in Marxist-Leninist Theory and Strategy* (Princeton,
NJ: Princeton University Press, 1984). Also see June Teufel Dreyer, *China's Political
System: Modernization and Tradition* (New York: Pearson, 2006), 279–303.

7. For China's Stalinized economic model, see Hua-yu Li, *Mao and the Economic Stalinization of China, 1948–1953* (Lanham, MD: Rowman & Littlefield, 2006).

8. For the CCP's interpretation, see *Minzu zhengce*, 5; for Lenin's views, see *V. I. Lenin Selected Works*, vol. 3 (New York: International Publishers, 1967), 172.

9. For a detailed analysis, see Minglang Zhou "Tracking Historical Development of China's Positive or Preferential Policies for Minority Education: Continuities and Discontinuities," paper presented at the International Symposium on Positive Policies in China, Carlisle, PA, Dickinson College, April 15-16, 2006. A revised version to appear in Minglang Zhou and Ann M. Hill, eds., *Affirmative Action in China and the U.S.: A Dialogue on Inequality and Minority Education* (New York: Palgrave Macmillan, 2009).

10. For the original documents and views, see *Minzu Zhengce*, 1–2; also see Lenin, 749.

11. *Minzu Zhengce*, 5. Jin Wen, Gongning Mao, and Tiezhi Wang, *Tuanjie jinbu de weida qizhi—Zhongguo Gongchandang 80 nian minzu gongzuo lishi huigu* [The great banner of unity and progress: a review of the CCP's 80 years of minority work] (hereinafter as *Tuanjie jinbu*) (Beijing: Minzu chubanshe, 2001), 11.

12. Jin Wen, Gongning Mao, and Tiezhi Wang, *Tuanjie jinbu*, 147–48. Joseph Stalin, *Marxism and the National-Colonial Question* (San Francisco: Proletarian Publishers, 1975), 153–56.

13. For the original CCP documents, see Binghao Jin, ed., *Minzu gangling zhengce wenxian xuanbian* [Selected collection of key minorities policy documents] (hereinafter as *Minzu gangling*) (Beijing: Zhongyang minzu daxue chubanshe, 2006), 7–20.

14. Binghao Jin, ed., *Minzu gangling*, 89–96.

15. *Minzu Zhengce*, 16–17; *Sulian Minzu Wenti Wenxian Xuanbian* [Selected soviet documents on the national question] (hereinafter as *Sulian minzu wenti*) (Beijing: Shehui kexue wenxian chubanshe, 1987), 10–11.

16. For the Russian Constitution, see Anna Louise Strong, *The New Soviet Constitution: A Study in Socialist Democracy* (New York: Henry Holt and Company, 1937).

17. For the open letter, see Jin Binghao, ed., *Minzu Gangling*, 169–71.

18. Jin Binghao, ed., *Minzu Gangling*, 198–200.

19. Jin Binghao, ed., *Minzu Gangling*, 205–9.

20. Jin Binghao, ed., *Minzu Gangling*, 238–46, 259–81.

21. Jin Binghao, ed., *Minzu Gangling*, 212–30.

22. Jin Binghao, ed., *Minzu Gangling*, 261-85.

23. Jin Binghao, ed., *Minzu Gangling*, 291–320.

24. Jin Binghao, ed., *Minzu Gangling*, 327–28.

25. For the Chinese version of Mikoyan's report, see "Migaoyan yu Mao Zedong de mimi tanpan" [The secrete talk between Mikoyan and Mao Zedong], *Dang de wenxian* [Party documents], no. 1 (1996), 90–96.

26. A. M. Ledovskii, *Sidalin yu Zhongguo* [Stalin and China], trans. Chunhua Chen and Zunkuang Liu (Beijing: Xinhua chubanshe, 2001), 85.

27. For this argument, see Liu Chun, *Liu Chun minzu wenti wenji* [Selected works of Liu Chun on the national question] (Beijing: Minzu chubanshe, 1996), 305–6.

28. For Mao's original speech, see Jin Binghao, ed., *Minzu gangling*, 221–26.

29. For more discussion, see Zhang Erju, *Zhongguo minzu quyu zizhi shigan* [A history of regional autonomy in China] (Beijing, Minzu chubanshe, 1995), 57–60.

30. For details on the three versions of the *Common Program*, see Han Dayuan, *Xin Zhongguo xianfa fazhan shi* [The history of the development of the PRC constitution] (hereinafter as *Xin Zhongguo*) (Shijiazhuang: Hebei renmin chubanshe, 1999), 1–35.

31. Gong Yuzhi was considered a top CCP historian who served as the vice president of the CCP Central Party School and executive vice director of the CCP Central Committee's Party History Research Department in the 1990s. Gong stated that the terms, federalism and self-determination, were deleted from some 1945–1949 CCP documents when they were republished during the PRC period. For his comments on the evolution from federalism to regional autonomy, see http://theory.people.com.cn/GB/40552/4046507.html.

32. For this account, see Luo Guangwu, *Xin Zhongguo minzu gongzuo dashi gailan* [An outline of major events in new China's nationalities' affairs] (hereinafter as *Minzu gongzuo*) (Beijing: Huawen chubanshe, 2001), 961.

33. For Zhou Enlai's speech, see Jin Binghao, ed., *Minzu Gangling*, 407–9.

34. For the complete document, see *Jianguo yilai Zhongyao wenjian xuanbian, dierce* [Selected important documents since the founding of the PRC, vol. 2] (Beijing: Zhongyang wenxian chubanshe, 1997), 24–25.

35. For the full version of the 1954 PRC Constitution and Liu Shaoqi's report, see *The Constitution of the People's Republic of China* (Beijing: Foreign Languages Press, 1962), 3–61, 63–94.

36. For a full analysis of the relationship between Mao and Stalin regarding the PRC Constitution, see Li Hua-yu, "The Political Stalinization of China: The Establishment of One-Party Constitutionalism, 1948–1954," *Journal of Cold War Studies* 3, no. 2 (2001): 28–47.

37. The reference list was worked out under Mao's direct supervision, see Han Dayuan, *Xin Zhongguo*, 46.

38. For a full discussion and the primary sources in Russian, see Shen Zhihua, *Sulian zhuanjia zai Zhongguo, 1948–1960* [Soviet advisors in China, 1948–1960] (hereinafter as *Sulian zhuanjia*) (Beijing: Zhongguo guoji guangbo chubanshe, 2003), 217–18.

39. For the details of Stalin's editorial work on the draft of the Polish Constitution, see Krzysztof Persak, "Stalin as Editor: The Soviet Dictator's Secret Changes to the Polish Constitution of 1952," *Cold War International History Project Bulletin* 11, 149–54.

40. For information on the distribution of Soviet advisors working in the PRC ministries, see Shen Zhihua, *Sulian zhuanjia*, 110. However, there was at least one Soviet advisor working in the Ministry of Foreign Affairs in 1954, according to Deborah A. Kaple, "Soviet advisors in China in the 1950s," in *Brothers in Arms: The Rise and Fall of the Sino-Soviet Alliance, 1945–1963*, ed. Odd Arne Westad (Palo Alto, CA: Stanford University Press, 1998), 117–40.

41. Minglang Zhou's interview with Dai Qingxia (July 2, 2003) and with Wang Jun (July 4, 2002), and personal communication with Sun Hong Kai.

42. For full discussion, see Minglang Zhou, *Multilingualism in China*.

43. For more information on G. P. Serdyuchenko's role in China, see Minglang Zhou, *Multilingualism in China*, 169–96; for a comprehensive list of Serdyuchenko's speeches made in China, see the reference section of *Multilingualism in China*.

44. Zhou Youguang made this statement in his book but gives no details. See *Xin yuwen de jianshe* [Language planning for the new language and script] (Beijing: Yuyan chubanshe, 1992), 373.

45. *Quanguo wenzi gaige huiyi wenjian huibian* [Collection of documents from the national script reform conference] (hereinafter as *Quanguo wenzi gaige*) (Beijing: Quanguo wenzi gaige huiyi mishuchu, 1955), 14.

46. G. P. Serdyuchenko, "Guanyu zhongguo wenzi de jige wenti" [On some issues in the Chinese script reform], in *Quanguo wenzi gaige*, 48–69.

47. The term "the alliance of writing systems" was originally used in Serdyuchenko's speeches. It symbolizes the theoretical equality among languages and nationalities, though not in practice.

48. For technical details, see Minglang Zhou, *Multilingualism in China*, 177–87.

49. Minglang Zhou's interview with Wang Jun, former vice chairman of the PRC State Language Commission, July 4, 2002.

50. G. P. Serdyuchenko, *Guanyu Zhongguo gezu renmin de yuyan wenzi* [On minority languages and scripts in China] (Beijing: Chinese Academy of Sciences, 1955).

51. Minglang Zhou's interview with Dai Qingxia (July 3, 2002) and with Wang Jun (July 4, 2002), and personal communication with Sun Hongkai (2002).

52. G. P. Serdyuchenko, "Sulian chuangli wenzi he jianli biaozhun yu de jingyan" [The Soviet experience in creating writing systems and establishing standard languages], *Yuyan yanjiu* [Language research], 1 (1956): 129–67.

53. For a full discussion, see Minglang Zhou, *Multilingualism in China*.

54. Jingchu Yang, *Mao Zedong minzu lilun yanjiu* [A study of Mao Zedong theory on the national question] (Beijing: Minzu chubanshe, 1995), 47.

55. *Zhongguo Gongchangdang guanyu minzu wenti de jiben guangdian he zhengce* [The CCP's basic views and policies on the national question] (Beijing: Minzu chubanshe, 2002), 10–38. Li Dezhu, *Zhongyang disan dai lingdao yu shaoshu minzu* [The third generation of CCP leaders and the minority nationalities] (hereinafter as *Zhongyang Disan Dai*) (Beijing: Zhongyang minzu daxue chubanshe, 1999), 6. For the numbers, see Guo Hongsheng, *Zhongguo yu qian sulian minzu wenti duibi yanjiu* [A comparative study of the national question in China and the former soviet union] (hereinafter as *Zhongguo yu qian Sulian*) (Beijing: Minzu chubanshe, 1997), 196.

56. Guo Hongsheng, *Zhongguo yu qian Sulian*, 1–11. Mao Gongning, *Minzu wenti lunji* [A collection of articles on the ethnic question] (Beijing: Minzu chubanshe, 2001), 113–19. Tiemuer and Wangqing Liu, eds., *Minzu zhengce yanjiu wencong, diyiji* [Studies of minorities policies, vol. 1] (hereinafter as *Minzu zhengce yanjiu, diyiji*) (Beijing: Minzu chubanshe, 2002), 136.

57. Guo Hongsheng, *Zhongguo yu qian Sulian*, 79–80.

58. Guo Hongsheng, *Zhongguo yu qian Sulian*, 228–29. Hua Xinzhi and Chen Dongen, *Sidalin yu minzu wenti* [Stalin and the national question] (Beijing: Minzu chubanshe, 2002), 186–87.

59. Guo Hongsheng, *Zhongguo yu qian Sulian*, 156–57.

60. For a full discussion on the effects of nativization on the composition of local party elites, see Mark Beissinger, "Ethnicity, the Personnel Weapon, and Neo-Imperial Integration: Ukrainian and RSFSR Provincial Party Officials Compared," in *The Soviet Nationality Reader: The Disintegration in Context*, ed. Rachel Denber (Boulder, CO: Westview Press, 1992), 211–26.

61. John H. Miller, "Cadre Policy in Nationality Areas: Recruitment of CPSU First and Second Secretaries in Non-Russian Republics of the USSR," in *The Soviet Nationality Reader: The Disintegration in Context*, ed. Rachel Denber (Boulder, CO: Westview Press, 1992), 211–26.

62. For a discussion of Gorbachev's policies, see Steven L. Burg "Nationality Elites and Political Changes in the Soviet Union," in *The Nationalities Factor in Soviet Politics and Society*, ed. Lubomyr Hajda and Mark Beissinger (Boulder, CO: Westview Press, 1990), 24–42.

63. Guo Hongsheng, *Zhongguo yu qian Sulian*, 129–32.

64. Zhang Zhirong, *China's Border Regions and Ethnic Nationalism* (Beijing: Beijing daxue chubanshe, 2005), 5–6.

65. For a thorough discussion, see Roman Szporluk, "The Imperial Legacy and the Soviet Nationalities Problem," in *The Nationalities Factor in Soviet Politics and Society*, eds. Lubomyr Hajda and Mark Beissinger (Boulder, CO: Westview Press, 1990), 1–23.

66. Guo Hongsheng, *Zhongguo yu Qian Sulian*, 1.

67. Xiaotong Fei, ed., *Zhonghua minzu yanjiu xintansuo* [New perspectives on studies of the Chinese nation] (Beijing: Shehui kexue chubanshe, 1991). Fei Xiaotong, ed., *Zhonghua minzu duoyuan yiti geju* [The pattern of diversity in unity of the Chinese nation] (hereinafter as *Zhonghua minzu duoyuan*) (Beijing: Zhongyang minzu daxue chubanshe, 1999), 13.

68. Fei Xiaotong, *Zhonghua minzu duoyuan*, 13.

69. Li Dezhu, *Zhongyang Disan Dai*, 158, 228.

70. *Zhongguo Gongchandang guanyu minzu wenti de jiben guandian he zhengce*, 18. Tiemuer and Wangqing Liu, eds., *Minzu zhengce yanjiu wencong diyiji*, 4–5.

71. Mao Gongning and Liu Wanqing, eds., *Minzu zhengce yanjiu wencong, disanji* [Studies of minorities policies, vol. 3] (Beijing: Minzu chubanshe, 2004), 14.

72. For Hu Jintao's speech, see Jin Binghao, ed., *Minzu gangling*, 926–41.

73. I still do not have any access to any official documents on this symposium, but several scholars in Beijing who participated told me about the symposium sponsored by the State Commission and the Institute of Nationalities Studies in the 1990s.

74. *Zhongguo Gongchangdang guanyu minzu wenti de jiben guandian he zhengce*, 41–44 and 126–46.

75. For a full report on the CCP's investigation of the conflicts between local laws and central laws on autonomy, see Mao Gongning, *Minzu wenti lunji*, 344–61.

76. Mao Gongning, *Minzu wenti lunji*, 344–61.

77. For the revised laws on autonomy, see *Zhongguo minzu quyu zizhi falufagui tongdian* [Collection of laws and regulations on minority regional autonomy in the PRC] (Beijing: Zhongyang minzu chubanshe, 2002), 13–28. For a comparison of the old version and the new version, see Wang Geliu and Chen Jianyue, *Minzu quyu*

zizhidu de fazhuan: minzu quyu zizhifa xiugai wenti yanjiu [The development of autonomy for minority regions: studies of the issues in the revision of laws on autonomy for minority regions] (Beijing: Minzu chubanshe, 2001).

78. For analysis of the minority population distribution in each province and autonomous region, see *Tabulation on Nationalities of 2000 Population Census of China* (Beijing: Minzu chubanshe, 2003), 4–27.

79. For the English version of this law, see Minglang Zhou and Hongkai Sun, eds., *Language Policy in the People's Republic of China: Theory and Practice since 1949* (Boston: Kluver Academic Publishers, 2004).

80. In the contemporary linguistic order there are at least three strata of languages, a super language, regional/national languages, and local languages. For more details on this analysis, see Minglang Zhou, "Globalization and Language Education in America and China: Bi/multilingualism as an Ideology and a Linguistic Order," invited speech at the GSE colloquium at the University of Pennsylvania, November 30, 2006.

81. Pamela Kyle Crossley, Helen F. Siu, and Donald S. Sutton, eds., *Empire at the Margins: Culture, Ethnicity, and Frontier in Early Modern China* (Berkeley: University of California Press, 2006). Steven Harrell, ed., *Cultural Encounters on China's Ethnic Frontiers* (Seattle: University of Washington Press, 1995).

82. Tamar Jacoby, ed., *Reinventing the Melting Pot: The New Immigrants and What It Means to Be American* (New York: Basic Books, 2004).

83. Mao and Liu, *Minzu zhengce yanjiu wencong, disanji*, 1–14.

84. For a large survey of the identity of Zhongguoren and thorough analysis, see Jian Zhang, *The Concept of Zhongguoren and Political Identities of Ethnic Minority People in Contemporary China*, unpublished Ph.D. dissertation, New York, Columbia University, 2007.

19

The Influence of the Collapse of the Soviet Union on China's Political Choices

Guan Guihai

A S TWO OF THE MOST IMPORTANT EVENTS in the last two decades, China's policy of reform and opening-up and the collapse of the Soviet Union have been analyzed and contrasted by many scholars. A good recent example is Christopher Marsh's new edited book, *Unparalleled Reforms: China's Rise, Russia's Fall, and the Interdependence of Transition.*[1] Actually, the Chinese reform is a process of discarding the Soviet model of socialism and building socialism with Chinese characteristics. Therefore and quite in contrast to scholars in other countries, especially those in the west, when examining the reasons for the Soviet collapse, Chinese scholars always bear in mind China's own reform and opening-up policy. As scholars have long recognized, since China absorbed much from the Soviet Union's political, economic and cultural systems, there were many similarities between the two. For nearly two decades of controversy and opposition, each tried to find out the weaknesses and faults of the other's system, policies and practices. Accordingly, Chinese leaders knew very well that there were serious problem in Soviet domestic and foreign affairs and they therefore understood the need for reform. As for Gorbachev's reforms, while he did promote the normalization of relations between two states and two parties, the CCP didn't approve of the *glasnost'* and democratization that he advocated. The CCP didn't approve of *glasnost'* and democratization, since this might lead to social turbulence, even to civil war, do harm to the process of economic reform, and threaten the stability and unity of the state.

Nevertheless, Chinese leaders did not predict that the CPSU could lose power so easily, and that the Soviet Union could disintegrate so quickly.

Without a doubt, the collapse of Soviet Union greatly influenced Chinese political choices.

Chinese Studies on the Reason for the Soviet Collapse

Due to its huge impact on China, Chinese leaders paid much attention to studies of the CPSU's failure and the collapse of the Soviet Union. They allocated considerable funds to support these studies. Generally speaking, it's very hard for Chinese scholars of social science to obtain national research funds, but if the research had something to do with the Soviet Union, getting money was much easier. So it's not surprising that some people used the same project to apply for funds again and again or did the same research many times.

From 1993 to 2006, scores of research programs related to the Soviet Union were approved and initiated by Chinese Academy of Social Sciences. The following are examples:

1. Lu Nanquan, "Study of the Rise and Fall of the Soviet Union," a key point program, Institute of Russian, East European and Central Asian Studies, CASS;
2. Xu Xin, "Study of the Historical Causes of Soviet Union's Collapse," an ordinary program of the Institute of Russian, East European & Central Asian Studies, CASS;
3. Wang Renzhi, "The History of the Rise and Fall of the Soviet Union," Institute of World History, CASS, an ordinary program;
4. Zhou Xincheng, "The Causes and Historical Lessons of the Evolution of the Soviet Union," Institute of East European & Central Asian Studies, Renmin University of China, an ordinary program;
5. Chen Fengxiang, "A Study of the Transitions of the Political Systems of the USSR and East Europe," Sixth Bureau of the International Department, Central Committee of CCP, an ordinary program;
6. Huang Lifu, "A Study of the Sudden Collapse of the Soviet Union," Institute of World History, CASS, an ordinary program;
7. Chen Pingping, "Nationalism and the Collapse of USSR," Central Compilation& Translation Bureau, an ordinary program;
8. Liu Shuang, "The Historiography of the Soviet Union's Collapse", Bureau of Scientific Research, CASS, an ordinary program.

Between 1992 and 2001, over 600 papers and 30 monographs were published that dealt with the causes of the USSR's collapse. The following books are examples:

Tan Suo, *Gorbachev' Reform and the Fall of the USSR* (Beijing: Social Sciences Academic Press, 2006, a special study paid for out of Social Science Funds); Chen Zhihua, Wu Enyuan and Ma Longshan, eds., *An Outline History of the Rise and Fall of the USSR* (Beijing: CASS Press, 2004); Lu Nanquan, ed., *On the History of the USSR's Rise and Fall* (Beijing: People's Publishing House, 2004); Zhou Shangwen, Ye Zongshu and Wang Side, *A History of the USSR' Rise and Fall* (Shanghai: Shanghai People's Press, 2002); Chen Xinming, *The Soviet Union's Evolution and the Reform of Socialism* (Beijing: The Press of the Party School of the Central Committee of C.P.C, 2002); Zhou Xincheng, *Reflections on the Century's Tragedy: The Nature of the SU's Evolution, Its Causes and Lessons* (Beijing: People's University Press, 2000); Zhou Xincheng and Guan Xueling, *Historical Lessons of the Evolution of the USSR & of Eastern Europe* (Hefei: Anhui People's Press,2000); Lu Nanquan, Jiang Changbin, eds., *A Study of the Deep Structural Reasons for the USSR's Collapse* (Beijing: China Social Sciences Press, 1999; Guan Haiting, *The Transition and Development of the Great Powers: A Comparative Study of the National Capabilities of China and Russia (SU) to Maintain Control, 1997*, written under the 1997 State Social Science Plan, (Beijing: China Yanshi Press, 1999); Zhou Xincheng, *An Evaluation of Humanistic Democratic Socialism* (Beijing: China Renmin University Press, 1998) written under the Program of the "8th Five-Year Plan" Philosophy and Social Sciences Research Plan (Beijing: China Xinshi Publishing House, 1999); Gong Dafei, chief editor, *A New Examination of the Sudden Soviet Transformation*, (Beijing: World Knowledge Press, 1998); Jiang Liu and Chen Zhihua, eds., *Historical Reflections on the Evolution of the USSR* (Beijing: China Social Sciences Press, 1994).

Within China, an 8 part DVD documentary, "Be Vigilant in Peacetime: the Historical Lessons of the Death of the Communist Party of USSR," elicited the greatest reaction. The series was shown internally for educational and reference purposes. It was the final product of a major CASS research program on this topic launched in 2000 and of a large National Social Science Foundation program on the "Rise and Fall of the CPSU and the Soviet State." It was perfected by a collective of specialist scholars from the National Party Construction Research Association and from CASS. The explanatory text of this TV film was edited, printed, and disseminated as an internal document by the Marxism Research Institute and the Center for Research on World Socialism of CASS. The core viewpoint in the explanations was that Gorbachev's "betrayal" was responsible for the fall of the Communist party and the collapse of the USSR. He abandoned Marxism, proletarian dictatorship, and renounced the existence of class struggle in international relations. Furthermore, he gave up Stalin's "sharp sword." This documentary produced a great shock at a critical moment in the Communist political system reform process. It had an intimidating effect.

Another important duty of Chinese studies of the USSR was to translate and publish the memoirs of famous leaders of the former Soviet Union and those of their assistants, as well as memoirs of former western diplomats who had been assigned to the Soviet Union. The memoirs of Gorbachev, Yeltsin, Yakovlev, Ryzhkov, Kliuchkov, Matlock and others were well-known in China. Different people with different statuses and backgrounds played different roles in the process of the Soviet collapse and they had distinct explanations for that part of history. These diverse explanations indicate that the political conflicts at the end stage of the USSR's collapse are far from over.

A new translation of a book, Run For Freedom: Comments on Gorbachev's Reform after Twenty Years, edited by the Gorbachev Foundation, appeared in May 2007 published by the Central Compilation & Translation Press). This book, with a preface by Gorbachev, contained important articles written over 20 years by people who had played key roles in the Soviet reforms in 1985–1991. The words in the title, "Run for Freedom," were added by the Chinese press, which referred to Gorbachev's original idea of letting the USSR have more freedom. Obviously, it was a kind of praise for Gorbachev.

Different Views on the Fundamental Cause of the Soviet Union Collapse

One quite popular viewpoint in China was that there was no single cause for the USSR's collapse, but that many complex factors were involved, which related to almost every aspect of the USSR's society. Once a thesis of the main or fundamental cause was advanced, however, other scholars always offered different opinions. Most people believed that we should look for answers by examining the historical roots. They emphasized that "the traditional defects and weaknesses of the system meant that it could not carry on as before and that it had come to a dead end."[2] In these scholars' opinion, the USSR's defects and weaknesses manifested themselves in the following four aspects:

Obsolete Thinking and Theories

The Communist Party of the Soviet Union became doctrinaire in the ideological field, which blocked theoretical innovation and ideological emancipation. Therefore, the CPSU could not catch up with societal developments and make social progress in the new era, not to speak of gaining the understanding and confidence of party members and the masses.[3] At the same time, natural sciences were blocked from advancement. Stalin insisted that Morgan's biological genetics, N. Wiener's cybernetics, Einstein's theory of relativity and organic synthetic chemistry were pseudosciences of the bourgeoisie. Due to ideological shackles of the CPSU, the Soviet Union lost a good chance to renovate its technology when the information revolution was spreading around the world in the second half of the 20th century.

An Inappropriate Economic System and Economic Development Strategy

The most serious problem of the Soviet economic system, which we also call the "Stalin model" was that it was extensive, closed to the outside world, and that it emphasized long-term preparation for war. This resulted in low economic efficiency, waste of resources, stagnation in technical innovation, and separation from the mainstream of world development. The worst problem was the threat that the masses might lose confidence in the Communist Party and the government because people's lives did not improve.[4]

An Ossified Political System

Some people thought that its ossified political system was the fundamental reason for the fall of USSR. The main problems of the system were the following: confusing the function of the Communist Party and the Government by relying on the party instead of the government; overemphasizing centralism but ignoring democratic participation; maintaining an unsound leadership and supervising mechanism; concentrating power in individuals, as well as the life-tenure and cadre appointments systems. All this led to terrible results, namely rule by man and not by law, abuse of power for personal gain, exclusion of dissidents and refusal to supervise.[5] This political system produced two kinds of cadres: one was mediocre and submissive; the other was slippery and trimmed its sails. A number of people with innovative minds were excluded by these cadres, who were already "divorced from the masses" and were even fearful of them. It's not surprising that these leaders could not stand the political test when upheaval took place, but went with the flow or fled in disorder.

An Unsuccessful Ethnic Policy

Without scientific argument, the ethnic policies of the Soviets simply equated ethnic problem with class conflict, ignored or even obliterated the differences between ethnic groups, crudely trampled on religious organizations, etc.[6]

In contrast to these systemic arguments, however, the authors of the documentary mentioned above insisted that Gorbachev's humanistic democratic socialism actually was revisionism, and therefore the decisive factor that caused the Party's failure. Gorbachev betrayed socialism, and the collapse would never have happened without him.[7] But, while some scholars agree that Gorbachev should take some of the blame for the collapse of the USSR, they also believe that we should learn more about his original intentions and the complicated background of his reforms.[8] In their essay, "Historical Doubt about 'Be Vigilant in Peacetime: The Historical Lesson of the Death of the Communist Party of USSR,'" Zuo Fengrong and Jiang Changbin pointed out that making Gorbachev alone responsible for the collapse is not in accord with historical materialism. He made some mistakes, should assume some of the blame, but quite a few policies were promoted by diversified forces, not just by himself. To give an example, Ligachev also played a very important role in the movement against drinking. At the beginning of the reform which was very complicated, Gorbachev greatly venerated Lenin and tried to carry out reforms according to the ideas that Lenin put forth in his later years. Actually, his slogan "All power belongs to the Soviet" just changed the leadership mode of the Communist Party, but never deprived it of its leadership. As the Secretary-General of the Party, Gorbachev was also the Chairman of the Supreme Soviet; Party secretaries at all levels served jointly as chairmen of the hierarchy of Soviets. Not until 1991 did Gorbachev adopt the separation of the three powers as a guide to reform. Some people attributed the fall of the CPSU to the constitutional amendment that repealed article 6, which concerned the leading role of the CPSU. But as we know this article did not exist in the constitution before 1977, yet, the CPSU was of course able to hold on to power without it. Therefore, when we talk about how the CPSU could gain mass support and confidence, we should pay more attention to policy instead of law. "Gorbachev forced the CPSU Central Committee to disband." How could this have happened? "How did Gorbachev accumulate so much power?" "Wasn't this a systemic problem?"[9]

However, because of traditionally strong left-leaning influences, the viewpoint of the documentary was accepted by many people and many responded to its message. The Associate Dean of the Marxism Research Institute, CASS, Wu Enyuan believed that Gorbachev's new thinking and the ideology of humanistic democratic socialism were the crucial cause of the CPSU's failure. We should affirm that Stalin and the social system that he created dramatically promoted the USSR's development. Wang Tingyou, from the School of International Studies, Renmin University, argued that the collapse of Stalin's economic model was not inevitable, as the examples of Vietnam and Cuba show. The crux of the matter is whether the reforms can be carried out correctly. The former Director of the Institute of Marxism, Leninism and Mao Zedong Thought, CASS, Ma Zongfu, thought that the disintegration of the USSR reflected the globalization of political struggle, the point of which is whether capitalism or socialism will in the end win out. To win this struggle, maintaining control over the media was a key factor. The Russian Bendalev commented on the Soviet media during the period of the USSR's reforms, "in these 6 years, some newspapers and journals managed to achieve the goal which in the 1940s Europe's best equipped army was not able to achieve by fire and sword when it invaded us. This army had the best technology and equipment, but lacked one thing—millions of infectious publications"[10]

In distinction to the black and white judgments characteristic of Chinese scholars, Russian leaders' attitudes were more nuanced. Before 2000, when he became the President of Russia, Putin said "one who does not bemoan the USSR's disintegration lacks a conscience; one who wants to restore the USSR is mindless," when answering the question, "what do you think about the disintegration of USSR" posed by a Russian reporter. Because it was the USSR led by Stalin that won the victory in World War II, Putin always prevailed over all dissenting views, insisting that Russians should not forget the history of the USSR. However, when someone tried to restore USSR, he responded sternly, "under the Soviets the nation did not thrive, society was not well-off nor were people free. No matter how hard it is to say this, we must admit that after 70 years our nation was moving toward a dead end and had already departed from the broad road of human civilization."

Influence of Academic Disputes on Political Choices

Generally speaking, Chinese scholars agree that "it is necessary to reflect on the processes and approaches in the selection of Chinese reforms in the context of analyzing the lessons of the USSR and its experience, especially those of Gorbachev's reforms," because the problems which had blocked Soviet reforms are also the key issues that China has to solve in the process of reform."[11]

The disputes about how to judge Stalin, Khrushchev, Gorbachev and other Soviet leaders and how to evaluate the Soviet system have gone beyond the realm of academic controversy. They have influenced Chinese choices with regard to question of social and political transition. Many important political journals like *Seeking Truth, Study Times, Scientific Socialism, Study of Socialism with Chinese Characteristics, Reference Materials on Reform, Hundred Year Tide*, have taken part in this debate on the judgment of history. One topic under dispute was whether the CCP would encounter the same problems. Actually, the comments on this dispute are quite different from Deng Xiaoping's remark, "if there are problems, they will arise within the CCP,"[12] spoken during his famous Southern Journey in 1992.

If problems did arise within the CCP, their sources would most likely lie in faulty ideology and theory. In the case of the CPSU, its problems began with Gorbachev's reforms: the abandonment of the dominance of Marxism, promotion of ideological diversification and the renunciation of the Communist Party's power in favor of democratization. For the sake of better explaining this point, these scholars repeated again and again to the public that "Russians regret not having taking part in the "August 19" incident or having being indifferent to it. They feel that nothing can make them feel more honorable and happy than to have lived in the USSR." Some even said that "51% of Russians thought CPSU did some good."[13]

Further, these scholars cited Chinese leaders' speeches and a talk by Gorbachev in order to make their view more persuasive. It is said that the former Secretary General of the CCP, Jiang Zemin, remarked that the change in the USSR and the East European countries was the result of giving up socialism but not due to the failure of socialism. It is also said that Secretary General Hu Jintao pointed out that there were many factors that explain the USSR's disintegration: Khrushchev's discarding of the sharp sword of Stalin and Gorbachev's betrayal of Marxism were pretty important ones (there was no reference in the original essay—author). It is reported that when Gorbachev was interviewed by a Chinese reporter, he said, "don't push democratization because there is no happy ending! Strengthening the party's leadership over the country and the reform process is crucial in the reform period. It would be very dangerous to carry on the reform without the Party's leadership, since chaos might result."[14] A researcher from the Institute of Studies on Party Construction in the Central Committee of the CCP, Shen Zongwu, argued that the main cause for CPSU's fall was ideological diversification, the introduction of the multi-party system and of private ownership. China should persist in Marxism, the system of multiparty cooperation and political consultation under the leadership of the CCP, and retain public ownership as the mainstay of the economy.

Another, contrasting viewpoint was that the problems of the CPSU were the result of the Party's excessive control over politics, the economy and culture. The Communist Party should have appropriately relaxed its relative domination.

Some disagreed with the condemnation of Gorbachev for giving up Marxism. They argued that ideology belongs to the field of social consciousness and spirit, which cannot be imposed by force. The CPSU used administrative methods to force the masses to accept its doctrine, the outcome being that neither the masses nor the elites themselves were persuaded. Consequently, in the face of the denunciations by dissidents and of various outside theories and thoughts, Soviet Marxist ideology was vanquished.[15] However, overemphasis on ideological liberalization as the cause of the collapse of the USSR, will lead to the conclusion that it was western "peaceful evolution" theory that was the chief culprit causing the collapse. Since this conclusion would do harm to the Chinese policy of reform and opening-up, and is counter to Deng Xiaoping's development theory which has already been proven in   practice, it is not acceptable.[16]

When criticizing those voices that defend Stalin, some raised a question, namely "what is it that Russians cherish?[17] Investigation indicates that Russians cherish the memory of the time when they had been the mightiest military power in the world and of the effective (*jingjing youtiao*) social order of the time. In a word, they yearn for the powerful country which had disintegrated, but not for the old social, political or ideological system. Obviously, the comment that "all the Russians want to go back to the period of USSR" is a myth. Even if 51% of the Russians think that the CPSU did some good, it does not mean that they identify with the leadership and domination of the CPSU.[18]

We should judge Gorbachev's merits justly: on the one hand, he reformed the socialism of the Stalin model; he ended the cold war; and achieved the normalization of Sino-Soviet relations. All of these should be affirmed. On the other hand, he tried to copy western political models and he gave up domination in the ideological domain. Finally, he was unable to prevent the collapse of the USSR. In this sense, as chief of the Party and the country, he was a failure. Consequently, after his visit to China in 1989, Gorbachev has never been to China again, although he gave lectures around the world. That can be seen as an indirect reaction of Chinese leaders to his passive behavior in the collapse of the Soviet Union.

Besides bemoaning the USSR's fate, Chinese leaders also paid attention to the question of why there was no one who said "no" when so powerful a party as the CPSU lost power. The best explanation is that the party had become separated from the masses and lost the people's confidence. In response, the CCP has in the recent period advanced some principles on management and governance. One of these is that in order to gain mass support, the party in power should "take people as the foundation," "govern on behalf of the people"; "persist in the scientific outlook on development" and "build a harmonious society."

In addition, already in 1990, the CCP approved a decision on keeping a close relationship with the people, maintaining that whether this can be achieved will directly influence the rise and fall of the Party and the country. The Party also insisted that the relationship between the CCP and the people, cadres and masses, together with the supervision and restrictions on power were two crucial issues in the process of political system reform in the last two decades. These principles and policies indicate that the CCP leaders know very well the essential reason for the collapse of the Soviet Union. The direction of Chinese reforms is therefore pretty clear. However, the leaders did not express their thoughts and intentions in great detail, following Deng Xiaoping's advice to "act more and say less, and never to engage in disputes." Maybe that is a lesson from Gorbachev's high-sounding style.

Notes

1. Christopher Marsh, ed., *Unparalleled Reforms: China's Rise, Russia's Fall, and the Interdependence of Transition* (New York: Rowman & Littlefield, 2005).

2. Lu Nanquan, "Sulian jubian de genben yuanyin" [The fundamental causes for the disintegration of the USSR], *Shijie jingji* [World economy], no. 9 (1996): 16–20.

3. Liu Keming, "Sulian jubian de lishi jiaoxun" [The historical lessons of the disintegration of the USSR], *Dangdai shijie de shehui zhuyi wenti* [Issues of contemporary world socialism], no. 1 (1994): 61–65.

4. Mou Zhengchun, "Lun Sidalin muoshi dui Sulian jieti de yingxiang" [The impact of Stalin model on the disintegration of the USSR], *Lilun xuekan* [Journal of theories], no. 5 (1999): 27–28.

5. Jiang Changbin and Zuo Fengrong, "Yingdang kexue di zongjie Sulian wang'dang de lishi jiaoxun" [A scientific analysis of the historical roots of the disintegration of the CPSU], *Kexue shehuizhuyi* [Scientific socialism], no. 3 (2007): 132.

6. Chen Jianyue, "Jiaoxun yu fansi: Sulian jiejue minzu wenti de shida shiwu" [Lessons and reflections: ten mistakes that the USSR had made on resolving ethnic minority issues], *Dong'ou zhongya yanjiu* [East European and Central Asian Studies], no. 1 (1994): 70–78.

7. Zhou Xincheng, *Dui shijie xinbeiju de sikao—Sulian yanbian de xingzhi, yuanyin he jiaoxun* [Commenting on the tragedy of the last century: characteristics, causes, and lessons of the collapse of the USSR] (Beijing: Renmin daxue chubanshe, 2000), 4, 19.

8. Lu Nanquan, "Xiqu Sulian jubian jiaoxun de ruogan zhongyao wenti de sikao" [Reflections on issues concerning the important lessons from the disintegration of the USSR], *Dong'ou zhongya yanjiu* [East European and Central Asian studies], no. 1, (1998): 42–49.

9. *Gaige neican* [Internal reference for reform], no. 2 (2007): 37–39.

10. Cao Changsheng, ed., *Sulian yanbian jinchengzhong de yishi xingtai yanjiu* [Studies of ideology in the changing soviet union] (Beijing: Renmin chubanshe, 2004), 273.

11. (E) Geerbaqiaofu jijinhui [Russian Gorbachev foundation], *Benxiang ziyou— Geer baqiaofu gaige ershinianhou de pingshu* [Moving toward freedom: commenting on Gorbachev's reform after twenty years] (Beijing: Zhongyang bianyi chubanshe, 2007), 2–3.

12. *Deng Xiaoping wenxuan, disanjuan* [Selected works of Deng Xiaoping, vol. 3] (Beijing: Renmin chubanshe, 1993), 380.

13. *Nanfang zhoumo* [Southern weekend], January, 14, 2007.

14. http://www.china.com.cn/xxsb/txt/2006-11/28/content_7420377.htm.

15. Jiang Changbin and Ma Shanlong, "Yi kexue shehui zhuyiguan renshi Sugong yishi xingtai de xiaowang (xia)" [Understanding the disappearance of the Communist Party of the Soviet Union with a scientific socialist view point, vol. 2], *Xuexi shibao* [Study times], March 19, 2007.

16. Huang Zongliang, "Sulian jubian yu zhongguo de gaige kaifang" [Change in the USSR and reform and opening-up of China], *Gaige neican* [Internal reference for reform] (hereinafter as "Sulian jubian yu zhongguo"), no. 2 (2007): 31–34.

17. Huang Zongliang, "Sulian jubian yu zhongguo," 31–34

18. Huang Zongliang, "Sulian jubian yu zhongguo," 31–34

Concluding Assessment:
The Soviet Impact on Chinese Society

Gilbert Rozman

O VER THE PAST FEW CENTURIES societies around the globe have become ever more influenced by the outside world, but rarely has one of the great powers become a testing grounds for the wholesale importation of another society's organizational and ideological blueprint. Without the impetus of defeat or occupation, China's leaders at the start of the 1950s embraced the Soviet model of socialist construction and the Stalinist worldview. Despite claims that in the 1960s and 1970s China had broken with what was then called "Soviet revisionism," its leaders acknowledged in the sobering environment of the 1980s that the "traditional" socialist system had actually endured and now would have to be "reformed," which increasingly meant "dismantled" with the exception of elements still regarded as essential for the Chinese Communist Party's maintenance of power. Looking back from this vantage point, we observe that many of the trappings of Soviet society had in fact been incorporated into China, but they failed to produce the same impact. Mao's inconsistent macro-level policies, the enduring character of China's micro-level social settings, and the rapid changes produced by Deng Xiaoping's multi-level initiatives all resulted in a society that looked significantly different from that of the Soviet Union.

In the second half of the 1980s Chinese and Soviet leaders alike called for reforms to dismantle "traditional socialism" with Deng Xiaoping placing priority on the economic system and Mikhail Gorbachev increasingly on the political system as his perestroika floundered. Both recognized the need for changes in society, but neither put those in the forefront. Yet, what they could accomplish depended heavily on the society in which they operated. Only by assessing how the two societies had diverged after importation of the Soviet model into China can we appreciate why their paths differed so much in the 1990s. The contrasts between the societies had secondary relevance when "traditional socialism" persisted, but they came to have great significance in the years of transformation to a new model of development. We are better able to recognize this by reviewing the importation of the Soviet model into Chinese society and then considering the factors that influenced the way Chinese society evolved, both in the period of the Sino-Soviet split and in the 1980s under the shadow of Soviet stagnation and then Gorbachev's dramatic reforms.

Importation of the Soviet Model

In the 1950s Mao Zedong led in modeling Chinese society on that of the Soviet Union. Guided by Stalin's interpretation of Marxist-Leninist theory on class struggle, he strove to eradicate class enemies, to make pariahs of bad class elements, and to mobilize workers through nationalization and tight control in enterprise communities, and peasants through collectivization and hierarchical nesting of rural communities, while forging bureaucratic and coercive command over specialists and officials that produces both "reds and experts." Through the mid-1950s "building of socialism" advanced along Soviet lines. Changes in labor force, urbanization, education, and, notably, the organization of political and economic life reinforced the Stalinist model that Mao had embraced. Twenty-some years later, this model remained mostly intact, despite the experiments of the Great Leap Forward and the Cultural Revolution that had appeared to shift China toward Mao's new conception of communism, where intense class struggle befitted a context of "continuous revolution." When Chinese analysts criticized the legacy of "traditional socialism," they cited meager material incentives, scant life opportunities, and stifled exploration of local options, failings inherited from the Stalinist model and shared with Soviet society. They also stressed dogmatic thinking that narrowed options for learning from experience to serve top-down, deliberate decision making. In rejecting deductive ideology, they were not, however, approving free-wheeling debate.

The Soviet model entered China fitfully as the Chinese Communist Party gained guerrilla havens and expanded control over base areas until it succeeded in proclaiming the People's Republic of China on October 1, 1949. The main objectives at a time of rebellion and civil war were to undermine existing authority and open the way to massive mobilization of resources, for example through land reform campaigns. Mao's reliance on peasants and on decentralized organization defied the early guidance of Josef Stalin and the Soviet agents in China; yet when Mao suddenly found himself in charge of the most populous state in the world he embraced Stalin's model for constructing a socialist society. Despite idealistic rhetoric about a "New People's Democracy," a crash course followed through translations of Soviet sources and the arrival of Soviet advisors who provided guidance on how to copy precedents in such areas as state administration, education, and industrial organization. Impatient to accelerate the pace of total socialist transformation, Mao forced collectivization of agriculture in 1955; and in 1956—twenty years after Stalin proclaimed that the Soviet Union had succeeded in constructing a socialist society—he followed the nationalization of industry with a similar proclamation for China. There was no doubt that in social control and mobilization of the population, China had essentially duplicated the Soviet achievement, guided by borrowed ideals and by many of the specific mechanisms that had been applied by the Soviet leaders.

In the uncertain years of 1956–60 China's leaders experimented with the openness of the "Hundred Flowers Movement," the purges of the "Anti-rightist campaign," and the radical social reorganization of the Great Leap Forward. They were competing with the reform spirit in the Soviet Union after Nikita Khrushchev's Twentieth Party Congress de-Stalinization speech, then reasserting their adherence to Stalin's totalitarian controls, and finally exploring radical social reorganization beyond anything the Soviets had even attempted. While reliance on intensive campaigns led by outside work teams and appeals to ideological themes inculcated through thought reform programs became a hallmark of China's radical eras, when Mao's frantic pace slowed after havoc had been wreaked, it became clear that the Soviet model had endured in the widespread construction of large industrial enterprises and cities. Although the failure of the Great Leap Forward led to a pause in social mobilization, structures left in place, especially in urban administration, industrialization, and education, kept China on the Soviet track. Even the disruptive decade of Cultural Revolution, after its hectic first three years, settled into a grudging tolerance for the status quo in many sectors with attendant administrative compromises to keep a minimum of order and to allow the economy in rural and urban areas to persist.

To the extent that the claim of having achieved socialism reflected comprehensive reorganization of state-society relations and successful realization of select indicators of development, it accurately conveyed the optimism of China's leaders and the qualified acceptance by the population of the early transformation that had occurred. Chinese society became strikingly different from what it had been. During the "golden age" of Sino-Soviet relations the model appeared to be working, With Soviet assistance growing rapidly in ways that made possible further application of the model and the emerging elite in China likely to adhere to the blueprint that facilitated their own social mobility, there is reason to think that China could have kept following the model and becoming more like the Soviet Union. Yet, a closer look at Chinese society reveals ample tensions that raised awareness of some of the costs of this model, as Khrushchev's candor made clear some of its serious inefficiencies and tendency to rely on coercion as discontent spread.

The Soviets had promoted a society of militant atheism, gender role adjustment centered on the fullest possible female participation in the labor force, and mobilized labor devoted to production targeted at fulfilling ever more ambitious state plans. China borrowed these ideals as set forth by Stalin and kept doing so even after Khrushchev's "thaw" revealed that many of them obscured a quite different reality. The desire for religious expression remained widespread, women were especially distressed by the conditions of life they faced, and raising labor efficiency required a new approach to management and the incentives offered to workers. Instead of following the Soviet path of correcting for the excesses that had resulted from pretending that the ideals were actually the reality, Mao chose to pursue the ideals more intensely. Thus, the Great Leap Forward took the mobilization of labor to levels unparalleled in Soviet experience, and over the next two decades criticisms intensified against the "Stakhanovite" incentives utilized by Stalin and the "revisionist" mechanisms such as "careerism" and a "worker aristocracy" attributed mostly to his successors. The Cultural Revolution carried "thought control" beyond anything seen in the Soviet Union, seeking to eradicate not only specific religious behavior but even the entire Confucian heritage that permeated Chinese culture. And strictures on daily life, covering such things as dress and courtship, accompanied by demands for "proletarian love" exceeded any of the limits on women in Soviet times. Even at the start of the 1980s visitors to China found that it had outdone Soviet attempts to deny individual traditions and preferences, leaving morale very low.

In the 1960s–70s China's leaders struggled with the consequences of this model. Generally, they resisted the tendency for class struggle to disappear, the rising influence of experts over "reds," the increasing materialist orientation of the elite as well as the masses, the growing attraction of the technology and culture in states with a capitalist economy, and the unquenchable thirst for information about their own country's past and present and the reality of the outside world. Finding that they could neither offer a satisfactory substitute for the Soviet model nor accept its unacknowledged persistence in their own society, they allowed the costs of the model to grow far beyond those seen in the Soviet Union from the 1950s while failing to provide the rewards that in the Brezhnev era tempered the lack of serious reform. After Mao's death in 1976 and Deng

Xiaoping's new direction at the Third Plenum in 1978, China reacquainted itself with Soviet society, as it had changed, in search of guidance for its own path of reform. Some had considered borrowing further in order to salvage the overall model, but the more they learned about recent Soviet stagnation in contrast to the dynamism of East Asian capitalist societies, the clearer they became on the need to jettison the model itself, both as a basis for economic development and as a structure for the organization of society. In the three areas noted above, China allowed individual religious expression in place of insisting on militant atheism, freed women to make many more of their own decisions about work and family, and opened the way to an economy in which labor responded to market incentives. The model was dead, even if controls persisted, such as political restrictions on organized religion, whether Tibetan Buddhism or Roman Catholicism, stringent family birth control policies, and limitations on private ownership of land or organization to lobby against the seizure of land or its environmental degradation without protection of local communities.

Chinese society at the end of the 1970s looked different from Soviet society in at least four critical respects for the transition ahead. First, it was less ethnically diverse and less tolerant of political representation based on ethnic areas. While in Xinjiang and Tibet the local interest in political rights was strong, these areas remained harshly subjugated and only a tiny force in the national polity in comparison to ethnic compromises reached in the fourteen non-Russian republics that preserved the peace in the Brezhnev era. Second, the Chinese populace overwhelmingly remained without major social contract benefits in the socialist system in contrast to the increasingly widespread education, health, pension, vacation, day care, and other benefits bestowed on Soviet citizens through the Brezhnev era. Third, Chinese society was in turmoil after the peripatetic pace of campaigns that reached a climax in the Cultural Revolution, while Russian society was stagnant in the absence of serious reform under Brezhnev's geriatric leadership. Fourth, Russian national identity was preoccupied with the United States, as one superpower facing another in quest of equal standing despite the enormous gap between the two, as opposed to China's national identity confused by Mao's radicalism but, at root, Confucian in its multi-level possibilities centered on family, community, and state in an East Asian context. China was less encumbered in its reform choices and better able to refocus national identity.

Factors Influencing the Evolution of Chinese Society

"Traditional socialism" did not have the same impact on Chinese society as it did on Russian society. There are many explanations. First, it was more consistent with past practices and ways of thinking in the country where it had originated. Second, it lasted for a shorter period and was more sporadically and crudely implanted in China. Third, in the thirty years after Stalin's death the context for it had greatly changed in Russian cities such as Moscow, where modernization and the flow of information had advanced rather far. On the one hand, educated Russians were disposed to press for unraveling the old system. On the other, far more Russians were dependent on that system and prone to find fault with reforms that did not maintain the benefits to which they were accustomed. The hold on the Chinese people of a model that had delivered so much less to them, no doubt, was far more precarious. Peasants had received few material rewards or welfare benefits, as per capita production and state inputs grew very slowly over two decades. Workers had experienced little social mobility as an award system that downplayed their diligence operated through the 1970s. And intellectuals and officials suffered from the anti-elitist and anti-education policies of the Cultural Revolution with no opportunity to feel secure in their careers or their children's prospects. Chinese society was left divided, insecure, and without any confidence in the future. No wonder the model was blamed, even as China's leaders forbade open calls to proceed beyond reform to change in the system.

While most explanations for the Sino-Soviet split center on leadership, ideology, and foreign policy, differences between the two societies warrant consideration. To explore these we should consider the following five points. One, the de-Stalinization speech by Nikita Khrushchev exposed severe social problems inherent in the Stalinist socialist model that resonated in China's awareness of the model. The bureaucratic nature of the model was found to be even less compatible with the dispersed structure of China's society, giving an impetus for the Mao leadership to switch course with implications for an ideological split over the nature of socialism. Two, the more mature Soviet socialist society faced different reform challenges that opened the way to alternative corrective measures in China, as Deng found it easier to unleash the energies of numerous Chinese. Three, the Confucian traditions of China, however much they may have been rejected by the Maoist leadership, created a basis for conflicting assumptions about society and how to involve it in the socialist enterprise. Essentially, China had a fallback worldview, while Russia, once shorn of the other fourteen republics, was little disposed to break away from the Soviet outlook. Four, the Chinese Communist Party had developed differently from the Bolshevik Party that had seized power in Russia and brought with it contrasting views of its constituency along with a wider perspective on how nationalism serves legitimacy. Five, the ambitions of China's leadership intent on regaining Taiwan and asserting influence had direct consequences for thinking about national identity as a force for rallying people behind social policies aimed at boosting China's comprehensive power.

When Khrushchev went further than Stalin in rejecting not only class struggle but also recourse to divisive purges of so-called enemies of the state, Mao turned toward a more radical emphasis on "continuous revolution." As Khrushchev's utopianism stressed a communist society of plenty able to meet expansive welfare needs, Mao's prioritized a mobilized society in which normative incentives substituted for material ones. In neither case did such adventurism satisfy the urgent concerns of ordinary citizens, and eventually more sober thinking prevailed—after an elite backlash in the case of China in response to the chaos that was unleashed and one in the Soviet Union that helped to topple Khrushchev. Utopian social programs failed to dislodge the overall Stalinist model; they were precursors to further deviations from the model that heightened consciousness of different orientations in the two societies.

Under its radical leadership during the Cultural Revolution China demonized the supposed "revisionist" nature of Soviet society, which in some ways led to distortions in the Stalinist model too. Referring to the Soviet elite as a "communist aristocracy," China undermined the security of its own elite and the material incentives as well as educational opportunities that accompanied social mobility under the model. Having borrowed the meritocratic features of the Soviet system, China nullified many rewards that greased the system and fostered loyalty and improved performance. At the same time, resort to class labels and punishing treatment of many who were capable of contributing to the system in China from the mid-1960s to late 1970s did at least as much to damage effective utilization of human resources as had Stalin in his purges. The skeleton of the Stalinist industrial and administrative system remained even as its functioning deteriorated, especially in contrast to the Soviet system that was tweaked to win popular compliance in the Brezhnev era.

Ironically, attempting to realize a higher form of socialism in every-day life, China failed to implant stable or deep-rooted changes. In pretending that the Chinese people surpassed the Soviets in their beliefs consistent with socialism, leaders ignored the structural requisites of changing beliefs. Superficial conformity, coerced or due to lack of alternative forms of expression, did not signify lasting acceptance of new social forms. To China's good fortune, however, the limited embeddedness of socialist dependency on the state gave it a far better foundation for the transition to a market economy. Frustrated by the chaotic conditions they had endured, Chinese of all types longed for a new course just as Deng's success in taking control of the leadership provided a new direction.

As Taiwan and Hong Kong's rapid modernization demonstrated, another model had been proven to bring extraordinary economic development to a Chinese society. If China's leaders long ignored such comparisons, they could not avoid at the end of the 1970s learning the lessons of the East Asian "economic miracles." The socialist model had little to say about a country's preceding social structure except the degree to which it had advanced into the capitalist mode of production. Indeed, by rejecting Confucian traditions and acting as if imperial China's entire social legacy was dispensable (family solidarity, educational competition focused on demanding examinations, local place networks in support of decentralized strategies for achieving an edge in various types of regional and national markets, etc.), Mao undermined China's foundation. The model, which relied on a command economy and centralized direction of every facet of social life rather than a market economy and the workings of a civil society, offered tantalizing early results. Yet, when two decades later it had produced meager results while neighbors influenced by the Confucian legacy had thrived, calls for reassessing how the promise of China's traditional society could be better utilized found a receptive audience.

Reintroducing entrance examinations and a meritocratic system of advancement, China could build on venerable traditions of study. Already when Chinese students had gone to the Soviet Union in the 1950s professors were in awe of their motivation along with their intellect. The responsibility system of farming coupled with the subsidiary household non-agricultural activities that spread quickly in the 1980s contrasted with the slow pace of agricultural reform and rural revitalization in Soviet society, heir to serfdom. Decentralization elicited diverse development strategies, particularly in Southeast China known for centuries of commercial specialization, in contrast to the stupor away from Moscow, as the stultifying impact of Tsarist overcentralization reinforced Soviet ways.

The Lingering Soviet Legacy

Today the debates about the suitability of Chinese society for rapid economic development and globalization have been resolved. The contrast between the troubled state of the society under the impact of the Soviet model and its vibrancy since the early 1980s has become indisputable. Mao's confused and inconsistent imposition of the model made it easier to dislodge. Deng's sustained, deliberate dismantling of the model quickly showed the way to replacing it. Yet, these two factors would not have been enough to stimulate a dynamic Chinese society if it were not for the enduring social practices and thinking that demonstrated positive results in a very short time. This is testimony to the bad fit between the Stalin model and the existing Chinese society.

It is also an indication of the remarkably good fit between core elements of that society and the requirements of rapid modernization. Of course, some features of the old society, as of any society, stood in the way. In launching sweeping changes, the Mao leadership may have contributed to their removal. Yet, over a quarter century it became clear that whatever the limited positive contribution that was made it was more than counterbalanced by the negative impact of implanting the Soviet model in a manner that undermined Chinese traditions. In eradicating many aspects of the Soviet model, China has accelerated its development even if other aspects of the model may arouse more ambivalence as they survive.

Deng's reforms unleashed much of the potential of Chinese society, but that does not mean that limitations on grassroots social forces do not remain. The Soviet model's impact is not necessarily over. Society is limited in how it can organize. As in Soviet times and in the Maoist era, environmental degradation was not countered by citizens' groups able to defend their community against insistence that economic development must be the priority and that decision-makers do not have to listen to any sort of public discontent. In areas of social life deemed sensitive for political control, other restrictions operate. The time may come when Chinese will look back on serious problems that they were unable to address in this age of stunning economic development and conclude that the Soviet model of socialism did not stop exerting a negative influence. Grass-roots society and other interest groups remain limited in their organization and leverage, as the state clings to authoritarian methods including censorship to maintain dominance.

National identity funnels attention to goals heightened in a society still grasping for normality: achieving economic development at the fastest possible pace; gaining world respect that would culminate in hosting the 2008 Beijing Olympics; building up comprehensive national power to put China on a par with the United States; and also confirming sovereignty in all respects, by recovering Taiwan as well as asserting China's voice in surrounding areas and the United Nations. Over time, however, the focus of national identity can change; many nation-centered goals that intensified in the second half of the twentieth century consistent with the Soviet struggle to remake the world may start yielding to middle-class quality-of-life interests and to global concerns in an age of new security threats. Chinese society, fortunate in its own traditions, has outgrown much of the Soviet legacy, but a half century after the Sino-Soviet split came to the surface some elements of the legacy remain.

Index

About the Contributors

Thomas P. Bernstein is emeritus professor of political science, Columbia University. He is the co-author, together with Xiaobo Lu, of *Taxation without Representation in Contemporary Rural China* (2003). He has also written on Chinese politics generally, on Chinese youth, and on comparisons of collectivization of agriculture and famines in China and the Soviet Union. He is currently working on Sino-Soviet comparisons, especially on reform processes.

Tina Mai Chen is associate professor in the Department of History at the University of Manitoba. Her recent publications include *Film, History, and Cultural Citizenship: Sites of Production* (co-edited with David S. Churchill, 2007), as well as articles on various aspects of film import and export in 1950s and 1960s China. They are published in *Cultural Critique, Journal of the Canadian Historical Association,* and *Journal of Chinese Cinemas.* Her general research interests include modern Chinese intellectual and cultural history; gender; nationalism; film; and lived experiences in China of global historical forces. She has two ongoing major research projects: one on Sino-Soviet film exchange in Maoist China; the other on migration of overseas Chinese between Burma, China, and India during the Japanese Occupation in the 1930s and 1940s.

Izabella Goikhman is research associate in the Institute of East Asian Studies, Chinese Studies, at the Free University Berlin. Her recent publications include "The Discourse on Jews in China" (*Berliner China Studien* 47, 2007) and various articles on academic research on Chinese Jews. Her current research interests are: Sino-Russian relations, intercultural knowledge transfer, history of Chinese science and humanities, Jews in China, and Gender-Studies.

Guihai Guan is currently associate professor and associate dean of the School of International Studies at the Peking University. He received his Ph.D. degree from Moscow State Institute of International Relations in 1997. His academic interests lie in the fields of Russian foreign policy, Sino-Russian relations, and Russia's political and social development. His publications include: *Da Ouzhou: guangrong yu mengxiang* (*Great Europe: Honor and Dream*, co-author, 1996), and *Yeliqin zhizheng shidai* (*Yeltsin's Years in Power*, co-author, 2000).

Donghui He is assistant professor of Chinese literature at Whitman College. She received her Ph.D. from the University of British Columbia, Canada, in Comparative Literature in 2000. She publishes on Chinese film and literature. And her recent publications include "Reconstructing 'God-Fearing Communities': Filming Tibet in the 21st Century," in Sheldon Lu and Jiayan Mi, eds., *Chinese Ecocinema* (forthcoming). Her current research interests include Chinese film, theatre (spoken drama), contemporary literature, and discourse analysis.

Xiaojia Hou is assistant professor in the Department of History at the University of Colorado Denver. She received her Ph.D. in history from Cornell University in 2008. She has published an article on the second Taiwan Strait crisis in 1958, and her chapter on the relations between the CCP central leadership and local agents in the early 1950s is included in a forthcoming conference volume (2009). Her research interests include comparison of communist developments in China and in Russia, the Chinese Communist Party's rural policies and China's transformation in the 1950s.

Hanbing Kong is professor in the School of International Studies at the Peking University. He received his Ph.D. from the same school in 1992. He has published ten books and his most recent books include *Zhong-Su guanxi yu dui zhongguo shehui fazhan de yixiang* (*Sino-Soviet Relation and its Influence on China's Social Development*, 2004); *Shijie shehui zhuyi lilun shi* (*History and Theories of World Socialism*, 2004); and *Zhijie liyong waizi de lilun yu shijian* (*Theories and Practices of Direct Utilization of Foreign Capitals*, 2003). Currently he is working on a book project, tentatively titled *The East and Central Europe in the Shadow of Big Powers*.

Hua-yu Li is associate professor in the Department of Political Science at Oregon State University. She received her Ph.D. in Comparative Politics from Columbia University in 1997. She is the author of *Mao and the Economic Stalinization of China: 1948–1953* (2006). She is an editorial board member for *The Journal of China in Comparative Perspective*. Currently she is working on a book concerning the evolution and change of the CCP between the 1940s and present.

Lorenz M. Lüthi is assistant professor in the History Department at McGill University. He is the author of *The Sino-Soviet Split: Cold War in the Communist World* (2008). He was a National Security Fellow at the Olin Institute at Harvard University between 2004 and 2005, and a member of the Institute for Advanced Studies in 2007. He is currently working on a book project concerning the rise of the post-Cold War world in East Asia, the Middle East, and Europe in the 1960s, 1970s, and early 1980s.

Elizabeth McGuire is a Ph.D. candidate in the history department at UC Berkeley. Her dissertation, "The Sino-Soviet Romance, 1921–1966," is about the relationship between the Russian and Chinese revolutions as seen through the biographies of Chinese communists who traveled, studied, and lived in the Soviet Union. Her second project, *Communist Neverland*, tells the history of a special children's home in Ivanovo, Russia, where the children of the international communist elite—from Mao to Tito—learned Soviet concepts of family, nation, and the individual, and formed their own international socialist family.

Gregory Rohlf is associate professor in the Department of History at the University of the Pacific. He is completing a book on agricultural resettlement to Qinghai province, China in the 1950s. He is currently researching a project on *Socialist Leisure and City Planning: Movie Theaters, Book Stores and City Parks in Small Cities in the Twentieth Century*. Other research interests include the global history of international voluntary service.

Gilbert Rozman is a Musgrave Professor of Sociology at Princeton University. He has published numerous books and his most recent books include: *Russian Strategic Thought toward Asia* (co-editor 2006); *Japanese Strategic Thought toward Asia* (co-editor, 2007); *Strategic Thinking about the Korean Nuclear Crisis: Four Parties Caught between North Korea and the United States* (2007); and *South Korean Strategic Thought toward Asia* (co-editor 2008). Currently he is working on a monograph concerning Chinese strategic thought toward Asia, and a comparative study of East Asian national identities.

Laurence Schneider is professor emeritus at Washington University in St. Louis. His most recent book is *Biology and Revolution in Twentieth Century China* (2003).

Douglas Stiffler received his Ph.D. in modern Chinese history from the University of California, San Diego, in 2002. He is associate professor of history at Juniata College in Huntingdon, Pennsylvania. During the academic year 2008–9, he was a Fulbright Research Scholar affiliated with Capital Normal University in Beijing, China. He is currently working on a book manuscript entitled *Socialist Modernity under Soviet Tutelage: the People's Republic of China and the Soviet Union, 1949–1960.*

Péter Vámos is senior research fellow at the Institute of History of the Hungarian Academy of Sciences. He received a Ph.D. from the Hungarian Academy of Sciences. He has authored and edited seven books and published numerous articles on the modern history and foreign relations of China, Sino-Hungarian relations, and the history of Christianity in China. His latest book, *Kína mellettünk? Kínai külügyi iratok Magyarországról, 1956 (Is China with Us? 1956)* (2008), contains the Hungarian translation of over 160 Chinese Ministry of Foreign Affairs documents on Hungary from 1956. The present chapter is part of an ongoing project which aims at documenting and analyzing the relations between China and East-Central European Soviet bloc countries between 1949 and 1989. Vámos is a recipient of both the Chiang Ching-kuo Foundation for International Scholarly Exchange (RG004-EU-05) fellowship, and OTKA (K 78484) fellowship for his research concerning Sino-Hungarian and Sino-Soviet bloc relations.

You Ji is reader/associate professor at the School of Social Science and International Studies, the University of New South Wales. He is author of three books and numerous articles. The most recent ones include *The 17th Party Congress and the CCP's Changing Elite Politics*, in ed. Dali Yang and Zhao Litao, *China's Reform at 30* (2009); "China's New Diplomacy, Foreign Policy and Defense Strategy," in ed. Pauline Kerr, Stuart Harris & Qin Yaqing, *China's New Diplomacy: Tactical or Fundamental Change?* (2008); "Revolution in Military Thinking," in ed. Bo Huldt & Masako Ikegami, *China Rising* (2008) "Symbiosis: Redefining Civil-Military Relations in China," in ed. Wang Gungwu & Yongnian Zheng, *China and the New International Order*, (2008). He is member of the editorial board of the *China Journal, Provincial China, Journal of Contemporary China* and the advisory board for the series on contemporary China.

Miin-ling Yu is associate research fellow in the Institute of Modern History at the Academia Sinica (Taipei, Taiwan). She has published a wide range of articles on the Sino-Soviet relations including Chiang Kai-shek's visit to the Soviet Union and the Soviet cultural impact on the PRC. Some of her articles are "Woman Holds the Plow?—Female Tractor Driver in the PRC," "A Soviet Hero, Pavel Korchagin, Comes to China," and "A Reassessment of Jiang Jieshi and the Policy of Alliance with the Soviet Union." Her research interests include comparative history, history of the Soviet Union and modern China, and Sino-Soviet cultural relations. Currently she is writing a book on making the new socialist man in the PRC.

Jian Zang is professor in the History Department at Peking University. She is the editor in chief of a prize winning book, *Jinbainian Zhongguo funu lunzhu zongmu tiyao* (*A Bibliographical Guide to Essays and Works on Chinese Women in the 20th Century*, 1996). She is also the co-editor of *Qingchun fangchengshi-50 ge Beijing nu zhiqing de zishu* (*Personal Stories Told by Fifty Beijing Sent-Down Female Students*, 1995). She has published numerous articles on a wide range of topics related to Chinese women and Chinese women in comparative perspectives. During the coming academic year, she will be a visiting scholar in the Chinese Department at the Free University Berlin, where she will work on an oral history book project concerning German women Sinologists and their research connections with China.

Shengfa Zhang is a professor at the Institute of Russian, Eastern European and Central Asian Studies, Chinese Academy of Social Sciences. His field of research is contemporary world history and the history of international relations. He was a visiting scholar at the Center of International Studies of Princeton University in 2003, and a visiting scholar at the Saint-Petersburg State University in 2005. He is the author of *Sidalin yu lengzhan* (*Stalin and the Cold War*, 2000 & 2007), and co-author of *Suweiai wenhua yu Suweiai renmin* (*The Soviet Culture and the Soviet People*, 1991). He has also edited *Sulian lishi dangan xuanbian* (*Collection of Historical Archives of Soviet Union*, vols. 17, 18, and 19, 2002). His new book, *Ershi shiji dongxifang guanxishi* (*The History of International Relations between the East and West*, is forthcoming).

Minglang Zhou is associate professor and director of the Chinese Program at the University of Maryland, College Park. He is the author of *Multilingualism in China: The Politics of Writing Reform for Minority Languages, 1949–2002* (2003), and editor of *Language Policy in the People's Republic of China: Theory and Practice since 1949* (2004), and *Affirmative Action in China and the U.S.: A Dialogue on Inequality and Minority Education* (2009). He has guest-edited an issue of *Journal of Asian Pacific Communication* (2006, vol. 16 [2]) on the theme of language planning and varieties of Modern Standard Chinese as well as an issue of *Chinese Society and Education* (2008, vol. 41 [6]) on the topic of linguistic diversity and language harmony in twenty-first century China. He has also published two dozen articles on the sociology of language in China. Recently he has won a 2009 American Philosophical Society Sabbatical Fellowship for his project on Between Integration and Segregation: Changing Models of Nation State Building and Language Education for Minorities in China.

Breinigsville, PA USA
20 December 2009
229513BV00003B/2/P

9 780739 142226